LOUISA S. McCORD

Political and Social Essays

THE PUBLICATIONS OF THE
SOUTHERN TEXTS SOCIETY

Michael O'Brien, Chair of the Editorial Board

An Evening When Alone: Four Journals of Single Women in the South, 1827–67
Edited by Michael O'Brien

Louisa S. McCord: Political and Social Essays
Edited by Richard C. Lounsbury

LOUISA S. McCORD

Political and Social Essays

EDITED BY RICHARD C. LOUNSBURY

University Press of Virginia
Charlottesville and London

THE UNIVERSITY PRESS OF VIRGINIA

First published 1995

Library of Congress Cataloging-in-Publication Data
McCord, Louisa Susanna Cheves, 1810–1879.
Louisa S. McCord : political and social essays / edited by Richard C. Lounsbury.
p. cm.—(Publications of the Southern Texts Society)
Includes bibliographical references (p.) and index.
ISBN 0-8139-1570-8 (cloth)
1. Southern States—Politics and government—1775–1865.
2. Slavery—Southern States. 3. Women—Southern States—History—19th century. 4. Southern States—Economic conditions.
I. Lounsbury, Richard Cecil. II. Title. III. Series.
F213.M35 1995
975.03—dc20 94-42013
CIP

Printed in the United States of America

Publication of this book has been supported by a grant
from the National Endowment for the Humanities,
an independent federal agency

Dis

Manibus

L. S. M.

Short of their promis'd height that seem'd to threat the Sky

Contents

Illustrations

Following page 155

Preface

Coming to write his parallel lives of Alexander the Great and Julius Caesar, Plutarch advised his readers that, as a biographer's task was to give "more particular attention to the marks and indications of the souls of men," so he claimed the freedom "to leave more weighty matters and great battles to be treated of by others."[1] One editing the writings of Louisa S. McCord may venture to claim something of the same liberty. Louisa McCord's life knew much of conflict; her legacy knows no less; but battles fought over that legacy are for others, not for her editor. His task, albeit it may be modest, comes first. Louisa McCord's writings are materials, materials immediately for critics and historians of the South, whether intellectual, political, or cultural, and materials more largely for critics and historians of literature, political economy, women, slavery. Yet these materials are more than a tomb to be rifled: they are also, and beforehand, utterance. It is their voice which, assisted from its teguments of marble and misunderstanding, the editor would call forth. But will the voice come when he does call for it? Perhaps he may invite its favor by the chance that he is native and citizen of the country which, a very young country, Louisa McCord chose for her exile, or refuge—without allegiance, either by descent or adoption, to causes struggling in battles long ago, but loyal only to the restoration of her voice. Moreover, being a student first of classical antiquity and its tradition, he is thus assured of a tranquillity, though it be to some an artless tranquillity, by education and tastes separate from the arena of scholarly enterprise in which it is customary to fight those remote battles anew.

Most of Louisa McCord's writings were published without her name; to establish what writings are to be assigned to her is not always a straightforward matter. Therefore, a Note on the Texts describes how the McCord corpus as a whole has been identified and explains why a few works that have been accredited to her ought to be rejected; it also sets out editorial policy in preparing the texts for this volume. The editor makes no claim to have

1. Plutarch *Alexander* 1, in *Lives of the Noble Grecians and Romans* 2:139

located all of her writings, nor would even speculate how many may remain to be identified and confirmed as hers. Rather, this collection of essays and its companion volume, *Louisa S. McCord: Poems, Drama, Biography, Letters* (Charlottesville, Va., forthcoming), together aim to be a comprehensive edition of all published works that have been determined to belong to Louisa McCord (with the exception of her translation of Frédéric Bastiat's *Sophismes économiques*), along with her manuscript "Memoir of Langdon Cheves," her deposition and fragmentary affidavit relative to the burning of Columbia, and all letters and documents that have been located. The essays in this volume are divided according to broad subject categories, categories which cannot be exclusive: for example, some essays devoted to slavery raise matters pertaining to women or to political economy; and, indeed, the author's intention is often to demonstrate how these three areas of investigation are, and must be, intertwined. Within each category, arrangement is chronological.

Louisa McCord read much, remembered much, liked to quote and (more often than the editor has been able to spot, probably even more often than he has come to suspect) to adapt and reshape citations from her favorite authors. Accordingly, the annotations aspire, if they cannot claim, to be (like the scholia accompanying a classical text) a guidebook united to the writings, animadverting upon background, context, the handsome and the austere, yet the welcoming, furniture of Louisa McCord's mind.

It is a pleasure to acknowledge help as cheerfully and astutely given as the help that I have enjoyed throughout my work with Louisa McCord. David Moltke-Hansen acted as host and nomenclator during my visit to Charleston and has remained a ready support to the preparation of this edition. Eugene Genovese and Elizabeth Fox-Genovese encouraged the project from the beginning. Happily chosen by the Southern Texts Society as its reader of the manuscript, Clyde Wilson contributed the experience and learning to be expected of the editor of *The Papers of John C. Calhoun;* no less valuable were his friendliness and kindness to me, a newcomer to Southern studies, while I was just commencing my researches in Columbia. To Alexander Moore few minutiae of Columbia society in the mid-nineteenth century proved to be inexplicable. In Charleston, Elizabeth Hanson conducted inquiries on my behalf, in particular securing an excellent photocopy of Louisa McCord's will. Geoffrey Harrison diverted a good part of a vacation into burrowing among the Sarah Wister Papers at the Historical Society of Pennsylvania. The staffs of the repositories which I visited, especially the South Carolina Historical Society, were unfailingly courteous.

At the National Archives in Washington, D.C., George Tate (assisted by

Nanci DeBloois and Evan DeBloois) secured crucial information for me concerning Louisa McCord's experiences during the Federal occupation of Columbia. He and Sue Elwyn provided helpful scrutiny of the Chronology. Alan Swanson and Patricia O'Brien accepted various arcane queries arising in the annotations. Miriam Pierce supervised and reviewed the transference of the essays to computer form, an enormous task accomplished always with care and patience. Garry Wickerd helped in locating illustrations. Brian McKibben untied puzzles of computer software in designing genealogical tables and in preparing the final manuscript. John Hall authorized a computer upgrade when it was most needed. More often than I can count now, I relied upon Kathleen Hansen and John Higginbotham, with the rest of the Interlibrary Loan department, at the Harold B. Lee Library. The Women's Research Institute of Brigham Young University assisted with research funding. A subvention toward publication was received from the Charles E. Merrill Monograph Fund in the College of Humanities, Brigham Young University.

This edition, were it mine and not Mrs. McCord's, must be dedicated to Michael O'Brien, who favored its inception, fostered its progress, and sighed, amazed perhaps, when it was done. He has shared his researches and his insights, never niggardly. More, the cast, the form, the demeanor of thought are to him not matters indifferent; yet he survives, example (and relief) in this age when scholarship is a perilous office. "Hunc ego Lepidum," wrote Cornelius Tacitus, who judged few persons to be worthy of praise, "temporibus illis gravem et sapientem virum fuisse comperior. Nam pleraque ab saevis adulationibus aliorum in melius flexit; neque tamen temperamenti egebat, cum aequabili auctoritate et gratia apud Tiberium viguerit."

Abbreviations

Chesnut	C. Vann Woodward, ed., *Mary Chesnut's Civil War* (New Haven, 1981)
De Bow	*De Bow's Review*
Duke	Manuscript Department, William R. Perkins Library, Duke University, Durham, N.C.
FOLS	Louisa McCord Smythe, *For Old Lang Syne: Collected for My Children* (Charleston, S.C., 1900)
Fraser	Jessie Melville Fraser, "Louisa C. McCord," M.A. thesis, University of South Carolina, 1919
Huntington	Henry E. Huntington Library, San Marino, Calif.
LC	Library of Congress
LSM	Louisa Susanna McCord
PDBL	Richard C. Lounsbury, ed., *Louisa S. McCord: Poems, Drama, Biography, Letters* (Charlottesville, Va., forthcoming)
PHS	Historical Society of Pennsylvania, Philadelphia
SCHM	*South Carolina Historical Magazine*
SCHS	South Carolina Historical Society, Charleston
SCL	South Caroliniana Library, University of South Carolina, Columbia
SHC	Southern Historical Collection, University of North Carolina, Chapel Hill
Simms, *Letters*	Mary C. Simms Oliphant et al., eds., *The Letters of William Gilmore Simms*, 6 vols. (Columbia, S.C., 1952–82)

SLM	*Southern Literary Messenger*
Smithsonian	Archives of American Art, Smithsonian Institution, Washington, D.C.
SQR	*Southern Quarterly Review*
Smythe	Louisa McCord Smythe, "Recollections of Louisa Rebecca Hayne McCord (Mrs. Augustine T. Smythe)" (typescript), South Caroliniana Library, University of South Carolina, Columbia
VHS	Virginia Historical Society, Richmond
Westminster "Enfranchisement"	[John Stuart Mill and Harriet Taylor Mill], "Enfranchisement of Women," *Westminster Review* 55 (July 1851): 289–311 [the American edition has different pagination]

LOUISA S. McCORD

Political and Social Essays

Introduction

Louisa McCord was among the most trenchant intellectuals of the Old South. No other woman wrote with more force, across such a range of genres, or participated so influentially in social and political discourse. She was, beyond the South, among the leading conservatives in American thought. Yet her writings have been inaccessible since her death and were not easy to find even in her lifetime. Since one of the purposes of the Southern Texts Society is the rediscovery and publication of such neglected intellectuals, it is particularly fitting that among our early volumes should be Richard Lounsbury's edition of her writings.

Yet Louisa McCord is a troublesome legacy. Even in her lifetime she was hard to approach, someone not to trifle with. Like the William Lloyd Garrison whom she abominated, she did not equivocate, she did not excuse, she did not retreat a single inch, and she would be heard. Her friend Mary Chesnut admired this flinty wholeness, embodying as it did something the diarist lacked. Even Sherman's soldiers learned to respect McCord and only fought her to a draw. They nearly strangled her, they destroyed most of her papers, but she had partially outwitted them. When others were laughing at the prospect of their invading Columbia, she already "had all the brick flooring of her carriage house taken up, and a large pine box sunk into the earth and filled with cornmeal and bacon." By the time the rampaging men came, "all traces of the digging had disappeared."[1] The McCords had enough to see

1. Smythe, p. 58.

them through, even enough to feed their less percipient neighbors. This was McCord's way: awareness of danger, intelligent forethought, then initiative. She concealed scars; it helped survival.

Everyone understood that she was remarkable, though many of her opinions were conventional to her culture. She believed in laissez-faire political economy, was proslavery, argued for woman's separate sphere, assailed Harriet Beecher Stowe, abhorred socialism, was a secessionist, and believed in the superiority of the white race. In these sentiments was little to ruffle her contemporaries in South Carolina. No doubt, at the Conversation Club in Charleston, whose discussions as a woman she was forbidden to attend, they thought Mrs. McCord a very reliable woman, one of us.[2] Her publications were satisfyingly sound, especially from someone known to be a good wife and mother, and an excellent plantation mistress. Still, she was a woman. Seldom did women write for the periodicals and participate directly in the political forum, as she did. This was so even in the North, as Sarah Hale noticed in 1855 when discussing McCord.[3] Usually, women were supposed only to nod in agreement when their husbands spoke at tedious length about the world of affairs, perhaps to add the odd supporting anecdote, at best to advise in camera. This was how Mary Chesnut did it. As Chesnut was to note of a conversation in June 1862, even such oblique influence could be frowned upon: "We discussed clever women who help their husbands politically. Some men hate every man who says a good word of or to their wives. They can't be helped. Just as well. These lady politicians—if they are young and pretty—always get themselves 'a little bit' talked about."[4] No doubt they talked about Mrs. McCord, not young, not pretty. However, she did write poetry, which was more conventional, even if it was odd stuff. Odder still was a play about the Gracchi; women were not usually dramatists. And, when you looked closely at her writings, they were far from ordinary. The usual conclusions were reached by unusual routes. And the prose was violent, polemical, defiant.

So no one was in doubt that Louisa McCord was a phenomenon. She had carved out her own special place, by force of mind and presence, a peculiar bonus to a culture that did not reckon on the necessity of such a woman, did not know what to make of her. Being a bonus, she was not closely scrutinized in her lifetime. Still, she did not go entirely unnoticed. The 1840s and 1850s

2. In the spring of 1853, Louisa and David James McCord called on Mitchell King in Charleston; that same afternoon King invited the husband but not the wife to attend the Literary and Philosophical Society of South Carolina. Entry for March 30, 1853, in Mitchell King Book of Memoranda, 1 Feb. 1852–8 April 1855, Mitchell King Papers, SHC.

3. Hale, *Woman's Record,* p. 894.

4. *Chesnut,* p. 365.

were anthologizing decades; she was given some due. Caroline May seems to have been the first to notice her, in *The American Female Poets* (1848), which reprinted two poems from *My Dreams,* published earlier in the same year ("Spirit of the Storm" and "'Tis But Thee, Love, Only Thee"), identified McCord's father and husband, and briefly described her residence, before observing that she had talents "of a superior order," a mind "by nature strong . . . richly cultivated by extensive reading of the best authors," a "vivid imagination and warm feeling" which were "not well disciplined by good taste and correct judgment."[5] Thomas Buchanan Read was next, in *The Female Poets of America* (1849), where she was said "to have no equal among the women of her native state. Her knowledge of the classics, and of the French and Italian languages and literature—and her intimate acquaintance with the best English authors, have richly stored her mind; while an unusual vigour and grasp of intellect, and power of apprehension, fit her for works of the highest order." Read reprinted three of the poems from *My Dreams:* "The World of Dreams," "The Voice of Years," and "Forget Thee!"[6] In 1852 John Seely Hart numbered her among *The Female Prose Writers of America,* "one of the few women who have undertaken to write on the difficult subject of political economy," and reprinted passages from her 1849 essays "Justice and Fraternity" and "The Right to Labor."[7] In 1853 J. D. B. De Bow reissued one of her essays in his *Industrial Resources, etc. of the Southern and Western States.*[8] In 1861 Mary Forrest included her among the *Women of the South Distinguished in Literature,* though with misgivings: "To combine the essential qualifications of a political writer, philosopher, and poet, would seem to require a mind of masculine calibre and resource: such a mind, certainly, as we have been accustomed to think incompatible with the temperaments and surroundings of southern women; yet Mrs. McCord . . . has presented to the world these several aspects, and won distinction in each." Evidently these aspects were too unusual to merit undue prominence: McCord was given only five pages, to the thirty-five lavished upon the literary flibbertigibbet of Mobile, Octavia Le Vert.[9]

Earlier than Forrest's publication, Evert and George Duyckinck of New York had put together their *Cyclopaedia of American Literature* (1856) for Charles Scribner; in it had been the sketch that was to prove the foundational portrait of McCord; most subsequent notices (including that of Forrest)

5. Pp. 420–22.

6. Pp. 207–16. It is of interest that Rufus Wilmot Griswold, ed., *The Female Poets of America* (Philadelphia, 1849), though acquainted with the anthologies of May and Read, omitted McCord.

7. Pp. 187–92.

8. "Negro-mania," 2:196–205.

9. Pp. 480–84.

were to rely upon or plagiarize it. The Duyckincks had good sources: they were friends to William Gilmore Simms, who knew the McCords, and there is evidence that David James McCord himself contributed to its writing. By the *Cyclopaedia* she was dubbed "a lady of strong natural powers," "with spirit and energy," whose writings were "of a conservative character." Many of her anonymous writings were listed and identified; "The Voice of Years" was given entire, in addition to a brief excerpt from her play *Caius Gracchus* (1851).[10] The Duyckincks, it is notable, though they had only reprinted her belletristic writings, had been careful to characterize McCord's political and social essays. The antebellum period had generally observed this variety of genre, as she had been numbered by Read and May among poets, by Hart and Hale among writers of prose. Once the Civil War was over, this balance began to disappear, as did significant recognition from non-Southerners. McCord survived best, almost only, as a minor figure to the scholars of Southern literature.[11]

In 1869 James Wood Davidson discussed her with some discrimination in his *Living Writers of the South;* he it was who first called her "altogether Doric." But he too built on the Duyckincks and used the same passages from *Caius Gracchus,* the same "The Voice of Years."[12] Mary Tardy in 1872 likewise included her among *The Living Female Writers of the South.*[13] This was a pattern, resisted only by Louise Manly in 1895, who declined to diminish McCord into a minor playwright, by using instead a snippet of her 1852 essay "Enfranchisement of Woman."[14] But the two great literary mausoleums of the early New South, the *Library of Southern Literature* (1907) and *The South in the Building of the Nation* (1909), reiterated the pattern. The former, with a brief sketch by Clelia P. McGowan, extended the Duyckincks' story into and beyond the Civil War, used the same passage from *Caius Gracchus,* but added others from the same play.[15] The latter managed a very brief sketch, which

10. 2:251–53.

11. An exception is S. Austin Allibone, *A Critical Dictionary of English Literature and British and American Authors,* 3 vols. (Philadelphia, 1870), 2:1163. One should also note, as a curiosity, that the American Free-Trade League republished McCord's translation of Bastiat, as part 1 (entitled "Sophisms of Protection: First Series") in Frédéric Bastiat, *Sophisms of the Protectionists* (New York, 1870); the volume contained translations by other hands of Bastiat's later writings.

12. Pp. 351–57. It would have been surprising if Davidson had omitted McCord, since he had once been tutor to her children.

13. P. 518. See also Sargent, *Harper's Cyclopaedia of British and American Poetry,* pp. 675–76, which printed two of McCord's later poems, "What Used to Be" and "Thy Will Be Done."

14. *Southern Literature from 1579–1895,* pp. 292–93.

15. McGowan, "Louisa S. McCord (1810–1879)," in Alderman and Harris, *Library of Southern Literature* 8:3505–7 (excerpts on pp. 3508–30). See also Wauchope, *Writers of South Carolina,* pp. 269–72, which reprints "The Voice of Years."

(remarkably, in twelve lines) made several blunders, including misspelling her middle name, mistaking her place of birth, misdating both the day and year of her death, and misunderstanding her sole place of residence to be her plantation, Lang Syne, rather than Lang Syne and Columbia alternated seasonally.[16]

So, by the time of the First World War, Louisa McCord's reputation was surviving by the most insignificant of threads. By the 1920s and 1930s, this had all but snapped, save for a mildly condescending entry written by a South Carolinian in the *Dictionary of American Biography,* which asserts that her writings were less important than her hospital duties during the Civil War and ominously calls *Caius Gracchus* a Victorian closet drama.[17] The literary critics, turning away from what they saw as intellectual provincialism, for which they particularly blamed ladies who did flower arrangements for the United Daughters of the Confederacy and wrote verse, began to ignore her. Even those with some interest in the Old South, like Allen Tate and Richard Weaver, forgot, or rather never knew.[18] In truth, they were never very interested in women writers and did not go out of their way on that score. Even Jay B. Hubbell, the most thorough student of Southern literature in his generation, though he had heard her name and knew she had written a play because he had browsed in late nineteenth-century anthologies, seems to have thought her only "the wife of a South Carolina newspaper editor" and read only her review of *Uncle Tom's Cabin.*[19] Outside of a 1919 M. A. thesis at the University of South Carolina and the odd piece of genealogy done by the family, the memory of Louisa McCord had all but vanished.[20]

She was rescued by a Yankee, which would not have pleased her. It is not clear why this was so, but the modern era of McCord studies began in 1949,

16. Julian A. C. Chandler et al., eds., *The South in the Building of the Nation,* 12 vols. (Richmond, 1909), 12:132.

17. [Robert Duncan Bass], s.v. "McCord, Louisa Susanna Cheves," in *DAB.* The preceding entry is for her husband; it was written by Robert L. Meriwether, later the first director of the South Caroliniana Library. Bass went on to write biographies of South Carolinian Revolutionary heroes; see, for example, *Swamp Fox: The Life and Campaigns of General Francis Marion* (New York, 1959).

18. Partly, this was because the dominant voices in Southern literary criticism were unsympathetic to the South Carolinian tradition; see Michael O'Brien, "'The South Considers Her Most Peculiar': Charleston and Modern Southern Thought," *SCHM* 94 (April 1993): 119–33.

19. *The South in American Literature, 1607–1900,* pp. 392, 607.

20. Fraser, "Louisa C. McCord," published as South Carolina University Bulletin, no. 91 (Columbia, S.C., 1920); Bennett, "McCords of McCords' Ferry, South Carolina," and "Cheves Family of South Carolina." Susan Smythe Bennett was Louisa McCord's granddaughter.

when Margaret Farrand Thorp published in New Haven a book called *Female Persuasion: Six Strong-Minded Women.* It was a book that celebrated various feminist pioneers, among them Catherine Beecher, Jane Swisshelm, Amelia Bloomer, Sara Lippincott, and Lydia Maria Child. This was a quirky list, the quirkier for being extended to Louisa McCord, who did service as "the opposition."[21] The book was unannotated, and Thorp made mistakes, chiefly by relying too much upon Louisa Smythe's *For Old Lang Syne* (a miscellany by McCord's daughter) and the 1919 thesis, but there is evidence of independent research, and she seems to have read through many of McCord's writings. Above all, savingly, Thorp's was a sprightly account, which communicated a sense that Louisa McCord was a mind that deserved consideration.[22]

So a new era began with a book that connected McCord contentiously to feminism and represented her most significantly as a social thinker. No more was McCord a poet or a playwright, however minor. This commenced the modern line, though for several decades there was more silence, until in 1976 Susan Phinney Conrad included McCord in *Perish the Thought: Intellectual Women in Romantic America, 1830–1860,* in a chapter that discussed how antebellum women found it easier to gain acceptance when, not urging feminist causes, they wrote history and literary criticism or translated foreign works. Indeed, it was in a section entitled "The 'Woman of Letters' as Translator" that McCord was introduced, for the sake of her 1848 version of Frédéric Bastiat's *Sophisms of the Protective Policy,* before Conrad suggested the South Carolinian had been "the Southern Elizabeth Cady Stanton," for, what is considered to be, a "biting, ironic, and colloquial style."[23]

While women's historians were making their way toward a rediscovery of McCord, other scholars following other logics were converging on her from different directions. These were the students of South Carolina history, who grew notable in the rewriting of Southern history, and the Southern intellectual historians.

For many years, when the "nationalist" school of interpreting the Civil

21. P. 10. Margaret Thorp was married to Willard Thorp, a leading scholar of American literature, among whose editions, though later, was *A Southern Reader* (New York, 1955). The Thorps lived for a while across Nassau Street from Allen Tate and Caroline Gordon in Princeton. This may help to explain Margaret Thorp's interest in the South, though scarcely in McCord, whom Tate and Gordon seem never to have mentioned, at least in print. See Thomas Daniel Young and Elizabeth Sarcone, eds., *The Lytle-Tate Letters: The Correspondence of Andrew Lytle and Allen Tate* (Jackson, Miss., 1987), p. 216.

22. "Altogether Doric: Louisa S. McCord," in Thorp, *Female Persuasion,* pp. 179–214. Thorp also wrote the sketch of McCord in *Notable American Women* 2:450–52.

23. Pp. 189–95.

War era was dominant, South Carolina had been something of a joke, the lunatic sponsor of secession, a special "problem" which it might require Freudians to understand.[24] It was easy to spot such interpreters; they were fond of quoting James Louis Petigru's tart observation, during the secession crisis, that "South Carolina is too small to be a Republic, and too large to be an insane asylum."[25] Even William Freehling, whose 1966 study of nullification dragged South Carolina out of its backwater and into a position of prominence in American historical literature, was not innocent of such a standpoint.[26] In time, however, partly under the influence of Eugene Genovese, it came to seem that the antebellum South was not unhinged but all too rational about its interests. South Carolinians, led by Calhoun, with their abundance of writings proved especially useful for understanding the self-awareness of Southern culture. So South Carolina attracted a remarkable number of interesting historians, more so perhaps than any other antebellum Southern state, not even excluding Virginia.[27] These writers, sometimes outsiders, had the opportunity to build upon a rich tradition of local history, whose most professional and graceful exponent has been George Rogers.[28] In turn, South Carolinian texts began to be republished, among which *Mary Chesnut's Civil War* was preeminent, in which Louisa McCord plays no small

24. James M. Banner, "The Problem of South Carolina," in Stanley Elkins and Eric McKitrick, eds., *The Hofstadter Aegis: A Memorial* (New York, 1974), pp. 60–93; see also Steven A. Channing, *Crisis of Fear: Secession in South Carolina* (New York, 1970).

25. Quoted in Sally Edwards, *The Man Who Said No* (New York, 1970), p. 164.

26. William W. Freehling, *Prelude to Civil War: The Nullification Controversy in South Carolina, 1816–1836* (New York, 1966).

27. A not-exhaustive list could include Drew Gilpin Faust, *James Henry Hammond and the Old South: A Design for Mastery* (Baton Rouge, La., 1982); Charles Joyner, *Down by the Riverside: A South Carolina Slave Community* (Urbana, Ill., 1984); Michael O'Brien, *A Character of Hugh Legaré* (Knoxville, Tenn., 1985); Orville V. Burton, *In My Father's House Are Many Mansions: Family and Community in Edgefield, South Carolina* (Chapel Hill, N.C., 1985); William H. Pease and Jane H. Pease, *The Web of Progress: Private Values and Public Styles in Boston and Charleston, 1828–1843* (New York, 1985); James Oscar Farmer, Jr., *The Metaphysical Confederacy: James Henley Thornwell and the Synthesis of Southern Values* (Macon, Ga., 1986); Michael O'Brien and David Moltke-Hansen, eds., *Intellectual Life in Antebellum Charleston* (Knoxville, Tenn., 1986); Theodore Rosengarten, *Tombee: Portrait of a Cotton Planter* (New York, 1986); Lacy K. Ford, Jr., *Origins of Southern Radicalism: The South Carolina Upcountry, 1800–1860* (New York, 1988); Peter A. Coclanis, *The Shadow of a Dream: Economic Life and Death in the South Carolina Low Country, 1670–1920* (New York, 1989); Rachel N. Klein, *Unification of a Slave State: The Rise of the Planter Class in the South Carolina Backcountry, 1760–1808* (Chapel Hill, N.C., 1990); Arthur H. Shaffer, *To Be an American: David Ramsay and the Making of the American Consciousness* (Columbia, S.C., 1991); Barbara L. Bellows, *Benevolence among Slaveholders: Assisting the Poor in Charleston, 1670–1860* (Baton Rouge, La., 1993).

28. A worthy tribute is David R. Chesnutt and Clyde N. Wilson, eds., *The Meaning of South Carolina History: Essays in Honor of George C. Rogers, Jr.* (Columbia, S.C., 1991).

role.[29] In time, South Carolina began to loom large in more general studies of the South.[30] Amid all this, the name of Louisa McCord began to be bandied about.

Like the literary critics, their contemporaries, the older generation of Southern intellectual historians had shown little awareness of McCord. She did not appear in Clement Eaton's early writing, though he gave her about a page in *The Mind of the Old South* (1967).[31] She was entirely absent from Jesse Carpenter's 1930 study of Southern political thought and mentioned only once in William Sumner Jenkins' influential 1935 book on proslavery thought. Rollin Osterweis and William R. Taylor were silent about her existence.[32] Even some of the new intellectual historians seem initially to have been oblivious.[33] In fact, I seem to have been the first modern intellectual historian to reprint anything by McCord, when in 1982 I edited her "Enfranchisement of Woman" in an anthology of antebellum writings by Southern intellectuals.[34] That I had spent several months at the University of South Carolina, was beginning a biography of Hugh Legaré, had a broader interest in Southern thought, and was among those who had just noticed the efflorescence of women's history helps to explain why McCord was included.

At the same time Eugene Genovese and Elizabeth Fox-Genovese began

29. See also, for example, Carol Bleser, ed., *The Hammonds of Redcliffe* (New York, 1981), and *Secret and Sacred;* Ward W. Briggs, Jr., *The Letters of Basil Lanneau Gildersleeve* (Baltimore, 1987); Richard J. Calhoun, ed., *Witness to Sorrow: The Antebellum Autobiography of William J. Grayson* (Columbia, S.C., 1990); Rayburn S. Moore, ed., *A Man of Letters in the Nineteenth-Century South: Selected Letters of Paul Hamilton Hayne* (Baton Rouge, La., 1982). There is also the multivolume edition of the Calhoun Papers, now under the editorship of Clyde N. Wilson.

30. For example, Drew Gilpin Faust, *A Sacred Circle: The Dilemma of the Intellectual in the Old South, 1840–1860* (Baltimore, 1977); Steven M. Stowe, *Intimacy and Power in the Old South: Ritual in the Lives of the Planters* (Baltimore, 1987); Kenneth M. Greenberg, *Masters and Statesmen: The Political Culture of American Slavery* (Baltimore, 1985); Eugene D. Genovese, *The Slaveholders' Dilemma: Freedom and Progress in Southern Conservative Thought, 1820–1860* (Columbia, S.C., 1992). Both the authors of a recent textbook on Southern history began as historians of South Carolina; see William J. Cooper, Jr., and Thomas E. Terrill, *The American South: A History* (New York, 1991).

31. Pp. 300–301.

32. Jenkins, *Pro-Slavery Thought in the Old South,* p. 114. See Jesse T. Carpenter, *The South as a Conscious Minority, 1789–1861: A Study in Political Thought* (New York, 1930); Rollin G. Osterweis, *Romanticism and Nationalism in the Old South* (New Haven, 1949); William R. Taylor, *Cavalier and Yankee: The Old South and American National Character* (New York, 1961).

33. There is nothing in Faust, *A Sacred Circle,* in John McCardell, *The Idea of a Southern Nation: Southern Nationalists and Southern Nationalism, 1830–1860* (New York, 1979), or in Allen Kaufman, *Capitalism, Slavery, and Republican Values: American Political Economists, 1819–1848* (Austin, Tex., 1982).

34. O'Brien, *All Clever Men,* pp. 17–20, 337–56.

to notice her, at first as a political economist. In 1984 they discussed her in a general essay on slavery and Southern political economists.[35] Fox-Genovese, in particular, made McCord peculiarly central to her important 1988 study of antebellum Southern women; in it can be found the most extensive and thoughtful analysis of her to date. Fox-Genovese's McCord is a representative woman, the shrewdest female intellectual of her culture, whose writings can be said to have laid bare the presumptions of her race, gender, and class in the Old South.[36]

From the neglect so marked in 1920, we have come to the point where Louisa McCord seems indispensable to understanding, not only the South, but even American culture.[37] A recent anthology of *The American Intellectual Tradition* puts her in the company of Jonathan Edwards, Margaret Fuller, Abraham Lincoln, and other luminaries; among Southerners before the Civil War, she is ranked with Thomas Jefferson, George Mason, James Madison, Sarah Grimké, John C. Calhoun, George Fitzhugh, and Frederick Douglass. It is claimed for her that she was "the most intellectually influential female author in the Old South and the only woman in antebellum America to write extensively about political economy and social theory."[38]

And yet, to this point, an absurdly tiny amount of Louisa McCord's writings has reached the public domain. This deficiency is swiftly, comprehensively remedied by this edition. All that she wrote, public and private, which a present and patient scholarship can discover and illuminate, will be available for readers to use as they will. Seldom does an author step from obscurity to daylight with such abruptness. Usually, there has been a volume or two, several anthologized essays, the old edition of selected works done by an acolyte, something in an Everyman edition or the World's Classics that turns up in a used bookstore; something usually botched, but something. Eventually, a comprehensive edition is undertaken. This has not been Louisa McCord's fate. Though others have talked about her, Louisa McCord has been, in effect, silent since her death in 1879. Now she will talk again. McCord the poet and dramatist, whom the late nineteenth century favored, will be reunited with McCord the social thinker, whom our own age has preferred.

35. "Slavery, Economic Development, and the Law," a lecture first given in 1983. McCord is absent from Fox-Genovese and Genovese, *Fruits of Merchant Capital: Slavery and Bourgeois Property in the Rise and Expansion of Capitalism* (New York, 1983), and does not seem to occur anywhere in Genovese's earlier work.

36. Fox-Genovese, *Within the Plantation Household.*

37. McCord has informed Fox-Genovese's analysis of modern American feminism: see her *Feminism without Illusions.*

38. Hollinger and Capper, *American Intellectual Tradition* 1:375–87. This anthology reprints "Enfranchisement of Woman."

Reading it all, as I have in the 1,400-odd pages of manuscript that will be transformed into two volumes, I can see we have understood some things clearly, but much else in error. Her story, it turns out, has been plagued by gossip set down as history. Many secondary accounts have built upon other secondary accounts, so that mistakes have accumulated and been perpetuated. Lounsbury has returned to the original sources, when they can be found, so that his Chronology of her life is the first accurate ordering of her biography. He has established many facts about her European travels, her Civil War, Canadian exile, and final years. We now know, for example, that she herself published *My Dreams,* not, as family legend had it, her husband without her knowledge. Lounsbury offers more accurate information on her financial affairs, including the circumstances and timing of her acquisition of Lang Syne plantation, and a firmer understanding that her marriage was not necessarily a happy one, from the evidence of both her writings and collateral testimony. His patient bibliographical research shows that, contrary to the conventional wisdom, the period of her authorship was not coterminous with her marriage. Further, it is evident how tangled and bitter were the affairs of the Cheves family. There is an astonishing sequence of letters, recounting her father Langdon Cheves' illness, senescence, and death, which cruelly lays bare the savage indignity sufferable by even a powerful woman in a patriarchal society. Much evidence has been lost forever, much will never be known, but this is what we can now know.

Above all, of course, we can read what she wrote and listen to her voice. The scale and extent of her oeuvre are the chief surprise. Over the years, but piecemeal, I had thought I knew what she had done; I can see I had underestimated her. These will be two substantial volumes. She was more experimental in genre than had been evident, at least to me. She tried her hand at most things, poetry, drama, biography, and social criticism. She was, in addition, a vigorous letter writer, often betraying a vulnerability previously unsuspected. I was misled by connecting her too rigorously to her husband, David James McCord, whose interests focused on the law and political economy. I was too much drawn by the pretty image that they had identical desks ranged around the fireplace at Lang Syne plantation. I once thought this Browning-like, but this was wrong.[39] In fact, her writings and interests ranged far beyond his. At the moment, because historians have paid more attention to her social criticism than recent literary critics have to her verse, it is easier to be confident about the significance of the social and

39. O'Brien, *All Clever Men,* p. 338. For a reading of McCord that stresses the strains within her marriage and explores unexpected points of sympathy with Northern feminists, see Eacker, "'A Dangerous Inmate' of the Antebellum South," forthcoming.

political writings that occupy the first volume of this edition. The second volume, which will contain *My Dreams* and *Caius Gracchus,* as well as her biographical writings and letters, will make possible a new estimate of her belletristic accomplishment. My guess is that we have erred in elevating the former too much above the latter. Words interested Louisa McCord; she tried to see what they could do; she had skills beyond political invective. Her editor is a Canadian and a student of—among other things—classical and Renaissance rhetoric. That he should have been drawn into a respect for McCord, sufficient to sustain him through his long task, may be an indication both that her reputation begins to reach beyond scholars of the South and that a mind accustomed to Suetonius and Tacitus can find satisfaction in her literary accomplishment.[40] But these are things that critics, in the convenience of their armchairs, will be able to measure.

To give Louisa McCord back to the world of intellectual discourse, as I began by observing, is to offer a vexed legacy. A conservative, slaveholding antifeminist is scarcely the woman for everyone in our times. The historian with an eye on the mid-nineteenth century need not be concerned by this. But her complexity was great, the legacy yet to be probed in all its angular sharpness. As there were, there will be disagreements about her. Now as then, we may be confident that she can hold her own. Louisa McCord is no straw woman, to be dismissed casually. Even the most hostile may acknowledge an intellect worthy of refutation. And, beyond the political icon, the representative she-devil, they will be able to see Louisa McCord the woman, troubled but determined. It turns out she secreted enough cornmeal and bacon to see her through.

Michael O'Brien
Chair of the Editorial Board
Southern Texts Society

40. Richard C. Lounsbury, *The Arts of Suetonius: An Introduction* (New York, 1987). His first interest in McCord was prompted by a study of classical influences in Charleston's culture; see Lounsbury, "*Ludibria Rerum Mortalium.*"

Chronology

1810 Born December 3, in Charleston, South Carolina, the second daughter and fourth of the fourteen children of Langdon Cheves (born September 17, 1776) and Mary Elizabeth Dulles Cheves (born May 27, 1789); is named Louisa Susanna after two daughters of her mother's aunt, Ann Heatly Reid Lovell, all of whose children died young. The son of Alexander Cheves, who emigrated from Scotland to Charleston in 1762 and became a trader to the Cherokees, Loyalist exile, and merchant in Charleston, Langdon Cheves is a prosperous lawyer, former attorney general of South Carolina, and lately elected to the United States Congress. Mary Cheves' father is a merchant in Charleston (he retires to Philadelphia in 1812), her mother a daughter of William Heatly, a planter with extensive holdings in St. Matthews Parish, about fifty miles north of the city.

1814 Langdon Cheves, now Speaker of the House of Representatives, returns from refuge in Germantown, Pennsylvania, to Washington, burned by the British in late August, where Cheves' congressional colleague William Lowndes, weary of political speculations, finds relief in Mary Cheves' parlor and "Louisa and Sophia propose no projects of a bank."[1]

1. Lowndes to Elizabeth Brewton Pinckney Lowndes, Nov. 6, 1814, William Lowndes Papers, LC.

1819 Langdon Cheves is appointed president of the Bank of the United States by President James Monroe. He moves his family to Philadelphia, where LSM and her elder sister Sophia are sent to William Grimshaw's school for young ladies, among whom LSM first confronts hostility to slavery; the sisters' manner of dress, "dark merino dresses high necked and long sleeved, and high, heavy, ugly boots," excites disdainful comment in contrast to the lighter fabrics, lower necklines, short sleeves, and slippers favored by their schoolmates—until their credit is repaired by a visit to the school from Mary Cheves arrayed in the height of fashion, her golden hair crowned by a chinchilla cap, a chinchilla pelisse enfolded about a frock of the most delicate muslin.[2] LSM studies French with Charles Picot and his wife, émigrés from France. According to family tradition, has been detected hiding behind the door, taking notes and working problems, while her brothers are being tutored in mathematics in the next room; her father therefore has decided that henceforth she should be instructed also in subjects taught more usually to boys.

1822–29 The architect William Strickland builds for Langdon Cheves a house on Washington Square in Philadelphia. Three stories high and of conspicuous splendor, it is soon known for its hospitality and for the brilliance of its guests, among them Hugh Swinton Legaré. When appointment to a commission investigating rival claims under the Treaty of Ghent takes Cheves more and more to Washington, he establishes his family on an estate of 73 acres, soon enlarged to 194, just outside Lancaster, Pennsylvania, where Lancaster's congressman, James Buchanan, is a frequent guest.

1829 The Cheves family returns to South Carolina (December). After sister Sophia is married on December 1, 1830, and because the health of Mary Cheves, never strong, is being enfeebled by her numerous confinements, LSM assumes more and more the management of the family household, which from 1830 begins to spend its summers, and from 1832 the whole year, at Pendleton in northwestern South Carolina, a village popular for its cool breezes and distance from the malaria of

2. Smythe, p. 100.

the coast. There LSM and her mother join the Social Library Society.

1833 Langdon Cheves purchases 1,530 acres adjacent to the plantation of LSM's sister Sophia and her husband Charles Haskell near Abbeville; this land is bestowed upon LSM, who brings to it thirty-eight slaves given her in 1830 by her grandmother Sophia Heatly Dulles and entrusts it to her brother-in-law's management. At Pendleton, LSM is set by her mother to making clothes for the domestic staff: "Louisa who had never before had any such business to attend to sat to work and cut and made a frock Coat (they call [them] Jackson Coats) and pantaloons in a day, sometimes 2 Coats a day and sometimes more[,] and the work I will answer for not to give way before the cloth. [I]n fact she made all the clothes for the men and children including shirts to all[,] with a few days work from an old woman hardly worth counting."[3]

1834 Near Portman Shoals, eight miles west of Pendleton, on the Seneca River, Langdon Cheves builds an ample, rambling house "to hold all the family and[,] in case of need, a dozen or two more." It is thirty-five miles to the Haskell plantation. "John and Louisa came down on horse back, and stayed with us for ten days. They both looked very well, and Louisa seemed quite pleased with their quiet winter in Pendleton"—quiet, but not idle, John teaching Latin to their younger brother Charles, LSM instructing Charles and younger sister Anna in English, French, writing, and arithmetic, and having charge of the illness of a servant whose mother has just died: "L[ouisa] is," her grandmother observes, "an uncommon Girl[;] I dont know how the [family] would make out without her."[4] From Mary Cheves' aunt Ann Lovell, who dies on October 16, Langdon Cheves inherits large properties, among them the plantation Home Place, now renamed Lang Syne, in Orangeburg County near Fort Motte, about thirty-five miles

3. Mary Cheves to Ann Heatly Reid Lovell, Nov. 28, 1833, Ann Heatly Reid Lovell Papers, Duke.

4. Sophia Cheves Haskell to Ann Heatly Reid Lovell [Spring 1834], ibid.; Sophia Dulles to Joseph Heatly Dulles, June 21, 1834, Langdon Cheves I Papers, SCHS.

south of Columbia. Cheves intends Lang Syne for his eventual retirement.

1835 Joins the family of James Hamilton, Jr., nullifier governor of South Carolina (1830–32), for a summer tour to New York City, Newport, and Ballston Spa, near Saratoga Springs.

1836 Amid plans to travel, with "Louisa as my companion," to seek medical advice in Philadelphia, thence to "the Falls, the Lakes, Canadas, etc. etc. . . . and thus dispose of the summer as much to her gratification as possible, for she did not reap much last summer," Mary Cheves dies at Lang Syne (April 5). LSM remains in charge of the plantation's management. "I feel as I wander about the house and have to take her place in a thousand things as if I were doing wrong all the time."[5]

1839 With her father, older brother Alexander, and sister Anna, spends the summer at resorts in western Virginia. "I have surmounted a summer at the Springs, which thank Heaven *est finie* and I am again released f[ro]m playing belle, which, nolens volens, seems some how or other to be my destiny when I go into company. Next time I go to matronise Miss Anna in the gay world, I vow it shall be in a cap, or some such distinguishing mark of old age. . . . I'll pin a piece of paper with '*aged twenty-nine*,' on my shoulder, and if that don't scare off the young seventeen-year-olders who come to flirt with me, the dear knows what will." At Asheville, North Carolina, during the journey home, the Cheves family finds Langdon Cheves' former pupil and old friend Robert Young Hayne mortally ill. "We staid to see him die" (September 24).[6] On Christmas Eve, LSM's younger brother Langdon Cheves, Jr., marries Charlotte McCord, eldest of the eleven children of David James McCord. Recently a widower, his wife having died in early August,[7] McCord (born January 13, 1797), a former newspaper editor and member of the state legislature,

5. Mary Cheves to Alexander Cheves, Feb. 26, 1836, Langdon Cheves I Papers, SCHS; LSM to Sophia Cheves Haskell, April 8 [1836].

6. LSM to Langdon Cheves, Jr., Portman Shoals, Oct. 7, 1839.

7. "Mrs. McCord is dead. She died in confinement. Poor children. I pity Charlotte." Francis Lieber to Matilda Lieber, Aug. 22, 1839, Francis Lieber Papers, SCL.

is a lawyer and president of the Bank of the State of South Carolina in Columbia, renowned for his fiery temper and ardent politics at least since his nullifier days.

1840 Is married to David James McCord (May 20); held at Lang Syne, the wedding, as sister Anna, baffled of beaux, complains, is "about as quiet an affair as could well take place."[8] There are three children of the marriage: Langdon Cheves (born April 17, 1841, in apartments above his father's bank in Columbia), Hannah Cheves (born September 18, 1843, at Fortress, a Sandhill village preferred by those summering from Fort Motte), and Louisa Rebecca Hayne (born August 10, 1845, in Pendleton). Son Cheves, "a fine intelligent lad, but whose health has from an infant been uncertain, and her greatest cause of anxiety,"[9] is stricken with a disease of the hip for his first two years and must use crutches for some years thereafter; his suffering, LSM thinks later, contributes to the firmness and composure characteristic of him throughout his life. LSM supervises her daughters' education carefully, in Columbia sending them three afternoons a week to the home of a Frenchwoman for practice in conversation, herself daily reading aloud to them in French as well as English, and at Lang Syne receiving regular shipments from John Pennington's bookshop in Philadelphia, many of the books ordered for the children being in French or German.

1841 Passing in their carriage through Lexington, South Carolina, the McCords recognize Matilda Lieber, a friend from Columbia, enjoying on a piazza the cool air of an August morning: "I was much pleased in having a momentary chat with Mr. and Mrs. McCord who with their infant were on their way to Pendleton, she looking miserable[;] she has been in very bad health."[10] With his family gathered at Lang Syne, Langdon Cheves divides his property among his children (November). LSM, asked to cede the land near Abbeville given to her in

8. Anna Cheves to Anna Dulles, May 24, 1840, Dulles-Cheves-McCord-Lovell Papers, SCHS.

9. Sophia Cheves Haskell to Eleuthera du Pont, Nov. 11, 1856, Langdon Cheves III Papers, SCHS.

10. Matilda Lieber to Francis Lieber, Aug. 5, 1841, Francis Lieber Papers, Huntington.

1833, receives the title to Lang Syne. Its library—located in a separate building until, in 1852, it is transferred into a room added to the main house—becomes the McCords' workroom, their identical writing tables standing on either side of the fireplace. The room is plainly furnished with bookcases homemade of pine (except one, more handsome, bought by LSM for her husband) and carpets woven on the plantation, and of the books many are bound by David James McCord, who also makes frames for the engravings placed on the mantelpiece; large windows open upon trees, among them a sycamore, its base surrounded with violets, and sweetbrier and lilacs. It is an agreeable isolation. "Such is the spirit of the day, that I seem no longer to belong to the community. My only companion is my wife, whose opinions, taste, reading, and prejudices are all in my own line."[11]

1845 Edward Dagge Worthington, physician, of Sherbrooke, Quebec, traveling for his health after service in the British army and practice in Edinburgh, visits Lang Syne (November) and stays for two months, an admirer of the plantation's order and of his hostess's horsemanship. When pneumonia breaks out he accompanies LSM during her regular morning inspections of the slaves' quarters. "Then she would take me off for a gallop through the open to some high point commanding a view of the country. . . . She was a tall *queenly* woman, and a very queen at heart; motherly and kind. She treated me as though I were an over grown boy."[12]

1848–54 Period of LSM's most intense literary activity. Publications include her translation of Frédéric Bastiat's *Sophismes économiques*, published as *Sophisms of the Protective Policy* in 1848, with a foreword by David James McCord and an introductory letter by family friend Francis Lieber, professor of history and political economy at South Carolina College; a collection of poems, *My Dreams*, dedicated to her father and published in 1848; dedicated to her son, *Caius Gracchus*, a tragedy in five acts, appearing in 1851; fugitive poems contributed to Paul

11. David James McCord to William Campbell Preston, Lang Syne, May 8, 1842, Preston Family Papers, VHS.

12. Worthington (1820–95) to David Ross McCord, 1894, in *FOLS,* pp. 4–5.

Hamilton Hayne's *Southern Literary Gazette*; and essays—which quickly gain for their author a reputation for energy, hard-driving argument, and invective—published in the *Southern Quarterly Review, De Bow's Review,* and *Southern Literary Messenger.* Building upon the translation of Bastiat, the essays concerning political economy uphold its intellectual claims against what LSM identifies to be the pernicious nostrums of competitors like socialism and communism. Other essays discuss the role and place and, especially, the duty of women; and, most numerous, slavery. An embattled and resourceful sequence of these last is initiated when William Gilmore Simms, editor of the *Southern Quarterly Review,* deciding that Harriet Beecher Stowe is best answered by another woman, invites LSM to review *Uncle Tom's Cabin*, "that abominable woman's abominable book. . . . It is one mass of fanatical bitterness and foul misrepresentation wrapped in the garb of Christian Charity."[13]

1849 Builds house in Columbia on a lot of one and a half acres at the northwest corner of Pendleton and Bull streets. Lays out a handsome garden with walks and, as soon as pipes carrying water are laid down in Columbia, many fountains. The house stands across the street from South Carolina College, of which David James McCord has served three four-year terms as a trustee (1829–40) and old friend William Campbell Preston is now president; the McCord family quickly becomes part of college life.

1850 Spends summer with family and brother Hayne at Narragansett Bay, Rhode Island; a journey to Niagara is cut short when in Boston son Cheves is struck by a heavy wagon and temporarily lamed. Making a tour of the Southern states with a wealthy friend also recuperating from illness, James Burrill Angell, lately graduated from Brown University in Providence, is entertained to tea by LSM in Columbia (late autumn), who, although "extremely cordial," tells her young guests, "We ought to fight you of the North."[14] On December

13. LSM to Mary Dulles, Oct. 9, 1852.

14. "We pray for the independence of the South, at any sacrifice of existing conditions and relations, as the greatest blessing that heaven could confer upon our beloved and almost

19 the two Northerners travel from Charleston to Lang Syne to spend the Christmas holidays with the McCords; the prosperity (Lang Syne now has 137 slaves), meticulous management, elegant mansion, and splendid grounds are recorded by Angell in his *Reminiscences*, published in 1912.[15]

1851 At White Sulphur Springs in western Virginia, author of *Swallow Barn* John Pendleton Kennedy encounters "several South Carolinians . . . ridiculously distempered with nullification and Disunion." David James McCord, predicting civil war, "is the most moderate of them—though I am told his wife, who has lately written a tragedy called 'Gracchus,' is not." At Red Sweet Springs, LSM meets diarist Jane Caroline North. "Mrs. M'Cord paid us a visit this afternoon. Aunt Harrie did not see her as she was lying down, with a headache—She made me quite a long visit—she is a masculine clever person, with the most mannish attitudes and gestures, but interesting and very entertaining. Mrs. [Langdon] Cheves[, Jr.,] is her step daughter and sister in law—her children are made to call her Aunt, Mrs. M'Cord not believing in the relationship of half sister—so I was told at least."[16]

1852 Summer finds the McCords restless in Columbia, the campus nearly deserted, the town emptied of most of its society. "I am glad to hear that you are all enjoying yourselves so well at Nar[r]agansett. What would I not give for a walk on the beach . . . with my brats tumbling along before me[?] I am almost sick of this horrid little place Columbia. I hope that Mr. McC. will get his fill of it some day. For surely I cannot see where the society he dreams of is. For myself, I do not care a fig for the society, but I long for a climate where a family can keep healthy and grow strong." Son Cheves' state of health continues worrisome; David James McCord "certainly does not look well, but I cannot see what is the matter with him. I

prostrate country." Chap. 5, "Diversity of the Races; Its Bearing upon Negro Slavery" (published in April 1851), p. 174.

15. Pp. 56–61.

16. Kennedy, Journal, 7 (July 14, 1851–June 1, 1852): entry of July 29, 1851, John Pendleton Kennedy Papers, Peabody Institute, Baltimore; North, "Journal of an Excursion to the Virginia Springs, No. 2," entry of Sept. 12, 1851, in O'Brien, *An Evening When Alone,* p. 174.

verily believe he is just sick, for want of company and a little excitement of some kind or another. He will have it that this is a charming place; but apparently it is charming for me to stay in, and for him to go away."[17]

c. 1853 Has portrait painted by William Harrison Scarborough, a Tennessean, who, having moved to South Carolina in 1830 and married to advantage, has settled in Columbia in 1843 (he is LSM's neighbor in 1865). The portrait does not find favor with the sitter, in general unsympathetic to representations of herself, on one occasion standing by, and smiling at the wreckage afterward, when her children toss out of a window a bust of her by Clark Mills, "a humbug,—a mere plaster-dauber, too ignorant even to be called an imposter."[18]

1855 Sally Baxter of Boston and New York visits Lang Syne (April): friend and correspondent of William Makepeace Thackeray, she has met the McCords while a guest of Francis and Matilda Lieber in Columbia and is full of praise for Lang Syne, which "is considered rather a model place even in South Carolina where there are so many fine ones," and commends to her father LSM's review of *Uncle Tom's Cabin*. "You must understand that the Cheves and McCord family is as much the stronghold of the slavery party as the Adams faction is of the Abolitionists. Mrs. McCord is hotly engaged in the strife and almost all her feeling and intellect seem to be expended on that one topic, and she and her husband warmly espouse the cause in every paper and periodical to which they can get admission."[19] Death of David James McCord (May 15). "Mamma and we little girls did not go to the church, but I recollect her taking us by the hands and walking very fast down to the bottom of the long garden path, where we could watch the procession going down the street and out of sight round the corner to Trinity Church."[20] Adducing LSM's considerable property held in her own right, David James

17. LSM to Mary Dulles, Aug. 25, 1852.

18. LSM to Hiram Powers, July 29, 1860.

19. Sally Baxter to George Baxter, April 15, 1855, in Hampton, *A Divided Heart,* pp. 20–23.

20. Smythe, p. 19.

McCord's will (dated February 21 the year previous) leaves nothing to his wife or to his three children by her. Francis Lieber reports to his son Oscar frictions between LSM and her stepchildren, two of whom refuse to call on her after their father's death; it is said that she means to cheat them of their inheritance. Oscar Lieber replies that "Langdon Cheves[, Jr.,] regards her as insane—the most charitable opinion that can be held of her actions" and, remembering David James McCord's kindness to him, concludes: "Poor old man, to think that he should have been so utterly without a friend in whom he was permitted to confide in all things. She must be a wicked woman indeed!"[21] After her husband's death LSM's health becomes cause for worry: in particular, symptoms of severe eyestrain grow more troublesome. Traveling to Philadelphia, loses her wedding ring into the sea.[22]

1856–57 Langdon Cheves has in 1852 retired to a house in the Sandhills near Columbia, convenient for visits, where he indulges his McCord grandchildren. Declining health in body and, more, in mind, and a stroke suffered after the death of his son Charles at the age of thirty, now require him, even against his will, to be removed to LSM's house in the city. "It is very painful and makes me feel like a jailer." Despite appeals to relatives, in particular to her brother Langdon Cheves, Jr., who has charge of their father's financial affairs, LSM is left largely alone to care for the old man. In the garden and near the greenhouses and their flowers beloved of his grandson Cheves McCord, LSM causes to be built a cottage of four rooms and a piazza: intended originally as a refuge "to go to if needed and to hide my children when he is as he has lately been," it is converted into private quarters for her father.[23] Impelled by medical warnings that her eyestrain may result in

21. Lieber to his parents, May 31, 1855, Francis Lieber Papers, SCL.

22. "The summer after my father's death she was sitting on the steamer with her hand hanging over the rail, and the finger being very thin her wedding ring slipped off and was lost. I remember the look on her face as it went." Smythe, p. 76.

23. LSM to Langdon Cheves, Jr., Jan. 16, March 7, 1856. "[Later in the war] fuel too began to fail—coal was not to be had, and with the scarcity of men and horses it was hard to get wood and what we got was green and worthless. One by one fires were given up and we went about much of the time in a striking costume of old faded calico dresses, and a blanket shawl pinned over our shoulders. . . . The little coal we had was saved and doled

blindness and that her son's vision appears to show incipient cataracts, and although she must call upon the reluctant help of her brother Langdon to assume the care of their father during her absence, LSM takes her children to spend the summer at Narragansett Bay, joined by her Dulles relations from Philadelphia; surprising the others present, breaks down and weeps at scenes of Charles Dickens' *David Copperfield* being read aloud in the family circle. Health not improving, travels with children to the White Mountains in New Hampshire; with the coming of winter, worsening eyesight constrains her to pass her days in a darkened room.[24] A Scotsman, his melodious conversation and love of reading soon making him a favorite of the family, is employed as a nurse replacing Langdon Cheves' servants, whose influence LSM suspects to encourage her father's agitation of mind, their behavior grown more unruly after their master has affirmed a desire to emancipate them; their leader is arrested, then sent down to Charleston to be sold out of the state "and in such manner as to prevent his return. This is a painful business to me, but my life or that of my children may depend upon proper action and I cannot hesitate." Her brother Hayne (born 1829), for many months ill of tuberculosis—"he belonged to me so young and so long, I cannot but feel that it is my child"—has died in Florence (August 14, 1856), news kept from their father, his mind collapsing into senile dementia; he dies June 26, 1857. A death mask is made by a workman summoned from Charleston by Langdon Cheves, Jr.; LSM never sees it. Besides certain residuary property to be shared equally with her sisters and posses-

out to keep alive the flowers in the greenhouse. They were so associated with your Uncle Cheves who was a great lover of flowers that we could not bear to let them go. After his death his man Tom returned to his old place as gardener and through all the trouble the garden and greenhouse were kept up as though their young master and lover were expected to come back to them. But at last the day came when Tom had to say that there was only coal enough to make the fire once more. It was a bitter cold evening and I well remember the look on Mamma's face and on poor Tom's as she said, 'Well, Tom, keep it up as long as you can.' The fire was lit but burned out before morning. . . . The doors of the two greenhouses were locked and we left them like graves. I never entered them again." Smythe, p. 55.

24. "I believe I wrote to you of Louisa. . . . Her health is not good, and her eyes are so much affected in some way, that she is entirely prohibited the use of them; not even to expose them to a strong light, night or day. It is a great trial, but the danger is so great, that she submits I believe in great measure to these directions." Sophia Cheves Haskell to Eleuthera du Pont, March 24, 1857, Langdon Cheves III Papers, SCHS.

sion of those slaves hitherto given to her conditionally, her father's will bequeaths to her "my house servant Priscilla, also, my house and the land whereon it stands in the Sand-Hills near Columbia, with my Library, Carriage and Horses, and the Household and Kitchen Furniture." In the summer of 1857, again in search of health, with her children LSM visits White Sulphur Springs, Sweet Springs, and Old Sweet Springs in Virginia, among her fellow guests being John Slidell and Judah P. Benjamin, and Francis W. Pickens in pursuit of Lucy Holcombe. At the end of the year, her "eyes continue almost useless."[25]

1858–59 A quarrel over the paternal estate between brothers Langdon and John and sister Sophia and her husband Charles Haskell begets ill will and resentments crowned by a lawsuit before the equity court of appeals in Charleston (May–June); LSM, although "quite willing to appear anywhere and do what is right in spite of blind eyes and straw flats pulled over them," is caught in the middle of the dispute.[26] Upon urgent advice from Dr. Eli Geddings, professor of surgery at the Medical College of South Carolina, on July 7 LSM sails from New York for Europe, on the paddle steamship *Persia* into Liverpool, accompanied by son Cheves and daughter Louisa and paying the expenses of her personal physician, John W. Powell, to attend the family. Tours Britain and Ireland, including Aberdeen, where she locates some Cheves connections, and the Orkneys, where at an inn daughter Louisa sees for the first time, and reads, *Uncle Tom's Cabin*.[27] In Paris, consults Jules Sichel and other ophthalmologists, who prescribe a course of treatment and the nurse of Empress Eugénie. Albeit a marked improvement follows in her son's health and her own,

25. LSM to Langdon Cheves, Jr., Dec. 18, Jan. 25, 1856; Langdon Cheves, "Last Will and Testament," Nov. 6, 1854, Langdon Cheves I Papers, SCHS; LSM to Langdon Cheves, Jr., Dec. 26, 1857.

26. LSM to Langdon Cheves, Jr., Feb. 5, 1858.

27. "Mrs McCord writes me from London discont[ent]ed with every thing even the climate of London!!! She has seen lots of sights[,] all Ireland Scotland and England, and poor lady it is all vanity and vexation of spirits. The garden culture of England has not enough green to show it off[;] Poets Corner at Westminster is a dirty hole,—how can England do any thing having no negro slavery[?]" William Campbell Preston to Francis Lieber, Oct. 20, 1858, Francis Lieber Papers, SCL.

from now on LSM must wear specially tinted spectacles. Rents an apartment on the Champs Elysées, engages two servants, a coach and pair with coachman, and a music master for the children, and attends the opera. Enters society, where an acquaintance from school days is the Princess Murat;[28] and John Smith and Caroline Martha Hampton Preston, friends from Columbia now resident in Rome, and Dr. Alfred Stillé and his wife, cousins from Philadelphia, are visiting also. Is entertained frequently at the house of the Virginian John Young Mason, American minister plenipotentiary to France, and is presented with son Cheves at the court of Emperor Napoleon III.[29] In late winter, travels in leisurely fashion to Italy. Arrives in Rome in time for Carnival. Meets Cardinal Bofondi(?),[30] who assists the McCord party in the minutiae of sight-seeing, among these the loan of a burly Irish priest to keep at bay the goat-skinned inhabitants of the Campagna; interview with the papal secretary of state, Cardinal Antonelli. Is granted a private audience with Pius IX. At the beginning of Lent, leaves Rome, and travels to Naples and in southern Italy, and ascends Vesuvius, before returning to Rome for Holy Week and happening upon John Taylor Rhett, nephew of Robert Barnwell Rhett, among the crush of tourists surging up the marble staircase into the Sistine Chapel for *Misereres*. In Florence, sits to sculptor Hiram Powers, who also entertains the McCord family at his home, once a monastery,

28. Carolina Georgina Fraser, daughter of Thomas Fraser, a commander of British and Loyalist troops in South Carolina during the Revolution, and Ann Loughton Smith Fraser, descended of one of Charleston's oldest families, was married in 1831 to Lucien Murat, then living in exile at Bordentown, N.J., second son of Joachim Murat and Napoleon Bonaparte's youngest sister Caroline, fleetingly king and queen of Naples.

29. "I was delighted at seeing my Mother for the first time in full evening dress. She wore a beautiful black moiré antique dress . . . trimmed with a profusion of black lace, some of which I have. It was in the days of hoop-skirts and the skirt of the dress was trimmed down the sides with panels of lace flounces, headed with ruchings of pansy colored ribbon. The neck was low, which rather shocked me, and was surrounded with a fall of lace and beautiful velvet pansies. Her hair was dressed too with pansies, and as I remember she was a splendid looking woman. . . . I remember being quite impressed with the fact that Mme. Poron [the dressmaker], who usually 'received' at home in state and superintended the work of her assistants, came in person to see *this* dress put on. I can see my dear young brother still, in his court dress, with his sword at his side, practicing court bows in our parlor, before they set off for the presentation and ball at the Tuileries." Smythe, p. 27.

30. See app. 4.

which, as he informs LSM, is haunted by pertinacious monks (late April–May). With Napoleon III moving his armies into Italy against an Austrian invasion of Piedmont, LSM returns to Paris by way of Marseilles; thence to London, where she sees Queen Victoria on her way to open Parliament. Sets out for the Netherlands and Germany, this part of the journey abbreviated by an ankle sprained at Schlangenbad, near Wiesbaden. Tours Switzerland and the Alps: Lucerne, the Rigi, Grimsel Pass, Interlaken, Geneva, Chamonix, Bern. After a third visit to Paris, departs for home on the *Persia*, out of Liverpool, being greeted as she disembarks in New York (October 26) by news of John Brown's raid on Harpers Ferry, Virginia. In Columbia the McCords find their house "in beautiful order—the silver standing bright and shining on the sideboard just where Mamma had forgotten it when she went away." The "last Christmas gathering at Lang Syne" is especially resplendent and populous: LSM's uncle and aunt Dulles with their three youngest children, Haskells, Thornwells, Barnwells, Reynoldses, and visitors from the neighborhood. The library, being "big and long," is chosen to house the dancing; there is a tournament, at which LSM's nephew Alexander Haskell, mounted on a handsome and unpredictable mare, cuts a fine figure, having "borrowed from Mamma a beautiful long white ostrich plume which had belonged to her mother."[31]

1860 In January, disposed to acquiesce in whatever settlement of her father's estate her brothers and sisters and brothers-in-law may decide upon, yet "as regards negroes I cannot consent to receive any more, for I am almost out of my senses with those that I have, and with my now permanently established defective vision, am entirely unfit for learning anything about planting concerns. Those that I have now, I must keep, only till Cheves is ready (which with *his* drawbacks of vision etc. will not be for years) to take them. To embarrass myself with more would be wretchedness to them and death to me."[32] Near Cashiers, in the Blue Ridge country of western North Carolina, where, "having horses, servants, and everything

31. Smythe, pp. 38–39.
32. LSM to Langdon Cheves, Jr., Jan. 18, 1860.

with us," the McCord family reckons to spend a few weeks of the summer, daughters Hannah and Louisa fall sick of typhoid fever; soon, under the care of a physician brought from Anderson, the most accessible large town, they seem to be convalescent—a convalescence almost amiable: from Alexander Ross Taylor, master of opulent plantations near Columbia and now resident with his family about four miles away, comes a daily emissary on horseback "carrying a basket with everything in it that could be wanted for the sick or the nurses. I was just able to be lifted out of bed and laid on a lounge in the piazza, and I remember the way that piazza looked with the dishes, bottles, etc., etc., ranged along it to keep cool and fresh. Wild turkeys and pheasants mixed up with gruel, beef tea, jelly, old brandy—*everything*."[33] But Hannah suffers a relapse, is gravely ill. LSM summons from Columbia Dr. Powell, who, having assessed the danger, returns home and orders a wagon to be built with a mattress fitted into its floor. "He took his own fast horses with this wagon and, feeling that snow would soon be on the ground, and it would then be impossible to bring Hannah over this road, he took her just as she was, and made a bed in the wagon, and with Mamma holding her head and my brother seated by him, he drove at full speed forty miles over the mountains" south to Walhalla in South Carolina, where a bed with springs has been prepared in a railroad car for the rest of the journey home.[34] Anticipating secession, LSM composes songs, one to the tune of "Gaudeamus," another adapting Robert Burns' "Scots Wha Hae wi' Wallace Bled," sung by the students of South Carolina College. When word arriving from Charleston of the Ordinance of Secession is announced by the pealing of the town bell (December 20), Columbia is a frenzy of bells, cannons, clamor; LSM joins the celebrations, riding with her daughters and future daughter-in-law in her new open carriage, a Brett lined with white silk just delivered from the James B. Brewster Company in New York, its quarters hung with banners

33. Smythe, p. 40. "Yesterday was such a lucky day for my housekeeping in our hired house. Oh, ye kind Columbia folk! Mrs. Alex Taylor, née Hayne, sent me a huge bowl of yellow butter and a basket to match, of every vegetable in season. Mrs. Preston's man came with mushrooms freshly cut. And Mrs. Tom Taylor's with fine melons." *Chesnut,* p. 629 (entry of Aug. 2, 1864).

34. Smythe, p. 40.

bearing inscriptions in honor of secession. After dark, the city lit by bonfires, a crowd of merrymakers, with band, serenade the McCord house, refusing to depart until LSM makes them a speech. "We are," she writes on Christmas Eve, "in the midst of a revolution. Our spirited little State has declared its independence . . . and now waits the result. A bloodless revolution (an unheard of event in history) can scarcely be expected; and yet some of us hope that such may be. . . . Even a Woman has the right to wake up when revolution is afoot, and when our Sons (even boys) throw aside their Greek, Latin and mathematics to practice rifles and study military tactics."[35]

1861–65 During the war, becomes famous for her energy, coolheadedness, unremitting labor, and outspoken dedication to the Confederacy, as such conspicuous in the diaries of close friend Mary Chesnut. Expecting, unlike many, the conflict to be long, turns over Lang Syne to the cultivation of provisions; outfits at own expense a company of Columbia Zouaves under son Cheves' command; manages tirelessly the hospital established in buildings of South Carolina College and a ward in her own house;[36] derides profiteers, blockade-runners, fashionable ladies who suppose nursing to be an opportunity for capturing admirers, and the "drill sergeants or military old maids" masquerading as generals of the Confederacy. "Mrs. Preston and I whisper. Mrs. McCord scorns whispers."[37]

1861 Going down "to see where the company with which Cheves is, was likely to be located," arrives in jubilant Charleston "just as the white flag was raised on Fort Sumter";[38] dines that evening with Mary Chesnut (April 13). In Columbia, becomes first president of the Soldiers' Relief Association (later

35. LSM to Hiram Powers, Dec. 24, 1860.

36. "I remember once saying to my husband[,] 'St. Julien, two ladies were here today, who said they wondered at your letting Mrs. McCord manage your Hospital.' He answered abruptly, 'The more she manages the better, every bit of her that isn't enthusiasm is common sense.'" Harriott Rutledge Ravenel to Louisa McCord Smythe, Jan. 2, 1899, in *FOLS,* p. 18. The hospital in the college was set up in June 1862, intended to last the summer only, that it might receive the overflow of wounded from Charleston and the coast; in October the arrangement was renewed, and remained in force to the end of the war.

37. *Chesnut,* p. 361.

38. LSM to Langdon Cheves, Jr., April 20, 1861.

relinquishing the office when pressed by nursing duties at the college hospital) and of the Soldiers' Clothing Association (July). On October 14 son Cheves marries Charlotte Reynolds, daughter of James L. Reynolds, professor of moral philosophy and sacred literature and criticism at South Carolina College. In order to be closer to her son and other Columbia men who after the Federal attack on Port Royal (November 7) have been moved to the coast, LSM brings her family for the winter to Charleston, staying at the Charleston Hotel and later, to her daughters' consternation, at the more sumptuous, but more staid, Mills House. From the roof of the house of a Reynolds kinsman, where they have taken refuge, the McCord family watch the fire of December 11–12 destroy much of the center of the city, five churches being lost including Charleston's largest, the Cathedral of St. John and St. Finbar: its steeple, two hundred feet high, topples "in one tall column of fire, just as a pine tree cut down falls its full length."[39]

1862 In April a dispute over the naming of a new Confederate gunboat: "Dr. Gibbes—Mrs. Pickens's knight errant (knight erran*d*, odd-jobber, says Mrs. McCord) and bodyguard in one—wants to call it Lucy Holcombe. We wanted to call it Caroline, for our old darling Mrs. Preston—but after Mrs. McCord's outburst we were mum. No Lydia Languish for her. 'No Lucy Long-tongue business for me. If we are to have a female name, let it be "she-devil," for it is the devil's own work it is built to do.'"[40] LSM's nephew John Haskell is severely wounded in the arm (it must be amputated); the wife of his brother Alexander dies in childbed, wrongly convinced that her husband is dead; Edward Cheves, only son of LSM's brother John, is killed in the Seven Days while serving as an aide to General Alexander Lawton (late June). "His sister kept crying, 'Oh, mother, what shall we do—Edward is killed!' But the mother sat dead still, white as a sheet, never uttering a word or shedding a tear. . . . While Mrs. McCord was telling me this terrible trouble in her brother's family,

39. Smythe, p. 47.

40. *Chesnut,* p. 329. Lydia Languish, character in Richard Brinsley Sheridan's *The Rivals* (1775), is besotted with the romantic expectations inculcated by sentimental comedy.

someone said, 'Alex Haskell died of grief!' 'Stuff and nonsense. Now you come with your silly sentiment. Folly! If he is not wounded, he is alive. Poor John may die of that shattered arm in this hot weather. Alex will never die of a broken heart.'"[41] Son Cheves is wounded at Second Manassas (August 29). Coming to Richmond, LSM learns from McCord cousin William Porcher Miles, Charleston's representative to the Confederate Congress and chairman of its Committee on Military Affairs, that the government has appropriated all trains and suspended the granting of passports. Ignoring these obstacles, hires special train, finds her son lying among other wounded in a church at Warrenton, and takes him back to Columbia, where he responds well to his family's nursing.

1863 Having returned to active duty before his wounds are fully healed, son Cheves dies suddenly in Richmond from a head wound thought not to be serious (January 23).[42] His only child, born less than two weeks later (February 3), is named, though a daughter, Langdon Cheves McCord after her father and great-grandfather. "A gentle sad letter [came] from poor Lou to your Aunt Charlotte announcing the birth of Lottie's baby, a fine little girl. This was of course a disappointment to all especially to Aunt Louisa and Lottie. . . . I hope your Aunt will be helped to bear her trouble by the necessity of supporting and caring for the two girls now entirely dependent upon her."[43] In July, LSM's brother Langdon Cheves, Jr., and nephew Charles Haskell are killed at siege of Battery Wagner in Charleston Harbor, a second nephew, Charles' brother William, at Gettysburg. "My girls seem to feel as if their

41. *Chesnut,* p. 406.

42. "Mamma was at the hospital—Lottie was with her mother—I was taking a music lesson from little Miss Garnett while Hannah was sitting chatting with Annie Hampton. I remember it all so well and yet I don't remember it for I cannot tell who brought the dispatch. I know that the boy who had it was searching for Mamma over at the hospital and in some way Lottie got it first—then it was brought to us and Mamma got it last of all—it was from Cousin William Miles and said that Cheves was dying. . . . All seemed blackness and confusion after that—the next thing I remember was a carriage at the door and Alex Haskell who had been at home wounded was putting her into the carriage and about to step in after her as he was to go on with her when someone handed her another dispatch. Cheves was dead." Smythe, p. 53.

43. Sophia Cheves Haskell to Sophia Haskell the younger, Feb. 8, 1863, Langdon Cheves III Papers, SCHS.

brother was lost a second time. Poor children, these shocks are very trying to them. This fearful war brings to our daughters a sadder fate than to their slaughtered brothers."[44]

1865 On Friday, February 10, word is brought to LSM at her home in Columbia that the enemy is at Orangeburg, a day's journey away. Flight from the city has begun. Having arranged for Hannah and Louisa to accompany Mary Chesnut, about to join the refugees, now LSM decides to keep her daughters with her. She has buried stores and valuables and ordered the staircase ascending to the back piazza on the upper floor to be removed, and the piazza enclosed, thus sealing off the rear of the house—a precaution which "gave the neighbors a good laugh at Mrs. McCord's fortification as they called it."[45] As the Federal army under William T. Sherman enters Columbia (February 17), soldiers pillage first shops and businesses, then private residences. Standing in the way of invaders who, having ransacked the main floor of her house, strive to move upstairs where her children are secluded, LSM is seized by the throat, and her son's watch, once her father's, torn from her dress. The plunder is interrupted by a staff officer sent to claim the McCord house for the headquarters of General O. O. Howard, deputed by Sherman to maintain order in the city. LSM and her daughters, together with her sister-in-law Rachel Cheves and Rachel's daughter Mary Elizabeth (they have sought refuge with LSM after the fall of Savannah),[46] continue to occupy the upper floor, although urged to flee by a lieutenant who, taking pity on them, has sent up to them by a servant a warning of what is to come "written upon a torn sheet of my dead son's note book, which, with private papers of every kind, now strewed my yard."[47] "As we stood on the upper piazza looking at the flames around, we could distinctly

44. LSM to Sophia Cheves Haskell, July 16, 1863.

45. Smythe, p. 59.

46. "I rec[eive]d the missing letter that Louisa wrote me before you went up[;] it expresses all that I expected from her well known kindness of feeling and nobleness of character." John Richardson Cheves to Rachel Cheves, Charleston, Feb. 11, 1865, Rachel S. Cheves Papers, Duke. John Cheves was in charge of a field hospital with the army of Gen. William Joseph Hardee, who commanded the Department of South Carolina, Georgia, and Florida.

47. "The Burning of Columbia," in *PDBL*.

see first one, and then another, of the houses in the environs of the town, and *quite out of reach of the fire*, blaze up, and burn down."[48] The McCord house survives the burning of Columbia;[49] but, after General Howard departs, the troops detailed to protect the house from looting loot it themselves, so completing the destruction of McCord family papers and most of the library; a like fate, "when the negroes were turned loose by Sherman upon my plantation residence with orders to destroy and ruin in any way they liked best," befalls the library and its contents at Lang Syne, the house itself being spared.[50] A few weeks before Sherman's approach, a woman claiming to be from Atlanta and destitute has been welcomed and given work as a seamstress in the homes of LSM and the Reynoldses. Now, as the invaders are departing from Columbia, this woman, richly dressed, reappears at the McCord house escorted by Federal soldiers, who, as the family watches, draw forth LSM's silk-lined carriage from the carriage house, where it has been stored beneath linen covers since the McCord horses were donated to the Confederacy;[51] after the soldiers have hitched to the carriage the horses brought with them, the woman gets in and, waving back at her benefactors, drives away in the train of the Federal army. Rachel Cheves and her daughter decide to move into a nearby house shared with the mayor of Columbia and others whose homes have been destroyed, for "we are anything but comfortable where we are and it requires all the patience and amiability one is

48. Rachel Cheves to James L. Reynolds [April? 1866], Rachel S. Cheves Papers, Duke. The letter encloses a draft of a statement, invited by Reynolds and John LeConte, describing Rachel Cheves' experiences of Sherman's troops in Savannah and Columbia.

49. "The house was twice set on fire and would of course have been burned had it not been for Gen[eral] Howard's regard for his own reputation. He couldn't afford to have his headquarters burned. But it was most evident the determination of the soldiers to burn it. They said over and over (to the servants) that it would burn. Burning cotton was found in the most extraordinary places, and Gen[eral] Howard would say in his suave manner that it was remarkable how the cotton was blowing about. On one occasion when a ball of it was found burning in the back entry, my Mother answered him, 'Yes, General, very remarkable, through closed doors,' and he said no more." Smythe, pp. 63–64.

50. LSM to Langdon Cheves III, April 6 [1876].

51. "When the call for horses was made, Mrs. McCord sent in her five bays. She comes now with a pair of mules—and looks *too* long at my ponies. If I were not so much afraid of her, I would hint: those mules would be of far more use in camp than my ponies. But they will seize the ponies, no doubt." *Chesnut,* p. 681 (entry of Dec. 2, 1864).

capable of to live here and avoid violent scenes daily about nothing at all."[52] On June 27 LSM's daughter Louisa is married to Charlestonian Augustine T. Smythe, to whom the same day LSM conveys, for the sum of five dollars, title to Lang Syne and the neighboring plantation of Goshen (formerly owned by her brother John, then by her uncle Joseph Heatly Dulles); also, in a separate transaction, a tract in the Pine Lands near Lang Syne. Smythe goes down to Fort Motte, to a Federal gunboat anchored there in the Congaree River; after taking the oath of allegiance to the restored Union, he is able to reclaim Lang Syne and the other lands conveyed to him, a total of about 3,315 acres. LSM talks of exile, a course adopted by her stepson Russell McCord, who departs for Brazil. In order to sell the Columbia house, which against her family's advice she insists on doing (September 23), LSM, also, is compelled to take the hated oath to the Union, persuaded finally by the father of her son's wife, Dr. Reynolds, who undertakes to submit to the oath along with her. "One of the saddest sights I ever saw was that couple walking arm in arm to the Provost Marshall's office, my mother in her shabby black dress and her rusty crêpe veil. It was like a pitiful, pitiful funeral."[53]

1866–68 LSM with daughter Hannah lives intermittently at Lang Syne, grim and ruinous; for a time with the Reynoldses, then at a boardinghouse, in Columbia; also at Abbeville, near to her father's birthplace and to Sophia and Charles Haskell; there are visits to Smythe relations in Charleston.

1867 Makes sworn affidavit to a committee of Columbia citizens, James Parsons Carroll chairman, appointed (April 22) "to collect evidence as to the burning of the city on the night of February 17, 1865."[54]

1869 Daughter Hannah is married to John Taylor Rhett (March 2). When a South Carolina Monument Association is founded

52. Rachel Cheves to John Richardson Cheves, March 2, 1865, Rachel S. Cheves Papers, Duke.

53. Smythe, p. 79.

54. Carroll, *Report of the Committee Appointed to Collect Testimony in Relation to the Destruction of Columbia, S.C., on the 17th of February, 1865* (Columbia, S.C., 1893), p. 3.

with the aim of building a memorial to the state's soldiers lost in the war, LSM, chosen its first president, composes a public appeal for subscriptions addressed not only to the bereaved but also to "all who cherish the name of Carolinian and cling with a fond love to whatever is left to us of our 'good old State.'"[55]

1870 In March, sends to Hiram Powers in Florence to inquire after the bust of her father commissioned—and, as she believes, completed—before the war; the letter, apologizing for the delay in writing—"truly it has seemed to me often, that I belonged to life no longer"—astounds Powers with its resentment of Northern victory: "Her letter is well written, but I fear that her head is not all right. Trouble has touched her reason."[56] Responds indignantly (April) to a character of Langdon Cheves published in the *XIX Century* as part of a series of "Reminiscences of Public Men" by Benjamin F. Perry. In June, resigns the presidency of the South Carolina Monument Association, refusing to cooperate (as her position demands) with "a powerful faction in our State, which seeks for her the degradation of negro equality," its motive being to attract votes of former slaves so as to unseat the Radical Republican government. "South Carolina is fast becoming to me, but as one great grave of the great past;—One proud memory which must pass away before the sweeping tide of corruption. . . . May God grant that some great head and heart shall yet arise to the rescue! But I see them no where."[57] On December 1 Lang Syne, together with Goshen and the tract in the Pine Lands, is sold, all except the family graveyard where David James McCord is buried.

1871–75 "By the sad results of our War, and our crushed out Liberties, now with no settled home, and much a wanderer,"[58] LSM lives largely away from South Carolina, mostly at various places in Canada, among them Cobourg and St. Catharines, whose

55. *FOLS,* p. 15.

56. LSM to Powers, March 20, 1870; Powers to Sidney Brooks, May 2, 1870, Hiram Powers and Powers Family Papers, Smithsonian.

57. LSM to the Board of Managers of the South Carolina Monument Association, June 17, 1870.

58. LSM, "Last Will and Testament," Feb. 12, 1876.

location on Lake Ontario makes them attractive for summer visits from her family, and Drummondville, Quebec, accessible to Montreal where she has McCord relations. From Charlottesville in Virginia expresses her dismay at Federal measures to suppress insurgency in South Carolina—"this Ku Klux inquisition despotism, will it not probably stretch its arms through the State?"—and her contempt for Carolinians who "get on their knees to lick the boots of Grant's drunken soldiery."[59] "To a people who have once been proud and great, and great because they were proud, a change in the national spirit is the most terrible of all revolutions."[60] In Drummondville, despite sullen times when she admires suicide, LSM can enjoy an excursion by sleigh to the Drummondville Falls but feels she must avoid sleigh rides on a Sunday, even if the weather is fine and the sun glittering on the snow, lest she be thought "a dissipated old character," and so attends church instead.[61]

1872 Daughter Hannah dies (November 24), six weeks after the birth of her second child. "Poor, dear Hannah had a long, fearful illness! God only knows the depth of her sufferings. I almost felt resigned when I closed the tired, wandering eyes. She was delirious nearly the whole time. She found it hard to leave those she loved."[62]

1873 Having "read carefully the testimony offered for the defence" against British subjects seeking redress before the Mixed Commission appointed, in accordance with the Treaty of Washington (May 8, 1871), to investigate claims for damages incurred during the late war, LSM deposes in Charleston

59. LSM to Augustine T. Smythe, Nov. 14 [1871].

60. Edmund Burke, *First Letter on a Regicide Peace* (1796), in *Writings and Speeches* 9:188. An unidentified newspaper clipping—too brief to determine its context—found in the Langdon Cheves I Papers, SCHS, quotes this passage from Burke (but reading, "to a people once proud and great, and great because proud"), thus introduced: "There is something very terrible in all this. It looks as if the heart of a once proud people was broken, and goes far to verify what Mr. Burke long ago said." There is an annotation to the clipping in LSM's hand: "Referring to France[;] Alas! to ourselves S[outh] C[arolina]. Dec. 1871."

61. LSM to Augustine T. Smythe, March 29, 1874; to Louisa McCord Smythe, Feb. 8 [1874].

62. [Sophia Haskell the younger?] to Rachel Cheves, June 27, 1873, Rachel S. Cheves Papers, Duke.

(May 3) an account of her experiences at the time of the burning of Columbia.[63]

1876 Although at first reluctant, and diffident of the result—"I wish you had thought of asking it of me a half dozen years ago"—at the request of nephew Langdon Cheves III, LSM writes a memoir of her father, carried down to his early career as a lawyer, and meditates a more ambitious memorial, in verse and prose, complementing the obelisk raised at last, "eight months after date of contract," in Charleston's Magnolia Cemetery.[64]

1876/77 Retires to Charleston, making her home with daughter Louisa and her husband Augustine T. Smythe at 25 Legaré Street.

1878 The war having arrested Hiram Powers' work on his bust of Langdon Cheves, LSM renews the commission, now to Hiram's son Preston Powers. The task is complicated, as before, by the want of reliable images to guide the sculptor: "When I sat to your Father, I indulged the faint hope, that he might retain from the family likeness, (which was said to be considerable in me, such as Woman may bear to Man) some far off glimmer of the grand head."[65]

1879 Purchases the house adjacent to the north of the Smythes (January 1) and plans extensive renovations with contractor (early November). An ailment diagnosed as "Gout in the stomach," which having troubled her for some time seems to have left her by late September, recurs abruptly; and after five days of suffering great pain, finally in agony, LSM dies (November 23) and is buried in Magnolia Cemetery next the graves of her father and son. "I do feel," her daughter writes, "in spite of husband children and all, very much alone—like the last of my own people."[66]

63. "The Burning of Columbia," in *PDBL*.

64. LSM to Langdon Cheves III, July 11 [1876].

65. LSM to Preston Powers, April 28, 1878. Hiram Powers had died on June 27, 1873.

66. Louisa McCord Smythe to Sophia Cheves Haskell, Charleston, Dec. 4 [1879], Langdon Cheves III Papers, SCHS. This letter is printed in app. 2.

Note on the Texts

Of LSM's writings published during her lifetime (apart from her translation of Bastiat's *Sophismes économiques*), only two are known to have appeared under her name: *My Dreams* (Philadelphia, 1848) and *Caius Gracchus* (New York, 1851). The rest were anonymous, although many carried the initials "L. S. M." Hence to establish the canon of her writings is, borrowing a favorite expression from textual editors of the classics, a *locus vexatissimus*. An editor lives in fear of an archive (or a descendant's house) not visited, a file not examined, a document not copied, a copy not read with enough care, which, if visited, examined, copied, or read, would furnish the clues opening up untold heaps of hitherto unattributed writings. The editor's task is aggravated by the loss of most of LSM's own papers relating to the period during which her anonymous contributions to periodicals were most frequent. Unable to help an historian inquiring in 1870 after a work by her husband, LSM explained: "Pamphlets, manuscripts, and every thing of the kind, formerly owned by me, were for the most part destroyed by our brutal invaders at the close of our Southern Struggle for Liberty. Whatever escaped *them,* was wantonly scattered by our ignorant negroes excited to join in their brutal Saturnalia. In our devastated homes little of value remained after the vandal like progress of Sherman." Her daughter Louisa recorded that the morning after the burning of Columbia the family set about destroying the personal papers still in their possession, lest these too be stolen, and described the scene when, after General Howard's departure and while their house was being plundered the second time (and more thoroughly), she and her sister—LSM refused to leave—were escorted from the house to a place of safety by the one guard left by Howard who was concerned for his charges: "As we went out of the house with our sergeant, the impression on my eye was that there had been a snowstorm. The street was white with paper—letters, legal documents—every kind of thing, valuable and worthless, strewed the ground."[1] An editor of LSM's writings has special cause to regret that blizzard in Columbia.

What are the grounds for attributing to LSM the writings assembled in this edition?

The most comprehensive source is the notice on LSM published in Evert A. and George L. Duyckinck, *Cyclopaedia of American Literature,* 2 vols. (New York, 1856), 2:251–53—familiarly referred to as Duyckinck—where footnotes give LSM's contributions to periodicals. This list is likely to be accurate (though not, as we know, complete), for it presumably derives from a questionnaire which William Gilmore Simms passed along from Evert Duyckinck to David James McCord;[2] and Duyckinck's notice on David James McCord, preceding that on LSM, concludes with a special note of thanks for "the friendly services of the late Colonel M'Cord. . . . We are indebted to his pen for much information of value relative to his literary associates at Columbia," of whom his wife was, of course, the closest. Some of LSM's periodical contributions are mentioned in John Seely Hart, *The Female Prose Writers of America* (Philadelphia, 1852), p. 187; and in Sarah Josepha Hale, *Woman's Record; or, Sketches of All Distinguished Women, from the Creation to* A.D. *1854,* 2d ed. rev. (New York, 1855), p. 894. (Later notices in anthologies and compendia seem to be derived wholly from Duyckinck; they demonstrate no independent knowledge.) There are a few references to LSM's contributions in the letters of William Gilmore Simms, editor of the *Southern Quarterly Review* from April 1849 to October 1854, and in the correspondence of others. Also persuasive, if not conclusive, is the appearance of the initials "L. S. M.," for although another writer contributing to Southern periodicals at this time might have had the same initials, none is known.

A list follows, in chronological order, of the anonymous published writings attributed to LSM, each item including the details of publication and the source(s) of attribution:

"Justice and Fraternity." *Southern Quarterly Review* 15 (July 1849): 356–74. Attributed: William Gilmore Simms to M. C. M. Hammond [June 1849],

1. LSM to Lyman C. Draper, June 3, 1870; Smythe, pp. 68–69.

2. William Gilmore Simms to Evert Augustus Duyckinck, July 17, 1854, in Simms, *Letters* 3:314.

and James Henry Hammond to William Gilmore Simms, July 9, 1849, in Simms, *Letters* 2:531–32; Duyckinck; Hart; Hale; signed "L. S. M."

"The Right to Labor." *Southern Quarterly Review* 16 (Oct. 1849): 138–60. Attributed: William Gilmore Simms to David James McCord, Jan. 15 [1850], in Simms, *Letters* 3:4; Duyckinck; Hart; Hale; signed "L. S. M."

"Diversity of the Races; Its Bearing upon Negro Slavery." *Southern Quarterly Review,* n.s., 3 (April 1851): 392–419. Attributed: Duyckinck; Hart; signed "L. S. M."

"Negro and White Slavery—Wherein Do They Differ?" *Southern Quarterly Review,* n.s., 4 (July 1851): 118–32. Attributed: Duyckinck; signed "L. S. M."

"Separate Secession." *Southern Quarterly Review,* n.s., 4 (Oct. 1851): 298–317. Attributed: William Gilmore Simms to Nathaniel Beverley Tucker, June 26, 1851, and to M. C. M. Hammond [Oct. 11, 1851], in Simms, *Letters* 3:133, 143.

"Enfranchisement of Woman." *Southern Quarterly Review,* n.s., 5 (April 1852): 322–41. Attributed: Duyckinck; Hale; signed "L. S. M."

"Negro-mania." *De Bow's Review* 12 (May 1852): 507–24. Attributed: Duyckinck; signed "L. S. M."

"Woman and Her Needs." *De Bow's Review* 13 (Sept. 1852): 267–91. Attributed: Duyckinck; Hale; signed "L. S. M."

"*Uncle Tom's Cabin.*" *Southern Quarterly Review,* n.s., 7 (Jan. 1853): 81–120. Attributed: Duyckinck; Hale; signed "L. S. M."; William P. Trent, *William Gilmore Simms* (Boston and New York, 1892), pp. 174–75.

"British Philanthropy and American Slavery." *De Bow's Review* 14 (March 1853): 258–80. Attributed: Duyckinck. *De Bow's* headnote to this article reports it to have come "from the pen of a Southern Lady," who contributed a "protest against the miscalled 'Woman's Rights' movement at the North, which we published in our September number of last year," an evident reference to "Woman and Her Needs."

"Charity Which Does Not Begin at Home." *Southern Literary Messenger* 19 (April 1853): 193–208. Attributed: Duyckinck; signed "L. S. M."

"A Letter to the Duchess of Sutherland from a Lady of South Carolina." Charleston *Mercury,* Aug. 10, 1853. Attributed: Duyckinck; Hale.

"Woman's Progress." *Southern Literary Messenger* 19 (Nov. 1853): 700–701. Attributed: Hale; signed "L. S. M."

"Carey on the Slave Trade." *Southern Quarterly Review,* n.s., 9 (Jan. 1854): 115–84. Attributed: LSM to Henry C. Carey, Jan. 18, 1854; William Gilmore Simms to Henry Carey Baird, Dec. 17, 1853, in Simms, *Letters* 3:267; Duyckinck; signed "L. S. M."

"Slavery and Political Economy." *De Bow's Review* 21 (Oct. and Nov. 1856): 331–49, 443–67. Author reported in the table of contents as "a South Carolinian." Attributed: LSM to James Henley Thornwell [July 1856]; James Henley Thornwell to George Frederick Holmes, July 30, 1856, and Holmes to Thornwell, Dec. 1, 1856, in Neal C. Gillespie, *The Collapse of Orthodoxy: The Intellectual Ordeal of George Frederick Holmes* (Charlottesville, Va., 1972), pp. 160–61.

"Langdon Cheves: Review of 'Reminiscences of Public Men.'" *XIX Century* 2 (April 1870): 885–88. Although the review is unsigned, internal evidence is conclusive. Besides the distinctive style and access to personal details, the reviewer laments "the times that have swept from life those worthy and able to undertake the scattering of insinuated aspersions; times which have left from the near watchers over the sunset of that noble life, not one survivor—save only a woman; . . . although it was only a woman, still there did live that one, who having clung with a daughter's love" to her father's last days might have supplied accurate material to his biographer, and proceeds to do so. Also, the reviewer cites, at the beginning and at the end of the article, the Latin phrase that LSM had engraved on her father's bust: *clarum et venerabile nomen*.

"To the Editor of *The XIX Century*." *XIX Century* 3 (June 1870): 83–84. Signed "Carolinian." Attributed: detached leaf of the journal found in Dulles-Cheves-McCord-Lovell Papers, SCHS, with "L. S. M. ?" written in pencil at end of article. Tone, style, habit of allusion, and what is known of LSM's sentiments at this period (in particular as expressed in her letter of June 17, 1870, addressed to the Board of Managers of the South Carolina Monument Association) suggest attribution to be not unlikely.

In addition, there are lyric poems, signed "L. S. M.," published in the *Southern Literary Gazette:* "Look Not Back," *Southern Literary Gazette,* n.s., 1 (Feb. 21, 1852): 94; "Constancy," n.s., 1 (March 6, 1852): 112; "Guardian Angels," n.s., 2 (Nov. 13, 1852): 226.

Also attributed to LSM:

"Stowe's Key to Uncle Tom's Cabin." *Southern Quarterly Review,* n.s., 8 (July 1853): 214–54. Attributed: Susan Phinney Conrad, *Perish the Thought: Intellectual Women in Romantic America, 1830–1860* (New York, 1976), pp. 265–66, n. 13; George C. Rable, *Civil Wars: Women and the Crisis of Southern Nationalism* (Urbana, Ill., 1989), p. 39 and n. 26. Although not without something of LSM's vigor, this article seems to demonstrate attitudes toward women not found in LSM's attested writings; it is not mentioned in Duyckinck (in itself not conclusive, however) or in Trent's *Simms;* without other evidence, therefore, it must be concluded that "Stowe's Key" is probably not by LSM. Jean W. Ashton, *Harriet Beecher Stowe: A Reference Guide* (Boston, 1977), p. 15, assigns "Stowe's Key" to William Gilmore Simms. In a communication to the editor (May 8, 1992), Michael O'Brien proposes tentatively Edward J. Pringle, whose pamphlet, "Slavery in the Southern States," reprinted in *Fraser's Magazine* 46 (Oct. 1852): 476–90, having taken Mrs. Stowe sternly to task, was in turn taken sternly to task by British reviewers, themselves doomed to be taken to task most sternly of all by LSM in "British Philanthropy and American Slavery" and "Charity Which Does Not Begin at Home."

"Rebecca Motte." In Sarah Butler Wister and Agnes Irwin, eds., *Worthy Women of Our First Century* (Philadephia, 1877; rpt. Plainville, N. Y., 1975), pp. 259–78. Author reported in the table of contents as "a Lady of S. Carolina." Attributed: card catalog, William R. Perkins Library, Duke University, describing detached leaves of *Worthy Women* bound in cardboard covers as a pamphlet; the connection to *Worthy Women* is not noted in the catalog entry or in the pamphlet. Other evidence supporting this attribution to LSM has not been located. No mention of LSM's authorship is to be found in her letters or those of her family; her daughter Louisa Smythe, when interviewed by Jessie Melville Fraser,[3] made no reference to any such attribution; finally, when asked in early 1876 by her nephew Langdon Cheves III to write a memoir of her father, LSM, allowing that "it would in truth be to me a labour of love," supplied some pieces of information to help her nephew's researches, but "as to your further request, something of a memoir, I am now quite unfit. A few scattered anecdotes and those[,] perhaps, already given to you by others, would be all I could do."[4] Although she changed her mind later and took up the requested "Memoir," any hesitation would be strange if she were lately, or at the time, composing a biographical treatment of Rebecca Motte. There is also evidence favoring another's authorship. In the Motte Family Miscellaneous Material, SCHS, is a handwritten transcript of "Rebecca Motte," headed by bibliographic information to *Worthy Women.* On the back of the last page of the transcript is written, in the same hand, "Copied by Rose P. Ravenel[,] Aug[ust] 1903—from manuscript lent her by Miss S. P. Frost her cousin"; then, an inch or so below, "Cousin Susan Pringle's house[,] 27 King Street[,] Charleston S. Ca." In the space between these two notes is a third, in a different hand: "Written by Miss

3. Fraser was gathering material for her M.A. thesis of 1919.

4. LSM to Langdon Cheves III, April 6 [1876].

Maria Middleton—1876." "Miss Maria Middleton" is presumably (there appears to be no other Middleton of that name, unmarried, and of a likely age in 1876) Maria Henrietta Middleton, born April 18, 1841, and known to be yet unmarried in 1900. The Sarah Butler Wister Papers, PHS, contain two letters (Nov. 28 and Dec. 8 [1875]) to Sarah Wister by Sophy G. Coxe, who had been asked to contribute a biography of a South Carolinian to the collection that Wister was preparing in honor of the American Centennial. Coxe, having no materials herself for such a task, undertook "to get for you some sketches of Carolina women from a friend there." In her second letter Coxe reports that her friend, who is indeed interested in the project, proposes Rebecca Motte; with this letter in the Wister Papers are handwritten transcripts of two Motte letters that appear in the published "Rebecca Motte." The name of the friend is not given in either letter. But Sophy Coxe's parents were Joshua Francis Fisher (1807–73) of Philadelphia, whose *Concessions and Compromises* (1860) had supported Southern grievances, and Elizabeth Middleton Fisher (1815–90), daughter of Governor Henry Middleton of South Carolina (1770–1846) and sister of John Izard Middleton (1800–1877), father of Maria Henrietta Middleton. Maria Henrietta Middleton and Sophy Coxe were thus first cousins. However, the attribution of "Rebecca Motte" to Maria Henrietta Middleton is compromised by the headnote to an unidentified newspaper clipping (also in the Motte Miscellaneous Material, SCHS) which reprints, sometime after 1887, "Rebecca Motte": its headnote assigns authorship to "a member of her family, a lady of Charleston." Maria Henrietta Middleton can claim no such connection to Rebecca Motte. But "Miss S. P. Frost," who lent the manuscript of which Rosa Pringle Ravenel (b. 1850) made the copy now at SCHS, is almost certainly Rosa Ravenel's cousin Susan Pringle Frost (1873–1960), whose mother, Rebecca Brewton Pringle (1839–1905), was a great-granddaughter of Rebecca Motte and sister of "cousin Susan Pringle" (1829–1917), whose house was neighbor to the Miles Brewton house at 25 King Street, inherited by Rebecca Motte and invoked with nostalgic familiarity in the first paragraphs of "Rebecca Motte." Therefore, that Maria Henrietta Middleton wrote "Rebecca Motte," although likely, cannot be taken as proved; but it seems to be proved that LSM—whose closest relation to the family of Rebecca Motte was that her sister Anna's husband, Thomas Pinckney Huger, was a great-grandson of Rebecca Motte—is not the author.

LSM is known to have composed two accounts of her experiences during the Federal occupation of Columbia. In accordance with articles 12–17 of the Treaty of Washington between Great Britain and the United States (May 8, 1871), a Mixed Commission was appointed to investigate and adjudicate claims (apart from the so-called *Alabama* claims) for damages incurred, by both British and American citizens, between April 13, 1861, and April 9, 1865. The commission met first on September 26, 1871, and for the last time on September 25, 1873; testimony and evidence for the claims submitted to the commission were gathered during this time. On May 3, 1873, at the British Consulate in Charleston, LSM made a deposition before Consul Henry Pinckney Walker. Walker certified on May 13 "that the deponents whose depositions are hereto annexed [including that by LSM] were duly by me sworn to tell the truth, the whole truth, and nothing but the truth; that said depositions were reduced to writing as nearly as practicable in the language of the witnesses; and that the said depositions were read to deponents respectively before being by them subscribed, and thereupon that the deponents respectively signed the same." LSM's deposition, reprinted in this edition with the added title "The Burning of Columbia," is taken from: Mixed Commission on British and American Claims Established under Article XII of the Treaty of Washington, *British and American Claims. Appendix: Testimony* (Washington, D. C., 1873), vol. 23, "*George Symmers* vs. *the United States* and *Frederick Ward* vs. *the United States,* cases no. 228 and 294, depositions in rebutting for claimants," bk. 2, pp. 26–29 (Walker's certification appears on page 1). A search of the case files of British claimants, held in the National Archives, Washington, D.C., has yielded no manuscript of the deposition.

A second account by LSM, written c. May 1867, was in the form of a sworn affidavit before a committee appointed, with James Parsons Carroll as chairman, to gather evidence relevant to the burning of Columbia. About sixty affidavits were assembled by the committee; all disappeared from the city council archives at some time during the Republican administration of Columbia (1870–78). Two fragments of LSM's affidavit survive, preserved in James Parsons Carroll, *Report of the Committee Appointed to Collect Testimony in Relation to the Destruction of Columbia, S.C., on the 17th of February, 1865* (Columbia, S.C., 1893), pp. 10, 17. The fragments are in this edition appended to LSM's 1873 deposition.

LSM's "Memoir of Langdon Cheves," together with fragmentary notes related to its composition, is published in this edition for the first time, from a holograph in the Langdon Cheves I Papers, SCHS.

This edition seeks to offer an inclusive or expanded transcription of LSM's writings: i.e., overt editorial intervention is reported at its place in the text, for instance by additional letters or words enclosed in square brackets or by a note immediately adjacent.[5] Manuscripts are not known to survive of LSM's published writings. For these, the first printed text forms the basis of the text furnished in this edition.[6] Substantives are preserved throughout; but accidentals—marks of punctuation, paragraphing, and so on—are modified when reading is measurably eased thereby, the editor striving, however, to be as conservative as possible: for example, a deposition, marked by long strings of semicolons in legal fashion, more accurately conveys the narrative structure when punctuated more variously; and in a piece published in the Charleston *Mercury* showing very light paragraphing, the movement of the argument is much improved by paragraphs used more frequently and more in accordance with paragraphing practice found in LSM's periodical essays. Emendation has been in general resisted (exceptions are clearly declared), although LSM noticed that she had "suffered enough from the impish fraternity of the printing-office to learn a most sympathizing fellow-feeling towards our co-sufferers in that line"; and we are told of *My Dreams* that its author "never liked it to be seen on account of the mistakes made in the printing."[7] No attempt has been made to reproduce features of the original typographic design. Typographical errors which are clearly such, and do not represent an oddity of usage or habit that may be LSM's, are silently corrected. When there is doubt in any change, a note alerts the reader.

The titles of the books and articles reviewed in LSM's periodical essays were listed variously, some in headnotes to the essays, some in footnotes, and with varying and inconsistent degrees of bibliographic detail. Such information has been regularized in this edition: a note at the first page of each essay contains, after the details of that essay's first publication, complete

5. In her periodical essays and elsewhere LSM frequently quotes other writers. Differences between her quotation and the original of the text which she quotes are indicated thus: (1) words or letters omitted by LSM are restored within square brackets; (2) words changed by LSM (or perhaps by the printer or the journal's editor, it being impossible to distinguish which) are inserted back into LSM's text within angle brackets (<>) immediately following the place where change was made; (3) if such a change is found to have been greater than of one or a few words, as for example not seldom when LSM is quoting poetry, the change is indicated in a note. The essays "Justice and Fraternity" and "The Right to Labor" contain numerous and often lengthy passages translated from the French. Differences of translation from original are indicated as above, with special attention to examples of addition and modification affecting tone or interpretation.

6. Chap. 8, "Negro-mania," was reprinted in De Bow, *Industrial Resources* 2:196–205. Chap. 3, "Enfranchisement of Woman," has been twice reprinted: O'Brien, *All Clever Men,* pp. 337–56; Hollinger and Capper, *American Intellectual Tradition* 1:375–87.

7. Chap. 4, "Woman and Her Needs," p. 128; Louisa McCord Smythe to William Porcher Miles, Feb. 26, 1880 (printed in app. 3). For example, the words *Christian* and *Christianity* are in Louisa McCord's writings sometimes capitalized, sometimes not; the inconsistency is preserved in this edition.

bibliographic documentation of the books and articles reviewed and of recent reprintings, if any, likely to be more available to the modern reader. Page references to the publications reviewed, when no ambiguity would arise and no additional information is supplied by the editor, are placed in the text of the essay, enclosed within square brackets; otherwise, page references are given in notes.

A note written by LSM is designated by [LSM] at its conclusion, any editorial interpolations within LSM's note being included inside square brackets. All other material in notes (with a few exceptions, so indicated) is the editor's. Of LSM's two favorite sources of quotation, Shakespeare is cited by act, scene, and line number as given in the New Arden Shakespeare, and the Bible, unless otherwise stated, in the Authorized (King James) Version.

Genealogical Tables

CHEVES

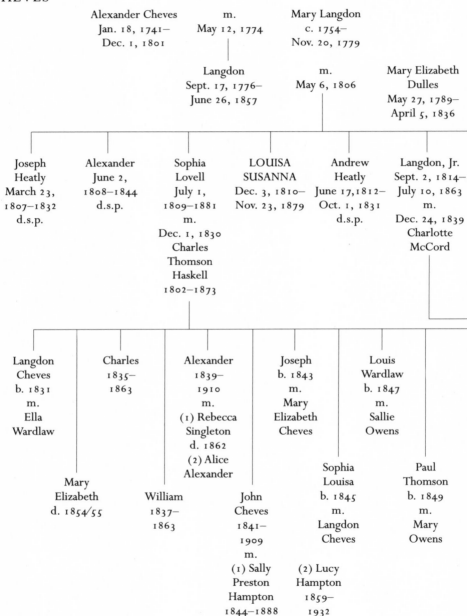

Alexander Cheves, Jan. 18, 1741–Dec. 1, 1801 — m. May 12, 1774 — Mary Langdon, c. 1754–Nov. 20, 1779

- **Langdon**, Sept. 17, 1776–June 26, 1857 — m. May 6, 1806 — Mary Elizabeth Dulles, May 27, 1789–April 5, 1836
  - Joseph Heatly, March 23, 1807–1832, d.s.p.
  - Alexander, June 2, 1808–1844, d.s.p.
  - Sophia Lovell, July 1, 1809–1881, m. Dec. 1, 1830 Charles Thomson Haskell, 1802–1873
    - Langdon Cheves, b. 1831, m. Ella Wardlaw
    - Mary Elizabeth, d. 1854/55
    - Charles, 1835–1863
    - William, 1837–1863
    - Alexander, 1839–1910, m. (1) Rebecca Singleton, d. 1862; (2) Alice Alexander
    - John Cheves, 1841–1909, m. (1) Sally Preston Hampton, 1844–1888; (2) Lucy Hampton, 1859–1932
    - Joseph, b. 1843, m. Mary Elizabeth Cheves
    - Sophia Louisa, b. 1845, m. Langdon Cheves
    - Louis Wardlaw, b. 1847, m. Sallie Owens
    - Paul Thomson, b. 1849, m. Mary Owens
  - LOUISA SUSANNA, Dec. 3, 1810–Nov. 23, 1879
  - Andrew Heatly, June 17, 1812–Oct. 1, 1831, d.s.p.
  - Langdon, Jr., Sept. 2, 1814–July 10, 1863, m. Dec. 24, 1839 Charlotte McCord

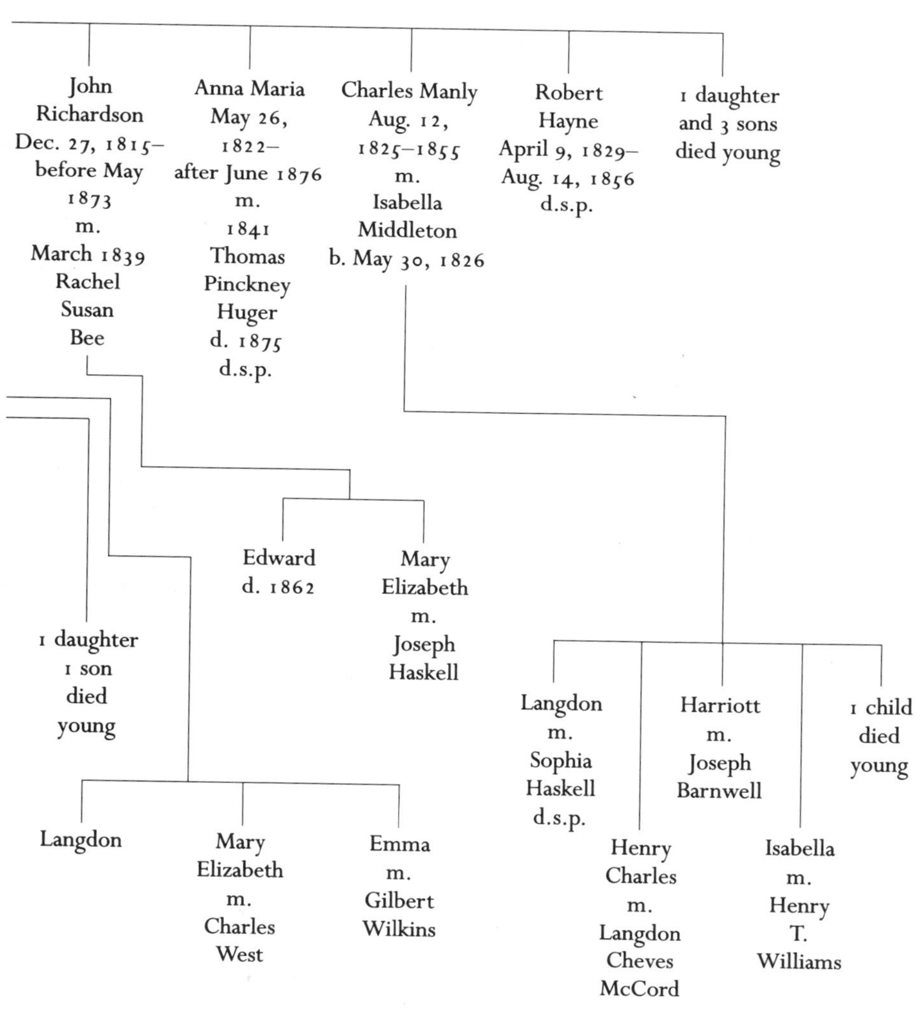
John Richardson Dec. 27, 1815–before May 1873 m. March 1839 Rachel Susan Bee
Anna Maria May 26, 1822–after June 1876 m. 1841 Thomas Pinckney Huger d. 1875 d.s.p.
Charles Manly Aug. 12, 1825–1855 m. Isabella Middleton b. May 30, 1826
Robert Hayne April 9, 1829–Aug. 14, 1856 d.s.p.
1 daughter and 3 sons died young
Edward d. 1862
Mary Elizabeth m. Joseph Haskell
1 daughter 1 son died young
Langdon
Mary Elizabeth m. Charles West
Emma m. Gilbert Wilkins
Langdon m. Sophia Haskell d.s.p.
Henry Charles m. Langdon Cheves McCord
Harriott m. Joseph Barnwell
Isabella m. Henry T. Williams
1 child died young

HEATLY-DULLES

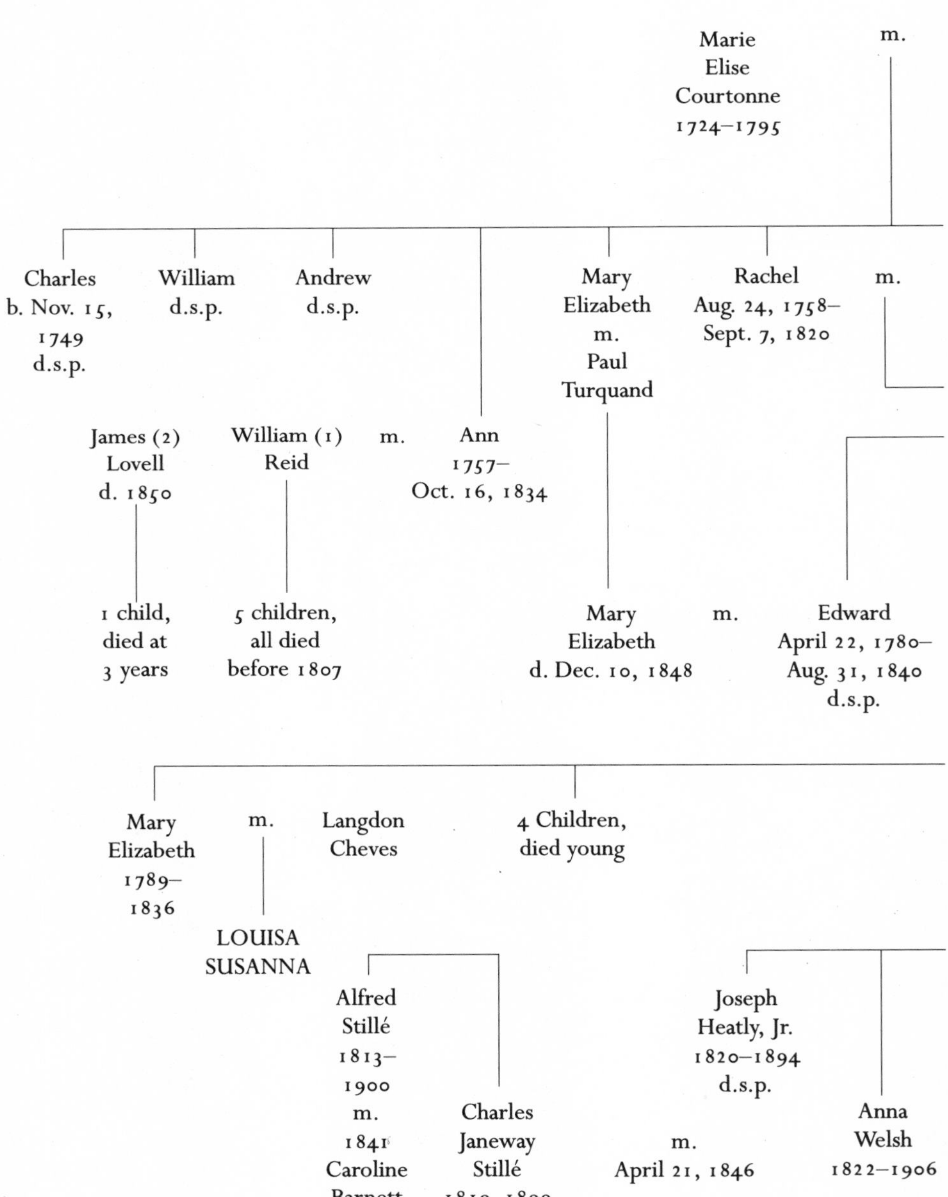

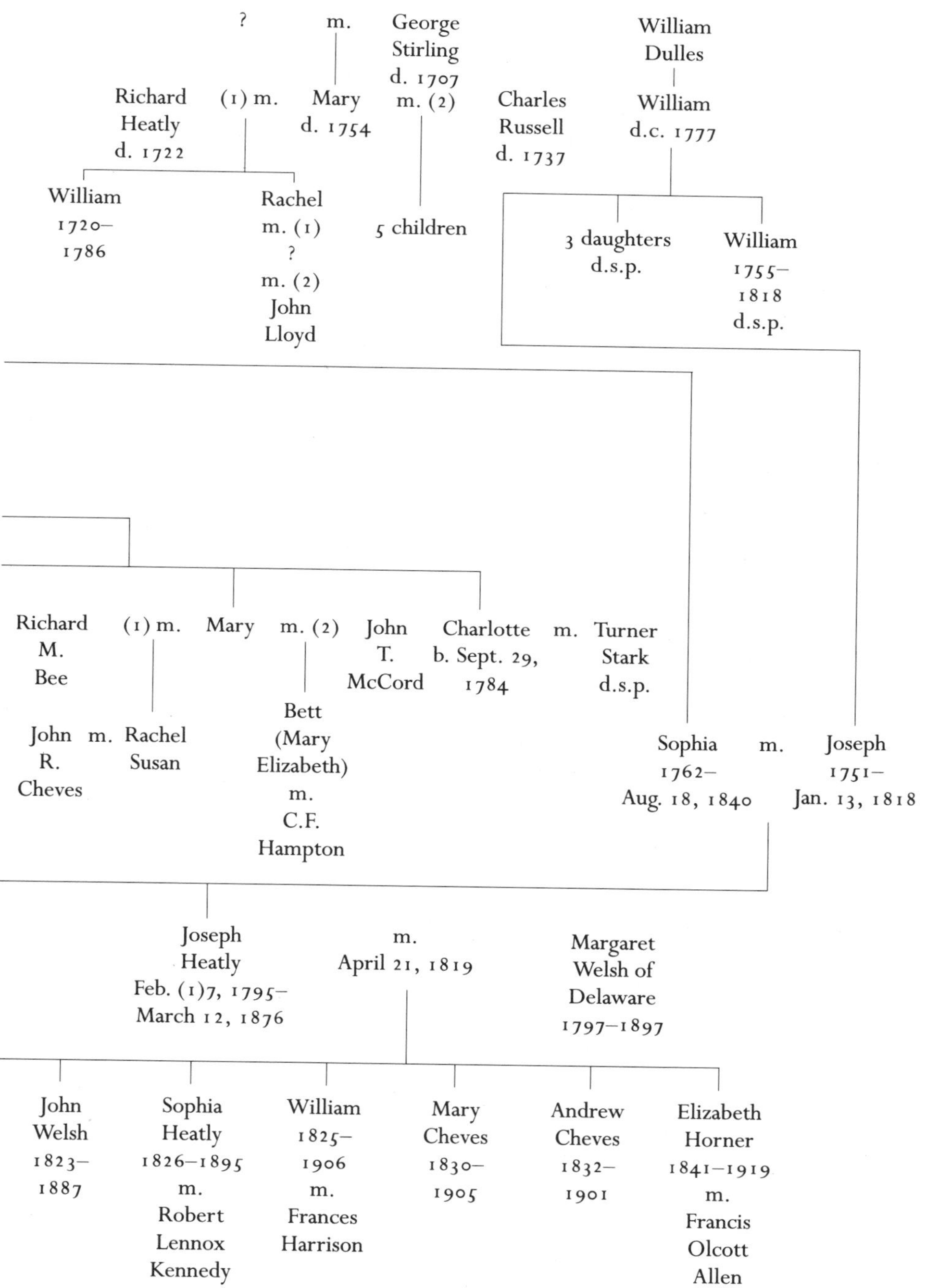
?
m.
George
Stirling
d. 1707
m. (2)
William
Dulles
Richard
Heatly
d. 1722
(1) m.
Mary
d. 1754
Charles
Russell
d. 1737
William
d.c. 1777
William
1720–
1786
Rachel
m. (1)
?
m. (2)
John
Lloyd
5 children
3 daughters
d.s.p.
William
1755–
1818
d.s.p.
Richard
M.
Bee
(1) m.
Mary
m. (2)
John
T.
McCord
Charlotte
b. Sept. 29,
1784
m.
Turner
Stark
d.s.p.
John
R.
Cheves
m.
Rachel
Susan
Bett
(Mary
Elizabeth)
m.
C.F.
Hampton
Sophia
1762–
Aug. 18, 1840
m.
Joseph
1751–
Jan. 13, 1818
Joseph
Heatly
Feb. (1)7, 1795–
March 12, 1876
m.
April 21, 1819
Margaret
Welsh of
Delaware
1797–1897
John
Welsh
1823–
1887
Sophia
Heatly
1826–1895
m.
Robert
Lennox
Kennedy
William
1825–
1906
m.
Frances
Harrison
Mary
Cheves
1830–
1905
Andrew
Cheves
1832–
1901
Elizabeth
Horner
1841–1919
m.
Francis
Olcott
Allen

McCORD

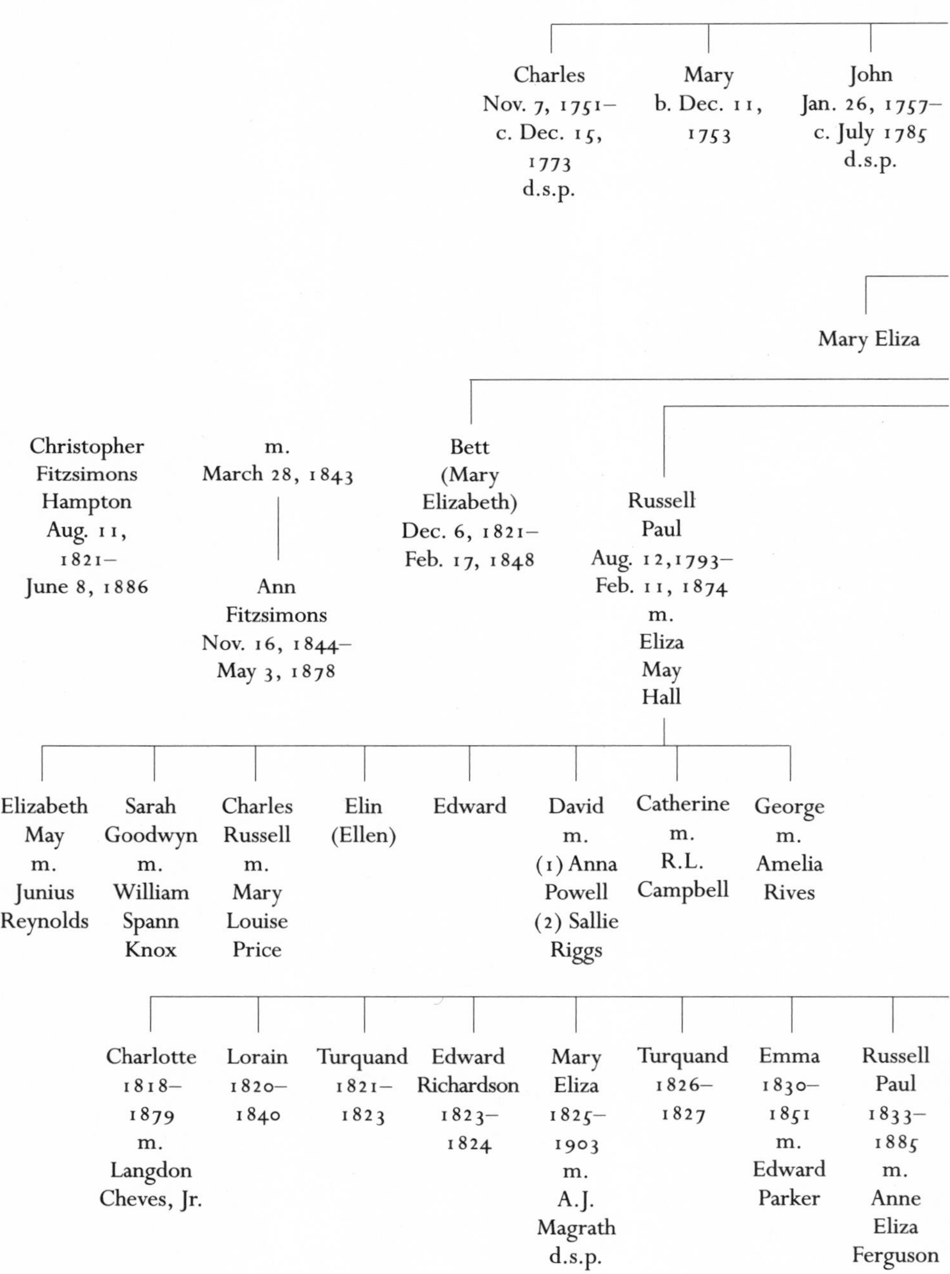

Charles
Nov. 7, 1751–
c. Dec. 15,
1773
d.s.p.
Mary
b. Dec. 11,
1753
John
Jan. 26, 1757–
c. July 1785
d.s.p.
Mary Eliza
Christopher
Fitzsimons
Hampton
Aug. 11,
1821–
June 8, 1886
m.
March 28, 1843
Ann
Fitzsimons
Nov. 16, 1844–
May 3, 1878
Bett
(Mary
Elizabeth)
Dec. 6, 1821–
Feb. 17, 1848
Russell
Paul
Aug. 12,1793–
Feb. 11, 1874
m.
Eliza
May
Hall
Elizabeth
May
m.
Junius
Reynolds
Sarah
Goodwyn
m.
William
Spann
Knox
Charles
Russell
m.
Mary
Louise
Price
Elin
(Ellen)
Edward
David
m.
(1) Anna
Powell
(2) Sallie
Riggs
Catherine
m.
R.L.
Campbell
George
m.
Amelia
Rives
Charlotte
1818–
1879
m.
Langdon
Cheves, Jr.
Lorain
1820–
1840
Turquand
1821–
1823
Edward
Richardson
1823–
1824
Mary
Eliza
1825–
1903
m.
A.J.
Magrath
d.s.p.
Turquand
1826–
1827
Emma
1830–
1851
m.
Edward
Parker
Russell
Paul
1833–
1885
m.
Anne
Eliza
Ferguson

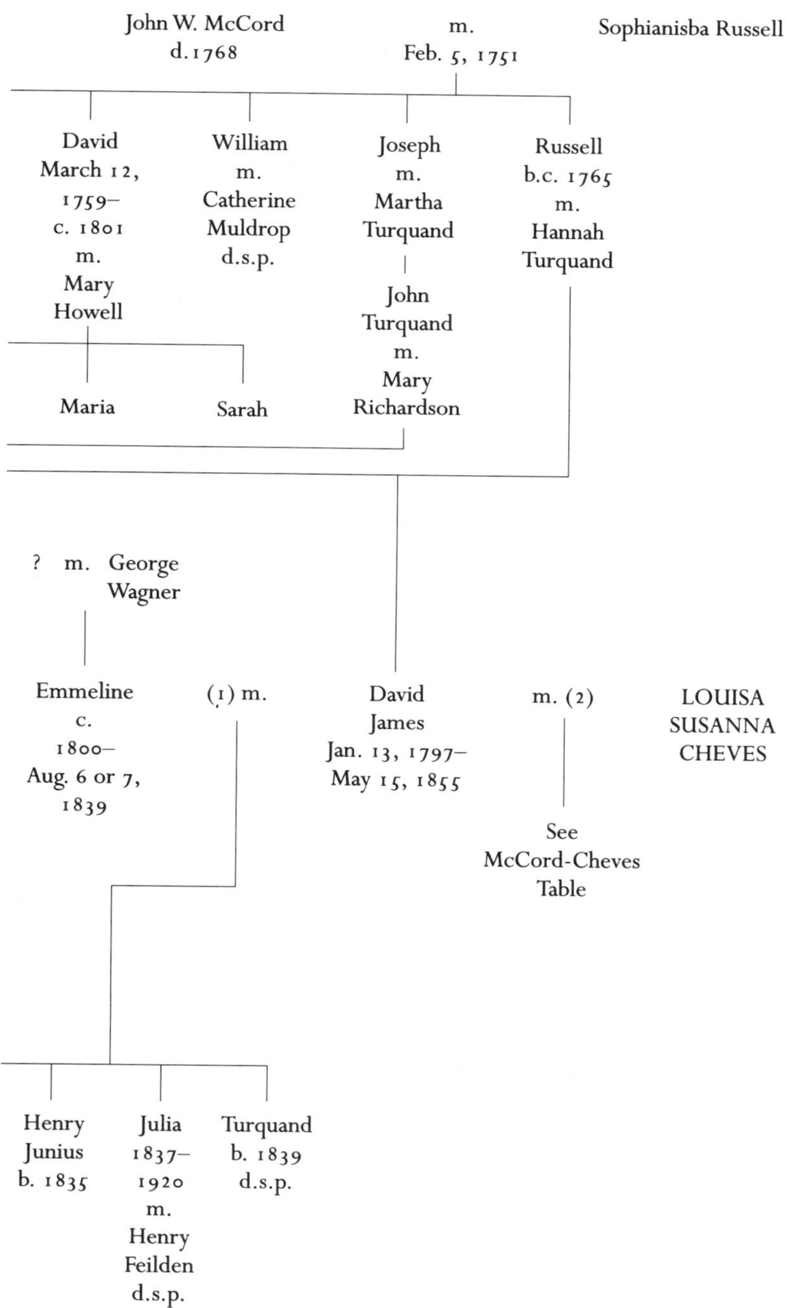
John W. McCord
d. 1768
m.
Feb. 5, 1751
Sophianisba Russell
David
March 12,
1759–
c. 1801
m.
Mary
Howell
William
m.
Catherine
Muldrop
d.s.p.
Joseph
m.
Martha
Turquand
Russell
b.c. 1765
m.
Hannah
Turquand
John
Turquand
m.
Mary
Richardson
Maria
Sarah
? m. George
Wagner
Emmeline
c.
1800–
Aug. 6 or 7,
1839
(1) m.
David
James
Jan. 13, 1797–
May 15, 1855
m. (2)
LOUISA
SUSANNA
CHEVES
See
McCord-Cheves
Table
Henry
Junius
b. 1835
Julia
1837–
1920
m.
Henry
Feilden
d.s.p.
Turquand
b. 1839
d.s.p.

McCORD-CHEVES

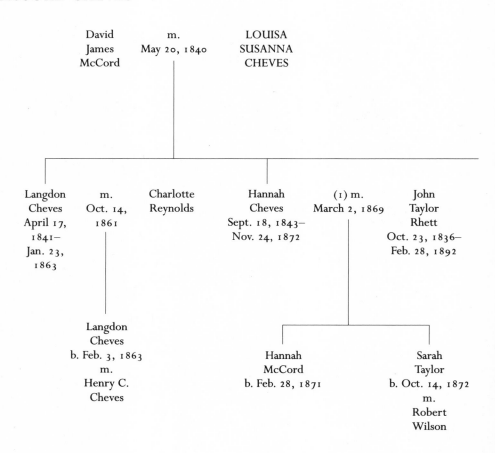

David James McCord — m. May 20, 1840 — LOUISA SUSANNA CHEVES

Langdon Cheves April 17, 1841–Jan. 23, 1863 — m. Oct. 14, 1861 — Charlotte Reynolds

Langdon Cheves b. Feb. 3, 1863 m. Henry C. Cheves

Hannah Cheves Sept. 18, 1843–Nov. 24, 1872 — (1) m. March 2, 1869 — John Taylor Rhett Oct. 23, 1836–Feb. 28, 1892

Hannah McCord b. Feb. 28, 1871

Sarah Taylor b. Oct. 14, 1872 m. Robert Wilson

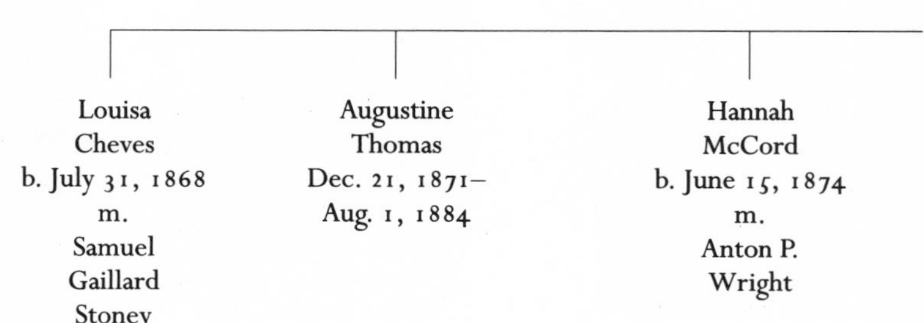

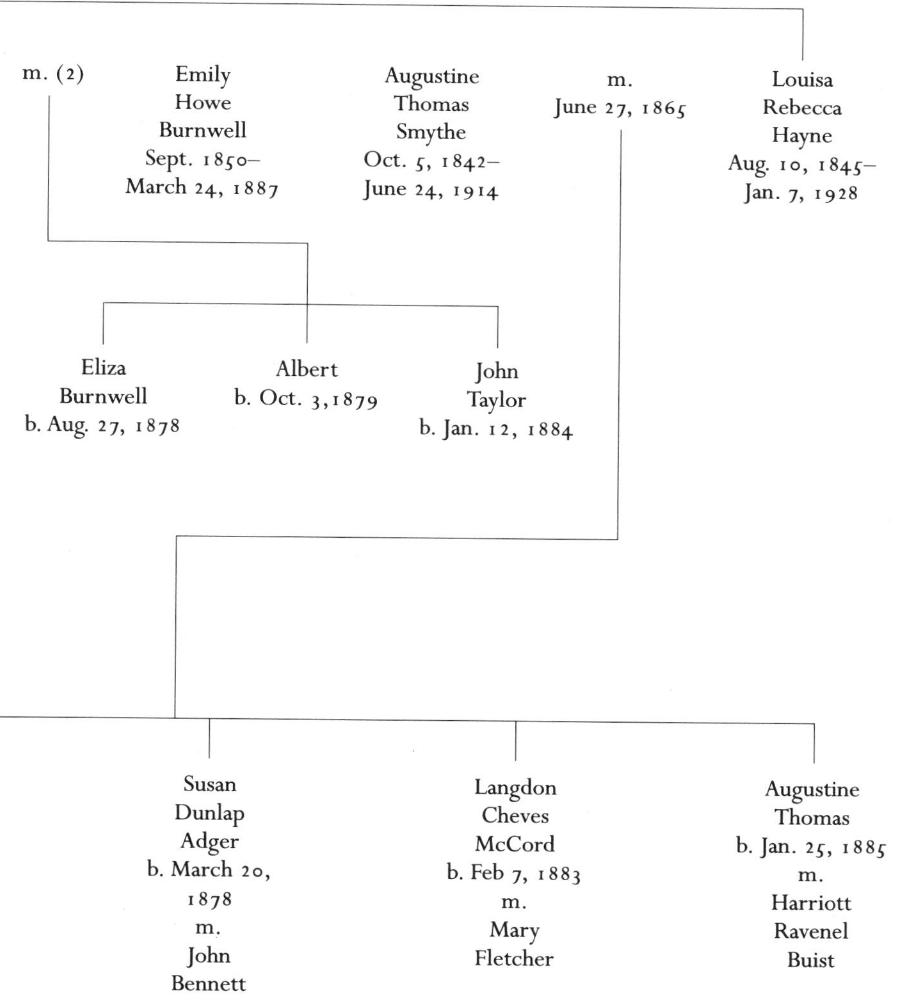
m. (2)
Emily Howe Burnwell Sept. 1850– March 24, 1887
Augustine Thomas Smythe Oct. 5, 1842– June 24, 1914
m. June 27, 1865
Louisa Rebecca Hayne Aug. 10, 1845– Jan. 7, 1928
Eliza Burnwell b. Aug. 27, 1878
Albert b. Oct. 3, 1879
John Taylor b. Jan. 12, 1884
Susan Dunlap Adger b. March 20, 1878 m. John Bennett
Langdon Cheves McCord b. Feb 7, 1883 m. Mary Fletcher
Augustine Thomas b. Jan. 25, 1885 m. Harriott Ravenel Buist

Part I

POLITICAL ECONOMY

1.

Justice and Fraternity

The valuable periodical with the name of which we head this article, is, we believe, less known than it deserves to be throughout the reading portion of our community. It is edited monthly, or semi-monthly, by many of the first writers in France; and, although maintaining occasionally principles in which we cannot entirely concur, it furnishes a series of brilliant and striking articles, generally well worthy of attention. From one of these, emanating from the pen of Frédéric Bastiat (already well known to us as the author, among other valuable publications, of the *Sophismes économiques*) we borrow our title, "Justice and Fraternity."[1] We do not intend to

SQR 15 (July 1849): 356–74. The second and third paragraphs (with some deletions) are reprinted in Hart, *Female Prose Writers of America*, pp. 187–89. Publication reviewed: *Journal des économistes: Revue mensuelle d'économie politique et des questions agricoles, manufacturières, et commercielles* 20 (June 1848): 241–360.

1. "Justice et fraternité," *Journal des économistes* 20 (June 1848): 310–27. Claude-Frédéric Bastiat (1801–50), French economist, member of the Constituent Assembly and National Assembly (1848). LSM translated his *Sophismes économiques* as *Sophisms of the Protective Policy* (New York and Charleston, S.C., 1848). Her translation appeared also as part 1 (entitled "Sophisms of Protection: First Series") in Frédéric Bastiat, *Essays on Political Economy* (Chicago, 1869; rpt. New York, 1870 [with new title, *Sophisms of the Protectionists*]); the preface, by Horace White (1834–1916), advised that "Mrs. McCord's excellent translation" was being reprinted "by permission of her publisher [G. P. Putnam], who holds the copyright," and noted that the "very few verbal alterations" made for this new edition "have no bearing on the accuracy and faithfulness of her work" (p. xvi).

stop here our pilferings, but will translate the greater portion of the article for the benefit of our readers, first venturing modestly to state our own position.

We are not ultra-reformists—far from it—and yet we are of those who see, in the present condition of the world, the waking up of a new era. We are of those who believe in—if not the perfectibility of man—at least his great, lasting, and boundless improvement. Thought is roused, mind is awakened, which never again can sleep. Vainly are we told that preceding ages have shown equal civilization and similar improvement. Vainly is our attention directed to the great Nineveh, to Egypt, to Greece and to Rome. These certainly do show—these have shown—progression and retrogression, rise and fall, as the great pulse of humanity has throbbed in its breathing of ages; but never has the world soul been roused, as now, by the expansion of thought, circulating to distant points of our globe, whose very existence was not dreamed of by the wise of ancient days. Never has the great heart of civilization cast, as now, by its every pulsation, its lifeblood to the farthest extremes of a universe, rousing itself from unconscious infancy to the full action of a reasoning being. Great as were the efforts of the ancients—great as were the results of those efforts—they were confined to little corners of a world, which now basks under the full radiance of extended and extending light. And yet, even of these efforts, nothing has been lost. The soul of their civilization, as each sank in its ruins, was breathed into the survivor, until at last, in the great crash of Roman power, the shattered remnants of its pride and its knowledge, scattering through Europe, laid the basis of modern civilization. *This* can never die—*this* can never be crushed. If driven from the East it would seek the West; crushed in the West still could it breathe in the East. A civilized *state* may fall back into barbarism; a civilized *world*—never! The diffusive spirit of Christianity, the wonderful invention of letters, the discovery of our Western world, the wide-spread power of steam, and now Heaven's lightning, by science tamed to be man's messenger—these put us on a pinnacle which Greece and Rome could never dream of. And yet the world is young! We look not into its future; veiled to us are its glories. But through the mist and mystery of forthcoming ages, interpreted by the awakening beam of the past, may we not read the one great hope—the one bright truth—man is improving, improvable, ceaselessly and boundlessly!

Yet not for this, alas! are we now exempt from the wildest follies, the grossest vices. France, in her present struggles, shows a mingling chaos of all that is best and wisest, of all that is maddest and worst. Among the most rampant of her run-mad fancies is this wild dream of "fraternity" and socialism, with their Icarias and Utopian worlds.[2] Would that these were confined to France alone. Unfortunately, we see their extravagant madness striding the Atlantic and stamping its too plainly marked foot-tracks on our own shores. That terrible fallacy compacted in the words, "the right to labor," is rapidly working its mischief. "The Right of Man to Labor, and of <to> Land whereon to Labor," in the words of the prospectus for 1849 of the New York *Tribune,*[3] what is it, as our communists interpret it, but the right to rob? They would not labor for nothing, nor yet for such compensation as the true value of their labor, given where it is wanted and paid for as it is needed, will produce. They have the right to labor, be it for good or for ill. They have the right to be paid for that labor, let the capital they force into their use be theirs or another's. You do not want my work—it matters not: "I have a right to work, and you, having capital, must pay me for such work, be it to your detriment or your benefit. I have the right to labor!"

Why, what is this but the highwayman's practice? "I cut your throat, sir, because I have nothing better to do, and, by way of compensation for the labor, will only make free with your purse." Too many of us, led away by the bright side of the dream, and without investigating its realities, catch only at the vague ideas of universal peace, self-sacrifice, fraternal union, etc., which it depicts. But the devil can quote Scripture to his purpose,[4] and under no form is mischief more insidious than when veiling itself in the garb of the purest feelings of the heart. "We have just read," says our *Journal,* "the profession of faith of many of our Parisian candidates, and find in them such phrases as the following: 'I am in favor of *a wise organization of labor.*' Citizens, the men who speak thus do not understand themselves, nor do they comprehend the weight of the formula, 'organization of labor.' They stand doubting between truth and falsehood. Give us rather the full-blooded socialist with his cut-and-dried system than this bastard breed who thoughtlessly tread without themselves knowing whither they lead us."[5]

But let us turn to M. Bastiat, who argues the question so clearly that we think we will be doing our readers a service in transferring the greater portion of his article to our sheets. "The school of political economy is," says he,

2. Besides Thomas More's *Utopia,* LSM refers to the novel *Voyage en Icarie* (1840) of the French socialist Etienne Cabet (1788–1856), who in 1849, under the influence of Robert Owen, founded a utopian community called Icaria in Nauvoo, Ill.

3. "Prospectus for 1849," New York *Daily Tribune,* Dec. 14, 1848.

4. *The Merchant of Venice* 1.3.92–97: "Mark you this Bassanio, / The devil can cite Scripture for his purpose,— / An evil soul producing holy witness / Is like a villain with a smiling cheek, / A goodly apple rotten at the heart. / O what a goodly outside falsehood hath!"

5. "Chronique," *Journal des économistes* 20 (June 1848): 291–96; 296 (LSM's italics).

on a crowd of questions, in direct opposition to the numerous socialist schools, which pretend to a newer light. We [the political economists][6] have for opponents Communists, Fourierists and Owenists—Cabet, Blanc, Proudhon, Leroux, etc.[7]—and it is worthy of remark, that these various schools differ among each other at least as much as they differ from us. One principle only, common to all, and in which consists our radical difference, they maintain: while political economy asks *from the law* universal justice and nothing more, socialism, in its divers forms, requires, over and above this, that *the law* should guaranty the realization of its favorite dogma of fraternity.

Socialism admits, with Rousseau, that social order exists entirely in the law. Rousseau based it upon a contract. Louis Blanc, in the first page of his work upon the revolution,[8] says, "The principle of fraternity is that which, looking upon mankind as one responsible body, has a tendency to organize society, which is *the work of man,* upon the model of the human body, which is the work of God."

Starting from this point, that society is *the work of man,* the *work of the law* [LSM's italics], socialists thence deduce the idea that there can exist in society nothing that is not pre-ordered and arranged by legislation.

Political economy asking from *the law* nothing but justice, justice every where and for all, they thence consider it as excluding fraternity [brotherly love, charity, benevolence. We have no exact synonyme for the French *fraternité.*][9] from all social relations. "Since," say they, "society exists in the law, and you ask from the law only justice, you thus exclude fraternity from the

6. LSM's interpolation.

7. François-Marie-Charles Fourier (1772–1837), French social theorist, in his *Théorie des quatres mouvements et des destinées générales* (1808) advocated a division of society into self-reliant phalanxes; settlements, called phalansteries, were founded upon his ideas in France and the United States. Robert Owen (1771–1858), Welsh socialist, proposed a completely environmental basis for human character; cooperative communities based on his ideas were established in Britain and the United States. Socialist, author of *L'Organisation du travail* (1840), and member of the Provisional Government formed after the abdication of King Louis Philippe on Feb. 24, 1848, Jean-Joseph-Charles-Louis Blanc (1811–82) secured a guarantee of employment to workers; in exile in England (1848–70). Also active in the Revolution of 1848, Pierre-Joseph Proudhon (1809–65) was editor of radical journals *Le Représentant du peuple* (1848–49), *La Voix du peuple* (1849–50), and *Le Peuple de 1850* (1850); most famous of his publications, favoring anarchism, is *Qu'est-ce que la propriété?* (1840), in the first chapter of which he enunciated his celebrated aphorism, "La propriété, c'est le vol." Pierre Leroux (1797–1871), journalist—among other publications, he founded with George Sand the *Revue Indépendante* in 1840—and socialist, was member of the Constituent Assembly (1848) and Legislative Assembly (1849); in exile after Louis-Napoléon's coup d'état (1851–59).

8. *Histoire de la Révolution française* (1847–62).

9. LSM's interpolation.

law and consequently from society." Hence follow imputations of coldness, harshness, heartlessness, which have been showered upon the science and professors of political economy.

But is this a true proposition, that society exists only in and by the law? If not, all such imputations fall to the ground.

And will you maintain that because absolute law, which acts always with authority and by force, backed by the bayonet and the dungeon, because law decrees neither affection nor friendship, love nor self-denial, nor yet the summing up of all these, fraternity, brotherly love, will you maintain that it annihilates or denies these noble attributes of our nature? Surely not. This only proves that society is more comprehensive than law, that an endless series of actions, a crowd of noble sentiments, are forever operating above and beyond the law. In the name of the science, I protest against this most unjust interpretation, which, because we acknowledge a limit to the law, would accuse us of denying every thing beyond this limit. . . .

Let us admit that the numerous writers who would smother in the heart of man every interested feeling, who, with no mercy for what they term individualism, have their mouths constantly filled with the words devotion, self-sacrifice, and brotherly love, let us admit that their hearts also are filled with them, that they are all disinterestedness and charity. We do not dispute their word, but only permit ourselves to say that we do not shrink from the comparison with them.

Each of these Decii[10] has a plan for perfecting the happiness of mankind, and each seems to say to us that if we oppose his system it is because we dread the periling of our property or other such advantages. But no! We oppose them because we look upon their ideas as false, their projects as not only puerile but fatal to society. . . .

We are not convinced of the possibility of forcing brotherly love upon the world. If this feeling, wherever it is manifested, excites our sympathy and admiration, it is precisely because it acts entirely free of all legal constraint. It exists spontaneously or not at all. To decree is to annihilate it. The law may force a man to be just, but vainly would it force him to be generous. [. . .]

When a number of families who, for their own comfort, wishing to labor either singly or in association, put in common a part of their power, what can they ask from this common power but the protection of the person, the labor, the rights, and the interests of each? And what is this but universal justice? It is plain that the right of each must have for its limit the precisely similar right of all the others. The law can do no more than acknowledge

10. See *Caius Gracchus* 3.4.76–77 and note in *PDBL*.

this limit and cause it to be respected. By permitting any to go beyond it the law would be unjust. And how much more so then, if, instead of tolerating such encroachments, it should command them!

Let us take for instance a question of property. Our principle is that to each individual belongs the produce of his own labor; and, in proportion as this labor has been successful, skilful or persevering, so is it productive. If any two choose to unite their power, and to divide the produce according to understood proportions, or should they choose to exchange their produce, or the one make to the other a loan or a gift, what has the law to do with it? Simply nothing—except to require the execution of agreements, and to hinder fraud and violence. Now, does this mean that the law thus interdicts acts of nobleness and generosity? Certainly not—but *has it a right to command them?* [LSM's italics] This is precisely the question in point, between political economists and socialists.

If socialists would merely maintain that, under extraordinary circumstances, and in urgent cases, the State should succour the unfortunate, or palliate the effects of disastrous change, most willingly we agree. This has been done, and we wish that it could be better done. But there is a point at which such efforts on the part of the State should stop—and this is, when governmental vigilance annihilates (by taking the place of it) individual vigilance. It is too well proved that, in such cases, organized charity produces a much larger proportion of permanent evil than of temporary good.

But exceptional measures are not what we at present have under discussion. The question we would examine into, is this: Is it the business of the law, generally, to prove and defend the limits of pre-existing reciprocal rights, or to seek, by direct legislation, the furtherance of the happiness of men by promoting acts of generosity, self-denial, and sacrifice?

The most striking effect of this last system [. . .] is the uncertainty which it cannot fail to cast upon the result of human effort, the doubt which it hangs over man's surest measures, paralyzing his every endeavor.

Justice—we understand what it is, and wherein it consists. It is a fixed immovable point. If the law takes it for its guide, we know well what we may expect, and arrange our measures accordingly.

But fraternity (brotherly love), where is its determined point? What is its limit? What its form? What is it but the undefined, limitless yearning of the heart to suffer and to labor for others? When free, spontaneous, voluntary, I understand and revere it. But when, in the heart of society, the principle is established that fraternity shall be *imposed by law* [LSM's italics]—that is to say, in plain English <en bon français>, that the produce of our labor shall be divided by law, without any reference or regard to the rights of labor itself—who can say where this fantastic principle shall stop, in what form the caprice of a legislator may invest it, or what institutions may be established by its whimsical decrees? On such conditions can society exist?

Self-sacrifice, unlike justice, has no marked limits. Beginning with the poor farthing thrown to the beggar, it may extend to the sacrifice even of life and more; *usque ad mortem, mortem autem crucis.*[11] The Gospel, which teaches brotherly love to man, thus explains its meaning: "Whosoever shall smite thee on thy right cheek, turn to him the other also. And if any man will sue thee at the law and take away thy coat, let him have thy cloak also."[12] It has done more than explain, it has given us the most complete, the most touching, the most sublime example of it on the summit of Golgotha.

And would you by legal code enforce upon society a fraternity so high as this? Or will you stop midway? Where shall be our bounds? These must depend upon the opinion of one censor today, and another tomorrow! . . . Can a people enjoy either moral rest, or physical prosperity, who, at the fancy of a legislator, may, at any hour, be called upon to assume such a stamp of benevolence as his whim of the moment may dictate?

Let us place in juxtaposition, for sober examination, the most striking consequences of the two systems in question.

We suppose, first, a nation, which, for its basis of legislation, adopts universal justice; whose citizens taking upon themselves the responsibility of their own support, worship, education, and business transactions, the only duty devolving upon the government is to watch over, and keep, each and all within the limits of their respective rights.[13] . . . Thus would each be secure of his future, in as far as that could in any way be dependant upon the law. Exact justice is of so certain a tenor, that a legislation taking it for its basis, would be, in effect, unchangeable, varying only as it might aim at higher perfection in defending individual rights. Thus might each, in his honest endeavors, seek, as he willed, his own prosperity, and, without fear of interruption, labor in whatsoever career might suit his circumstances, inclination, and interest, independent of all privileges, monopolies, and restric-

11. Phil. 2:8: "et habitu inventus ut homo, humiliavit semet ipsum factus oboediens usque ad mortem, mortem autem crucis." "And being found in fashion as a man, he humbled himself, and became obedient unto death, even the death of the cross."

12. Matt. 5:39–40.

13. LSM's text, here somewhat awkward, translates the following ("Justice et fraternité," p. 314):

"Supposons d'abord une nation qui adopte pour base de sa législation la Justice, la Justice universelle.

"Supposons que les citoyens disent au gouvernement: 'Nous prenons sur nous la responsabilité de notre propre existence; nous nous chargeons de notre travail, de nos transactions, de notre instruction, de nos progrès, de notre culte; pour vous, votre seule mission sera de nous contenir tous et sous tous les rapports dans les limites de nos droits.'"

tions. . . . Property thus secured, whatever the nature of the services which each individual might render to society or to his fellow-citizen, or exchange for foreign produce, these services could not fail to bear their *natural value*. This value would certainly depend much upon circumstances, but at least could not be affected by the caprices of law, the exactions of imposts, or by parliamentary intrigues, pretension, and influence. The prices of things and of labor would be subjected to the lowest possible minimum of fluctuation, and, under such circumstances, it would be impossible but that industry would be developed, riches increased, and capital accumulate with unexampled rapidity.

From this increase of capital would follow, as a consequence of the competition thence resulting, that its remuneration would diminish, or, in other words, the rate of interest would become lower. In proportion as this would weigh less and less upon the price of production, the share claimed by capital in the general result would, of course, consequently also become less and less. This agent of labor, more extended, would now be within the reach of a larger number of individuals, while the prices of all articles of consumption would be diminished by so much, as they would be relieved of the demand of capital. Thus the means of subsistence, one of the first requisites for the relief of the working classes, would become cheap. At the same time, and from the same cause (rapid increase of capital), wages would necessarily rise. Capital is in truth absolutely valueless unless employed, and the larger and more employed it is, in proportion to the number of workmen, so must wages of course increase.

Thus the necessary result of this government of simple justice (of, in consequence, liberty and security) is to relieve, in two ways, the suffering classes. Giving them the means of existence cheap, it raises likewise the rate of wages. Their physical condition thus relieved, it is impossible that their moral condition also should not be raised and refined. Here, then, are we not upon the road to equality? Not simply legal equality, but equality of fact, physical and moral, resulting from the fact that the remuneration of labor augments in proportion as, and because, that of capital diminishes. [310–16]

M. Bastiat goes on to argue that, in foreign relations, this country of exact and simple justice must also be peaceful, its commercial relations free and extensive, and its governmental expenses reduced to a point which would almost entirely obviate the necessity of taxation. "When," he remarks,

a nation is overloaded with taxes, nothing is more difficult, or rather impossible, than to equalize them. Financiers have given up the effort as futile. And yet one thing there is, even more impossible: and this is, to cast the load upon the *rich*. Governments can only obtain superabundant funds by exhausting the resources of the whole community, and most particularly of *the poor.* [316–17; LSM's italics]

He continues:

> We will be answered perhaps by our opponents: "We see indeed, in the government you describe, justice, economy, liberty, riches, peace, order, and equality, but where is fraternity?" Once more let me ask: Is the heart of man moulded only by the legislator? Does it know nothing, and feel nothing, but what is written "in the bond"? Must benevolence be enforced upon you by censorial surveillance? And does the law forbid charity, because it enforces justice? [. . .] The law, which is force, can be employed usefully only in repressing injuries and maintaining rights. [318]

M. Bastiat then goes on to exemplify the other side of the question, and supposes a nation where "the law, not limiting itself to enforcing rights, would also enforce fraternity" [318]. What do we see?

> First, a frightful uncertainty, a mortal insecurity, shadowing the whole domain of individual effort. For, from the thousand unknown forms that fraternity may assume, what thousand unforeseen decrees may there not spring forth to menace and destroy every pre-established form of society? One, in the name of fraternity, steps forth to demand *uniformity of wages;* and behold the industrial classes at once transformed into Indian castes. Neither skill nor courage, assiduity nor intelligence, can redeem them thence; a law of lead is upon them, weighing down their effort and their hope. This world is thus, to them, become like the Hell of Dante, over which runs the inscription *Lasciate ogni speranza, voi ch'entrate.*[14]
>
> Again, in the name of fraternity, comes another who requires that the hours of labor should be reduced to ten—to eight—to six—to four hours; and here we have production suddenly checked. Bread is scant, clothing is scant, and to feed the hungry, and clothe the naked, a third Solon proposes *forced paper money.* "Do we not," says he, "procure food and clothing with money? Increase the circulation of money, and you increase food and clothing. Circulate paper—paper is money." A fourth decrees the abolition of competition; a fifth, of self-interest. Here stands one, who demands that the State shall furnish work; another that it shall give education; and, while a third asks a pension for each and every of its citizens, there starts up yet another who requires that royalty shall be abolished throughout the globe, and that in the name of fraternity, war, universal war shall be proclaimed in order to this effect. Enough! What end to these Utopian dreams? Such

14. *Inferno* 3.9. "Abandon all hope, ye who enter."

propositions, say you, would be rejected. Very likely; but it is *possible* that they might not, and such a possibility is enough to create mistrust <*incertitude*>—mistrust, the enemy of labor and its direst scourge.

Under such a government, capital could never increase, but would, on the contrary, become scarce and concentrated. Wages would of course fall, and equality would, at every step, dig deeper and deeper the abyss which separates class from class.

Public finances must be in complete confusion; for, government being called upon to furnish every thing to every body, the people would soon find itself crushed by taxes, and the State, forced from loan to loan, would, after exhausting the present, devour its own future.

Finally, as it is an acknowledged principle that the State must show its fraternity in favor of its citizens, the entire people is transformed into petitioners. Landed property, agriculture, commerce, shipping, mechanics, industrial associations, all crowd to claim favors from government. The public funds are literally held up for pillage. Each brings excellent reasons to prove that the just interpretation of legal fraternity must give him the profits, let who will pay the expenses. The effort of each is to snatch from the legislature some fragment of this *fraternal* privilege. The suffering classes, despite their better claim, cannot always be successful: their numbers increase without end, and each stride of the country is from revolution to revolution.

Then becomes developed, in all its fearfulness, the dismal spectacle of which we already see the mournful preface, in such modern societies as have adopted the fatal watchword, *legal fraternity!* [318–19]

That the idea of fraternity may be founded in generous sentiments, M. Bastiat cheerfully acknowledges. But, for this very reason, is it the more fatal. Acting thus upon the better feelings of men, it conciliates the sympathies of the mistakenly good and misleads by its plausibility. That the State should be able to give every thing to every body, yet require nothing from anybody, is certainly an unfathomable enigma. That it should, in the words of M. Bastiat,

take upon itself all care, all responsibility, every duty which Providence, in its inscrutable designs, has left of laborious and difficult execution to man, that it should assume these, and leave to individuals only the delights, pleasures, and calm existence, a happy present, a promising future; fortune without effort, family without care, and life without struggle! Who but would willingly aid in the rearing of such a system? But can this be? "That is the question." [. . .] What is this personified *State,* which so generously takes

> upon itself the execution of every virtue and duty? Whence these abundant resources which are to be so freely scattered among the people? Whence can they be derived but from the people themselves? [320–21]

It is they who must sweat and drudge to provide them, and, as we have seen, not from the rich only, but more particularly from the poor, must bloated governments draw their superabundance. This "juggling fiend,"[15] *the State,* pampered with the life-blood of its own children, can only gain an hour of sickly popularity—petting the ten to starve the million—by sucking out the existence of the masses.

From a "letter to workmen" (*lettre aux ouvriers*) by Amédée Gratiot (one of the working classes), entitled *Organisez le travail, ne le désorganisez pas,* we will make a short extract to exemplify this remark. M. Gratiot attacks the two decrees, passed shortly before his writing, by the Provisional Government: the one promising to furnish work, the other suppressing one hour from the working day. "We cannot," says he,

> count at less than a million the number of citizens who will be daily forced to ask work from the republic, and as the *minimum* of wages for these would be an average of two francs per head, this would amount to 2 millions daily, or 600 millions yearly. We have in France about ten millions of workmen. The daily hour of labor suppressed may be averaged at 25 centimes per hour. Ten millions of hours at 25 centimes amount to 2,500,000 francs daily, which, by the year (of 300 days), makes 750 millions of drawback upon French industry! Now let us count up: 600 millions for the guaranty of labor, 750 millions for the suppression of the working hour, makes in all 1,350,000,000, one thousand, three hundred and fifty million that France must pay to indulge her governors with an hour's popularity![16]

But to return to M. Bastiat, he glances at divers subjects of human legislation—religion, education, the press, foreign intercourse—and proves that justice and only justice can suffice to regulate them all. Touching religion: "However desirable," he observes,

15. *Macbeth* 5.8.19–22: "And be these juggling fiends no more believ'd, / That palter with us in a double sense; / That keep the word of promise to our ear, / And break it to our hope."

16. This passage is quoted in the review of Amédée Gratiot, *Organisez le travail, ne le désorganisez pas: Lettre aux ouvriers* (Paris, 1848), in *Journal des économistes* 20 (June 1848): 288–90; 289 (LSM's italics). Amédée Gratiot (1812–80), printer and poet; secretary of the Chamber of Printers; judge on the Tribunal of Commerce (1850).

unity may be, diversity—that is to say, investigation and discussion—is better, so long as we have no infallible sign by which this *true faith* may be stamped upon the mind. The intervention of the State, even with the plea of fraternity, would, if endeavoring to establish unity, be an act of oppression and *injustice;* for who can certify that the State may not be mistaken? Unity can only result from the universal consent of freely judging intellect, untrammelled by aught but the natural attraction exercised by truth upon the mind of man. Law can have nothing to do with belief—it may guaranty liberty; it may forbid it; it can neither make nor unmake it.[17]

Concerning intercourse with foreigners, our essayist observes:

I see still, no other rule, prudent, fit to become law, but *justice.* To subject such intercourse to the dictation of legal fraternity would be to decree universal and perpetual war. It would be forcing us to place our strength, our blood and fortunes, at the disposal of whoever might claim them in any cause calculated to excite the sympathy of the legislator. Singular fraternity! Quixotism, established and imposed by law!

But above all is this dogma of fraternity dangerous when, contrary to the very essence and nature of the idea, we seek to introduce it, with its accompanying penal sentence for the *regulation of labor* <avec accompagnement de la disposition pénale qui sanctionne toute loi positive>, to our legal code. . . .

Fraternity (let us once for all take the word in the full extent of its French signification) is a *voluntary sacrifice dictated by our own feelings.* Enforce it by the power of the law [. . .] and what remains of this definition? One thing truly: it is still a sacrifice; but a sacrifice involuntary, forced and dictated by the fear of punishment. And what is in truth such a sacrifice, forced upon one for the benefit of another? Is this fraternity? Or is it not rather robbery, and robbery of the most fatal kind? Robbery systematized, permanent, inevitable, in as much as it is legalized!

This principle Barbès put into practice when [dans la séance du 15 mai] he decreed a tax of a thousand million in favor of the poorer classes, and Sobrier, in his proclamation to the same effect, commences with these words, "As it is right that fraternity should no longer be a vain word, but

17. "Justice et fraternité," p. 321. The last sentence appears to be a free translation, or condensation, of: "Tout ce qu'on peut donc demander à la loi, c'est la liberté pour toutes les croyances, quelque anarchie qui doive en résulter dans le monde pensant. Car qu'est-ce que cette anarchie prouve? que l'Unité n'est pas à l'origine, mais à la fin, de l'évolution intellectuelle. Elle n'est pas un point de départ, elle est une résultante. La loi qui l'imposerait serait injuste, et si la justice n'implique pas nécessairement la fraternité, on conviendra du moins que la fraternité exclut l'injustice."

should manifest itself by actions, be it decreed that all capitalists shall contribute etc."[18]

You exclaim at this, but why? Barbès and Sobrier were only a little more consistent than yourselves in their endeavor to put your own principle into action.

I repeat it, when this principle is introduced into legislation, let it make its approach with however timid a step, its apparition must paralyze at once both labor and capital. Unknowing the limits of its action, men, in doubt whether they will be permitted to enjoy the fruits of their own labor, naturally cease to work, or at least work less. Insecurity drives off capital, hinders its accumulation, and what then becomes of the very classes whose relief was the plea for such injustice? Truly this tyranny of fraternity would, in itself, suffice to rapidly drive the most prosperous nation below the condition of despot-ridden Turkey. . . .

The law, thus imposing upon men mutual sacrifice, can still not deprive humanity of its nature, and the effort of each is, of course, to bring as little, and to claim as much as possible, in the mass of fraternal sacrifice. In the struggle and scramble which follows, are the needy and the wretched winners? Or rather does the pampered rapacity of intrigue and power find here its harvest?[19] . . .

Vainly would this legal robbery borrow the name of fraternity, with its form and its formulas; never can it be other than a principle of discord and confusion, terror and wretchedness, of unjust pretension, jealous hatred, and effortless languor. [322–24]

"Again," continues M. Bastiat,

another grave objection is made by our opponents. "Simple justice," say they, "remains entirely neutral between the rich and the poor, the strong and the

18. Sigmund-Auguste-Armand Barbès (1809–70), French revolutionary, condemned to death for treason under Louis Philippe in 1839; the sentence commuted to life imprisonment, he was released after the king's abdication; made president of the Club de la Révolution at the instigation of Marie-Joseph-Camille Sobrier (1812–54), radical leader, who had been briefly prefect of police in Paris in February 1848. Barbès and Sobrier were arrested for their part in the invasion of the National Assembly and the Hôtel de Ville and in the proclamation of a new provisional government on May 15, 1848; each was sentenced to seven years' imprisonment.

19. Cf. the original French of this paragraph: "Quand, sous prétexte de fraternité, le Code impose aux citoyens des sacrifices réciproques, la nature humaine ne perd pas pour cela ses droits. L'effort de chacun consiste alors à apporter peu à la masse des sacrifices, et à en retirer beaucoup. Or, dans cette lutte, sont-ce les plus malheureux qui gagnent? Non certes, mais les plus influents et les plus intrigants." (324) We observe here LSM's tendency, when translating, to build a richness and vigor of style upon hints suggested by the original.

weak, the learned and the ignorant, the landed proprietor and the houseless beggar, fellow-citizen or foreigner. Now, *interests being naturally antagonist,* thus to leave men their liberty without any intervention but laws simply just, is to sacrifice at once the poor and the needy, the weak and the ignorant, who, thus disarmed, present themselves for the combat."

"What could result," asks M. Considérant,[20] "from this industrial liberty, on which so much stress has been laid, from this famous principle of *untrammelled competition,* which was supposed to be so strongly gifted with the character of democratic organization? What could result from these but general subjection, complete enfeoffment of the masses, who, without capital, tools, instruments of labor, or even education, are launched into the struggle? 'The lists are open,' we are told, 'all are equally called, with equal conditions, to the combat.' This sounds plausibly enough; but it is forgotten that in this great battle for life some are well trained, instructed, armed to the teeth, possessing abundant supplies, materials, munitions and machines of war, occupying and monopolizing every commanding position, while others, naked, ignorant, hungry, and exposed, are obliged to save themselves, their wives and children from starvation, to beg from day to day, even from their *adversaries,* work which may bring them in some scanty pittance of wages."

And does M. Considérant regard this as a just comparison? Are capital, tools, intellect, education, which are used to conquer natural obstacles and smooth the way of life—are these, by a wretched sophistry, to be compared to offensive arms and ensanguined weapons? Why stamp with all the vocabulary of battles the routine of labor and industrial order? The great, irreconcilable difference which exists upon this point between socialists and economists is this: socialists believe in a natural and essential antagonism of interests; economists, in a natural harmony of interests, or rather in the possession, by them, of a necessary and progressive harmonizing tendency. Socialists, starting with this proposition, that interests are naturally antagonist, are thence logically led to seek for them an artificial organization <une organisation *artificielle*>, or even, if possible, to extinguish all interested feeling in the heart of man. . . .

Doubtless, if interests are, as they suppose, naturally antagonist, it thence follows that it is necessary to trample under foot justice, liberty, and legal equality. The world must be re-made, or, to use their own expression, *society must be re-modelled* upon some one of the numerous systems which they are constantly inventing. For self-interest, that disorganizing principle, must be

20. Victor-Prosper Considérant (1809–93), French disciple of Fourier, member of the Constituent Assembly (1848); wrote, among other works, *Le Socialisme devant le vieux monde* (1848).

substituted self-sacrifice, imposed by law, involuntary, forced—in a word, organized spoliation; and, in order that this new principle may be swallowed with the least possible resistance, it is very well to blazon its first appearance with the deceitful name of fraternity, even while law and power are called in to enforce it.

But if Providence has not blundered in the making of our world, and has so arranged affairs that, under the natural law of justice, interests will of themselves assume the most harmonious combinations—if equality of rights is the most certain path to equality in fact—then we need only justice and liberty, that is to say, the removal only of unnatural obstacles, in order to allow things to assume their own natural level, as does each unobstructed drop of water that forms the ocean. [324–25]

"This," says M. Bastiat, "is the conclusion that political economy finds, rather than seeks. It comes in the natural course of events, and needs no forcing system to produce it."[21]

He then compares the two opposing systems to two chemists, the one of whom declares that he has just made the discovery that the world is threatened with a great catastrophe.

"Providence," says he, "has not properly arranged matters. I have analyzed the air ejected by the human lungs, and I find that it is quite unfit, entirely destroyed for the purposes of respiration. This being the case, how soon must the supply of atmosphere be exhausted! I can, by calculating its volume, infallibly predict the day on which it must become entirely vitiated and mankind will perish for want of breath, unless, as a remedy, there is immediately adopted a respiratory apparatus, which, in anticipation of this evil, I have been fortunate enough to invent."

"You are mistaken," answers his brother chemist. "The air, it is true as you state, is, when ejected by the human lungs, unfit for maintaining human life,

21. These two sentences are a condensed translation of:

"Et c'est là la conclusion à laquelle arrive l'économie politique. Cette conclusion, elle ne la cherche pas, elle la trouve; mais elle se réjouit de la trouver, car enfin, n'est-ce pas une vive satisfaction pour l'esprit que de voir l'harmonie dans la liberté, quand d'autres sont réduits à demander à l'arbitraire?

"Les paroles haineuses que nous addressent souvent les Socialistes sont en vérité bien étranges! Eh quoi! si par malheur nous avons tort, ne devraient-ils pas le déplorer? Que disons-nous? Nous disons: Après mûr examen, il faut reconnaître que Dieu a bien fait ce qu'il a fait, en sorte que la meilleure condition du progrès, c'est la justice et la liberté.

"Les Socialistes nous croient dans l'erreur; c'est leur droit. Mais ils devraient néanmoins s'en affliger; car notre erreur, si elle est démontrée, implique l'urgence de substituer l'artificiel au naturel, l'arbitraire à la liberté, l'invention contingente et humaine à la conception éternelle et divine." (325–26)

but it is precisely suited for vegetable life; and that, reciprocally, which is exhaled by vegetables is suited for the breathing of man. You have looked only on one side of the question. A deeper research will prove to you that *God* has put order into all his works. Let us then go on breathing as *God* and nature have designed. We do not need your breathing apparatus, which is troublesome, expensive, and mischievous."[22]

"Heartless man!" exclaims the first, "cruel! unnatural! dead to the sufferings of humanity! You advocate the horrible *Laissez-faire* system. You reject this great blessing to mankind, this wonderful breathing apparatus I have discovered."

Thus stands our dispute with the socialists. We wish, both of us, for harmony and order. They seek it in the innumerable restraints which they would by law impose upon mankind; we find it in the nature of men and things. [. . .] We find it because we do not, with socialism, stop our investigations at the immediate consequences of the phenomena of human nature, but seek farther into their ulterior and definitive effects. The two schools differ exactly as our two chemists: the one sees a part, the other the whole of the system. . . . In the domain of political economy *there is much to learn, little to do.* Much to learn, because the chain of effects can only be followed up by close application; little to do, because, from its own final action, this chain of effects produces the general harmony of events. [326–27]

"Let me finish," says M. Bastiat,

by assuring our socialist friends that if they have really been under the belief that political economy rejects association, organization, and fraternity they are entirely mistaken.

Association! Society itself, forever seeking to perfect itself, what is this but association?

Organization! Do we not know that in this exists all the difference between a heterogeneous mass of elemental matter and the most perfect masterpieces of nature?

Fraternity! Do we not feel that this is to justice what the spontaneous impulse of the heart is to the cool calculation of reason?

We agree with you, gentlemen, we applaud your efforts, and would labor with you to scatter through the broad field of human nature a seed of which the future shall bear abundant fruit.

22. These last four sentences translate: "Une étude incomplète avait induit à penser que Dieu s'était trompé; une recherche plus exacte montre qu'il a mis l'harmonie dans ses oeuvres. Les hommes peuvent continuer à respirer comme la nature l'a voulu." (326)

But from the moment that you would bring law and taxes, constraint and spoliation, to second your efforts, from that moment we oppose you. Thus, at once, you prove that you rely not upon human nature, but upon your own systems, for success. And thus, also, you entirely destroy the very spirit and nature of the principle which you seek to realize. [327]

To the reader who has patiently followed us through M. Bastiat's argument it is, we believe, unnecessary to apologize for the length of our extracts. The subject is an important one, and we here find it discussed by an able man, who has seen the system in as full operation as has ever yet been tried. Heaven grant that past experience may give future wisdom! But the system, although for the moment on the decline in France, is far from extinct. The terrible declaration of Proudhon, "Property is Robbery," "La Propriété, c'est le vol," will yet, we fear, among the ignorant masses, who grasp at present license, thoughtless of future consequences, work out its terrible effects.

In our own country, we see too plainly at every turn the insidious effects of this fearful fallacy. Free-soilers, barn-burners, anti-renters, abolitionists stare us in the face at every turn, and frightful to the thinking mind is the anarchy which must follow could they have their way.[23] Anarchy, M. Proudhon boasts, is the rule—if rule it may be called which rule has none[24]—which we are daily nearing. "Anarchy," says he, "absence of master, sovereign—people ordinarily attribute to the word *anarchy* the sense of absence of principle, absence of rule, and thus it has become a synonyme for *disorder*—such is the form of government that we approach every day."[25] And what principle, what rule can be, when, every form of natural justice

23. The Antirenters were a group of tenant farmers in New York State, who protested (1839–47) against paying rents for land which they had cultivated for generations and regarded as their own; their protests were often violent, forcing a new state constitution in 1846 to guarantee to them ownership of their lands. Given their name (about 1843) from the fabled farmer who burned down his barn to rid it of rats, the Barnburners were the radical, antislavery faction of the Democratic party in New York State; having split from the state party in 1847 and from the federal Democrats in 1848 over the extension of slavery into the western territories obtained after the war with Mexico, they were absorbed into the Free Soil party, which, formed in New York, shared their antislavery aims. The Free Soil party ran unsuccessful candidates in the presidential elections of 1848 and 1852; in 1854 it merged with dissident Whigs and Democrats to found the Republican party.

24. John Milton, *Paradise Lost* 2.666–67 (of Death): "The other shape, / If shape it might be called that shape had none."

25. *Qu'est-ce que la propriété?* (Paris, 1848), chap. 5, pt. 2, sect. 2, p. 242. LSM has within the dashes incorporated into the text what Proudhon placed in a footnote.

abolished, fantastic visions of fraternity domineer in each brain-sick fancy which struts upon the stage its little hour of rule?[26] when each,

> Drest in a little brief authority,
> Most ignorant of what he's most assured—
> His glassy essence—like an angry ape,
> Plays such fantastic tricks before high Heaven
> As make the angels weep.[27]

What can follow, but, on one side, that most crushing of all tyrannies, the tyranny of dominant and bigot opinion, which tramples out even the right of thought, or, on the other, the wildest license, most lawless anarchy, sweeping in its whirlwind progress every vestige of civilization, every footmark of man's better life—the life of reason and improving mind. That such must be the fate of some now flourishing empires is, under the excitement of this fearful question, much to be dreaded. Thank God! the bulwarks of civilization are too well established for us to anticipate a general retrogression of the world. A civilized State may, as we have remarked, fall back into anarchy; a civilized world—never! But fearful examples there have been—more fearful there yet may be—marked-out States, who, in their own folly, shall constitute themselves the terrible beacon-marks of man's impious madness, when, combatting Providence, he rails at the workings of its high behests.

Our own country is perhaps among those which now stand most prominent in this peril. Her wide-extended and extending domain, her active, thinking population—thinking, as all beginners must do, superficially, rushing to their end, the means unweighed, the cost uncalculated—these are her merits, but these also are her dangers. This noble people, still in its infancy, is, as such, easily led astray. The child of wide and expansive mind, grasping thought, and eager apprehension needs to be more carefully guarded in the associations and guidance of its youthful promise than the duller and more plodding, who, in the regular routine of its life, is less calculated for the extremes both of good and of evil. To our legislators, to our politicians, to our periodicals, and to our press generally, a serious task has fallen. Wake and watch! Ye are the preceptors, ye the guides of this budding intellect, this giant power, whose yet undeveloped strength is appointed to stamp with its world-waking spirit the destinies of human nature. Mind is free, but mind is swayable. Legislation cannot force it, but argument may

26. *Macbeth* 5.5.24–26: "Life's but a walking shadow; a poor player, / That struts and frets his hour upon the stage, / And then is heard no more."

27. *Measure for Measure* 2.2.119–23.

guide it. And you, whose position gives you almost unlimited power in its guidance, should beware what use you make of the "talent" which Heaven has placed in your hand. "To whom much is given, from him also shall much be expected."[28] Be men, with hearts of men, thinking, acting for your country and eschewing the petty spirit of demagogueism which, for its hour of paltry triumph, would recklessly work the ruin of millions. Wake and watch, that yourselves be not led astray by the plausibility of these most mischievous of theories. That the crowd, eager for change, discontented with their position, should grasp at licence, thinking to grasp at some imagined, unattainable excellence of liberty, is natural enough; but to you who have opportunity, whose business it is, or at least should be, to think, to study out the truth, to winnow the wheat from its chaff, to you the question is one which, if thoughtlessly argued, hastily acted upon, must bring upon your heads the curse of generations.

One more extract, before taking leave of our subject, we will give, from an article by A. Clément, in the *Journal des économistes,* entitled "Socialism and Liberty."[29] "The socialists," says our author,

> in proposing that the State shall guarantee the *right of labor,* imply that the government must be constantly provided with the means of furnishing labor to all who are notable by their own exertions to procure it. This is evidently one of the divers means by which they hope gradually to place in the hands of government the entire direction of labor. To be able to furnish occupation to all, whatever the number or profession of its applicants, it is evident government must acquire, in every part of the country, extensive lots of land, with innumerable workshops, forges, etc., furnished with utensils, circulating capital, and all the necessary materials for the progress of each profession. All these must, by means of taxes, be forced from the overburthened industry of the country, which, thus daily drained of its life-blood, must soon sink from exhaustion, unable to struggle against the increasing extent of these national work-shops, whose growth would be in exact proportion to the drain upon individual industry. The State thus become, as it soon inevitably must, sole proprietor, capitalist, and dispenser of labor, then, at last, would the reign of these disorganizers exist without control, each setting to work to re-model society according to his own notions. Already have we

28. Luke 12:48: "For unto whomsoever much is given, of him shall be much required: and to whom men have committed much, of him they will ask the more."

29. "Le Socialisme et la liberté," *Journal des économistes* 20 (June 1848): 241–51. Ambroise Clément (1805–86), disciple of Jean-Baptiste Say; general secretary of the town council of Saint Etienne (1838–48); among other works, *Des nouvelles idées de réforme industrielle et en particulier du projet d'organisation du travail de M. Louis Blanc* (1848).

been enlightened by some twenty or thirty different systems for the organization of labor; thousands of others would bud forth in this springtime of their fortunes; and, in order that each might have its fair trial, society would be called to pass successively through the crucible of each of these alchymists, until, victim to their experiments, its ashes alone would indicate a past existence.

The half way socialists <les socialistes *indécis*>, who yet adhere to no regular system [mongrel half-breed, almost more mischievous than those who, declaring their position, put the world upon its guard],[30] may doubtless maintain that this is carrying the right of labor too far; that the extent of national workshops might be limited, so as to prevent the ruin of individual industry, by giving their workers only the minimum of wages necessary to keep them from starvation, and that in order to avoid the effects of competition, they might be devoted exclusively to such labor as would not come within the range of individual industry. Without discussing the practicability of these conditions, we will only remark that the establishment of such limits is at once *the negation of the rights of labor;* for if this right exists—if it is founded upon justice—to render it thus illusory is a fraud upon those who, claiming labor from the national workshops, have, if *any right* [LSM's italics], the *full right* [LSM's italics] to exercise their profession with every advantage possessed by individual industry. To thus lower wages and force every man to a species of labor for which he may be entirely unfit and unprepared, is certainly to deny, at least in part, the right <*droit*> of labor, and to subject this right to such restrictions as might in the end effectually annul it.

Farther, even were such a reduction of this pretended right to labor feasible, this limited assistance, given by the State to all who could not depend upon their individual industry, would still produce the evil effect of encouraging and multiplying this exuberant and necessarily parasitical portion of its population. It would, like the poor laws in England, cause a rapid increase in the class of unfortunates which it would aim at relieving, and, at the same time, aggravate the sufferings, by augmenting the burthen, of the usefully laborious part of the community.

If society, which owes to every individual nothing but justice with the certain and complete guaranty of person and property, determines thus to take upon itself the charge of all those who fail to maintain themselves, *inevitably* it multiplies the numbers of this class, enervates every useful faculty, propagates every vice generative of misery and wretchedness, and endlessly increases its idle and parasitical population, at the expense of those who, courageously taking upon themselves the responsibility of their own maintenance, furnish at the same time the necessaries of the State.

30. LSM's interpolation.

> "Heartless doctrines!" we think we hear our socialists exclaim: "heartless doctrines! of that unfeeling science <cette science *sans entrailles*>, political economy, which, coldly submitting every thing to calculation, measures suffering by lines and figures, and weighs human misery by cool argument!" Wretched quibblers! mock philanthropists! Which, then, will you tell us are the most humane, the most benevolent, the most charitable doctrines: those which, seeking out wretchedness in the sources of its existence, endeavor to impress on every individual the feeling of his own dignity and responsibility, seeking to raise him to habits of labor, order, intelligence, and foresight, by purging our institutions of every thing which detracts from the advantages naturally attached to the practice of these virtues; or those who, wilfully forgetting every cause of voluntary indigence, BURTHEN VIRTUOUS HABITS WITH THE RESULTS OF VICE, and thus force on society to progressive misery and degradation? [250–51]

We have said that the tracks of this insidious policy have shown themselves in our own country. We are pained farther to declare, that they are even beginning to show themselves in our own State, in that South Carolina whose principles, we had fondly persuaded ourselves, were among the most conservative in all the country. Demagogueism is at work among us. Mischievous politicians, for their own, or party purposes, are busy in the endeavor to mislead or distract us. There has recently been put into circulation an artful pamphlet—an "Address to the Citizens of South Carolina"—most iniquitous in purpose and most mischievous in tendency. It is a bold and impudent effort to rouse the poorer classes against the rich. That this is done fraudulently, and with evil purpose, appears from the fact that the blow is aimed in the dark, and every effort made to conceal the writer and the publishers of it. Accident has perhaps revealed the name of one of its more active agents. We hope for farther revelations. The whole tenor of the paper in question is in accordance with the system which, throughout this article, we have been endeavoring to combat. It is an attempt to put dissension between the different classes of our State, and thus weaken the whole. Our people need not to be assured that "an enemy hath done this."[31] Let them guard against this wolf in sheep's clothing, nor allow themselves to be misled. Poor, or rich, our interests are with our State—the prosperity of one, is the prosperity of all, for wealth, once introduced and established in a country, must be diffused through it. It is not in its nature to stagnate. The law of its existence is circulation. One common interest should then bend our citizens in one common effort. Believe it, the levelling system of socialism gives no

31. Matt. 13:28.

equality but that which is found in one general ruin. It is the system of anarchy, disorder, misery, and death—death political, moral, and physical. Our existence as a State, our existence as men, depend equally upon the maintenance of order and unanimity in our councils. The apple of discord is among us. Hungry politicians, to seize a little and a merely momentary good—and that only in seeming—would plunge us unhesitatingly into anarchy and blood. Let us take warning from the wretched experience of those who have trodden this path before us—we have only to look to France for our beacons—and, true to ourselves and to each other, shoulder to shoulder, poor and rich, maintain the rights, the liberties and constitutional privileges belonging to all.

L. S. M.

2.

The Right to Labor

Within this specious formula—"the right to labor"—lie concentrated the greater number of those terrible fallacies which now threaten to overrun and devastate civilized society. The hydra of communism holds struggling in its deadly folds the Hercules of truth. That the latter conquers, who can doubt? Man's nature, his soul, and instinct, alike lead him to the light. The world is progressive. The past shows, the present hopes for, and the future promises this; but fearful are the doubts, the despondencies, and the agonies, through which society must pass to attain its highest tone! Around each great truth is gathered a crowd of errors—deceitful reflections of its beauty—giving to the mischievous a pretext for ill, and often, with *ignis fatuus* light, misleading even the true-hearted and the good.

There are crises in the world's course, when, rousing from temporary

SQR 16 (Oct. 1849): 138–60. The first seven paragraphs are reprinted in Hart, *Female Prose Writers of America,* pp. 189–92. Publication reviewed: *Journal des économistes* 21 (Aug.–Nov. 1848). "It gives me pleasure to mention that in a recent letter from Hon. B. Tucker of Virginia he spoke in language of high compliment of the last article of Mrs. McCord—'Praise from Sir Hubert!' The favorable opinion of such a good writer and admirable thinker as Tucker, is no small proof of success, and should be grateful" (William Gilmore Simms to David James McCord, Jan. 15 [1850], in Simms, *Letters* 3:4). Nathaniel Beverley Tucker (1784–1851), from 1834 professor of law at the College of William and Mary; among his works, the novel *The Partisan Leader* (1836) and writings on law and political economy. "Sir Hubert" is Sir Hubert Stanley, the upright, albeit impoverished, squire in *A Cure for the Heart Ache* (1797), a comedy by Thomas Morton (1764–1838). In scene 2 of act 5, Sir Hubert says to Young Rapid that "by asserting your character as a man of honour, in rewarding the

lethargy, reason seems more than usually wide awake to the influence of truth and light. But, in this very waking, is she also more subject to the misleading influence of error. The craving heart—the longing, seeking, hungering for truth—is roused; and, in its eager search, how often, alas! is the will-o'-the-wisp mistaken for the star-beam! Through one of these crises are we now struggling. The world is in labor of a great truth, but its sick fancy is cheated with the bewildering dazzle of its own delirious dreams.

One of society's closest guards—a kind of shepherd's dog, as it were, of the flock—stands political economy. Watching, barking, wrangling at every intruder, suspicious of outward show, nor satisfied with skin-deep inspection, it examines, before admitting all pretenders as true prophets, and strips many a wolf of his sheep's clothing. The evil-inclined, thus, naturally, hoot and revile it. The ignorant mistrust it. What do we, its advocates, ask in its defence? Simply nothing, but that the world should learn to know it. We wish no law for its imposition—no tax for its protection. Let truth be but heard: there is in the heart of man an instinct to know and to seize it. Error is simply negative; like shadow, it is only want of light. Heaven's sunbeam on the material world—reason's effulgence on the thinking soul—alone suffice to work *God's* purposes. Man, his humble instrument, cannot *make* the light; he can but strive to remove the obstacles which intercept its abundant flow.

We ask, then, only to be heard. Let the world know us. Let the *people* know us. Let political economy be the science of *the crowd.* It is neither incomprehensible nor abstruse. It requires but that each individual man should think—think, not imagine, not dream, not utopianize—but think, study, and understand for himself. Where the masses are ignorant, what more natural than that they stumble into wrong? Mind must act; and more and more, as the world advances, does it call for the right of exerting and developing its power. In earlier ages, learning, information, thought being limited to the few, the masses took the word from these high-priests of reason, whose veiled holy of holies was sacred from the intrusion of the crowd. But, now, the veil is rent asunder. Not you, nor we, nor he—nor any chosen one—nor ten, nor twenty—but *man*—now claims the right to think for himself. He claims it; he will have it; he ought to have it. Let but those who are ahead in the race of knowledge give to those who need; guide those who stumble in the dark; and each, thus putting in his mite of well-doing in the cause, ward off, as much as possible, the calamities which necessarily hover round the great and progressive change through which the world is passing. Great

---

affections of this amiable woman, you command my praise;" to which Young Rapid replies, "Approbation from Sir Hubert Stanley, is praise indeed."

changes are oftenest wrought out only through great convulsions. It is a man's work, and man's heart is in it, when the humblest individual, with shoulder to the wheel, stands boldly and honestly forth, to raise his hand in warding off the avalanche of evil.

France, which now stands before the world, in the agonies of her struggles—great alike in truth and in error—France has experimented, and written for us, in her sufferings, a mighty lesson. May we but read and learn it! Revelling in the madness of newly-gained freedom, her people not knowing the use of what they had seized, for them it became the synonyme of license. Rushing from extreme to extreme, they forgot that liberty was but enfranchisement, and, with "democracy" for their watchword, exercised a despotism much more fearful than that of the single tyrant, because its power, like its name, was "legion."[1]

And what is the result? Credit dead; industry paralyzed; commerce annihilated; her starving people now sinking despondent under their difficulties—now driven to the madness of revolt, against they know not whom—asking, they know not what. France, terrified at her own acts, calls out for succor, and on every side resound the answers of her best and wisest citizens: "Step back from your errors; give truth its way"—*laissez passer*—*laissez faire*.

Amidst the throng of confused theories, each of which burns into the very vitals of the suffering state its brand of crime and folly, while

> lean-look'd prophets whisper fearful change,[2]

political economy alone, with its great and simple truths, seems to hold forth some hope of a real regeneration. It alone enjoins upon its disciples to follow, step by step—to sift to the bottom its theories and their remotest effects—before launching the world upon untried experiments. It alone gropes patiently its way, grappling with doubts and difficulties, making sure and clear its footing, before calling upon society to follow. Its opponents—socialists of every grade—leaping blindfold to their conclusions, and taking impulse for inspiration, recklessly drag on their devotees from one wild dream to another, until

> contention, like a horse
> Full of high feeding, madly doth break loose,
> And bears down all before him.[3]

1. Mark 5:9.
2. *Richard II* 2.4.11.
3. *2 Henry IV* 1.1.9–11, reading "hath broke" for "doth break."

They do not mean the evil which they do. Very possibly, their hearts are of the purest—but their ideas, unfortunately, not of the clearest. Without examining into the practicability of their own schemes, they give way to a misty vision of goodness—a kind of foggy virtue—which, often but the rushlight of their own unregulated fancy—too indolent or too cowardly to probe to its source, and follow to its end—they imagine an inward light, a transmitted beam of heaven, and so dream on!

Many, too, who would shrink from the broad notions of communism and forced fraternity, most unwittingly often assist in scattering the poison through society. Something they find out of joint: the world might be better certainly; and, forthwith, they set about preaching the vague ideas of fraternity, equality! Heaven knows the while (for they themselves do not) what it is all aiming at! Such a writer as Carlyle, for instance, popular and plausible, forever holds up to view the wretchedness of the masses, with threats of undefined evil to the better classes, if this is not remedied, scoffing bitterly, the while, at the *laissez faire* system. His heart, we believe, is good, his intentions pure; but does he himself know—has he ever put the question to his own heart, and answered it fairly?—where he is leading? We mistake much, if Carlyle would not shrink from forced legalized fraternity, from communism, or from Owenism; and yet to such do his vague generalities drag us. Working up discontented, and even well-intentioned minds, to a restless feeling of the need of something better, he does not sufficiently impress upon them that if, in his own beautiful words, "always there is a black spot in our sunshine, it is even the shadow of ourselves,"[4] and that "he who seeks *out of himself* what is found *in* himself, will seek forever and find nothing"—(Z[s]chokke).[5] Many, to save themselves the trouble of thinking (and do not ninety-nine in the hundred shirk this when they can?), take it for granted that *he has* his idea—that *he has* his plan; and, as it seems to be philanthropic, well rounded with groans and appeals for suffering humanity, they range themselves under his banner. But to what does all this complaining lead? There is sorrow—ay, and wretchedness and suffering, oppression and injustice, trampled misery and heartless power, enough, too much—in this world of ours; we see this as well as he—but where is *his remedy*? While he is continually telling us that the *laissez faire* of political economy is treason against the rights of the poor, and that something must be done; *that some-*

4. Thomas Carlyle, *Sartor Resartus* 2.9 ("The Everlasting Yea"), in *Works,* Ashburton ed., 17 vols. (London and Philadelphia, 1885–88), 3:130: "Always there is a black spot in our sunshine: it is even, as I said, the *Shadow of Ourselves.*"

5. Johann Heinrich Daniel Zschokke (1771–1848), born in Magdeburg; settled in Switzerland in 1796; playwright, novelist, journalist, historian.

thing he never indicates, never hints at. The crowd, having taken his dictum so far—"something is wrong, it must be righted"—when he comes to a halt, for which they are totally unprepared, are almost forced to rush on a little farther, into the arms of some better revolutionizer—Cabet, Proudhon, etc.

It might be well for this energetic writer to con over more frequently his own humorous fable:

> Once upon a time, a man, somewhat in drink belike, raised a dreadful outcry at the corner of the market-place, that the world was turning all <all turned> topsy-turvy; that the men and cattle were all walking with their feet uppermost; that the houses and earth at large (if they did not mind it) would fall into the sky; in short, that unless prompt means were taken, things in general were on the high road to the devil. As the people only laughed at him, he cried the louder and more vehemently; nay, at last, began objuring, foaming, imprecating, when a good-natured auditor, going up, took the orator by his haunches, and, softly inverting his <*his*> position, set him down upon <on> his feet. The which upon perceiving, his mind was staggered not a little. "Ha! deuce take it," cried he, rubbing his eyes; "so it was not the world that was hanging by its feet, then, but I that was standing on my head!" Censor, *castigator morum,*[6] radical reformer, by whatever name thou art called, have a care—especially if thou art getting loud![7]

And how correct this habit of half way thinking? this grasping at superficialities? By teaching the masses to think rightly. *Popularize* (allow us the word) popularize political economy. Most truly and beautifully does the distinguished writer whom we have just ventured to animadvert upon remark: "All misery is but faculty misdirected, strength that has not yet found its way. [. . .] No *smoke,* in any sense, but can become flame and radiance."[8] All the confusion and turmoil which we now see bubbling up in restless discontent upon the troubled surface of society, has its mission, has its result. There is much of great, much of good under it. Let but now the true thinker, he who thought

> Till thought is standing thick upon the brain
> As dew upon the brow—for thought is brain-sweat,

let him not grudge the fruit of his study, but *popularize* it for the crowd.

The valuable periodical, with the last completed volume of which we

6. "Chastiser of morals" (Latin).

7. Thomas Carlyle, "Four Fables," in *Critical and Miscellaneous Essays,* vol. 1, in *Works* 15:627.

8. Thomas Carlyle, "The Gifted," *Past and Present,* in *Works* 2:244.

head this article, and of some of the earlier numbers of which, in a preceding article, we took large notice, developes most usefully the nerve of the politico-economical party in France. Many of the strongest men of that gifted but erring country, here exhibit their efforts and energies in her cause. Her great struggle is between the truths of political economy, as advocated by them, and the opposing concentrated formula of communism: "the right to labor."

It would be impossible, in such limits as are here assigned to us, to gather together, even in half-rate strength, the many arguments and examples, which the four months, included in the volume under review, offer to our attention; but we will at least endeavor to do enough to rouse to the subject the attention of our drowsy community, which sleeps on, while, like the poisoned majesty of Denmark, a traitorous hand

> Into the porches of our ear doth pour
> Its leperous distilment.[9]

"Nothing," says Guizot, "has a more certain tendency to ruin a people than a habit of accepting words and appearances as realities."[10] The fashion of our age is *cant,* a whining pretension to goodness. Ultra in every thing, it condemns and tosses aside, as scarcely worth the hearing, each sober thinker, who without "ahs!" or "ohs!", without groaning over the heavy and unparalleled suffering, and exulting in the great and unexampled enlightenment, of his time, sees the world, in steady progress, advancing by almighty behest, through its destined changes, to its appointed might of developed reason and civilization. This man is too cold, exclaims the one side; he has no heart for sympathy, or he would join with us in revolutionizing this world where crime and vice play so dominant a part. He is dull, says the other; he cannot see the glorious progress of the age, and keeps plodding along at his old jog-trot, instead of leaping at once to perfection. And then both extremes, meeting, join in their loud "hallelujahs" for fraternity and equality. But a little of the old jog-trot prudence might be useful here. Would our improvers but pause and think, nor trust quite so much to the inspiration of impulse, perhaps they might find that they are foisting up "words and appearances" instead of "realities." "Life has one virtue," beautifully remarks

9. *Hamlet* 1.5.61–64: "Upon my secure hour thy uncle stole / With juice of cursed hebenon in a vial, / And in the porches of my ears did pour / The leperous distilment."

10. François Guizot, *Democracy in France. January, 1849* [trans. of *De la démocratie en France*] (London, 1849; rpt. New York, 1974), p. 15. François-Pierre-Guillaume Guizot (1787–1874), French historian, foreign minister (1840–47) and first minister (1847–48) to Louis Philippe, forced from public life by the Revolution of 1848.

George Sand, "*the eternal sacrifice of self.*"[11] Pure and chaste thought!—which we quote from Mme. Dudevant, but which beamed upon the world in the softening influence of christianity, eighteen centuries before her birth! "Give to him that asketh of thee, and from him that would borrow of thee, turn not thou away."[12] But he who preached this lesson to man, taught him also, to "render unto Caesar the things which are Caesar's."[13] Far from the tone of charity and benevolence thus inculcated, is the wide-spread spirit of tyranny and spoliation which now usurps its place; and Mme. Dudevant has learned but half her lesson. Charity can only go hand-in-hand with justice, and he who robs to give is scarcely less culpable than he who robs to enjoy. In the volume under review (page 56) we find Mr. Proudhon exclaiming before the French assembly; "Why talk about property? Property does not exist; it is abrogated; the provisional government in recognizing *the right to labor* has annulled it. If lodgers now pay their rent, farmers their leases, or debtors their creditors, it is simply because it is agreeable to them to do so."[14] And this is fraternity! This the right to labor! Take, keep, borrow, and do not return, is the lesson of these ultra-sympathizers, who thus crush all morality in their wild interpretation of the gentle maxim, "Love ye one another."[15]

Even so well intentioned a man as Lamartine[16] (and after his famous free-trade speech at Marseilles) declared (p. 219): "If in such questions as these [Politico-Economical] we find our limits, it would be necessary to efface from our constitution the three sublime words, liberty! equality! fraternity! to replace them by the two low, filthy [*immondes*] substitutes, *buying and selling*."[17] Ah! M. Lamartine, if you would live in the clouds, keep to poetizing and let alone legislating! Fancy delights, but sober reason must rule the world. Buying and selling—service and compensation—are at the basis of the world's law of action, its great foundation stone. We must possess before we can give. Property must precede charity and individual superiority exists before the very idea of benevolence can have birth. Your fanciful equality, may, in truth, drag all down to one level of starvation and beggary; but although this may the better suit the poetic fancy of M. de Lamartine, for

11. Amandine-Aurore-Lucile Dupin Dudevant (1804–76), French novelist under the pen name of George Sand.

12. Matt. 5:42.

13. Mark 12:17.

14. "Chronique," *Journal des économistes* 21 (Aug. 1848): 50–56; 56.

15. John 13:34, 15:12, 17.

16. Alphonse-Marie-Louis de Prat de Lamartine (1790–1869), French poet, minister of foreign affairs in the Provisional Government set up after the abdication of Louis Philippe.

17. "Chronique," *Journal des économistes* 21 (Sept. 1848): 219–24; 219 (LSM's interpolations and italics).

this work-day world of ours, perhaps the old plan may be the best. At least as M. Amédée Gratiot says to his compeers (p. 162), "Workmen, let us go to our work, our spinning machines, our presses, and our forges; let us leave our friends, the socialists, to make up their minds, and experiment upon systems among themselves; next year perhaps they will have determined how to make us all happy."[18] For *God's* sake, gentlemen, you, our socialists of America, Mr. Horace Greely, Albert Brisbane, etc.,[19] make up your minds—in the words of M. Gratiot, "une solution s'il vous plait," before you plunge us deeper into this quagmire of unexplored utopias. Leave us to our old vulgar practices of "buying and selling" until at least you shall have invented some feasible substitutes for them.

This constant dwelling upon ideal perfection and visionary improvement does much harm. The masses, familiarized by constant repetition to the terms "organization of labor," etc., naturally look for their farther signification. To these words and appearances they would next attach "realities," and when the word comes to their turn they at once interpret it to mean "immediate amelioration of their condition, that is to say, increase of wages and diminution of labor." Such was the course of things in France (p. 378, vol. 20th, of *Journal des économistes:* Joseph Garnier). "That the state could not regulate all this in their favor, never came into their heads. They never doubted that the State, led by organizers and Associa[tio]nists, was all powerful to guaranty labor."[20] The Provisional Government being equally misled, thence followed their proclamations guarantying labor to such as could not procure it for themselves; thence the insurrections and barricades of June,[21] and then the excuse of them by Proudhon and others. The State had madly undertaken what it could not accomplish.

18. *Messieurs les socialistes, une solution, s'il vous plaît* (Paris, 1848), cited in "Bibliographie," *Journal des économistes* 21 (Sept. 1848): 162–63; 162. LSM condenses the original text.

19. Horace Greeley (1811–72), journalist and reformer, founded the New York *Tribune* in 1841 and promoted, among other causes, the Free Soil movement and abolitionism. Albert Brisbane (1809–90), author of *Social Destiny of Man* (1840) and *Association* (1843), established in 1843 a Fourierist phalanx at Red Bank, N.J.

20. "Quelques mots d'explication et d'histoire au sujet des principales formules socialistes," *Journal des économistes* 20 (July 1848): 375–80; 378. Joseph Clément Garnier (1813–81), political economist; senator from 1876; among his works, *Traité de finance* (1882) and *Traité d'économie politique* (9th ed., 1889).

21. Angered by what they saw as the unresponsiveness of the Constituent Assembly to their needs, finally by government action in effect closing the national workshops—these had been established by the Provisional Government on February 26, 1848, to provide work for the unemployed—on June 23, 1848, between 40,000 and 50,000 workers rose in revolt in Paris. The insurrection was crushed within four days by the minister of war, Louis Cavaignac, to whom had been assigned supreme command of the armed forces in and around Paris.

And this "State," this personified power, which socialism invests with such inordinate authority, "this monopolizer of wealth, organizer of labor, regulator of consciences,—this impalpable power, what is it?" Some superhuman guide to dictate to, and control us? Or rather, is it not still men—men only[22]—who, even while they talk most of the people and their rights, would crush out the faintest trace of man's individuality, to subject the whole conglomerated mass to their own rule? Let us always remember that in proportion as governmental power increases, the individual is necessarily effaced from the direction of affairs.

> One or the other, the government or the individual, must increase and develop itself. What is gained by the one, must be lost by the other, and the oppressive and plethoric centralization of national workshops, national banks, national securities, could only be obtained by the entire obliteration of the individual. (p. 233. Alcide Fonteyraud)[23]
>
> Socialism supposes, also, a dualism between the individual and society. Instead of considering society as a reunion of forces and intelligences, it is, as it were, transformed into a reasoning being, a power to itself, a fantastic personage, a kind of fairy possessed of hidden treasures and unlimited powers, ever giving, never receiving. Each individual asks more than he brings, forgetting that only through individual possession can the State be rich; that it only produces by the labor of each and all, and that its power is the result of the number and concert of individual wills. (p. 360. Léon Faucher)[24]

The "right to labor," then, guarantied by the State, throws all power into the hands of the government. The individual becomes only the bold beggar, the claimant of governmental protection. No longer dependant upon himself, his *right* is to demand from government what, enfeebled by this individual imbecility, it is more than ever incapacitated from giving—and neither small nor limited are the demands thus entailed upon it.

22. Cf. Bastiat, "Justice et fraternité," 321: "Qu'est-ce donc cet Etat qui prend à sa charge toutes les vertus, tous les devoirs, toutes les libéralités? D'où tire-t-il ces ressources, qu'on le provoque à épancher en bienfaits sur les individus? N'est-ce pas des individus eux-mêmes?"

23. "La Vérité sur l'économie politique," ibid., 21 (Aug. and Oct. 1848): 1–15, 225–48. Alcide Fonteyraud (1822–49), political economist; born in Mauritius; studied free trade in England; disciple of David Ricardo, of whose works he was an editor and translator (1847); writings collected by Joseph Garnier in *Mélanges d'économie politique* (1853).

24. "Opinion sur le droit au travail," *Journal des économistes* 21 (Oct. 1848): 345–68. Léon Faucher (1803–54), political economist and politician; minister of the interior and of public works (1848–49) and of the interior (1851); among his works, *Recherches sur l'or et sur l'argent* (1843) and *Etudes sur l'Angleterre* (1845).

> The "right to labor" includes the right to capital, the right to wages, the right to comfort. It is the most unlimited claim with which individuals can be armed against the public treasury. To such a system the equal division of property <le partage des biens> would be infinitely preferable, for this <la communauté des biens> does nothing more than place all upon the same footing, and the rich, the provident and successful, once despoiled for the benefit of their poorer brethren, may at least count with some certainty upon their future gains. But the "right to labor" goes farther. Its demands are insatiable. Its claim extends not only to what *is* but to what *may be*. It implies community, not only of *existing wealth,* but of all *future effort*—a perpetual servitude imposed upon the better part of society for the benefit of all idle vagabonds whom the State takes into its pay. (p. 359. Léon Faucher)[25]

The "right to labor" thus proclaimed, what next? Do its advocates go on to demonstrate the existence of such a right? Oh no! *that* is quite unnecessary. Let political economists weary their brains with seeking proof and demonstration; the heaven-inspired socialist acts from impulse. A dream, an inspiration, an instinct, these are his guides—what needs he demonstration?

> And yet the thing was worth the effort. As these social Archimedes would, by means of their fulcrum, turn the world,[26] surely it was worth their while to see it firmly fixed. Why, then, have they contented themselves with simply stating the right, and attempting no proof of it? Why, unless, indeed, the existence of this right to labor is incapable of proof? But, proof or no proof, it is all one to these gentlemen. They make their premises, draw conclusions and build their consequences accordingly. (p. 65. G. de Molinari)[27]
>
> Society, in its present condition, displeases them, and, instead of a manly effort to ameliorate it, they call in the convenient specific of organization. They seek an amulet, where there is needed a virtue. (p. 239. Alcide Fonteyraud)

We may be told by some, "You are combatting a chimera, the whim of a few madmen, which cannot have weight in any community." This is an unfortunate mistake, which lulls us to the danger, but does not thence lessen

25. "Its demands are insatiable" is LSM's addition. The original of the last sentence, after the dash, reads: "une servitude perpetuelle imposée aux chefs de la société dans l'interêt des prolétaires nombreux que la République prend à sa solde."

26. The Greek mathematician and philosopher Archimedes (c. 287–212 B.C.) asserted that he could move the world with a lever, were there a plaçe to set the fulcrum.

27. "M. Proudhon et M. Thiers," *Journal des économistes* 21 (Aug. 1848): 57–73. Gustave de Molinari (1819–1911), Belgian political economist; professor from 1851 at the University of Brussels; author of *Etudes économiques* (1846), *Le Droit de la paix et de la guerre* (1887), *Les Problèmes du XXe siècle* (1901).

it. Few go to these extremes, but many, very many, walk blind-fold upon their brink. "I do not fear," remarked Mr. Faucher, in addressing the French Assembly,

> or at least fear but little, the socialism which, moving openly to its extreme object, declares boldly, "No family! No property!" Much more to be dreaded is the indirect, bastard, half-way socialism, which constantly tempts downward and downward upon the descent, still hiding the abyss that yawns at its foot. A member of the provisional government recently remarked, "Socialism is the plague!" Ay, it is the plague, but who of you is quite free from the infection? (p. 222)[28]

The venom has extended far and wide. The whole tone and spirit of society is tinged with it.

> The ranks of socialism have increased, and will increase if their error and falsehood be not speedily unmasked. There is no need of study in order to dream, to hope, to build castles in the air and pictures of social felicity. The most untaught and simplest mind may group these around it, and thus for a while raise itself upon this stepping-stone to felicity. But alas! at how high a price must these fleeting visions, so eagerly grasped at, be paid. In the deepest sincerity we believe that a little light thrown upon the subject would speedily lead back from these wanderings every true heart, every upright mind, to be found among the people, and these are many, very many. (p[p]. [14–]15. Alcide Fonteyraud)

In all questions between free trade and protection, socialism of course sides with the latter, whose every principle is based upon its favorite system of crippling the individual to increase governmental power.

> Mr. Billault, a friend of the "right to labor," very logically proved its necessary connection with the theory of protection, as Mr. Proudhon had already exhibited a similar connection with the violation of property (p. 220).[29]

Political economy answers still with its constant *laissez faire, laissez passer. Laissez faire* to thought, genius, labor; *laissez passer,* food, capital, ideas!

Labor will find its way. The nature of production pushes it to the supply of demand.

28. Cited in "Chronique," *Journal des économistes* 21 (Sept. 1848): 219–24; 222.

29. Ibid., 220. LSM adds, from context, "a friend of the 'right to labor.'" Adolphe-Augustin-Marie Billault (1805–63), French politician and moderate advocate of the right to labor; argued, especially in a speech of September 1848, that workers must recognize that this right imposed responsibilities; minister of the interior under Napoleon III (1854–58).

> *Labor for labor* is the law of production. [231] . . . When we hear, upon the banks of the Mersey or the Rhone, the groans of a manufacturing population, with the bitterness of conviction we feel that these groans too surely find their echo among the agricultural population of Poland, Russia, Egypt. The sufferings of Lyons and Manchester find their way to the heart of the fellah or the coolie; and let the cotton jenny but anywhere cease to work, it is a certain sign that somewhere else the plough and the hoe are idle. [230–31] . . .
>
> We confess that we are utterly unable to comprehend what is meant by the words, "fatal competition," "antagonism of labor and capital." We believe [. . .] that there has never existed in this world such a thing as superabundant supply, inordinate production. The horn of abundance, the lamp of Aladdin, the wonders of Cana, the wand of the enchanter Merlin, and more powerful perhaps than all, the steam machine, might act in concert for a long time before they could give lodging, clothing, fire, food, and light to all mankind. England, that industrial Titan, whose hundred arms work every lever of production, and whose extensive machine power does the work of one hundred and twenty millions of men, accomplishes but a fraction of what is wanted for the fulfillment of the above enumerated simple wants. . . . Where, then, is this unlimited competition, this overproduction which we hear of?
>
> Is it the result of industrial freedom, or rather, is it not the result of privileges and monopolies, that Ireland, like a Lazarus in rags, lies in the agonies of its death-pang near the overburthened stores of Leeds and Coventry? that corn becomes almost valueless in Poland, while Silesia, Flanders, and the Alps echo but one cry of starvation? (pp. 231–[3]2. Alcide Fonteyraud)[30]

Among the innumerable points of difference between the two systems we have under review, a very important one lies in the opposing views which they take of capital. While socialism regards capital as inimical to labor, and cries out against its tyranny, political economy, with clearer view, considers it as the circulating life-blood of society, the prop, and stimulant, and life of labor. Socialism attacks riches as monopolized capital; political economy, wisely, sees capital consisting, not alone in accumulated possessions or money, the mere representative of value, but in every thing possessing value in itself, in every auxiliary to labor. Not only tools and machines, but earth,

30. The last paragraph reads: "C'est au nom des privilèges et non des franchises industrielles, que l'Irlande, Lazare en haillons, râle auprès des magasins encombrés de Leeds et de Coventry, que le blé est à vil prix en Pologne, tandis que la Silésie, les Flandres, les Alpes s'éteignent dans la faim."

air, water, steam, when once called into requisition, and, by man's mind and power, turned to man's benefit—all valueless, but by his exertion—are, as soon as used, capital. The very exertion, too, and power of calling these into use—that is to say, energy, industry, skill—these also are capital. The head that thinks and the hand that acts, both are capital; both having value, as capable of contributing their share in man's service; both laboring in his cause—for surely labor is not, as socialism interprets it, mere manual exertion.

The experience of France has proved the disastrous consequences of this mistake of the socialists. Capital every where attacked for the benefit of labor—which interpreted by them meant simply and solely manual labor—as a necessary consequence, credit, which can only exist with confidence, sank under the meddling dictation of the State. Mr. A. Clément, in the volume we are reviewing (p[p]. 181–82), remarks:

> The sudden check received [depuis la révolution de Février] by the credit of the State can easily be explained by the acts of the provisional government. What solid guaranties could be offered by a government which, beginning by proclaiming *the absolute right of labor* and *its claims to assistance,* thus took upon itself the charge of maintaining all who either could not or would not do this for themselves; which organized national workshops to spend 170,000 francs per day, to produce nothing <sans rien produire>; which was contemplating gratuitous instruction, numerous benevolent institutions, the liberation of slaves and indemnity to the colonists, the loan of capital to workmen, the creation of new establishments of credit, the formidable increase of army and navy, the suppression of taxes;[31] and all this while the principal sources of the public revenue were rapidly becoming extinct? Was it not plain enough that it was rushing to inevitable bankruptcy? . . .
>
> Public and private credit can only be re-established when public authority will have completely abandoned the perilous path into which socialism has drawn it; when society can find some security for the maintenance of those conditions which are the basis of its existence, viz: respect for property, family, liberty of labor and business transactions; and when government shall seriously set about seeking the true means for ameliorating its financial condition by the reduction of its expenses, and the re-arrangement in the most perfect simplicity of a just system of taxation.
>
> As long as on any other conditions it seeks to re-establish credit, it pursues

31. "The suppression of taxes" translates: "qui, en même temps, promettait et accomplissait la suppression ou le dégrèvement de plusieurs impôts" (181).

> only impalpable chimeras, and prepares a cruel deception for all who place their trust in it.[32]

This opposition to capital has found its climax in the often quoted saying of Proudhon, "Property is robbery." It may seem to many almost ludicrous to meet such an assertion by grave argument, and yet, even in our own country, it is received by some as true, by many as partially true; and countless numbers give more or less into its folly, arguing against accumulation of funds, exaction of interest, etc. To all such we would say: pause before you step—you are on a dangerous path.

> Once raise the cry against competition and capital, you give up the whole at once. For the honor of your logic, you are forced to sweep on from conclusion to conclusion, from negation to negation, down to the bottomless pit of communism. You give your hand to the solemn figure, which moving towards you invites to its splendid banquet. The hand is icy! The figure marble! You shudder and would fly from this contact with death! But its grasp is upon you; you are forced to follow your guide and sup, like Don Juan, with annihilation. (p. 241. Alcide Fonteyraud)

Political economy strikes boldly at this shallow fallacy. If my life belongs to me, so also must the result, the proceeds of that life. To give an hour, to give a day, these are common expressions, and no one denies the right existing in me of thus disposing of my time. On what principle then can I be denied the right of disposing of the labor, or the proceeds of the labor of that hour? I may give my life to my country or my friend, and this is acknowledged to be a noble or generous action. I may give it by a sudden and abrupt sacrifice of life, or by a long, patient, and laborious one. The last I do for my wife or children, when passing a life of toil in their service. What matters it whether I give it in the form of food or raiment, immediately grasped from my labor, and as immediately consumed in their service, or whether, from the representative of this labor, put aside for the time of need, they are enabled to procure future necessities, comforts, or luxuries? In either case it is equally my life devoted in their service; honestly mine to give, honestly theirs to receive. Charity, benevolence, generosity, may, if the proceeds are large, suggest a wider circulation of them. I may give to the needy, I may share with the suffering, but still it is *mine* which I give, *my life* thus freely distributed—law and justice can have nothing to do in such a question.

It has cost me a year of toil and effort to amass a certain sum, the repre-

32. "Le Crédit—ses avantages—ses inconvénients—ses conditions," *Journal des économistes* 21 (Sept. 1848): 169–82; 181–82.

sentative of this toil and effort. This sum, if I give to my child, I, in so doing, give him a year of my existence. Perhaps I see fit to put up this year of my strength and youth, for the uses and necessities of age; or perhaps, in dying, see fit to transfer it to my dependant child or necessitous friend; who, if my life is my own, can dispute with me the right of so doing?

> If, in dying, I leave to those whom I love, house, merchandise, land, money, what you will <le vêtement, le meuble, la marchandise, la maison, la terre, le contrat, l'argent>, have I not given a part of the time I had to spend upon earth, in order to obtain these? Do I not, in reality, thus bequeath a portion of my life and my faculties? I might, by avoiding the effort requisite to their production, have made life easier, or by consuming the result of that effort, have increased my enjoyments, but I am happier in bestowing upon those I love this portion of my existence. Generous and consoling idea, which inspires courage, [charme le coeur,] sustains virtue, prompts to noble sacrifices, and uniting generation to generation leads to the amelioration of mankind by the gradual *increase of Capital*! (p. 305. Louis Leclerc)[33]

Mr. Proudhon, in his efforts to enforce his system in France, in order to suppress interest and rents on land, proposed the establishment of what he terms "a bank of exchange," which was destined to furnish gratuitous loans to all who might need them! (See p. 58.) "Individuals, instead of borrowing from each other at interest, would naturally go to the bank, which, absorbing gradually the capital of the nation, would finally be all-sufficient for the demands of production."[34] The State, be it understood, was expected to furnish the first capital of this bank. But how, in the depressed and disastrous condition of France, could this be done? This establisher of banks must surely have had in reserve, for the use of the State, some Fortunatus' purse[35] or alchymist power. He must command

> Gold! gold! and gold without end!
> Gold to lay by, and gold to spend,

33. "Simple observation sur le droit de propriété," ibid., 21 (Oct. 1848): 300–306; 305 (LSM's italics). Louis Leclerc (b. 1799), after a time in the ironworks, graduated from L'Ecole de Commerce in Paris (1830); professor there of literature and geography; coauthor of *Etudes sur les vins français et étrangers* (1842); author of *La Caisse d'épargne et de prévoyance* (1848) and *Les Vins malades* (1853).

34. Molinari, "M. Proudhon et M. Thiers," pp. 58–59.

35. A hero of European folklore (perhaps the earliest version was published at Augsburg in 1509), Fortunatus receives from Fortune a purse that, however much he should draw from it, can never be emptied.

Gold to give, and gold to lend,
And reversions of gold *in futuro*![36]

But, no—Mr. Proudhon's system seems to have been based much more upon

the good old rule
. . . the simple plan,
That they should take, who have the power,
And they should keep who can.[37]

Let quittance, says he, be given to all debtors of one-third their debits, on condition that one-half of this third, amounting to seven hundred and fifty millions, or even less, say five hundred millions, shall be put into the treasury of the State. Of this five hundred millions, let three hundred be employed in indemnification of certain taxes—salt tax, custom-house, etc.—which weigh heavily upon the poor. The two hundred remaining millions would serve to found the "Bank of Exchange." Let this quittance be renewed for the remaining portion of debt, in the same manner, for the second and third year, and thus at the end of three years the "Bank of Exchange" will find itself with a capital of six hundred millions. (See p. 59.) Admirable invention for the manufacture of capital! All debtors would no doubt be loud in praise of the liberality and judicious management of so generous a government. And creditors? Ah! never mind creditors, hard-hearted accumulators of capital as they are! Besides, Mr. Proudhon grants to *them,* too, a "certain compensation" [59]. Surely, says he, they will find it, in the reduced price of produce, etc.!

What says political economy? "Certainly," remarks Mr. de Molinari (p. 66),

> certainly, it is all important to production, that interest, rents, and the accessories of labor generally, should be procurable at the lowest possible rate.
>
> It is certain [. . .] that high interest, rents, and prices seem to be <sont> obstacles to the development of labor and increase of production.
>
> But why are these *obstacles*? Is it because they oblige the laborer to divide more or less equally with the capitalist and the landed proprietor the fruits of his labor? By no means. Nowhere do men labor with more spirit than in the United States—and yet nowhere is interest higher. The obstacle, then, does not exist in that portion of the proceeds of his labor which the high rate

36. Thomas Hood, *Miss Kilmansegg and Her Precious Leg: A Golden Legend,* ll. 53–56, reading: "Gold! and gold! and gold without end! / He had gold to lay by," etc.

37. William Wordsworth, "Rob Roy's Grave," st. 9.

> of interest takes from the laborer, but in the *scarcity of capital* which such a rate indicates. Suppose, for instance, twenty laborers, who, needing each his spade, go to hire them from the manufacturer of tools. If the latter should own only ten spades, and others not be procurable,[38] it is very evident that he will ask a larger compensation for each than if owning twenty. The rate of interest or hire would here be high. But a Proudhon of the band persuades the proprietor to let his spades go for nothing. What follows? Will production be thus either facilitated or increased? By no means. Ten spades can only do the work of ten spades, and can turn no more earth when loaned gratis than if hired at 20 per cent. Moreover, the spade proprietor will hardly find sufficient inducement to manufacture ten more, in the promise that they, too, shall be borrowed from him gratis! Here, then, lies the error. You have said, production is easy, in proportion as interest is low—*ergo,* by suppressing interest entirely, production will have acquired its maximum of facility. You have not reflected that the rate of interest is not so much an obstacle in itself as the *indication* [LSM's italics] of an obstacle—which obstacle is scarcity of capital. Suppress interest entirely, you would not in the slightest degree facilitate production, unless you could at the same time scatter over the land such a mass of capital as would, by its existence, naturally produce that suppression of *interest* which you propose to force upon the country.[39]

"You have," continues Mr. de Molinari,

> been the dupe of a similar illusion to that by which the promoters of an unlimited paper currency have imagined that capital could be indefinitely multiplied by the emission of paper, its representative. By an analogous turn of thought, you have imagined that capital can be indefinitely increased by the suppression of interest—the representative, not the cause, of its scarcity <représentation, indice du degré d'abondance des capitaux>.
>
> Dupe of this illusion, you have conscientiously labored to destroy interest and rents; and, to succeed in this, you have adopted the surest means. You have denied their right; you have endeavored to prove them robbery. [. . .]
>
> [. . .] This you have, we believe, done in good faith, and honestly, perhaps, have uttered the monstrous falsehood, "Property is robbery." Whence thus deceived? Only for want of having sufficiently studied the nature of loans and interest, and the causes and existence of capital <la *raison d'être* de l'intérêt des capitaux>. (p. 67)

38. "And others not be procurable" is added by LSM.

39. The last sentence, beginning from "such a mass of capital," translates: "la masse de capitaux que cette suppression suppose."

Mr. de Molinari then goes on to show that interest is merely the compensating representative of the risks run in the loaning of property. These risks are two: first, that of entire loss of capital loaned; and, second, the risks of loss or inconvenience resulting from the temporary absence of that capital from its owner. These, in the natural and free circulation of interest, balance themselves with the benefit accruing to the borrower, in their exact representative, the current rate of interest. Perhaps, in an individual loan, there may be nothing lost, but the risks are not, therefore, the less real. I may lose a part, or even my entire capital, by thus putting it out of my hands. I may lose some opportunity for employing it conveniently or advantageously, by thus holding it subjected to the commands of another. These risks undoubtedly exist, and I have no certainty that they shall not fall upon me. There may be individual gain by the loan at interest, but there is no general gain.

> In society, as God has created it, [et telle qu'elle existe depuis le commencement du monde,] the risks which interest serves to cover have never ceased to exist—only acting with more or less intensity in different countries and under different contingencies. The greatness of the risk being proportioned to the scarcity of capital and the insecurity of men and possession, invariably we find interest lowered with abundance of capital and security of person and property.
>
> But is it not possible that a society should exist where abundance of capital and complete security should cause all risk to disappear? We can only answer, such we have never seen, such certainly is not ours, and such could only be possible under the supposition that the annihilation of interest should never interfere with the accumulation of capital, the great spur to progress. Men do not accumulate to lend, but *to dispose of at their need and convenience,* or to give, for the benefit of those dependant upon them, the fruit of their labor. Capital is nothing more than the *accumulation of labor* [LSM's italics], reserved *for an indefinite period,* for eventual use, whether foreseen or unforeseen, and interest is intended, not for the increase of capital, but to preserve it from the risks of this *voyage into time* <à le préserver des risques du voyage>. Suppress interest without suppressing the risks of capital, and capital will never embark. All motive for accumulation disappears, and society retrogrades into barbarism. . . . (p. 70)
>
> . . . By such suppression, unless at the same time you suppress all risks, of which it is simply the compensation, you *rob* the receivers of it.
>
> Your *bank of exchange,* [. . .] not diminishing in any degree the risks, but only destroying the compensation which served to cover them, would, as its only result, hinder the accumulation and circulation of capital thus *transported forward into time* <n'aurait d'autre résultat que d'empêcher la circulation des

> capitaux dans le temps>, and, as a necessary consequence, suddenly suspend all vital movement in the arteries of society. (p. 71)

Mr. de Molinari thus continues his argument to prove that, the risks of capital being neither ameliorated nor yet guarded against, the consequence would inevitably be that the six hundred millions of capital of Mr. Proudhon's bank must, in the end, be swallowed up by its losses. Terrible perturbations in the industrial world would inevitably follow, and the gulf of social inequality yawn deeper than ever.

But enough for our limits. Volumes would be requisite did we undertake to combat the results of all the Alnaschar visions which have ambitiously foisted themselves up in a vain attempt to regulate society.[40] Alas! their regulation is but destruction. Mr. Fonteyraud (p. 248) borrows a Grecian fable in illustration of the unfortunate rage for regulating and improving the ways of God and nature, against which we have been directing our arguments. "A certain Athenian, to save his bees the trouble of a long journey to Mount Hymet[t]us, cut off their wings and put within their reach the most beautiful flowers he could gather. *The poor bees made no honey*."[41]

The allegory needs no interpretation. Gentlemen, socialists, be-rule us not into imbecility. You have your dreams, visions, theories—who of us has not? Who has not built his wondrous systems, where his hope and fancy paint all as beautiful and feasible? All is easy, all is simple, in these ecstasies. A breath scatters the cloud of our horizon. A wave of the hand, a stamp of the foot, summon around us the good and the rich, as fairy castles spring into existence with the raising of a wand. But the world is not governed by these dreams.

> Face to face with obdurate reality, we see what has been man's labors. We see how he has sweated, struggled, labored, and saved. . . . We keep our hope, we believe in tomorrow, because we see the result of yesterday; but our illusions disappear, and manfully and patiently we set about our daily task. (p. 242)[42]

40. Alnaschar is a beggar in *Arabian Nights' Entertainments* who neglects his own means by indulging in unattainable fantasies of prosperity. The work became well known as *Mille et une nuits* (1704–17), the French translation of Antoine Galland (1646–1715); an expurgated English version by the Arabic scholar Edward William Lane (1801–76) appeared in 1839–41.

41. Fonteyraud, "La Vérité sur l'économie politique," p. 248.

42. Fonteyraud's original of this quotation reads: "Mais quand on se trouve face à face avec la réalité implacable; quand on voit ce que fut le patrimoine de l'homme au début, ce qu'il a fallu de sueurs, d'épargnes, de luttes acharnées pour défricher, peupler, civiliser quelques lieues de pays, et pour constituer surtout ce fonds de sciences, d'arts, d'instruments, de monnaie, de capital—gage insulté du travail—on garde ses espérances, sans doute; on croit au lendemain, parce qu'on voit l'oeuvre accomplie hier; mais on déchire ses illusions, comme un voile menteur, et on se remet virilement à la tâche quotidienne."

We are happy to remark, in the volume which we have been endeavoring to introduce to the attention of our readers, the first number, from the pen of Mr. Bastiat, of what he apparently intends as a series of papers, under the title of "Harmonies économiques" (Concordances of Political Economy).[43] Not only from this gentleman's well known power as a writer, but also from the striking views here presented, in his usual terse and concise diction, we anticipate a treat of instruction in what is to follow. Our readers will forgive us for detaining them a little longer in this discussion.

In the article in question we see political economy in its full strength, nerving itself to the great struggle against its pernicious enemy, the "right to labor." "If," says Mr. Bastiat,

> nature has been mistaken in making *personal interest* the great spring of human society (and if, as socialism supposes,[44] interests are fatally antagonistic, the conclusion is self-evident), how is the evil remediable? Men as we are, where can we find the cure for this evil tendency of man's nature? Shall we invoke the police, the magistracy, the State, the legislature? But these are all men, and laboring under the common infirmity. We appeal to the universal suffrage. What then? Do we not thus only open wider the gate to the exercise of this universal tendency?
>
> Only one resource remains to these (our new light) reformers <à ces publicistes>, and that is to pass themselves off [pour les révélateurs,] for prophets, formed of a different clay, and drawing their inspirations from different sources from the rest of mankind. Thence follows the mystic phraseology in which they frequently envelop their counsels to the world. But if they are the emissaries of heaven, let them at least prove their mission. They ask nothing less than absolute power, the most complete despotism imaginable, governing not only our actions, but aiming even at the subversion of the very essence of our being <l'essence même de nos sentiments>. [. . .] Can they hope to be believed upon their bare affirmation, and that, moreover, when they differ very essentially among themselves?
>
> But before examining their systems of artificial society, let us satisfy ourselves whether they are not mistaken from the very starting point. Is it certain that *interests are naturally antagonistic*? that an irremediable cause of inequality is thus fatally developed in the natural order of human society? and that *God* has manifestly made a mistake in ordaining that the tendency of man should ever be towards well-being?

43. Fréderic Bastiat, "Harmonies économiques," *Journal des économistes* 21 (Sept. 1848): 105–20. The series of papers, left incomplete at Bastiat's death, was published as *Harmonies économiques* in 1850.

44. "As socialism supposes" added by LSM.

This is what I propose examining into, taking man as it has pleased God to make him, capable of foresight and experiences, perfectible, loving himself certainly, but with an affection tempered by a sympathetic tendency in his nature, and every where held under restraint by the contact with an analogous sentiment, universally pervading his theatre of action. My inquiry is, what social order naturally results from the combination and untrammelled tendencies of such elements?

If we find the result to be a constant and progressive advance towards well-being, perfection, and equality; a continual approximation of all classes towards a physical, intellectual, and moral level [en même temps qu'une constante élévation de ce niveau]; then will the work of *God* [LSM's italics] be justified, and we convinced [avec bonheur] that social order does not stand alone in creation, blotting its perfection, and[45] devoid of that harmony and regulation of forces <ces forces harmoniques> before which Newton bowed in admiration, and which drew from the psalmist the cry: *Caeli enarrant gloriam Dei!*[46] (p[p]. 106 and 107) . . .

It has been a fashion of late to reproach political economy that it occupies itself solely with the consideration of wealth <*richesse*>, instead of considering every object which, in any way, contributes to the happiness or suffering of mankind; accusing it even of denying every feeling, and impulse to action, which, not falling under its particular province, it has failed to notice. As well accuse the mineralogist of denying the existence of the animal kingdom. [. . .] If the conclusions of the economist should ever be found clashing with those [de la politique ou] of the moralist, the accusation would be conceivable. It might be said to him, "In limiting your research you have deceived yourself, for it is impossible that two truths should oppose each other." My present aim is to prove that the science of riches is no exception, but harmonizes with the general system of all great truths. (p[p. 109–]110)

We have not room to follow the argument of Mr. Bastiat, proving that in its early struggles for self-development political economy, by an unfortunate nomenclature, attached to *value* the idea of *materiality;* which idea, rejected by J. B. Say,[47] has still left upon this science the confusion of its early vocabulary. "Starting," says our author,

from this point, that *value* is *immaterial,* one of my objects in the present work is to prove that *services* are not *products* because they have *value,* but on the

45. "Blotting its perfection, and" added by LSM.

46. Ps. 19:1: "The heavens declare the glory of God."

47. Jean-Baptiste Say (1767–1832), French economist, author of *Traité d'économie politique* (1803) and *Cours complet d'économie politique pratique* (1828–30). Say's law, which states that supply creates demand, and demand supply, is named for him.

contrary that *products* have *value* only because, and in so much as, they are *services*. . . . [112]

Sensations, efforts, satisfactions, make up man's life. Of these three terms, the first and last are always necessarily confounded in the same individual. It is impossible to conceive them as existing separately. We can very well imagine an unsatisfied sensation, unsatisfied want; but certainly, never a *want* in one man and its *satisfaction* in another.

If the middle term, *effort,* were in the same category, man would be an entirely solitary creature. The economic phenomenon accomplishing itself entirely in the isolated individual, there might be juxtaposition of persons but no society; *personal* economy, but no *political* economy.

Thus, however, is it not; for constantly the *want* of one owes its *satisfaction* to the *effort* of another. [. . .] The majority of our satisfactions are due to the efforts of others, while our own labor, each in his profession, goes for the most part to satisfy the wants of others.

Then not in wants, nor their satisfactions (essentially personal and intransmissible phenomena), but in human *efforts,* must we seek the social principle, the origin of political economy.

This faculty given to men, and to men alone among all creatures, to *labor for each other;* this transmission of efforts, this exchange of services, with all its infinite and complicated combinations in time and space—this is precisely what constitutes political economy, shows its origin and determines its limits.

[Je dis donc:]

The domain of political economy includes, then, every *effort* capable of satisfying <susceptible de *satisfaire*>, for an equivalent, the wants <*besoins*> of a person different from him who accomplishes the effort, and consequently the wants and satisfactions relating to such effort.

Thus, for instance, the action of breathing, although containing the three terms (sensation, effort, satisfaction)[48] does not belong to the domain of political economy, because it is an *effort* generally intransmissible. We require no assistance to breathe. There is no service either received or rendered. It is an *individual* [LSM's italics], not a *social* act.

But if, under particular circumstances, men are obliged to assist each other to breathe, as when a man <ouvrier> descends in a diving bell, a physician acts upon the pulmonary organs, or the police takes measures to purify the air, then there is a want satisfied by a person distinct from him who receives the satisfaction; there is a service rendered, assistance given, and remuneration received; and, to the extent of such service, breathing becomes a legitimate subject for political economy. [. . .]

48. LSM's interpolation.

> An effort accomplished in the cause of another is a *service* rendered. If a service is stipulated in return it is an exchange of services <*services*>, and this being most commonly the case, political economy may consequently be defined: *the theory of exchange*.
>
> Whatever may be the intensity of want in the one party, or the strength of effort in the other, if the exchange be voluntary, the exchanged services may be considered as equivalent <*se valent*>. *Value* [LSM's italics], then, consists in the comparative appreciation of reciprocal *services*, and political economy may also be termed, *the theory of value*.
>
> Allow me here a remark which proves how sciences may mingle and be confounded with each other.
>
> I have just defined *service*, as the effort of one agent, while its want and satisfaction <le *besoin* et la *satisfaction*> exist in another. Sometimes a service is rendered gratuitously, [. . .] from a sympathetic principle, rather than an interested one. This is gift and not exchange, and consequently belongs not to political economy (which is the theory of exchange) but to the domain of morals. [. . .] We will see, however, that, in their effects, they still refer to the science in question, while, on the other hand, services rendered for a recompense, and with a condition, are, nevertheless, not on that account foreign to ethics.
>
> These two sciences, then, have constant points of contact; and as two truths cannot be antagonistic, if the political economist be ever found assigning to any phenomenon consequences, either for good or for evil, in which the moralist is opposed to him, certain it is that one or the other wanders from the truth. Thus do sciences verify each other. (p[p. 113–]114)

Mr. B. then goes on to discuss the undoubted existence of human wants, the suffering resulting from their non-satisfaction, and the necessity under which man exists of seeking such satisfaction, as well as the sickly sentimentality of those who scoff at *bodily wants* and *bodily comforts,* as though *God* had not created man under these necessities. Granted that moral perfection is a much higher point of aspiration than the gratification of physical wants; but once for all, "to perfect himself man must live [116]. . . . He cannot devote himself to the satisfaction of moral wants, the highest and the noblest, until he has first provided the necessities of existence" (p. 117). Hence, all that contributes to elevate the habits of man and his wants above the level of mere brutal wants, gives to the mind a free play and contributes to raise and enlarge it. "The wants of a man cannot be fixed as a fixed quantity. They are not of a stationary, but of a progressive nature." (p. 117) Wants, ever changing with circumstances and condition, thus constantly goad man on towards improvement. A constant "something more" urges him on from step to step, and with every change of situation still his restless soul is the same—forever hungering, forever seeking. It would seem that nature designed thus,

> that man, forever pushed towards something higher, should never stop in his career of civilization. [118] . . .
>
> Certain it is that human wants are never stationary.[49] Whether as to food, lodging, locomotion, or instruction, the wants of the fourteenth century were indisputably not ours; and it may be safely predicted that ours are below those to which our descendants will be subjected. (p[p]. 119[–20])

This point of view is important; many errors originate in the fact that human wants are frequently considered as a given quantity. As for instance:

> All the general satisfactions of our own time counted up, the conclusion is drawn that, here, humanity satisfied admits nothing farther. Then, if the liberality of nature, the power of machinery, or other cause <ou des habitudes de tempérance et de moderation> should for a time paralyze some portion of human labor, [. . .] forthwith come these absurd but specious formulas: "Production is superabundant." "We are perishing of plethora." "The power of production exceeds that of consumption," etc., etc. It is impossible to find a solution to these difficulties <à la question des *machines,* à celle de la *concurrence extérieure,* à celle de *luxe*>, so long as wants <le *besoin*> are considered as a fixed quantity and their indefinite expansibility forgotten.
>
> But if, in man, want is indefinite, progressive, gifted with increase <*croissance*> like desire, the source whence it forever feeds, it follows that (without discordance and contraction in the economic laws of society) nature must have placed, in and around man, indefinite and progressive means of gratification <*satisfaction*>, equilibrium between the means and the end being the first condition of all *harmony.* [120]

Not to exhaust the patience of our readers, we here check all farther remarks, proposing, should we be so fortunate as to interest them in our subject, at some future opportunity to renew its consideration, by examining such other volumes of the *Journal des économistes* as may fall beneath our notice.

L. S. M.

49. This sentence reads in the original: "Au surplus, que la philosophie le trouve bon ou mauvais, le besoin humain n'est pas une quantité fixe et immuable. C'est là un fait certain, irrécusable, universel."

Part II

WOMEN

3.

Enfranchisement of Woman

Glancing lately over a quaint old history of the Albigenses, by Pierre de Vaulx Cernay, we were amused by a remark of the author, that "dès ce moment, le Seigneur qui semblait s'être endormi tant soit peu, se reveillait au secours de ses serviteurs."[1] To judge from the movements of certain portions of society just now, one is led to suppose that they agree with the warlike Pierre as to the disposition of *Le Seigneur* to nap, "tant soit peu," now and then; and are, like the savages of certain of the Pacific islands, who, as we have somewhere read, endeavour, with drums, rattles, and other hideous noises, to rouse their sleeping Deity, now attempting, by all manner of singular commotions and bustle extraordinary, to effect a similar end. To this laudable aim the ladies seem at present disposed to lend a helping hand, and,

SQR, n.s., 5 (April 1852): 322–41; reprinted in O'Brien, *All Clever Men*, pp. 337–56; Hollinger and Capper, *American Intellectual Tradition* 1:375–87. Publications reviewed: [John Stuart Mill and Harriet Taylor Mill], "Enfranchisement of Women," *Westminster Review* 55 (July 1851): 289–311 [hereafter cited as *Westminster* "Enfranchisement"; the American edition of the *Westminster Review*, cited in the notes of O'Brien's edition, has different pagination], reprinted in John Stuart Mill and Harriet Taylor Mill, *Essays on Sex Equality*, ed. Alice S. Rossi (Chicago, 1970), pp. 91–121; *The Proceedings of the Woman's Rights Convention, Held at Worcester, October 15th and 16th, 1851* (New York: Fowler and Wells, 1852). The *SQR* headnote gives this last title as: *Proceedings of the Third Session of the Woman's Rights Convention, Held at Worcester, Mass., Oct. 15, 1851;* it is not clear whether this was a separate publication.

1. Vaulx-Cernay, *Histoire de l'hérésie des Albigeois*, in *Collections des mémoires relatif à l'histoire de France*, ed. François Guizot (Paris, 1824), 14:90. This passage is marked, possibly by LSM, in the copy found in the Thomas Cooper Library, University of South Carolina.

if Providence is not to be roused, evince no little disposition to take the arrangement of affairs into their own hands.

> C'est dommage, Garo, que tu n'es point entré
> Au conseil de celui que prêche ton curé;
> Tout en eût été mieux.[2]

We must try, however, to rectify, since we are too late to have things made to order. So, go it, ladies! On, for "the whole hog!" while your hands are in for it. Let's have no half-way measures, sickly things, "at war 'twixt will and will not."[3]

> Now o'er the enemy's battlements we'll stride,
> And cry our loudest war-cry in his ear,
> Nor pause until each coward drop of blood
> To tell the story of its fears hath run
> And, whispering to the panic-stricken heart,
> Quick bids it summon forth the cringing knee
> And own its victor's might.

Universal equality! *Fraternité* extended even to womanhood! And why not? Up for your rights, ladies! What is the worth of a civilization which condemns one half of mankind to Helot submissiveness? Call ye this civilization, with such a stained and blurred blot upon it? "Out, damned spot! Out, I say! One; two; why then 'tis time to do it!"[4] The knell of injustice has sounded! The world is awake! All men (and women too) are born free and equal. Every man shall have his rights, according to his own reading of them. Let A knock down B, and B trip up C. *Vogue la galère!*[5] Reform! Reform! If the world should be turned somewhat topsy-turvy thereby, and chance, in the hustle, to be kicked back to barbarism and the dark ages, or even to something worse, perchance, than man has yet the memory of—never mind. *Fiat Justicia ruat Coelum.*[6] Capital motto that, by the way. Like the

2. Livre 9, fable 4, in La Fontaine, *Fables, contes, et nouvelles,* ed. René Groos and Jacques Schiffrin (Paris, 1954), p. 220. Jean de La Fontaine (1621–95), French poet, playwright, librettist, official, and courtier, most famous for his *Fables* (1668–94). "Garo" is derived from Matthieu Gareau, a character in Cyrano de Bergerac's *Pédant joué.*

3. *Measure for Measure* 2.2.33.

4. *Macbeth* 5.1.33–34.

5. French idiomatic expression, meaning "Arrive ce qui pourra." It forms the title of chapter 6 of Charles Kingsley, *Yeast* (London, 1851), cited below by LSM.

6. Cf. David Hume, "Of Passive Disobedience," in *Essays Moral, Political, and Literary,* ed. Eugene F. Miller, rev. ed. (Indianapolis, 1987), p. 489: "The maxim, *fiat Justitia et ruat Coelum,* let justice be performed, though the universe be destroyed, is apparently false, and by sacrificing the end to the means, shews a preposterous idea of the subordination of duties."

prince's tent of the fairy-tale, it is capable of limitless extension, and all can find shelter under its interpretations. *Justicia,* says the communist beggar—*Justicia* means, whip me down those rich fellows and let me revel in their luxuries. Why should not I too ride in the king's carriages? *Justicia,* says Louis Napoléon, means, that I shall do what I please in this realm of France. Shoot down the beggarly rascal who disputes it.[7] *Justicia,* says Austria, means that Hungary shall not breathe without my permit. *Justicia,* growls the Russian bear, means imperial might. *Justicia,* answers Kossuth, means democratic might.[8] *Justicia,* shouts Cuffee, means that I am a sunburned white man. *Justicia,* responds Harriet Martineau,[9] means that I may discard decency and my petticoats at my own convenience; and *Justicia,* echo her Worcester Convention sisters,[10] means extinction to all law, human and divine. God is a bugbear—decency a dream. *Fiat Justicia ruat Coelum.* The beggar shall have his *patés de foie gras;* the negro shall be christened a white man; and woman—surely she, too, shall profit by this general revolution! Stand to your colours, ladies! Take for your flag the whole animal, *in extenso,* from snout to tail, with the motto, *ab actu ad posse valet consecutio;*[11] i.e. if a man swallows the head, surely he may take in the tail also. Follow close, ladies. The door of privilege is open pretty wide for the admission of Cuffee. Should *he* get in, surely *you* might follow.

Woman is awake. "You see, her eyes are open." "Ay, but their sense is shut."[12] Forgive us, you true women; you, the noblest of practical philosophers; you, who bear and forbear, humbling yourselves, that others may rise upon your efforts, and yet ceasing those efforts, never; you, who see, with

7. President of France, Charles-Louis-Napoléon Bonaparte (1808–73), according to the constitution of the Second Republic unable to succeed himself, after an attempt to amend the constitution failed, made a coup d'état on Dec. 2, 1851, and with a loyal army suppressed all resistance through imprisonment and execution; the coup d'état was approved by plebescite, with 7.5 million in favor, 640,000 opposed, on Dec. 20.

8. Lajos Kossuth (1802–94), leader of Hungarian revolt against the Austrians (1848–49), during which he was made governor of an independent Hungary; the revolt crushed, he resigned (August 1849) and fled into exile.

9. Harriet Martineau (1802–76), English political economist, abolitionist, and women's rights advocate; author (among other works) of *Illustrations of Political Economy* (1832–34) and *Society in America* (1837); LSM supposed, incorrectly, that she was the author of *Westminster* "Enfranchisement."

10. The first Woman's Rights Convention, organized by Elizabeth Cady Stanton (1815–1902) and Lucretia Coffin Mott (1793–1880), had met at Seneca Falls, N.Y., on July 19–20, 1848. Of later meetings of the convention, two had been held at Worcester, Mass., on Oct. 23–24, 1850, and on Oct. 15–16, 1851.

11. Legal Latin: "An action implies the capacity to repeat it."

12. *Macbeth* 5.1.23–24. The subject of the exchange is Lady Macbeth.

love and without envy, husband, brother, or son, too often in the pride of manhood, with slight and sneer contemning his "womankind," and holding her, even in his love, as

> Something better than his dog, a little dearer than his horse;[13]

you, who can see this, feel it, and yet strive on; you, whose heart may ache, and yet lovingly labour still, seeking no reward, knowing no reward, save the fulfillment of that high duty, of that great mission of love, which is woman's mission on earth. *Your* eyes are indeed open, nor is their sense shut. A true woman, fulfilling a woman's duties (and do not let our masculine readers suppose that we would *confine* these to shirt-making, pudding-mixing, and other such household gear, nor yet even to the adornment of her own fair person), a high-minded, intellectual woman, disdaining not her position, nor, because the world calls it humble, seeking to put aside God's and Nature's law, to *her* pleasure; an earnest woman, striving, as all earnest minds *can* strive, to do and to work, even as the Almighty laws of nature teach her that God would have her to do and to work, is, perhaps, the highest personification of Christian self-denial, love, and charity, which the world can see. God, who has made every creature to its place, has, perhaps, not given to woman the most enviable position in his creation, but a most clearly defined position he *has* given her. Let her object, then, be to raise herself *in* that position. *Out* of it, there is only failure and degradation. There be those, however, and unfortunately not a few, who look upon these old-fashioned ideas as exploded. God's and Nature's laws have nothing to do with the question. A Harriet Martineau, or a Fanny Wright,[14] would prefer a different position in the picture, and many a weak sister is misled by them.

In every error there is its shadow of truth. Error is but truth turned awry, or looked at through a wrong medium. As the straightest rod will, in appearance, curve when one half of it is placed under water, so God's truths, leaning down to earth, are often distorted to our view. Woman's condition certainly admits of improvement (but when have the strong forgotten to oppress the weak?), but never can any amelioration result from the guidance of her prophets in this present move. Here, as in all other improvements, the good must be brought about by working with, not against—by sec-

13. Tennyson, "Locksley Hall," ll. 47–50: "As the husband is, the wife is: thou art mated with a clown, / And the grossness of his nature will have weight to drag thee down. / He will hold thee, when his passion shall have spent its novel force, / Something better than his dog, a little dearer than his horse."

14. Frances Wright (1795–1852), Scottish reformer who settled in New York in 1829; author of *Views of Society and Manners in America* (1821); traveling lecturer advocating, among other causes, emancipation of women and slaves; established in 1825 a short-lived colony for freed slaves in Nashoba, Tenn.

onding, not opposing—Nature's laws. Woman, seeking as a woman, may raise her position; seeking as a man, we repeat, she but degrades it. Every thing contrary to Nature is abhorrent to Nature, and the mental aberrations of woman, which we are now discussing, excite at once pity and disgust, like those revolting physical deformities which the eye turns from with involuntary loathing, even while the hand of charity is extended to relieve them. We are no undervaluer of woman; rather we profess ourselves her advocate. Her mission is, to our seeming, even nobler than man's, and she is, in the true fulfilment of that mission, certainly the higher being. Passion governed, suffering conquered, self forgotten, how often is she called upon, as daughter, wife, sister, and mother, to breathe, in her half-broken but loving heart, the whispered prayer, that greatest, most beautiful, most self-forgetting of all prayers ever uttered, "Father, forgive them, [for] they know not what they do."[15] Woman's duty, woman's nature, is to love, to sway by love; to govern by love, to teach by love, to civilize by love! Our reviewer may sneer—already does sneer—about "animal functions" and the "maternity argument."[16] We fear not to meet him, or rather her (for we do not hesitate to pronounce this article to be the production of one of the *third* sex; that, viz., of the Worcester Convention petticoated would-be's); true woman's love is too beautiful a thing to be blurred by such sneers. It is a love such as man knoweth not, and Worcester Conventionists cannot imagine. Pure and holy, self-devoted and suffering, woman's love is the breath of that God of love, who, loving and pitying, has bid *her* learn to love and to suffer, implanting in her bosom the one single comfort that she is the watching spirit, the guardian angel of those she loves. We say not that all women are thus; we say not that most women are thus. Alas! no; for thus would man's vices be shamed from existence, and the world become perfect. But we do say that such is the type of woman, such her moral formation, such her perfection, and in so far as she comes not up to this perfection, she falls short of the model type of her nature. Only in aiming at this type, is there any use for her in this world, and only in proportion as she nears it, each according to the talent which God has given her, can she contribute to bring forward the world in that glorious career of progress which Omniscience has marked out for it. Each can labour, each can strive, lovingly and earnestly, in her own sphere. "Life is real! Life is earnest!"[17] Not less for her than for man. She has no right to bury her talent beneath silks or ribands,

15. Luke 23:34.

16. *Westminster* "Enfranchisement," pp. 297–98.

17. Henry Wadsworth Longfellow, "A Psalm of Life," st. 2: "Life is real! Life is earnest! / And the grave is not its goal; / Dust thou art, to dust returnest, / Was not spoken of the soul."

frippery or flowers; nor yet has she the right, because she fancies not her task, to grasp at another's, which is, or which she imagines is, easier. This is baby play. "Life is real! Life is earnest!" Let woman so read it—let woman so learn it—and she has no need to make her influence felt by a stump speech, or a vote at the polls; she has no need for the exercise of her intellect (and woman, we grant, may have a great, a longing, a hungering intellect, equal to man's) to be gratified with a seat in Congress, or a scuffle for the ambiguous honour of the Presidency. Even at her own fireside may she find duties enough, cares enough, troubles enough, thought enough, wisdom enough, to fit a martyr for the stake, a philosopher for life, or a saint for heaven. There are, there have been, and there will be, in every age, great hero-souls in woman's form, as well as man's. It imports little whether history notes them. The hero-soul aims at its certain duty, heroically meeting it, whether glory or shame, worship or contumely, follow its accomplishment. Laud and merit is due to such performance. *Fulfil* thy destiny; *oppose* it not. Herein lies thy track. Keep it. Nature's sign-posts are within thee, and it were well for thee to learn to read them. Poor fool! canst thou not spell out thy lesson, that ever thus thou fightest against Nature? Not there! not there! Nothing is done by *that* track. Never; from the creation of the world, never. Hero-souls will not try it. It is the mock-hero, the dissatisfied, the grasping, the selfish, the low-aspiring, who tries *that* track. Turn aside from it, dear friends—there is no heaven-fruit there; only hell-fruit and sorrow.

We regret to believe that this move for woman's (so called) enfranchisement is, hitherto, entirely (at least in its modern rejuvenescence) of American growth. Thank heaven! our modest Southern sisters have held aloof from the defiling pitch, and Worcester Conventions are entirely a Yankee notion. Not a little surprised have we been to see, in so long-established and respectable a periodical as the *Westminster Quarterly* [*Review*], a grave defence of such mad pranks as are being enacted by these petticoated despisers of their sex—these would-be men—these things that puzzle us to name. They should be women, but, like Macbeth's witches, they come to us in such a questionable shape, that we hesitate so to interpret them.[18] Moral monsters they are; things which Nature disclaims. In ceasing to be women, they yet have failed to make themselves men. Unsexed things, they are, we

18. *Macbeth* 1.3.39–43, 45–46: "What are these, / So wither'd and so wild in their attire, / That look not like th' inhabitants of earth, / And yet are on't? Live you? or are you aught / That man may question?. . . / . . . you should be women, / And yet your beards forbid me to interpret / That you are so." The ghost of Hamlet's father comes "in such a questionable [= questioning] shape / That I will speak to thee" (*Hamlet* 1.4.43–44).

trust—like the poor bat in the fable, who complains, "neither mouse nor bird will play with me"—destined to flit their twilight course, alone and unimitated.

Such is the point of view in which we have hitherto looked upon this subject, that we feel as though to attack it seriously were scarcely less ridiculous than to defend it. But the poison is spreading; and, truly, except that the fashion of the thing is a little newer, it is but a piece with negro emancipation; a subject with which the world has been stunned for many a year, until, at last, it now seems ready, with fanatic zeal, to sacrifice all that it has gained, of good, of beautiful, and of true, at the shrine of this fearful phantom. Madness becomes, sometimes, contagious; and, to judge from the symptoms, society labours, at present, under a high state of brain-fever—delirious, decidedly—raving over one fantastic dream or another. Communism and abolitionism have been dancing their antics through its bewildered brain; and now behold the *chef d'oeuvre* of folly! Mounted on Cuffee's shoulders, in rides the lady! The genius of communism bows them both in, mouthing over Mr. Jefferson's "free and equal" sentence, and banishing the motto, *par nobile fratrum.*[19] Woman! woman! respect thyself and man will respect thee. Oh! cast not off thy spear and thy shield, thine Aegis, thine anchor, thy stay! Wrapped thou art, in a magic cloud. Cast it not off to destroy thine own divinity. Man worships thee and himself; he knows not why. Ignorantly, in thee he bows to his "Unknown God."[20] The benevolent, the true, the holy, the just; in a word, the God of Love speaks to him through *thee.* Woman, *cherish thy mission.* Fling thyself not from the high pedestal whereon God has placed thee. Cast not from thee thy moral strength—for, lo! what then art thou! Wretchedly crawling to thy shame, thy physical meekness trampled underfoot by a brutal master, behold thee, thou proud mother of earth, to what art thou sunk!

We have said that this move is entirely of American growth. Our reviewer tells us, exultingly, that "there are indications" of the example being followed in England, and that "a petition of women, agreed to by a large public meeting at Sheffield, and claiming the elective franchise, was presented to the House of Lords by the Earl of Carlisle."[21] Heaven bless the mark!—surely our poor world is moon-struck! Let us, however, hear some of the reviewer's arguments, though we confess it is with a sickening loathing that we turn them over.

19. Horace *Satires* 2.3.243. "A notable pair of brothers."

20. Acts 17:23.

21. *Westminster* "Enfranchisement," p. 311. On Carlisle, see chap. 5, "Diversity of the Races; Its Bearing upon Negro Slavery," n. 1.

What first do these reformers ask? "Admission, in law and in fact, to equality in all rights, political, civil, and social, with the male citizens of the community." "Women are entitled to the right of suffrage, and to be considered eligible to office." "Civil and political rights acknowledge no sex, and therefore the word 'male' should be struck from every state constitution." "A coequal share in the formation and administration of laws—municipal, state, and national—through legislative assemblies, courts, and executive offices." Then follows the memorable quotation from the "memorable document" about all men being created free and equal, the ladies arguing, with some reason, that "men" here certainly stands for human beings, and thereby prove their right at least equal to Cuffee's.[22] In fact, the reviewer remarks that, such being American principles,

> the contradiction between principle and practice cannot be explained away. A like dereliction of the fundamental maxims of their political creed has been committed by the Americans in the flagrant instance of the negroes; but[23] of this (she charitably remarks) they are learning to recognize the turpitude. After a struggle which, by many of its incidents, deserves the name of heroic, the abolitionists are now so strong in numbers and influence that they hold the balance of parties in the United States. It was fitting that the men whose names will remain associated with the extirpation, from the democratic soil of America, of the aristocracy of colour, should be among the originators, for America and for the rest of the world, of the first collective protest against the aristocracy of sex; a distinction as accidental as that of colour, and fully as irrelevant to all questions of government.[24]

This is certainly taking a position, and we are glad to see that the advocates of this move class themselves exactly where they should be, cheek by jowl with the abolitionists. We thank them, at least, for saving us the trouble of proving this position. Of the first Worcester Convention, that of 1850 (which is, in fact, the second Woman's Rights Convention, the first having been held somewhere in Ohio),[25] "the president was a woman, and nearly all the chief speakers women—numerously reinforced, however, by men, among whom were some of the most distinguished leaders in the *kindred cause* of negro emancipation." One of the resolutions of this meeting declares "that every party which claims to represent the humanity, the civilization,

22. *Westminster* "Enfranchisement," pp. 289–91.

23. The word "but" is not in *Westminster* "Enfranchisement."

24. *Westminster* "Enfranchisement," p. 292 (LSM's parenthesis).

25. Following ibid., p. 289, LSM omits the Woman's Rights Convention at Seneca Falls, N.Y. "Somewhere in Ohio" is Salem; its convention was held on April 19–20, 1850.

and the progress of the age, is bound to inscribe upon its banners, equality before the law, *without distinction of sex or colour*."[26] Oh! there are things so horrible that man, in sheer terror, will mock at what he hates, and think to sneer the scoffing fiend away. We laugh at this, but it is frightful—frightful to think that thousands of women, in these United States, have signed, and thousands more, if these accounts be correct, are willing to sign their names to such a document. Oh! woman, thou the ministering angel of God's earth, to what devil's work art thou degrading thyself!

But, their reasoning in all this? for they have an argument. First, then, as we have just seen, they claim that the distinctions of *sex and colour are accidental and irrelevant to all questions of government.* This is certainly clinching the argument, and that by an assumption which is so extremely illogical that we are forced to say, if this reforming sisterhood can advance no better ground for their pretentions, it shows them but ill-fitted for the reins of state which they propose taking in hand. The distinction of colour has for many years been a point in discussion, and science has now settled that, so far from being accidental, it is an immutable fact of creation, that the black skin and woolly head are distinctive marks of race, which no age, climate, nor circumstance, has ever been able to efface; and there is no more accident in a negro's not being born a white man, than there is in his not being born a baboon, a mouse, or an elephant. As to the distinction of sex being accidental, this is a remarkable discovery of the present enlightened and progressive age. Sex and colour are severally so essential to the being of a woman and a negro, that it is impossible to imagine the existence of either, without these distinctive marks. We have hitherto understood that the sex of a human being was fixed long before its entrance into this world, by rules and causes, which, entirely unknown to man, were equally beyond *his* reach and that of accident. Such has, we believe, been the received opinion of the learned; but Miss Martineau (who is, we take it, our reviewer) has determined to assume the position of vice regent to Deity (a power, by the way, which she seems inclined entirely to depose) and, like Sganarelle in Molière's witty play of the *Médecin malgré lui,* she arranges things to suit her own ignorance. Sganarelle, having assumed the fact that the heart was on the right side of the human system, has the suggestion made by one of his bewildered admirers[27] that the generally received opinion of science and experience has universally placed it on the left. Oh! answers the ready quack, "cela était autrefois ainsi; mais nous avons changé tout celà."[28] If Miss Martineau and her

26. Ibid., p. 290 (LSM's italics).

27. The original reads "bewildered admired admirers."

28. Molière, *Le Médecin malgré lui* 2.4.

sisterhood should prove powerful enough to depose *Le Bon Dieu,* and perfect their democratic system by reducing *His* influence to a *single vote,* we do not doubt that, according to the approved majority system, it will be clearly and indisputably proved that Cuffee is Sir Isaac Newton, and Mrs. Cuffee, Napoleon Buonaparte, and Miss Martineau herself may stand for Cuffee, unless, indeed, she should prefer (as some of her recent works seem to indicate) to have it decided that she is *Le Bon Dieu* himself. She could probably carry the votes, with equal ease either way, and get rid of these little accidental distinctions. We, however, must, at this point of the question, be old-fashioned enough to declare ourselves conservatives. We cannot entirely shake off old prejudices, and still, spite of Dr. Sganarelle and Miss Martineau, are inclined to look for our hearts on the left side of our bodies, and for our God in the glorious works of his creation. We prefer His rule to Miss Martineau's, and believe that He has given the distinctions of race and sex, not accidentally (with Omniscience there is no accident), but distinctively, to mark the unchanging order of His creation—certain beings to certain ends.

All the further arguments of our reviewer are based upon the assumption we have been discussing, and with it fall to the ground. If beings are created to different ends, it is impossible to consider in them the point of equality or inequality, except in so far as their differences are of a kind to still allow them to be cast in the same category. As, for instance, the man, as animal, is superior to the beast, whose subordinate intellect makes him, as co-labourer of the soil, or as rival candidate for its benefits, inferior to man. The white man is, for the same reason, superior to the negro. The woman, classed as man, must also be inferior, if only (we waive for the moment the question of intellect) because she is inferior in corporeal strength. A female-man must necessarily be inferior to a male-man, so long as the latter has the power to knock her down. In womanhood is her strength and her triumph. Class both as woman, and the man again becomes the inferior, inasmuch as he is incapable of fulfilling her functions. A male woman could as ill assume the place and duties of womanhood, as a female-man could those of manhood. Each is strong in his own nature. They are neither inferior, nor superior, nor equal. They are different. The air has its uses, and the fire has its uses, but these are neither equal nor unequal—they are different.

"A reason," says the reviewer, "must be given why anything should be permitted to one person and interdicted to another."[29] A reason!—a reason why man cannot drink fire and breathe water! A scientific answer about hydrogen and oxygen will not answer the purpose. These are facts, not rea-

29. *Westminster* "Enfranchisement," p. 293.

sons. Why? Why? Why is anything on God's earth what it is? Can Miss Martineau tell? We cannot. God has made it so, and reason, instinct, and experience teach us its uses. Woman, Nature teaches you yours.

"The speakers at the Convention in America have," says the reviewer, "[. . .] done wisely and right, in refusing to entertain the question of the peculiar aptitudes either of women or of men, or the limits within which this or that occupation may be supposed to be more adapted to the one or [to] the other."[30] In the name of all that is foolish, what shall we consider, if not the aptitude of a person or thing to his or its uses? It is fortunate that Miss Martineau has never descended from her high sphere, to allow herself to be burthened with the cares of a family; for had she, in that capacity, forgotten to consult the aptitudes of things to their uses, she might, in some inauspicious fit of philosophic experiment, have committed the unlucky blunder of packing her children in December ice to warm them, or, perchance, cast the little unfortunates into the fire, by way of cleansing their dirty faces. And what might the philosophical and reforming world have thus lost! The ignorant mob, who persist in judging of the uses of things by their aptitudes, might have committed the egregious mistake of taking this doughty[31] philosopher—this Wilberforce[32] of women—this *petit bon Dieu*—for a murderess, and hung her for the interesting little experiment of burning her brats.

We, of the conservatives, who judge of the uses of things by their aptitudes, can read woman's duties anywhere better than in an election crowd, scuffling with Cuffee for a vote. Imagine the lovely Miss Caroline, the fascinating Miss Martha, elbowing Sambo for the stump! All being equals, and no respect for persons to be expected, the natural conclusion is, that Miss Caroline or Martha, being indisputably (even the Worcester conventionalists allow that) corporeally weaker than Sambo, would be thrust into the mud. "Hello da! Miss Caroline git two teet knock out, and Miss Marta hab a black eye and bloody nose!" "Well, wha' faw I stop fa dat? Ebery man must help hisself. I git de stump anyhow, and so, fellow-citizens, Sambo will show how Miss Marta desarve what she git." Or, let us suppose them hoisted through this dirty work. The member is chaired—some fair lady, some Mrs. or Miss Paulina Davis, who, we see, figures as President of the last convention, or one of her vices, Angelina Grimké Weld,[33] or Lucretia Mott—let us imag-

30. Ibid., p. 295.

31. "Doubty" in original.

32. William Wilberforce (1759–1833), English politician (member of Parliament from 1780 to 1825), evangelical Christian, and a leader of the antislavery crusade.

33. Paulina Kellogg Wright Davis (1813–76), born in Bloomfield, N.Y.; with her first husband helped organize an antislavery convention in Utica, N.Y. (October 1835), their

ine the gentle Paulina, Angelina, or Lucretia fairly pitted, in the Senate, against Mr. Foote, for instance, or Mr. Benton, or the valourous Houston,[34] or any other mere patriot, whom luck and electioneering have foisted there. We do not doubt their feminine power, in the war of words—and again we beg to defer a little the question of intellect—but are the ladies ready for a boxing match? Such things happen sometimes; and though it is not impossible that the fair Paulina, Angelina, and Lucretia might have the courage to face a pistol, have they the strength to resist a blow? La Fontaine tells us a fable of a wax candle, which, being ambitiously desirous of immortality, and seeing a handful of clay, that, hardened by the fire into a brick, was enabled to resist time and the elements, turned the matter over for a while in its waxen brains, and finally determined to try the experiment in its own person. A fire being conveniently near, and concluding, we presume, like the lady conventionalists, that all argument on aptitudes and uses was quite *de trop,* in so clear a case of logical induction,

> Par sa propre et pure folie
> Il se lança dedans. Ce fut mal raisonné;
> Ce cierge ne savait grain de philosophie.[35]

The fact that women have been queens and regents, and filled well these positions, as cited by the reviewer in the cases of Elizabeth, Isabella, Maria Theresa, Catharine of Russia, Blanche, etc.,[36] proves that woman, as a woman and a monarch—with the double difference that the habits of the

---

house in consequence attacked by a proslavery mob; lectured on health reform, having imported from Paris an anatomically correct female manikin whose frankness of cast brought notoriety; president of the October 1850 and October 1851 Woman's Rights Conventions at Worcester; in 1868 helped found the New England Woman Suffrage Association. Angelina Emily Grimké Weld (1805–79), like LSM a native of Charleston but, after conversion to Quakerism and persuaded of the evil of slavery, having moved to the North in 1829; wrote *An Appeal to the Christian Women of the South* (1836), published by the American Anti-Slavery Society; prepared, with husband Theodore Dwight Weld and sister Sarah Grimké, *American Slavery As It Is: Testimony of a Thousand Witnesses* (1839), also published by the American Anti-Slavery Society; though elected to the Central Committee of the October 1850 Woman's Rights Convention at Worcester, was unable to attend but attended later conventions at Rochester and New York.

34. Henry Stuart Foote (1804–80), senator (1847–52), then governor (1852–54), of Mississippi; Thomas Hart Benton (1782–1858), senator from Missouri (1821–51) until opposition to extension of slavery into the territories cost him reelection; Samuel Houston (1793–1863), victor over the Mexican army under Antonio López de Santa Anna at the battle of San Jacinto (April 21, 1836), twice president of the Republic of Texas, its senator after admission into the Union, then its governor.

35. Livre 9, fable 12, in La Fontaine, *Fables, contes, et nouvelles,* p. 229.

36. *Westminster* "Enfranchisement," pp. 296–97. Elizabeth I (1533–1603), queen of England from 1558; Isabella of Castile (1451–1504), queen of Castile from 1474, joint sover-

civilized world accord to these positions—has had the intellect to fill the position well; but it does not prove, and rather goes to disprove, her power of struggling with the masses. As woman and queen, doubly isolated from those masses, she kept her position simply because of such isolation—because, supported by the laws and habits of society, none dared insult or resist her. But suppose those laws and habits abrogated, what would have become of the virago, Elizabeth, when she gave the lordly Essex a blow on the ear? If ever it should happen to the fair Paulina, Angelina, or Lucretia to try, under the new *régime,* a similar experiment on any of their male coadjutors or opponents, it is rather probable that they may receive, upon the subject of aptitudes and uses, a somewhat striking lesson. Of the combatant ladies, similarly cited,[37] the same remark is to be made. Ladies of the feudal ages, they generally were petty monarchs: that is to say, defending their strongholds. These were always supported and strengthened, rather than impeded, by their sex, the *prestige* of sex seconding and doubling the admiration accorded to their remarkable actions. Joan of Arc (decidedly the most remarkable of heroines, and, strange to say, not cited by the reviewer) was a wonderful woman; great as a woman; a phenomenon in her way, certainly, but still a woman phenomenon. Her deeds were unusual for woman, but, nevertheless, done as a woman, and claiming for their sanction, not the rights and habits of manhood, but divine inspiration. She never levelled herself to man, or, so doing, must have sunk to the rank of the coarse *femmes de la Halle* of the French revolution.[38]

---

eign of Castile and Aragon with her husband Ferdinand from 1479; Maria Theresa (1717–80), archduchess of Austria, queen of Hungary and Bohemia, empress from 1745, when she caused her husband, Francis of Lorraine, to be elected Holy Roman emperor; Catherine II of Russia (1729–96), born Sophie Frederike Auguste of Anhalt-Zerbst, sole empress after the deposition and murder of her husband, Peter III, in 1762; Blanche of Castile (1188–1252), granddaughter of Henry II of England, daughter of Alfonso VIII of Castile, wife of Louis VIII of France, whose help she secured with an attempt to seize the English crown after the death of her uncle King John; regent during the minority of her son, Louis IX (1226–36), and when he was absent on crusade (1248–52).

37. Ibid., p. 297, carrying examples down to the seventeenth century with the Royalist heroine Charlotte de La Trémouille, daughter of the duc de Thouars, married in 1626 to James Stanley (1607–51), Lord Strange, seventh earl of Derby. During the Civil War, her husband absent, the countess of Derby sent raids from the family seat of Lathom House in Lancashire against neighboring Parliamentarians; defied a siege (February to May 1644) brought by the Parliamentary general Sir Thomas Fairfax until it was raised by Prince Rupert; and held the Isle of Man for Charles II until Charles' defeat at Worcester (Sept. 3, 1651) and the execution of her husband, arrested after escaping from the battlefield, six weeks later.

38. On Oct. 5, 1789, about 7,000 "women of the Market," infuriated by unstable prices and food shortages, marched from Paris to Versailles and, joined by other sympathetic Parisians, compelled the royal family to return with them to the capital. The incident was not

Such, too, would of necessity be the case with the man-woman that our conventionists would manufacture. Deprived of all which has hitherto, in separating her from man, wrapped her, as it were, in a veil of deity; naked of all those observances and distinctions which have been, if not always her efficient, still her only, shield; turned out upon the waste common of existence, with no distinctive mark but corporeal weakness, she becomes the inevitable victim of brutal strength. The reviewer acknowledges (or rather, remarks, for she does not seem to be conscious that it is an acknowledgment) that to account for the subjection of woman, "no other explanation is needed than physical force."[39] Setting aside, then, for the moment, all other differences, we would be glad to have the lady explain how she would do away with the difficulty arising from this acknowledged physical inferiority? Man is corporeally stronger than woman, and because he, in the unjust use of his strength, has frequently, habitually (we will allow her the full use of her argument), even invariably, oppressed and misused woman, how does she propose to correct the abuse? Strangely, by pitting woman against man, in a direct state of antagonism; by throwing them into the arena together, stripped for the strife; by saying to the man, this woman is a man like yourself, your equal and similar, possessing all rights which you possess, and (of course she must allow) possessing none others. In such a strife, what becomes of corporeal weakness? Perhaps we will be told how man conquers the wild beast, and, by knowledge and intellect, holds in sway the mighty elephant and the forest's king. True, by *intellect.* He has the superiority of intellect, and he uses it. It is God's and nature's law that he should use it. Man, generally, uses it to subdue his inferior, the beast. The white man uses it to subdue his inferior, the negro. Both are right, for both are according to God's law. The same argument has been used, to prove the necessity of woman's subjection. This, we think, is taking mistaken ground, and unnecessarily assuming a doubtfully tenable position. Woman's bodily frame is enough to account for her position. The differences of mind between the sexes we are, ourselves, inclined to regard rather as differences than inequalities. More of this anon, however. Granting, for the moment, exact mental equality, how will the conventionists redeem corporeal deficiencies? They do not pretend that woman is the superior mind, only the equal. Still, then, man—where they are matched against each other; where woman assumes

---

without violence; the palace was invaded and guards killed; to Edmund Burke, the royal family's terror and humiliation were compounded by "the horrid yells, and shrilling screams, and frantic dances, and infamous contumelies, and all the unutterable abominations of the furies of hell, in the abused shape of the vilest of women." *Reflections on the Revolution in France,* p. 122.

39. *Westminster* "Enfranchisement," p. 294.

manhood, and measures herself hand to hand with him—has, of necessity, the superiority—a brutal superiority, if you please, but still the superiority—and, in proportion as it is brutal, will the triumph it gives be brutal. Woman throws away her strength, when she *brings herself down* to man's level. She throws away that moral strength, that shadow of divinity, which nature has given her to keep man's ferocity in curb. Grant her to be his equal, and instantly she sinks to his inferior, which, as yet, we maintain she has never been.

Many women—even, we grant, the majority of women—throw themselves away upon follies. So, however, do men; and this, perhaps, as a necessary consequence, for woman is the mother of the man. Woman has allowed herself to be, alternately, made the toy and the slave of man; but this rather through her folly than her nature. Not wholly *her* folly either. *Her* folly, and *man's* folly, have made the vices and the punishment of both. Woman has certainly not her true place, and this place she as certainly should seek to gain. We have said that every error has its shadow of truth, and, so far, the conventionists are right. But, alas! how wide astray are they groping from their goal! Woman has not her true place, because she—because man—has not yet learned the full extent and importance of her mission. These innovators would seek to restore, by driving her entirely from, that mission; as though some unlucky pedestrian, shoved from the security of the sidewalk, should, in his consternation, seek to remedy matters by rushing into the thickest thoroughfare of hoofs and wheels. Woman will reach the greatest height of which she is capable—the greatest, perhaps, of which humanity is capable—not by becoming man, but by becoming, more than ever, woman. By perfecting herself, she perfects mankind; and hers, we have said, is the higher mission, because, from her, must the advance towards perfection begin. The woman must *raise* the man, by helping, not by rivalling, him. Without woman, this world of mankind were a wrangling dog-kennel. Could woman be transformed into man, the same result would follow. She it is who softens; she it is who civilizes; and, although history acknowledges her not, she it is who—not in the meteoric brilliancy of warrior or monarch, but in the quiet, unwearied and unvarying path of duty, the home of the mother, the wife, and the sister, teaching man his destiny—purifies, exalts, and guides him to his duty.

"Under a nominal recognition of a moral code common to both," says our reviewer,

> in practice, self-will and self-assertion form the type of what are designated as manly virtues, while abnegation of self, patience, resignation, and submission to power, unless when resistance is demanded <commanded> by other

> interests than their own, have been stamped, by general consent, as preeminently the duties and graces required of women—the meaning being merely, that power makes itself the centre of moral obligation, and that a man likes to have his own will, but does not like that his domestic companion should have a will different from his.[40]

Now, all this means, if it means anything, that woman, in the present condition of the world, is a self-denying, patient model of Christian love and charity; while man, unable to conquer his harsher passions, still benefits by her virtues. The reviewer, envying him the lordly privilege of getting into a passion, raving and ranting, would advise all womankind to disturb him in his monopoly, and to rave, rant, and be selfish along with him. We confess, for ourselves, that where a poor woman, borne away by human weakness, and restive under oppression, catches the raving malady a little, we seldom feel inclined to be harsh in our judgments of her. Nature is frail—we pity her, and confess that her case is a hard one. Even Zantippe, "the famous old scold,"[41] could, no doubt, have shown cause for exasperation; and it is not unlikely that, as philosophers are men, the good dame had no little reason on her side. Still, if she had borne life meekly, although her present great renown in history and spelling-book, spreading the knowledge of her name as far as that of old crooked back Z himself, would never have been attained; even Miss Martineau, we think, must confess that, while less celebrated, Mrs. Zantippe would have been a more perfect and more amiable character; and we, while we feel a deep interest in the sorrows of this far-famed personage, would hardly deem her a desirable model for our daughters. Wrath and power are hideous and fearful; wrath and weakness are hideous and contemptible. We trust that such of our sisters as may have attained the beautiful point of perfection, which our reviewer rather contemptuously refers to, will be sufficiently rewarded by the proud consciousness of duty fulfilled, to induce them to work on, in their righteous course—if not a flashing beacon of light to a benighted world, at least a holy ray of God's own sunlight, to purify and to bless. If ladies fear that these concessions are too great, and the pride of sex inclines them to rebel a little, let them remember that they are concessions, not to man, but to God; not to the husband or the brother—who, if he raves too hard, it is not in human weakness not to feel a little spiteful against—but to nature and mankind. Each—the lowliest individual woman—is in bearing and forbearing, in earnest striving and in patient suffering, doing her share towards softening and civilizing this hard world. Such is God's task to her, and she must fulfil it, or pass away

40. Ibid., p. 301.

41. Xanthippe was the wife of Socrates. LSM uses the French spelling.

either the frivolous plaything of a day, or the scorned abortion of a misplaced and grovelling ambition.

As regards the question of intellect, it is a most difficult one to argue. We are ourselves inclined to believe that the difference of intellect in the sexes exists, as we have said, rather in kind than degree. There is much talk of the difference of education and rearing bestowed upon individuals of either sex, and we think too much stress is laid upon it. Education, no doubt, influences the intellect in each individual case; but it is as logically certain that intellect, in its kind and degree, influences education *en masse*—that is to say, Thomas, the individual man, may be better suited to woman's duties, than Betty, the individual woman, and *vice versa.* Thomas might make a capital child's nurse, in which Betty succeeds but badly, while Betty might be quite competent to beat Thomas hollow in a stump oration; and yet we have a fair right to argue, that Thomas and Betty are but individual exceptions to a general rule, which general rule is plainly indicated by the universal practice of mankind. The fact that such relative positions of the sexes, and such habits of mind, have existed, more or less modified, in all ages of the world, and under all systems of government, goes far to prove that these are the impulses of instinct and teachings of Nature. It is certainly a little hard upon Mrs. Betty to be forced from occupations for which she feels herself particularly well qualified, and to make way for Mr. Thomas, who, although particularly ill-qualified for them, will be certain to assert his right; but laws cannot be made for exceptional cases, and if Mrs. Betty has good sense, as well as talent, she will let the former curb the latter; she will teach her woman-intellect to curb her man-intellect, and will make herself the stronger woman thereby. The fact that less effort has been made to teach woman certain things, is a strong argument that she has (taking her as a class) less aptitude for being taught those certain things. It is difficult to chain down mind by any habit or any teaching, and if woman's intellect had the same turn as man's, it is most unlikely that so many myriads should have passed away and "made no sign."[42]

In the field of literature, how many women have enjoyed all the advantages which men can command, and yet how very few have distinguished themselves; and how far behind are even those few from the great and burning lights of letters! Who ever hopes to see a woman Shakspeare? And yet a greater than Shakspeare may she be. It may be doubtful whether the brilliant intellect which, inspiring noble thoughts, leaves still the great thinker grovelling in the lowest vices and slave of his passions, without the self-command to keep them in sway, is superior to that which, knowing good and evil,

42. John Milton, *Paradise Lost* 6.24–25: "of so many myriads fallen, yet one / Returned not lost"; Shakespeare, *2 Henry VI* 3.3.29: "He [Cardinal Beaufort] dies, and makes no sign."

grasps almost instinctively at the first. Such, in its uncorrupted nature, is woman's intellect—such her inspiration. While man *writes,* she *does;* while he imagines the hero-soul, she is often performing its task; while he is painting, she is acting. The heart, it is sometimes argued, and not the brain, is "the priceless pearl of womanhood, the oracular jewel, the 'Urim and Thummim,' before which gross man can only inquire and adore."[43] This is fancy and not reasoning. The heart is known to be only a part of our anatomical system, regulating the currents of the blood, and nothing more. It has, by an allegory based upon exploded error, been allowed to stand for a certain class of feelings which every body now knows to be, equally with other classes, dependant upon the brain; and, in a serious argument, not the heart and the brain, but the difference of brain, not the feeling and the intellect, but the varieties of intellect, should be discussed. We consider, therefore, the question of preeminence as simply idle. We have already endeavoured to prove that, whatever the intellect of woman, it would have no influence in altering the relative position of the sexes; we now go farther, and maintain that the nature of her intellect confirms this position. The higher her intellect, the better is she suited to fulfil that heaviest task of life which makes her the "martyr to the pang without the palm."[44] If she suffers, what is this but the fate of every higher grade of humanity, which rises in suffering as it rises in dignity? for is not all intellect suffering?

We have, throughout this article, made no reference to the biblical argument, because, with those who receive it, it is too well known and too decisive to need farther comment. To those who reject it, it is of course no argument. We have endeavoured to prove that common sense, quite independently of revelation, marks the place of woman, and that while the Scriptures confirm, they are by no means necessary to decide, the question.

The resolutions of the last Worcester Convention are taken so entirely (in many sentences verbatim) from the article in the *Westminster* which we have been reviewing, that very evidently the same mind has inspired both, showing thus a systematizing of the subject, that proves, we fear, some truth in the assertion of the reviewer that this movement is a political one, and "carried on in a form which denotes an intention to persevere."[45] A letter was read to the meeting from Miss Martineau, and, putting two and two

43. Kingsley, *Yeast,* chap. 10, p. 145, reading: "the heart, and not the brain, enshrines the priceless pearl of womanhood. . . ." On "Urim and Thummim," see Exod. 28:30.

44. Elizabeth Barrett Browning, "The Cry of the Children," 41–44: "They know the grief of man, without its wisdom; / They sink in man's despair, without its calm; / Are slaves, without the liberty in Christdom, / Are martyrs, by the pang without the palm." The final line is cited in Kingsley, *Yeast,* "Epilogue," p. 321.

45. *Westminster* "Enfranchisement," p. 289.

together, we conclude that Miss Martineau was the *de facto* composer of these resolutions, in which morbid vanity, "that brawl-begotten child of struggling self-conceit and self-disgust,"[46] so painfully exhibits itself. Should we prove mistaken, we can only regret that there should be two women in the world capable of such a composition. The reviewer thinks, farther, that this move "is destined to inaugurate one of the most important of those <the> movements towards political and social reform, which are the best characteristics <characteristic> of the present age."[47] When a grave periodical allows such sentiments to soil its pages, it is time for us to cease to laugh. It is time for man to open his eyes to the mischievous effects of a progressive system of reform, which allows, not illogically, such a bud to be grafted upon it. It is time for woman, in right earnest, to take up arms in her own cause, ere she be hurled by traitors of her own sex from the high pedestal where God has placed her. Let her wield those weapons of love, charity, affection, firmness, and fortitude, with which Nature arms her, and, though her path be through sorrow, even through sorrow climbs she to perfection. Richter somewhere compares a young bride to the sleeping child of Garofalo, over which an angel holds a crown of thorns.[48] The angel of sorrow shall indeed wake her by pressing that crown upon her brow; but let her not shrink from the waking. "Life is real! Life is earnest!" and its duties are not to be shunned because our weakness relishes them not. Let woman make herself free, in the true sense of the word, by the working out of her mission. "Liberty is duty, not license;" and woman is freest when she is the truest woman, when she finds the fewest difficulties in the way of conforming herself to her nature.

Not enjoyment, and not sorrow,
   Is our destined end or way;
But to live <act> that each tomorrow
   Find us farther than today. . . .

Let us, then, be up and doing,
   With a heart for any fate;
Still achieving, still pursuing,
   Learn to labour and to wait.[49]

46. Kingsley, *Yeast,* chap. 10, p. 145.

47. *Westminster* "Enfranchisement," p. 290.

48. Johann Paul Friedrich Richter (1763–1825), *Leben des Quintus Fixlein,* in *Werke,* ed. Norbert Miller, 6 vols. (Munich, 1960–63), 4:33. Benvenuto Tisi, called da Garofalo (1481–1559), prolific painter of the school of Ferrara.

49. Longfellow, "A Psalm of Life," sts. 3 and 9.

Woman is not what she might be, not what she ought to be. Half persuaded, as she is, that her position is one of degradation and inferiority, she becomes, as a matter of necessity, degraded to that opinion, just in so far as she is convicted of its truth; and hence, too often, folly becomes her pleasure, vanity her pride. But this is man's blotting of God's fair work. Woman is neither man's equal nor inferior, but only his different. It would indeed be well if man, convinced of this, could, in his relations with her, "throw aside his instruments of torture," and aid rather than oppress her. Thus, we firmly believe, it will be, in the perfection of time, worked out by woman's endurance and patient labouring in her own sphere; but never, certainly, by her assumption of another, equally ill-adapted to her mental and her bodily faculties. For her it is (God's apostle of love) to pass through life with "the cross, that emblem of self-sacrifice, in her hand, while her pathway across the desert is marked by the flowers which spring beneath her steps."[50] Life's devoted martyr she may be—man's ministering angel she may be; but, for heaven's sake, mesdames, the conventionists—not Cuffee's rival candidate for the Presidency!

L. S. M.

50. Kingsley, *Yeast,* chap. 10, pp. 149–50: "The sketch was labelled, the 'Triumph of Woman.' . . . In front of the sun, down the path of the morning beams, came Woman, clothed only in the armour of her own loveliness. Her bearing was stately, and yet modest; in her face pensive tenderness seemed wedded with earnest joy. In her right hand lay a cross, the emblem of self-sacrifice. Her path across the desert was marked by the flowers which sprang up beneath her steps; the wild gazelle stept forward trustingly to lick her hand; a single wandering butterfly fluttered round her head."

4.

Woman and Her Needs

Myriads on myriads of men, before the time of Isaac Newton, must have sat under apple-trees; and vast numbers of them, too, undoubtedly, had apples to drop upon their heads; while not a few, it is likely, puzzled themselves to know why the apple should fall plumb down (thereby entailing upon them the evils of a headache) instead of flying off at a tangent, a right angle, or a curve. Many a one of these myriads might, perchance, just as well as the great philosopher, have guessed out the wonderful law of gravitation; only—not one of them did it. Why was this? Not want of intellect, surely. No doubt there were many men, before as well as since Sir Isaac Newton, quite his equals in mental power. But they did not solve the riddle, and *he* did. The time for the solving of it being come, even then came the man to solve it. Perhaps the day may yet arrive, when all puzzling questions in physics and metaphysics, in morals and in ethics, may be as clearly disposed of; but in the meantime we must be content, like the non-Newtons of the past world when the apples came tumbling about their ears, to scratch our heads and bear the penalty of our ignorance. To be sure, we will still, in the midst of this head-thumping process, look up inquiringly and ask, "Why?" Why are

De Bow 13 (Sept. 1852): 267–91. Publication reviewed: E. Oakes Smith, *Woman and Her Needs* (New York: Fowler and Wells, 1851). Elizabeth Oakes Prince Smith (1806–93) first published as a series in Horace Greeley's New York *Tribune* the papers later collected into *Woman and Her Needs.* See Wyman, *Selections from the Autobiography of Elizabeth Oakes Smith,* pp. 151–53.

some things hard and other things soft? some things square and other things round? Man has a great propensity for asking "Why?" and, upon the whole, it is a fortunate tendency. By perpetual knocking at a closed door, sometimes a hand comes to open it.

Why, then, among the darkest of life's problems, constantly recurs to us the question: Why is there evil in this world? and how is it to be remedied? "Why?" "why?" "why?"—has the weary thought of man constantly interrogated of Nature, appealed to Reason, and searched Revelation to discover. But ever there has come back to him only the dull echo of his own inquirings: "Why?" What is Evil? Can any man put his hand upon it? Can any man explain it in its nature, its birth, or its causes? Is it truly a Lucifer breath, a blast from hell, sent to poison our world, that God's mercy may find scope to redeem us from it? Is it the inspiration of some great Satanic creation, which strides our earth in mystic significancy of unimagined mysteries? Is it an active power, or a passive one? an existence, or only a deficiency? a something that is? or rather, a something that is not? a virtue left imperfect? a good not filled up? even as darkness, ignorance, and error are in themselves nothing—only deficiencies, *minus* quantities of light, knowledge, and truth? These are the questions—and such as these—over which, age after age, the wise and the good have thought themselves weary; while the imaginative and the weak have sought among the stars, and thought to read their destinies from leaves and flowers; and listened to their dreams, and believed that it was God who called them. But all have passed away, and, one after another, they have resigned their gray hairs and wearied hearts to the dust, while still upon their expiring lips quivered the great, unanswered, "Why?"

Today, in this great age of "new lights," we have solutions numberless offered to this our world-wide problem. Every "*ism*" upon earth has got its explanation of, and its remedy for, this monster Evil, which the poor, ignorant world has so long imagined inexplicable and incurable. What is this bugbear of the world? this sin—this pain—this suffering? Nothing, forsooth, it would now appear—nothing but a nightmare dream; a kind of world dyspepsia; at worst, a species of toothache, which, by some socialistic, communistic, feministic, Mormonistic, or any other such application of chloroform to the suffering patient, may be made to pass away in a sweet dream of perfection. If we will only believe our doctors and open our mouths wide, we are cured at once. Down goes their nostrum, as glibly as the new-fashioned *capsule,* by help of which the lucky individual to whom a nauseous dose of castor-oil is prescribed may (so declareth to us the immaculate truth of advertisements) luxuriate in a dainty something, resembling a luscious piece of turtle-fat; one luxurious gulp, and, lo! the deed is done.

Startled by the loud-mouthed Eurekas of each new sect as it starts into being, we turn to investigate their discoveries—but alas! like the fabled fruit of the Dead Sea, these are but dust and ashes to the taste.[1] Their great discoveries, forsooth, end in the tautologous declaration that the world is evil, simply because it is not perfect. They write books, and they make speeches; they plan and they counterplan; they fancy they have found a perfect mine of thought, and they dig away at it valorously. But, behold! the fancied jewels which they dive at prove to be but cast-off glass—the refuse offal of those great laborers who have preceded them; while still, in its fullest development, the same great mystery of evil, for which neither man nor woman has yet found a cause or a cure, looms out, not only in spite of, but even in bolder prominence from, their ignorant meddling. Quacks they are, whose salve fires the wound, whose potion poisons the blood, and the sick world writhes under their ill-judged medicaments. Back, fools! to what ye were made for!—your plow and your loom, your spindle and your shears; these, and these only, are the tools Heaven destined for you. *Ne sutor ultra crepidam.*[2] Wo to the world which seeks its rulers where it should but find its drudges! Wo to the drudge who would exalt himself into the ruler! Nature is vigilant of her laws, and has no pardon for the breakers of them. The sentenced wretch appeals in vain; and the hair-brained Phaeton, who would guide the chariot of the sun, must perish amidst the suffering he has caused.[3]

The world has supped full of horrors under such false guides. Blind leaders of the blind, they have led us through dirty slough and miry way, until filth and corruption seem almost our natural element. But we are about to touch upon womanhood, and must, in courtesy, somewhat soften our language, though we are by no means sure that the feminine reform corps may not take our deference, thus offered, as an invidious distinction, maliciously bestowed upon their sex. Strong, however, in the purity of our intentions, the defender, not the libeler of the sex, we must, while we will do our "spiriting" as gently as the circumstances of the case allow, endeavor to show the false position in which the innovators have placed themselves, as

1. Thomas Moore, *Lalla Rookh,* "The Fire Worshippers," 2.484–85: "Like Dead Sea fruits, that tempt the eye, / But turn to ashes on the lips." Byron, *Childe Harold's Pilgrimage* 3.301–4: "But Life will suit / Itself to Sorrow's most detested fruit, / Like to the apples on the Dead Sea's shore, / All ashes to the taste."

2. Pliny *Natural History* 35.85: "ne supra crepidam sutor iudicaret" ("the cobbler should make no judgments away from his last").

3. When his father, the Sun, promised any gift he should ask, Phaethon begged to be allowed to drive his father's chariot; insisting despite the Sun's advice, Phaethon was unable to manage the horses, which dragged the chariot out of control, scorching the earth, until Phaethon was hurled to his death.

well as the slanderous assertions which their course is calculated to throw over the true cause of womanhood.

The reforming ladies have not yet got an "*ism*" for their move; but have nevertheless come forward scarcely less boldly than their masculine coadjutors—or, perhaps, we should rather say competitors—in the world-doctoring system. We have had some curiosity to see their arguments; and being, we confess, both unable and unwilling to plow through the mass of declamation with which they favor the world, have endeavored to limit our studies, in this line, to selections. Following this course, our attention has happened to fall upon Mrs. E. O. Smith, who is, we are informed, among the most moderate of the feminist reformers! Tolerably fair specimens of the other extreme have been made public in the sundry women-convention reports which have appeared, and also in a very remarkable article which graced, or rather disgraced, the pages of the last July number of the *Westminster Quarterly*.[4] We have not, with a superficial view of criticism, limited ourselves to a glance over title-page and final flourish, with a hurried glimpse or two at the intervening pages of the little work we have undertaken to review, but, with a sober spirit of inquiry, have set about finding whatever we could find in it of true or of false, marking and remarking everything noteworthy in our progress, and are, we think, ready to give the authoress credit for any merit of thought or style which she may have exhibited.

We will say little of the last—simply remarking, that if the lady is not a very careless writer, she has to complain of a very careless printer, her thoughts (or vacancies of thought, we cannot quite determine which) being not unfrequently given in a form which fairly puzzles our grammar as well as our logic. How many of these discrepancies belong to the printer, we will not undertake to say, having ourselves suffered enough from the impish fraternity of the printing-office to learn a most sympathizing fellow-feeling towards our co-sufferers in that line. We take it, moreover, for granted, that many worse literary delinquencies must be frequent among the reformist sisterhood (the lady in question ranking, we are informed, among their literati), and we have cause to thank our stars that we have not, in the boldness of our exploring expedition through these unknown regions, fallen into worse hands. If we are, as we frankly confess ourselves, somewhat mystified even now, by the irregular currents and the confusion of words and ideas around us, what might have been our fate had we become entangled midst the overwhelming icebergs of female-convention polemics? Would the

4. *Westminster* "Enfranchisement," reviewed by LSM in chap. 3, "Enfranchisement of Woman."

world have immortalized in us a second Sir John Franklin?[5] Upon the whole, we have laid down our little volume with a most sympathizing consciousness of the truth of a remark we encountered in a recent number of *Blackwood*. The reviewer there observes, that the fashion of the day, among a certain class of writers, is to dwell with great emphasis and a kind of inspired frenzy upon the word "infinite," which they have appropriated to their use in a peculiar, mystified, indefinite, indefinable signification. "They have made the discovery that this poet or that painter talks or paints the 'infinite.' They find in every obscurity of thought, in every violence of passion, the 'infinite.' There is no such thing as 'sound and fury signifying nothing.' They always signify the 'infinite.'"[6] Very decidedly Mrs. Smith deals largely in the "infinite"; and we confess ourselves matter of fact enough to wish that she had, instead, confined herself to the much more distinct, as well as more succinct, explanation of a certain Mrs. Mehitable Haskell, who, rising to make a speech at the first Worcester Convention, frankly acknowledges that "she does not know what are woman's rights, but for forty, nay, fifty years, she has known what woman's wrongs are, for she has felt them."[7] Now there is something right hearty—something earnest and downright—in the declaration of this good lady. We feel that *she, at least,* did not frequent the conventions for the purpose of displaying her graces, whether of person or rhetoric. We fancy we can see the good Mrs. Mehitable before us: broad, square-shouldered; somewhat raw-boned; sharp gray eyes; teeth deficient (she would disdain to mend her oratory or her looks by false ones); a bony hand which hath shown service over the washtub, and well calculated, in its mere appearance, to excite admonitory twinges in the flagellatable parts of luck-

5. Sir John Franklin (1786–1847), English explorer, led several expeditions into the Arctic in search of the Northwest Passage; in the last (1847–48) was lost with his entire company.

6. [William Henry Smith,] "Miss Mitford's *Recollections,*" *Blackwood's Edinburgh Magazine* 71 (March 1852): 259–72; 263.

7. *Proceedings of the Woman's Rights Convention*—reviewed by LSM in chap. 3, "Enfranchisement of Woman"—pp. 95–96, reports in direct speech the words of "Mehitable Haskell, of Gloucester," of which a part is: "This meeting, as I understand it, was called to discuss the question of Woman's Rights. Well, I do not pretend to know exactly what woman's *rights* are; but I know that I have groaned for forty, yea, for fifty years, under a sense of woman's *wrongs.* I know that, even when a girl, I groaned under the idea that I could not receive as much instruction as my brothers could. I wanted to be what I felt that I was capable of becoming; but this I could not do, for public opinion denied to females the intellectual culture that was granted to males." The speech is also given, with some changes of wording, in Elizabeth Cady Stanton et al., eds., *History of Woman Suffrage* 1 (Rochester, London, and Paris, 1887): 232. The Woman's Rights Convention of October 1851 was the second held at Worcester, Mass.

less youth, said hand being used with some vehemence of gesticulation. All her motions angular; all her forms angular. Worthy Mrs. Mehitable, vastly rather would we shake hands with thee in all amicable companionship, than stand a few of those angular motions, energetically applied about our ears. In very truth, too, we confess to something of sympathy with thee. Evidently, thou art an earnest soul. Earnest, doubtless, in thy washtub, as in thy flagellatory duties; and earnestly, too, frequentest thou these conventions, hoping that some good may be hatched out of them. Alas! good Mrs. Mehitable, take home that earnest soul of thine. There is work for it elsewhere, but none here. Here is Babel-confusion, brawling presumption, restless vanity; no room for truth. Thy woman's wrongs, borne for fifty long years, canst thou not bear yet a little longer? Let suffering teach thee patience. Let patience teach thee love. Let love teach thee gentleness, charity, forbearance; and although we will not warrant thee a disfranchisement from woman's wrongs—for our world is far from perfect, and ever the strong hand must abuse its power—credit us, worthy Mrs. Mehitable, thus thou hast done more to put down the abuse of that strong hand—more in the true cause of woman—than scores of conventionists can accomplish. Thus all that one woman can do, thou hast done. For hast thou not shown that gentleness can master passion? Bowing before the strong hand, hast thou not shamed it? And doth not thus thine earnest soul teach to all within the circle of its influence, the true lesson of Christian charity and philosophical forbearance?

But let us return to Mrs. Smith, who, being a literary lady, a "woman of genius" [44, 88], as we understand her occasionally to intimate, would in all probability spurn the idea of comparison with so humble a sister reformer as this most excellent Mrs. Mehitable, the charm of whose name and eloquence has drawn us off from our more immediate subject of discussion. We have confessed that Mrs. S. is too high in "the infinite" for our clouded intellects to penetrate her dream-land. We have done our best, but cannot exactly find out what she would be after. We even doubt whether, in the full flow of inspiration, her genius could condescend to settle so trifling a point in her own mind. When folks are in "the infinite," they are of course, and ought to be, incomprehensible to other people; very likely, also, to themselves. She, too, preaches love and gentleness; but it is with a reservation: a resistance reservation, a conventionist reservation, a right-of-voting reservation, a spontaneity reservation, an intuition reservation. In short, her argument, rushing to and fro on every varying gale, from communism to socialism, from Christianity to free-thinking, from real woman-thought to conventionist woman-thought, is as impossible to follow as an *ignis fatuus*. We can only say that it has, in all its veerings, a most distressing tendency to the "higher law" fallacies, and our authoress has, much more than she is herself probably aware of, exhibited to us the undeveloped Louis Blanc in petticoats. We must however here do the ladies the justice to remark, that the feminine move has at least this advantage over the various masculine ones, that, more than any theory yet advanced, it logically carries principles to their climax. Granted that A is B, and B is C, inevitably then A must be C. The ladies jump to their conclusion boldly, while men stand higgling with the relics of old prejudice. Given the premises that "all men[8] are born free and equal;" that "intuition is God's law," and that "aptitude is no argument of use," they are right, and have the merit of bringing out their principles in unadulterated perfection. A strange *pot pouri* of a world must indeed result from such premises!

Our authoress complains of the degradation of woman in society: that she is out of her place, unappreciated, having her talents and powers not only hidden under a bushel, but absolutely thrown away, while she becomes either the slave or the toy of man. Now this is all true of some women—many women—perhaps, we must even confess, of a majority of women. (We are not quite ready to concede this position in its full force, but for the sake of argument will give our antagonists the furthest point to which they can possibly lay claim.) Yet we will not allow the universality nor the necessity of such an effect, from the operation of the actual laws of existing society. It is not woman, as a class, who is thus degraded, but only so many individual women, each one of whom is separately, and from causes quite extraneous from her position as woman, so degraded. Many, noble (and we believe increasing in proportionate numbers with the advance of civilization) are the examples of high, self-relying, heaven-depending, duty-fulfilling women in every position of life, who, by a noble self-abnegation, and a faithful adherence to the laws of God and nature, are daily showing that woman is not inherently, either in her nature or her position, what our authoress would wish to prove her. Many women (we have already said we will even grant an unfortunately large proportion of women) are degraded, not because they have submitted themselves to the position which nature assigns them, but because, like Mrs. Smith, they cannot be content with the exercise of the duties and virtues called forth by that, and in that, position. They forget the woman's duty-fulfilling ambition, to covet man's fame-grasping ambition. Woman was made for *duty,* not for *fame;* and so soon as she forgets

8. It would be, as the ladies have justly remarked, mere quibbling, to contend that the word "men" in this oft quoted sentence does not mean (if it means anything) human beings, and includes them as well as Cuffee. [LSM] The ladies had justly remarked this in *Westminster* "Enfranchisement," pp. 291–92, and *Proceedings of the Woman's Rights Convention,* p. 12.

this great law of her being, which consigns her to a life of heroism if she will—but quiet, unobtrusive heroism—she throws herself from her position, and thus, of necessity, degrades herself. This mistaken hungering for the forbidden fruit, this grasping at the notoriety belonging (if indeed it properly belongs to any) by nature to man, is at the root of all her debasement.

Look at the ballroom belle for instance. Why is she a flirt, a coquette, a heartless trifler with hearts? Not because there is harm in the ballroom enjoyment of youth; in the joy-waking music, or the spirit-rousing dance; but because she would be *talked* of, and forgets duty, conscience, and heart, in the love of notoriety. Why does the young mother forget the sick baby in its cradle, to listen to the whispered inanities of those bewhiskered fops who surround her? Why, but because she cannot resign to duty that petty fame to which she degrades herself. Why does the gray and wrinkled matron, whom nature and duty would keep at her fireside corner to wake the young hearts round her to the love of God, nature, and virtue, rush out with her be-rouged cheek and stained locks, to try and play the belle a little longer? Still she grasps at her shame. It is her ambition that degrades her. Why does the literary lady leave too often her infant to the hireling, her sick and her poor to chance charity? What is it that stocks the world with Harriet Martineaus, George Sands, and Lady Bulwers?[9] Is it not the same hungering love for notoriety, the same misdirected ambition; misdirected still, though in another track? There is nothing unwomanish in the fullest exercise by woman of the thought and mind, which, if God has given, he has given for use. There is nothing unwomanish in the writing of such thoughts; nothing unwomanish even, we think, in the publishing of them. Society has accordingly permitted, and does permit, unblamed and unchecked, woman's fullest liberty in the exercise of her literary powers in every line; and she has, equally with the man, as far as she is able to use it, this theatre of effort open to her. If she has not, equally with the man, distinguished herself in it, it is because her talents and disposition do not indicate this as the career best suited to the fullest exercise of her faculties and virtues. It is *not her highest destiny*. It is *not her noblest life*. Nevertheless many women, with great and true woman-minds, have written, have published, and have done good, by so expanding the brighter developments of woman-thought. But so soon as

9. Rosina Doyle Wheeler Bulwer-Lytton (1802–82), having been legally separated (April 1836) from her husband, the novelist Edward George Earle Lytton Bulwer-Lytton—her children were removed from her two years later—turned novelist herself with *Cheveley, or the Man of Honour* (1839), containing a hostile portrait of her husband, whom she continued to pursue with recriminations until his death in 1873.

woman strives with man's ambition, so soon as she forgets the ruling thought of duty, letting its throne be usurped by the illegitimate hungering for fame and notoriety which so fatally misleads her, her writings, as her nature, become corrupted in the struggle. She has resigned herself to an *ignis fatuus* guide, which fails never to plunge her into the mire of degradation. Man, like woman, may fall, and does fall, through similar causes, to similar degradation. But as the woman's fall is from a higher and a purer elevation, even so grovels she lower in her debasement, and closer and heavier clings to her its consequent soil. Because women have thus sinned, we behold their punishment. Degraded they are, even in that proportion wherein they have erred. The ballroom coquette, in the midst of her triumph, is degraded in her heart and in her being. The brilliant George Sand, bold in her impudence and her talent, is degraded to the dust before the blushing mother, who watches that her innocent child shall not lay its hand upon the foul productions wherein France's brilliant novelist often competes in obscenity with the nauseous filth spewed forth, as though in devilish scorn, by her compatriots, a Sue and a Dumas, upon a community sufficiently degraded to admire them.[10] In a steady pursuit of duty such names would be perhaps entirely unknown. But dares any one say that they are better for being thus known? or is there anything but a sickly appetite for notoriety which could make such a position to be coveted? Is a Ninon de l'Enclos, a duchess of Pompadour,[11] or a George Sand (indisputably celebrated women all of them) so good, so pure, or so noble in the eye of God, as the unknown mother who strokes to sleep the weary eye of her baby, and whispers to its waking thought her never-to-be-forgotten lessons of duty and of truth. Brilliant fallen ones the world have seen; but nature turns from them in sorrow. She glories not, but weeps for her fallen children.

It is this same misguided love for notoriety which now misleads women to insist upon political rights, as they word their demand—that is to say, admission to the struggle for political distinction. And what is this that they ask? What, but that like the half-barbarous, half-heroic Spartan maid they may be permitted to strip themselves to the strife, and wrestle in the public arena? Can civilized, Christianized woman covet such a right? They pretend,

10. Eugène Sue (1804–57), French writer, some of whose novels, set in the Parisian underworld, promote socialism; Alexandre Dumas father and son (1802–70 and 1824–95), French novelists and playwrights, of whom LSM elsewhere (chap. 9, "*Uncle Tom's Cabin,*" p. 247) singles out for blame the former's *Le Comte de Monte Cristo* (1844) and may have in mind also the latter's *La Dame aux camélias* (1848) and *Diane de Lys* (1851).

11. Anne, called Ninon, de Lenclos (1620–1705), French courtesan; Jeanne-Antoinette Poisson, marquise de Pompadour (1721–64), made duchess (1752), mistress of Louis XV of France, exerting strong political influence.

or they mislead themselves to the belief, that they are actuated by a pure desire to ennoble the sex. Let them look honestly and calmly to the bottom of the question, and they will see that it is but notoriety, not elevation, which they seek. In all derelictions from the right, the just, the holy, and the true, woman is responsible for her own degradation, inasmuch as it entirely proceeds from her own act, in casting herself out from her true position. She is herself, we repeat, the sole cause of it; and we wish to lay a stress upon this, because we maintain her to be a responsible, reasoning being, and not man's puppet. It is no excuse for her that man tempts her into folly. Man is unfortunately ready enough to tempt woman to err, and does not always stop to calculate the possible evil resulting from his pleasures and amusements. It amuses him to see the performances of the circus-clown or the monkey-man. It pleases him to have woman for his toy. He will pay the former with his money, the latter with his flattery, and thus tempt to degradation, but he cannot degrade. The degradation can be accomplished only by the consent of the degraded. The accessory to murder cannot be held guiltless because tempted by his principal. No reasoning being can be made an accessory but by his own consent. We may pity the weakness that falls by temptation, but cannot receive it as exculpation from the crime, except by acknowledging, in so far as it is thus received (as in the cases of infants or maniacs), a defect or inferiority in the reasoning powers of the person misled. We allow no such defect or inferiority to woman, and therefore hold her fully responsible for her own course. Seeking notoriety and applause, if (as too often she does) she stoops to conquer, she stoops with her own free will.[12] Man's wishes cannot degrade her. She degrades herself to man's wishes. Let her feel her duty as a woman, avoiding alike an undue valuation of man's applause, and an unworthy grappling with him for notoriety, and there is no shadow of degradation in her position. There may be no publicity, no far-spread reputation, no fame; but certainly there is no degradation in the holy, full, conscientious, and unguerdoned fulfilment of duty.

There are, undoubtedly, many false positions in which woman may be placed, where the fault is not so entirely her own as in the classes above noticed. But none of these are of the same vital importance, for by none of them is the woman-nature so entirely neutralized and destroyed. Our authoress attacks the established laws of society as defective, as not sufficiently protecting woman in the right of holding property; not sufficiently upholding her in the right of laboring for its acquisition; and, last and greatest, not sufficiently checking her in the right of getting married before she has the sense to know what she is about. We are far from maintaining that our laws

12. Oliver Goldsmith, *She Stoops to Conquer* (1773).

are perfect in the varied system of checks and balances required, or that they may not exhibit some ill-jointed legislation upon these and many other subjects; but strongly suspect, from the legal instinct (intuition) displayed by Mrs. Smith, that, if she and her compeers were set to put the laws to rights, we should have a strong compound of the Draconian and the barn-burner systems. Tyranny here, license there—lock doors and bolt windows on this side of the street, but over the way throw all open, pray for "the good time coming,"[13] and trust to "the law of our own intuitions." We should like to see Mrs. S. at the head of a family of some half-dozen young ladies of sixteen and there about, who had made up their minds to get married with or without permission. What system of restrictions and legal checks she could devise to keep her unruly little community in order, we think would be a vast puzzle to her genius, requiring a higher exercise of mind, of Christian charity, of philosophy, and of every noblest intellectual characteristic, than the writings of some scores of such volumes as that wherewith she has now seen fit to edify the public. We strongly suspect that much more could be effected in such a case by one sensible, matronly, gentle, and judicious mother or aunt, kindly watching and counseling from that throne of woman, her own chair, by her own fireside, than by troops of voting and speech-making conventionist lawgivers.

"If," says Mrs. Smith,

> any woman of genius is so untrue to herself as to say she should have been happier as an in-door, painstaking, fireside woman; careful for the small savings of a household, holding the rod *in terrorem* over unruly urchins, and up in the morning early to scold the servants, her nature satisfied with this ordinary manifestation of sex, she is from some cause disqualified for the holding of God's beautiful and abundant gifts in reverent stewardship—she is the Jew, better pleased with the worship of Apis than the sublime mysteries of Jehovah, looking to the flesh-pots of Egypt, and turning from the heavenly manna.[14]

Mrs. S., we presume, considers it a mark of *genius* to make oneself as happy as convenient, leaving duty to knock, unheeded, outside the door. We can only say, that the highest and most intellectual specimens of womanhood we have ever seen, scorning not the duty of managing children and servants, took into their hands and hearts the task which nature gave them, and ful-

13. Smith, *Woman and Her Needs,* p. 34; Charles Mackay, "The Good Time Coming," st. 1: "There's a good time coming, boys! / A good time coming." Charles Mackay (1814–89), Scottish songwriter, poet, and journalist.

14. *Woman and Her Needs,* p. 88. Cf. Exod. 16:3, 14–35, 32:4–6.

filled it, with the fullest powers of a God-given, soul-beaming intellect. If these were Jews worshiping Apis, Heaven preserve us from the *sublime mysteries* with which Mrs. S. would replace such worship!

> We must and will feel the stirrings of a great nature if it be great, and we are happy only as we obey its monitions. We are not happy in a half life, a half utterance; for the wealth struggles for its power; the smothered fire burns and consumes till it finds <find> room for its healthful glow. A thousand women are ill-natured and miserable, not from positive ills about them, but from compression; they have that within, demanding space and indulgence, and they pine for its freedom—the laws of their life are not comprehended, and they sink into <to> imbecile complaints, only because there is no voice to call them forth to freedom and light. [89–90]

Still the question seems, not "what ought I to do," but "what would I like to do?" It is, apparently, in the opinion of our authoress, sufficient excuse for a woman to be *ill-natured* and *miserable,* that she suffers *from compression.* A man, too, may, we suppose, suffer from compression as well as a woman. He may be as ill suited to the plow or the counting-house, as she is to the spindle or the nursery; but has he, therefore, the right to be "ill-natured and miserable"? Has he the right to say, "I am a genius, and it is an unjust fate that places me here"? Men, as well as women, certainly do follow such a course not unfrequently, grumbling very unnecessarily and very uselessly at the defects of this God-made world, which they would have made so much better. But we, until enlightened by these recent new-light developments, have always supposed that the old fable of the child crying for the moon, was the most usual, as well as most reasonable, mode of answering such complaints against the orderings of life and destiny. Human cravings soar high. Perhaps there is no human being, not born in a state of imbecility almost as cramped as that of the oyster in his shell, who does not suffer, or fancy that he suffers, from compression. Shall we all begin to pout for the moon? to be ill-tempered and miserable over our state of compression? Such are they, who

> By the road-side fall and perish,
> Weary with the march of life.[15]

Such are they who wantonly waste the talent which God has given them. The true soul, the strong soul, with shoulder to the wheel, asks not, "How

15. Longfellow, "Footsteps of Angels," st. 4: "He, the young and strong, who cherished / Noble longings for the strife, / By the roadside fell and perished, / Weary with the march of life."

shall I be happy?" but "How shall I do right?" and, choosing its course, strives forward bravely, cheerily, and God-fearingly, to its goal.

> Sorrow and silence are strong, and patient endurance is God-like.[16]

Sisters, is it we who preach unto you degradation? Is it we who point you from the "heavenly manna" to "the flesh pots of Egypt"?

In the little book before us, we find many a glimmering of the true consciousness of what woman ought to be—glimpses of genuine woman-nature, showing how difficult it is, even embroiled among such sophistries, to entirely corrupt it. But every where comes the adjunct, the unlucky reservation which spoils everything that is good and truthful in the thought. For good and truth there are, even here, struggling, as ever they do struggle, at the groundwork of every error. Good and truth there are in the thought which says that woman is not what she should be; but falsehood and mischief in the cry which hounds her on to these most unwomanish proceedings, by way of bettering a condition which needs not *change,* but *cure;* not *reform,* but *perfection.* Never spake prophet truer words than these of Mrs. Smith:

> There is a Woman's sphere—harmonious, holy, soul-imparting; it has its grades, its laws from the nature of things. [28]
>
> There is <I know of> nothing more holy, more God-serving, ay, and more beautiful, than the steady, self-denying labor of the large class of women in the middle ranks of life, who, with woman-like dignity and solid sense, pursue a calling humble and painstaking to earn an honest subsistence for their families. The lives of these women are often truly heroic, are silent, beautiful epics, breathing the best aspirations of poetry and romance. [39]
>
> I see no way in which harmony can result in the world without entire recognition of differences, for surely nothing is gained upon either side by antagonism *merely.* [28; LSM's italics]

Alas! for that unlucky little word "*merely.*" Therein lies snugly hid away the mischievous devil who is whispering his reservations to the ear of our modern Eves.[17] Antagonism is all right, we may suppose, though not *antagonism merely.* Happy would we be, however, did the reservation of our authoress end here; for, unfortunately, the mass of her little volume is one succession of bitter antagonism, illogical reasoning, romantic dreaming, and half-understood truths. We regret this the more, as she is evidently not one of the deepest-dyed reformers; and if (as we think not at all unlikely) she sports the "Bloomer," we will wager our newest gold pen that she "wears it with a

16. Longfellow, *Evangeline* 2.59.
17. Milton, *Paradise Lost* 4.799–809.

difference."[18] She is not "perfectly certain" of the efficacy of woman's rights conventions; but she rejoices in the fact, that this "stirring of woman-thought originates in our own country,"[19] and sees no reason why women should not "associate, as do our compeers of the other sex, for the purpose of evolving better views, and of confirming some degree of power" [14]; nor why "those [of ours] who have a fancy to tinker a constitution, canvass a county, or preach the Gospel, should not be permitted to do so, provided they feel this to be the best use of their faculties" [27].

> Hereafter, in the progress of events, I see no reason why the influence of woman should not be acknowledged at the ballot-box. [90]
>
> I do not know that I am prepared to say, as has been said, that women have a right to our halls of legislation, our courts of justice, our military posts, and each and all spheres where men "most do congregate."[20]

She doubts; but why? Not because woman is there entirely out of her place, but because (here the lady takes a plunge into the *infinite*) she thinks that a "pure state of society" is approaching wherein "these needs will pass away" [45]. "But," she continues, "but till 'the good time coming' arrive, let her be free to her own intuitions" [45].

> Merrily swim we; the moon shines bright.[21]

Verily, at this rate, we will soon be in the deep of the waters.

A step or two further we will venture, under the guidance of Mrs. Smith's moonlight; warily, however, lest we find ourselves over head and ears in the bog, before we are ready for the plunge. The lady's own mind, as our readers may have perceived, does not appear to be quite determined on many of the most important points of her subject. She "sees no reason;" she is "not perfectly certain," etc., etc. What guide then does she propose to herself and us, through these labyrinthian mazes? "*Our intuitions are to be trusted*" [9; LSM's italics]. Here we are, then. Behold it: the mystery of mysteries!—the inspiration!—the intuition! In a word (although she does not just give it the fashionable name, perhaps because her mind is not quite made up), the higher law! "Emancipate from external bondage, and the internal law writ-

18. *Hamlet* 4.5.180–81 (Ophelia to Claudius): "You must wear your rue with a difference."

19. *Woman and Her Needs,* p. 31: "I am glad this peculiar stirring of womanly thought upon womanly requirements originated in our own country."

20. Ibid., p. 45; *Merchant of Venice* 1.3.44.

21. Sir Walter Scott, "Fording the River," l. 1 and later refrains; the song, perhaps deriving "the moon shines bright" from *Merchant of Venice,* 5.1.1, appears in chapter 5 of *The Monastery* (1820).

ten upon every human heart makes itself audible. Thus the most free are the most bound" [34], e.g., the Mormon governor, with his score or threescore (we really forget which it is) of wives.[22] Verily, *he is bound,* being most free.

Our authoress continues: "A woman is better when she acts *out of* her own spontaneity, tenfold, than when she attempts to conform to any theory" [111; LSM's italics]. This somewhat dubious expression, we take it, would be more clear if the "out of" we have italicized were replaced by "from"; and as to the merit of the sentiment, let it be judged of by what follows. Referring to the *duty* of a wife, she exclaims:

> Duty! why it is the spontaneous, the natural action and privilege of her soul, not her cold duty; she, the true wife, does not say "it is my duty"; the law of God in her heart teaches a nicer view than this, a more intimate and sacred relation. [111–12]

Good! if such be her spontaneity. But what if the spontaneity lean on the other side? Wo, then, to the household over which she presides. Duty has gone to the dogs; the husband may go to the devil; and should there be any unlucky brats of things called children, which the feminine individual's spontaneity leaneth not kindly towards, let them also betake themselves to Old Nick, or wherever luck may send them, while the lady spontaneously turns herself to the constructing of some woman's rights constitution in readiness for "the good time coming."

> Can they not, will they never learn, that the Good Father is wise in the bestowal of his gifts; that he does not impart a superfluous intelligence; that he does not create a desire <need> without its appropriate, safe, and harmonizing medium of gratification? [36]

Have we then no desires which we have not the right to gratify? This is a dangerous doctrine, which the most run-mad reformer of the day will, we think, scarcely undertake to carry to its extreme, without consigning the actor of it either to the gallows or the madhouse. Besides, we must remember that there are male spontaneities and intuitions as well as female ones; the former possessing the indisputable advantage of being backed by physical force, which will secure, as it always has secured, male supremacy, in case of a clash between contending spontaneities. Man's "higher law" must certainly override woman's. What then is the necessary result to woman of such a combat of intuitions? What but the most fearful oppression exercised by an

22. Brigham Young (1801–77), head of the Mormon church from 1844, its president from 1847; led Mormon migration to Great Salt Lake valley in Utah; first governor of the territory of Utah (1849–57).

exasperated tyrant over a conquered foe; or, at best, the degrading kindness of the master-husband with his threescore wives? EXCELSIOR! Is this the height of Mrs. Smith's vision of perfected civilization? Why, the world is but just emerging from such a rule; and even the Grand Turk[23] throws not the handkerchief so boldly as did his fathers. Let the weak cling to the law. For him or for her, the worst legislation is better than none. The rule of intuitions is the rule of brute force. What doth it benefit, that my intuition is clearer, brighter, truer than his? What matters it that my impulses are good while his are evil? If the evil be strong, if the dark be mighty, even evil will sweep away good; even darkness will conquer the light. Cling therefore to the law; for the law, however faulty, is still the feeble effort of right to embody itself into a rule which time and experience may perfect. It is the struggling forward of the spirit of good. It is the concession of the powerful evil to the weaker good. Ye who are feeble, ye who are oppressed! cling to the law, even although that very law may oppress you. That it does oppress you, is proof in itself that the strong were the makers of it. How then can you wrest it from them? How then can your feebleness better it? The law is a concession from the strong to the weak; and because the concession is but a lame one—is but a half-accorded justice—will the weak gain by its rejection? Will he not act more wisely to nurse and cherish it, if possible, to a nobler growth. Woman! thou whom Nature hath made to persuade and not to combat—to entreat but not to force—cling thou then to the written law. Ay, e'en as to thine ark of safety, amid the surging billows, the deluge of brute force—cling even to its very letter.[24] Better it, if thine influence may; but as thou valuest the rule of reason and of God, abolish it not to make way for intuitions and spontaneities.

Our lady reformers will answer, that they do not reject, that they would only reform, the law. But stumbling in their darkness, they talk of they know not what. What becomes of written law, when such impertinent twaddle as the following is listened to?

> In our Integrity we stand poised in our own Unity, a Law, a Life. [117]
>
> Yes, the sin about which so much is vaguely preached, is the violation of this great light within us. It is the putting out of the light in God's temple, that we may not see the requirements of his laws, all violations of which shall be revealed, as from the house-tops of our being. We must look within to learn these laws, and go forth in holy obedience. [119–20]

23. The Ottoman sultan.

24. Cf. Byron, *Heaven and Earth* 1.3.272–73: "God hath proclaimed the destiny of earth; / My father's ark of safety hath announced it."

Such was the law of a Robespierre,[25] who looked within himself, and went forth in holy obedience to slaughter and to drown his country in blood. Such is the law of the Mormon, who, in holy obedience, takes to himself his threescore wives; such the law of the communist, the socialist, the Fourierist; and such finally of this new sect, as yet but limitedly known, which is, we learn, springing up in the interior of the State of New York, and proving itself, even more than all these, grossly ready to follow "intuitions," in "holy obedience" to which its members speak and act in a way to make common decency veil her eyes.[26]

However, the ladies are aggrieved; let us return to them, and examine how they propose to right themselves. "When our Fathers," says Mrs. Smith, "planted themselves upon the firm base of human freedom, claimed the inalienable rights of life, liberty, and the pursuit of happiness, they might have foreseen that at some day their daughters would sift thoroughly their opinions and their consequences, and daringly challenge the same rights" [10]. Warlike this, rather. Again, elsewhere, in advocating marriage reforms, and woman's right to hold property, she remarks: "Allow woman the rights of property, open to her the avenues to wealth, permit her not only to hold property, but to enter into commerce, or into the professions, if she is fit for them. In that case she would assuredly take the stand that her forefathers <fathers> took, that taxation without representation is oppressive," etc. [75] And of course, we presume, fight for that stand as her fathers did. The *voie de fait*[27] is, after all, the only way of defending disputed rights in this world; and at this rate, ladies, it is time to throw aside your kid gloves, and accustom yourselves to something even more manlike than your satin and

25. Maximilien-François-Marie-Isadore de Robespierre (1758–94), French revolutionary politician; a leader of the Jacobin Club; member of the second Committee of Public Safety (1793), instituted Reign of Terror as instrument of policy; guillotined.

26. In 1848, fleeing charges of adultery in Putney, Vt., John Humphrey Noyes (1811–86) founded with his followers a colony in Oneida, N.Y. Noyes endeavored to remove distinctions of labor, dress, and conduct between the sexes; but the Oneida Community gained its unwelcome notoriety from its practice of "complex" (i.e., communal) marriage, which relied on *coitus reservatus* (male continence) to permit sexual relations without procreation and, thus, a sexual freedom designed to copy that of the angels (Mark 12:25). Local complaints against the community made in 1850 and 1851 were relieved by its members' frugality and sober deportment; but in 1852 a crusade was preached against the community's sexual practices by the New York *Observer* and other religious newspapers, causing a temporary cessation of complex marriage. The Oneida Community was dissolved in 1881 (and its flourishing business interests converted into a joint-stock company), partly because of outside hostility to such sexual experiments as "stirpiculture" (begun in 1869), which was designed to make a progeny of superior spirituality.

27. Assault and battery.

muslin Bloomer equipments.[28] Your fair hands must harden themselves to the management of Colt's revolvers, of bombs, grenades, and whatnot. But, ladies, room, if you please, for one little thought. You know we had *mothers* as well as *fathers*—pilgrim mothers and patriot fathers. Women, true women they were; women of the home and of the hearth; women of true hearts and earnest faiths; of bold councils—ay, and when need was—of bold actions, too. And yet these, disdaining neither their duties nor their petticoats, had nothing to do with votings and conventions, nor ever claimed the right "to our halls of legislation, our courts of justice, and our military posts." *Quaere,* whether our fathers or our mothers, with all due reverence for both, were the truest models for their daughters' imitation.

A glimmering of common sense seems to come over our authoress when she remarks that "the 'proud stomach' of the manish Bess had something to command respect, at least; and unless we can do, as well as talk, it were better to be silent."[29] Here has an evident little truth, plain enough for the comprehension of the simplest dairy-woman or cook-maid, escaped the pen

28. One word *en passant* of "the Bloomer." We really mean nothing disrespectful of the dress, which, as far as we know anything about it, is not only entirely unobjectionable, but we decidedly think, from description (we have never ourselves been so happy as to encounter a real live Bloomer), a great improvement upon the dirty length of skirt wherewith our fashionables sweep the pavements and clear off the ejected tobacco of our railroad cars. The *dress* is not only convenient, but entirely modest; and could the same be said of its *wearers,* we would decidedly be of the number of its advocates. We object to it, not as intrinsically wrong in itself, but only in so far as it is used for wrong purposes. The Bloomer dress has been adopted as a kind of flag of rebellion against established usage, and when some good-tempered peacemakers, endeavoring to excuse it on the score of health and neatness, ventured to advance the plea that it was nothing new, inasmuch as a similar garb had been worn for centuries by eastern womanhood, forthwith a meeting of the Bloomers inform these ignorant meddlers, that they do not know what they are talking about; that the Bloomer is no eastern dress, but the chosen garb of such ladies, who consider themselves as having a full right to consult their own sense of propriety, and to indulge the freedom of their nature in the pursuit of health, happiness, and humbug! It is the rallying standard of woman's rights advocates, and as such unfit for a modest female. Had it been but the invention of some Parisian *modiste,* or some country, field-tripping milk-maid, or of any other womanish thing, imagined womanishly and worn womanishly, we would not have hesitated to recommend it to our daughters. But indifferent things become vicious entirely by their uses; and the uses to which the Bloomer dress has been applied condemn it *in toto.* [LSM]

29. Smith, *Woman and Her Needs,* p. 106. Prov. 16:18: "After a proude stomake there foloweth a fall" (trans. Miles Coverdale). "What gives the unhappy Man this Peevishness of Spirit, is, that his Estate is dipp'd, and is eating out with Usury; and yet he has not the heart to sell any Part of it. His proud Stomach, at the Cost of restless Nights, constant Inquietudes, Danger of Affronts, and a thousand nameless Inconveniences, preserves this Canker in his Fortune, rather than it shall be said he is a Man of fewer Hundreds a Year than he has been commonly reputed" (Richard Steele, *Spectator,* no. 114).

of our reformist lady. But surely her mind, used to higher speculations, cannot stoop to comprehend it clearly, or she would cease to talk of woman's *daringly challenging her rights.* These ladies forget, when they cite their favorite exemplifications of woman's abilities in such characters as Shakspeare's Portia [41, 91], and wise or warlike queens, that the first class are so entirely poetic as to require all Shakspeare's genius to cause them to be tolerated even on the stage; the simple truth, quoted above, that it is necessary to *do* as well as to *talk,* being sufficient to prevent their appearance in real life. Imagine Mrs. Smith, or any other real Bloomer or non-Bloomer, attempting the role of a Portia at the New York bar. Does it need an argument to prove the certainty of her most egregious failure? The hissings of the street boys would soon settle the question in spite of her fancied logic. She may argue that the street boys are thus exhibiting a great want of decorum; that such a course is contrary to the philosophy of things and the higher law; and that she being the *equal* ("all men are born free and equal") of the street boys, she has as good a right to hiss as they. Verily, the philosophy of things and the higher law must cede to the nature of things and the divine law. We deny that Mrs. Smith is the *equal* of the street boys. If she consent to degrade herself by the comparison, she sinks far below them; for while *they* are in their place, acting more or less perfectly in accordance with their being, *she,* in aiming to reverse the laws of nature, becomes an inferior in a position for which nature unfits her; a crawling counterfeit of man, instead of that noble, pure, and exalted being which Nature intended when, bestowing upon her woman's being and woman's instincts, she gifted her also with perhaps somewhat more than ordinary woman's intellect. Examples from poetry are no proofs of fact; and if ladies will borrow arguments from imaginary characters, why not take at once the powerful Minerva springing full-armed from the brow of Jove, and contend that the world is not, cannot, and shall not be considered as properly managed, until all the female sex shall have reached that point of perfection?

As regards the position of governing queens, who with the "manish Bess have something to command respect," whence, we would ask, get they that something? Does their case show any power in the woman, whether different in its nature or differently exercised, at all deviating from that exhibited by the ordinary individuals of her sex in the ordinary duties of life? Have they anything inherent in their characters which enables them to conquer and maintain their position? or does their so maintaining it simply show, that when men are *willing* to be ruled, when they have *established laws for their own government,* they will submit to be reined even by the hand of a woman?—ay, and frequently the feeblest of women. Surely no one will contend that Queen Victoria, for instance, keeps her place either through talent, energy, or any other characteristic of her own, whether natural or acquired. If a woman becomes anywhere man's inferior, it is in such a position; which, being by nature unsuited to her faculties, makes her, in so far as she is the tool of the active and acting man, simply his puppet—a dressed-up doll, if you please, a worshiped statue; but still, only a doll and a statue. There is perhaps no woman in the world whose natural expansion of true woman-intellect and woman-nature is more shackled by circumstance and cramped by position than that of England's Queen. Her limited faculties are of a kind which are crushed rather than developed by her position. As a *queen* she receives the homage of her place, but as a *woman* she is certainly neither exalted nor perfected by it. Like all inefficient monarchs, who form but the centre points of acting governments, she stands a mere figure-head, which men have chosen to place at the head of the vessel of state, having no more agency in her own position than the literal wooden block from which we draw our figure. "The manish Bess," and others of her stamp, have, we grant, been something different. But besides the impossibility, which even they would have found, to retain their positions, had not the *prestige* accorded by man to their place separated them from the rest of their sex, the very epithet *manish* shows how far nature had isolated such from the mass. God forbid that we should look upon such isolation as a merit or a source of admiration! Rather do we regard it as a kind of moral monstrosity which may suit the queen, but not the woman. A hive thrives under its one queen-bee; but a community of such could never exist. A single queen Elizabeth might be tolerated, and, if suited to the taste of the nation over which she ruled, even admired; but a race of such monster-women could only exist as a race of Amazons. *Men* must disappear from a world where *men-women* should gain the ascendancy.

This may be a very faulty arrangement, and perhaps the world would have been improved by some difference in the relative position of the sexes. Thus, no doubt, think our lady-champions. For our part, we have never allowed ourselves to speculate upon the propriety or impropriety of an arrangement, so evidently marked by the Almighty hand that we have resigned ourselves to it as a fixed necessity, taking it for granted that here, as elsewhere, he has made all things good. When God created man, "male and female created he them."[30] Male and female nature requires that they remain, not only in body and form, but in act and deed. We are sorry to be obliged so to offend the delicate sensitiveness of Mrs. Smith as to use, and repeatedly use, the "obnoxious word *female*" [84], which she considers so objectionable as to deem it necessary on one occasion to make an apology for its use, even when introduced in a quotation [91], and in another remarks, "The persistent use

30. Gen. 1:27.

of the obnoxious word *female* in our vocabulary is proof of the light in which we are regarded" [84]. Now, we confess to the existence in ourselves of more blunted sensibilities. We—even we, the reviewer—must acknowledge ourselves of the feminine gender, of the female sex—woman; and can, in the fullest exercise of any intellect with which God has gifted us, feel, see, or discover no possible reason why we should find anything "obnoxious" in any of the above epithets. They can only become a reproach, they can only become obnoxious, by being applied where they ought not to be merited. They are insulting to men, because the characteristics which accompany them are generally unsuited to man; and their application implies that he has failed to bring himself up to the character which nature intended men generally to fulfil. They are becoming—they are suited—they are fitting to the woman (be she true woman), and the shame is not when she suits herself to, but when she avoids, them. An epithet is objectionable only when the nature that it indicates is objectionable; and therefore the word "female," as indicating woman-nature, can only be obnoxious to the woman who mistakenly aims to rank herself in a position antagonistic to her nature. There is something out of joint in her reasoning, when she can come to the conclusion that "female" is an obnoxious epithet, or "manish" a flattering one. It is the high duty of every reasoning mortal to aim at the perfecting of his kind by the perfecting of his individual humanity. Woman's task is, to make herself the perfected woman, not the counterfeit man.

We have been obliged to confess ourself woman, because only as woman can we take the defensive in this question. Man is excluded from the discussion as a party interested against this female move, and the question is assumed to be one in which the sexes are placed in antagonism. Only as woman, therefore, can we attempt the defence of woman against a move calculated in every step of its progress to lower her from the position which nature has accorded to her. Only as woman can we efficiently enter our protest against the folly and madness of ideas of which, we do their woman-advocates the justice to believe, that there is not one in a thousand degraded enough to maintain them, could she logically deduce the inference from her own premises. There is enough of pure, enough of holy in the God-created and heaven-endowed woman-nature, to make it shrink from contact with the foul chaos which such a deduction would develop. In their ignorance they have done this.[31]

31. Acts 3:13–17: "His son Jesus . . . ye delivered up, and denied him in the presence of Pilate, when he was determined to let him go. But ye denied the Holy One and the Just, and desired a murderer to be granted unto you; and killed the Prince of life, whom God hath raised from the dead. . . . And now, brethren, I wot that through ignorance ye did it, as did also your rulers."

Mrs. Smith (of whom, once for all, we know nothing personally, and only in so far as she has published her theories feel at liberty to take her as the exponent of the more quiet class of reformers) has in advance considered not only the antagonistic animal, man, as opposed to her theories, but also deprecates the admission of a large portion of her own sex to this argument. She divides womankind into three classes; and as we have confessed our womanhood, we will endeavor to satisfy ourselves, and let our readers judge, to which of these categories we shall be consigned, or whether we have the right, in the name of the female sex, to claim a different classification:

> There is a large class of our sex so well cared for, "whom the winds of heaven are not allowed to visit too roughly,"[32] who are hemmed in by conventional forms, and by the appliances of wealth, till they can form no estimate of the sufferings of their less fortunate sisters . . . a class [. . .] delicate, amiable, lovely even; but limited and superficial. These follow the bent of their masculine friends and admirers, and lisp pretty ridicule about the folly of "Woman's Rights" and "Woman's Movements." These see no need of reform or change of any kind; indeed, they are denied that comprehensiveness of thought by which they could hold the several parts of a subject in the mind, and see its bearings. Society is a sort of grown-up mystery which they pretend not to comprehend, supposing it to have gradually developed to its present size and shape from Adam and Eve, by *natural gradation,* like Church Bishops. [11–12; LSM's italics][33]

Need we enter our disclaimer against being included in this category? We believe, if our readers have followed us thus far, that they will need no argu-

32. *Hamlet* 1.2.139–42: "So excellent a king . . . / . . . so loving to my mother / That he might not beteem the winds of heaven / Visit her face too roughly."

33. Our thanks, by the way, to Mrs. S. for this piece of information, quite new to us, with regard to the Bishops. We did not know that these Rev. gentlemen were *gradually developed* by *natural gradation.* We shall, in future, study with a double zest the beautiful developments of natural history, in hopes of further enlightening ourselves upon so interesting a question. The great Agassiz must hide his diminished head before this wonderful discovery of Mrs. Smith. What are his fish and his polypi to her Bishops? [LSM] Jean Louis Rodolphe Agassiz (1807–73), Swiss-born American naturalist; professor of natural history at Harvard University (1847–73), of comparative anatomy at the Medical College of South Carolina, in Charleston (1851–53); author of, among other works, *Contributions to the Natural History of the United States* (4 vols., 1857–62) and *Essay on Classification* (1857). LSM had herself heard Agassiz speak (see chap. 8, "Negro-mania," p. 232), perhaps when he lectured in Columbia in 1850; in chap. 5, "Diversity of the Races; Its Bearing upon Negro Slavery," she reviewed Agassiz's "The Diversity of Origin of the Human Races," *Christian Examiner* 49 (July 1850): 110–45.

ment to convince them that we are not of the above class of pretty lispers, and will credit our assertion when we claim to have lived long enough, and to have suffered enough, to learn that life is an earnest duty, and woman's share in it one of deep and soul-searching responsibility.

> Then there is another class doomed to debasement, vice, labor of body and soul, in all their terrible manifestations. Daughters of suffering without its ennobling influence; too weak in thought, it may be, to discern the best good; or, it may be, too strong in passion to resist the allurements of the immediate; or, it may be, ignorant only, they wake to the sad realities of life too late to find redress for its evils. These are the kind over whom infinite Pity would weep, as it were, drops of blood. These may scoff at reform, but it is the scoffing of a lost spirit, or that of despair. It is the blind utterance of regions denied the light of infinite love, and condemned to the Fata Morganas of depraved vision. [12–13]

Again we beg leave to plead "not guilty." Among these "lost spirits," condemned to "blind utterances" and "Fata Morganas," believe us, gentle reader, we are not. The affections, as well as the duties of life, have laid upon us their guiding hand, teaching us to love, to suffer, and to hope. When our feet stumble in the path, as in all humility we confess right often they do, truly it is by human weakness, and no "Fata Morganas," that we are misled. Let us pass now to class No. 3, the elect of the sex, according to reformist creeds.

> Then come the class of our sex capable of thought, of impulse, of responsibility—the worthy to be called Woman. Not free from faults any more than the strong of the other sex, but of that full humanity which may sometimes err, but yet which loves and seeks for the true and the good. These include all who are identified with suffering, in whatever shape, and from whatever cause; for these, when suffering proceeds from their own acts even, have that fund of greatness or goodness left, that they perceive and acknowledge the opposite of what they are. These are the ones who are victims to the falseness of society, and who see and feel that something may and will be done to redeem it. They are not content to be the creatures of luxury, the toys of the drawing-room, however well they may grace it—they are too true, too earnest in life, to trifle with its realities. They are capable of thinking, it may be far more capable of it than those of their own household who help to sway the destinies of the country through the ballot-box. They are capable of feeling, and analyzing too, the evils that surround themselves and others—they have individuality, resource, and that antagonism which weak men ridicule, because it shames their own imbecility; which makes them

> obnoxious to those of less earnestness of character, and helps them to an eclectic power, at once their crown of glory. [13–14]

We quote literally, that our readers may, should they possess sufficient profundity of intellect, seize the whole mysterious beauty of this sublime extract. For ourselves, credit us, O most indulgent reader—so little are we, in our humility, akin to this class of elect who sit crowned in eclectic power—that we really cannot even feebly comprehend the mystic signification of the "eclectic power, at once their crown of glory," here so mystically sketched. These reformist saints, as well as their sinners, are, we are free to confess, entirely beyond our matter-of-fact comprehension; and if we were more than bothered to grasp the idea of blind utterance and Fata Morgana ladies, we are now doubly mystified in our attempt to catch even the faintest outline signification of these beatific and inspired eclectics. Behold us, therefore, according to Mrs. Smith's classification, as we belong to none of her categories, fairly ousted, not only from our womanhood, but in no little danger of finding ourselves ultimately pushed altogether out of our humanity; for of the bearded species (Heaven help us!) we are, if we may trust our looking-glass, certainly not. Under penalty, therefore, of being classed among apes and elephants, or being picked up as a specimen of some new and undefined family of the vertebratae, it will, we trust, be permitted us to enter our humble protest in favor of such of the female sex as, without having reached the sublime height of the eclectic crown of glory, may yet feel that they are neither "lost spirits," nor yet "toys of the drawing-room."

There certainly are, unless this world has been to us a dream, true women, of every grade of intellect, who belong to none of Mrs. Smith's categories. We find them varying, of every type, from the simple, confiding woman-heart, which, knowing little but the instinct of its nature, feels only that such instinct is to lean, and that its being is dependent, up through every nicely changing shade of individual loveliness and intellectuality, to the less happy, perhaps, but nobler existence, the highest model of womanhood—the woman of thought, of mind, of genius, and yet filled with deep-brooding woman-love and woman-nature. She, the earnest striver, wrestling with life's cares, but contemning not its duties, feels so sensibly her noble nature, that she scorns to degrade it by placing it in an unnatural antagonism with man's, and presents in her pure woman-existence, we truly think, the highest model to which humanity is capable of attaining. But, spirits of eclectic womandom! most certainly such a woman is not of *you;* for while she speaks neither in "blind utterances" nor pretty lispings, yet is she innocent of ballot-boxes and conventions. Such a woman needs not to make any man feel "shame of his imbecility;" nor to place herself in antagonism with any, whether weak or strong. Her mission is one of love and charity to all. It is the very essence of her being to raise and to purify wherever she touches. Where man's harder nature crushes, her's exalts. Where he wounds, she heals. The lowest intellect, be it but combined with a sincere nature, shrinks not from her, for in her it perceives, reflected and ennobled, its own virtues; the highest, worships, for it understands her. In every grade, then, between these two extremes, there are women—and we are proud to believe, in spite of the world's vices and its follies, the majority of women—whose very existence Mrs. Smith has, in her classification, entirely ignored; and these are the women in defence of whose true womanhood we now venture to enter our disclaimer in opposition to the assumed position of our lady-reformers, that, as the world is, woman "must use mean weapons because the nobler are denied her; she cannot assert her distinctive individuality, and she resorts to cunning, and this cunning takes the form of cajolery, deception, or antagonism in its many shapes, each and all as humiliating to herself as it is unjust to man" [35]. No true woman feels that the nobler weapons of life are denied her, because she cannot tinker at constitutions and try her hand at law-making. Her's are the noble weapons of philosophy and Christianity. She may find it difficult to wield them, and, in her human weakness, sometimes murmur at the hardness of that lot by which a mysterious Providence has assigned a task so difficult to her feeble frame; but she cannot, she dare not, call degrading a task which, executed in its perfection, would make her the truest personification of our great Christian law. One advantage, at least, to cheer her in her path, she has over man. Her duty is always clear, while *his* may be doubtful. Her's is the Christian law of love and charity, to which (however passion may tempt) unvarying points the finger of duty. His is too often a divided struggle. She has but to strive and to pray; while he has to strive and to fight. She *knows* that to soothe, to comfort and to heal, is her highest duty. He *doubts* whether to wrangle, to strike and to wound, be not his. God, man, and nature alike call upon her to subdue her passions, to suffer, to bear, to be meek and lowly of heart; while man, summoned by nature, and often by duty, to the whirl of strife, blinded in the struggle, forgets too often where wrath should cease and mercy rule. What, then, more beautiful than woman's task to arrest the up-lifted arm, and, in the name of an all-pardoning Heaven, to whisper to his angry passions—"Peace, be still!"[34]

"I long," says Mrs. Smith, "to see my own sex side by side with man[35] in every great work, and free to see the light, when his vision is dimmed with

34. Mark 4:39.

35. "Men" in both Smith's and LSM's original.

the dust of his chariot-wheels in the mighty race in which he is engaged" [101]. And how will she do this, if she throws herself even in the thick of the dust beside him? Let her stay where she is, out of the blinding cloud of struggling passion, where, from the beautiful eminence on which nature has placed her, she looks down like some pitying saint, some angel of mercy, some ray of God's own sunlight glancing over a bloody battlefield, to soften, to cheer, and to bless. God forbid that ever she should sink to wallow in dust and blood beside him whom it is her duty and her privilege to rescue from the soil to which his nature clings! Woman the civilizer! woman the soother! how is your holy mission forgotten, striving thus to degrade itself!

"If," says our authoress, "if she be a simple, genial, household divinity, she will bind garlands around the altar of the Penates, and worship in content. If more largely endowed, I see no reason why she should not be received cordially into the school of Arts, or Science, or Politics, or Theology, in the same manner as the individual capacities of the other sex are recognized." [26–27] And this, in Mrs. Smith's opinion, would be *raising* her condition. Too *largely endowed* for a household divinity, she casts aside that divinity, and who dares contemplate the struggle into which her feeble ignorance precipitates her? These reforming ladies have pushed forward in their move from the instigations of a most egregious vanity, which has induced them to consider themselves as so superior to the rest of their sex, that they have finally (as our quotations a few pages back may show) come to the conclusion, and quietly assumed the ground, that they alone—they, the throned in "eclectic power" [14]—are the thinkers of their sex. Our effort, through this article, has been to prove to them that they may perhaps be mistaken. We would now entreat them to look a little forward into the practicability and operation of their system. Allowing, for a moment, the fulfilment of their demands to be desirable, how do they propose enforcing it? Why have men always legislated, but because they have the power? and by what process is this power to be wrenched or coaxed from them? We presume our authoress, when the point of action should come, would hardly advise the sisterhood to so far imitate the deeds of their fathers, as to shoulder muskets in the cause. What then can they do, but ask the proposed reform through men, their legislators? Here then we have woman, by her own voluntary act, as seeking to graft man's nature upon her own, reduced to the degrading position so much deprecated by Mrs. Smith, wherein she "must receive happiness not as the gift of her Maker, careful for the well-being of the creature he had made, but as a boon from Man—who had the *right* to make her miserable, but forebore the exercise of his prerogative" [33]. Herself, grasping at rights not naturally belonging to her, places herself in the position of receiving, as a "boon from man," what her Maker has in his wisdom seen fit not to gift her with. Mrs. Smith vainly may answer that her improved system would make woman her own legislator. This is impossible. Power exercised through the tolerance of another is never a free power, but only in fact the delegated authority of him who tolerates. Woman legislators could thus act only under the influence and authority of men, because men would at any moment have the power, the might, to depose them. As we cannot fight, so we cannot enforce our claims—so we cannot insist. We can but entreat, we can but sway, we can but receive as a boon. If woman is to be admitted as co-legislator with man, it can only be through man's prior legislation. He must *give* the right, which she has not the power to *take*. Is this condition of things wrong? Go then, if it be, and cavil with the God who hath thus dictated it. *He* gave to the man the right, even as He gave him the power. *He* laid upon his strong right arm those folds of muscle by whose might he can rule, must rule—ay, and in all physical right ought to rule—all that God in his wisdom hath made weaker. Ought to rule, we say; because whatever God has made ought to be. Where *He* has seen fit to give checks and balances to the various powers of various beings, there we see Nature forces such checks and balances into action. To the man, for instance, pitted against the corporeally stronger beast, has been given the governing reason which forces the brute to crouch before him; and here, as elsewhere, *power* is the stamp and seal of God to indicate His will—the only real right of His creature. Man has then the corporeal, physical right to rule the woman, and she combats God's eternal law of order when she opposes it; combats it to her own undoing; for who can strive against God? Physically, then, she must be ruled, and submit her "proud stomach," be it her curse to bear one, to the necessities of her case.

Morally, physically, let us next consider, what is woman's destiny? We believe, the highest. The beautifully developed soul is hers; and truly has Mrs. Smith said that woman is man's "superior in the elements that most harmonize life" [26]; and only in her self-wrought debasement (a debasement brought about by her forgetfulness of her own individuality and her natural position) has she been forced to beg "for tolerance where she before had a right to homage—pleaded her weakness as a motive for protection, because she had laid aside her own distinctive powers, and become imbecile and subservient. Women must recognize their unlikeness; and then, understanding what needs grow out of this unlikeness, some great truth must be evolved." [26] This is as wisely said, as if the spirit of the great Solomon himself had placed itself at the lady's elbow, and made her his medium to knock out this spiritual truth for our benefit. But, alas! the spirit of wisdom is wearied soon of its work of charity, for even in the same paragraph follows the sentence we quoted above. Woman, she says, must seek her sphere; "if she be a simple, genial, household divinity, she will bind garlands around the altar of [the] Penates, and worship in content. If more largely endowed, I see no reason why she should not," etc. [26–27]

Now, *we* contend that to be a divinity, a genial, household divinity—not in that character, at least, to *worship* (which by some confusion of thought Mrs. Smith has assigned as the occupation of a household divinity), but to *be worshiped* at that holiest altar of the Penates, the home hearth; to be the soul of that home, even as our great Father-God is the soul of creation; to be the breath, the life, the love-law of that home; the mother, the wife, the sister, the daughter—such is woman's holiest sphere, such her largest endowment. This is the natural position from which she has stepped; this the individuality which she has forgotten; these the distinctive powers which she has laid aside, to become imbecile and subservient in the exercise of others unsuited to her nature. This beautiful recognition of her unlikeness to man, is the sole mystery of her existence; the one great truth which must be evolved to make woman no longer the weak plaything of a tyrannic master, no longer the trampled thing, pleading for tolerance at the foot of her conqueror, but the life, the soul, the vital heart of society; while in her and through her thus circulates the every throb of this great living world. She does not rule, she cannot rule, by stump-speech, convention, or ballot-box; but she can rule, and she does rule, by the great quiet soul-power, which, silent as the blood through the arteries of life, throbs on forever, ceasing but with the existence of the body which it vivifies.

Such is woman's noble task. Can any be nobler? What disgrace and degradation have ever fallen upon her, whether individually or in the mass, have been the result of, and in proportion to, her neglect or contempt of this her God-marked mission. "If more largely endowed!" [26]—Is it from largeness of endowment, or is it from the cramping guidance of an ill-ordered intellect, that she is induced to throw herself out of such a position, to become a suppliant and an inferior in one whose duties are inconsistent with her nature? If woman will fulfil her destiny, let her put away from her head and heart the idea that she is man. Let her abandon the thought of an equality or superiority, or inferiority, between the sexes, which exists neither in nature or fact, but simply in the mistaken views which men and women have both taken of the subject. Each is inferior, when attempting to fulfil a part destined to the other. A horse or an ass is certainly not the superior of man; and yet let man, or woman either, attempt to fulfil the duties of the poor brute, and how immeasurably inferior is he to the quadruped he rivals. We assure our conventionist sisters, that they are as ill qualified to perform the part of the man as the ass, and would advise them to attempt neither. The celebrated monkey-man, whose wonderful performances attract roars of applause from delighted audiences, is still far behind the veritable baboon whom he apes. Woman, in emulating man in his own sphere—and consequently out of hers, even though she succeed to the height attained by "the manish queen Bess," with "her proud stomach," so often quoted as proof of the powers of woman—holds still to man the second rate, inferior, and imitative position, which the poor actor does towards the baboon; the belittling ambition of the monkey-man and the man-woman being equally but a sad model for the general imitation of society. Woman's sphere is higher, purer, nobler. She ought *not* "to be received [cordially] into the schools <school> of Arts, or Science, or Politics, or Theology, in the same manner as the individual capacities of the other sex are recognized" [27].[36] She ought not to be so received, because her individual capacities are different. We do not bid her be ignorant of these matters. We do not say that her mind is incapable of grasping them. On the contrary, we believe that her capacities are fully suited to them, and that it is not only her right, but her duty, as it is that of every intelligent being, to forward the world's progress by the accumulative impulse of individual progress. Every mind has a thought which may be of benefit in the circle of its influence, and we sin in cramping that thought. Woman's mind is made for improvement, and her duty would lead her to seek that improvement, according to the inclination and capacities of her intellect. But that improvement must be gained and used in a manner consistent and in harmony with her nature. Her arts and science are *not* for the public schools. Her theology is not for the pulpit; nor are her politics for those arenas of strife where rougher man is soiled by the polluting struggle, and shrinks often in disgust from the stifling contamination. She may counsel, she may teach, she may uphold the weary arm of manhood—of the husband, the brother, or the son—and rouse him to the struggle for which nature never designed her; but she may not (without foregoing her nature) rush into the combat of blood, shouting man's war-cry and the victim's death. Side by side she may stand with man, to guide, to strengthen, to check, or to soothe; but let her keep clear of the blinding "dust of his chariot wheels" [101], that her eye may see and her tongue may counsel, by the clear dictates of her unstained soul, while *his* eye and spirit are alike dimmed in the strife. Woman, we believe, is designed, by nature, the conservative power of the world. Not surely, therefore, useless, because comparatively inactive in the tumultuous rush and turmoil of life, she checks oftener than she impels. The lock-chain which arrests the downward rushing

36. Our readers, we trust, do not hold us responsible for the halting grammar of our authoress (or her printers), which has, we confess, puzzled us in more sentences than the remarkable eclectic glorification one, though we have not always stopped to note it. [LSM]

and precipitously destructive course of the ever forwardly impelled vehicle, is not useless because temporarily allowed to rest in the uphill tug. Life and limb are saved by the proper use of that which, injudiciously applied, would be in itself destruction.

That "good time coming," the political millennium towards which Mrs. S. looks forward, when "the lion will lie down with the lamb, and the sting shall be taken from whatever is noxious, and the dragon of restrictive and retributive law loosen its folds upon human society" [100], will certainly never be brought about by woman's conventions, woman's speeches, nor woman's votes. Rather, if the world shall ever see it, will it be perfected by the home divinity of woman, whispering her truths to the heart of man, wrapping his soul in the inspiration of a revealed duty, and bearing him upward and onward to the fulfilment of that duty. Is it a degradation to *her,* if, while thus ennobling man by her all-pervading influence, he fail, as much as he might, to profit by it, and sometimes in his error may even scoff and sneer at her? No; only when that scoff and sneer rouse her to unfeminine resistance, or still more unfeminine imitation, is the evil done. Then, indeed, are both degraded in the sin of both. Thus woman's weakness in its human imperfection truly often errs; but, again, nobly often, spite of scoff and sneer, does woman's strength soar almost above humanity, whilst, bending beneath ills too great for man's endurance, she humbly joins in that Godlike prayer of resignation, "Father, if it be thy will, let this cup pass from me; nevertheless, not as I will, but as thou wilt."[37] Can there be degradation in bearing the cross of patient endurance midst rebuff and wrong, even to the great Calvary of self-abnegation and triumphant love? Woman! if man forgets his duty, what nobler lesson than to recall him to it, by remembering yours? What more degrading, at once to yourself and to him, than to fight and squabble like hungry dogs over a bone, for a something which, even could its acquisition be proved desirable to your sex, you are still called to, not by duty, but simply by wish and appetite. We are no enemy of woman, but rather have ventured, as her champion, upon this her defence; believing that the recent demonstration, among certain members of her own sex, is at once the most degrading, the most insulting to her, and the most dangerous attack that can be made upon her true liberty. Liberty is never license. It is the freedom to fulfil, in their highest perfection, the duties of our God-given being. The true defender, therefore, of woman's rights and woman's liberty, asks only that she may be permitted to perfect, not to alter, her nature.

In conclusion, let us remark, for those of the masculine gender who (if

37. Matt. 26:39.

there be any such) may perchance think our authority worth quoting against womandom, that we beg not to be misunderstood. Our argument being solely against the female move, our effort has been to show its false assumptions and ludicrous inefficacy; but we have not, therefore, intended to signify that man is sinless towards woman. Far from it. If we have endeavored to lay upon woman the burden of her own sin, as a reasonable, responsible being, and to prove to her how necessary is the exercise of her own inward strength for the performance of life's duties, and how doubly necessary it becomes to her, through physical weakness, that she should guard herself in the position where God and nature have placed her—we have endeavored to be the more forcible in so doing, because we consider her danger doubled through man's constant thoughtless and often heartless oppression. She must guard not only against her own folly and her own weakness, but also against his. If we have pointed out her aberrations from duty, and blamed or ridiculed her short-comings, it is not that we would make her the butt of man's ridicule, who has sinned both with her and against her, but because we consider her as more than him disinterested, more than him swayable by the purer instincts, and more than him exalted above the passions of our common nature. If woman has erred, to man, clamorous in her accusation, we would say—"He that is without sin among you, let him first cast a stone at her."[38] Man the oppressor, man the tempter, will he dare to strike? or rather, checked by the holy word of reproof spoken to the repentant Magdalene, will he not take to his bosom the lesson intended for her? Happy would it indeed be for both, could each, in the holy fulfilment of the duties of their differing spheres, "*go, and sin no more*."[39]

L. S. M.

38. John 8:7.
39. John 8:11.

Louisa Susanna McCord. (*From the Collections of the Georgia Historical Society*)

Langdon Cheves, bust by Clark Mills, 1844. (*Courtesy of the South Carolina Historical Society*)

Mary Elizabeth Dulles, miniature by Edward Greene Malbone, c. 1806. (*Courtesy of Lenora Cheves Brockinton*)

David James McCord. (*From the Collections of the Georgia Historical Society*)

Langdon Cheves McCord. (*From the Collections of the Georgia Historical Society*)

Left to right: Louisa Rebecca Hayne McCord, Charlotte Reynolds, Hannah Cheves McCord, Elizabeth Horner Dulles, 1860. (*From the Collections of the Georgia Historical Society*)

Tuesday night March 5th [1856]

I send the above my dear Brother as an excuse for what I fear you will consider my persecution of you. It is an attempt of our dear old Father to write something; I believe a letter to you.— He is very anxious to hear from you & evidently much irritated with me because he does not do so. He seems to think it is my fault. I offered to write for him but he would not allow me to do so & says when he found he could not write, that he will send down June with a message. Indeed he wished to send him today, and with difficulty has been prevented. He is much irritated, much displeased, & is altogether in a far more painful condition than when you saw him.— Could you not my dear brother, write or even cause Charlotte to write, if it be but 2 lines, say every week? It would I think assist in soothing Father.— My position is here so intensely distressing that you must excuse me if I press upon you more urgently than you think right.— I know you have troubles, I know you have

Louisa Susanna McCord to Langdon Cheves, Jr., March 5 [1856]. (*Courtesy of the South Carolina Historical Society*)

Indian Rock, Narragansett, c. 1862/63, ink and wash over graphite on paper, by William Stanley Haseltine. (*Courtesy of the M. and M. Karolik Collection, Museum of Fine Arts, Boston*)

The British and North American Royal Mail Steamship *Persia*. (*Courtesy of the National Maritime Museum, Greenwich, London*)

The McCord house in Columbia. (*Courtesy of the South Carolina Historical Society*)

Gravestone of Louisa Susanna McCord, Magnolia Cemetery, Charleston.

Louisa Susanna McCord, bust by Hiram Powers, 1859. (*Courtesy of Lenora Cheves Brockinton*)

Part III

SLAVERY AND THE SOUTH

5.

Diversity of the Races; Its Bearing upon Negro Slavery

Slavery. We are not afraid of the word, although Lord Carlisle (late Morpeth), in a recent lecture upon America, speaks of "what they (South Carolinians) term their *peculiar institution* <institutions>, which is their euphonious description of slavery." The honourable gentleman has, like most of his predecessors in the travelling and book-making line, jumped at some sudden and frequently rather fantastic conclusions. We are not, we believe, so mealy-mouthed as he would imply. We are not ashamed of our "peculiar institution," nor do we need any sugared epithets to cloak an iniquity of which we are entirely unconscious. One would certainly imagine that we, of this Southern United States of America, must be of more obtuse intellect than other men. We have not the same inspirations, the same heaven-breathing warnings. Witness, for instance, the enthusiastic exclamation and high-wrought feelings of the illustrious traveller we have just named, as, when passing Mason and Dixon's line, he first finds himself in a slave State: "Declaration of Independence which I read yesterday—pillar of Washington

SQR, n.s., 3 (April 1851): 392–419. Publications reviewed: Samuel George Morton, *Letter to the Rev. John Bachman, on the Question of Hybridity in Animals, Considered in Reference to the Unity of the Human Species* (Charleston, S.C.: Walker and James, 1850); Samuel George Morton, *Additional Observations on Hybridity in Animals, and on Some Collateral Subjects; Being a Reply to the Objections of the Rev. John Bachman, D.D.* [subheading: "from the *Charleston Medical Journal and Review*"] (Charleston, S.C.: Walker and James, 1850); [Louis Agassiz,] "The Diversity of Origin of the Human Races," *Christian Examiner* 49 (July 1850): 110–45; Robert Knox, *The Races of Men: A Fragment* (Philadelphia: Lea and Blanchard, 1850; rpt. Miami, Fla., 1969).

which I have looked on today—what are ye?"[1] What are ye, mystic emblems of an unknown faith? What mystery dwells in these magic symbols, beyond the ken of our comprehension? The exalted imagination of the noble Lord seems to have read the enigma which, to our simple intellects, is unintelligible. Truly, it would appear to us that the Declaration of Independence is precisely nothing more nor less than it was when, upwards of seventy-four years ago, it was signed by the representatives of *thirteen free and independent* SLAVEHOLDING *States.* As the history of America is not very closely studied on the other side of the Atlantic, it may possibly have escaped the observation of the noble traveller, that *all* were then *slaveholding* States. As to what Washington's monument is, we ought perhaps to be ashamed to confess that we are by no means certain whether it is of brick or granite. If the question were, what was Washington, we could more easily answer it. He was indeed a great and a good man, a true patriot, a pure man, and, withal, a *slaveholder.* Fie upon the humbug cant of the day!

But we are not reviewing Lord Morpeth, and must pass on to our more immediate subject.

> Man clings to error, as a dormant bat
> To a dead bough.

The bough breaks at last, however, and the poor bat is doomed, *nolens volens,* to move his lodgings. It is not our object here to discuss the vexed question concerning the "unity of the races." This has been done, and, in our opinion, the question decided, by wiser heads than ours. We confess ourselves entirely unfit for argument upon the subject. It is only the learned naturalist who has the right to mingle in such a discussion. He whose studies have not long and laboriously led him in this direction, has the right only to listen, to read, to weigh authorities, and thus, from the learning and investigation of others, to find his own belief.

The great and distinguishing superiority of the human mind over the brute is the capacity, which reason gives it, of thus seizing and profiting by the conclusions of other men. In the beginning of any science, the mind starts tremblingly, doubtingly, creeps forward from conclusion to conclusion, fearfully retraces its steps, and again and yet again measures the same

1. Earl of Carlisle, *Travels in America. The Poetry of Pope. Two Lectures Delivered to the Leeds Mechanics' Institution and Literary Society, December 5th and 6th, 1850 . . .* (New York, 1851), pp. 51 (LSM's parenthesis and italics), 34. George William Frederick Howard (1802–64), Viscount Morpeth, seventh earl of Carlisle; member of Parliament (1826–41, 1846–48); Irish secretary (1835–41); chancellor of the duchy of Lancaster (1850–52); viceroy of Ireland (1855–58, 1859–64); promoted reforms in public health, education, rule in Ireland, slavery, woman's rights.

path, before it can trust its own deductions and stamp them with the certainty of belief. That certainty once gained, daylight opens upon it. No longer groping in the gloom, it boldly pushes forward; its progress is by leaps, and, with the exulting might of manhood, it rushes to the full effulgence of knowledge. Slow, indeed, would be the progress of the world, were each individual mind obliged to laboriously retrace these steps, instead of grasping and appropriating, so far as its individual intelligence is capable, the labour of its predecessors. The great mind, which first draws its conclusion from the darkness of error and forces it upon the world, has then a high and noble, but oftenest, alas! an ungrateful task to perform. The voice of error, when the attempt is made to rout her from her stronghold, is ever loud and clamorous—"Crucify him! Crucify him!"[2]

> For millions never think a noble thought;
> But with mute hate of brightness bay a mind
> (Which drives the darkness out of them) like hounds.

The history of Galileo every schoolboy knows. Error, building her defenses upon a literal, unauthorized, and dogmatic interpretation of Scripture authorities, screeched anathemas; and, backed by imprisonment, the wheel, and the inquisition, she triumphed. *God's* own prophet (such a prophet as yet, in every age, he sends to enlighten the world, and speak his thought, and interpret his ways—for genius is the voice of *God*), *God's* own prophet was hushed—Galileo recanted! "E pur si muove." Yes, still it moves, and, spite of infallible popes and bigot priests, *will* move, so long as the Almighty fiat destines it a place in *God's* glorious universe.

Geology has been forced to fight its way against persecution and revilings. The superstition of the church (the noblest things may be abused, and the highest polluted to foul purposes), the *superstition* of the church everywhere armed itself, and the hue and cry of "infidelity" was again raised. The light emanating from the investigation of *God's* own works was most painfully forced aside, and superstition gloried in her achievement; but

> Thought sprang from *God;* and all bestained with earth,
> Struggling and creeping still, at last the truth
> Is forced upon the day.[3]

Geology triumphs, and baffled error hides her head.

A fresh subject of discord has again risen, in the question of the "unity of

2. Luke 23:21; John 19:6.
3. *Caius Gracchus* 2.4.22–24 in *PDBL*.

the races," and again the cry is, "to the rescue."[4] The church declares herself in danger; the pious are called upon to close their ranks and gird themselves to the fight; the banner of the holy faith is raised, and sentence of excommunication fulminated against the innovators.

> I can scorn nothing which a nation's heart
> Has held for ages holy.

Even error becomes, to a certain degree, sacred, when it has been stamped for centuries with the approbation of the world, and should be touched lightly, gently dealt with, and led rather than shoved aside. But it is carrying too far this prerogative, to claim exemption from question; and he who demands such exemption weakens the cause which he endeavours to defend. The sincere and humble Christian should rather invite than repel investigation. A touchy shrinking from inquiry implies a consciousness of fallibility. *Facts* must have their way. There is no power, in heaven or earth, to make an accomplished fact cease to be a fact. Stern as destiny, immovable in truth, it *is*. Had the truths advanced by Galileo really clashed with the Christian faith, as its early and imprudent defenders imagined, even *that* faith (pure and beautiful as it is) must have bowed before the stern and unbending veracity of fact. Such, however, cooler judgments and calmer investigations proved to be far from being the case. All that was holy, chaste, and pure in that purest of creeds, stands as sacred, more sacred, perhaps, than ever. The coward fear, that shrinks the searching eye, but proves the weakness of its faith.[5] There is "something rotten,"[6] where the tenderest touch can cause such wincing. If it be a fact that man originates from various sources, not the less are we brethren—not the less bound to consult the good of all, and to endeavour to contribute, in so far as *God* has put it in our power, by just and righteous means, to the well-being and happiness of all. Man is man, and to man venerable, as the highest created work (so far, at least, as our intelligence extends) of the Almighty. If there are differences in grade of intellect and stamp of character, which fit men for differences of rank and position in life—if these extend from individuals to races, marking the course of each as with the finger of destiny—then, by investigating those differences, by searching into those peculiarities of character, we best enable ourselves to second, as well as lies in the power of feeble man, the great behests of the all-wise Ruler, who, in his wisdom, directing the world not

4. *1 Henry VI* 4.3.19.

5. *Richard II* 3.2.37: "the searching eye of heaven;" Caroline Anne Bowles Southey, "It Is Not Death," ll. 1–2: "It is not Death—it is not Death, / From which I shrink with coward fear."

6. *Hamlet* 1.4.90.

always in accordance with the Utopian plans of man, oftenest guides us by facts, which no reasoning, no theorizing, can set aside. If there are differences in the races of men, stamped ineffaceably by the hand of *God* and nature, we, by determining, in our blind and feeble judgments, to force upon all one mould and one stamp, can succeed only in blotting out much of the beautiful order of creation; but one mite we can never add to it by such a course. Man's improvement must advance in accordance with, not in opposition to, Almighty order.

It is, then, no light question upon which we are called to decide. Long, patient, and laborious have been the investigations of those who have now ventured to express their opinion against the unity of descent; and no prejudice, no dogmatic assumption (no foolish fear that *God's* word may be found in opposition to *God's* works!—revelation to fact!), should induce us to cast aside, as false, the thus matured opinion of wise and good men, much less, in our ignorance, to raise against them the cry of "infidelity." We know that there are also strong defenders of the unity of descent, and the name of Prichard[7] is unknown to no one who has thought even lightly upon this subject. But it cannot be denied that the most recent investigations and authorities are opposed to it. We have in the United States two names too well known to need comment—Agassiz and Morton.[8] Our champions of the old faith are less widely known. The city of Charleston has furnished two, whose zeal and sincerity are unimpeachable, and who are warm in defence of a belief which they consider as a part of their religious creed. Habit has made it venerable, even sacred to them, and we respect the feeling by which they instinctively hug and protect it. But, with all deference for the purity of their intentions, for their capacity and learning, which far be it from us to underrate, the Rev. Messrs. Bachman and Smyth will scarcely, we presume, feel themselves aggrieved if we rank their names, as *naturalists,* below the world-known ones of Agassiz and Morton.[9] Dr. Bachman has, we know, in addition to his useful labours as a teacher of the Christian faith, devoted

7. James Cowles Prichard (1786–1848), English physician and ethnologist; proposed a single origin of the human species in *Researches into the Physical History of Man* (1813) and *Natural History of Man* (1843).

8. Samuel George Morton (1799–1851), American physician and naturalist; author, among other works, of *Human Anatomy* (1849); president of the Academy of Natural Sciences in Philadelphia; exerted great influence on Louis Agassiz.

9. John Bachman (1790–1874), naturalist; Lutheran pastor in Charleston; collaborated with John James Audubon on *The Viviparous Quadripeds of North America* (1845–49); author of *The Doctrine of the Unity of the Human Race Examined on the Principles of Science* (1850). Thomas Smyth (1808–73), Irish-born pastor of the Second Presbyterian Church of Charleston (1834–70); author of *The Unity of the Human Races Proved to Be the Doctrine of Scripture, Reason, and Science* (1850); *Complete Works* in ten volumes (1908–12); in 1865 his son Augustine married LSM's daughter Louisa.

much time to the study of zoology; but we have said, and say again, that the world-wide fame of Agassiz and Morton must set *their* authority on much higher ground. Besides, Dr. Bachman *has been answered,* and we presume that few who have read Dr. Morton's *Additional Observations on Hybridity in Animals, etc.* will need further proof to convince them that the reverend, learned, and most estimable gentleman has, in this discussion, got a little beyond his depth. Dr. Bachman should, before entering upon it, have thrown aside his fear of "being biassed by authorities," and have ceased to shrink from reading the numerous works written upon this subject. It is by authorities that the mass of our knowledge is attained, and, if we allowed ourselves to be balanced by no authorities, the a b c of science would not yet be passed. Cast aside authority, and what an effulgence of light becomes suddenly extinct for man!

The question of race must, to be honestly and calmly discussed, be considered entirely distinct from its theological bearing. It is a question of fact to be first decided, and then referred to the theologist, that his judgment and learning may reconcile it with the higher doctrines of a creed whose friends are, by their injudicious sensitiveness, doing more to call it into doubt than could be effected by its bitterest enemies. Nothing can more strongly mark the strength and invulnerable purity of this creed, than its capacity for resisting such support. It stands firm, and beautiful in its firmness; not because it has been well defended, but because the beautiful and the good in it stand out too boldly to be smothered or crushed by the mistaken zeal of its defenders. Virtue is equally virtue, and the creed which exhibits it in its highest form is equally venerable, whether mankind be descended from Adam and Eve, created some 6000 years since, in the garden of Eden, or whether, in times unknown, in regions unknown, from ancestors unknown, they sprang into being, under circumstances as various as *God* has seen fit to show them to us, in their present existence. We mean no attack upon a religion which only the bitterest enemy of mankind could wish to enfeeble. To the philosopher and the philanthropist, independent of personal belief, christianity is equally sacred. With it modern civilization walks hand in hand; from it proceed all those softening influences which make us feel, spite of the *chefs d'oeuvres* of ancient art, now inimitable, that the world is better and wiser than it has been. It stands, after a trial of eighteen centuries, the purest code of philosophy and morals that the history of man has ever developed. But there are those who undertake to interpret and explain it in a manner to which, we must confess, our judgments do not so entirely submit. There is, to the best of our belief, nothing in pure christianity which in any way clashes with the settlement of the question of the races; and we see no reason for the extreme tenderness required in touching this point where it appears to differ from the literal and verbal biblical text, which has, in cases equally strong, been already waived. None but a madman or half idiot would, with the universal opinion of the civilized world against him, now maintain that the earth is the centre of the universe, and that the sun revolves round it. Few, among well-informed men, are bigoted enough to contend for the long-established biblical chronology and six days creation. Not only learned and good men, but christian preachers, honest teachers of Christ and his doctrines, have read, in that greatest of Bibles, *God's* Holy book of nature, that these are the errors of a past and mistaken faith, and have, like great and true men, recanted and confessed them.

Speaking of the period of man's creation, Dr. Morton says:

> There is nothing in geology to disprove the existence of man upon the earth for a period vastly longer than has generally been supposed. Dr. Prichard, who bestowed a part of his great learning and remarkable talents in the investigation of chronology, arrived at the conclusion that the Hebrew annals afford no data of this kind beyond the epoch of Abraham. Hence, according to his <this> view, there can be no antagonism between the Sacred Records and the discoveries of Dr. Lepsius.[10]

The remark of Dr. Prichard here alluded to is (speaking of the arrival of Abraham in Palestine): "Beyond that event we can never know how many centuries, nor how many *chiliads* of years may have elapsed since the first man of clay received the image of *God* and the breath of life."[11]

Dr. Morton believes that the evidence of his existence may yet arise, in the alluvial deposits, and even in the older deluvial beds.

In answer to the question whether the deluge was a universal cataclysm, Dr. Morton says: "Geologists began their investigations with the full belief in a universal deluge; but the irresistible evidence of the facts of nature is wholly opposed to such a theory, and it is now, by almost universal consent, abandoned" [*Observations,* p. 44]. He quotes the authority, to this effect, of Prof. Hitchcock, Rev. Adam Sedgwick, Mr. Greenough,[12] and then remarks:

10. *Observations,* pp. 47–48. Karl Richard Lepsius (1810–84), Egyptologist; professor at Berlin from 1846; among his works, *Totenbuch der Ägypter* (1842) and *Chronologie der Ägypter* (1849).

11. Cited in Morton, *Letter,* p. 18 (LSM's italics).

12. Edward Hitchcock (1793–1864), American geologist, professor and president at Amherst College; Adam Sedgwick (1785–1873), English geologist, professor at Cambridge; George Bellas Greenough (1778–1855), English geographer and geologist, founder and first president of the Geological Society of London, president of the Royal Geographical Society.

"Buckland, Lyell, Élie de Beaumont, Murchison,[13] and, as <so> far as I am informed, every other distinguished geologist of the day, have arrived at the same conclusion; and the Rev. J. Pye Smith[14] has shown, with great probability, the proximate barriers by which the Hebrew deluge was circumscribed in Western Asia" [*Observations,* p. 45]. After sundry quotations, which want of space will not allow us to transfer, Dr. Morton continues:

> I can only further refer to this most learned and elaborate work [*The Holy Scriptures and Geolog. Science,* by Rev. J. Pye Smith][15] for a vast mass of additional zoological and geological testimony in relation to this highly interesting question. But I may add that the evidence is designed to prove, and it is convincing to my judgement, that the *Creation,* as described in Genesis, only relates to one of the various independent zoological centres; while the Mosaic deluge <*Mosaic deluge*> describes the submersion of that locality only, and the destruction of all its inhabitants, excepting those who were preserved in the ark; and such was also the opinion long ago expressed by Bishop Stillingfleet.[16]

Here, then, we have the honest opinion of more than one enlightened preacher of the Christian faith, that the literal and cramped interpretation of Genesis to which some would confine us, is utterly untenable, and that the existence of the world, if not of man, is of millions and millions of years. Only after the most violent persecution was astronomy allowed to enfranchise itself from such an interpretation. Geology is even yet fighting against the giant superstition. Has the world become no wiser, that the same battle must be fought by ethnology?

It is a strange assertion of Dr. Bachman, that "if the Scriptures could, by any possibility, be tortured to prove the plurality of origin for the human species, philosophers and men of science would become infidels" [*Observations,* p. 50]. Rather, we should say, if the Scriptures can be proved to agree

13. William Buckland (1784–1856), English, professor of mineralogy at Oxford (from 1813), dean of Westminster (from 1845); Charles Lyell (1797–1875), Scottish geologist, author among other works of *Travels in North America, with Geological Observations* (1845); Elie de Beaumont (1798–1874), French geologist, professor at the Collège de France (from 1832); Roderick Impey Murchison (1792–1871), Scottish geologist, secretary and twice president of the Geological Society, director general of the Geological Survey, director of the Royal School of Mines.

14. John Pye Smith (1774–1851), English nonconformist divine; lecturer and tutor at Homerton College (1800–1851); among other works, *Relation between the Holy Scriptures and Some Parts of Geological Science* (1839).

15. LSM's interpolation.

16. *Observations,* pp. 45–46. Edward Stillingfleet (1635–99), English prelate and controversialist; dean of St. Paul's, London (1678); bishop of Worcester (from 1689).

with what appears to such men an evident and necessary fact, would the difficulty to faith be removed. Science and learning would thus be brought to corroborate instead of opposing it. It would be a sorry argument in favour of the revealed word, to maintain that philosophers and men of science are forced to abandon it, as inconsistent with revealed fact. Far be it from us to pronounce a judgment so inconsistent with Almighty wisdom. The Rev. J. Pye Smith, a clergyman *in favour* of the *unity side* of the question, and, as we have already shown, frequently referred to by Dr. Morton for his learned but liberal opinions, remarks:

> If the two first inhabitants of Eden were the progenitors, not of all human beings, but only of the races whence sprang the Hebrew family, still it would remain the fact, that *all* were formed by the immediate power of *God* [LSM's italics], and all their circumstances, stated or implied in the Scriptures, would remain the same as to moral and practical purposes.
>
> Some difficulties in the Scripture history would be taken away—such as the sons of Adam obtaining wives who were their own sisters; Cain's acquiring instruments of husbandry, which must have been supplied by miracle immediately from heaven, upon the usual supposition; his apprehensions of summary punishment; his fleeing into another region, of which Josephus so understands the text as to affirm that Cain obtained confederates and became a plunderer and a robber, implying the existence of a population beyond his own family; and his building a 'city,' a considerable collection of habitations.[17]

"Is our faith shaken," asks Dr. Morton,

> because Galileo has shown that the sun does not revolve round the earth, but the earth round the sun? Does it detract from our admiration of Creative Wisdom to be told, as Geology teaches, that past time is an eternity? Should it lessen our admiration of the past, or our hope in the future, to be told that mankind have existed thousands of centuries upon the earth? Or does our religion suffer detriment, because the great Lepsius has deciphered the legends of Memphis, and proved that they date back three thousand five hundred years before Christ? Yet these things are true; and, if the pride of man feels humiliated at his past ignorance, let him be thankful that he has yet lived to see so much light. [*Letter,* pp. 18–19]

17. *Letter,* pp. 15–16, citing Smith, *Relation between the Holy Scriptures and Some Parts of Geological Science,* 3d ed. (London, 1843), pp. 398–400. Flavius Josephus (c. 37-c. 100), historian; among his works, *History of the Jewish War* and *Antiquities of the Jews.*

We have said that the greatest weight of authority is opposed to the unity of descent. Prichard himself, the great defender of it, says: "If the elucidation of doubts on subjects of physical inquiry were to be sought for, in preponderance of authorities or opinions of celebrated men, I am afraid that the problem which I have endeavoured to investigate would receive a solution different from that I have obtained." The authority of Prichard is a very high one; but besides the acknowledgment just quoted, we must remember that the subject of diversity is one upon which the world is, but recently, full awake. Late investigations have added vastly to the strength of argument in its favour, and Prichard closed his labours at a period when light was breaking in, almost in floods, upon the science of ethnology.

Dr. Morton's opinions on the subject are so well known, that it is only necessary for us further to quote what has a particular reference not only to the difference but to the inequality of men.

> I believe in a plurality of origin for the human species; that they were created not in one pair, but in many pairs; and that they were adapted, from the beginning, to those varied circumstances of climate and locality which, while congenial to some, are destructive to others. Hence the differences in their physical characteristics, and in their mental and moral endowments. [*Letter,* p. 14]

Mr. Agassiz, in common with Dr. Morton, not only disclaims all wish and idea of clashing with scriptural belief, but considers his opinions as entirely conformable with, and confirmatory of, such belief. He impresses upon us the distinction between the question concerning the "Unity of Mankind" and that of the "Diversity of Origin of the Human Races."

> The unity of species does not involve a unity of origin, nor does a diversity of origin involve a plurality of species.[18] . . . Do we cease to recognize the <this> unity of mankind because we are not of the same family? because we originate in various countries, and are born in America, England, Germany, France, Switzerland? Where the relationship of blood has ceased, do we cease to acknowledge that general bond which unites all men of every nation? By no means. This is a bond which every man feels more and more, the further he advances in his intellectual and moral culture, and which, in this development, is continually placed upon higher and higher ground—so much so, that the physical relation arising from a common descent is finally entirely lost sight of in the consciousness of the higher moral obligations. It

18. "Diversity of Origin," p. 113: "The writer . . . would therefore insist upon this distinction, that the unity of species does not involve a unity of origin, and that a diversity of origin does not involve a plurality of species."

> is this consciousness which constitutes the true unity of mankind. . . . The comparisons made between monkeys and men by comparative anatomists, when tracing the gradations in nature, have been greatly misunderstood by those who have concluded that, because there were no other types between the highest monkeys and men, these highest monkeys were something intermediate between men and beasts; or that some race particularly disagreeable to those writers was something intermediate between monkeys and human beings. These links between mankind and the animal creation are only the great steps indicating the gradation established by the Creator among living beings, and they no more indicate a relation between men and monkeys, than between monkeys and beasts of prey, or between these and the ox, or between the ox and the whale.[19]

Mr. Agassiz goes on to remark, that however important it is that the unity of mankind, as he has just explained it, should be recognized and defended, such unity does in no wise exclude diversity.

> Diversity is the complement of all unity; for unity does not mean oneness, or singleness, but a plurality in which there are many points of resemblance, of agreement, of identity. This diversity in unity is the fundamental law of nature. . . . and [. . .] becomes gradually more and more prominent throughout organized beings, as we rise from their lowest to their highest forms. . . . This law of diversity, therefore, must be investigated as fully, as minutely, and as conscientiously, as the law of unity which pervades the whole. . . . Those who contend for the unity [of the human race, on the ground] of a common descent from a single pair, labour under a strange delusion, when they believe that their argument is favourable to the idea of a moral government of the world, and of the direct intervention of Providence in the development of mankind. Unconsciously, they advocate a greater and more extensive influence in the production of those peculiarities by physical agencies, than by the Deity himself. If their view were true, *God* had less to do directly with the production of the diversity which exists in nature, in the vegetable as well as the animal kingdom, and in the human race, than climatic conditions and the diversity of food upon which these beings subsist. . . . Whether the different races have been from the beginning what they are now, or have been successively modified to their present condition (a view which we consider as utterly unsupported by facts), so much is plain—that there are upon earth different races of men, inhabiting different parts of its surface, which have different physical characters; and this fact, as it stands, without reference to the time of its establishment and

19. Ibid., pp. 110–11, 119–20.

> the cause of its appearance, requires further investigation, and presses upon us the obligation to settle the relative rank among these races, the relative value of the characters peculiar to each, in a scientific point of view. It is a question of almost insuperable difficulty, but it is [as] unavoidable as it is difficult; and, as philosophers, it is our duty to look it in the face. . . . *It seems to us to be mock philanthropy and mock philosophy to assume that all the races have the same abilities, enjoy the same powers, and show the same natural dispositions, and that in consequence of this equality they are entitled to the same position in human society.* History speaks here for itself. Ages have gone by, and the social developments which have arisen among the different races have at all times been different, and not only different from those of other races, but particularly characteristic in themselves, evincing peculiar dispositions, peculiar tendencies, peculiar adaptations in the different races.[20]

Our Declaration of Independence was a great and noble act. It showed the world that a people capable of self-government has the right of self-government, and will, almost of necessity, seek the exercise of that right—that a thinking and intelligent people cannot be kept under subjection by a dogmatically assumed power. Physical strength may be—ought to be—curbed and governed; and submits willingly and naturally to such government. Our negro, for instance, feels by instinct that his condition is suited to his powers; and would, but for mischievous interference, never seek, never wish to change it. Intellectual strength, conscious of the power and right of self-government, can no more be crushed, than could the fiery Pegasus be broken to plough and wagon.[21] The Declaration of Independence was, then, a great and noble act; but never was a greater or more mischievous fallacy contained in six unlucky words, than in the blundering sentence, "*all men are born free and equal.*" *No man is born free.* What is freedom, but the power of exercising a will? the right and ability to act independently of the dictates and control of others? Will any man contend that the infant "mewling and puking in its nurse's arms" is a free agent? or the school-boy, "creeping like

20. Ibid., pp. 132–34, 141–42 (LSM's italics).

21. Those familiar with Retch's outlines will understand our allusion. [LSM] For "fiery Pegasus," see *1 Henry IV* 4.1.108–10: "As if an angel dropp'd down from the clouds / To turn and wind a fiery Pegasus, / And witch the world with noble horsemanship;" Matthew Prior, "Carmen Seculare, for the Year 1700," ll. 212–13: "The fiery Pegasus disdains / To mind the Rider's Voice, or hear the Reins." *1 Henry IV* is among the plays receiving line drawings ("outlines") in Moritz Retzsch, *Gallery to Shakspeare's Dramatic Works in Outlines* [cover title: *Outlines to Shakspeare*] (New York, 1849). Friedrich August Moritz Retzsch (1779–1857), born in Dresden; draftsman and painter; besides Shakespeare, illustrated works by Goethe and Schiller.

snail / Unwillingly to school?"[22] The madman or the drivelling idiot—what law can make free agents of *them*? Here, we will no doubt be answered, is a subjection instituted by the order of nature, for the regulation and benefit of the feeble and unformed intellect. Undoubtedly it is; and we contend, upon precisely similar grounds, that the subjection of the negro (he being once brought into contact with the higher and governing intellect of the white man) is equally just, equally natural, equally beneficial, and equally necessary. No man is born free, and no two human beings, perhaps, were ever born equal. Privileges and capacities of endless shade and variety chequer their lives with endless shades of difference, forming thus the beautiful "diversity in unity." Man everywhere, but everywhere the distinct, individual man; nowhere the machine, stamped by the thousand copies upon one model and never varying construction. Men are not, never were, and never can be, born free and equal. And so certainly was this felt, so meaningless were the words, that at the very moment of signing the Declaration all the States composing the confederacy were *slaveholding* States, and those which afterwards ceased to be so, only liberated their slaves when, in the progress of events, and from the effect of climate, negro labour proved valueless, and the slave became a burthen to his master. Let us not be accused of casting slur or slight upon the great men who signed our Declaration of Independence. They were men, and, therefore, liable to mistake or oversight. That such was the case here, cannot be denied. If any, in zeal for their honour, maintains the contrary, he only casts himself upon the sharper horn of the dilemma. Our patriot fathers, if they took these words in their full and literal sense, put the negro altogether out of the pale of humanity. Either the expression, "all men were born free and equal," means nothing, or the negro was, in their estimation, *not a man*.

But we have wandered far from Mr. Agassiz. Let us return to our quotations. Speaking of Africa, he remarks:

> This compact continent of Africa exhibits a population which has been in constant intercourse with the white race, which has enjoyed the benefit of the example of the Egyptian civilization, of the Phoenician civilization, of the Roman civilization, [of the Arab civilization,] and of all those nations that have successively flourished in Egypt and in the northern parts of Africa, and nevertheless there has never been a regulated society of black men developed on that continent, so peculiarly <particularly> congenial to that race. Do we not find, on the contrary, that the African tribes are today what they were in the time of the Pharaohs, what they were at a later period, what they are

22. *As You Like It* 2.7.144, 146–47.

probably to continue to be for a much longer time? And does not this indicate in this race a peculiar apathy, a peculiar indifference to the advantages afforded by civilized society?[23]

After speaking of the peculiarities of divers races, he continues:

The indomitable, courageous, proud Indian—in how very different a light he stands by the side of the submissive, obsequious, imitative negro, or by the side of the tricky, cunning, and cowardly Mongolian! Are not these facts indications that the different races *do not rank upon one level in nature*—that the different tendencies which characterize man in his highest development are permanently brought out in various combinations, isolated in each of these races, in a manner similar to all the developments in physical nature [and,] we may also say, similar to all the developments in the intellectual and moral world, where in the early stages of development we see one side predominant, which in the highest degree of perfection shows itself combined <is combined> with all others, in wonderful harmony, even though the lower stages belong to the same sphere as the highest? So can we conceive, and so it seems to us to be indeed the fact, that *those higher attributes which characterize man* in his *highest development* are exhibited in the several races in *very different proportions,* giving, in the case of the inferior races, prominence to features which are more harmoniously combined in the white race, thus preserving the unity among them all, though the difference is made more prominent by the manner in which the different faculties are developed.

"What," continues Mr. Agassiz,

would be the best education to be imparted to the different races in consequence of their primitive difference, [if this difference is once granted,] no reasonable man can expect to be prepared to say, so long as the principle itself is so generally opposed; but, for our own part, we entertain not the slightest doubt that human affairs with reference to the coloured races would be far more judiciously conducted if, in our intercourse with them, we were guided by a full consciousness of the *real differences* <difference> *existing between us and them,* and a desire to foster those dispositions that are eminently marked in them[, rather than by treating them] on terms of equality. We conceive it to be *our duty to study these peculiarities,* and to do all that is in our power to develop them to the *greatest advantage of all parties.* And *the more we become acquainted with these dispositions, the better,* doubtless, *will be our course with reference to our improvement, and with reference to the advance of the coloured*

23. "Diversity of Origin," p. 143.

> *races.*[24] For our own part, we have always considered it as a most injudicious proceeding to attempt to force the peculiarities of our white civilization of the nineteenth century upon all nations of the world.[25]

Here, with regret, we leave Mr. Agassiz. Surely we have quoted from him enough to waken every thinking mind. Men are different—of different races, different capacities; necessarily, therefore, of different desires, different wants. The circumstances and position in life which to the individuals of the one race would be the sole endurable existence, to those of another might present a very different aspect. Happiness and wretchedness, independent of absolute bodily suffering, cannot be predicated of any particular routine or position in life. They depend entirely upon the suitableness of the character to the circumstances in which fate has cast it. We have somewhere seen an extract from (we think) an old sermon, of which we remember neither the where, nor the how, the author, nor the circumstances of its delivery. The preacher compares life to a board filled with holes, of various size and form. To each of these holes, some particular individual is exactly suited and fitted. If every man could find his right place, life would indeed be happy, passing as "merry as a marriage bell";[26] but, "alas! my hearers, how often do we find the *round man stuck into the square hole!*"[27]

The white man, made for liberty (i.e., for self-government, of which the instinct is implanted in his bosom), rebels at what "the submissive, obsequious, imitative negro" finds, perhaps, his happiest existence. Could our innovators succeed in displacing the negro from his present position, they would very soon learn from his turbulent restlessness, that all their fancied philanthropy had for sole achievement, terminated by the cramming of the poor fellow into the *square hole*. It would be well for us all, if the motley crew which is now working to revolutionize the world—to upset *God's* rule, and establish their own patent discoveries for its government—could only be-

24. The italics throughout these quotations from Mr. Agassiz are ours; we have taken the liberty of so marking certain passages from this very high authority. [LSM]

25. Ibid., pp. 144–45.

26. Byron, *Childe Harold's Pilgrimage* 3.188.

27. Sydney Smith, *Elementary Sketches of Moral Philosophy, Delivered at the Royal Institution, in the Years 1804, 1805, and 1806* (New York, 1850), pp. 109–10: "If you choose to represent the various parts in life by holes upon a table, of different shapes—some circular, some triangular, some square, some oblong—and the persons acting these parts by bits of wood of similar shapes, we shall generally find that the triangular person has got into the square hole, the oblong into the triangular, and a square person has squeezed himself into the round hole. The officer and the office, the doer and the thing done, seldom fit so exactly, that we can say they were almost made for each other." Sydney Smith (1771–1845), English; canon of St. Paul's, London (from 1831); a founder of the *Edinburgh Review;* wit and essayist.

lieve the simple truth, that when men are fit for liberty, they need *no promptings to make them claim it.* Officious interference may, under other circumstances, drive them to rebellion and bloodshed, but never to the attainment of liberty. Men who need to be driven on by the excitement and promptings of others ask, when roused to exertion, not for self-government, but no government; not for liberty, but license.

This question of race is, then, most important in the consideration of negro slavery. The whole world seems to have joined in a crusade against us; and while we would resist to the uttermost the encroachments of our northern (not brethren, but) aggressors; while we would back not one step, give up not one *iota* of our right; while we say to them, just or unjust, right or wrong, pure as heaven or black as hell, *you* have no right to interfere with us; while we pray for the independence of the South, at any sacrifice of existing conditions and relations, as the greatest blessing that heaven could confer upon our beloved and almost prostrate country; yet we are willing, and anxious, to show that our cause is just. The consciousness of right is a shield of proof, but not, therefore, need we entirely despise the opinion of the world. Let us, if possible, convince others, also, of the justice of our cause. Were it merely as an act of charity, it would be a praiseworthy deed towards those unfortunate individuals, who seem to think it their duty to take the world under their charge, and who, constituting themselves *God's* vice-gerents, have determined as their *coup d'essai,* in correcting the faults of the universe, to begin with this black spot of American negro slavery, and have, accordingly, so fixed their eyes upon it, that the dark speck has, to their diseased imaginations, gradually expanded itself, until like the cloud at first no bigger than a man's hand, it now envelopes and darkens their whole horizon. Talk of oppression, they groan "poor negro!" Starvation; again, "poor negro!" Destitution, misery, unutterable wretchedness! "Poor negro!" "negro!" "negro!" There stands the spectre, and ever,

> Like some tormenting dream,
> Affrights them with a hell of ugly devils![28]

These people, could they only be brought to use their common sense instead of screaming, starting, and fainting at the ghosts of their wandering imaginations, might discover that they are playing the fool in this combat of shadows, and that they manufacture miseries much as Don Quixote did his giants out of wind-mills. Could the civilized world be convinced that all the races do

28. *Richard III* 1.3.225–27: "No sleep close up that deadly eye of thine, / Unless it be while some tormenting dream / Affrights thee with a hell of ugly devils."

not have the same abilities, enjoy the same powers, or show the same natural dispositions, and are not, therefore, entitled to the same position in human society; could the subject be fairly brought before the white man, and investigated as a great philosophic question deserves to be investigated, we verily believe, so well is the negro fitted for his position, that the philanthropist of every nation would arm in defence of our institutions, and presumptuous ignorance which seeks to force out *God's* law, in order to displace it by some "Icarie" of its own invention, would be hooted from the position which it now so impudently assumes.

This most important question it is, then, a sad mistake for us to allow to be pushed aside, or dogmatically determined upon by religious sectarians, whose sincerity is generally superior to their judgment; who blind themselves with a prejudice, and shrink with horror from the hand which would withdraw the veil from their eyes. We have already, however, disclaimed the intention of discussing it. This is a task to which we might prove entirely incompetent; we have convinced ourselves, and would have others do it as we have done. Authorities without number are open to them. The articles which form the subject of our present comments are so short that none can say he has not time, so clear that few can say they have not capacity, to investigate them. Dr. Nott[29] has, both in the pages of the *Southern Quarterly* [*Review*] and *De Bow's Review,* laid the question frequently before us, and we hope will continue his useful labours. This subject is one which, until lately, has been sacred to the learned; but the time has arrived when, like all other similar questions, it must, after due discussion, become vulgarized to common opinion. The question has been started, and as well might one try to stop the waters of the Mississippi with a mud-bank, as to attempt, with the old notion of Adamic descent, to prevent the current of thought which flows in upon it: men *will* think, argue, and familiarize themselves with the idea; will consult authorities and, according to the weight of those authorities, and the bias of their intellects, form their conclusions, without being sufficiently learned ethnologists to argue conclusively upon the subject. Many, who know with certain conviction that our earth revolves around the sun, as its great centre, might find it extremely difficult to advance any argument or proof of the fact, other than those received from the most approved authorities upon the subject. The discovering mind, bursting like sun-beams

29. Josiah Clark Nott (1804–73), born in Columbia, S.C.; physician and ethnologist; M.D. from the University of Pennsylvania (1827); settled in Mobile, Ala.; author, with George R. Gliddon, of *Types of Mankind* (1854) and *Indigenous Races of the Earth* (1857), both urging the diversity of the human races.

through the clouds of ignorance, reveals the light, which it is easy for common men to see and follow, though through ages of darkness they might fail to originate it.

While writing this article, quite a startling work has fallen into our hands: *The Races of Men, a Fragment,* by Robert Knox, M.D.[30] We presume this volume will hardly obtain favour with the advocates of either side of this question. The author's bold speculations leap ahead of argument in a manner little calculated to satisfy the wary philosopher, while he bombards the unity theory with a boldness of assertion which staggers even its opponents—and yet we have read the work with much interest. Its original and startling views have already attracted, and will, no doubt, further attract, both attention and animadversion from the learned, and to them we leave the discussion of its merits and demerits, contenting ourselves with some extracts, which strike us as worth making.

> Race is everything. Seign[i]ories and monkeries, nunneries and feudality, do not form, neither do they modify, the character of any people; they are an effect <*effect*>, not a cause <*cause*>, let chroniclers <*chroniclers*> say what they will. They indicate the character of a race—they do not make that character. [90–91] Race is everything: science, literature <literature, science>, art, in a word, civilization, depend on it. [7]

This is a sweeping stroke against the common idea, that man is so completely the creature of circumstance, that national characteristics are the result of location, institutions, etc., and yet it is by no means entirely new with Mr. Knox. The learned Arnold lays, occasionally, much stress upon race, and the difference of power in different races. Speaking of the Sclavonic and German races, as having respectively effected the changes in Eastern and Western Europe, he expresses an opinion, which, while we confess it is not entirely consistent with the general tone of his writings, is, we think, worth quoting:

> The changes which have been wrought have arisen out of the reception of these elements by new races, races endowed with such force of character that what was old in itself, when exhibited in them, seemed to become something new. But races so gifted are, and have been from the beginning of the world, few in number: the mass of mankind have no such power; they either receive the impression of foreign elements so completely that their own indi-

30. Robert Knox (1791–1862), Scottish anatomist. His eminence now derives from his regular purchase of cadavers from William Burke and William Hare, who supplemented their meager supply by murder; hence Knox's place in a couplet dear to aficionados of true crime stories: "Burke's the murderer, Hare's the thief, / And Knox the boy who buys the beef."

> vidual character is absorbed, and they take their whole being from without; or, being incapable of taking in higher elements, they dwindle away when brought into the presence of a more powerful life, and become at last extinct altogether.[31]

Mr. Knox contends that permanent amalgamation of race is impossible, and, as may be seen from the quotation just made, in this, too, he is to a considerable extent supported by Arnold; who, as we have just seen, speaks of the *weaker races as dwindling away when brought into the presence of a more powerful life, and becoming, at last, extinct altogether.* This, in our own country, has been fully exemplified in the case of our native American Indians; is actually being exemplified among the negroes located in our free States; and will be exemplified in the whole transplanted race, if abolition, folly, and madness continue their unchecked career without producing a more awful and sudden catastrophe.

We must allow ourselves one more extract from Arnold; we quote from his miscellanies commenting on Thucydides, and referring to habits of ancient Greece.

> The mixture of persons of different races <race> in the same commonwealth, unless one race had a complete ascendancy, tended to confuse all the relations of life, and all men's notions of right and wrong; or, by compelling men to tolerate, in so near a relation as that of fellow-citizens, differences upon the main points <point> of human life, led to a general carelessness and scepticism, and encouraged the notion that right and wrong have no real existence, but are the mere creatures of human opinion.[32]

Slavery, if this be true, is the only safeguard of our morals and manners, when races so entirely opposed to each other as the negro and the Saxon are thrown together.

Of the dark races generally, Knox remarks, "No one seems much to care for them. Their ultimate expulsion from all lands which the fair races can

31. Thomas Arnold, *Introductory Lectures on Modern History,* 2d London ed., ed. Henry Reed (New York, 1845), pp. 46–47. Thomas Arnold (1795–1842), eminent Victorian; headmaster of Rugby School (from 1828); Regius Professor of Modern History at Oxford (from 1841); among his works, many volumes of sermons, an edition of Thucydides in three volumes (1830–35), and *Introductory Lectures on Modern History* (1842).

32. Ibid., p. 88, where the editor Reed is quoting a passage from the preface to volume 3 of Arnold's edition of Thucydides. This passage from "the learned and pious Dr. Arnold" is quoted (with the same errors in transcription, but converting the past tenses into present) by David James McCord in "How the South Is Affected by Her Slave Institutions," *De Bow* 11 (Oct. 1851): 349–63; 352; he quotes also the last lines (from "being incapable of taking") in the previous passage from Arnold cited by LSM.

colonize seems almost certain." [210] If, in America, the Saxon "will not allow a black man to be a free man, in Australia he deems him entirely below his notice; in Tasmania he swept him at once and entirely <him, and at once, entirely> from the land of his birth. No compunctious visitings about the 'fell swoop'[33] which extinguished a race." [186] This is a painfully true observation. The mock philanthropy which is now so much the fashion as regards American slavery will expend itself upon a fugitive Mr. and Mrs. Crofts, or a Rev. Fred. Douglas;[34] will hone and wail over the dreams with which its diseased imagination has enveloped our "peculiar institution," but forgets to look at the slaughtered Tasmanian, the starved Australian, the enslaved Coolie, and even the fast-perishing negro of our own free States, who, in the home of the agitator and the abolitionist, starves for want of a friend and a master.

"Look," exclaims our author,

> at the Negro, so well known to you, and say, need I describe him? Is he shaped like any white person? Is the anatomy of his frame, of his muscles, or organs, like ours? Does he walk like us, think like us, act like us? Not in the least. What an innate hatred the Saxon has for him, and how I have laughed at the mock philanthropy of England? [161] The Dutch at the Cape [(Saxons)] have a perfect horror for the coloured races; it extends to the Mulatto, whom they absolutely despise. The placing a coloured man in an important official situation in South Africa, has caused to Britain the loss of some millions, and laid the basis for the ultimate separation of that colony from Britain. [318]
>
> Wild, visionary, and pitiable theories have been offered respecting the *colour* of the black man, as if he differed only in colour from the white races; but he differs in everything as much as in colour. He is no more a white man than an ass is a horse or a zebra: if the Israelite finds his ten tribes amongst them I shall be happy. But what has flattened the nose so much—altered the shape of the whole features, the body, the limbs? Some idle, foolish, and, I might almost say, some wicked notions have been spread about of their being

33. *Macbeth* 4.3.217–19: "All? / What, all my pretty chickens, and their dam, / At one fell swoop?" The speaker is Macduff, upon hearing of the slaughter of his entire family and household.

34. William (d. 1900) and Ellen Craft (c. 1826-c. 1897) fled in disguise from Macon, Ga. (December 1848) to the North, later (1850) to Canada and England; toured with antislavery lecturer William Wells Brown; settled in London; *Running a Thousand Miles for Freedom, or the Escape of William and Ellen Craft from Slavery* (1860) told their story; having returned to the United States after the abolition of slavery, both died in Charleston. Frederick Douglass (1817–95), abolitionist; born a slave in Maryland, escaped to the North (1838); author of *Narrative of the Life of Frederick Douglass* (1845).

> descended from Cain; such notions ought to be discountenanced; they give a colour to <for> oppression. [163; LSM's italics]

With all our hearts we endorse this last sentiment of Dr. Knox. This race, so markedly our inferior, placed by providence among us in the position of all others best suited to their comfort and happiness; whom (considering the mutual social ties established between us) we regard it not only as a right, but as a sacred duty, to *protect* and *govern*—how often have we heard them stigmatized as a race accursed! a wicked and perverse generation whom it was almost a virtue to persecute! The natural aversion of race in the white man, strengthened and legitimatized by the fancied curse of *God,* stamps the poor outcast with a brand ineffaceable indeed, until nowhere finds he a protector, nowhere a home, save under the sheltering arm of that master hooted at and slandered by the ignorant and the bigoted, as his tyrant and oppressor.

> In Central Africa the true black or negro race seems to have attained its ultimatum centuries ago. He has his own form of civilization, but, unfortunately, it includes neither literature, art, nor science. Yet he is industrious, good-tempered, energetic, accumulative, a lover of order and of finery; a fatalist and a worshipper of Fetis[c]hes. . . . When the race attempts to imitate the civilization <attempts the civilization> of another, Celtic or Saxon, for example, the whole affair becomes a ludicrous farce, and even grave men laugh at it. The after-piece is being played in St. Domingo, where they have elected a black emperor![35] In Liberia they will elect a sham president.[36] It can come to nothing in either case. Each race must act for itself, and work out its own destiny; display its own tendencies; be the maker of its own fortunes, be they good or evil. A foreign civilization they cannot adopt, calling it national, native; but the imposture, like all impostures, becomes manifest in time, whether practised by the negro or the Saxon. They elect a president in Hayti; in recollection of Napoleon, he declares himself emperor, standing in the same relation to that name which the ourang-outang <oran-outan> does to the Apollo. [303–4][37]

35. Such an election being not unique, it is not clear to whom Knox refers, or whether the mention below of the "president in Hayti" applies to the same occasion; perhaps Knox has in mind Faustin Elie-Soulouque, former slave, declared Emperor Faustin I of Haiti in 1849.

36. Joseph Jenkins Roberts (1809–76), born of free parents in Virginia; settled in Liberia in 1829; made governor in 1842; proclaimed independence of Liberia in 1847; its first president (1847–56); president again (1871–76).

37. I.e., the Apollo Belvedere.

Incapable of civilization, but good-tempered, and with considerable intelligence and activity, destined to extinction if coming unprotected into contact with the white races, what better destiny could *God,* in his merciful wisdom, have marked out for him than the one which he occupies under our institution of slavery? Transplanted from his natural soil, and without the possibility (were it desirable) of being re-transferred to it; cast into the midst of a flourishing white population, the negro would be trampled from existence, without the refuge of slavery; in which, good-tempered, unambitious, unintellectual, incapable of civilization, and unfit for amalgamation, he finds, when unexcited by the mischievous meddling of ignorant fanaticism, his comfort and his happiness.

The possibility of communicating to the negro the civilization belonging to the white race being set aside, the question presents itself, "What, then, is his probable destiny?" "He seems [to me]," says Mr. Knox,

> to have qualities of a high order, and might even reach a *certain point* of civilization. . . . Africa is his real country—Central Africa. It is here that climate enables him to set the Celtic and Saxon races at defiance. [163; LSM's italics]
>
> I incline[, then,] to the opinion that the dark races may for many ages hold the tropical regions; that many countries now in the military occupation of the fair races may and will revert to the dark; that it would be a better policy, perhaps, to teach them artificial wants and the habits and usages of civilization. Commerce alone, I think, can reach Central Africa; the Negro must be taught the value of his labour. When this happens, the slave-trade will of necessity cease. [209]

It would be difficult to imagine a system better calculated than ours, for teaching to the "submissive, obsequious, and imitative negro" [Agassiz, p. 144], in his transplanted condition, the wants, habits, and usages of civilization. As regards his condition in Africa, the door is open wide. Philanthropists, colonize, colonize, colonize; establish commercial depots, inland trading societies, central mission societies, anything! If you do no good, the chances are, at least, you can do no harm.[38] Our abolitionists, unfortunately, like their comfort too well for such undertakings, and prefer the petty and

38. No harm, if we of the South are not forced to pay for experiments which we consider as childishly futile and inefficient. Our Congressional legislation seems now to find no limit to its action, other than "the good old rule . . . , the simple plan, / That they may take who have the power, / And they may keep who can" [Wordsworth, "Rob Roy's Grave," st. 9, reading "should" for "may" in each case]. The proposed measures upon this subject now before Congress, are unjust and iniquitous: plans for picking our pockets to pay for ridding the Northern States of a troublesome and dangerous population, which their own mischievous meddling with our institutions has brought upon them. The negro population of the

mischievous notoriety of making "it the business of their lives," as Lord Morpeth assures us some of them informed him they did, "to superintend the passage of [the] runaway slaves through the free States; they reckon[ed, at that time,] that about one thousand yearly escaped into Canada," and his lordship doubts "whether the enactment and operation of the fugitive slave law will damp the ardor of their exertions."[39] We do not doubt, we are sure, that it will not; but we should like to have the true and faithful history of these escaped bondmen. Verily, there is more than sufficient reason to fear, that their last state is worse than their first.

Our author gives us, however, a glimpse at the kind of colonization to which the negro is most probably destined. Of South Africa, he remarks: "A new element of mind had appeared, about to create a new South African [a]era: the Saxon or Celtic element, bringing with it the semi-civilized notions of Europe—the power of combinations, fire arms, discipline, laws. Before this [new] element, antagonistic of nature, her works are doomed to destruction, in as far as man can destroy." [311] Forests and plants are swept before it.

> The antelope [is exterminated or disappears;] the zebra, the gnoo, the ostrich, the bustard, escape from the land, or are shot down; the mighty onslaught of an antagonistic element, seemingly too strong for nature, defeats even the rhinoceros, the elephant, the lion. . . . Last of all comes <Last comes> man himself, the coloured man, the man placed there by nature; he also must of necessity give way; his destiny apparently is sealed, and extinction in presence of a stronger race seems inevitable. The yellow race, the

---

Northern States would be so nearly extinct, as to render all special legislation on its account quite unnecessary (so rapidly does it "dwindle and die out"), were it not kept up by the constant influx of fugitives, tempted on from the South. [LSM] The Charleston *Mercury* of Feb. 15, 1851, reported that on Feb. 11 Stephen A. Douglas had presented to the U.S. Senate "the petition of the Mayor, Board of Aldermen, and Board of Common Council of Washington City, in favour of the scheme of mail steamers to Africa, as a means of forwarding the colonization of free negroes." On Feb. 24 the *Mercury* reported similar petitions from Georgetown and Brooklyn. The *Mercury* of March 13, reprinting from the *Southern Press* (Washington, D.C.), reported that "it is proposed to colonize free negroes on the coast of Africa, by the aid of Government," and opined that "the Ebony line of steamers, which is proposed as the great instrument of colonization, . . . is extravagantly consistent with such a scheme, and the other chimeras of the age. Mr. [Asa] Whitney insists on building a railroad where there are no people; this is a line of mammoth steamers to a place where there is no trade—of mail steamers to a place that has no correspondence." "At the late session" of Congress, complained James L. Orr in a speech printed in the *Mercury* of May 30, "Seward introduced a bill appropriating a large sum of money to purchase all the slaves in the District of Columbia, and slavery will be abolished in that way."

39. Carlisle, *Travels in America,* p. 36, reading "Fugitive Slave Bill."

> feebler, will naturally yield first; then the Kaffir—he also must yield to the Saxon Boor, on whose side is right, that is, might; for, humanly speaking, might is the sole right. [311–12]

Slavery, then, or extermination, seems to be the fate of the dark races, when invaded by or otherwise brought into juxtaposition with the white. We need not go further than our own aboriginal tribes for a case in point, illustrating the exterminating mode of procedure. Are our opponents such devoted admirers of all the acts of the "Pilgrim Fathers," and their immediate descendants, that they would set up such a course as the model method to be pursued by us towards our negroes? Extermination or slavery, we have said, is their fate; not by man's will, but *God's* will; who, for his own purposes, and in his impenetrable wisdom, has so formed the weaker race that they dwindle and die out by contact with the stronger; has so formed the stronger that they instinctively repel the thought of amalgamation with the weaker; has so formed both, that amalgamation leads to extinction. Extermination, then, or slavery; and a slavery not such as ours, which, softened by christianity and civilization, by the ties of dependence and propinquity, shows us the subjection of race by race in the mildest, most humanizing form in which it is possible for this necessary subjection to exist, but hard and crushing. "If we are to hold India," says Dr. Knox,

> it can only be as *military masters, lording it over a slave population.* It is the same with Jamaica, Cuba, even Brazil, tropical Africa, Madagascar, the northern coasts of Australia, and all the islands of the Indian Ocean situated as Borneo, Sumatra, etc. (p. 194 [LSM's italics]) The policy of the European nations <of European races> would be [in Cuba and Jamaica] to expel the Negro and transplant the Coolies, Hindoos, Chinese, or other feeble races, as labourers and workmen—*bondmen,* in fact. Why not call everything by its right name? Over these the Saxon and Celt might lord it, as we do in India, with a few European bayonets, levying taxes and land rent, etc. (p[p. 178–]79 [LSM's interpolation and italics]).

Algeria needs a working class—the climate does not admit of white labour. "The French would do well, perhaps, to encourage the immigration of Coolies or Negroes, as we do to the West Indies. The trade (a modified slave-trade) is free to all. Call them *apprentices,* as we do—there is much in a name." (p. 209) Of the Caffres, he says: "We are now preparing to take possession of their country, and this of course leads to their enslavery and final destruction, for a people without land are most certainly mere bondmen. *Ascripti glebae*[40] —they would, but they cannot, quit it. The old English yeo-

40. "Bound to the land," i.e., in the manner of a serf.

man and the modern Dorsetshire labourer, the local tenant of Sutherlandshire and the peasantry of Ireland, are simply bondmen or slaves; there is no avoiding the phrase." (p[p]. 160[–61]) Of America, he remarks: "The hottest actual war ever carried on—the bloodiest of Napoleon's campaigns—is not equal to that now waging between our descendants in America and the dark races; it is a war of extermination—inscribed on each banner is a death's head and no surrender; one or other must fall." [162]

There is one check, and one only, to this bloody climax, and that we find in our slandered, reviled, but, we believe, providentially established institution of slavery, blessed, thrice blessed and beautiful in its harmony with creation! Almost, were it not profanation to thus, as it were, thrust ourselves into the councils of Deity, we would call it an emanation of the Almighty wisdom, a reflected thought of Deity, so beautifully does it mingle together, in softened communion, the otherwise clashing and antagonistic characteristics of race, each race thus using and profiting by those peculiar traits which, being in itself deficient, are more fully developed in the other. The dark, as we have endeavoured to show, needs, and in slavery obtains, the governing mind and protection of the white, necessary to secure him his position, even in existence. The white, in and near the tropics, cannot live and progress without the labour and bodily endurance of the dark race. Thus, each finds in each that which he lacks, and through the beneficent institution of slavery a hitherto unknown phenomenon in history occurs: a barbarous people lives peaceably, happily, and improvingly, in connection with a superior one. Has the history of the world ever furnished a similar example? Has it, on the contrary, not always shown, what experience still shows us, the inferior race, if not strong enough to drive out the superior, suddenly exterminated, or gradually crushed from existence?

What, then, is the destiny of the negro, supposing the success of the present fanatical crusade against slavery? We say nothing just now of the white man; for the new-light prophets and dealers in inspiration have rhapsodies and sympathies only for the black skin. What, we ask, would be the result of their schemes upon the negro?

Peaceable emancipation (could such a thing be) would consign the race to that gradual extinction which is already rapidly advancing upon that portion of it located in our Northern States. But it is a farce to talk of the peaceable emancipation of millions of human beings without land, without property of any kind, without habits of foresight and self-dependence, and without the capacity for attaining these; without the knowledge even of what liberty means, and attaching to the word "freedom" only the idea of *idleness*. Inconceivable to them the brain-workings and the heart-struggles of the white man; they think of liberty as of a long holiday, and would be surprised to find that hard work, scant pittance of food, sickness without help, rags for clothing, and shivering cold, without fire or house-room, are often the lot of the so-called freeman. What know they of labour? We see the sneer which curls the lip of the abolitionist as he answers, "The life of the slave is labour." But we deny it. What knows he of labour? Nothing. Nothing, compared to the anxious thought, the brain-sweat, the sleepless night and weariness without rest, without hope, which breaks down the sorrow-scourged life of millions of—shall we say freemen? Is he a freeman who, under the lash of hunger, walks to the gallows to escape it? Is he a freeman who, continually stared in the face by the wretched alternative between vice and starvation, rushes to the grave to forget it? In courtesy, let us, however, say *freeman,* and grant him the sorry superiority which undoubtedly he has over the slave—of superiority of wretchedness! The peculiarity of the negro character is, we grant, one cause of their total exemption from care. Overgrown children, living only in today, thoughtless of tomorrow, living only in the moment as it flies, they are, both in their virtues and their weaknesses, eminently fitted for their position. Children in mind, with the bodily strength of the man, what a gigantic corporeal power, unsubdued by intellect, would, by the emancipation of such a people, be let loose upon the community. Bread, food, raiment, they must have. The privileges of the freeman (i.e., in their vocabulary, the right to live idle and luxuriously), they would grasp at; need we paint the scenes of robbery, murder, devastation, and riot that would follow!

Could the negro be excited to rebellion, it is evident enough that a sudden fate would terminate his career in all countries where the climate would allow the white man to live and thrive without him. The only question, then, that remains, is as to the result where his labour is necessary to the soil. The result of attempts to cultivate Jamaica with white labourers is sufficiently known. Mr. Knox cites failure upon failure of a similar kind in similar climates, and then asks: "Is it[, then,] that there exists a vast region of the earth, the richest in all respects, the most productive, which the European cannot colonize, cannot inhabit as a labourer of the earth, as a workman, as a mechanic? From which, should he expel the coloured aboriginal races, he also must quit or cease to live? which he requires to till with other hands? It would seem so; and all history proves it." [193] Then, it must follow as a certain corollary that, in all such portions of the globe in which the white races are established, either the two races must continue in juxtaposition (and such juxtaposition can only be maintained by slavery), or the white race must be expelled to make way for the black.

Is this, then, the consummation aimed at? It is well when a great move is contemplated upon the grand chess-board of the world, that such a move should be weighed, meditated upon, and examined in its bearings. The plans of abolitionism carried to their climax lead inevitably to negro dominion wherever negro labour is necessary for the cultivation of the soil. The steps to this will be through blood. Only wading knee-deep in the blood of the white man can negro rule be established. St. Domingo is a case in point. Is it one which shows so brightly on history's page, that the civilized world should combine to produce facsimiles of it? Can it indeed be that "were a million of slaveholders cut off in cold blood tomorrow, there would fall no tear of sympathy"?[41] By what fanaticism can it be that in order to establish new empires of Hayti, civilized men would seek to inundate in blood the fairest portions of *God's* earth! Their madness would light the torch of the most fearful servile war that ever imagination could paint—and for what? That barbarism may sweep back into her fold the half-redeemed negro, who, after destroying his white rulers, and aping for a while the pageants of their power, sinks back into his natural insignificance, and slaughters, fights, and starves in lawless brutality.

And the white races—the civilized world—this secondary portion of humanity, upon which fanaticism has no time to think—do we not see that it too must stagger beneath the blow, like the stricken victim staggering to its death? Dares any man look into the future, and say what would be the result, upon the civilized world, of the failure of two cotton crops? and dares any man who has spent six months of his life in attending to the growth and management of that crop, pretend that the cessation of it would not be the certain result of negro emancipation? These things are below the consideration of fanatic visionaries who, seeing wreck and ruin hurled over the universe, would take the confusion wrought by their own folly only as a sign, perhaps, of the coming day of judgment, and, arrayed in white robes, would go upon hill tops to wait for immediate ascension to heaven as the reward of their zeal. But sober men, who cannot believe that this beautiful world was made to be upset by the Utopian dream of every madman, can they not see, and seeing, can they not cease to sit listlessly contemplating the deluge of barbarism which blind fanaticism is drawing down upon the world? Is this a point to be put in the balance with the privilege of shuffling the cards, or casting the die in a game of President-making? These are no freaks of fancy, but things of sober thought, which come upon us in the midnight watch, and make us shudder at the coming ills which lower o'er us, as the wildest threats of some unlicensed dream.

A more momentous question has never before agitated the world. Rather

41. Knox, *Races of Men,* p. 163: "A million of slave-holders cut off in cold blood tomorrow would call forth no tear of sympathy in Europe."

too large it is, for the comprehension of gentlemen who "make it the business of their lives to superintend the passage of [the] runaway slaves"[42] from State to State; rather too large for the petty optics of interested politicians, who, burrowing in the blind paths of selfish policy, know not that, in their eager and unprincipled plottings, they may, like the mole under the princely castle, be drawing down over their own heads a ruin too vast for their cramped and grovelling policy to understand. Yet thus it is; while he who foresees, can, alas! do but little to prevent the princely wreck. *God* only knows the future. Our harassed minds, cast to and fro, 'twixt hope and fear,[43] vainly would pierce its mysteries, vainly interrogate the heavens and the earth. Cast back upon ourselves, we can only gaze and tremble at the lowering darkness of our threatened destiny.

Solemn before us,
Veiled, the dark portal:
Stars silent rest o'er us;
Graves under us, silent.[44]

L. S. M.

42. Carlisle, *Travels in America,* p. 36.

43. *1 Henry VI* 5.5.84–86: "I feel such sharp dissension in my breast, / Such fierce alarums both of hope and fear, / As I am sick with working of my thoughts." *Antony and Cleopatra* 4.12.6–9: "Antony / Is valiant, and dejected, and by starts / His fretted fortunes give him hope and fear / Of what he has, and has not."

44. Johann Wolfgang von Goethe, *Mason-Lodge,* ll. 11–15, as translated by Thomas Carlyle in "Morrison Again," *Past and Present,* in *Works* 2:192, 196, 199–200. LSM omits l. 13: "Goal of all mortal."

6.

Negro and White Slavery—Wherein Do They Differ?

"There are," as a recent writer in the *Edinburg[h] Review* remarks,

> two classes of philanthropists—the feelers and the thinkers—the impulsive and the systematic—those who devote themselves to the relief or [the] mitigation of existing misery, and those who, with a larger <longer> patience, a deeper insight, and a wider vision, endeavour to prevent its recurrence and perpetuation by an investigation and eradication of its causes. The former—in imitation, as they imagine, of their Master—go from house to house assuaging wretchedness, but, alas! not always "doing good"; relieving present evils, but too often leaving an increasing crop ever springing up under their footsteps; attended and rewarded by blessings, but doomed, probably, at length to feel that they have ill deserved them. Far different is the course of the latter class: their life is spent in a laborious research into remote and hidden causes; in a patient and painful analysis of the operation of principles from the misapplication or forgetfulness of which our social disorders have sprung; in sowing seeds and elucidating laws that are to destroy the evil at a distant day <date> which they themselves may never see—while sometimes its pressure may be aggravated during the period which they do see. They are neither rewarded by the gratitude of those for whom they toil—

SQR, n.s., 4 (July 1851): 118–32. Publication reviewed: Charles Kingsley, *Alton Locke, Tailor and Poet: An Autobiography* (New York: Harper and Brothers, 1850); numerous later printings; page numbers added in the text refer to the edition in Everyman's Library (London, 1910).

> since the benefits they confer are often blessings in disguise and *in futurum*—nor gratified by beholding the fruit of their benevolent exertions—for the harvest may not be ripe till all of them have passed away and till most of them have been forgotten. Nay, more, they are misrepresented, misconstrued, accused of hardness of heart by a misconceiving generation, and too often cursed and thwarted by the very men in whose service they have spent their strength. And while those who have chosen the simpler and easier path are reaping blessings in return for the troubles they have ignorantly stimulated and perpetuated by relieving, these men—the martyrs of philanthropy—must find their consolation and support in unswerving adherence to true principles and unshrinking faith in final victory; and must seek their recompense—if they need one—in the tardy recognition of their virtues by a distant and [a] wiser time. While therefore the warm and ardent natures, which can find no peace except in the [free] indulgence of their kindly impulses, are worthy of all love, and even, amid all the mischief they create, of some admiration for their sacrifices and zeal—and while we fully admit that they also [may] have their <a> mission to fulfil—we cast in our lot with their more systematic fellow labourers, who address themselves to the harder, rougher, more unthankful task, of attacking the source rather than the symptoms—of eradicating social evils rather than alleviating them.[1]

The author of *Alton Locke*[2] is of the well-meaning but mischievous class included under the head of "the feelers." In sympathy for the wretchedness which he so vividly describes, he cannot think coolly upon the chances for remedying it; and, because evil very evidently exists, he falls foul of the first fancied obstacle he meets and, shutting his eyes, fights away, without taking breath to consider if, perchance, he may not be drubbing the wrong subject.

Political economy seems to be the special bugbear of all such sentimental reformers. Because this science cannot extirpate evil, they rail against it as not only inefficient but mischievous; because the grand rule of *laissez faire*

1. [William Rathbone Greg], "English Socialism, and Communistic Associations," *Edinburgh Review* 93 (Jan. 1851): 1–33; 3–4.

2. Charles Kingsley (1819–75), English novelist; a founder of the Christian Socialist movement; chaplain to Queen Victoria (1859); professor of modern history at Cambridge (1860–69); canon of Westminster (1873). His early novels *Yeast* (1848), cited by LSM in chap. 3, "Enfranchisement of Woman," and *Alton Locke* (1850) promoted, with increasing reservations, Chartism, a movement, mostly working class, advocating reforms—such as universal suffrage for men, a secret ballot, abolition of a property qualifications for members of Parliament, and annual elections—intended to make government responsive to all classes.

cannot cure all ills, they blame it as the parent of all; because God Almighty has not seen fit to make this world suited to their ideas of right and wrong, they would revolutionize it to some devil's rule, which one half of them, in their gentle beneficence (for they are "good easy men,"[3] well-meaning folks, this half of them), deem some model-work of heaven, specially confided to them, the heaven inspired. The other half, mixed up of madman and fanatic, care not what devil's brood may be let loose upon the world, provided the "higher law" be exalted, and reason and common sense forced back before their visionary schemes.

Alton Locke, most decidedly a work of talent, is throughout sprinkled with the impracticable spirit of reform which now sets the world agog after some unfound and unknown system of improvement, which its seekers seem to imagine is to prove, as it were, some great strengthening plaister, to be clapped upon all weak places in our sick and sorry world, where, God's providence having failed to make all perfect and healthy, wise prophets and new lights stand ready to better his works with their *nostrums* and *emplastra.* Like all quacks, however, do they not aggravate the evil, even unto death? The civilized world seems struggling almost in its death throes, while, like some poor patient, sweating under a Thomsonian steam-practice,[4] and gasping for God's air and God's sun, we stand bolstered up with dreams of "phalansteries," "rights of labour," and "all men are free and equal" systems, vainly the while interceding "*Laissez faire!*" *Laissez faire,* God's glorious providence; *laissez faire,* the beautiful system which he has established; and where he has seen fit to leave us subjected to the fearful influence of a Vesuvius or an Etna, what boots it that we go about, in a panic, to block up the volcanic might of evil with a cart-load of sand! Deeper research must make us acquainted with the cause, and larger, more far-seeing remedies must—if any can—alleviate the evil.

3. *Henry VIII* 3.2.352–58 (the speaker is Cardinal Wolsey):

> This is the state of man; today he puts forth
> The tender leaves of hopes, tomorrow blossoms,
> And bears his blushing honours thick upon him:
> The third day comes a frost, a killing frost,
> And when he thinks, good easy man, full surely
> His greatness is a-ripening, nips his root,
> And then he falls as I do.

4. Samuel Thomson (1769–1843); born in Alstead, N.H.; originated a system of medical treatment which included administering the herb *Lobelia inflata,* cayenne pepper, and a steam bath; sold franchises to societies founded to promote his methods; several Thomsonian journals; among his books extolling the Thomsonian system were *New Guide to Health, or Botanic Family Physician* (1822) and *Learned Quackery Exposed* (1824).

The civilized world seems, we have said, to be struggling in its death throes; not yet is "the strong man laid low,"[5] but "how long, oh! Lord, how long" can we resist the fearful influence which stands ready to sweep over us its desolating night of barbarism![6] Communism and Socialism, in their various forms and divers masks, now showing themselves in bald and fiend-like horrible indecency, with their bold cry of "no property," "no family"; now, again, with almost angelic gentleness insinuating the same ends, in sentimental wailings and tearful remonstrance—Communism and Socialism are the doctors, the soul and body healers, to whom our future destiny seems in too much danger of being subjected; and, if they succeed in once shutting the door upon our true and patient friend, political economy, it will not, it is to be feared, take them long to steam us to death under their patent processes.

Alton Locke is, we repeat, a work of talent. There is a vivid reality about his descriptions which too well vouches for their truth, and touches us home—we of these Southern United States—by the great contrast which such a state of society presents with the far happier, and every way more elevated, position of *our* labouring classes. Aye, negro and slave though these be, the white slave of England—great, proud, glorious England—has sunk far lower than they, in the weltering abyss of misery and hopeless wretchedness. After a few further remarks upon the general tenor and merits of the volume, we will proceed to give some quotations calculated to prove this assertion.

There are, in the various characters of this volume, few who interest us strongly. The heroines (one of whom is intended as a very prominent personage) are distressingly vapid; and when, toward the conclusion, this most prominent one—this beau ideal of perfect womanhood—begins to prate of "Emancipation of Labour" [369], and a "Holy War [. . .] against the fiend of competition" [361], we feel that we have had quite enough of her.[7] There

5. Cf. Matt. 12:29; Mark 3:27.

6. Robert Southey, *Roderick, the Last of the Goths* 8 ("Alphonso").1–6:

> Fain would Pelayo have that hour obey'd
> The call, commencing his adventurous flight,
> As one whose soul impatiently endured
> His country's thraldom, and in daily prayer
> Imploring her deliverance, cried to Heaven,
> How long, O Lord, how long!

7. In the final chapters of *Alton Locke,* Eleanor Staunton, widow of Lord Lynedale, whom the hero often calls "the dark lady," delivers—after the fashion of Diotima in Plato's *Symposium* (to whom Eleanor is explicitly compared [338])—a series of speeches summing up the conclusions of the novel.

is, indeed, a "vast machinery of good" in the world, needing only guidance to turn itself to some useful purpose in the end and destiny of man; but it is not the "dark ladye" [150, 153, 163] of *Alton Locke* who has yet let in light upon the enigma of earthly sin and earthly sorrow. There is certainly nothing very novel in the discovery that a perfectly virtuous world would cease to be a sinful one; but how to bring about so desirable a climax is an enigma which the "dark ladye" does not solve. Individual virtue and self-sacrifice, beautiful devotion to truth and duty, are of daily, hourly occurrence in this God's world of ours—for God's world and no devil's world it is—but a self-sacrificing community, where every clashing interest sways under and cheerfully submits to the good of all, making one mind and one soul of opposing thoughts, sentiments, and wishes—such a community the world has not yet seen, and *Alton Locke* certainly does not teach us how to manufacture it.

In the widowed mother of Alton, we have a fine specimen of a human heart, welling forth all the better feelings of humanity, but crushed down by grinding bigotry, and smothering all its gentleness in conscientious fanaticism; and our heart aches at the glimpses given of his young and gentle sister, subdued by the same annihilating process. One sterling character gives life to the whole book. Old Sandy Mackaye would be enough to tempt us through a dozen volumes of far inferior merit. We see the kindly heart which has broken loose from its trammels, after having been bred up by a "right <richt> stern auld Cameronian sort o' body" [304], as he describes his father.

> I was unco drawn to the high doctrines ance, when I was a bit laddie, an' sat in the wee kirk by my minnie and <an'> my daddy; [. . .] but as I grew, and grew, the bed was ower short for a man to stretch himsel' thereon, and <an'> the plaidie ower straight for a man to fauld himsel' <himself> therein; and so I had to gang my gate a' naked in the matter o' formulae, as Maister Tummas has it. [304]

But though naked in the matter of formulae, not the less was auld Sandy clothed with all true Christian graces, and we feel that he was on safe ground when he tells us, midst his deathbed wanderings, that:

> There was a gran' leddy, a bonny leddy, came in, and talked like an angel o' God to puir old Sandy, anent the salvation o' his soul. But I told <tauld> her no['] to fash hersel'. It's no my view o' human life, that a man's sent into the warld just to save his soul, and <an'> creep out again; an' I said I wad leave the savin' o' my soul to him that made my soul; it was in richt good

> keeping <gude keepin'> there, I'd warrant. An' then she was unco fleyed when she found I didna haud wi' the Athanasian creed. An' I told <tauld> her, na'; if he that died on the cross <on cross> was sic a ane as she and I teuk him to be, there was na that pride nor spite in him, be sure, to send a puir auld sinful, guideless body to eternal fire, because he didna a'thegither understand the honour due to his name. [303–4]

A higher philosophy and religion was Sandy's than either Cameronian or Athanasian creeds: the philosophy and religion of true Christian charity.[8] "Ah! boy, boy," he exclaims to young Alton, "do ye think that was what ye were made for: to please yoursel' <yersel'> wi a woman's smiles, or e'en a woman's kisses—or to please yersel' at all? How do ye expect ever to be happy, or strong, or a man at a', as long as ye go on looking to enjoy yersel'?" [87]

The duties of life are its only legitimate enjoyments to the reasoning, thoughtful mind. And this brings us back to our caption: "Negro and White Slavery—Wherein Do They Differ?"

One grand point of difference presents itself as a corollary to the sentence we have uttered: the duties of life are its only legitimate enjoyments. These duties lie so plainly before every slaveholder, that there is no necessity for his travelling out of his way, and losing himself in philosophic and philanthropic mazes, to find them. We do not pretend to say that to the aristocratic master of the white (*de facto*) slave duties are not rife, and the means of fulfilling them scattered at every step. But he may easily blind himself to them; he does not feel so intensely as the master of the negro (acknowledged) slave the strong call for, the necessity of, curtailing his luxuries to supply the wants of his subordinate. In the case of the white (*de facto*) slave, each individual who uses his labour may say, and with some truth, "This is no affair of mine. It is no more my duty than that of A, or B, or C, to relieve this suffering. This is the duty of the community, not mine. Society is, I am not, answerable for this wretchedness." And so, with a recommendation to a charitable society, or an alms, which may serve, at most, to hold life together for a few weeks, the rich man has done his duty, and passes on to his business or his pleasures. The poor victim of society, too, passes on, to toil, starve, and die—forgotten. Not so with the black (acknowledged) slave. In his case, individual responsibility cannot thus fling itself off upon society. "*Thou art*

8. Richard Cameron (1648–80), Scottish preacher, killed after renouncing allegiance to Charles II in 1680, was leader of a group of dissenters called Cameronians or Reformed Presbyterians. Although called after Bishop Athanasius of Alexandria (c. 293–373), the Athanasian Creed, adopted as part of the service of the Church of England, was not formulated until the sixth century.

the man."[9] And public opinion, with its raised finger of scorn, combines with conscience to shame the cruel or negligent master. Yes—marvelous as, to many, the statement may appear—the slaveowner (acknowledged) has, very generally, a conscience, which, combining with the kindliness of feeling resulting from propinquity, produces a strong tie between master and slave, unknown and, to judge from his speech and actions, utterly inconceivable to the slaveowner (*de facto*)—the white slave driver. We love our negroes. They form to us a more extended bond for human sympathies. We love our negroes: not as a miser loves his gold, but rather as a father loves his children. The tie, if not so close, is still of the same kind. As a larger family, associated in the same home interests, the same hopes and the same fears, they are *of us*—a part of ourselves. The grey-haired negro, who watches with pride the growth of his baby-master, exulting in his lordly air and glorying, more perhaps even than the parent, in the progress of that young thing, the object of so many hopes and fears—does he find no tender point in that parent's heart, which extends its sympathies to the faithful negro, his children, and his grandchildren? That toddling boy, so watched and cared for, has he no soul to return, with growing years and expanded feelings, the affections of negro as well as parent? Thank God! the slaveholder is (spite of slander and reviling) still a man, and often, perhaps, a kinder, gentler, truer man, because, with so many to look up to him, so many to help and to be helped, so many to guide, his nature has educated itself to sympathy and kindness; he has learned in the school of experience, not theory, that "he prayeth well, who loveth well."

> He prayeth best, who loveth best,
> All things, both great and small;
> For the dear God that loveth us,
> He made and loveth all.[10]

The lesson is forced upon him. He dare not turn away from suffering, and say, "Go to the poor-house," "Go to the authorities," "to the relieving officer," "the medical officer." He *dare* not—for the sorrow is his, the sickness is his. It is no merit to him that he heeds and soothes them. Society would mark him as a nuisance, if his sick or starving negro were driven forth, to seek charity from others. He dare not refuse. No merit, then, to *him*, because he relieves; but much merit to *the system* which thus puts a check upon individual selfishness and, while it relieves the sufferer, softens and raises the

9. 2 Sam. 12:7.

10. Samuel Taylor Coleridge, "The Rime of the Ancient Mariner," ll. 612, 614–17; reading "the dear God who loveth us."

heart of him who relieves. Public paupers, "street folks," are unknown to such a system. The charity of alms and of poor-rates is unneeded, while every day calls for the exercise of that higher charity, which "suffereth long and is kind," and without which, "though I bestow all my goods to feed the poor, . . . it profiteth me nothing."[11]

In contrasting the situation of the white and black slave, we mean no attack upon those institutions where the larger evil, as we consider it (white slavery), exists. The evils caused by governmental blunders and mistaken policy are usually the work of ages, deep-seated, and requiring much time and prudence to correct. Too often the gangrened sore, which is beyond all hope of remedy other than a patient trusting to the powers of nature, is increased to agony by officious but kind-hearted interference, equivalent in efficacy to an old woman's "yarb-teas" and bark-plasters, prescribed for a sick heart. Such communities are indeed sick at heart, and can only, in their own patient efforts, find a chance of cure. There is a God above us, and He it is who sends the earthquake as well as the sunshine, the tornado as well as the zephyr, evil as well as good. He has made the white man for *his* place, the negro for *his.* The white man, with his larger brain, and more highly developed faculties, is unfit for the position of the negro—could never be suited to it—and therefore, in contrasting the condition of these differing classes, we only show the contrast: we defend our institutions, without ill-will to others. Alton Locke, speaking of an assembly of proletarians (white slaves), remarks: "We, for our part, shall not be ashamed to show foreheads against your laughing House of Commons—and [then] say, what employment can such <those> men find, in the soulless routine of mechanical labour, for the mass of brain which they almost universally possess?" [92] Our black slave is not troubled in this way. Admirably suited to his position, he is happy in it, if only let alone.

In turning over the pages of *Alton Locke,* we may everywhere find the most vivid descriptions of wretchedness, and scenes where, to use old Mackaye's words, "all around ye, in every ginshop and costermonger's cellar, are God and Satan at death-grips" [101]. Human nature, struggling in the lowest degradation and, only in its almost extinguished glimpses of humanity and god-like energies, not sinking to bestiality—truly, indeed, "God and Satan at death-grips!"

> It was a foul, chilly, foggy Saturday night. From the butchers' and green-grocers' shops the gas-lights flared and flickered, wild and ghastly, over haggard groups of slipshod, dirty women, bargaining for scraps of stale meat

11. 1 Cor. 13:3–4.

> and frostbitten vegetables, wrangling about short weight and bad quality. Fish-stalls and fruit-stalls lined the edge of the greasy pavement, sending up odours as foul as the language of sellers and buyers. Blood and sewer water crawled from under doors and out of spouts, and reeked down the gutters, among offal, animal and vegetable, in every stage of putrefaction. Foul vapours rose from cowsheds and slaughterhouses, and the doorways of undrained alleys, where the inhabitants carried the filth [out] on their shoes from the back-yard into the court, and from the court up into the main street; while above, hanging like cliffs over the streets—those narrow, brawling torrents of filth, and poverty, and sin—the houses with their teeming load of life were piled up into the dingy, choky night. A ghastly, deafening, sickening sight it was. [95]
>
> We went on through a back street or two, and then into a huge, miserable house, which, a hundred years ago, perhaps, had witnessed the luxury and rung to the laughter of some one great fashionable family, alone there in its glory. Now every room of it held its family, or its group of families—a phalanstery of all the fiends—its grand staircase, with the carved balustrades rotting and crumbling away piecemeal, converted into a common sewer for all its inmates. Up stair after stair we went, while wails of women, and curses of men, steamed out upon the hot stifling gush of air from every doorway, till, at the topmost story, we knocked at a garret door. We entered. Bare it was of furniture, comfortless, and freezing with cold <freezing cold>; but, with the exception of the plaster dropping from the roof, and the broken windows, patched with rags and paper, there was a scrupulous neatness about the whole, which contrasted strangely with the filth and slovenliness outside. There was no bed in the room—no table. On a broken chair by the window sat a miserable old woman, fancying that she was warming her hands over embers which had long been cold, shaking her head, and muttering to herself, with palsied lips, about the guardians and the work-house; while upon a few rags on the floor lay a girl, ugly, small-pox marked, hollow-eyed, emaciated, her only bedclothes the skirt of a large, handsome, new riding-habit, at which two other girls, wan and tawdry, were stitching busily, as they sat right and left of her upon <on> the floor. The old woman took no notice of us as we entered; but one of the girls looked up, and, with a pleased gesture of recognition, put her finger [up] to her lips, and whispered "Ellen's asleep." [97]

The two poor girls were not only working their fingers to the bone, but—far worse—"that other <ither>," as old Mackaye exclaims, "prostituting hersel' to buy food for her freen. Is there no <na> poetry there?" [101] Aye, and tragedy too. "Look, there's not a soul down that yard but's either beggar, drunkard, thief, or warse! [95] . . . Drunkards frae the breast! harlots frae the cradle! damned before they're born! John Calvin had an inkling o' the truth there, I'm a'most driven to think, wi' his reprobation deevil's doctrines." [96]

What man can read these, taken at random from amidst scores of similar passages, with which this work abounds, and compare the condition of such freemen(?) with that of the negro slave of these United States? And these scenes are not peculiar to England. Our Northern cities, in their filthy crowded cellars and dirty lanes, show scenes which may begin to compete with them. We have meetings of distressed needle-women in New-York, as well as London. Would to God that restless philanthropists, on both sides of the water, would learn to look at home for suffering brethren and sisters—to open their eyes upon the misery nearest them—to give bread to the hungry, comfort to the sick—rather than squander their means and sympathies, they know not where or upon what. "What do ye ken about <anent> the Pacific?" [96] asks old Mackaye of the young aspirant in poetry who has been exercising his imagination in some faraway scenes. What, we would ask of our abolitionist versifiers, what do you know about our slaves? "Which is maist to your business?—the <thae> bare-backed hizzies that play the harlot o' the other side o' the warld, or these—these thousands o' bare-backed hizzies that play the harlot o' your ain side, made out o' your ain flesh and blude? You a poet! True poetry, like true charity, my laddie, begins at hame." [96]

Our quotations[12] would grow to a volume, were we to endeavour to transcribe one-fourth of those which make us shudder in the reading. We have no room for the horrible descriptions of the "sweaters' dens,"[13] with their hollow-eyed, sallow, starved, and naked ghosts of humanity, who, until death relieves them, find no release from "the bond" which their misery signed in entering. *Free-men! Slaves!* Ha! ha! verily the English language would seem to need a new dictionary. We have no room for the scenes of agricultural wretchedness, with their "crowds of wan and haggard faces, lacklustre eyes and drooping lips, stooping shoulders, heavy dragging steps, and crushed, dogged air."[14]

One picture more:

> [And what] a room! A low lean-to with wooden walls, without a single article of furniture; and through the broad chinks of the floor shone up, as it

12. "Questions" in original.

13. "The Sweater's Den," title of chap. 21 of *Alton Locke*.

14. *Alton Locke,* p. 251: "As we pushed through the crowd, I was struck with the wan, haggard look of all faces; their lacklustre eyes and drooping lips, stooping shoulders, heavy, dragging steps, gave them a crushed, dogged air."

were, ugly glaring eyes, staring at us. They were the reflections of the rush-light, in the sewer below. The stench was frightful, the air heavy with pestilence. The first breath I drew made my heart sick <sink>, and my stomach turn. But I forgot everything in the object that <which> lay before me, as Downes tore a half-finished coat off three corpses, laid side by side on the bare floor.

There was his little Irish wife—dead—and naked. The wasted white limbs gleamed in the lurid light; the unclosed eyes stared, as if reproachfully, at the husband whose drunkenness had brought her there to kill her with the pestilence; and, on each side of her, a little, shrivelled, impish child-corpse. The wretched man had laid their arms round the dead mother's neck.[15] The rats had been busy with them already <already with them>—but what matter to them now?

"Look!" he cried, "I have watched 'em dying! Day after day I saw the devils come up through the cracks, like [little] maggots and beetles, and all manner of ugly things, creeping down their throats; and I asked 'em, and they said they were the fever devils."

It was too true; the poisonous exhalations had killed them. The wretched man's delirium tremens had given that horrible substantiality to the poisonous fever gases.

. . . "If you had taken my advice, my poor fellow," I said <went on>, [. . .] "and become a water-drinker[, like me—]"

"Curse you and your water-drinking! If you had had no water to drink or wash [with], for two years, but that—that," pointing to the foul ditch below; "if you had emptied your <the> slops in there with one hand, and filled your kettle with the other. . . . Drink? and who can help drinking, with his stomach turned with such a hell-broth <such hell-broth> as that—or such a hell blast as this air is here, ready to vomit from morning to night with the smells?"

. . . Ugh! it was the very mouth of hell, that room! [317–19]

Great God! and in this very town of London there are men who turn from such scenes, to preach a crusade against negro slavery! Is it ignorance? Is it satanic malevolence? What devil-born propensity can it be, which would drag our inoffensive negro down to this? And for what? That his master may be ruined in his downfall, and one flood of barbarism desolate this beautiful portion of God's earth. This portion? Is it *this portion* that alone would suffer? Can the Southern States of this Union fall alone? Must not our Northern sisters, now blinded by party violence, led astray by unprincipled demagogues and fanatical enthusiasts, must they not too sup of the bitter potion?

15. Omitted here (without notice): "and there they slept, their hungering and wailing over at last for ever."

Can they survive our fall? Can England, with all her pride of might and power, survive us? The restless, wretched population, with which, in all her glory, still she swarms, would not, certainly, be bettered or quieted by the cessation of her cotton supply. Who can calculate the effects of such a cessation? A tenfold accumulation of wretchedness, and certain revolution, would be its first effect upon England. What upon the world? Our limited sight fails to penetrate the chaos which would be the inevitable result. The cloudy future stands before us, a terrible uncertainty of horrors, and, like the mystery of some fearful dream, frights us the more from its undefined magnitude:

Without me and within me; not imagined—felt.[16]

This only sure—the accumulated civilization of eighteen centuries must fall, and one sweep of barbarism cast back the world to the blind struggle, in which physical force is the only might, and the strong arm the only law. It may be said that God, in his wisdom, sees fit to sweep the moral world with something similar to those cataclysms which have operated his great crises in the physical. As one race of beings has followed upon the destruction of another, thus our civilization, religion, existence, must, perhaps, give way to some hidden rule, some mystery of mind, which must sweep us into utter annihilation, ere itself can struggle into being. It may be thus; for thus, only, can we explain to ourselves the fearful progress of the annihilating principle which advances upon us. Destruction hangs over us, like the sword of Damocles, suspended by a single hair; and yet we look at it, and laugh, and play with the fatal point, whose fearful vibrations threaten, with every instant, to bring down upon us our doom. Negro emancipation would be inevitably the death-blow of our civilization. By *ours,* we mean not ours of Georgia, Alabama, Mississippi, or Carolina—nay, nor of these Southern United States—nay, nor of this whole great empire, this young giant, whose infant strength startles its European forefathers with its newborn might; but *ours*—our civilization of this world of the nineteenth century, *must fall* with negro emancipation.

Who, in the hue and cry of abolition, remembers (it were well for each to condescend to remember) that the weapon they are sharpening against the slaveholder must cut both ways? Ruin is the no more certain result of their course to us than to themselves. But a game is playing for a premiership or a presidency, and to cast some weight—to load his die—the unprincipled politician joins with the fanatic and, glorying in a majority of votes, or a casting of his opponent, rushes on blindfold, neither knowing nor caring, in his selfish triumph, for the terrible results, which *his day* may not see quite

16. *Cymbeline* 4.2.306–07: "The dream's here still: even when I wake it is / Without me, as within me: not imagin'd, felt."

accomplished. Prater of frothy patriotism and philanthropy, but really dead to both of these virtues, he carries his point, and is happy, so far as triumph can make him so.

Another work, which we have not seen, *London Labour and the London Poor,* by Dr. Mayhew,[17] presents, we understand, a similarly harrowing collection (with the one which we now have under review) of the statistics of wretchedness. Of "street-folk," who pick up their livelihood from charity and accident, in the city of London, coster-mongers, bone-grubbers, old clothes men, etc., there are, according to his computation, no less than 50,000. These are, in habits and morals, of the lowest order of humanity—ready-made communists, as we read them, without the assistance of Louis Blanc and Co.—a population as inferior in decency, comforts, and usefulness, to our negro population, as they are superior to them in race and natural capabilities. By what strange anomaly in reasoning can the illogical conclusion be drawn, that a system so degrading to the white man could possibly raise the black?

It is scarcely now a subject of dispute, that the black man is of inferior race to the white. Five thousand years of captivity, slavery, and barbarism prove him incapable of civilization. Could any imaginable circumstances crush down, for that space of time, into such perfect stagnation, any people capable of improvement? In his natural home, Central Africa, what has existed to prevent his progress? Nothing, but natural incapacity. He has enjoyed, equally with the white races which have raised themselves to civilization, the undisturbed advantages of all the intellect which God Almighty has seen fit to bestow upon him. The white man, by his nature, has sought and found improvement. The negro, by *his nature,* has crouched contented, in the lowest barbarism. Only under the guidance of the white man has he, with a kind of monkey imitativeness, sometimes followed, to a very limited extent, the white civilization, seizing often its follies, but never its higher points of development. Soulouque can order his coronation gear from Paris; but therein consists his closest imitation of his white models.[18]

17. Henry Mayhew (1812–87), English journalist; a founder and coeditor of *Punch* (1841–43); wrote farce *The Wandering Minstrel* (1834), tales, and *London Labour and the London Poor* (1851–62).

18. Faustin-Elie Soulouque (1782?–1867), born a slave in Haiti; active in revolt against the French (1803); elected president of Haiti (1847); proclaimed himself emperor as Faustin I (1849); deposed (1859), fled into exile. "Even now, Soulouque, the fantastic savage that Mr. Walsh describes in his correspondence with Mr. Webster, compels the negroes to work to buy vulgar finery to cover his majesty's dusky person" (David James McCord, "Practical Effects of Emancipation," *De Bow* 18 [April and May 1855]: 474–96, 591–602; 597). LSM cites from Robert Moylan Walsh's correspondence with Daniel Webster in chap. 10, "British Philanthropy and American Slavery."

Negro-like and ape-like, enveloped in slavery, he is satisfied with his height of greatness, and quite indifferent as to whether his subjects regale themselves with a cannibal feast of roasted Dominicans, or ride naked about his dominions, in palm hats and golden spurs (two amusements to which, we are informed, they are occasionally addicted), or occupy themselves in any similarly innocent and enlightened manner. Oh! there are things so fearful in their folly, terrific and yet comically mad, we laugh even while we shudder, in the gazing. "There is nothing more frightful than active ignorance." A Grace Greenwood, a Whittier, an Abby Folsom, a Thomson, a Sumner, or a Garrison, may, in their ignorant fanaticism, set the world on fire.[19] They play with sheathed lightnings, careless at what moment these may burst from their confinement to light the funeral pile of all that is good and great upon our earth. To point a stanza or a paragraph, they rouse nations to madness. Too late, in the sweeping desolation which must follow, will they see the evil of their ways. The curse of Timon upon Athens but faintly paints what the world must see exemplified in the horrible results of their mad and ignorant interference, should it, in God's wrath against our world, prove successful. Almost in plain words do they give the shameful counsel:

Matrons, turn incontinent!
Obedience fail in children! Slaves and fools,
Pluck the grave wrinkled senate from the bench,
And minister in their stead[s]! To general filths
Convert, o' th' instant, green virginity!
[Do 't in your parents' eyes!] Bankrupts, hold fast!
Rather than render back, out with your knives,
And cut your trusters' throats! Bound servants, steal!
Large-handed robbers your grave masters are,
And pill by law. Maid, to thy master's bed;
Thy mistress is o' th' brothel! Son of sixteen,

19. Grace Greenwood, pseudonym of Sara Jane Clarke Lippincott (1823–1904), journalist; regular contributor to the antislavery *National Era*. John Greenleaf Whittier (1807–92), poet, Quaker, abolitionist. Abby Folsom (c. 1792–1867), English-born abolitionist; indefatigable speaker at meetings of the American Anti-Slavery Society; called by Ralph Waldo Emerson "that flea of conventions." Edward Thomson (1810–70), bishop of the Methodist Episcopal church; first president of Ohio Wesleyan University; antislavery advocate in the *Ladies' Repository* (editor 1844–46) and other journals. Charles Sumner (1811–74), U.S. senator from Massachusetts (from 1851); antislavery advocate in Congress. William Lloyd Garrison (1814–79), a founder of the American Anti-Slavery Society (1831), its president (1843–65); published leading antislavery journal the *Liberator* (1831–65).

Pluck the lin'd crutch from thy old limping sire;
With it beat out his brains! Pity and fear,
Religion to the gods, peace, justice, truth,
Domestic awe, night-rest, and neighbourhood,
Instruction, manners, mysteries, and trades,
Degrees, observances, customs, and laws,
Decline to your confounding contraries;
And let confusion live![20]

All this, and worse (if worse can be) is included in their system of negro emancipation—for negro emancipation is the emancipation of brute force. Necessarily, upon it would follow, in those regions where the negro race outnumbers its masters, a barbarism tenfold worse than Gothic or Vandal. Upon that, again, inevitably follows the extinction of the cotton crop; and upon the extinction of the cotton crop—certain and uncontrollable as fate—the extinction of civilization.

If such be the Almighty fiat—if only from the chaos which must ensue from such a wreck God will deign to execute his designs for this world—we are indeed pigmies in his hands, and must bow to the overwhelming destiny. But need we, in our blindness, work out our own destruction? A higher fate may be our destiny. The glorious mind of man—of the white man—which, in meridian vigour, now leaps forward to the grandest scientific discoveries, and throws open, almost daily, some new mystery of nature, may pause in its career, and hesitate to crush into oblivion the beautiful result of its own great works. God, in his mercy, grant that it may, and

What in us is dark,
Illumine; what is low, raise and support;
That to the height of this great argument
We may assert Eternal Providence,
And justify the ways of God to men.[21]

Pending the fearful doubt, we stand "even as men wrecked upon the sands, that look with the next tide to be washed off,"[22] and the world totters

Upon the very brink of gaping ruin.[23]

20. *Timon of Athens* 4.1.3–21.

21. *Paradise Lost* 1.22–26, reading "what in me is dark" and "I may assert."

22. *Henry V* 4.1.97–98: "Even as men wracked upon a sand, that look to be washed off the next tide."

23. Edward Young, *The Revenge* (1721), 4.1.13–14: "O forbear! / You totter on the very brink of ruin."

"Time was!" "Time is!"[24] But play the laggard yet a little longer; and yet a little longer—on the verge of this so frightful steep, sit dallying with our doubts—then comes the end:

Of comfort no man speak.
We'll talk of graves, of worms, and epitaphs,
Make dust our paper, and with rainy eyes
Write sorrow on the bosom of the earth.
We'll choose executors and talk of wills.
And yet, not so—for what can we bequeath,
Save our deposèd bodies to the ground? [. . .]
And nothing we can call our own but death.[25]

L. S. M.

24. Robert Greene, *Friar Bacon and Friar Bungay* (c. 1589), scene 11, in *Elizabethan Drama: Eight Plays,* ed. John Gassner and William Green, rev. ed. (New York, 1990), pp. 216–17: "*The Brazen Head.* Time is! . . . Time was! . . . Time is past! . . . / *Friar Bacon.* 'Tis past indeed. Ah villain! time is past: / My life, my fame, my glory, all are past."

25. *Richard II* 3.2.144–50, 152; reading "Let's choose executors" and "nothing can we call our own but death."

7.

Separate Secession

Separate secession! Terror thrills us at the thought. Ay, though fiery and rampant valour may hiss disgrace at a word so inconsistent with the fashion and spirit of the day, yet must we confess, terror thrills us at the idea of a course so suited, we solemnly believe, to crush our dearest hopes for liberty, and plunge into anarchy, ruin, and slavish bondage all that is nearest and dearest to us. If any step be well calculated to retard the hopes of the South, making us the patient hewers of wood and drawers of water for our Northern aggressors, we believe it to be this well-meant, but mistaken expedient. We have no love for the Union; we have no fear of its dissolution. Welcome as summer shower to the sun-parched earth—welcome as heaven's free air to the heart-sick tenant of a dungeon—would come to us the voice of freedom, the word, the deed, which would tend to burst our bonds and, in earnest faith, contribute to the disruption of this proud fabric (once beautiful, but now rotten to the core) which, under the name of Union, threatens to crush us beneath its unholy power. As *God* is true, we believe that we speak truth when we say that there is no risk of life or property that we

SQR, n.s., 4 (Oct. 1851): 298–317. Publication reviewed: *Proceedings of the Meeting of Delegates from the Southern Rights Associations of South Carolina* [subheading: "held at Charleston, May, 1851"] (Columbia, S.C.: Johnston and Cavis, 1851). A convention of the Southern Rights Associations of South Carolina met on May 5, 1851, in Charleston's Military Hall and on May 8 voted its approval of proposals to the effect that South Carolina should secede from the Union "whether with or without the co-operation of other Southern States" (ibid., p. 20).

would shrink from, in the accomplishment of so desirable an end; for, albeit most certainly a noncombatant, in every legal and customary application of the word, we believe that we, too, could be roused, if need were, to give our mite of strength, in a struggle for hearth and home. Our little mock-bird (Carolina's nightingale) will, at the risk and sacrifice of life, fight for its nest, against odds the most fearful! Is there a heart in Carolina less bold than that of our poor fluttering song bird? But where hearth and home, child and country, are to be heedlessly thrown into the balance, against a vaunting spirit, a headlong rashness, which mocks the counsels of our wisest and our best, methinks the *God* of battles is against us, and terror is not too strong a word, when we contemplate the countless woes, the fathomless abyss of ills, which may ensue.

In all revolutions, impulse is undoubtedly the motive cause, with the masses; but thinking men, who act by reason, and well-weighed, long-considered, deeply-studied motives, must—unless *God* has marked out a people for destruction—sway and direct that impulse to its proper course. If, then, the voice of the convention of delegates held in Charleston, in the beginning of May last, were indeed the voice of the State, it would present a fearful crisis in our history. *Quem Deus vult perdere, prius dementat.*[1] Has *God* made us cast aside all the counsels of wisdom, that he may thus crush us under the weight of our own madness? We trust not; we believe not. The voice of the convention of May was *not* the voice of the State; its members were *not* the delegates of the State; they were the delegates of certain associations of the State, useful in their way, no doubt, but who have gone a step too far, who have assumed too much, in the course which they have pursued. Violent, enthusiastic (we speak, of course, of the majority, whose voice has alone been heard), actuated by the best motives, but misled by impulse—impatient and sore under insufferable oppression, but excited by the heat of unripe counsels—they have thought, by this display of passion, to bind the State to a course which *they* believe the safest for her interests, and to thus influence the action of her proposed State convention.[2] This unauthorized step is calcu-

1. "Whom God wishes to destroy, he first makes mad." Unattributed Latin motto.

2. A convention was called (June 3–12 and Nov. 11–18, 1850) at Nashville, Tenn., to discuss Southern grievances arising, for the most part, from Northern attempts to prohibit slavery in the territories acquired after the Mexican War (1846–48). At the end of the Nashville Convention's meeting in November a call was issued for a congress of slaveholding states to be held, at which resistance and possible independence might be considered. On Dec. 20, 1850, the legislature of South Carolina passed a bill endorsing a Southern congress, setting Oct. 13 and 14, 1851, as dates for the election of delegates to this congress, and providing for a constituent convention (to which LSM here refers) in South Carolina; the legislature also elected four delegates-at-large to the proposed congress, among them Langdon Cheves.

lated to do much harm. Efforts to have it accredited, as an act of the State, have, to a considerable extent, been but too successful, both at home and abroad. Our object is, before going farther, to show the fallacy of such an impression.

The intrinsic nature of the elective bodies to this convention ought, perhaps, to be sufficient to convince us of such a fallacy. District associations, got up by individuals, are, necessarily, from their very qualities of being, most regularly attended by their more active and violent members. Sober and orderly men, however patriotic, are apt to tire of such meetings, which, although they may be occasionally useful in keeping up the flagging spirit of the people, or bringing the doubtful to the mark, will be found too often to degenerate in their tendency (like the revolutionary clubs of France) into a factious disposition to mob-rule.

We mean no slur upon the high-spirited people of our gallant and noble State;[3] but such is the general tendency of all similar associations. They fall, necessarily, into the hands, and under the management, of the restless and violent, and are thus, even in a good cause, liable to rush into dangerous extremes. Not only, then, were the elections, in each district, made by this portion, alone, of its citizens; but from the very irregular numbers of the delegates we easily perceive that each district, or rather, each district association, was represented without regard to the population, property, or representative force of such respective districts. Lancaster, with a legislative representation of *two,* and a population of 5,794 free, and 5,014 slave, sent *nineteen* delegates; while Laurens, with a similar legislative representation, and a population of 11,453 free, and 11,953 slave, sent *seven.* Georgetown (comprised in parishes of All Saints and Prince George, Winyah) and Greenville, with each a legislative representation of *four,* sent, respectively, *eight* and *nine* delegates; while Richland and Barnwell, with each a similar legislative representation, sent, respectively, *twenty-seven* and *thirty-three.* Marion, Orangeburgh, and Fairfield have each a legislative representation of *three.* The population of Marion is 9,888 free and 7,720 slave; of Orangeburgh, 8,199 free and 15,425 slave; of Fairfield, 7,164 free and 14,246 slave. The delegates of Marion to the convention of May were *three,* from Orangeburgh, *twenty-one,* and from Fairfield, *thirty-five*!! Pickens had *one* delegate, for a population of 13,228 free and 3,679 slave. Besides sundry of the parishes, as St. James, Goose Creek, St. James, Santee, St. Thomas and St. Denis, St. George, Dorchester, St. Pauls and St. Lukes, we find not only the whole district of Horry, with a population of 5,824 free and 2,082 slave,

3. The nature of our article compels us to write, more than is desirable for a *Southern* Quarterly, in the limited view of South Carolinian rather than under the wider designation of Southron. [LSM]

entirely unrepresented, but the populous district of Spartanburgh, whose inhabitants number 18,358 free and 8,038 slave, entitled to a legislative representation of *five* (almost double that of Fairfield, which sent *thirty-five* delegates), stands in the same category—not one voice from Spartanburgh. Will any man who can add two and two together contend, for one instant, that such an assembly has the shadow of a right to speak for the State, or can, in the smallest degree, bind or compromise her by the expression of its opinions? On the contrary, ought not its bold action and spirit of dictation to startle us into prudent watchfulness? These men mean well, perhaps. The majority of them, no doubt, do. But so, we are told by veracious historians, did Robespierre. A good man was Robespierre, a kind-hearted man, say these, and *he thought* he was doing the best for his country, when he was bringing upon her a "desolation of desolations," for there was death, "and hell followed with him."[4] He was her guide and protector. *God* shield us from such self-constituted guides and protectors!

But permit us here to ask, what was the power of a Robespierre or a Danton,[5] other than the gift of such clubs as these very associations which formed the convention we are discussing? They were but the agents of a similar power, pushed to a further extreme. Let us here, once for all, disclaim any wish to cast the taint or shadow of a doubt upon the sincerity of men whose zeal, alone, we regard as their stumbling-block. They love their State, but *qui amat non semper amicus est.*[6] Their love is death. Robespierre and Couthon,[7] at the height of their assumed power, *thought themselves right,* and acted for the weal of their country. It is somewhat startling to find that our convention intends not to resign the power (whatever it may be) that it swayed in May last. Its members have declared themselves a permanent body, "*preserving its organization, under the same officers.*" We have seen how, and by whom, these officers have been elected. They have appointed a "Central Committee," to "promote the [common] cause," and thus govern the State; and they have pronounced that all future members shall be elected—not by the people—but by district associations, and by *district associations* ALONE![8]

4. Rev. 6:8.

5. Georges-Jacques Danton (1759–94), French revolutionary politician; president of the Jacobin Club; member of the Committee of Public Safety; arrested by his rival Robespierre; guillotined.

6. Seneca *Epistulae morales (Moral Letters)* 35.1: "Qui amicus est amat; qui amat non utique amicus est." "Who is a friend, loves; who loves, is not always a friend."

7. Georges Couthon (1755–94), French revolutionary politician; member of the Committee of Public Safety; supplied legal foundation to the Reign of Terror; guillotined with Robespierre.

8. *Proceedings of the Southern Rights Associations,* p. 21 (LSM's italics).

Carolinians, are you awake? Will you sanction the proceedings of such a body, as the *proceedings of the State*? Will you take the voice of unruly faction for the voice of the people? Heaven save us from ourselves, if *this* be Southern patriotism! But it cannot be. When faction speaks, let it speak in its own name, nor pass its dictates for the fiat of a people.

We are glad to believe that the convention, formed and elected as we have above shown, was, even under such circumstances, by no means so unanimous as we are led to suppose from printed accounts. Five and six dissentient voices, even to the most objectionable of its resolutions, is the report we receive; but, in the triumph expressed concerning this most astonishing unanimity, we are not told, but are left, from accident, to gather the fact, that many of the more moderate members, who were members elect to the State convention, abstained, upon principle, from a vote, which was calculated to compromise them, and to shackle their action, as servants of the State.[9] Hon. Mr. Butler, in his speech before the convention, remarks: "The measures intimated in the draft of the address, and in some of the resolutions, will not allow many of this convention to vote upon them. All who are members of the constitutional convention of the people cannot give a vote to control their future judgment. They ought not to be required to do so. I have conversed with several of them, and they have come to a common conclusion: to give no vote upon any matter upon which they will have to deliberate when there shall be a real occasion for their officially responsible judgment."[10]

Here, then, we are brought to a stand. We see the graver men, even of this meeting, not only shrinking from the violence of its course, but advising, imploring, headstrong valour, to check itself by prudence, and heed "the pauser, Reason."[11] Alas!

But older men are monitors too dull
For passionate youth.

And in

That season when the fancy is a god,
Hope a conviction,

9. We are informed, upon the best authority, that this meeting refused to allow the yeas and nays to be called. [LSM]

10. Andrew Pickens Butler (1796–1857), U.S. senator from South Carolina (1846–57), spoke at the morning session on May 7. His speech is printed in the Charleston *Mercury,* May 17, 1851.

11. *Macbeth* 2.3.109.

wild work may be made upon unwary faith by the spirit of party, faction, and demagoguism. Cassandra-like rise the warnings of our long-tried counsellors. *Young* Carolina heeds them not. The opinions of men whom the State delighted to honour are trampled upon, as not worth the hearing. The eloquent appeals, the labored reasonings, of a Barnwell[12] or a Butler are cast aside, for the passionate declamations of some new Camille Desmoulins.[13] The opinion of the venerable Cheves, in whom

> old experience doth attain
> To something like prophetic strain;[14]

whose voice, at Nashville, startled the country, and half roused the South from its lethargy,[15] meets with less respect than that of the noisiest gabbler of "drawn swords and bloody bones" whom the convention could produce.[16]

Scarcely had his last words of warning been spoken (we will not say listened to),[17] when the chairman "from the Select Committee of Twenty-one" submitted *his* resolutions and address, evidently cut and dried for the occasion.[18] There was little intention to make the meeting a deliberative

12. Robert Woodward Barnwell (1801–82), born in Beaufort, S.C.; president of South Carolina College (1835–41); delegate to the Nashville Convention, where he advocated cooperative secession; a commissioner sent to negotiate with President James Buchanan after South Carolina's secession in December 1860; member of the Confederate Senate. Barnwell spoke at the afternoon session on May 7. His speech (not a strict transcription but, as Barnwell's headnote states, recalled imperfectly from memory and recast) is printed in the Charleston *Mercury,* May 27, 1851.

13. Camille Desmoulins (1760–94), French revolutionary politician, pamphleteer, and journalist; Danton's secretary in ministry of justice; guillotined with him.

14. John Milton, *Il Penseroso,* ll. 173–74.

15. Langdon Cheves was chosen as delegate to the Nashville Convention by a caucus of the legislature of South Carolina. At the November session he delivered a speech of nearly three hours, recommending the secession of a united South; the speech was immediately published as a pamphlet, a second edition in 1851. Andrew Pickens Butler, in the speech from which LSM quotes above, also referred to her father as "the venerable Cheves."

16. Samuel Butler, *Hudibras* 3.2.677–82: "For Zeal's a dreadful Termagant, / That teaches Saints to Tear, and Rant; / And Independents, to profess / The Doctrine, of Dependences; / Turns meek and sneaking Secret ones, / To Raw-heads fierce, and Bloody Bones." Raw-head and Bloody Bones were bugbears used by nurses to frighten children.

17. We know that an afterthought sought to cover the appearance of want of respect, and that the letter, to which a reading was first refused, was afterwards voted to be printed; but the facts are as we state them. [LSM] Cheves, although elected a delegate from Charleston to the May meeting of South Carolina's Southern Rights Associations, did not attend but sent a letter containing his views opposing separate secession; the letter, which was read out to the convention at its afternoon session on May 6, is printed in *Proceedings of the Southern Rights Associations,* pp. 8–12; also in the Charleston *Mercury,* May 7, 1851.

18. *Proceedings of the Southern Rights Associations,* pp. 12–17.

assembly, for it is scarcely possible to suppose that the committee of twenty-one, whatever the genius and talent of its members, had taken sufficient time, since its nomination, to compose so important an address, and mature such momentous resolutions, when we remember that its nomination had only been on the morning of the same day. The committee, or at least the acting portion of it, had very evidently decided itself a committee, and determined its measures, before the assemblage even of the convention. Such is universally the action of clubs and club-meetings. They are never governed but by caucus and demagoguism. Let, then, the action of this convention be taken for what it is worth, i.e., for the action of certain associations, who have most undoubtedly a right to the expression of their own opinions; but none, whatever, to endeavour to give to those opinions the impression of State action. Few as there are of submissionists and Union men in our State, still there is, even of these Yankeeized Southrons, some small sprinkling to be found. These men might, with equal propriety as the convention to which we refer, gather themselves together, as district delegates, pass their resolutions, write their addresses, and claim to be exponents of the spirit of South Carolina. Difference of numbers would make no difference in legality of action. Both of these meetings are, or rather would be, the representatives only of party, and both would be, we regret to say, in our opinion, equally mischievous, could they succeed in giving to their voice the impress of State sovereignty. When the State speaks, let it be through her proper authorities, and with the due solemnity of legalized assemblies, not the party violence of club-meetings. We think it will be a question worth the consideration of our approaching legislature, whether men who have prematurely committed themselves to any decisive mode of action, independently of future events, have not thus incapacitated themselves as members of a grave deliberative body such as our State convention, should it ever assemble, ought to be; and whether it might not be the wisest course of such legislature to abstain from calling the meeting of so important a body, under circumstances which would so much shackle, and contribute to prevent, its discreet and sober action. Faction and party-spirit have worked hard, and done much, since the elections to the proposed convention have been made.[19] To such a meeting, its members ought to come with clean hands and clear heads.

19. Elections for South Carolina's constituent convention were held on Feb. 10 and 11, 1851. Langdon Cheves was head of the Charleston delegation. The Charleston *Mercury* calculated 127 of the 169 delegates elected to be in favor of separate secession. By the time of elections in October for delegates to the proposed Southern congress, however, the opponents of separate secession had rallied; they won decisive victories in twenty of the state's twenty-nine judicial districts and by an aggregate vote of about 25,062 to 17,617. When the constituent convention met, after numerous postponements, on April 26, 1852, Lang-

The present is a crisis of vital importance, not to South Carolina alone, but to the South generally. Indissolubly are we united, for weal or for woe, with our Southern sisters. As Ruth clave unto Naomi, so we to them.[20] Surely, their people should be our people, and their *God* our *God*. One we are in interests, one in hopes, and one in dangers; and one we *must be*—unless the Almighty has frowned upon us his darkest measure of reprobation—one we must be in effort. Surely, so important a consummation is worth years of patience and of striving. Shall we, then, throw away our last chance, in the violent excitement of party dispute, and to maintain the honour of inconsiderate heroism?

We have talked enough—more than enough—of "Palmetto banners," "bleaching bones," and "Southern chivalry." Such boasts have become a bye-word, and a taunt, in the mouths of our opponents. It were well to let them sleep. When a man talks much of his own valour, we are aptest to doubt it, and the truly brave and great need not trumpet their own merits. There is a self-respect to be exercised, as well by communities as individuals; and is there not, in this continual vaunting, an implied disgrace—a doubt, at least, of the spirit of our people, which would thus appear to need such a system, to keep it to the point of action? This "blood and ashes" style of oratory suits only the schoolboy, or the vaunting Bobadil.[21] The continual exercise of it has placed us somewhat in the position of the champion in the Eastern tale who, having it in aim to conquer some magic spell of evil, is suddenly introduced into a capacious and mysterious abode, where are suspended before him a sword and a horn, with an accompanying inscription, importing that victory will fall to him who chooses rightly between these implements. The rash, nervous, and, if we may so express ourselves, *timorous valour* of the would-be hero, induces him to seize the horn; but, as he blows, troops of armed knights rush upon the unfortunate and defenceless wight, felling him to the ground, and leaving the victory to be gained by the wiser and braver champion, whose cool courage and deliberate reason prompt him to *draw the sword* before he blows the horn.

We have boasted too much—quite too much—already. An act of separate secession would be but a continued boasting—a farther blowing of the

---

don Cheves moved that a Committee of Twenty-one be appointed to oversee the convention's business and to draft its report; Cheves was appointed its chairman. The convention approved the committee's two measures, which together asserted South Carolina's right to secede from the Union; no further action was taken. The proposed Southern congress never met.

20. Ruth 1:14.

21. John Milton, "Sonnet 18: On the Late Massacre in Piedmont," l. 10. Captain Bobadill is the boastful soldier in Ben Jonson's *Every Man in His Humour.*

horn. Every reasoning man feels that it would be so, and if he, for a moment, sincerely maintains the contrary, it will be found, we think, to be because he has not fairly weighed and sifted his own words. He advocates separate secession, not because he believes in the efficacy of separate secession *per se,* but only so far (in his own mind, at least) as he regards it as a means of precipitating the course of our sister States, and dragging them into action. The talk about San Marino republics,[22] English alliance, and so forth, is merely a glittering bait, to amuse the crowd—a new way of blowing the horn. We speak of thinking men, for no doubt there are thousands of unfledged lads, whose green reason exudes in boiling wrath and illogical conclusions, who would contend, and believe too, in the sincerity of their enthusiasm, that South Carolina can live and flourish by the mere chivalry of her sons, a Lilliput empire, with the spirit of the world against her and her institutions. But this can never do. As we love the South, as we love our State, as we cherish her institutions, her honour, her very existence, let us cease this trumpeting, nor again blow the horn before we draw the sword—ay, even before we have the sword to draw! Is it the part of valour, or of prudence, thus weaponless to give the taunt, hoping that others may be roused to redeem our pledge?

And will they thus be roused? This is a fearful throw, and the advocates of separate secession are playing a game of brag, too alarming to contemplate with composure. Desperate gamesters, they cast into the stake not only property and life, but children and country—and for what? "*Because the State cannot recede, without dishonour.*" Ay, say they so, these men of valour? Truly, we love our State as devoutly, and shrink from her shame with as nice a sense of honour, as they; but we deny that our honour is engaged, to the breaking of our own necks, by this worse than Curtius-like leap.[23] There has been no oracle, to promise us that this self-devotion shall save our country. On the contrary, the voice of wisdom calls a halt. The State, thank heaven! is *not* pledged to separate action and, we trust in *God,* will not be driven to a measure so suicidal. The State has declared that the South ought to act, and holds herself in readiness to act, according to the pledge given by her best and boldest sons, at Nashville and elsewhere, so soon as she sees opportunity for doing so, without breaking her own neck by a desperate plunge and, at

22. San Marino, a tiny (24 sq. mi.) independent republic, southwest of Rimini, twelve miles from the Adriatic coast, traced its existence back to the fourth century. It maintained its independence by treaty in 1862 with the lately consolidated kingdom of Italy.

23. In his account of the year 362 B.C. the Roman historian Livy records (7.6.1–5) that, a chasm having opened in the Roman Forum, a young soldier named Marcus Curtius, commanded by an oracle, rode fully armed, his horse likewise, into the gulf as a sacrifice to secure the safety of the republic.

the same time, stabbing to the heart, in her blind struggles, the last hope for liberty of her Southern sisters. The State is ready to redeem every pledge she has ever given, and will only fail to do so if driven on by party, which thus coolly assumes her dictatorship. She would prove false to the cause by committing herself to a move so treasonable, as is separate State secession, to Southern interests. By pausing with dignity, in an effort to unite, instead of alienating the South, South Carolina is *not receding;* she takes no step backward but, on the contrary, firmly stands precisely where she did when, at the last session of her legislature, she stood, proud of the counsels of him, her "old man eloquent,"[24] who, confident alike in her boldness and her prudence, brought to her legislative halls the pledge which, in *her* name, he had just given at Nashville, and received the only reward suited to his merit, the hearty "well done, thou good and faithful servant,"[25] echoed by the true representatives of his native State. Has the State changed, since this period? and, while South Carolina holds such a position, resolute and unflinching, has she the traitor-son who will dare accuse her of receding from her pledges? If such there be, let the mother who bore him shrink from his kiss, for would the Judas who defames his country spare even his mother's blush?

"Faithful and true,"[26] South Carolina stands to her pledges. We pause, but we do not recede. The South bids us pause, and she has *a right* so to do. Each and every Southern State has a right to deliberate and investigate, before taking a step so momentous in our history as a disruption of this Union, foul and rotten though it be. We are convinced that disunion is the only remedy for our ills. Gladly would we persuade our Southern sisters to the same belief; but, pending their decision, they have a right to bid us pause. We pause, not to yield, but to maintain our position, while our hosts are gathering. They have never told us that they will desert us; they have never surrendered their arms; and we will win their confidence by admitting that they will not prove recreant to their duty—that they are not slavishly apathetic to their rights. We differ from them in time and expediency of action, but must allow something to their judgment, nor endeavour to gag them with our ideas of right. We will never make a man our friend by calling him a rascal, and giving him a kick to prove it; nor, we believe, will the plan be likely to prove at all more effectual with States than with individuals. The former,

24. John Milton, "Sonnet X: To the Lady Margaret Ley," ll. 6–8. This quotation, referring to the Athenian orator Isocrates (436–338 B.C.), appears also in LSM's defense of her father, "Langdon Cheves: Review of 'Reminiscences of Public Men,'" in *PDBL*.

25. Matt. 25:21.

26. Rev. 22:6.

like the latter, may feel that they have a right to the guardianship of their own honour, and be rather revolted than convinced by the dictatorial *ipse dixit* of another.

One of the arguments of the separate secessionists is, that the State is now ready for action, and it is doubtful whether it will bear delay. They think it necessary to keep up an eternal puffing and blowing, for fear the fire will burn out, and the glowing iron cool. Fie upon it! Is it so hard to keep "our courage to the sticking point"?[27] and cannot we be trusted to keep our honour's truth, but we must, like some poor coward, dragged up to the lists, be held there at the bayonet's point, lest we may turn and run? If such were the spirit of our State, then indeed were it time to bow ourselves in the dust—then indeed is "the glory departed from Israel."[28] Such courage is fear, such fire but cowardice! If our spirit of resistance has not strength to survive prudent delay, it is but a mocking semblance of firmness, and failure becomes certain. But we have a higher opinion of our people. We need not fight today, for fear that, ere tomorrow, our bottled up courage will evaporate, and leave the trembling slave to crouch to the yoke. The firm spirit can "bide its time," and the truly brave among Carolina's statesmen do not fear to trust Carolina's sons.[29] They feel that these are ready for duty when the fitting time shall come, and will not need to be whipped up to the cannon's mouth, as an alternative to a regular *stampede.*

Let us give up the "Hercules' vein,"[30] and confess—for there is no shame in it—that we are not strong enough, we of South Carolina alone, to maintain our cause. We can die! ay, and bury our children beneath the ruins of our hearthstones, that our enemies may triumph and our names be forgotten. But it would be desperation, not courage, which would prompt us to this. True courage can bear and forbear, can wait and watch, and strive and endure. It is impatience, not courage—it is coward shrinking, not resolution—which casts itself upon the sword point to terminate its struggles. The ancient Roman was half a barbarian, when he sought death as a cure for life's evils; a higher civilization—a nobler philosophy—teaches us to *bear* and *conquer* them.

27. *Macbeth* 1.7.60–62 (the speaker is Lady Macbeth): "We fail? / But screw your courage to the sticking-place, / And we'll not fail."

28. 1 Sam. 4:21–22.

29. George Croly, "The Woe upon Israel," in *Scenes from Scripture, with Other Poems* (London, 1851), ll. 35–40: "Israel, where are now thy wise? / Woe to those who live by lies, / Calling (all their souls deceit) / Evil good, and bitter sweet, / Selling justice, pampering crime, / But revenge shall bide its time!"

30. *Midsummer Night's Dream* 1.2.36–37: "This is Ercles' vein, a tyrant's vein: a lover is more condoling."

Because we are weak, our enemies have trampled us. Because we are weak, yet a little longer must we endure their insult. But because we are weak, not therefore are we cowards. Rather is the sense of our wrongs keener, from the sense of our weakness, and, if we pause, we pause that our strength may grow with our endurance. The South *must* unite, and our spring will be the more vigorous and resistless from the gathered might of our temporary crouch. We have much faith in our legislature. We cannot believe that this body, upon the eve of so momentous a step, will move without due consideration. When great events require great minds to work them out to their conclusions, such minds are generally found to rise, as it were, heaven-inspired from the chaotic mass which surrounds them. We trust in *God,* that He has not so shut us out from all hope of mercy that our every beacon-light is to be dashed aside and extinguished by the roar of passion which environs us. We trust in *God,* that the legislature, upon the prudence of whose action so much depends, will (although a majority of its members may be young in years) act like grave men, upon whose decision the destinies of a nation hang, and not like some rabble-rout of school-boys, impatient to rid themselves of the supervision of their preceptors, and who fancy that noisy bragging can be mistaken for heroism. The members of such a body have assumed to themselves, on entering it, heavy duties and responsibilities, well calculated to make men pause in the acting. All their boldness they will need; but should it not be purged from the very shadow of rashness? Men upon whom a nation's fate depends have no longer the right to be young. Deep thought, which sits like dew upon the brow—"for thought is brain-sweat"—should

> From the table of their memory
> All trivial records wipe,
> Leaving the book and volume of the brain
> Unmixed with baser matter.[31]

There is, in the question which we discuss, and the decision of which must virtually fall upon our legislature, matter

> To make the brow to ache, the eye turn dim,
> And resolution search itself for rashness,
> Or ere it dares to plunge.

We have faith in our legislature, and *God* grant that we be not deceived.

The *right* of secession we are not inclined to discuss—we consider it too

31. *Hamlet* 1.5.98–99, 102–4: "Yea, from the table of my memory / I'll wipe away all trivial fond records, . . . / And thy commandment all alone shall live / Within the book and volume of my brain, / Unmix'd with baser matter."

well established to need argument. The *risk* of it, to life, limb, and property, not one who deserves the name of man will shrink from. The *mischievous folly* of separate secession, acting as an alienating medium between ourselves and our true and natural allies, is alone what we fear. If the step be taken, our life for it, you have no truer soldiers than those who now warn you from action. "Our country, right or wrong,"[32] will be the watchword of our State. (Alas! alas! that our own blind precipitancy should oblige us to limit this certainty to *our State,* rather than extend it to *our country,* our *Southern Union,* our home of hope!) If there is to be any "bleaching of bones" upon our battle-fields, the names and families of such men as Cheves, Barnwell, and Butler will have as full a share in the anticipated sacrifice as those of any other more fiery heroes of all the State rights associations in the country. "These men are cautious, fearful; we will not listen to their arguments; this is a time to act, and not to reason," say our hot-headed and unripe counsellors. These men, we answer, *are* cautious, fearful; but of what? Cautious of *self*? Fearful of *personal* risk? If there be tongue of slander vile enough to utter, if there be ear of folly senseless enough to listen to, so vapid a charge, we will not disgrace our pen by referring to it. They are cautious for their country; fearful of *her* perils; and, while their blood boils beneath oppression, they have the courage and self-possession to plead with us: patience, prudence, even for the sake of that cherished country. They have the courage to raise their voices against the stormy cry of faction, to warn that faction against its own rashness. They have the courage of that Aemilius who, at Cannae, after vainly striving to check the hot zeal of an imprudent colleague, when that colleague had, in spite of all remonstrances, made such a disposition of his troops as completely to place himself in the power of the enemy, was yet ready to die nobly, in the desperate struggle, brought on by the headlong rashness of another. While the boastful Varro fled from the slaughter consequent upon his own obstinate folly, Aemilius died upon the field. "My part is chosen," exclaimed the expiring hero when urged to flight. "My part is chosen. Go and tell the Senate, from me, to fortify Rome against the approach of the conqueror."[33] If the State needs victims, she will find, perchance, the firmest not among her noisiest politicians.

32. From a toast given at Norfolk, in April 1816, by Marylander naval hero Stephen Decatur (1779–1820).

33. Lucius Aemilius Paullus and Gaius Terentius Varro, the consuls of 216 B.C., were in personal command of the Roman army when it met the Carthaginian forces, under the command of Hannibal, near the town of Cannae in Apulia. Tradition held that Varro rashly committed his troops to battle without consulting his colleague, who was compelled by events to come to his aid; Paullus, with most of the Roman army, was killed, Varro being among the survivors. LSM follows Livy (22.45–49).

We were at first inclined to believe that the expression of opinions made by the "meeting of delegates of Southern Rights Associations," of May last, was calculated not only to do much, but unmitigated, evil. The rashness and dogmatic assumption of its course (we begin, however, to hope) is bringing its own antidote. Men are startled at the idea of being thus over-ridden; and the warning, we hope, will prove salutary. Leaders of clubs are seldom the best leaders for nations; and a revolution effected by mere animal excitement is inevitably a failure. Revolutions ought not to be made too easily: they are fierce remedies, for fiercer ills, and, when rashly applied, they become, like the knife of the surgeon in the hands of the quack, instruments, not of healing, but of death. Revolutions, to be efficient, must be the work of intense thought, grave effort, systematized action, and, consequently, of time. They ought not, we repeat, to be made too easily. Witness France, where revolutions have become the bloody toy of the multitude; who fight for they know not what; spurning today the idol of yesterday, and calling for revolution as they would for a parade or "un spectacle." Hasty revolution (and it were folly to deny that we are on the eve of revolution, for, however legalized, still it is revolution at which we aim) must always be inefficient, if not mischievous. Give us time: time to arrange our forces; time to bring our people to the point of action (by people we mean our Southern people, not simply Carolinians); time to show them the necessity and the right of that action; time to accustom themselves to the idea of severing old ties—for, even when such ties are chains, the habit of wearing them is to be conquered. No people roused by a fit of momentary passion (and years are but moments, in the history of nations) has ever accomplished great deeds. Oh! you, our too hasty brethren, to whom, in our heart of hearts, we cling—for one aim, one thought is ours—pause yet, ere the Rubicon be passed, which is to sever us not only from foes but from friends; pause, ere we throw down the gauntlet of defiance, not to our oppressors alone, but to those, our sisters in endurance, who (give them but the time) must yet be with us in our struggle. Pause, were it but for unanimity in our own State, at a crisis when division were death. Give us time!—time!

"Time," you answer, "we have had time enough! This storm has been brewing for a quarter of a century." Most truly, and in very deed, it hath! The seeds of it were planted even with the forming of that constitution to which we have vainly clung, and looked for aid, and fain would have called sacred, while our opponents have sneered at our credulity, and trampled it in the dust. This storm has, of a truth, been brewing long; but who among us have been fully awake to the muttering wrath of its insidious approach? awake to the consciousness of danger? awake to the point of resistance? It is but of very recent date that the word "disunion" has ceased to be (even in

South Carolina) a word almost of treason. Has there been, until within the last three or four years, more than one voice in the country which dared to boldly predict, and warn us of the possible necessity of, such a measure. Mr. Cheves, we know, as far back as the year 1830, publicly expressed the opinion that joint resistance of the Southern States was the only hope for the preservation of the Union in its integrity, and, that hope failing, disunion, if not our choice, might be "our necessity."[34] But did not Mr. Cheves stand alone? Did not even the nullifiers, of that date, against whose expedient he argued as a partial and inefficient measure, shrink from the word "disunion"? We have ourselves heard a Hayne and a Hamilton,[35] then among the most active resistants to governmental oppression, and personal intimates of Mr. Cheves, answer the arguments of the latter by the avowal that they were not prepared to go so far. They believed his remedy to be more severe than was needful. Time, alas! has proved but too fully the correctness of Mr. Cheves's position; and the same voice which, in 1830, exclaimed, "Submit? Why, the question is, whether we shall <will> bear oppression or not!"—the same voice which counselled us then that "any measure, by one of the suffering states alone, will be a measure of feebleness, subject to many hazards; any union, among the same states, will be a measure of strength, almost of certain success"[36]—twenty years after echoed itself at Nashville, "Submit? Submit? The very sound curdles the blood in my veins! But O! great God, unite us, and a tale of submission shall never be told!"[37]

Mr. Cheves, then, foresaw the necessity which has fallen upon our times, but stood alone in so doing. How long is it (three or four years, we think) since Mr. Calhoun, decidedly the most popular man in the State of South Carolina, declared that, if there were any man in the Union sincerely attached to it, that man *was himself.* We cannot doubt the perfect sincerity of Mr. Calhoun, in this declaration, and certainly there was, at that time, no single voice in the State so potential, or so well calculated to speak the spirit

34. Langdon Cheves to John Taylor et al., Charleston, Sept. 15, 1830, reprinted from the Columbia *Times and Gazette* in *Niles' Register* 39 (Oct. 1830): 129–32; 131–32: "Disunion will not be her [South Carolina's] choice, but her necessity." At a States' Rights Dinner given in Charleston on July 1, 1830, at which prominent nullifiers were the speakers, Langdon Cheves had spoken in opposition to nullification, favoring instead united action by all Southern states. This opposition he reiterated in the letter cited above, replying to an invitation to attend another States' Rights Dinner, to be held in Columbia on Sept. 20, 1830.

35. Robert Young Hayne (1791–1839), Cheves' law partner and close friend. James Hamilton (1786–1857), governor of South Carolina (1830–32); president of its convention adopting an Ordinance of Nullification (November 1832).

36. Cheves to Taylor et al., p. 130.

37. *Speech of the Hon. Langdon Cheves in the Southern Convention at Nashville, Tennessee, November 14, 1850* ([Nashville?]: Southern Rights Association, 1850), p. 30.

of the majority, as his. Progress is never found in rapid change, and the sudden and fierce desire of a large portion (we will not believe it the majority of the State) to throw itself "o' the other side"[38] speaks impulse rather than reason. We must not attempt (time and space—our editor being stringent against long articles—forbid it) to sum up our authorities in favour of waiting upon a Southern Union, as opposed to hurried separate State action; neither have we space to dwell upon the inevitable evils, the bitter feuds, the heart-burnings and jealousies, which the opposite measure entails upon us, terminating in long if not permanent estrangement among States whose prosperity, whose very existence, depends upon union among themselves; neither can we dwell upon the crushed hopes, the bitter remorse, the angry revilings which must ensue, even among the now united advocates of this hasty measure, to make our State a very hell of discord, and passion, violence, and rancour the rulers of its fate. Such thoughts would swell our article into a volume. They have been profoundly discussed and, we hope, will be as profoundly studied. But, having mentioned the popular name of Calhoun, and as our violent party have made large use of it, delighting in rhetorical flourishes about his "guardian spirit," which they suppose to be looking down sympathizingly upon their course, we must be allowed to quote the authority of this distinguished statesman himself against these worshippers and desecrators of his name. In a letter addressed to Mr. Foote in August, 1849, and recently published in the New Orleans *Delta,* Mr. Calhoun, after stating his desire, which he presumes to be that "of every true hearted Southern man, [. . .] to save, if possible, the Union, as well as ourselves; but, if both cannot be, then to save ourselves at all events," remarks,

> *Without concert of action, on the part of the South, neither can be saved;* by it, if it be not too long delayed, it is possible *both yet may be.* Without it, we cannot satisfy the North that the South is in earnest, and will, if forced, choose resistance; and, until she is satisfied of this,[39] the causes which have brought the question between the two sections to its present dangerous stage from a small beginning, will continue to operate, until it will be too late to save the Union, and nothing will be left us but *to dissolve the connection. To do that, concert of action would be necessary,* not to save the Union, for it would be too late; but *to save ourselves.* Thus, in my <any> view, *concert is the one thing needful.*[40]

38. *Macbeth* 1.7.25–28: "I have no spur / To prick the sides of my intent, but only / Vaulting ambition, which o'erleaps itself, / And falls on the other."

39. "Of this" added by LSM.

40. John C. Calhoun to Henry Stuart Foote, Fort Hill, Aug. 3, 1849, in the New Orleans *Daily Delta,* May 29, 1851; reprinted from the *Delta* in the Charleston *Mercury,* June 4, 1851 (LSM's italics).

From the above extract we may draw two conclusions, most important to our argument. First, that Mr. Calhoun had, at this period, become entirely concurrent in the opinions of Mr. Cheves, expressed nearly twenty years before, concerning the necessity of a *concert of action* among the Southern States, which, as we see, he here pronounces to be "*the one thing needful;*" and, secondly, that, at so late a period as August, 1849, but a few months before his death,[41] he had by no means abandoned the hope of seeing the Union preserved in its integrity. In favour of this hope we are not inclined to argue. The measure of our sufferings has long been full, and new injuries have heaped it to overflowing. We feel, with Mr. Cheves, that "the Union is already dissolved," and the constitution a "*caput mortuum*"—a "shape of dead formalities," wherein we have no farther interest than had "free Rome" in that constitution by which "Caligula made his horse a Roman consul."[42] We argue not for the Union—"the glorious Union"—at whose chariot-wheels we have long been dragged, the victims of its triumphal progress; but we notice the above-quoted opinion of Mr. Calhoun, as showing how rapid a change has come over the spirit of our State—for we presume there is no man to dispute that Mr. Calhoun was, from his extreme popularity, as much as any one man could be, the exponent of that spirit. Certainly South Carolina was not, at the date of this letter, prepared for disunion—still less for separate secession. Two short years have since passed over us. And are two years enough to so entirely change the sentiments of her people as to authorize not only the great and momentous revolution which we contemplate (and which may heaven speed!), but such an eagerness for forcing on that revolution that we, in our hot haste, must throw overboard all hope of uniting our sister States and, calling them traitor and recreant because they think as we did two years ago, rush headlong upon separate secession? True, we have suffered new injuries since that time; but does the tumultuous and unregulated action by which it is proposed to right these injuries not better suit a schoolboy rebellion, and barring out (in which the actors, as a matter of course, are not only destined, but expect, to be punished and whipped back into submission), than the grave action of grave men, legislating for the most important crisis which the history of their country could present?

It cannot be that this disgrace has come upon our time.

Our *true leaders,* resolute in resistance, are opposed to violent and sepa-

41. John C. Calhoun died in Washington, D.C., on March 31, 1850.

42. *Speech of the Hon. Langdon Cheves in the Southern Convention at Nashville, Tennessee, November 14, 1850,* p. 17. The Roman biographer Suetonius records only that the emperor Caligula (A.D. 12–41) was reported to have intended to confer the consulship upon his favorite racehorse Incitatus (*Gaius Caligula* 55.3: "consulatum quoque traditur destinasse").

rate action. Among the party in favour of such action, there is scarcely a single man to whom the State has hitherto been accustomed to look for advice. All whom South Carolina has hitherto held dear and venerable in authority are opposed to this movement. She will, she must, be guided by the kindly, calm, and rational counsels of her long-tried advisers. We will not believe otherwise of the State we love so well!

The question is not, with us, one between resistance and submission. We are unanimous for resistance—resistance to the death—and the wariest of our counsellors, when the struggle comes, will be found shoulder to shoulder with the warmest. The doubt is not *whether,* but *how* shall we resist? and our leading men plead with us, even as a father pleadeth with his children,[43] to use wisely those means which God and nature have given us, rather than throw them away in weak, futile, and misguided effort. If there is, as we have suggested, a hope in the spirit of reaction caused by the dictatorial tone of the May convention and its evident desire to force the State into premature action, there is also, we cannot deny to ourselves, the fear of a result much to be dreaded and, should it occur, never too deeply to be deplored. This reaction may become too extreme. There is, in every country, and amidst the most enlightened population, a large proportion whose natural instinct leads them, in difficult political questions, to submit the guidance of their judgments to stronger minds, whose power and truth experience has taught them to venerate. There is danger that such men, misled by the opprobrium which the violent party endeavours to cast upon the more prudent, may become, to a certain extent, embarrassed between the submissionist and the *bona fide* resistance party. The principles, the faith, and the men of these parties are, indeed, wide as the poles asunder; but an error or a slander, constantly and emphatically repeated, obtains finally, in the ears of unthinking men, a familiarity which stamps it with a semblance of truth. There are many men who will have sufficient diffidence of their own judgments, and sufficient respect for such names and opinions as we have cited, to induce them, very much, to regulate their course by these opinions. If, then, the vituperation of party violence can succeed in convincing such individuals that the almost dying words of a Calhoun, that the earnest and prophet-like appeals of a Cheves, that the advice of a Barnwell, a Butler, besides a host of true and noble men, fire-tried in our political struggles, are in favour of submission, is there not danger that such vituperation is doing much to the manufacture of submissionists?

As we believe that there are many, very many, true and earnest hearts among those against whom we argue, those our only too zealous brethren,

43. Job 16:21.

we would beg them, in God's name, to beware of such a result. Then, indeed, might South Carolina be in danger of receding from her pledges; then, indeed, might there be fear that she would hold out her hands to the shackles; and then, when trampled under the heel of the oppressor, would the sin and the shame be upon those who have deceived her people into believing that this was the voice, this the advice, of her wise men, her seers and her prophets! Hush the voice of passion and of slander; let the people judge for themselves, rather than through the dictation of party associations; and we have no fear that they will be misled by the opinions of those very men whose trumpet-call to freedom has been the first to rouse them to the consciousness and defence of their rights. We have no fear that they will be deceived, by *ignis fatuus* lights, from the flame of those altars, where the fire of their patriotism has first been lighted! *Pro patria! Fide et Fiducia.*[44]

44. "For our country! With loyalty and confidence." The collocation of *fides* and *fiducia* is very old, dating at least from Plautus (d. c. 184 B.C.).

8.

Negro-mania

This is too useful a work to be lightly passed over with the short notice we gave it in our December number.[1] A most valuable compilation it is on the subject of the races; a work of which it would be difficult to show all the merits in a review, for almost every line and word of it deserves to be paused upon. It is itself a review of, and selection from, sundry distinguished authors who have boldly dared to face the storm of fanaticism, and in spite of the almost universal prejudice of the world, to roll back its tide of error, and with the godlike power of intellect to pronounce the almighty fiat, "Thus far, and no farther!"[2] Some names unknown to science are introduced, to prove by arguments of common sense the necessity of those relations which science shows to be inevitable.

The author of this compilation makes no pretence to originality, but his

De Bow 12 (May 1852): 507–24; reprinted in De Bow, *Industrial Resources* 2:196–205. Publication reviewed: John Campbell, *Negro-mania: Being an Examination of the Falsely Assumed Equality of the Various Races of Men . . .* (Philadelphia: Campbell and Power, 1851). John Campbell (1810–74), born in Points Pass, Armagh, Ireland; emigrated to the United States in 1843; founded publishing and bookselling firm of John Campbell in 1850; author also of *Campbell's Democratic Song and Recitation Book* (1842); *A Theory of Equality, or, The Way to Make Every Man Act Honestly* (1848); *Unionists versus Traitors: The Political Parties of Philadelphia; or, The Nominees That Ought to Be Elected in 1861,* its author described as "a Douglas Democrat" (1861).

1. "Equality of the Races—Negro Mania," *De Bow* 11 (Dec. 1851): 630–34. This article, anonymous, from tone and style was not written by LSM.

2. Job 38:11.

work is not therefore the less meritorious, and perhaps it is even the more useful, as he has in many of his authorities given such names as only the grossest ignorance can refuse to bow to. A collection of judicious selections, judiciously commented upon, forms in itself a volume of infinite value; and while we disclaim the ability of laying before the public, in a short review, all its merits, we are anxious, as far as we can, to draw popular attention to it. The aim of our author is to *popularize* his subject, to make attainable to the everyday reader the results of learned investigation, and to let every man find within his reach a compendium of such authorities as he often could not afford to purchase, or may not have leisure to study in full. Most warmly do we wish him success in his experiment, and most heartily recommend his work to all. It is time that the subject should be investigated in all its bearings.

Among the authors cited by Mr. Campbell, we find advocates both for the unity and the diversity of man's origin. Prichard, etc. have been boldly quoted, while Morton, Lawrence, Knox, Smith, Browne, Gliddon, etc. are called upon, and most triumphantly, to prove the fallacy of their conclusions.[3] Many strong names which the author might have summoned on his own side of the question, he has (partly perhaps from superabundant material) left aside. From among ourselves, Nott—no mean authority—should perhaps not have been entirely forgotten; but such oblivion may well be pardoned in consideration of what he *has* given us, and he has from a very proper motive drawn his resources less from Southern men than from Englishmen and Northerners, among whom certainly no one can look for any weakness or bias towards our Southern institutions, in the decision of a ques-

3. Sir William Lawrence (1783–1867), anatomist; surgeon at St. Bartholomew's Hospital, London; sergeant-surgeon to Queen Victoria; wrote, among other works, *Lectures on Physiology, Zoology, and the Natural History of Man* (1819), excerpted in Campbell, *Negro-mania,* pp. 79–160. Charles Hamilton Smith (1776–1859), English soldier and naturalist; his *Natural History of the Human Species, Its Typical Forms, Permanent Distribution, Filiations, and Migrations* (1848) is excerpted in Campbell, *Negro-mania,* pp. 161–88. Peter Arrell Browne (1782–1860), L.L.D.; "a scientific gentleman of Philadelphia" (Campbell, *Negro-mania,* p. 78); his *Classification of Mankind, by the Hair and Wool of Their Heads, with an Answer to Dr. Prichard's Assertion, That "The Covering of the Head of the Negro Is Hair, Properly So Termed, and Not Wool"* (1850) is reprinted in Campbell, *Negro-mania,* pp. 339–64. George Robins Gliddon (1809–57), Egyptologist; author, among other works, of *Discourses on Egyptian Archaeology* (1841) and, with Josiah Clark Nott, of *Types of Mankind* (1854) and *Indigenous Races of the Earth* (1857); his commentary on Herodotus' description of the Egyptians is quoted in Campbell, *Negro-mania,* pp. 16–49. Campbell, *Negro-mania,* cites James Cowles Prichard, Samuel George Morton, and Robert Knox (all discussed by LSM also in chap. 5, "Diversity of the Races; Its Bearing upon Negro Slavery"), at pp. 50–77 (Prichard), 198–338 (Knox), and 379–429 (Morton).

tion which is of such vital importance to *us.* It is singular, however, that the great Agassiz should not have been named by him. The opinions of Mr. Agassiz upon this subject are well known, and it shows the richness of material, the overwhelming mass of proof, that such a supporter could be dispensed with.

Our author enters only incidentally upon the question of the origin of the races, and rather turns the force of his argument to prove their inequality. The races exist, and exist with different powers, different instincts, and different capacities. These differences are inalienable and unchangeable. Such are, in few words, the propositions of his argument, and every authority quoted (even that of Prichard, the principal upholder of the unity theory) tends to confirm this position. Whenever and however men have appeared upon this earth (we, in common with our author, consider the diversity of origin proved beyond dispute), here they now are: unlike in all things, with the marks of race stamped ineffaceably upon them, in body and in mind, in form, color, instinct, and reason—differing in all, and having differed, as is most indisputably proved by historical monuments for four thousand years, and by every philosophical deduction must continue so to differ. Man's handiwork will scarce bring about a revolution in despite, as Carlyle would say, of "the immortal gods."[4] Should he try to force it, forgetting the necessary conditions of his existence, "which Nature and the Eternal Powers have by no manner of means forgotten, but do at all moments keep in mind," these they will "at the right moment, [. . .] with [the] due impressiveness, perhaps in rather a <a rather> terrible manner, bring again to our mind also."[5]

The highest capacity of man, and its noblest use, is the discovery and execution of the Almighty behests, thus enabling him to second instead of opposing the beautiful order of God's developed thought in creation. If the negro be an inferior man, the struggle against God's will, which aims at putting him upon the same footing as the superior, is only not an impious work in so far as it is a blind and a foolish one. Folly, unfortunately, often leads to consequences fatal as vice, and there is nothing more mischievous than active ignorance. In the fanaticism which now actually desolates some of the most favored and beautiful parts of our globe, threatening others even at the risk of dragging to earth the high-reared monuments of man's civiliza-

4. Campbell, *Negro-mania,* p. 515 = [Thomas Carlyle], "Occasional Discourse on the Negro Question," *Fraser's Magazine* 40 (Dec. 1849): 670–79; 675.

5. Campbell, *Negro-mania,* p. 514 = [Carlyle], "Occasional Discourse," p. 675. Campbell, *Negro-mania,* reads "rather a terrible manner," hence LSM's change from Carlyle's wording.

tion, we find vicious malevolence and ignorance combining their power to raise some higher law than any which God has sanctioned; and because the black man cannot reach the level of the white, they would even drag down and degrade the white to *his* capacities.

Can it be that in an age when science walks abroad, astonishing the world by a progress hitherto unequaled in her annals—when no longer, with snail-like advance, she labors the ascent to knowledge, but rather leaps forward to her magnificent conclusions—when she girdles the world with steam, and flashes her lightning thought, even with lightning speed, through the expanse of a continent—when we see her votaries (in the eloquent language of Professor Lieber), "like priests of nature, revealing [some of] her great <greatest> mysteries and showing thought, one thought, the thought of God, pervading the universe and its phases"[6]—oh! can it be that this is to be swept aside, or rather crushed down to the level of a Haytien civilization? Can it be, that the great *one thought,* that *thought of God,* so beautifully pictured out even in the lowest, as in the highest, of his works, is to be tinkered at and defaced, patched and plastered, by a set of madmen, whose one idea seems to be built upon some whining, Wilberforcian, Clarksonized[7] wail of "black brethren" and "negro improvement"? Verily, nature "suffereth long and is kind,"[8] or, ere this, had her curse fallen upon us. We struggle against her, we fiercely resist her teachings, and fancy that these poor heads of ours—to say nothing of black Sambo's and Cuffee's—can regulate matters by a higher law than hers. But the time cometh when our probation can last no longer. Then, and in "rather a terrible manner," it is to be feared, we will receive our lesson! Is it not even now, alas, beginning? What is this cry over Europe, echoing even to our own shores? What means this darkly-shadowed caricature of good—this horrible disfigurement of Christian charity—which, but that it stalks in terrible reality before us, would seem like the mockery of some fearful dream? The angel form which we have gazed upon and worshiped as Christian charity and brotherly love, now suddenly starts forth, grinning upon us in hideous deformity of vice, and gibbering out its horrible obscenities of "socialism" and "communism," drags along upon its track the shouting mob, who, in their ravings for "negro abolition" and

6. Francis Lieber, *The Necessity of Continued Self-Education: An Address to the Graduating Class of S.C. College, at Commencement, on the First of December, 1851* (Columbia, S.C., 1851), p. 10. Francis Lieber (1800–1872), German-born political economist; professor at South Carolina College (1835–56); at Columbia College in New York City (1857–65) and Columbia Law School (1865–72).

7. Thomas Clarkson (1760–1846), English abolitionist; associate of William Wilberforce; author, among other works, of *History of the Abolition of the African Slave-Trade* (1808).

8. 1 Cor. 13:4.

"universal equality," trample under foot at once God's law and man's law—virtue and decency. The demon is unchained. This widespread and wider-spreading evil figures forth, not badly, the beast of the Apocalypse, unto whom "was given a mouth speaking great things and blasphemies; . . . and he opened his mouth in blasphemy against God, to blaspheme his name, . . . and power was given him over all kindreds, and tongues, and nations."[9]

The strength of this hideous power is now interesting itself largely in the negro cause; and because the innovators find the impossibility of putting into execution their crude theories among their white brethren, and more nearly equalized population, they, in their agony for action, look about for something tangible, something less impossible, and fancy that it is found in the abolition of negro slavery. Alas! for the mistaken folly of those who, in thus acting, act sincerely. Their well-meaning and officious ignorance is pushed on by the powerful lever of fanaticism to ends from which they would shrink in affright could they see them in full development, but which, in half-way execution, they rejoice over, as the poor idiot gazes in delighted wonder and warms his fingers by the blaze which is demolishing his dwelling, fancying the while that he has done a wise thing in the application of the spark which has lighted to their destruction his own and his neighbors' homes.

Alas for their folly! But wo! wo! a wo of darkness and of death! a wo of hell and of perdition to those who, better knowing, goad folly on to such an extreme! This is indeed the sin not to be forgiven, the sin against the Holy Ghost and against the spirit of God.[10] The beautiful order of Creation, breathed down from Almighty intelligence, is to be moulded and wrought by fanatic intelligence! until dragged down at last to negro intelligence!!

The Almighty has thought well to place certain of his creatures in certain fixed positions in this world of ours, for what cause he has not seen fit to make quite clear to our limited capacities; and why an ass is not a man, or a man an ass, will probably forever remain a mystery to our limited intellects. One thing, however, he has in his mercy made clear enough, viz., that by no manner of education; no stocks, braces, nor regimental drillings; no problems, theories, nor definitions; neither by steam nor by telegraph, neither by mesmerism nor by chloroform, can our unfortunate brother ass, whether mentally or corporeally, be induced to consider himself as a gentleman, and act accordingly. *He,* at least, is not capable of attaining the *white* civilization

9. Rev. 13:5–7.

10. Matt. 12:31: "All manner of sin and blasphemy shall be forgiven unto men: but the blasphemy against the Holy Ghost shall not be forgiven unto men."

of this our nineteenth century. We hope that our philanthropic friends will allow us this. We would fain have some sure ground to stand upon, but do not feel quite certain that they may not come with some new-fangled theory of communism to knock this platform also from under our feet. Believing, however, that (until the spirit of improvement rises a step or two higher) they will allow us our position, we would beg them to instruct us upon what principle of justice this unfortunate brother ass—this hirsute relative—should be so bedeviled and trampled upon. Why should he not lie amidst feathers and velvet, as well as the best in the land? And why, above all, must he help work to make such feathers and velvet comfortable lodgings for his so-called betters? God-given intellect and power to attain count for nothing in this modern system of arguing. The ass has as good a right to the possession of intellect as the man; and if God has not given it to him, we must remedy the injustice by some patent "free-and-equal" system. The process is easy enough. If the ass cannot stand on two legs, knock the man down to all fours (nothing is simpler), and *vive la fraternité!* Why did not the Almighty save us all this trouble, and make the ass a man, or the man an ass, from the beginning? Truly, 'tis a problem hard to solve, and poor donkey, with his lamentable braying, comes as near an explanation as all our philosophizing can do. God made the world—God gave thee there thy place, my hirsute brother; and according to all earthly probabilities and possibilities, it is thy destiny therein to remain, bray as thou wilt. From the same great power have our sable friends, Messrs. Sambo, Cuffee, and Co., received their position also; with which position, allow us to remark, the worthy ancestors of Messrs. Sambo, Cuffee, and Co. have continued perfectly satisfied for some four thousand years (longer, perchance, but records go no farther), and their descendants would, most undoubtedly, have so continued; but behold, Satan, as when

> Squat like a toad, close at the ear of Eve,
> Assaying by his devilish arts to reach
> The organs of her fancy,[11]

comes now in the likeness of an "all men are born free and equal" advocate, to raise "vain hopes, vain aims, inordinate desires"[12] in poor Cuffee's hitherto quiet brain!

Alas, "my poor black brother!" thou, like the hirsute, must do thy braying in vain. Where God has placed thee, there must thou stay. "You, Quashee, my pumpkin—not a bad fellow either, this poor Quashee, when tolerably

11. John Milton, *Paradise Lost* 4.800–802.
12. Ibid., 4.808.

guided!—idle Quashee, I say you must get the devil *sent away* from your elbow, my poor dark friend! In this world there will be no existence for you otherwise."[13] To the immortals, perchance, this tempest in a teapot, this little hubbub on our little globe, may look trifling enough, they seeing very certainly that at the end of some score of centuries all things will go right again. Quashee will either have gone back to his quiet corner in this world's civilization or, perchance, have vacated it forever in favor of some higher claimant. It matters little in all likelihood to the supreme spectators of this world's game, what confusion of checking and checkmating may be going on in our little ant-hill. The thought of God must conquer finally, and the score or so of centuries more or less would be but a moment in its development. But to us, my brothers, and our children, these twenty centuries, what are they? White and black, were it not well to think on this a little? Truly to us, my biped brethren of all complexions, this abolitionist Satan is preparing (if so be we chain him not in time) a sorry chase through this world's existence. Only the hirsute can flourish then: ranging at will through beauteous regions, cast back again to wildness and the desert. There nature's bounty may furnish grass to the hirsute, but, truly, no bread to the biped. Black Quashee cannot understand this; God has not given him the intellect for it; and if we teach him to bray out for liberty, i.e., for idleness, verily it is as easy for him to bray to that tune as to any other. But the white man! Of what is he dreaming, when he listens even for a moment to such cant? To him God *has* given intellect (would he but use it!) to see the truth. Brother (for if acting conscientiously, and no devil's firebrand sent by Satan to our undoing, even as a brother, although differing, we hail thee), brother, thou speakest, perchance, in ignorance. Hast thou ever lived along side of Quashee? noticed his habits, his mind, his character, his tastes, his virtues, and his vices? clothed him in health, and nursed him in sickness? cheered him in merriment, and comforted him in sorrow? rejoiced with him, and suffered with him? laughed with him, and wept with him? Thou *hast not;* but there be those who have. "Go thou and do likewise,"[14] and when (if ever) thou dost, *thou wilt cease to be an abolitionist.* The white man, whose heart truly warms to the fate of the negro, would cease to agitate this question in that moment that he would become well acquainted with him, for thus would he learn its utter impracticability. At the hideous thought of amalgamation, even the abolitionist white-blood shudders. The white and the black race can only exist together in their present relations. Abolition is the extinction of the one or the other.

13. Thomas Carlyle, "Model Prisons," *Latter-Day Pamphlets,* in *Works* 5:58.
14. Luke 10:37.

I to herd with narrow foreheads, vacant of our glorious gains,
Like a beast with lower pleasures, like a beast with lower pains!
Mated with a squalid savage—what to me were sun or clime?
I the heir of all the ages, in the foremost files of time![15]

The civilized man must retain his position, or perish.

We beg pardon of Mr. Campbell, however, whom we have, like a garrulous host, kept for a long time, hat in hand, ready to make his bow to the reader, while we, instead of remembering our duty of introducing him, have been prosing away upon his text. Mr. Campbell is, he tells us, a member of the Social Improvement Society of Philadelphia; at divers meetings of which society, "various and talented speakers" (we use Mr. C.'s words), *white and black,* joined in the discussion of this question—"Can the colored races of men be made mentally, politically, and socially equal with the white?" [4] This is a rather startling outset; and judging from the results usually emanating from such parti-colored associations, our first impulse was to withdraw from Mr. Campbell's extended hand. Gulping down the doubt, however, we boldly enlist under the motto he adopts—"Prove all things; hold fast that which is good"[16]—and we are rewarded by finding that he honestly and manfully meets the question. Here, then, we have a collection of extracts, selected by a northern man, who has entered freely into the discussion of the subject with minds of all hues, "black spirits and white, blue spirits and gray,"[17] enthusiast and fanatic; whose important scientific authorities are all, without exception, Englishmen or northern United States men. Surely no bias should be here expected in favor of southern United States institutions, and yet a stronger defence of them it would be difficult to find.

In answer to the question, "Can the colored races of men be made mentally, politically, and socially equal with the white?" our author first states the indisputable fact that never, from the most remote antiquity until now, has there appeared a "race of negroes, that is, men with woolly heads, flat noses, thick and protruding lips, which <who> has ever emerged from a state of savageism or barbarism to even a demi-civilization. Look to the West Indies, to Brazil, to Australia, to the Gold Coast, to Zanguebar, to Congo, to Senegambia, to Ashantee, nay to the civilization under his imperial highness Faustin the First, Emperor of Hayti, and answer me, ye Garrisons, and Phil-

15. Tennyson, "Locksley Hall," ll. 175–78.

16. *Negro-mania,* pp. 5 and 549, citing 1 Thess. 5:21.

17. *Macbeth* 4.1.44 (from Thomas Middleton, *The Witch* 5.2), reading "red spirits and gray."

lipses, and Burleys, and Folsoms, and Smiths,[18] what has this race done in five thousand years?" [6–7] To those who advance the argument that the negro has never had an opportunity for development because the white man has always oppressed him, our author says:

> They forget that the latter portion of this proposition refutes the former. If the white man has always oppressed the negro, it goes to establish the fact claimed by me that the white man is mentally superior, because, if the white man has been always powerful enough to debar the negro from improving his intellect, it establishes the complete force of my views—"that no amount of education or training can ever make the negro equal in intellect with the white;" "knowledge is power," and it is evident to all that under no circumstances <circumstance> has the negro race ever been able to compete with the white.
>
> We see around us, in every direction, evidences of the fact that the negro is naturally inferior to the white; but it is unfair to institute comparisons where this race is held in bondage by the white. We will give them all the advantages of a fair examination. We will travel to that quarter of the globe which seems to be the native land of this race, and to which they appear to be indigenous. We will go where the white man has never oppressed them <oppressed this race>. [7–8]

And what do we find?

> Monumental ruins of Dahomey, forty ages do not look down upon you![19] Strewn columns of Ashantee, where shall we find you? [and] echo answers, "Where?" Decaying towers of Zanguebar, shall any traveler ever discover your <thy> nameless and undiscovered and undiscoverable foundations? Sculptured temples of Guinea, what hierologist shall be able to decipher your extinguished hieroglyphics? . . . [I said before,] if only one great negro name could be produced to redeem a whole race, then <that> I will retract all I have ever said of negro inferiority. But this one only name, this *rara avis,* this white blackbird, this phoenix, is not forthcoming; "you cannot make a silk purse out of a sow's lug," is an old and homely adage, but not the less true;

18. Wendell Phillips (1811–84), abolitionist; associate of William Lloyd Garrison; president of the American Anti-Slavery Society (1865–70). Charles Calistus Burleigh (1810–78), born in Plainfield, Conn.; abolitionist; contributor to William Lloyd Garrison's *Liberator;* edited the *Pennsylvania Freeman;* his brother, William Henry Burleigh (1812–71), from 1836 lectured for the American Anti-Slavery Society; active in the temperance movement. Gerrit Smith (1797–1874), associate of William Lloyd Garrison; friend of John Brown.

19. At the Pyramids, on July 21, 1798, Napoleon Bonaparte is said to have told his troops, "From the summit of those Pyramids, forty centuries look down upon you."

> so can you not make anything from a negro but negroism, which means barbarism and inferiority. . . . Have the woolly-headed races of men ever produced one, even only one man famous either as lawgiver, statesman, poet, priest, painter, historian, orator, architect, musician, soldier, sailor, engineer, navigator, astronomer, linguist, mathematician, anatomist, chemist, physician, naturalist, or philosopher? [8–10]

Not one, in the whole expanse of the world's history, for 4,000 years; and yet there are men who dare to babble of circumstance, disadvantage, oppression, and universal equality. What might the negro have done, if—and if—and if? What might the jackass have done, if—and if—and if? The proof is as fair in the one case as in the other—the same in kind, differing only in degree. As God made them, so they have been, so they are, and so they will be; the white man, the negro, and the jackass, each to his kind and each to his nature; true to the finger of destiny (which is the finger of God), and undeviatingly pursuing the track which that finger as undeviatingly points out. Where rebel reason in its little pride of might would try to change that track, there does the restless vehemence of disorganized nature prove its own avenger. The negro, become master, extinguishes that civilization which his nature abhors, to revel in savageism to which his instincts limit him. Philanthropy, or rather philo-donkeyism, has never yet experimented how the ass would act under similar circumstances; but we are fully authorized, from logical induction, to conclude that green grass and the wilderness would be the order of the day under his *régime,* and humanity, both black and white, would be fairly kicked out of existence. To the white man then, the philosopher, poet, orator, historian—to him "the heir of all the ages, in the foremost files of time," it matters little whether donkeyism or negroism predominate; either, to him, would be extinction.

To return to the question of inferiority of the negro, we have, then, in all honest reasoning, the full right to deduce it from constant, unvarying, and unstruggling inferiority of position; and the observations of naturalists all go to confirm this position by his anatomical inferiority. Mr. Campbell quotes largely to this effect, and gives us extracts even from Dr. Prichard acknowledging that, by a comparison with the highest of the simiae, the chimpanzee and the orang, there is apparent, in certain parts of the skeleton, "an approach towards the forms of these latter species" [54].[20] Lawrence, after enumerating the various points of anatomical difference, continues: "In all the particulars just enumerated, the Negro structure approximates unequivo-

20. Our quotations, let it be understood, are henceforward invariably taken at second hand from Mr. Campbell. It is our object to show what he has done, and to give his book, as far as in our power, the circulation which it so well deserves. [LSM]

cally to that of the monkey. It not only differs from the Caucasian model, but is distinguished from it in two respects: the intellectual characters are reduced, the animal features enlarged and exaggerated." [117] Knox, of the dark races generally, remarks: "The whole shape of the skeleton differs from ours; and so, also, I find, do the forms of almost every muscle of the body" [264–65]. Of the Hottentots, he says: "Their skeleton presents, of course, peculiarities, such as the extreme narrowness of the nasal bones, which run into one in early age not unfrequently, as we find in apes. But it is the exterior which is the most striking; and this, no doubt, is wonderful. No one can believe them to be of the same race with ourselves; yet, unquestionably, they belong to the genus man." [273]

The now exploded assumption, that the ancient Egyptians were negroes, is met by Mr. Campbell with such a mass of authorities that we must refer the reader, who is curious on the subject, to his book. One can but smile in reading them, at the idea that such an error could ever have obtained credence enough to make it worth combating. "Now that we distinguish the several human races by the bones of the head," remarks Lawrence, "[and that we possess so many of the ancient Egyptian embalmed bodies,] it is easy to prove that, whatever may have been the hue of their [the Egyptians'][21] skin, they belonged to the same race with ourselves; . . . that they formed no exception to that cruel law"—a cruel law! which God has made! and shall *we* better it?—"which seems to have doomed to eternal inferiority all the tribes of our species which are unfortunate enough to have a depressed and compressed cranium." [113–14] The great Cuvier[22] had already long before pronounced, that "neither the Gallas [. . .] nor the Bosjesmen, not any race of Negroes, produced that celebrated people" [113]; and Morton[23] (a name at which we bow our heads in sorrow, that so early should have been closed a life whose labors science can ill spare)[24] gives a stream of decisive evidence on the subject. "A translation of a deed on papyrus of the reign of Ptolemy, Alexander First <Ptolemy Alexander I>," giving a description of the persons, parties to a sale of land at Thebes, describes one of them as of a dark complexion, the remaining five as sallow [400–401]. The Egyptians themselves, on their monuments, have represented the men red, the women yel-

21. LSM's interpolation.

22. Georges, Baron Cuvier (1769–1832), French naturalist, official, and professor at the Collège de France; founder of paleontology.

23. It is but justice to this distinguished man to remark that we have ourselves heard Agassiz (himself the greatest of living naturalists) say that he was an authority inferior to *none* in ethnology. [LSM] Agassiz lectured in Columbia in 1850 and was professor of comparative anatomy at the Medical College of South Carolina, in Charleston (1851–53).

24. Samuel George Morton died in Philadelphia on May 15, 1851, at the age of fifty-two.

low; and both with features entirely distinct from the negro, who appears among them with all the characteristic features of his race, and always in a condition of bondage or inferiority. "Negroes," observes Morton, "were numerous in Egypt, but their [social] position in ancient times was the same that it now is, that of servants and slaves. . . . The hair of the Egyptians resembled, in texture, that of the fairest Europeans of the present day." [426–27]

Equally futile and equally rejected by science is the assumption that climate or habit of life can account for the differences of race. "The physical or organic characters which distinguish the several races of men, are as old," says Morton, "as the oldest records of our species." We frequently find one race inhabiting an extent of country which serves, at once, to prove the irrationality of the conclusion that climate can have had any influence in stamping upon it its characteristic differences. "The flat face of the Chinese," observes Lawrence,

> not only extends throughout that vast empire, which covers nearly forty degrees of latitude and seventy of longitude, but also over the neighboring regions of Central and Northern Asia, the north of Europe and of America; over a very large portion of the globe, including every possible variety of heat and cold, elevation and lowness, moisture and dryness, wood, marsh, and plain.
>
> That European Creoles in the West Indies, in America, and in the East, have preserved their native features in all instances where no intermixture of blood has occurred, is proved by the uninterrupted experience of the Spaniards, Portuguese, and English, who have had foreign colonies, in climates most differing from their own, longer than any other nation. [. . .] The modern Gipseys, and the Jews, afford examples of peculiar and distinctive casts of countenance being preserved in every climate. [119–20]

Volney has attempted to account for the peculiarities of the negro features in the following whimsical manner. We translate, for the benefit of those to whom the French may not be quite familiar. "I observe that the features of the negro represent precisely the state of contraction which our faces assume when struck by the light and a strong reverberation of heat—then the brow frowns, the ball of the cheek rises, the eyelid contracts, and the mouth draws itself together (*fait la moue*). Is it not natural that this contraction which takes place continually in the naked and hot country of the negro, should become the permanent characteristic of his face?"[25] "Unfortunately,"

25. Campbell, *Negro-mania,* pp. 120–21. Constantin-François Chasseboeuf, comte de Volney (1757–1820), French traveler and politician; visited Egypt and Syria (1782–85) and the United States (1795–98); imprisoned during the Reign of Terror; created count and peer under Napoleon I.

answers Lawrence, "for these speculations, the Negro features occur in numerous tribes spread over a very great <over a great> extent of country, with various climates, and in many instances where the heat is by no means excessive; the character, too, is permanent, after any number of generations, when the negro is <the Negroes are> taken into other climes" [121]. Blumenbach seriously quotes some wiseacre, even more fanciful than Volney, who would fain account for the flat mouth and swollen lips by the fact that, the mothers carrying their children on their backs, "in the violent motion <motions> required for their hard labor, as in beating and pounding millet, etc., the face of the young one is constantly thumping against the back of the mother."[26] *Povero bambino!* One would imagine that thumps violent enough to flatten its poor little nose must keep the juvenile martyr in a state of constant depletion from that important organ. What, moreover, becomes of this theory in a barbarous country like our own, where, when the mother goes to work, the child is, by order of her brutal master, actually taken from her until her labor is done, and consigned to its cradle, or to the arms of a nurse, who holds it in the ordinary fashion for the carrying of such commodities, while basking in the sun or sitting by a comfortable fire, according to circumstances. Farther—to call in science to our aid—"all the peculiarities of the Negro cranium," says Lawrence, "exist in the foetus; . . . the prominent jaws, flat nose, and [all] other characteristics <characters>, are found as strongly marked in the youngest embryo as in the adult" [123]. That climate has no transmittible effect on the skin is evident from the fact that

> the children of the husbandman, or of the sailor whose countenance bears the marks of other climes, are just as fair as those of the most delicate and pale inhabitants of a city. Nay, the Moors, who have lived for ages under a burning sun, still have white children, and the offspring of Europeans in the Indies have the original tint of their progenitors. . . . [138]
>
> On the hypothesis, which assigns the varieties of mankind to the operation of climate as their cause, we should expect to find in Africa all tribes under the equator of the most intensely black color; the tinge should become lighter and lighter as we proceed thence towards the south, and the complexion ought to be white when we arrive at regions which enjoy a <an> European climate. This, however, is by no means the case. The Abyssinians on the east, with dark olive color and long hair, are placed near the equator, and surrounded by Negroes. In the same part, also, the Gallas, a great and barba-

26. Campbell, *Negro-mania,* p. 121. Johann Friedrich Blumenbach (1752–1840), founder of anthropology as a modern discipline; professor of medicine at Göttingen (1778–1835); introduced the classification of the human species into Caucasian, Mongolian, Ethiopian, American, and Malayan.

> rous nation, having, according to Bruce,[27] long black hair, and white skin verging to brown, occupy extensive regions under the equator itself. On the other hand, as we proceed from the equator towards the south, through tribes of Negroes, we find the black color continue with undiminished intensity. It is known in the West Indies that the Congo Negroes, in the blackness of their skin and woolly hair, equal any tribe <race> of Africans. [. . .]
>
> The island of Madagascar, which is cooled by the mild breezes of the Indian Ocean and ought, therefore, to continue a white race, has two kinds of natives: one of olive color with dark hair, the other true Negroes. [. . .]
>
> When we consider how large an extent of Africa is occupied by the black woolly-haired Negroes, and that these regions vary in their latitude, their elevation, and every other point; that they include sandy deserts, coasts, rivers, hills, valleys, and very great varieties of climate, the conclusion that these adventitious circumstances do not influence the color or other properties of the race is irresistible. [149–51]

Knox says: "My esteemed friend, Dr. Andrew Smith, informs me [. . .] that he attentively looked at a family descended from forefathers who came to South Africa with the first settlers. Three hundred years, then, had elapsed since their first arrival. Their descendants at this moment are as fair as the fairest of Europeans." [335] Cases there are of white families, under similar circumstances, being lost to the whites and only known in their negro descendants; but there is abundant proof that this is the result of constant mingling with negro blood, until the white has run out; which the commonest observer knows must be the case where the supply of white blood is not constantly renewed. We in the United States of America, whether North or South, seem to be in little danger of changing our skins; and our children are as fair as their Saxon or Celtic ancestors, although occupying the very grounds on which the red man lived and died, leaving his scattered graves as memorials of ages of possession.

The wool of the negro, another mooted point, our author most satisfactorily settles for us, through the minute and learned argument of P. A. Browne. Most unwillingly do we pass over a discussion showing such close research, and so triumphantly carried through. Our bounds will not, however, allow its insertion, and we can only entreat our readers to study it for themselves. The garbled view which our very limited extracts could give would be doing it injustice. Suffice it to say, that Mr. Browne not only proves his point by producing fact upon fact in a way which it is difficult for a candid mind to oppose, but gives us also an insight of the extremely slovenly and

27. James Bruce (1730–94), Scottish explorer; wrote *Travels to Discover the Source of the Nile in the Years 1768, 1769, 1770, 1771, 1772, and 1773*, 5 vols. (1790).

careless manner in which Prichard occasionally pushes forward his positions. The covering of the negro-head is most indisputably *wool*. "Hair will not felt, but wool will; and the covering of the Negro's head will felt—has been felted" [363]. With reference to the color of the skin, which, a few lines back, we were discussing, Mr. Browne cites the authority of "M. Flourens, an eminent French physiologist,"[28] who

> found four distinct layers between the cuticle and the cutis; the second of which, he says, is a mucous membrane—a distinct organized body, underlaying the pigment, and existing in persons of dark color only. M. Flourens sought, in vain, for this membrane between the cutis and outer lamina of the epidermis of the <a> white man; and yet this is the seat of the discoloration produced in his complexion by exposure to the sun. From these examinations, this distinguished naturalist and anatomist was able to pronounce, definitely, that the discoloration in the skin of the white man is totally different in kind from the cause of blackness in the Negro, and, therefore <; he, therefore>, justly concludes that the Negro and [the] European are separate species of beings. [363–64]

Have we yet given enough proof of difference of race and negro inferiority? Lawrence remarks that the difference of color "between the white and the black <and black> races is not more striking than the pre-eminence of the former in moral feelings and in mental endowments." The negroes "indulge almost universally in disgusting debauchery and sensuality, and display gross selfishness, indifference to the pains and pleasures of others, insensibility to beauty of form, order, and harmony, and an almost entire want of what we comprehend altogether under the expression of elevated sentiments, manly virtues, and moral feeling. The hideous savages of Van Dieman's Land, of New Holland, New Guinea, and some neighboring islands, the Negroes of Congo, and some other parts, exhibit the most disgusting moral as well as physical portraits <portrait> of man." [135–36] And yet, we repeat with Carlyle, "not a bad fellow either, this poor Quashee, when *tolerably guided*." Guidance, however, he does need. Colonel Charles Hamilton Smith, whose predilections are, as Mr. Campbell remarks, "in favor of the oppressed and degraded races" [161], who resided long in the West Indies, and continued for years his investigations on the subject of the races, says of the negroes, "War is a passion that excites in them a brutal disregard of human feelings; it entails the deliberate murder of prisoners, and victims are slain to serve the manes of departed chiefs. Even cannibalism is frequent

28. Marie-Jean-Pierre Flourens (1794–1867), professor at the Collège de France from 1832.

among [the] tribes of the interior. The perceptive faculties of the children are far from contemptible, bearing good comparison with the white, but they drop behind about the twelfth year, when the reflective powers begin to have the ascendancy"[29] and when the mind of the white is just developing itself. Is this not an approach to the state of the brute, whose mind, or instinct—call it as you will—is certainly, in early infancy, more developed than the human being? A lamb, a calf, or a colt, of a day or a week old, shows to much greater advantage than an infant of the same age. "Collectively," continues Col. Smith,

> the untutored Negro mind is confiding and single-hearted, naturally kind and hospitable. *Both sexes are easily ruled,* and appreciate what is good under the guidance of common justice and prudence, . . . [but][30] they have never comprehended what they have learned, nor <or> retained a civilization taught them by contact with more refined nations[, losing it][31] as soon as that contact has ceased. [. . .] Conquest with them has been confined to kindred tribes, and produced only slaughter. Even christianity, of more than three centuries in Congo, has scarcely excited a progressive civilization.
>
> Thus even the good qualities given to the Negro by the bounty of nature have seemed only to make him a slave trodden down by every remorseless foot, and to brand him for ages with the epithet of outcast. . . . And true it is that the worst slavery is his lot [even] at home, for he is there exposed to the constant peril of becoming also a victim, slaughtered with the most revolting torments. Tyrant of his blood, he traffics in slavery as it were merchandise, makes war purposely to capture neighbors, and sells even his own wives and children. [172–73]

Is the negro made for slavery? God in heaven! what are we that, because we cannot understand the mystery of this Thy will, we should dare rise in rebellion and call it wrong, unjust, and cruel? The kindness of nature fits each creature to fulfill its destiny. The very virtues of the negro fit him for slavery, and his vices cry aloud for the checks of bondage. Would it not be more worthy of thinking men, instead of endeavoring to brand with infamy a system so evidently marked out by the finger of God, rather to combine their efforts to make that system what it should be? Instead of driving the

29. Campbell, *Negro-mania,* p. 172. The last sentence reads, as cited in *Negro-mania:* "Notwithstanding the listless torpidity caused by excessive heat, the perceptive faculties of the children are far from contemptible; they have a quick apprehension of the ridiculous, often surpassing the intelligence of the white, and only drop behind them about the twelfth year, when the reflective powers begin to have the ascendancy."

30. LSM's interpolation.

31. LSM's interpolation, without notice.

slaveholder, by an interference which puts his property and life in danger, to acts of harshness and restraint entirely unnecessary by the laws of nature, would it not be more wise, more human, and more philanthropic, to aid in removing obstacles, to soften difficulties, and thus prevent the abuses of a system which, sanctified by the laws of nature, needs but the fair operation of those laws to be like every other result of God's thought, beautiful in the undeviating order of creation? Beautiful it is in its fulfillment; hideous only in the unnatural struggle which, opposing man's law to God's law, rouses the evil passions of men in a vain effort to correct the works of Omniscience. But let us sum up this branch of our subject in the words of Dr. T. D. English, from a letter addressed to the author of *Negro-mania:*

> The steady advance of the white species meets with no parallel in the black. The latter has proved itself, when left to itself, to be incapable of progress. Even when taught by a superior species, it soon retrogrades to hopeless barbarism. To give it dominance is to extinguish agriculture, destroy the mechanic arts, and root out science. Such an apparent exception as may be seen in Liberia, gladly as the philanthropist may hail it, proves only the power given by the infusion of other blood. The mulattoes there, as here, have the most intellectual force. When these wear out, as they will in time, a recurrence to the characteristics of the predominant original race will reproduce <reintroduce> barbarism—unless, indeed, this calamity be averted by a renewed amalgamation. Nor do the isolated cases of Negro smartness, in this country, prove anything more than the value of a Caucasian <of Caucasian> admixture.[32] Nature has marked, by unerring lines, the distinction between the species; and her tokens cannot be wiped out by either the sophistry of the negrophilist or the cant of the fanatic. The manifest moral, intellectual, and physical inferiority of the Negro issues from the decree of God, which no efforts of man can either alter or abrogate. Even modification must be but partial, at least. It is the destiny of the Negro, if *by himself, to be a savage,* if *by the white, to be a serf.* He may be a savage in name and in fact, as in Africa, or in fact only, as in Hayti; he may be a serf in name and in fact, as in the Southern States, or in fact only, as in the Northern States; but savage or serf he must be.
>
> No man who values himself, who has any regard for sound morality, or who feels any desire to see intellectual progress made certain, can join in the absurd attempt to raise the Negro to his own level. A movement for such ends is necessarily impotent, and can only result, at the best for the Negro, in the degradation of the white. Kindness to these unfortunate beings is the

32. Omitted here, without notice, is: "I doubt much whether there be a pure Negro in the whole United States of America. Where such a one is found, he will also be found to be, body and soul, a barbarian."

> duty of every man. They may be styled human beings, though of an inherently degraded species. To [attempt to][33] relieve them from their natural inferiority is idle in itself, and may be mischievous in its results. Calculated as it is to arouse evil passions, it may one day provoke a necessity, not to be contemplated without horror. It may lead to a war between the species, which must <will> result in the extirpation of the Negro. True philanthropy—not that sickly sentiment which neglects the interests <interest> of the white laborer to cant about the black—but a true and honest regard for the best interests of mankind, will maintain the Negro undisturbed in the relation which God has marked out for him.[34]

What that relation is, can, we think, be pretty fairly deduced from such testimony as we have here seen advanced. The alternatives are serfdom or savagedom, a state of equality being, we think, honestly proved impossible. The antagonism of races is working itself out, in every instance where two races are put in collision, by the quicker or slower extinction of the inferior and feebler race. The only exceptions to this rule which the world has ever seen are where the beneficent system of serfdom (i.e., slavery) has come to the rescue and protection of the weaker race; and nowhere has this system been exhibited in more perfection, and freer from the abuses (for every system has its abuses) with which it is stained, than in the negro slavery of our Southern States. Knox has shown us everywhere the white blood treading down and exterminating the darker races. "The Saxon," he remarks,

> will not mingle with any dark race, nor will he allow him to hold an acre of land in the country occupied by him. . . . Already[, in a few years,] we have cleared Van Dieman's Land of every *human* aboriginal; Australia, of course, follows, and New Zealand next. There is no denying the fact that the Saxon, call him by what name you will, has a perfect horror for his darker brethren. Hence the folly of the war carried on by the philanthropists of Britain against nature. . . . [266–67]
>
> The Anglo-Saxon has already cleared out Tasmania. It was a cruel, cold-blooded, heartless deed. Australia is too large to attempt the same plan there; but, by shooting the natives as freely as we do crows in other countries, the population must become thin and scarce in time. [243–44]

"It would be revolting," says Col. C. H. Smith, whom we have already quoted as the advocate of the dark races, "to believe that the less gifted tribes were predestined to perish beneath the conquering and all-absorbing covet-

33. LSM's interpolation, without notice.

34. Campbell, *Negro-mania,* pp. 430–32 (LSM's italics). Thomas Dunn English (1819–1902), born in Philadelphia; physician, lawyer; wrote songs, plays, novels, poems.

ousness of European civilization without an enormous load of responsibility resting on the perpetrators. Yet this fate appears to be sealed in many quarters, and seems by a pre-ordained law to be an effect of more mysterious import than human reason can grasp." [166] Revolting though it may be to our eye, which pierces but the outer thought of creation's plan, if this be really the pre-ordained law of our existence, shall we better matters by struggling against it? One only door seems opened by nature to prevent such a catastrophe, and that is through the beneficent system of serfdom or, otherwise, slavery. The word is of little import: the thing is the same. The negro, docile in subjection, attached, like the household dog, to his master—only, in proportion to his intellect, in a far higher grade of being—is satisfied and happy in the half-civilized condition which, with us, his imitativeness enables him to attain. Liberated—in other words, unprotected—and starving for want of protection, the dog, as the negro, returns to the untaught habits and instincts of nature. Thievish and wolfish, the dog, poor fellow, is easily disposed of, and a gun, or a rope, settles the difficulty—as far as he is concerned. The negro is, it seems, according to Mr. Knox, occasionally disposed of by the same summary process. In more civilized communities, where law protects him, he will still, if the black population be comparatively small, dwindle and disappear before the antagonism of race, as we see now in the process of exemplification in our Northern States. But where the proportion is in an opposite ratio, the negro, whose individual is, as a man, protected by the law, becomes soon, in the aggregate, too powerful for the law. Then comes the clash of race, hideously developed in all its horrible proportions. The brutish propensities of the negro now unchecked, there remains no road for their full exercise (unless the white man voluntarily retreats before him) but in the slaughter of his white master, and through that slaughter he strides (unless he himself be exterminated) to the full exercise of his native barbarity and savageism. And this, then, is the consummation so devoutly to be wished![35] Congo civilization! Hottentot civilization! Haytien civilization!!!

Jamaica is fast treading on the tracks of Hayti. British philanthropy has already succeeded in making the rich lands of that fair isle so utterly valueless, that the white man must soon abandon his right to live in it. And the vast and beautiful territory composing the southern and southwestern states of America—this territory, whose giant youth is governing the world by its vast produce, which holds the reins of Europe and spins round it, even with the fine web of its cotton fibre, a network the destruction of which is the destruction of civilization—is this country, too, to be abandoned to the desert and the waste, to negroism and barbarity, that abolitionism may chaunt its *Io paeans* over our ashes?

35. *Hamlet* 3.1.63–64.

Abolition is not the abolition of slavery. Equality is no thought nor creation of God. Slavery, under one name or another, will exist as long as man exists; and abolition is a dream whose execution is an impossibility. Intellect is the only divine right. Intellect seeks freedom from its own proper impulses, and attains it by its own proper power. The negro cannot be schooled, nor argued, nor driven into a love of freedom. His intellect cannot grasp it, nor can he love an abstraction which it is beyond his intellect to understand. The apostle of freedom can to the negro be nothing more than the apostle of temporary license and permanent savageism. "Heaven's laws are not repealable by earth, however earth may try."[36]

We have in our article entirely forgotten the odious plea for amalgamation—a thought from which nature shrinks; but as all points are to be met, we are glad to find it in Mr. Campbell's book most ably discussed by more than one learned author. Knox, over and over again, strongly pronounces against the possible permanent existence of a hybrid race, and as such he unhesitatingly classes all mulattoes. "Nature's laws are stronger than bayonets. . . . No mixed race will she support."[37] P. A. Browne, whom we have already noticed as so triumphantly meeting Prichard on the question of the woolly-head, comes here to our assistance in a manner equally decisive; confuting him from his own words, and proving his utter incapacity for the argument he undertakes. Let us remark, *en passant,* of Prichard, that he has been hitherto strangely overrated. His ponderous tomes are calculated, from their imposing appearance and their real merit as a collection of facts, to make a great impression upon that large proportion of readers who read without close observation, and adopt without dispute the conclusions of their author; but we are glad to believe that a more just appreciation is now being formed of his labors. We have seen a notice, among other similar articles, of a review of his works, in the form of a treatise, by Dr. Caldwell (Cincinnati: James),[38] by which the false positions of Dr. Prichard are said to be ably exposed, and the unphilosophical tendency of his work thoroughly combated. We have not room for the argument of Mr. Browne, but he satis-

36. Campbell, *Negro-mania,* p. 519 = [Carlyle], "Occasional Discourse," p. 677, capitalizing "Earth" in both instances.

37. Campbell, *Negro-mania,* p. 280, reading: "But Nature's laws are stronger than bayonets—she made the Saxon and she made the Indian; but no mixed race called Mexican will she support."

38. Charles Caldwell, *Thoughts on the Original Unity of the Human Race,* 2d rev. ed. (Cincinnati, 1852). Charles Caldwell (1772–1853), born in Caswell County, N.C.; studied medicine under Benjamin Rush at the University of Pennsylvania; M.D. in 1796; in 1819, a founder, then professor, of the Medical Department of Transylvania University in Lexington, Ky.; professor at Louisville Medical Institute (1837–49); author of more than two hundred books and papers.

factorily proves, what many of us know from our own unlearned observation, that no mulatto race is self-perpetuating. They are subject to the law of hybrids, and can only continue to exist so long as they continue to receive supplies from the original races whence they sprang. These ceasing to flow in, with equipoised proportions, the predominating race gains the ascendant. Could we suppose, therefore, the possibility of a general amalgamation of the races, the certain result would be that, as the dark races by far outnumber the white, the white must, by the course of nature, become in time extinct. But such "is not the ultimate issue; no, not that."[39] God has implanted in the white races, for their own preservation and for the perfecting of their high destiny, that strong antagonistic feeling of race which holds them aloof in their purity. The white and the dark races can never amalgamate. "Nature's laws are stronger than bayonets"—stronger than the full tide of abolition and colonization societies, with all their old women and negro men, Lucretia Motts and Fred. Douglasses to boot. Wilberforce was a good man, no doubt, a well-meaning, sentimentally good man; but all the vice and all the crimes of all the hardened and ruffianly criminals whom the gallows has disposed of for the last century, could not, if allowed the full scope of their career, have accomplished one-tenth of the ill—one shadow of the evil—which this same sentimental goodness has occasioned. The first piddles in little murders, the last sweeps away nations. Goodness, which in its well-meaning ignorance assumes an antagonistic position to nature's laws, becomes infinitely mischievous. Those laws, embodying, as they do, the thought of God, must finally prevail; but alas for the generations upon whose destinies such antagonistic influences act! For them at least the beautiful thought of God, the all-conquering order of nature, becomes a fearful scourge. Placed in antagonism with it, they cannot destroy it—it must destroy them. The thought of God prevails, and generations are swept away. "*Depart ye quack-ridden, incompetent!*"[40]

"Every one knows," says *Blackwood,* "how easy it is to get up a shout upon any vague pretext of humanity, and how frequently the credulity of the people of England has been imposed on by specious and designing hypocrites. With this set of men Africa has been for many years a pet subject of complaint. They have made the wrongs of the negro a short and profitable cut to fame and fortune, and their spurious philanthropy has never failed to engage the support of a large number of weak but well-meaning individuals, who are totally ignorant of the real objects which lie at the bottom of the

39. Campbell, *Negro-mania,* p. 517 = [Carlyle], "Occasional Discourse," p. 676, reading: "No; that is not the ultimate issue; not that."

40. Campbell, *Negro-mania,* p. 520 = [Carlyle], "Occasional Discourse," p. 678.

agitations <agitation>."[41] "An abolition meeting," remarks Mr. Campbell, "is held at some <a> town in Ohio, New York, or Pennsylvania; speeches are made, negro wrongs are dwelt upon, Burns is quoted, 'A man's a man for a' that,' and Terence also, *Homo sum et nihil a me alienum puto,*[42] 'My black brother,' and 'All men are born free and equal.' The meeting terminates; an impression is made, and frequently even upon strong minds. There are no libraries within reach [of them]; the different authors' works are too expensive, and the abolition poison runs through the mental system [precisely] as hydrophobia [does] through the physical, until the patient becomes a rabid, raving fanatic." [546] The author goes on to say that his volume is intended to popularize the subject, and thus to counteract this evil. Most heartily do we wish him success. Full time it is that something were doing—sinking as we are, to use the words of Carlyle,

> in deep froth oceans of "Benevolence," "Fraternity," "Emancipation-principle," "Christian Philanthropy," and other most amiable looking, but most baseless and, in the end, baleful and all-bewildering jargon. . . . Never, till now[, I think,] did the sun look down on such a jumble of human nonsenses. . . . We have a long way to travel back, and terrible flounderings to make, and in fact an immense load of nonsense to dislodge from our poor heads, and manifold cobwebs to rend from our poor eyes, before we get into the road again, and can begin to act as serious men that have work to do in this Universe, and no longer as windy sentimentalists that merely have speeches to deliver and speeches <despatches> to write. . . . Our own white or sallow Ireland, sluttishly starving from age to age on its act-of-parliament freedom, was hitherto the flower of mismanagement among nations; but what will this be to a Negro Ireland, with pumpkins themselves fallen short <scarce>, like potatoes? Imagination cannot fathom such an object; the belly of Chaos never held the like. The human mind, in its wide wanderings, has not dreamt yet of such a "freedom" as that will be. . . . Terrible [must be][43] the struggle to return from <return out of> our delusions, floating rapidly on which, not the West Indies alone, but Europe generally, is nearing the Niagara Falls.[44]

41. Campbell, *Negro-mania,* pp. 522–23 = [W. E. Aytoun], "Our West Indian Colonies," *Blackwood's Edinburgh Magazine* 63 (Feb. 1848): 219–38; 224.

42. Robert Burns, "For A' That and A' That," l. 12; Terence *Heauton timorumenos* 77: "Homo sum: humani nil a me alienum puto" ("I am a human being; I think that nothing human is alien to me").

43. LSM's interpolation, without notice.

44. Campbell, *Negro-mania,* pp. 505–6, 508–9 = [Carlyle], "Occasional Discourse," pp. 671–73.

We agree with Mr. Campbell that a full and open discussion on the subject of the races is the likeliest mode of warding off the terrible evil which hangs over us. We are hardly sanguine enough to believe with him that "there is a rapid change going on in the public mind of our northern states <public mind in the North,> favorable to negro slavery" [469]; but we do believe that nothing would go farther towards expediting such a change than the bold expression of such fair and honorable views as he has not hesitated to advance. "Let our citizens," he says, "understand the real merits of the question at issue, and there is no fear but a healthy tone will be given to public opinion, and that maudlin, silly humanitarianism will give way to true ideas and plain, practical common sense. . . . It is only necessary to demand discussion, open, fair, and free discussion, to prove to our working citizens the extreme wickedness of freeing the Negro under any pretext at all." [456, 459] Fain would we believe this; and from our hearts we thank Mr. Campbell for his manly effort in the true cause of civilization and humanity. It is indeed a noble cause; and high the meed of praise to those who contribute to unmask the hideous form which now, under the assumed name of philanthropy, covering like the veiled prophet of Khorassan its fearful loathsomeness with the garb and appurtenances of divinity, claims the worship of the world.

Not the long-promised light, the brow whose beaming
Was to come forth all-conquering, all-redeeming,
But features horribler than hell e'er traced
On its own brood. . . .
There, ye wise saints, behold your light, your star,
Ye *would* be dupes and victims, and ye *are*.[45]

L. S. M.

45. Thomas Moore, *Lalla Rookh,* "The Veiled Prophet of Khorassan," in *Poetical Works* (New York, 1867), p. 401.

9.

Uncle Tom's Cabin

Truly it would seem that the labour of Sisyphus is laid upon us, the slaveholders of these southern United States. Again and again have we, with all the power and talent of our clearest heads and strongest intellects, forced aside the foul load of slander and villainous aspersion so often hurled against us, and still, again and again, the unsightly mass rolls back, and, heavily as ever, fall the old refuted libels, vamped, remodelled, and lumbering down upon us with all the force, or at least impudent assumption, of new argument. We anticipate here the answer and application of our charitable opponents. We, too, have studied our mythology, and remember well, that the aforesaid Sisyphus was condemned to his torment for the sins of injustice, oppression, and tyranny.[1] Like punishment to like sin will, no doubt, be their corollary.

SQR, n.s., 7 (Jan. 1853): 81–120. Publications reviewed: Harriet Beecher Stowe, *Uncle Tom's Cabin or, Life among the Lowly,* 2 vols. (Boston: J. P. Jewett, 1852); [Rufus W. Griswold?], "Contemporary Literature of America," *Westminster Review* 58 (July 1852): 272–87. *Uncle Tom's Cabin* has been frequently reprinted. The Library of America edition of Harriet Beecher Stowe, ed. Kathryn K. Sklar (1982), comprising three novels, reprints the first American book edition of *Uncle Tom's Cabin* (listed above). This in turn has been issued separately as a paperback, retaining the pagination of the hardback Library of America Stowe and adding an introduction by James M. McPherson (New York, 1991), from which the page references supplied below are derived.

1. More precisely, Sisyphus, king of Corinth, suffered for insulting the gods (*hubris*). Sentenced to die for betraying one of Zeus' love affairs, Sisyphus instructed his wife Merope to refuse his body proper burial. In the Underworld he persuaded Hades to permit him to visit earth, so that he might punish Merope for her impiety before returning to the Under-

Boldly, however, before God and man, we dare hold up our hand and plead "not guilty." Clearly enough do we see through the juggle of this game. It is no hand of destiny, no fiat of Jove, which rolls back upon us the labouring bulk. There is an agent behind the curtain, vulnerable at least as ourselves; and the day may yet come when, if this unlucky game cease not, the destructive mass shall find another impetus, and crush beneath its unexpected weight the hand which now directs it, we scarce know whether in idle wantonness or diabolic malice.

Among the revelations of this passing year, stand prominent the volumes we are about to review. In the midst of political turmoil, Mrs. Harriet Beecher Stowe has determined to put *her* finger in the pot, and has, it would seem, made quite a successful dip. Wordy philanthropy—which blows the bellows for discontent, and sends poor fools wandering through the clouds upon its treacherous breezes, yet finds no crumb of bread for one hungry stomach—is at a high premium nowadays. Ten thousand dollars (the amount, it is said, of the sales of her work) was, we presume, in the lady's opinion, worth risking a little scalding for. We wish her joy of her ten thousand thus easily gained, but would be loath to take with it the foul imagination which could invent such scenes, and the malignant bitterness (we had almost said ferocity) which, under the veil of christian charity, could find the conscience to publish them. Over this, their new-laid egg, the abolitionists, of all colours—black, white, and yellow—foreign and domestic—have set up so astounding a cackle, it is very evident, that (labouring, perhaps, under some mesmeric biologic influence) they think the goose has laid its golden egg at last. They must wake up from their dream, to the sad disappointment of finding their fancied treasure an old addle thing, whose touch contaminates with its filth.

There is nothing new in these volumes. They are, as we have said, only the old Sisyphus rock, which we have so often tumbled over, tinkered up, with considerable talent and cunning, into a new shape, and rolled back upon us. One step, indeed, we do seem to have gained. One accusation at least, which, in bygone times, used to have its changes rung among the charges brought against us, is here forgotten. We see no reference to the old habit, so generally (according to some veracious travellers) indulged in these Southern States, of fattening negro babies for the use of the soup-pot. This, it would appear, is a species of black broth which cannot be swallowed any longer. If, however, Mrs. Stowe has spared us the story of this delectable

---

world. Hades agreed; Sisyphus then was careful never to punish Merope. But when he came to die of old age, Hades had not forgotten the trick and sentenced Sisyphus eternally to roll up a hill a boulder which, at the summit, eternally rolls back down again.

soup, with the small *nigger paws* floating in it by way of garnish, truly it is all that she *has* spared us. Libels almost as shocking to humanity she not only indulges herself in detailing, but dwells upon with a gusto and a relish quite edifying to us benighted heathen, who, constantly surrounded (as according to her statements we are) by such moving scenes and crying iniquities, yet, having ears, hear not, and having eyes, see not[2] those horrors whose stench become[s] an offence to the nostrils of our sensitive and self-constituted directors.

Most painful it is to us to comment upon a work of this kind. What though "our withers be unwrung"?[3] Does slander cease to be painful because it is gross? Is it enough for us to know that these obscene and degrading scenes are false as the spirit of mischief which dictated them? and can we, therefore, indifferently see these loathsome rakings of a foul fancy passed as current coin upon the world, which receives them as sketches of American life by an American citizen? We cannot; and loathsome as is the task; little as we hope to be heard in any community where such a work can be received and accredited, and where the very fact of such reception proves at once that our case is prejudged; yet will we speak and sift the argument of this fair lady, who so protests against vice that we might think her, like that "noble sister of Publicola," that "moon of Rome,"

> chaste as the icicle
> That's curdied by the frost from purest snow
> And hangs on Dian's temple,[4]

were it not that her too vivid imagination, going so far ahead of facts, shows too clearly that not now, for the first time, does it travel the muddy road. Some hints from the unfortunately fashionable reading of the day, some flashes from the French school of romance, some inspirations from the Sues and the Dumas', have evidently suggested the tenor of her pages.

The literary taste of our day (i.e., the second-rate literary taste, the fashionable novel-reading taste) demands excitement. Nothing can be spiced too high. Incident, incident, and that of the vilest kind, crowds the pages of those novels which are now unfortunately all the vogue. *The Mysteries of Paris, Monte Cristo, The Wandering Jew,*[5] *et id genus omne,*[6] leave the diseased taste of the reader, who has long subsisted on such fare, sick, sick and palled as it is

2. Ps. 115:5–6; Jer. 5:21.

3. *Hamlet* 3.2.237–38: "Let the galled jade wince, our withers are unwrung."

4. *Coriolanus* 5.3.64–67.

5. *Les Mystères de Paris* (1842–43) and *Le Juif errant* (1844–45) by Eugène Sue; *Le Comte de Monte Cristo* (1844) by Alexandre Dumas the elder.

6. "And all that sort" (Latin).

with the nauseous diet, still with a constant craving, like that of the diseased palate of the opium eater, for its accustomed drug. For such tastes, Mrs. Stowe has catered well. Her facts are remarkable facts—very. Let us see on what authority she bases them. This is a question worth examining, as she here assumes to have given us an exhibition of slavery in its "*living dramatic reality*" [513; Stowe's italics]. In her "concluding remarks," appended to the second volume of the edition (seventh thousand) which we have, she says:

> The writer has often been enquired of, by correspondents from different parts of the country, whether this narrative is a true one; and to these enquiries she will give one general answer.
>
> The separate incidents which <that> compose her <the> narrative are, to a very great extent, authentic, occurring, many of them, [either] under her own observation, or that of her personal friends. She or her friends have observed characters the counterpart of almost all that are here introduced; and many of the sayings are word for word as heard herself, or reported to her. [510]

We can only say, in answer to this, that "she and her friends" are far from being, in our minds, decisive authority. If she says "it is," just as emphatically do we answer "it is not." What vender of falsehood but vouches for the truth of his own fabrications? She tells us, "Some of the most deeply tragic and romantic, some of the most terrible incidents, have also their parallel in reality" [510]. And again, of one of her most horrible inventions, she remarks: "That this scene <the tragical fate of Tom, also,> has too many times had its parallel, there are living witnesses, all over our land, to testify" [510]. Living witnesses all over our land are such intangible antagonists that it would be a worse combat than that of Don Quixote against the windmills for us to undertake them, and therefore we must let them pass. One stray sheep, however, she does introduce; and as we cannot be cheated, by the clouds of dust she has kicked up, to mistake him for a giant, we will not need, to encounter him, the courage exhibited by the celebrated Don in his attack upon a flock of the same animals. She says, with reference to a story of brutal persecution and slow murder:

> The story of "old Prue," in the second volume, was an incident that fell under the personal observation of a brother of the writer, then collecting-clerk to a large mercantile house, in New Orleans. From the same source was derived the character of the planter Legree. Of him her brother thus wrote, speaking of visiting his plantation on a collecting tour: "He actually made me feel of his fist, which was like a blacksmith's hammer, or a nodule of iron, telling me that it was 'calloused with knocking down niggers.' When I left

the plantation, I drew a long breath, and felt as if I had escaped from an ogre's den." [510]

The testimony of this brother is the only one which she cites, except in the general "all over the land" style which we have noticed; and we think any one who has spent six months of his life in a southern city will recognize the type of this her solitary authority. Who has not seen the green Yankee youth opening his eyes and mouth for every piece of stray intelligence; eager for horrors; gulping the wildest tales, and exaggerating even as he swallows them? Why, this fellow is to be met with in every shipload of candidates for clerkships who come out like bees to suck our honey; but so choke-full the while of all they have heard of the horrors and dangers incident to these latitudes, that they wink their eyes and dodge a fancied pistol or bowie-knife whenever a man but raises his hand to touch his hat to the stranger. Having made up their minds that Southerners are all brutes, what earthly power can cure the moral near-sight? Not reason, certainly, nor fact either. Their school dame taught it to them with their catechism; and surely those green eyes could never be expected to see across the catechism and the school-dame's teachings far enough to learn the truth. Pity that this gentle Balaam[7] of a brother had not possessed a little of the cunning and courage of those favourite heroes of our childish days, "Puss in Boots," and "Jack the Giant Killer," that he might have decisively disposed of this redoubtable ogre with nodules of iron hands, instead of sneaking out of his den and leaving him there, like a great "Giant Despair," to devour all unfortunate pilgrims who fell in his way. How poor Balaam summoned courage to feel *of* that fist, "calloused with knocking down niggers," we cannot imagine. Verily, there are trials by land, and trials by water, and poor Balaam, apparently, cared not to put his delicate person in danger from any of them. Seriously, is it not easy here to perceive that a raw, suspicious Yankee youth, having "happened" (as he would say) in contact with a rough overseer, a species of the *genus homo* evidently quite new to him, has been half gulled by the talk of the fellow who has plainly intended to quiz him, and has half gulled himself with his own fears while in the vicinity of this novel character, whom he, poor gentle specimen of Yankee humanity, has absolutely mistaken for an ogre because his hand is hard. That the fellow himself made the speech quoted by Balaam, viz., that his fist was "*calloused* by knocking down niggers," we more than doubt—that elegant word "calloused" being one entirely new to our dictionary, and savouring, we think, much more of Yankee clerk origin and Noah Webster, than of Southern birth.

7. Num. 22–24.

Upon the whole, the authorities of our authoress put us in mind of one of our earliest trials in life. Our first entrance upon school being made in one of our Northern cities, we found ourselves, before the first week of probation was over, the object of some comment among the younger members of the establishment, and were finally accused, by the leader of the little faction, of coming from the land of negrodom. To this charge, we, of course, could but plead guilty, wondering, in our little mind, what sin there could be in the association. A portion of our iniquities we soon had revealed to us. "Father's cousin's wife's sister was at the South once, and she knows all about how you treat your negroes! She knows that you feed them with cotton-seed, and put padlocks on their mouths to keep them from eating corn while they are in the field." Vainly we protested; as vainly reasoned. Authority was against us, and the padlock story vouched by "father's cousin's wife's sister, a very nice lady, that always told the truth," was swallowed by the majority, and received in our Lilliput community with as undisputed credence as Mrs. Stowe's brother's account of the fist "calloused by knocking down niggers" will be gulped down by her admirers. A lady-friend of ours, travelling northward a summer or two since, was similarly enlightened as to some of the iniquities constantly practiced round us, but which, blinded creatures that we are, we have to leave home to discover. Miss C., she was informed, had a cousin who had gone school-keeping to Georgia, and that cousin told Miss C., on her word, as a lady, that she had often and often seen baskets full of ears and noses cut and pulled from the negroes by way of punishment and torture. Miss C. couldn't say whether they were big baskets or little ones; she supposed they were not very big ones, because the supply of ears and noses would be exhausted, and she did not suppose it was a case to call for miraculous increase. She could not account for it all exactly, but she knew that it was true—she did. Her cousin was a lady, and had seen it herself. Pity it is that Mrs. Stowe had not made acquaintance with Miss C.'s cousin; the ears and noses would have made a fine picturesque point, graphically introduced among her "dramatic realities." The Balaam brother, however, seems to answer her purpose pretty well, and upon his testimony about the nodule-fisted gentleman, and some enlightenments from a speech of the freesoil Massachusetts senator, Horace Mann, she has manufactured a character which would shame the Caliban of Shakspeare.[8] That great master of the human mind, when he imagined a being devoid of all human feeling and yet possessed of something like human form, remembered that, in the

8. *Uncle Tom's Cabin,* pp. 511–12. Horace Mann (1796–1859), lawyer and educator; member of the Massachusetts legislature (1827–33), and senate (1833–37); of U.S. House of Representatives (1848–53); Free Soil candidate for governor in 1852.

wildest flights of imagination, there must still be kept up a semblance of probability, and painted him, therefore, free also from human parentage. Shakspeare's Caliban was a monster of devilish origin, to whom Sycorax, his dam, bequeathed but little of humanity. Mrs. Harriet Beecher Stowe, however, gives to *her* Caliban a human mother; a gentle, fair-haired, loving mother, and does not shame to pass upon us as a man this beast, this brute, without conscience and without heart, devoid equally of common sense and common feeling.

The *Westminster Review,* in noticing, with high approbation, these volumes of Mrs. Stowe, takes upon itself to pronounce that she has therein exhibited the "concealed realities" of the system of slavery, "without falling either into vulgarity or exaggeration."[9] The opportunities of the writers of the *Westminster* to judge of our habits and manners must, we should suppose, be small; and whence they may have received the capacity for so dogmatically determining the point at issue, we cannot well guess.[10] Simple assertion is easily answered by counter-assertion. *We* assert that there is in this dramatic sample of abolitionism not only vulgarity and exaggeration, but gross vulgarity and absolute falsehood. The *Westminster* goes on to remark of this infamous libel upon our people, that the "darkest part of it is *possible within the law,*" that "the slave-code *authorizes these very enormities,*" and, therefore, whether these things be true or not, it is the "privilege of the artist" so to represent them.[11] We answer, that such transactions are *not possible within the law,* that murder of the slave is equally punishable with murder of the free man; that the slave-code does *not authorize these enormities;* that our laws protect, as far as legislation can, the very beast from cruelty and barbarous treatment. How much more the slave! Cruelty cannot always be prevented. The parent may ill-treat his child, the man his wife, without giving tangible cause for prosecution. But where such cause can be found, an individual may

9. "Contemporary Literature of America," pp. 282–83.

10. If Rufus W. Griswold (1815–57)—born in Vermont, Baptist clergyman, editor and critic in New York, and notorious libeler of Edgar Allan Poe—is the author of "Contemporary Literature of America," *Westminster Review* 58 (July 1852): 272–87, which LSM reviews here, his opportunities to judge of Southern "habits and manners" were not so small, or at least not so remote, as LSM supposes from their publication in an English journal. "Will Southern gentlemen still continue to subscribe to such British Reviews [as the *Westminster Review*], while they neglect those at home, which are engaged, one-third of their time, in answering and refuting the slanders of the very British Journals that are so popular with us? We really trust that there will be a change soon, in this matter, or it will be too late. If we do not encourage our own press, we must go to the dogs, and deserve to go there." David James McCord, "American Institutions—the Monroe Doctrine—Intervention—etc.," *De Bow* 15 (Dec. 1853): 584–95; 585.

11. "Contemporary Literature of America," p. 283; italics in original.

with us, precisely as in any other well-governed country, be indicted for unjust oppression of any kind, whether of beast, of child, or of slave. The public feeling with us is, we believe, as delicate, and as much on the alert upon such points, as in any part of the world. Indeed, the existence of a system of slavery rather tends to increase than diminish this feeling, as, leaving a larger portion of society in a state of tutelage, naturally and necessarily greater attention is turned to the subject. If, therefore, the shadow of such enormities as these volumes describe may sometimes be, we deny that it is "the artist's privilege" to cull out the most horrible exceptional cases, and to represent them as forming the manners and habits of a whole people, vouching for them as *fac simile* representations of real life. What would the *Westminster* say if one should take the celebrated murderer Burke (whose notorious name has given a new word to our language), with some half dozen other such desperadoes easy to imagine, and write a novel thereon, to depict English manners of the nineteenth century, only using so far "the privilege of the artist" as to represent Mr. Burke as an accomplished gentleman, circulating freely in English society, and his satellites as tolerated and everyday frequenters of the same?[12] What would Mrs. Stowe herself say should we take the Parkman tragedy (a much better foundation, by the way, than anything she has raked up in her Southern investigations), and represent such gentlemen as of daily frequency in the pure New England society, the morals of which she would contrast with our own.[13] If the lowest vices of the lowest men, if the darkest crimes of the darkest villains—actions which the vilest of mankind, only in their moments of blackest passion, can perpetrate—are to be culled out with care, and piled upon each other, to form a monster disgusting to humanity, let the creator of so unnatural a conception give to his Frankenstein the name as well as the character of the monsters of fable. Let the creature stalk before us as some ghoul or afrite, and we shudder at the supernatural might of evil, which does not strike us as unnatural because it does not claim to be of the nature of anything with which we are acquainted. But let the same creature be represented to us as a man—above all, as one of many men, forming an integral part of a community of civilized men—and the effect becomes simply ridiculous where it is not disgusting.

12. William Burke (1792–1829), with accomplice William Hare, killed at least fifteen people in Edinburgh in order to sell the cadavers to anatomy schools; executed.

13. The physician George Parkman (uncle of the historian Francis Parkman) disappeared in Boston on Nov. 23, 1849. Remains identified to be his were found in the laboratory of John White Webster, Erving Professor of Chemistry and Mineralogy at Harvard and lecturer at Massachusetts Medical College, who owed Parkman money. Convicted of murdering Parkman, Webster was hanged on Aug. 30, 1850.

God made man in his own image; Mrs. Stowe has very decidedly set up a rival manufacture in the devil's image.

The *Westminster* says that this work "cannot be accused of presenting a one-sided view <picture>;" that "it is rather remarkable <remarkable rather> for its breadth of view, . . . its genial charity." There are some good men and women, it thinks, among the characters represented. "St. Clare is a humane and cultivated gentleman."[14] We must make our readers acquainted with this model Southern gentleman before answering this observation.

In the meantime, permit us to ask whether, in the results of governmental systems, as in all else, it is not a fair criterion to judge the tree by its fruit?[15] Shall we cut down the fruitful and flourishing tree because, theoretically, it was ill-planted, or because its roots do not grow by rule as A., B., or C., or even as whole communities of A's, B's and C's, judge most decorous and most productive? If there is any community whose system of government works better for *all classes* than our own, we are willing to abandon the defence of ours. But if, after all honest investigation, it has to be conceded—as, in spite of travellers' slanders, is conceded, has been proved by many an able essay, and can easily be proved again, whenever space and time are allowed for the subject—if, we say, it be acknowledged that no where are the higher classes more elevated—no where are the lower more comfortable—no where do both and all work together in their several positions with less of bitterness or more of the genial spirit of christian love and charity—that no where is there less misery and less vice exhibited than under the working of our system; if cases of wrong and oppression (which exist in every system, and must exist so long as man is not perfect) are, as in all good governments they must be, exceptional cases, and not cases in rule; if all this is, as we contend it is, proved and conceded, what matters it if Mrs. Stowe's theory, or Mr. Horace Mann's, or Mr. Giddings's,[16] or Mrs. Stowe's store-clerk brother's theory points it out as iniquitous? It is *not* enough to condemn such a system, even were it true, as the *Westminster* falsely states, that the horrors imagined by Mrs. Stowe are "possible within the law." Evils, to be felt, must be tangible and not theoretic evils. It is not enough that a master *might* do this, and *might* do that. The question is, what *does* he, in the majority of

14. "Contemporary Literature of America," p. 283.

15. Matt. 12:33: "Either make the tree good, and his fruit good; or else make the tree corrupt, and his fruit corrupt: for the tree is known by his fruit."

16. Joshua Reed Giddings (1795–1864), Ohio member of the U.S. House of Representatives (1838–42, 1842–59), was censured by the House in 1842 for violent antislavery activities; opposed the Compromise of 1850.

cases, do? How does the system work? not how *ought* it to work, according to my theory, or your theory, or his theory? Theory has done, and is doing, wild work in our world, of late years. The French universal equality and fraternity theory, for instance, after inundating the country in blood, and trying its wing in every variety of communistic and socialistic flight, has finally theorized itself away into as hard a despotism as tyrant could desire. The Mormon theory has introduced regular and legally established polygamy into these United States. The woman's rights theory is putting the ladies into their husbands' pantaloons; and Mrs. Stowe's theory would lead them, Heaven knows where! All spirit of joking leaves us as we look shudderingly forward to *her* results. Amalgation is evidently no bugbear to this lady.

But let us look a little into the drama of our romance. The book opens with the introduction of "*two gentlemen,*" seated at a table in a house, of which the general style "indicated easy, and even opulent circumstances." The master of the house is one of the "gentlemen." The other, "when *critically* examined, did not seem, *strictly* speaking, to come under the species." [11; LSM's italics] This gentleman, who proves to be a slave-trader, but who must be so *critically* examined to discover that he is not *strictly a gentleman,* seems, however, quite at his ease, and rattles his watch-seals like a man of consequence, hale fellow well met with the opulent signor, whom he constantly and familiarly terms Shelby (leaving off the form of Mr.) and occasionally slaps on the back, to make his conversation more impressive. Into what society can Mrs. Stowe have been admitted, to see slave-traders so much at their ease in gentlemen's houses? We have lived at the South, in the very heart of a slave country, for thirty years out of forty of our lives, and have never seen a slave-trader set foot in a gentleman's house. Such a début argues somewhat queerly for the society with which madame and her clerk-brother have associated, and prepares us for some singular scenes in the elegant circles to which she introduces us.[17]

To give some idea of the style of these volumes, we will presently quote a page from the conversation of these two *gentlemen.* Mr. Shelby, the opulent owner of the house, is, it appears, in debt to an amount not stated, but, as he proposes paying his debt by the transfer of *one* negro, we are to presume that it does not exceed a thousand dollars. Strange to say, this opulent Ken-

17. "In no State in the Union is a negro-trader less respected, than in South Carolina. It has always been so within the recollection of the writer, which extends to more than half a century. Familiar with most of the Southern States, he believes the same feeling of dislike exists everywhere in the slaveholding country. They are always contemptuously called by the negroes, 'speculators'; and it would astonish Cuffee to see 'a speculator' at a gentleman's table, no less than to see a black face like his own taking wine with 'mauser.'" David James McCord, "Life of a Negro Slave," *SQR,* n.s., 7 (Jan. 1853): 206–27; 209.

tucky gentleman has no resource in so pressing a difficulty but the sale of a favourite negro, the manager of his farm and his companion from childhood. There are, apparently, neither banks nor friends who could loan so enormous a sum as one thousand dollars to rescue the opulent gentleman from this difficulty, or Mr. Shelby is of the same opinion, perhaps, as our little girl of six years old, who shakes her head gravely and exclaims, "One thousand dollars! Why, there is not so much money in this world, I think." At any rate it is so insurmountable a difficulty that, for this one thousand dollars, our opulent gentleman forgets that he is a gentleman—forgets that he is a man—forgets honour, principle, gratitude, and common sense, and offers his old black friend, his father's slave, his childhood's companion and guardian, the manager of his farm, the husband and father of a whole family of attached servants, to this brute of a slave-dealer, with decidedly more coolness than we could command in ordering the whipping of a thievish cur. To heighten the value of the commodity offered, this gentleman is praising his wares in rather singular language, by the way, for an educated man: "Tom is a good, steady, sensible, pious fellow. He *got religion* at a camp-meeting, four years ago" [12; LSM's italics]. To which remark the gentleman negro trader, who must be so *critically* examined to discover that he is not *strictly* of the first stamp, responds (we beg our readers to notice the elegant familiarity of his style):

> Some folks don't believe there is pious niggers, Shelby, [. . .] but *I do.* I had a fellow, now, in this yer last lot I took to Orleans—'twas as good as a meetin', now, really, to hear that critter pray; and he was quite gentle and quiet like. He fetched me a good sum, too, for I bought him cheap of a man that was 'bliged to sell out; so I realized six hundred on him. Yes, I consider religion a valeyable thing in a nigger, when it's the genuine article, and no mistake. [12]

To this, instead of kicking the scoundrel out of doors, our opulent gentleman answers, politely falling into the tone of his companion:

> "Well, Tom's got the real article, if ever fellow had, [. . .] You ought to let him cover the whole balance of the debt; and you would, Haley, if you had any conscience."
>
> "Well, I've got just as much conscience as any man in business can afford to keep—just a little, you know, to swear by, as 'twere," said the trader, jocularly; "and, then, I'm ready to do anything in reason to 'blige friends; but this yer, you see, is a leetle too hard on a fellow—a leetle too hard." [12]

O tempora! O mores! This is a *leetle* too hard to swallow. But let us go on. After a little more conversation of the same kind, "a small quadroon boy, four or five <between four and five> years of age," makes his appearance. Evidently this "small quadroon" is a gentleman at large, and a pet in the family, for he enters unsummoned, is patted on his "curly head," and "chucked [. . .] under the chin" by his master, who receives him in whistling and "*snapping* a bunch of raisins at <towards> him." The gentleman master then, for the amusement of his gentleman visitor, causes his "small quadroon" to go through sundry funny exhibitions, such as imitating "Uncle Cudjoe when he has the rheumatism," showing "how old Elder Robbins leads the psalm," etc., during which exhibitions "both the gentlemen laughed *uproariously*." [13–14; LSM's italics] On their termination, the gentleman visitor bursts out anew:

> "Hurrah! bravo! what a young 'un! [. . .] that chap's a case, I'll promise. Tell you what," said he, suddenly clapping his hand on Mr. Shelby's shoulder, "fling in that chap, and I'll settle the business—I will. Come, now, if that ain't doing the thing up about the rightest!" [14]

The mother of the child, at that moment making her appearance, carries him off; and as soon as she leaves the room, our facetious and gentlemanly trader, struck with *her* saleable qualities, takes a new start.

> "By Jupiter! [. . .] there's an article now! You might make your fortune on that ar gal in Orleans, any day. I've seen over a thousand, in my day, paid down for gals not a bit handsomer." [14]

The *Westminster* finds no vulgarity nor exaggeration in these volumes! In answer to this vulgar insolence, the master of the house can apparently find no better way of showing his disapprobation than by uncorking a fresh bottle of wine, of which he politely asks the opinion of his polished guest.

> "Capital, sir—first chop!" said the trader; then turning, and slapping his hand familiarly on Shelby's shoulder, he added: "Come, how will you trade about the gal?" [14–15]

But enough of this disgusting vulgarity. Need we say to any reader who has ever associated with decent society anywhere, that Mrs. Stowe evidently does not know what "a gentleman" is. We will pass over the one who, upon *critical* examination, shows that he is somewhat deficient; but what will any gentleman or lady say to Mr. Shelby? Mrs. Stowe has associated much, it would appear, with negroes, mulattoes, and abolitionists; possibly, in her exalted dreams for the perfection of the race, she has forgotten the small punctilios of what, in the ordinary parlance of the world, is called decent society. She will, therefore, perhaps, excuse a hint from us, that her next dramatic sketch would be much improved by a somewhat increased decency of deportment in her performers. Whatever may be the faults, the vices, or the crimes of any man holding the position of gentleman (at least we vouch for a southern community), he would be above such coarse vulgarity. We would suggest, too—as she, no doubt taken up with her glorious aspirations and high and *uncommon* feelings, has forgotten what portion of *common* ones more ordinary creatures have—that it would be well to allow the appearance of the shadow of such even to us wretched slaveholders. If we are brutes, we usually try to appear a little more like human beings; and it would decidedly look more "nateral like" so to represent us. She describes this Mr. Shelby as "a fair average kind of man, good-natured and kindly" [19]; and yet, after the above scene, and a great deal more of discussion as to how a mother bears to have her children taken from her, in which the negro-trading gentleman, Haley, edifies the opulent gentleman, Shelby, with sundry descriptions in the taste and tone of the following:

> "I've seen 'em as would pull a woman's child out of her arms, and set him up to sell, and she screechin' like mad all the time—very bad policy—damages the article—makes 'em quite unfit for service sometimes. I knew a real handsome gal once, in Orleans, as was entirely ruined by this sort o' handling. The fellow that was tradin' <trading> for her didn't want her baby; and she was one of your real high sort, when her blood was up. I tell you, she squeezed up her child in her arms, and talked, and went on real awful. It kinder makes my blood [run] cold to think on't; and when they carried off the child, and locked her up, she jest went ravin' mad, and died in a week. Clear waste, sir, of a thousand dollars, just for want of management." [15–16]

After this, we say, the "good-natured and kindly" Mr. Shelby determines to sell the child in a quiet way, to avoid the *screechin'*, by stealing it away from its mother. Upon this very probable and natural incident, as Mrs. Stowe and the *Westminster* pronounce it, turns the principal romance of the story. The woman runs away with her child, and after adventures infinite, finally arrives among the Quakers and in Canada, etc.

In the next scene, the authoress introduces us to one of her high and noble characters, one of those whose hearts, uncontaminated by the debasing effects of our system, rise above it. We will see whether she understands this class better than the gentlemanly, "good-natured and kindly": "Mrs. Shelby was a woman of a high class, both intellectually and morally," with "magnanimity and generosity of mind, . . . high moral and religious sensibility and principles, carried out with [great] energy and ability into practical results" [20–21]. This very sensible, moral, and religious lady, when made acquainted with her husband's brutal conduct, is very naturally distressed at it. But what remedy does she find? Does she consult with him as a wife should consult? Does she advise as a woman can advise? Does she suggest means and remedies for avoiding such a crisis? Does she endeavour to show her husband the folly and madness, as well as the wickedness, of his course? No. After a few remonstrances, feebly advanced, she, too (the high intellectual woman!), seems to be struck dumb with the insurmountability of that terrible debt which is to be paid by the sale of *one elderly man and a little child;* she, too, seems to think there is no imaginable way for a comfortable farmer or planter to get round that enormous sum of the one thousand dollars or thereabouts; and neither she nor her good-natured and kindly husband seem[s] to imagine or to care whether it might not be possible—quite as easy, perhaps—should they be forced to part with a negro or two, to dispose of them in families to some humane neighbour (such servants as these are described to be seldom go begging for owners), instead of tearing them apart and selling to a brutal slave-dealer, whom Mr. Shelby himself describes as "cool and unhesitating, and unrelenting as death and the grave" [49]. No; she thinks she fulfills her Christian duty much better by letting the "faithful, confiding, excellent creature, Tom," who is willing "to lay down his life" for his master, "be torn in a moment" from all he holds dear,[18] the petted and delicate child from its petted and delicate mother, while she, the magnanimous woman, who carries out her high principles with energy into practical results, bursts out into a tirade which, if anything could, might excuse the cold brutality of her husband, by the supposition that the poor man had gone crazy under similar lectures:

> "This is God's curse on slavery!—a bitter, bitter, most accursed thing!—a curse to the master and a curse to the slave! I was a fool to think I could make anything good out of such a deadly evil. It is a sin to hold a slave under laws like ours—I always felt it was. . . . Abolitionist! If they knew all I know about slavery, they *might* talk!" etc., etc., etc. [48]

Poor Mr. Shelby! Perhaps we have blamed him too soon. It would not have been astonishing if, with so inspiring a sample of femininity about him, he should have gone raving mad, and after cutting, selling, and slashing, wound up in a lunatic asylum. This worthy couple, however, go quietly to bed; and such was their philosophical equanimity of mind, that "they slept somewhat later than usual the ensuing morning." And so little is Mrs. Shelby troubled

18. Stowe, *Uncle Tom's Cabin,* p. 47, reading: "I do believe, Mr. Shelby, that if he were put to it, he would lay down his life for you. . . . How can I ever hold up my head again among them [the servants], if, for the sake of a little paltry gain, we sell such a faithful, excellent, confiding creature as poor Tom, and tear from him in a moment all we have taught him to love and value?"

by the impending evil (having, we presume, set her conscience at ease by the cursing steam-burst of the preceding evening) that, on waking up somewhat later than usual, she quietly lies in bed, ringing her bell to summon Eliza (the unfortunate mother of the "small quadroon," who is this morning to see her son transferred to Mr. Haley's tender mercies); and "after giving repeated pulls of her bell <giving her bell repeated pulls> to no purpose," coolly exclaims: "I wonder what keeps Eliza!" [57] Oh! blessed composure amidst life's whirl! *She* has apparently no sins upon *her* mind, nor cares either, dear, virtuous lady! She cursed them all off upon her husband and slavery last night!

But enough of this incomprehensible family. This Mrs. Shelby is one of Mrs. Stowe's "first chop" ladies. Let us now look a little into the *model* gentleman slaveholder of the work, Mr. St. Clare, who is pronounced by the *Westminster* to be a "humane and cultivated gentleman." He is first introduced to us joking familiarly with the fascinating Mr. Haley (who seems to have a wonderful facility in making his vulgarity acceptable to real gentlemen) concerning the purchase of Uncle Tom, of whom having taken possession, "soul and body" (to use a favourite expression of Mrs. Stowe, to the propriety of which we are far from prepared to accede), we follow him into the home of an elegant New Orleans family. The household consists of the master, who, having been partly educated in New England, cannot be entirely corrupted by the system of things round him; a New England cousin, with some prejudices, but very sensible of course, and

> e'en her failings lean to virtue's side;[19]

a wife, of whom more anon; and a very angelic little daughter, who, being destined to die early, is, according to approved rule in such cases, represented as a terrible piece of precocity, and a kind of ministering, guiding angel to the whole family.

The wife had been, "from her infancy, [. . .] surrounded with servants, who lived only to study her caprices; the idea that they had either feelings or rights [had] never dawned upon her, even in distant perspective" [185–86]. Heartless, selfish, foolish, and entirely corrupted by "the system," this strangely obtuse person still appears before us as an elegant woman of fortune. She seems to have no object in life but by continued fretfulness to torment her husband, servants, and household generally, just as much as one person can well manage. Yet, as she is at the head of a princely establishment, and has been all her life accustomed to the elegances, indulgences,

19. Oliver Goldsmith, *The Deserted Village,* l. 164: "And even his failings leaned to virtue's side."

and luxuries of the highest style of living, we must, it is to be presumed, take it for granted that she has the manners of a lady, whatever inherent defects of character, selfish or even cruel, might exist. Indeed, the authoress seems anxious to impress upon us a high opinion of the elegant ease and grace of this voluptuously educated lady, whom she describes as "so graceful <slender>, so elegant, so airy and undulating in all her motions" [213], who has been cradled and grown up in such luxurious elegance as would become some Eastern sultana.

Such a woman, it may be well imagined, might be selfish in the extreme. Spoiled and indulged from her birth, she might snub her husband, neglect her child, be peevish and exacting with her servants; but she *could not* be the vulgar virago. We do not deny that our Southern character has its faults—faults, too, which take their stamp, in part, from our institutions and our climate, as do those of our Northern neighbors from theirs; but we do deny that any Southern woman, educated as a lady, could sit for such a portrait as Mrs. Stowe has drawn. Shrinking timidity, and an almost prudish delicacy, is perhaps a fault of our Southern women—at least, it is certainly a characteristic, which, in the opinion of many, is a fault, and which, whatever merits it may possess at a home fireside, makes them necessarily less prominent to the public gaze, less remarkable to public inspection, and gives a quietness of manner which, when compared to the much more free and easy ways of our Northern sisters, sometimes amounts to insipidity. Such, at least, are the faults which we have heard found by Northern critics. With its disadvantages, however, this manner retains also its advantages; and a Southern lady, even in her faults—aye, term them, if you will, her vices—retains still the shadow of that delicacy which is inherent in her education, if not in her nature.

With what Southern society Mrs. Stowe and her clerk-brother have associated, we leave to be guessed by any Southern lady or gentleman who reads her description of Mrs. St. Clare. To judge from a variety of New England idiomatic expressions, such as: She asked him "to smell *of* hartshorn" [185]; "I can't sleep nights;" "She offered to take care of me nights;" "I don't see *as* any thing ails the child" [320]; etc., etc., we should have a shrewd suspicion that she had found her character somewhat nearer home than New Orleans. These are expressions which are almost as foreign to the idioms of our Southern tongue as Greek or Hebrew. And again, when speaking of an incorrigible servant, this lady is made to say (vol. ii, p. 99):

> "She has been talked to and preached to, and every earthly thing done that any body could do, and she's just as *ugly as always*."[20]

20. Stowe, *Uncle Tom's Cabin,* p. 335, reading: "If she hasn't been talked to, and preached to, and every earthly thing done that anybody could do—and she's just so ugly, and always will be."

We doubt if one Southern person in a hundred, who has not taken an enlightening journey to New England, would imagine the meaning of the expression. The word ugly, with us, is applied entirely to physical, never to moral, deformity. However trifling these verbal faults may appear, we deem them worthy of note, as showing that Mrs. Stowe does not even know the language of the society she undertakes to depict.

The spirit of it is still farther beyond her. *Vide* Mrs. St. Clare's elegant discussion (vol. ii, p. 81), as to whether she or her daughter *sweats* most:

> "Very often, night after night, my clothes will be wringing wet. There won't be a dry thread in my night clothes, and the sheets will be so that Mammy has to hang them up to dry! Eva doesn't sweat any thing like that!" [321]

And again, to a negro girl (vol. ii, p. 97):

> "What now, you *baggage!*—what new piece of mischief! You've been picking the flowers, hey?" and then Eva <and Eva> heard the sound of a *smart slap.*
>
> "Law, Missis! they's for Miss Eva." [. . .]
>
> "Miss Eva! A pretty excuse! You suppose she wants your <*your*> flowers, you *good-for-nothing* nigger! Get along off with you." [334; LSM's italics]

Elegant Southern gentleman, however curtain-lectured or hen-pecked, will you acknowledge this as a picture of your wife? *You baggage! You good for nothing nigger!* Southern language in select society! Mrs. Stowe, by way of showing the effect of "the system," endeavours to make the maids and their mistresses speak as much alike as possible. Her mulatto ladies are at times as unnaturally elegant as their mistresses are vulgar. We have no time for them, however, but must exhibit Mrs. St. Clare a little farther. The coarse indifference which this elegant lady constantly expresses for the feelings of her dependents, and particularly for those of "Mammy," an old family servant, who has tended her from childhood, and whom she has separated from husband and children, can find its parallel in no rank of society. *Never,* we contend, was there the Southern woman, brought up in decent associations, at once so heartless and so foolish that, supposing it possible for her to feel nothing in such a case, would not, for mere fashion and gentility sake, imitate those feelings of which she would know it to be her shame to be devoid. It is not the *fashion* with us to hang out the flag of hard-heartedness. If "*the system*" necessitates in us that short-coming from virtue (as the omniscient Mrs. Stowe most dogmatically asserts that it does, has done, must and ever will do), at least we have learned the hypocrisy to conceal the calamitous deficiency under which we labour. No woman but would, by the tacit moral sense of any Southern community, be excluded from all decent society, did she dare to talk as this lady, the spoiled child of elegance and luxury, is represented as doing.

> "Just as if Mammy could love her little dirty babies as I love Eva! Yet St. Clare once really and soberly tried to persuade me that it was my duty, with my weak health, and all I suffer, to let Mammy go back, and take somebody else in her place. That was a little too much even for *me* to bear. [. . .] I did break out that time." [207]

This is bad enough—ridiculous enough; but we did not break out till some half page farther, at which point we did break out into most uncontrollable laughter when this elegant, spoiled, lounging Southern lady remarks:

> "I keep my cowhide about, and sometimes I do lay it on (!!!); but the exertion is always too much for me. If St. Clare would only have this thing done as others do, . . . send them to the calaboose, or some of the other places, to be flogged. That's the only way." [207; LSM's exclamation points]

Ye gods! we do not believe that there is a lady's maid south of the Potomac who would not blush through her black or yellow skin, at hearing her mistress use such language, however much she might think it her right to occasionally indulge in it herself. An elegant Southern lady keeping a *cowhide,* and *laying it on sometimes*!

Mon Dieu! Mein Gott! We feel like a little one we have known, who, learning the French and German languages simultaneously with the English, used the several tongues indifferently, until she got into a passion, and then, the French and German sounding, we presume, more *cursing-like* to her ear, she whipped out those in high style. We could use French, German, Hebrew, or Cherokee—anything, *mein Gott!* except our own native tongue, which this lady (?) has so defiled.

We wish Mrs. Stowe would undertake an English high-life novel, and give the *Westminster* a home sample of the "privilege of the artist" for which it contends. Should she carry through her characters with a consistency similar to that exhibited in the present work, we might perchance be introduced to Queen Victoria and her ladies drinking beer or gin and water at the first convenient "exchange" (as dram shops are elegantly termed out West), and, when they should get a little tipsy, royalty might amuse herself by boxing the ears of her satellites. Prince Albert, the while, should stand by with a gentlemanly simper, or perhaps offer the "cowskin" to royalty, that she might assert her prerogative *à l'Américaine*. All this, if we mistake not (we humbly defer, however, to the judgment of the *Westminster*), is "*possible within the law,*" and if it be the "privilege of the artist" to consult only possibilities, and leave probabilities out of the question, Mrs. Stowe, with her vivid imagination, might revel in such a subject.

If our readers have a fancy for another scene in the same style, we refer them to vol[ume] two (p[p]. 146–7), where our same elegant lady, become[21] a widow, after *slapping the face* of her maid writes an order in her "delicate Italian hand, to the master of a whipping-establishment, to give the bearer fifteen lashes" [373], the bearer being a sensitive, delicate, and beautiful quadroon girl, as white as her mistress, whom the lady declares it her intention to have whipped until she "brings her down." "I'll teach her, with all her airs, that she's no better than the raggedest black wench that walks the streets" [374]. Reader, we gasp for breath, and are happy, once and forever, to take leave of this elegant Southern lady. We confess to being almost as much frightened as was the clerk-brother in the "ogre's den."

We must return to the gentleman specimen, from whom we have been drawn off by his wife. Mr. St. Clare's New England education, we should say, had marked, whether or not his virtues, certainly his English, very decidedly—unless, indeed, as Mrs. Stowe has put a similar phraseology in the mouth of his wife, she intends to pass upon us such expressions as the following for the English of educated Southern society: "Isn't it dreadful tiresome." "They arn't." "That isn't my affair *as* I know of." "I don't know *as* I am." "I've travelled in England some," etc., etc. This (according to the *Westminster*) humane and cultivated gentleman, besides an occasional habit of being "helped home [. . .] in a condition when the physical had decidedly attained the upper hand of the intellectual" [241], seems to do very nearly nothing but lie upon sofas, read newspapers, and indulge himself in occasional abuse of a system by which he holds a property the possession of which he considers as iniquitous in the extreme, and yet never takes one step to correct this iniquity. The whole tenor of Mrs. Stowe's book implies that all benevolent slave owners are benevolent only because they feel that they have no right to be slave owners at all, and, therefore, endeavour, by kindness and indulgence, to, in some sort, pay the slave for that of which, in their own opinions, they are habitually defrauding him. Verily, this is a sickly kind of goodness enough, and one of which, we are happy to state, we have met with but few instances. To rob a man and pay him back a moderate percentage on the spoils of his own pocket, is not Southern honour.

We are not such votaries of the convenient and the expedient that it has become the habitual life of our "humane and cultivated gentlemen" to daily and hourly continue in the commission of a flagrant act of injustice, because it suits their convenience so to do. If such be the Stowe and *Westminster* idea

21. "Became" in original.

of a gentleman, we are unfortunate enough to have less convenient consciences; and, singular as the fact may appear to this knowing fraternity, we are willing to state upon oath, or in any other, the most veracious manner possible, our fixed belief and certain opinion, that there *really are* a good many among our Southern inhabitants, men and women, who do what they think right, and are not living with a constant lie on their lips and in their hearts; who own slaves because they believe "the system" to be the best possible for black and white, for slave and master; and who can, on their knees, gratefully worship the all-gracious providence of an Almighty God, who has seen fit, so beautifully, to suit every being to the place to which its nature calls it. Ay, Mrs. Stowe, there are pious slaveholders; there are christian slaveholders; there are gentlemanly slaveholders; there are slaveholders whose philosophic research has looked into nature and read God in his works, as well as in his Bible, and who own slaves because they think it, not expedient only, but right, holy, and just so to do, for the good of the slave—for the good of the master—for the good of the world. It is not only a New England "Miss Ophelia" who "would cut off her right hand, sooner than keep on from day to day doing what she thinks wrong."[22] There are men, and women too, slave-owners and slaveholders, who need no teachings to act, as closely as human weakness can, to such a rule. Southern hearts and Southern souls can beat high, and look heavenward, with noble and pure aspirations, blessing God for his mercies, blessing "the system" through which His wisdom obviates what to man's little intellect might seem insurmountable evils, and blessing that beautiful order of creation which ignorant bigotry, vainly, as yet, has striven to cast back into chaos. We believe that there is not, in the whole of these United States, one solitary instance of a Southern gentleman owning slaves and using or even *thinking* such language as the following:

> "The short of the matter is, cousin, [. . .] on this abstract question of slavery there can, [as] I think, be but one opinion. Planters, who have money to make by it—clergymen, who have planters to please—politicians, who want to rule by it—may warp and bend language and ethics to a degree that shall astonish the world at their ingenuity; they can press nature and the Bible, and nobody knows what else, into the service; but, after all, neither they nor the world believe in it one particle the more. It comes from the devil, that's the short of it; and, to my mind, it's a pretty respectable specimen of what he can do in his own line." [261]

22. Stowe, *Uncle Tom's Cabin,* p. 260, reading: "It seems to me I would cut off my right hand sooner than keep on, from day to day, doing what I thought was wrong."

Was there ever a more impudent, wholesale accusation, at once of bold iniquity and crouching meanness, than is here coolly put forward by this humane gentleman in this work so "remarkable for its breadth of view" and "its genial charity." A whole population, not cheating themselves but, with open eyes, living in iniquity, educating their children to it, praying to their God for it, and not one prophet rising in the midst of this glaring, this heinous offence, to cry "Wo! wo!"[23] Why, this is worse than heathendom. The idol-worshipper, crouching before his gods of clay and of wood, believes at least in the Mumbo Jumbo whom he worships, and seeks to make his adoration agreeable to it. Covered with blood and bathed in crime, he still brings to his deity a sincere sacrifice. But *we* dare to kneel before a christian God, mocking him with prayers of which we know the hollowness, and, boasting of the sin which we pray him not even to pardon, content ourselves with claiming Omnipotence as a kind of partner in the concern! "The short of it is," then, to sum up the gentleman's words a little more concisely, that slaveholders are, without exception, the greatest set of, at once, bold rascals and sneaking fools that ever lived. No exception, we presume, can be claimed in favour of such characters as Mr. Augustine St. Clare himself, for, surely, there are few who, entertaining such liberal views as the *Westminster,* would set him down as a humane and intelligent gentleman.

As concerns his humanity, let us examine a little farther. Constantly repeating such opinions as we have just quoted, and adding thereto, frequently, the most vituperative abuse of every thing connected with "this monstrous system of injustice," hoping that there yet "may be found among us <among us may be found> generous spirits, who do not estimate honour and justice by dollars and cents" [365–66], he yet continues to hold the iniquitous possession and, without the courage of a Pilate to wash his hands clean of the sin, he continues to receive the price of blood, and idly luxuriates in the income of his slave-labour, in as matter-of-course a manner as Queen Victoria does in hers, and finally dies suddenly without having ever taken the trouble to secure his dependents from the unlimited control of their supremely elegant and brutal mistress. It is singular enough, too, that this conscientious gentleman, who, converted to religious views very much through the instrumentality of the faithful Tom, dies a true christian death; holding in his own the hand of this devoted black friend; conscious of his situation; knowing Tom perfectly; entreating him to pray for his parting spirit; joining in those earnest prayers sent for him to Heaven's throne from the very depths of this generous, devoted, self-forgetting heart, yet dies forgetting his duty, his solemn promise of liberation to this humble friend, and leaves him hope-

23. Ezek. 16:23: "Woe, woe unto thee! saith the Lord God."

lessly separated from all that he has dear upon earth, in the power of the worst of owners, under this (according to his own statement) "monstrous system of injustice." Strange conduct, to say the least, for an intelligent, humane, christian gentleman.

Apropos of Tom's liberation, what does our authoress mean by talking as she does, at sundry different times, about his master "commencing the legal steps necessary to Tom's emancipation" [356]? Is it so hard to get rid of a negro in New Orleans, that one cannot tell the fellow in three words, or by a stroke of the pen give him a permit to be off? In some of our Southern States there is, we know, a law forbidding liberation within the precincts of the State; but, besides that this is not the case in Louisiana, even in the States where such a law does prevail there is no difficulty whatever in letting the individual take himself off, as Tom desired to do, to "Kentuck," or any where under Heaven, where he could be admitted; and we are quite mystified by these incomprehensible "legal formalities for his enfranchisement" [356] which were the root and cause of all Tom's subsequent difficulties. Do they tattoo negroes in New Orleans when they want to liberate them? Or is there a kind of Freemason ceremony to go through? Or what was the difficulty, that Tom could not take himself off to Kentucky in half an hour, after his master chose to permit him to do so? *We,* in our ignorance, should have supposed that, not only could it have been done at any hour within the many weeks during which the subject was in agitation, but that, even if previously neglected, one word from the master to the physician or any other reliable witness, as he lay upon his death-bed, soothed by the negro's devoted care, would have been quite sufficient to secure the execution of his desires on this point. But the *Westminster* determines that all the horrors and difficulties of the actors in Mrs. Stowe's *dramatic realities* are strictly and entirely according to the laws of the divers States wherein they are stated to have occurred. *Westminster Review* contributors must, of course, be well versed in Southern United States laws. So high an authority cannot be disputed by poor folks, who have not been enlightened on the subject of their own laws and customs by having "travelled in England some," as Mr. St. Clare would say.

We have laboured through the painful task we have given ourselves, to the middle of the second volume of Mrs. Stowe's dramatics, and are heartily sick of our task; yet the most disgusting part of the work is left untouched. We confess, our courage fails us. Not that there is a single argument to answer or a single fact proved against us. But what argument avails against broad, flat, impudent assertion? The greatest villain may swear down an honest man: and the greatest falsehoods are oftenest those which it is impossible to disprove. Mrs. Stowe, among those of her accusations which are the most revolting at once to decency, truth, and probability, puts constantly and nauseously forward, the object for which *she* chooses to assert, that mulatto and quadroon women are particularly valued at the New Orleans market. If, as the only way of answering it, we give this charge the lie, the *Westminster* responds it is "possible within the law;"[24] and it would seem, according to *Westminsterian* logic, for an author who professes to give the dramatic realities of life, a legal possibility is fair material, and human nature's probabilities and possibilities not worth considering. If we answer that there is no more moral population in the world than that of our Slave States (few, indeed, equally so), we are answered with a sneer of derision. We, who live at home in the midst of it, cannot know as well as Mrs. Stowe, who gets her intelligence from "personal friends," and "collecting clerks," or as the *Westminster* reviewer, who know[s] all about it from Mrs. Stowe. We can but meet false evidence by counter evidence; we can but meet false assertion by counter assertion. If Mrs. Stowe, the *Westminster,* and their followers, are willing to listen, we will give them as much of that as would satisfy any reasonable human being. But no. They have had a vision of the truth. It is possible within the law to sell babies and to ill-treat women; therefore it is done, is their sapient conclusion.

So let us, also, imagine a novel of legal possibilities. Here we suppose is a father, his wife, and some half dozen children under age, consequently subjected to his authority. The poor wife, broken down by cruelty, privation, exposure, and hard labour (throw in here much pathetic reading about fascinating beauty, female delicacy, etc.), falls into a consumption, and is dying of want in a wretched cellar. A skeleton infant, hanging on her withered breast, sucks up disease instead of nourishment; while a child of some two summers old, whose emaciated limbs, projecting cheek bones, and eager, ravenous eye, show too plainly that starvation is the disease of which it is dying, as it lies moaning by the bundle of rags which forms its mother's pillow (not even a handful of straw has she to keep her from the cold, damp ground), gnaws, eagerly as its prostrate strength will permit, a mouldy crust which an elder brother has raked from the filth in the street. Other spectres of famine move languidly about the apartment, while the brutal father amuses himself by mocking their staggering steps, and then, pausing by his dying wife, rattles in his pocket some certain amount of cash which he has this instant received from a burly, comfortable looking citizen, who stands coolly looking on at the agonies of the dying woman as her husband, with a diabolical sneer, informs her that not one penny of the contents of his pocket shall she or her brats ever touch. She points to the starving child, which her

24. "Contemporary Literature of America," p. 283.

husband only pushes aside contemptuously with his foot and then, snatching from it the mouldy crust, flings it back into the street, as he exclaims, "Let the little devil die! The sooner the better. I can't kill it, for the laws would catch me; but damn it if I won't be glad to see the whole set of you in your graves." The burly citizen seems too much amused with the progress of events to think of interrupting them by calling in assistance to the sufferers. One of the wretched boys starts up as though he would do something; but the father, striking him back, asks him what he means by his insolence, and the almost idiotic creature (brutalized as he is, and stupified by long suffering) creeps back to the corner where he has heretofore crouched. The dying struggles now come upon the woman, and both the men amuse themselves by mimicking the contortions of her agony, as she lies upon the cold ground. The husband, kicking away from her head the bundle of rags which has hitherto supported it, tells her the sooner she goes to the devil the better, and then carries on in her hearing an infamous bargain with the other brute, for the sale of his second daughter (beautiful girl, shrinking innocence, etc.—these may be much expatiated upon), with the understanding that, should the law by chance enquire into the affair, the assumed ground is, that the child is sent for benefit of education, etc.; and in case of resistance or attempt to escape insanity can be easily sworn to. The mother, who has already seen her elder daughter torn from her by a similar bargain of infamy, now, vainly endeavouring to utter a remonstrance, groans her last; and, as her dying words are checked by the death-rattle, the husband, pushing aside the almost corpse, tears the terrified girl from that last embrace, which seems as though it would drag her away from the hell that hangs over her young and innocent life, and, turning to the citizen, bids him count out his cash. He comments on the beauties of the child, tells how it is a young, fresh thing, and should pay well; while the other looks—

But *God* forgive us! It is too horrible thus to follow out imaginations whose only aim is to blacken *God's* creatures, and

> Little knowing how to value right
> The good before us, thus pervert best things
> To worst abuse, or to their meanest use.[25]

Shall we abolish the relations of husband and wife, of parent and child, because they are sometimes abused, and because some foul imagination delights in painting them as ten-fold worse perverted than ever truth has shown

25. John Milton, *Paradise Lost* 4.201–4: "So little knows / Any, but God alone, to value right / The good before him, but perverts best things / To worst abuse, or to their meanest use."

them? Shall we abolish every tie that can by possibility be abused? Shall we take such a scene as the above, and because it is possible, as the *Westminster* might say, "within the law," or rather, to speak more correctly, by *evasion* of the law (and just as possible and just as natural it is, as Mrs. Stowe's disgusting dramatics), because such things might, by an imaginary possibility, come to pass in England or any other civilized country, under existing laws, shall we, therefore, declare that they *do* exist in fact, and exist not as exceptional cases merely, but as the daily habit and general custom of such countries, and that, therefore, every system of government shall be reversed and "chaos come again"?[26]

It is the habit of a certain class of Gospel-quoting writers, so to quote those beautiful maxims that they are turned to wrath rather than charity. The scriptures may be quoted, as we once heard it remarked by a venerable divine, to sound very much like cursing. Such persons seem to themselves to rise in virtue, just in such proportion as they can degrade their fellows. They do not mount the ladder of righteousness; but, fixing themselves sturdily on a certain round, they do their best to keep off all competitors, quite sure of being saints, so soon as they can transform their brethren into devils. They discover, imagine, invent blots on the robes of others, that they may boast their own saintly purity, and thank God that they are not as other men. And lest the Omniscient hear them not, then do they cry aloud in remonstrance: "Cry aloud, for He is a God; either he is talking, or he is pursuing, or he is in a journey, or peradventure he sleepeth, and must be awaked." Thus has Mrs. Stowe lifted up her voice, and with a furious onslaught on the mote of her brother's eye noteth not, perchance, the beam in her own.[27]

To disprove slanders thus impudently uttered, and obstinately persevered in, is impossible, unless those who are to judge the question had some little insight into the facts of the case and could know something of our habits and our laws, thus being enabled to judge of the respective worth of the testimony brought before them. So far from this being the case in the present question, not only is our cause prejudged, but our very accusers assume to be our judges. They make the assertion; they swear to its truth; they pronounce sentence; and then, at once judge, jury, witness, and plaintiff, they set up the most lamentable wailings over the horrible creations of their own fancy. To those who are determined to credit such assertions, in spite of all

26. Shakespeare, *Venus and Adonis,* l. 1020; *Othello* 3.3.93.

27. Luke 18:11: "The Pharisee stood and prayed thus with himself, God, I thank thee, that I am not as other men are"; 1 Kings 18:27; Matt. 7:3: "And why beholdest thou the mote that is in thy brother's eye, but considerest not the beam that is in thine own eye?"

testimony, no argument can be of avail. To such as are willing to hear both sides, we have endeavoured to invalidate Mrs. Stowe's testimony by proving that, so far from being well acquainted with our habits and manners, she has probably never even set foot in our country, and is ignorant alike of our manners, feelings, and even habits of language. She makes her Southern ladies and gentlemen talk rather vulgar Yankee-English. Her Louisiana negroes all talk "Kentuck." She is probably not aware that the negro dialect varies even more than the white, in accordance with the local bringing up of the speaker. No negro, we believe, except a Virginia or Kentucky one, uses "thar," for there; "har," for hair; "that ar," for that; "hev," for have, etc. They have a *patois,* much more unintelligible frequently, but not the Kentucky lingo which she puts into their mouths. We doubt if Mrs. Stowe has ever crossed the line of a slave state at all. If she has, it has evidently not been further south than the mere crossing of the Kentucky border. There, with all her prejudices wide awake, she has seen slavery (if, indeed, she has seen it anywhere), in the worst condition in which it can exist. In a border state, constantly open to the attacks of meddling fanaticism, every man feels that his property (while the legal institutions of his state, formed for its protection, are staggering) stands but by a very doubtful tenure, and he naturally looks forward to parting with it in some way or other. Peaceably or forcibly, at a loss or a profit, in some way or the other the thing must come. By this habit of mind, a severance of old ties and affection soon springs up. The child is no longer educated to think that the slave is almost a part of himself, a dependant to live and die with. The idea is constantly held forward of some necessary change; and how to make that change, at the least loss to himself, will, of course, be a frequent question with the property holder. Then comes the clash between interest and humanity, and, the old link of mutual affection broken, too often the sick and weak negro becomes a burden, the strong one simply a property. *This* is no longer the slavery we love to defend. This bastard growth of abolitionism grafted on selfishness, is *not* Southern United States Slavery. It is border state slavery, from which, thanks to abolitionism, have sprung *some* (thank God! only *some,* only a few) of those horrors which abolition writers delight to depict. Here, more than elsewhere, may exceptional cases be seen, that abuse of power which occurs when affection is blotted out, humanity weak, and selfishness strong.

These cases are still comparatively rare; but they are a melancholy proof of what may be effected, when man opposes himself to his God. God directs and man perverts. Make a law perverting nature by which (as our woman's rights reformers would have it) woman and man are equal, and created with similar rights; and what ensues but bloody barbarity and tyrannic force, trampling to earth the beneficent, though often abused, relations which now exist between them? Make a law by which (because the parent sometimes abuses his authority) the child shall become the free and equal competitor for that parent's privileges, to aim at a general home democracy and, on true free soil principle, to take what suits him of house or land; and what again follows but the extinction of all affection, the early murder of infants, the reign of blood and brute force, instead of charity, affection, beautiful dependance, and christian love? Make your laws to interfere with the God-established system of slavery, which our Southern States are beautifully developing to perfection, daily improving the condition of the slave, daily waking more and more the master to his high and responsible position; make your laws, we say, to pervert this God-directed course, and the world has yet to see the horrors which might ensue from it. The natural order of things perverted, ill must follow. The magnitude of that ill, may heaven protect us from witnessing! Mrs. Stowe has seen, on the border lands, where something of a clash has arisen between the rival powers of abolitionism and slavery, a shadow of those evils which would result to the slave when, the natural boundaries of the system being broken down, the master would retain the powers without the affections belonging to his position. These evils her imagination has multiplied an hundred fold; but yet are to be depicted those scenes when the slave, struggling with his destiny, shall force into opposition the rival might of civilization and barbarism, of brute force and intellectual power. Imagination has not yet depicted *those*. She threatens us with a second Haytien tragedy. Hayti! She knows not of what she talks. As the ocean to the wave—as the rill to the torrent—as the zephyr to the whirlwind—would any such scenes, if possible among us, be to those of Hayti, fearful as they were; and as ocean's gulf to a rain-puddle, would be the ensuing barbarism. Mrs. Stowe has a fertile imagination, and has got up quite a respectable collection of "tales of wonder," which would rival in horrors those of Monk Lewis;[28] yet, though she should go on, and on, and on, till even *her* thought should quail, and even *her* heart sink at the fearful picture, yet will she not have touched, yet can she not have begun to imagine, the fearful penalties which indulgent nature would attach to her so outraged laws.

"Thus far shalt thou go, and no farther,"[29] hath God said, not to the great ocean only, when he chained it within its bed, but equally to every creature within the limits of its uses and its intelligence. To the white man, he has given *his* place; to the negro, *his*. The white man who abuses his God-given power, is indeed criminal, both to God and to man. Hitchings there are,

28. Matthew Gregory Lewis (1775–1818), famous for his Gothic novel *The Monk* (1796), was editor of, and largest contributor to, *Tales of Wonder* (London, 1801).

29. Job 38:11.

and disorders numberless, in the great world-system of machinery, which Omniscience has not seen fit to make perfect; but what are these, compared to the general crash which would follow, should man, with his tinkering, upset the whole fabric that he may rectify its errors by his puny wisdom? The civilized world must totter to its foundations, when, if ever, African slavery in America ceases to exist.

As Mrs. Stowe seems to forget, or rather to deny, the possibility of all human feeling in slaveholders, we will not pretend to argue against her grossest imaginations on that ground, but will base what further we have to say upon the moral impossibility of her facts, and their improbability as connected with the one question of "dollars and cents," which she represents as the all-absorbing one of the system. This consideration would, certainly, be alone sufficient to prevent a man from whipping to death a property, a chattel, an ox, or an ass, for which he had paid, and for which he could obtain a large equivalent by a simple transfer of the property to other hands. By Mrs. Stowe's own argument, the slave, being a chattel and a property, would, in the natural law of things, fall under the same rule. But her ingenious malignity, cleverly as it generally works, sometimes, in the zeal of argument, forgets its logic. While her effort is, constantly, to represent the slave as a mere chattel in the eye of the master, occasionally, in order to exhibit the action of some demoniac cruelty, she suddenly forgets her own reasoning and argues upon the supposition of a rivality of feeling; a hatred, not simply as of man to man, even in the indifferent positions of life, but such a hatred, such a rivality, as could only exist among individuals whose clashing ambitions and contending interests should have cast them struggling together in the closest juxtaposition, in one arena, with similar aims, similar hazards, similar hopes, and similar jealousies. In the ordinary relations of master and slave, such feelings are not only impossible, but the mere supposition of them becomes ludicrous, to any one who has looked into the institution as it exists in the United States, between the white man and the African. Such human links as exist between the races under this system are, necessarily, all of a softening character. The natural antipathies of race are checked, and almost obliterated, by the peculiar relation which, at once, unites and separates the races, acting in social life like the disjunctive conjunction in grammar, linking, yet severing so distinctly, that there is no possibility of confusion among the objects thus connected. The master gives protection; the slave looks for it. Interest combines with humanity to tighten these bonds, and it would be impossible for the most satanic malignity of disposition to imagine laws which, under this system, could sever these two great incentives to action. Occasional acts of cruelty, of maiming, or of murder, when they do occur (as undoubtedly, in all relations of life, the nearest, the dearest, they do and must occur), are always, when exercised from master to slave, the result of violent passion and impulsive anger. A man will, perhaps, in a fit of rage, shoot the horse which has thrown him; but can it be imagined that he would subject to a long course of torture, with the purpose of disabling or subjecting to a lingering death, in cold-blooded revenge, the animal which, if he have taken a dislike to it, he can more easily rid himself of, by sale of transfer, with pecuniary profit to himself. Mrs. Stowe forgets that even the vices of men are so arranged by an Omniscient Providence, that they are frequently found to balance one another, and even were the slave-owner the devil she imagines him, his malignity must be checked by his avarice.

We have not room for the story of George Harris, a remarkably intelligent mulatto, perfectly orderly, submissive, and obedient, who is, by his ingenuity and talent, making immense profits for his master at a neighbouring factory. The master, without the slightest provocation on the part of his slave, suddenly becomes jealous of his extraordinary capacity, and determines to put him down. Purposely, therefore, to *force him to be good-for-nothing,* he withdraws him from the only kind of service to which he is adapted, and puts him to the most degrading drudgery, expressly with the intention of destroying the value of his labour. Not satisfied with this, he uses every means that "tyrannical ingenuity can <could> devise," to render his condition "more bitter by every [little] smarting vexation and indignity;" and what reason, forsooth, does this reasonable master give for such a course? "The man is <man's> *mine,* and I do what I please with him—that's it!" [25]

Let us imagine similar conduct towards a horse, an ox, an ass, and what would be the universal comment? That the man is cruel—hard-hearted—brutal? No—that he is fit for Bedlam. Did ever a man in his senses ruin his property, because he is jealous of it? "Dollars and cents! dollars and cents!" Mrs. Stowe, you have rung the changes upon these so often, you should have surely remembered them still. What sends men to the California diggings? What sends them to Australia? What sends them to the devil? Dollars and cents; dollars and cents; dollars and cents. We argue nothing for the conscience, the humanity, the charity, the decency of these abominable slave-owners, given up, as they are, to Satan and his devices; but—dollars and cents, Mrs. Stowe; there is no getting around that difficulty. George Harris's master, if he had taken a dislike to George Harris, would have sold him for as many dollars as he could bring, and not by a slow process of torture have undertaken to ruin and make thoroughly valueless the animal which he held in such fine saleable order. We have here adopted Mrs. Stowe's own manner of reasoning, and in her own style, and following up her own arguments, prove, we think, her conclusions somewhat illogical. No man will, in cold blood, burn down his house, because he has got out of temper with its manner of construction; no man will torment to death, or uselessness, whether his beast or his slave, simply because he has taken a prejudice against the structure of body, or turn of mind, of the article. In either case, however much as he may dislike the concern, he will very much prefer handing it over to the first purchaser for a reasonable equivalent in dollars and cents. The malignity of jealous spite can only arise in cases where rivality has existed. The deadly venom of smothered hatred may rise in the bosom of rival against rival; of friend against friend; of brother against brother; but not—of master against slave.

But our argument is becoming so prolix, that we must cut it short. We could run on for fifty pages, showing our author's blunders and inconsequences. Let any one look at the strange system of management she attributes to her Caliban, Legree; and say how long it would be, with such a system of mingled brutality and familiarity, before a man would be murdered by his own negroes. It would be wonderful if his very horses and oxen, similarly treated, should not learn to gore and kick him to death. Look at her brutal slave-trader, who, after enlightening the reader with sundry horrible tales of mothers driven to suicide or insanity, by having their infants torn from them, finally, by way, apparently, of illustrating his lectures, sells a child of *ten months* old, from a woman whom he has just purchased, and has the pleasure, accordingly, a few hours after, of hearing that she has (as, we are to presume, he, of course, intended, from his experience in former cases) drowned herself. This man must, we should presume, have been some disguised student of the anatomy of the human feelings, who experimented thereon, much as young surgeons do upon the agonies of their cats and dogs. Surely, he was no simple negro-trader, carrying on his barbarous traffic for its accruing gains, or he would have better learned how to cast up his balance of profit and loss. Look again at the wonderful accumulation of instances she offers of *quadroons* and *mulattoes,* so fair as to be almost mistaken—frequently, quite mistaken—for white; with glossy brown curls, fair soft hands, etc., etc. Indeed, seeming to forget that her principal task is the defence of the negro, decidedly the majority of the persecuted individuals brought forward for our sympathy are represented as whites, of slightly negro descent, not negroes. We cannot forbear copying a page to illustrate her manner of exhibiting such characters. Cassy, one of these unfortunates who has made her escape from hellish bondage, appears in a steamboat under the protection of Mr. George Shelby, a young Kentucky gentleman:

> She sat upon the guards, came to [the] table, and was remarked upon in the boat as a lady that must have been very handsome. [. . .]

The next [state-]room to Cassy's was occupied by a French lady, named De Thoux, who was accompanied by a fine little daughter, a child of some twelve summers.

This lady, having gathered, from George's conversation, that he was from Kentucky, seemed evidently disposed to cultivate his acquaintance; in which design she was seconded by the graces of her little girl, who was about as pretty a plaything as ever diverted the weariness of a fortnight's trip on a steamboat.

George's chair was often placed at her state-room door; [. . .]

"Do you know," said Madame de Thoux to him, one day, "of any man, in your neighbourhood, of the name of Harris?"

"There is an old fellow, of that name, lives not far from my father's place," said George, "We never [have] had much intercourse with him, though."

"He is a large slave-owner, I believe," said Madame de Thoux, with a manner which seemed to betray more interest than she was exactly willing to show.

"He is," said George, looking rather surprised at her manner.

"Did you ever know of his having—perhaps you may have heard of his having—a mulatto boy, named George?"

"Oh certainly, George Harris, I know him well; he married a servant of my mother's, but has escaped, now, to Canada."

"He has?" said Madame de Thoux, quickly. "Thank God!"

George looked a surprised enquiry, but said nothing.

Madame de Thoux leaned her head on her hand, and burst into tears.

"He is my brother," she said.

"Madame!" said George, with a strong accent of surprise.

"Yes," said Madame de Thoux, lifting her head, proudly, and wiping her tears; "Mr. Shelby, George Harris is my brother!"

"I am perfectly astonished," said George, pushing back his chair a pace or two, and looking at Madame de Thoux.

"I was sold to the South when he was a boy," said she. "I was bought by a good and generous man. He took me with him to the West Indies, set me free, and married me. It is but lately that he died; and I am <was> coming up to Kentucky, to see if I can <could> find and redeem my brother." (2d vol., p. 291 [493–95])

Some further conversation shows that the wife of this brother is the daughter of the quadroon lady, Mrs. Cassy, who is passing herself off for a Spanish lady of rank and who, thereupon, falls insensible upon the floor. Forthwith, the cabin is crowded with ladies, and all proper bustle, and other accompaniments of fainting-fits, occur; but, strange to say, nobody on this

Southern steamboat ever seems to divine that the mulatto ladies are anything but the French and Spanish dames for which they pass themselves off. Verily, we can inform the *Westminster* that whether such scenes be possible, or impossible, "within the law" according to *Westminster* readings, they are most certainly impossible within the law of nature; and if we of the South had wished to pass a good hoax upon our northern or transatlantic brethren, we could not easily have imagined a more ridiculously improbable scene than that of the woolly-headed and yellow-skinned mulatto, Madame de Thoux (for the woolly-head and yellow skin must have been there, in spite of Mrs. Stowe and the *Westminster*), established as, and passing for, a lady in the cabin of a Southern steamboat.

Earlier in the work, this same "mulatto boy named George" is represented as boldly entering into a hotel in Kentucky, within a few miles of his master's residence (from which he has just made his escape), as a "well-dressed, gentlemanly man," who drives up in his buggy, escorted by his negro servant, having assumed no other disguise than the *dyeing* of his hair and face, to pass himself for a Spanish complexioned gentleman.

> He was very tall, with a dark, Spanish complexion, fine, expressive black eyes, and close-curling hair, also of a glossy blackness. His well-formed aquiline nose, straight thin lips, and the admirable contour of his finely-turned limbs, impressed the whole company instantly with the idea of something uncommon. He walked easily in among the company, and with a nod indicated to his waiter where to place his trunk, bowed to the company, and, with his hat in his hand, walked up leisurely to the bar, and gave in his name, etc., etc.

In the meanwhile, although "the whole party examined the newcomer with the interest with which a set of loafers in a rainy day usually examine every newcomer," this elegant gentleman seems to pass muster, as true white blood.

> The landlord was all obsequious, and a relay of about seven negroes, old and young, male and female, little and big, were soon whizzing about, like a covey of partridges, bustling, hurrying, treading on each other's toes, and tumbling over each other in their zeal to get massa's <Mas'r's> room ready, while he seated himself easily in <on> a chair in the middle of the room, and entered into conversation with the man who sat next to him. (vol. 1, p. 160 [131–32])

These quotations are so delightfully racy, that we find it difficult to abridge them. But we are fast nearing the utmost limits of our article, and must stop. The readers of these volumes will find in them one mass of gross misrepresentation and ridiculous blundering. The authoress is so ignorant of Southern life and slave institutions, that she does not know how very far she leaves behind her the track of probability, and her vouchers of the *Westminster* might, perhaps, if induced to reconsider the matter, be gracious enough to acknowledge that there are some things quite "possible within the law," and yet impossible in nature. We know of no human law forbidding the moon to be green cheese, and the inhabitants of this globe from establishing a balloon communication and furnishing the universal market with the commodity, thereby seriously conducing to the detriment of all future generations, who would thus, by our greedy avarice, be seriously curtailed in their due allowance of moonshine. And yet it will hardly be contended that it is the "privilege of the artist" to make such the material of anything but a "Mother Goose" fairy tale. Mrs. Stowe has wandered almost as far from the possible. If she has not given us moons of green cheese, she has given what is just as far from God's creation: a nation of men without heart, without soul, without intellect; a nation, too (strange incongruity!), of cultivated human beings, so ignorant of right and wrong, so dead to all morality, that it were an insult to Deity to believe in their existence. So anomalous a creation was never sent by God upon this earth, and Satan or Mrs. Stowe must claim the honour of the invention.

We thought we had done; but one point more we must glance upon. Mrs. Stowe, in spite of experience, in spite of science, determines that the negro is intellectually the white man's equal. She "has lived on the frontiers of a slave State <, for many years, on the frontier-line of slave states>," "she has [also] the testimony of missionaries," etc., and "her deductions, with regard to the capabilities of the race, are encouraging in the highest degree" [517]. Bravo! Mrs. Stowe! Your deductions are bold things, and override sense and reason with wonderful facility. Perhaps they would become a little more amenable to ordinary reasoning if, instead of living "on the frontiers of a slave State," you should see fit to carry your experience, not theoretically, but practically, into the heart of one; or still better, perhaps, avoiding the contaminating system, to explore at once the negro nature in its negro home, and behold in native majesty the *undegraded* negro nature. In native and in naked majesty, the lords of the wild might probably suggest more appreciable arguments, for difference of race, than any to which Mrs. Stowe has chosen to hearken. The negro alone has, of all races of men, remained entirely without all shadow of civilization.[30] It is a mere quibble to talk of

30. We speak, of course, of the *real negro,* and not of the African. All Africans are no more negroes, than all fish are flying-fish. The real woolly-headed and thick-lipped negro is as distinct from many African races as he is from the Saxon. And when Mrs. Stowe tells us that Tom "looked respectable enough to be [a] Bishop of Carthage, as men of [his] color were, in other ages" [212], either she chooses to forget that all men of colour are not negroes, or she is lamentably ignorant of the facts to which she refers. [LSM]

his want of opportunities and instruction. Where were the white man's opportunities and instruction, when the power of mind guided him to the destiny for which Heaven created him? when, by the sunlight of reason, he burst the bonds of ignorance, and, echoing the Almighty fiat, "let there be light," saw the day beam, which still to the negro was darkness? What guide had he? what opportunities? what instruction? further than the God-given intellect which nature has denied to his lowlier fellow? The white man needed no leading strings. God created him for the leader and the teacher. The mind of the white man sprang by its own power to that eminence which to the negro nature is unattainable.

Mrs. Stowe herself has, evidently most unintentionally, shown that, however her theories and her fanaticism may lead her opinions, instinct, even in her mind, is endeavouring to point her right. Every where in her book is the mulatto represented as the man superior to, and suffering in, his position. She has been obliged, wherever she has introduced her fugitives into the hearts of white families, and *fraternized* them with their white protectors, to represent these fugitives as white, with the slightest possible negro tint. Even she has not dared to represent the negro in those scenes where she has boldly introduced the mulatto. Even she would not have dared to paint a pretty little Quakeress liberator snatching up a negro bantling and covering it with kisses, and putting the mother into her own bed, and "snugly tucking her in," as she does by the white mulattoes whom she introduces [168]. Even in *her,* the instinct of race is too strong. She dares not so belie her nature. She takes the mulatto as an approach to the white man, gives scope enough to her fancy to make him a thorough white, and then goes ahead with her romance. The real unfortunate being throughout her work is the mulatto. The negro, except where her imagination has manufactured for him such brutes of masters as are difficult to conceive, seems well enough suited to his position. It is the mulatto whom she represents as homeless and hopeless; and we confess that, in fact, although far below her horrible imaginings, his position is a painful one. Nature, who has suited her every creation to its destined end, seems to disavow him as a monstrous formation which her hand disowns. Raised in intellect and capacity above the black, yet incapable of ranking with the white, he is of no class and no caste. His happiest position is probably in the slave States, where he quietly passes over a life which, we thank God, seems, like all other monstrous creations, not capable of continuous transmission. This mongrel breed is a most painful feature, arising from the juxtaposition of creatures so differing in nature as the white man and the negro; but it is a feature which, so far from being the result of slavery, is rather checked by it. The same unhappy being must occasionally exist wherever the two peoples are brought in contact, and much more frequently where abolition license prevails, than under the rules and restraints of slavery.

To conclude. We have undertaken the defence of slavery in no temporizing vein. We do *not* say it is a necessary evil. We do *not* allow that it is a temporary makeshift to choke the course of Providence for man's convenience. It is *not* "a sorrow and a wrong to be lived down." We proclaim it, on the contrary, a Godlike dispensation, a providential caring for the weak, and a refuge for the portionless. Nature's outcast, as for centuries he appeared to be, he—even from the dawning of tradition, the homeless, houseless, useless negro—suddenly assumes a place, suddenly becomes one of the great levers of civilization. At length the path marked out for him by Omniscience becomes plain. Unfit for all progress, so long as left to himself, the negro has hitherto appeared simply as a blot upon creation, and already the stronger races are, even in his own land, threatening him with extinction. Civilization must spread. Nature seems to require this, by a law as stringent as that through which water seeks its level. The poor negro, astounded by the torrent of progress which, bursting over the world, now hangs menacingly (for to the wild man is not civilization always menacing?) above him, would vainly follow with the stream, and is swept away in the current. Slavery, even in his own land, is his destiny and his refuge from extinction. Beautifully has the system begun to expand itself among us. Shorn of the barbarities with which a slavery established by conquest and maintained by brute force is always accompanied, we have begun to mingle with it the graces and amenities of the highest Christian civilization. Have begun, we say, for the work is but begun. The system is far from its perfection, and at every step of its progress is retarded by a meddling fanaticism, which has in it, to borrow a quotation from Mrs. Stowe herself, "a dread, unhallowed necromancy of evil, that turns things sweetest and holiest to phantoms of horror and affright" [434]. Our system of slavery, left to itself, would rapidly develop its higher features, softening at once to servant and to master. The satanic school of arguers are far too much inclined to make capital of man's original sin, and to build upon this foundation a perfect tower of iniquitous possibilities, frightful even to imagine. Men are by no means as hopelessly wicked as Mrs. Stowe and others of this school would argue; and these would do well to remember, that when God created man, "in the image of God created he him;" and though "sin came into the world and death by sin,"[31] yet is the glorious, though clouded, image still there, and erring man is still a man, and not a devil.

We, too, could speculate upon the possibilities of this system, and present

31. Gen. 1:27; Rom. 5:12.

a picture in beautiful contrast with Mrs. Stowe's, as purely bright as hers is foully dark; but, as we remarked earlier in our argument, the fairest reasoning is not from what a system might be, but from what it is. We grant that there is crime, there is sin, there is abuse of power under our laws; but let the abolitionist show us any rule where these are not. Utopias have been vainly dreamed. That system is the best which, not in theory, but in practice, brings the greatest sum of good to the greatest number. We challenge history, present and past, to show any system of government which, judged by this test, will be found superior to the one we defend.

"Oh liberté!" exclaimed Mme. Roland, when led to the scaffold, "que de crimes a-t-on commis en ton nom!"[32] *Theoretic* virtues are more dangerous than open vice. Cloaks for every crime, they are pushed boldly forward, stifling our natural sense of practical right, and blinding men with the appearance of a righteousness, which dazzles like the meteor, but warms not like the sun. Theoretic liberty and theoretic bread satisfy neither the hungry soul nor the hungry stomach, and many a poor fugitive to the land of freedom, sated full with both, has wept to return to the indulgent master and the well filled corncrib. The negro, left to himself, does not dream of liberty. He cannot indeed grasp a conception which belongs so naturally to the brain of the white man. In his natural condition, he is, by turns, tyrant and slave, but never the free man. You may talk to the blind man of light, until he fancies that he understands you, and begins to wish for that bright thing which you tell him he has not; but vainly he rolls his sightless orbs, unhappy that he cannot see the brightness of that beam whose warmth before sufficed to make him happy. Thus it is with the moral sunbeam of the poor negro. He cannot see nor conceive the "liberty" which you would thrust upon him, and it is a cruel task to disturb him in the enjoyment of that life to which God has destined him. He basks in his sunshine, and is happy. Christian slavery, in its full development, free from the fretting annoyance and galling bitterness of abolition interference, is the brightest sunbeam which Omniscience has destined for his existence.

L. S. M.

32. Jeanne-Marie Philipon Roland de La Platière (1754–93), French revolutionary; her husband was a Girondin leader, her salon a center of Girondin activity; guillotined with other Girondins.

10.

British Philanthropy and American Slavery

An Affectionate Response to the Ladies of England, etc., from the Ladies of the Southern United States; Together with Some Remarks for the North British Review*—by a Southern Lady.*[1]

"Fire! fire! fire!" bawled, one day, an officious neighbor, as he pointed to the heavy smoke, whose black volumes rose somewhat threateningly from an adjacent chimney. "Fire! fire! fire!" Street boys soon echoed the cry. Town-bells rang. Rattling on rushed the engines. "Fire! fire! fire!" There stood the officious neighbor, watching the smoke, and rather in hopes that the greedy flame might start up at last to prove him a true prophet. "Fire! fire! fire!" The cry continues, though he vainly strains his eyes to catch a glimpse of the red flash. "Fire! fire! fire!"—The flash, the noise, the crash is behind him. While he, poor meddling fool![2] is watching for it in his neighbor's house, his own is blazing.

De Bow 14 (March 1853): 258–80. Publications reviewed: [Alicia Hill with Richard Whately and Samuel Hinds], "American Slavery and *Uncle Tom's Cabin,*" *North British Review* 18 (Nov. 1852): 235–58; "The Affectionate and Christian Address of Many Thousands of the Women of England to Their Sisters, the Women of the United States of America." For a complete text of "The Affectionate and Christian Address," which was published in many newspapers in Britain and the United States, see app. 1.

1. We recommend this spirited and able paper, from the pen of a Southern Lady, to the attention of our readers on both sides of the Atlantic. The author, though known to fame, prefers the discharge of domestic duties to the noisy applause of the world. Her protest ["Woman and Her Needs"] against the miscalled "Woman's Rights" movement at the North, which we published in our September number of last year, asserted and maintained the dignity, the elevation, the beauty of female character in its relation to that of the male, in the present constitution of society, and without any resort to Amazonian conventions. [*De Bow* headnote]

2. Prov. 20:3: "It is an honour for a man to cease from strife: but every fool will be meddling."

Most noble and honorable ladies! most sapient and learned reviewers! fortunate would it be for your own sakes and ours, could you but fix your eyes upon the stifling smoke issuing from your own homes, instead of keeping them busy with your spy-glasses in watching *our* motions across the Atlantic. These spyglass reports, by the way, play wild work sometimes. We have lately had a droll explanation from a learned professor,[3] of a report concerning certain views of the inhabitants of the moon. It seems that the learned gentleman, while indulging a pretty young lady with a peep at that luminary through his telescope, chanced to mention in conversation with a bystander that, in casting his telescopic sight over the surrounding sublunary landscape, he had once chanced to bring into the view a washerwoman at her tub, whose evolutions had much amused him. The wonder-loving young lady understood this remark to refer to the moon; and forthwith behold in circulation a perfectly well-authenticated story of washerwomen in the moon, and for aught we know to the contrary, the world might have been soon agog for the improvement of the condition of these ladies, and some philanthropic society would have imagined a method for sending them the last invention in washing-kettles, if unfortunately the learned professor had not spoiled the wonder by revealing the truth. Ladies and reviewers, may it not be worth inquiring whether the "Uncle Tom" view of your transatlantic brethren be not as wide of the truth as this young lady's lunar washerwomen? Let us advise you to cast aside your "Uncle Tom" spy-glasses. Look with your own eyes, hear with your own ears, and do not too easily credit stories about washerwomen in the moon.

"Fire! fire! fire!" When the cry is in your ears, look at your own house first. Perchance you may see the sorrow and the anguish there. Perchance you may see the black smoke of suffering steaming forth from the sweltering sacrifice of broken hearts within your own soil! Hangs it not over you, that great sorrow-cloud—thick, dark, dense—even as the fog of your own great London, casting its gloom over pomp and palaces? Sin and sorrow are the badge of mortality; and, gentle ladies, believe us, if you would act the good Samaritan, you will find your sick and wounded, even as you pass along by your own road side. For heaven's pity, then, crush not beneath your chariot wheels, in a wild chase after phantasmagoric evils, those whom God has given you to relieve. You trample over real flesh and blood, while you gaze weepingly toward the painted pictures of a magic lantern.

3. Professor Olmsted, of Yale College. [LSM] Denison Olmsted (1791–1859), professor of mathematics and natural philosophy (1825–36), then of natural philosophy and astronomy (1836–59), at Yale College; author of many textbooks, including for a general audience *Letters on Astronomy, Addressed to a Lady* (1840).

Evils there are, alas! God knows, strewn thick enough through our world; and prophets too there are, whose God-inspired genius may sometimes help to guide us through the labyrinth, and point a ray of hope, shining midst the darkness. But, fair ladies, they are not such as you who can grapple with God's mysteries. Nor, learned reviewers, are ye yet learned enough for the holy task. Your conventions and your appeals, your Uncle Tom corollaries and Wilberforcian apings, are but the filthy scum which, forcing itself uppermost, hides the deep truth beneath. There is evil in God's blessed world (why, God only knows), but there is also good—deep, earnest good—for those who will seek it deeply and earnestly. Below the nauseous froth-scum of sickly philanthropy and new-light Christianity, runs, quiet but clear, the pure stream of God-given reason and common-sense humanity. Ladies and reviewers, *God* is *God,* but *ye* are *not* his prophets. Deeply must the heart have felt, deeply must the brain have thought, laboriously must its problem be worked out by the giant mind whose destiny it is to turn the fate of nations. Who are these who now start up with gibbering, mopping, and wringing of hands, to guide the peoples of the earth to righteousness, and to dictate to the consciences of nations? What know the Duchess of Sutherland, Bedford, or Argyle—what knows the Countess of Shaftesbury or the Viscountess Palmerston,[4] or any Hon[ora]ble Lady A. B. or C. of all who thought fit to convene at Stafford House for the benefit and instruction of the benighted of this land[5]—what know any of these of the workings of great political

4. Harriet Elizabeth Georgiana (1806–68), third daughter of George Howard, sixth earl of Carlisle, by Georgiana Dorothy, first daughter of William Cavendish, fifth duke of Devonshire; married in 1823 to George Granville Sutherland-Leveson-Gower (1786–1861), second duke of Sutherland; mistress of the robes to Queen Victoria. Her daughter Elizabeth Georgiana (1824–78) was married in 1844 to George Douglas Campbell, eighth duke of Argyll (1823–1900), at this time Lord Privy Seal. Anna Maria (1783–1857), first daughter of Charles Stanhope, third earl of Harrington, and Jane, daughter and coheir of Sir John Fleming, Bart.; married in 1808 to Francis Russell (1788–1861), from 1839 tenth duke of Bedford, nephew to the eighth duke, who was Edmund Burke's victim in *A Letter to a Noble Lord* (1796). Emily Caroline Catherine Frances (1810–72), first daughter of Peter Leopold Louis Francis Nassau Clavering-Cowper (1778–1837), fifth Earl Cowper; married in 1830 to the seventh earl of Shaftesbury. The countess of Shaftesbury's mother, Emily Mary (1787–1869), first daughter of Peniston Lamb, first Viscount Melbourne, by Elizabeth, daughter of Sir Ralph Milbanke, Bart. (grandfather of the poet Byron's wife), was married a second time, in 1839, to Henry John Temple (1784–1865), third Viscount Palmerston, who at this time had been three times foreign minister, soon to be prime minister (1855–58, 1859–65).

5. Stafford House, the London residence of the duchess of Sutherland, was a center of abolitionist sentiment in England; there "The Affectionate and Christian Address of Many Thousands of the Women of England to Their Sisters, the Women of the United States of America" was conceived and written, hence being generally known as the Stafford House Address. It carried the signatures of the duchess of Sutherland, the other ladies whom LSM

systems? What know they of American slavery? They have read *Uncle Tom's Cabin* forsooth, and they have seen that the authoress thereof vouches for the accuracy of her facts, even as did the veracious Baron Munchausen for his.[6] They have read *Uncle Tom's Cabin,* and without further question they take it for their gospel, and Mrs. Stowe for their Messiah; and, with the zeal of new converts, start a crusade to the land where their Peter the Hermit (the Hon. the Earl of Shaftesbury) points them.[7] With hallelujahs to liberty, and dolorous laments over negro bondage, they commence the attack; not in person, with the cross of suffering upon their shoulders, but comfortably lolling upon their sofas, they issue their appeals to their sinning sisters of this sinful land with most pharisaical humility. "Lord, we thank thee that we are not like unto these!"[8]

"Fire! fire! fire!" Most loving sisters, be not too much startled by the cry, but retain, if possible, your gentle sympathies and nervous terrors sufficiently within bounds, to enable you to look with the necessary presence of mind to your own premises. "Fire! fire! fire!" This stifling sorrow-smoke, still slowly rising always as though in solemn appeal to the God of Heaven against heart-breaking, body-crushing agony; this constant dumb prayer of remediless suffering, whence is it? Is it only from our sugar fields and cotton plantations? Is it the negro alone whose weary shoulders bend beneath their load? England is a proud country—a great country—a noble and a glorious country; but, proud Pharisee, beware! You may fast twice in the week, you may give tithes of all you possess, and yet you may find, even in happy England, most stringent duties that you leave unfulfilled. The suppliant at your own door is forgotten, while you weep over the unredressed wrongs of foreign lands. Were it not better, gentle ladies, to nurse your own sick, to feed your own hungry, and to trust to the instincts of woman's heart in her own land to relieve her own weary and her own suffering. Can it be that, midst

---

names just above, and, in time, more than 560,000 others. For LSM's direct response to the duchess, see chap. 12, "A Letter to the Duchess of Sutherland from a Lady of South Carolina."

6. Karl Friedrich Hieronymus von Münchhausen (1720–97), soldier; tales of his exploits, e.g., *Vademecum für lustige Leute* (1781–83), became proverbial for their exaggerations and untrustworthiness.

7. Anthony Ashley Cooper (1801–85), seventh earl of Shaftesbury; promoted Catholic emancipation, factory reform, the Mines Act (1842), Ten Hour Act (1847), Lunacy Act (1845), and the work of Florence Nightingale, among many other causes; he was probably the author of the Stafford House Address, of which his wife, as LSM has noted, was a prominent signatory. Peter the Hermit (c. 1050–1115) preached the First Crusade and led a party of Crusaders as far as Asia Minor, where, Peter being absent on a mission to seek aid from the emperor in Constantinople, his followers were annihilated by the Turks.

8. Cf. Luke 18:11.

the millions of America, Mrs. Stowe's is the only true woman's heart which has dared to remonstrate against such scenes of horror as you suppose to exist among us. Belie not thus your sex, noble ladies. If duchesses and countesses can sufficiently descend from their high rank to feel like ordinary women, with everyday hearts, and everyday woman sympathies, will they not blush to think what a slander their "Affectionate and Christian Address" casts upon so large a portion of their civilized sisterhood? Ladies of Stafford House, believe us, you have not the monopoly of woman-feelings, and were the evil of our institutions so "enormous," and prevailing with "such frightful results" as you suppose, long ere this would we women of the Southern United States, "as sisters, as wives, and as mothers," have raised "our voices to our fellow-citizens and our prayers to God for the removal of this affliction from the Christian world." Believe us, ladies, we have not waited for your appeal "to ask council <counsel> of God how far such a state of things is in accordance with His holy word, the inalienable rights of immortal souls, and the pure and merciful spirit of the Christian religion."[9] We can think as women, and feel as women, and act as women, without waiting for the promptings of your appeals, or of Mrs. Stowe's imaginative horror. It seems to us, that you should receive it as a strong proof of how much you have mistaken our system, that so many millions of women—mothers, sisters, and daughters, loving and beloved, civilized women, Christian women—have contentedly lived in the midst of it, and yet the common woman-heart among us has not risen up to call it *cursed.* Are ye women and mothers, and yet believe that these millions of women and mothers, bearing their babes upon their breasts, could teach their own beloved ones, even with their earliest breath, a constant lie? that for the paltry dollar's sake we would bid them suck in falsehood with their mother's milk and teach them to barter their consciences for money? Nay, if ye have not, in the luxuries of rank, ceased to know the mother's love for her nurseling, and the pure welling forth of a mother's hope for the child of her bosom, rather will ye suppose that we will tip those breasts with arsenic, and drug their milk with hemlock. However exceptional cases may shock the world, never did a nation of women systematically rear their sons to be villains. Yet such, and no less, is the charge conveyed against us in your "Affectionate and Christian Appeal." If we have tolerated the system of iniquity that you describe, if we have taught our children to love it, if we are willing to bid them defend it, even unto blood should it be necessary, as man should defend the dearest rights of his hearth and home, what are we? The heathen kneeling to his "Moloch, horrid king, besmeared with blood / Of human sacrifice," and offering his

9. App. 1, pp. 477–78.

child upon the altar of "his grim idol,"[10] has, at least, the excuse of ignorance and superstition for his brutal worship. Not so we. Knowingly and with open eyes, without one twinge of conscience, one *mea culpa,* we fling the offspring of our own flesh and blood into this seething abyss of abominations. This is, in fact, unless we advance the plea of a general national imbecility, the crime of which we are guilty, if there is any foundation for the universal jeremiades which it is now the fashion to wail over negro slavery.

It is useless for us to tell the benevolent ladies and gentlemen who have undertaken to instruct us in our catechism of humanity, that they have quite mistaken our case and are entirely ignorant of the condition of the negro. *Uncle Tom's Cabin* tells them differently. It is useless for us to tell them that our slaves are not interdicted "education in the truths of the Gospel and the ordinances of Christianity;"[11] it is useless for us to repeat that their family ties and social affections are respected and indulged in a greater degree than those of any laboring class in the world. *Uncle Tom's Cabin* says differently; and the negrophilists have very nearly reached the point of pronouncing sentence of excommunication, on the ground of infidelity, against all who dispute the authenticity of so high an authority. It is useless for us to point to the comparative census of the divers nations of the earth; it is useless for us to show that in none are the tables of crime, of deformity and insanity, so low as in our slave population. Mrs. Stowe and Uncle Tom! Mrs. Stowe and Uncle Tom! Mrs. Stowe and Uncle Tom! ding, ding, dong. What is the use of reasoning, what is the use of facts, when those who should hear us deafen themselves with this eternal "ding, dong" of superstitious prejudice and pharisaical cant? As regards the condition of our slaves, compared with that of the white population of our own free states (than which, avowedly, no population in the world enjoys higher advantages), ten minutes' investigation of our late census returns, with about so much arithmetical knowledge as any boy of ten years old can command, will suffice to show that for every insane slave there are from eight to nine insane whites; and that this is not an exception resulting from any physical peculiarity of the negro, is proved by the fact that among the *free* blacks the proportion of insane is, within a very small fraction, equal to that among the whites. This fact alone speaks volumes. The numbers of deaf mutes and of blind, although the disproportion is not so great, show largely in favor of the slave, and are worth dwelling upon as indicating the comforts of his position; but, would men consent to open their eyes and hearts to the truth, volumes of argument and cart-loads of *Uncle Tom's Cabins* would not weigh a feather against the indisputable fact

10. John Milton, *Paradise Lost* 1.392–96.
11. App. 1, p. 478.

which we have just noted of the disparity in the numbers of the insane presented in the different positions referred to. Will the ladies of Stafford House favor us with some corresponding facts among their manufacturing and mining populations? They cannot. They dare not. The statistics of the poor are a fearful study. Duchesses and countesses can only read of them in novels, and weep over them when well draperied in romance.

But our brethren of the reviews, hard-handed and hard-headed folks as they are, venture sometimes deeper, and we are accordingly a little amused, and not a little instructed, by an article in the *North British,* which happens, by accident we presume (though the close juxtaposition looks almost like a mischievous design on the part of somebody), to have its place immediately following the one with which we have headed our remarks. We are amused by the contrast between the two articles. Here stands "American Slavery and *Uncle Tom's Cabin,*" treated of with all the gall and prejudice which the subject always seems to awake in those who ignorantly meddle with it; and immediately annexed is "The Modern Exodus in Its Effects on the British Islands,"[12] wherein the sufferings leading to this Exodus (as the enormous emigration from the British islands is aptly termed) are treated of with a philosophic insight, a coolness of argument, and an apparent careful investigation of fact, which present a strange contrast to the sentimental slang, the careless assertion, and broad misstatements of the negrophilist article. The two together put us strangely in mind of the often-quoted joke of the reverend wit: "Orthodoxy is my doxy, and heterodoxy is your doxy."[13]

In the article on the "Exodus," it is acknowledged of the laborers of certain districts of England (Dorsetshire and Devonshire) that they are "permanently wretched." "In Buckinghamshire and Bedfordshire[14] wages are seldom such as adequately to support life;" and as a whole it is "indisputable that the usual earnings of the rural day-laborer are not sufficient to provide his family with food, clothing, and habitation, of fitting kind and quantity." [264] Of artisans, the reviewer states that "the hand-loom weavers of Lancashire, Paisley, and Spitalfields are either always or periodically in distress. . . . Their toil is so incessant and severe, as to leave no time nor wish for anything but sleep, and to render their life an alarming approximation to that of the brutes that perish." [265] Of "distressed work-people of large towns," needle-women, etc., he says: "These classes are said to number [some] thou-

12. [William Rathbone Greg], "The Modern Exodus in Its Effects on the British Islands," *North British Review* 18 (Nov. 1852): 259–302.

13. Ascribed to William Warburton (1698–1779), bishop of Gloucester, friend and editor of Alexander Pope, in Joseph Priestley, *Memoirs* (1807), 1:372.

14. Her Grace the Duchess of Bedford, it would appear, might find something at home to occupy her special charity. She is second in the lists for the American Crusade. [LSM]

sands in the metropolis alone, and their sufferings and privations are <privations to be> such as can scarcely be credited in a civilized and Christian country. Nor, whatever may be our opinion as to the causes of their wretchedness, or the undue coloring thrown over it, can we refuse to believe in the general fact of its existence." [265] Let our readers remember that we are not quoting from a novel. The writer has no wish to make up a picture. There is no call for the sympathies of readers, no necessity for embellishment. Simple facts are stated in the simplest manner, and that not of misgoverned colonists or degraded Irish, but of the laboring classes of great and happy England. Such as these naturally emigrate largely. Let us turn now to Ireland and guess what must be her condition, even had we no other data from which to argue, when we find that her emigration considerably more than doubles that of the whole of England and Scotland combined. "Of 335,966 who left the United Kingdom in 1851," it is stated that 257,372 were Irish [268]. If the emigration is proportioned to the suffering, what is the condition of Ireland? "By the combined effect of emigration and famine," says the reviewer, "the population of Ireland was reduced from 8,175,124 in 1841, to 6,515,794, in 1851." In 1851 the number of Irish emigrants had risen to 257,000; and in the first six months of 1852 already 125,000 had gone. "Ireland is being depopulated at the rate of a *quarter of a million* per annum, a process which, if continued, will empty her entirely in the course of *twenty-four years*." [273] So much for the happiness of the subjects of Britain. God knows, not in triumph but in self-defence do we dwell upon such facts. We are accused of supporting a system heinous beyond comparison, oppressive beyond conception. What defence have we farther than to show (while we acknowledge suffering and oppression under every system) that ours is certainly not the worst? Let England, if it be possible, cure this, her own heart-disease, before prescribing for others. If it be *impossible,* let her bow to the mystery of God and patiently work out her destiny, leaving us to accomplish ours.

The reviewer of the "Exodus" goes on to remark with regard to Ireland that not only is it necessary "to remove redundant numbers, but to replace them by a more energetic, more aspiring, and more improvable race." The poor Celts must be pushed out, or starved out, to make place for more improvable Saxons: and why? Because their nature requires them to be "controlled, disciplined, and guided <disciplined, guided> by others. [. . .] Left to their own devices, a prey to their own indolent, slovenly, and improvident tendencies, all history shows how helpless and prone to degenerate they are." They are "deficient also in that faculty of self-government and self-control in the absence of which free institutions can never flourish or be permanently maintained." [275] The poor Celt, then, must be unhoused, turned forth upon the world—to work, beg, steal, or die, it matters little;

for the powerful and "improvable" Saxon needs his land. He is incapable of self-government; ergo, he must be governed. Or, the governing power being deficient, he must even make himself scarce in just such proportion as will establish the equilibrium between the *minus* and the *plus* quantities. He must emigrate or die, according to circumstances. The world must progress and his place is wanted. There is no longer room for him. Let him vanish! Amen! Is this wrong? We dare not say so. It seems rather a hard necessity than a wrong. The inferior people always have, always must, it would appear, pass away before the wants of the superior, and the necessities of progress. "Begone, ye incompetent!"[15] is surely the stern law of man's existence. Begone, from your land, from your home—ay, if it be necessary, from your life! The short spasm of a being, or of millions of beings, counts low in these calculations. We shudder at the thought, and yet, we repeat, we dare not call it a wrong. A necessity is never a wrong. A necessity of God's making—is it not a right? From such a dilemma where is the escape? Heaven only knows, and to its high mystery we bow.

Our brethren of England see and feel the necessity of this iron logic when the evil comes home to them, but find a quite different philosophy when the question is of their neighbors. While their Irish slave is turned shivering and houseless forth upon the bleak, cold world, their sentimentalists, as though in compensation for the philosophic coolness of this veritable edict for the extinction of a nation, weep floods of sympathy for the oppressed negro!—the negro, whose happy lot of ease and plenty would, to the wretched of their land, present an almost Elysian bliss. What would they have us do? Even allowing that the condition of the negro were such as they represent, how would they better it? The negro surely is not a superior man to their outcast Celt. If the Irishman be incapable of self-government and self-control; if his indolent, slovenly, and improvident tendencies need the control, discipline, and guidance of others, who that has the slightest knowledge of the negro character will deny that these difficulties present themselves in him in a tenfold *ratio*! Our reviewer finds his only hope for the Irish in a scattering of them among the other nations of the earth. "Wherever they settle singly among Americans or British, they improve, advance, and civilize; wherever they *congregate,* so as to carry Ireland about with them, they continue what we see them at home."[16] This adherence to the peculiarities

15. Cf. [Carlyle], "Occasional Discourse," p. 678.

16. [Greg], "Modern Exodus," p. 275, continuing: "We do not, in saying this, by any means wish to imply that they are an *inferior* race, but simply that they are a *peculiar* one, and not fitted *to stand alone,* being deficient in that restless energy, those indefinite desires, which are the very mainsprings of successful colonization—deficient also in that faculty of self-government and self-control, in the absence of which free institutions can never flourish or

of race is of course not singular to the Irish. The negro, too, has *his* peculiarities, which are kept in abeyance by his association with, and subjection to, the white man. Check that association and subjection, and how rapidly do we see him falling back to *fetishe* and barbarism! Wherever the Irish *congregate,* they carry Ireland about with them, for the simple reason that the peculiarities of one race can only be washed out by the commingled blood of others. The negro, under similar circumstances, brings to us, then, all the dark horrors of Negro-land; and not many decades will elapse ere the imperial Soulouque will (unless the rapid downward progress of himself and his nation be arrested by the mastery of the white sovereigns who are now closing round him) present to us some pretty scenes of negrodom of the fashion perhaps of that which we are told the grandees of Dahomy recently treated her majesty's commissioners—*une jolie fête*! a pretty pastime!—consisting of the hunting down and roasting of a few of their free and happy negro brethren made prisoners among the neighboring nations.[17]

What then is to be done with the negro? The Irish, to prevent this formation of little Irelands all over the world, are very judiciously advised to scatter themselves, and thus, by a proper distribution of their peculiar traits, the Irish blood, as a kind of salt to the earth, distributes itself not uselessly through the civilized world. Will our reviewer maintain that the same course is practicable, conceivable even, with regard to the negro? Can the ladies of Stafford House coolly contemplate the feasibility of such an unraveling of this Gordian knot? Will their admiration for Mrs. Stowe not stop short of amalgamation? We answer for them boldly. We do them more justice than they have done to us. As Christian and civilized women, they shrink with horror from the idea. What then, we repeat, can be done with the negro? Amalgamation cannot be thought of. Barbarism then—cannibal barbarism—slavery or extinction—is his fate. Will our self-constituted teachers in the A, B, C, of humanity have the goodness to inform us which of these alternatives they would advise as a first experiment?

---

be permanently maintained. But when their peculiarities have become modified, and their capacities developed, and their activity directed by an adequate amount of Scotch and English colonization of their country, we may hope to see all their good qualities brought out and *utilized,* and all their bad ones repressed and controlled."

17. That human sacrifice was practiced in the kingdom of Dahomey was regularly noticed, and as regularly deplored, in the accounts of visitors. Accompanying John Beecroft (1790–1854), British consul for the Bights of Benin and Biafra, to the Dahoman capital in 1850, Frederick Edwyn Forbes described the killing to which the embassy was witness in *Dahomey and the Dahomans: Being the Journals of Two Missions to the King of Dahomey, and Residence at His Capital, in the Years 1849 and 50,* 2 vols. (London, 1851), 2:49–54. LSM may refer to this incident, although there is no mention of cannibalism (as her "roasting" implies) in Forbes.

Even were the condition of the negro with us such as the wailings of negrophilists have described it, however much it might need a remedy, that remedy would never be found in emancipation. Jamaica shows what, under the best auspices, is the rapid tendency of this people, when set free from control. It will not need a century more to convince England that Jamaica, but for her greater distance and thus more convenient facility for being shaken off, would be a worse sore upon her system than ever Ireland has been. If the one be the disgusting boil, which stains and soils with its constantly emitted pus, the other (unless Coolie emigration and common sense puts the negro back into his natural position or, as is likeliest, drive him from existence) will prove the black and incurable gangrene to be got rid of only by speedy amputation. Supposing then slavery to be even such as it has been described, what escape is there for the negro? Literally none. If there be upon him a curse (which we are not inclined to allow), the curse is of God's laying on—not of ours. But, we repeat, we believe it not a curse. Inferiority is not a curse. Every creature is suited for its position, and fulfilling that position can certainly not be called cursed. What God has made, dare we to call it cursed? No, ladies. As He has made you to be women and not men—mothers and sisters, and not (according to the modern improvement system) soldiers and legislators, so has He fitted the negro for his position and suited him to be happy and useful in it. The negro's civilization—his only civilization—is slavery, serfdom; call it what you will, the condition and not the epithet is the point in question. Were the disease of our system such as you, ladies, and others have, we believe, in thoughtlessness rather than in malice described it, your rose-water appeals, as a contemporary editor well calls them, could have but slight effect; a sticking-plaster to a cloven skull, a pack-thread to guide an elephant, would be equally efficient.

But our decriers have, we now go on to maintain, entirely mistaken our case. They have trusted to Mrs. Stowe's spectacles, whose strange power of distortion shows everything under a false view. The *North British* expatiates upon the power of pathos and other admirable qualities of this authoress, and cheers her on to the work, recalling the fact that "it was a woman, Elizabeth Heyrick, who wrote the pamphlet that moved the heart of Wilberforce, to pity, and to pray over, the wrongs of the oppressed sons of Africa."[18] We can only say that, if so, Elizabeth Heyrick was almost as mischievous a woman in her day as Mrs. Stowe now threatens to be; for those tears

18. "American Slavery and *Uncle Tom's Cabin*," p. 235. Elizabeth Coltman Heyrick (1769–1831), English Quaker and abolitionist; wrote, among other antislavery pamphlets, *Immediate, Not Gradual Abolition; or, An Inquiry into the Shortest, Safest, and Most Effectual Means of Getting Rid of West Indian Slavery* (1824).

of Wilberforce have caused more shedding of blood, more anguish of soul, more agony of body and of mind, than it often falls to the lot of one man to give scope to. He attacked crime, not with the philosophic coolness which examines, compares, probes causes and effects, and thus has at least the fairest chance for cure; but with a species of feminine pathetics and wailings, caught perhaps from Mrs. Heyrick, he set the example, and opened that sluice, of sickly sentimentality which too often, taking the place of sound sense and argument, now inundates the world, causing agonies of body and soul, to which the worst scenes of the slave trade, heinous as they were, stand but as dust in the balance. The tears of blind enthusiasm are oftenest paid for, more than drop for drop, in blood. Wilberforce was, we believe, a good man, so far as *intentions* go; but a more mischievous man in *deeds* has seldom existed. The maniac may be pardoned for his follies, but it is hard to call upon the world to kneel and worship him. To Mrs. Stowe it is difficult to extend the same charity. We rejoice to believe, from sundry indications, that the mania of Uncle Tomism has nearly run its course; but it is a fearful sign of the times that such a truckling, money-seeking speculation—such a Judas-like sale of truth and conscience—should, even for the short space of a few weeks or a few months, have raised its author to the position of a heroine and prophetess. The sudden accession of philanthropic *furor* which has been waked up in the cause of negrodom, catches its flame from an altar lit up by no fire from heaven; its prophetess no sibyl, but rather some fortune-seeking gipsy who, her hand once crossed with gold, laughs at the simple fool who credits her tales, while she pockets the reward of her falsehood.

The *North British* remarks:

> Among <Amid> all the tributes to this appeal of Mrs. Stowe to every human feeling and every Christian principle, there is, perhaps, no greater tribute to its power than the kind and multitude of *answers* that have issued, and are [still] issuing, from the upholders and abettors of the slave-system, of whose horrors this *tremendous revelation* <tremendous revelation> has been made. We have said that the power of the book lies in its truth, directed to the consciences of men—and, accordingly, we find that the consciences of men are dealing with it as <*as*> truth. And perhaps it is in its being an appeal to conscience, and in its being responded to as such, that the book stands out from the class to which it nominally belongs. When did an army of journalists, and novelists, and pamphleteers—in fact, all the legal organs of society—ever before so set themselves in battle array to contend against the truth of a so-called "work of fiction"? . . . The fact is, that Mrs. Stowe has told the truth fearlessly; and therefore is she not only answered, but answered wrathfully; and should these answers not teach us to doubt her

> statements, they will, at least, teach us to estimate the degree of moral courage, the power of Christian principle, required to enable her to speak the truth in America. [237]

In the days of witchcraft, among other ordeals, one, which was, we are told, much used, consisted in casting the accused, bound hand and foot, into the water. Should the unfortunate being sink, a quiet death was his (or oftenest her) best fate. Should the unstruggling wretch float, no farther proof of crime was necessary, and pricking to death, or burning, or torturing in any and every imaginable way, was the certain result. We are placed, it would appear, in a somewhat similar position to that of the accused witch. Here is a "*tremendous revelation*" stated to have appeared against us. If we are silent, we acknowledge the sin and our accusers proceed accordingly. If we speak in exculpation, it proves that we feel the "appeal to conscience," and shrink before the prick. And if, unfortunately, the slightest impatience, the slightest warmth of expression, enters into our defence, behold! it is proof positive and indisputable! The devil's mark upon us. The poor witch is condemned while the righteous accuser pockets at once the honor and the profits of our conviction. We should like to summon before us in bodily entity the intangible existence shrouded under the reviewer's "we," and ask him, as a *man,* whether, on receiving a slap on the face, or a tweak of the nose, the involuntary impulse which moves his arm to knock down the aggressor be a proof of his deserving said slap, or said tweak? Or whether, when some insolent puppy gives him the lie, it be a verification of the charge, that the indignant motion of the flexor and extensor muscles of his leg gives the assailant a somewhat angry response to the remark? It is false, too, to say that *all* this indignation is excited by a "so-called 'work of fiction,'" if by this it is intended to say an *acknowledged* work of fiction. Mrs. Stowe expressly states, both in her work and out of it, that it is a representation of *fact*. The reviewer himself calls it a "tremendous revelation." "Mrs. Stowe has told the truth fearlessly," etc., etc. Are we then, in combating her assertions, combating a *so-called* fiction or a *so-called* fact? The world of Europe has chosen to take on trust, because it strikes in with the sentimental whim of the day, the account of a woman every page of whose book shows that she has seen little, and knows nothing, of our institutions. Still she calls them fact, and Europe takes them as fact. What more natural than that we should attempt to check the progress of the slander, by declaring its falsity. A little further on, the reviewer quotes what he calls "the heart words of this true-hearted woman." She writes of her book: "There has been hardly a day since it has been published that confirmatory voices have not come from southern slaveholders, men who have long waited for an opportunity to speak, and who now come out to attest its truth; for alas! they know what I know, and they must perceive that I know it, that the half is not told in that book. A book that should tell all, would not be credited—*it could not be read*. . . . I have only wondered some moments, in the anguish of the survey, that the firm earth does not collapse to hide such horror from the sun!"[19]

This, certainly, from the sound, indicates something horrible! most horrible! and considering the prevalence of cholera there is something peculiarly alarming in the idea of threatened collapse of the firm earth which should come to visit our sins, particularly as the lady tells us that she has so many confirmatory voices to bear witness to the iniquities of our land.[20] Now, to assuage the terrors of our reviewer and others, who, in case of our old mother earth being "taken so bad," might, as well as ourselves, suffer in the catastrophe, we must inform them, that Mrs. Stowe's published letters have not always had that regard for veracity which would be desirable in so distinguished a lady. We have not room here for the details of a correspondence, threatened suit, etc., etc., with and about the Rev. Dr. Parker, who happened to be brought in by name as a "confirmatory voice" by the lady, and who, not submitting quietly to the charge, forced an investigation and confession, which proved the publication, by Mrs. Stowe, of sundry letters which had in fact never been sent, received, nor even written, by the persons from whom they purported to have come.[21] In short, they were utterly false and what would, in the usual language of the world (whatever milder term Mrs. Stowe and her coadjutors might make use of), be called forged letters. The lady has, we believe, been more careful since this transaction, and following the safer plan of not naming names, speaks indefinitely of "confirmatory voices," which, like those "airy tongues which <that> syllable men's names,"[22] are too intangible to be brought in witness against her,

19. "American Slavery and *Uncle Tom's Cabin*," p. 244, quoting a letter from Stowe of which "we have ourselves been favoured with the sight."

20. After the cholera epidemic of 1848–49 in the United States, there were lesser, though no less alarming, outbreaks in 1850 and 1851; 1852 saw virulence nearly matching that of 1849, with 1,320 deaths in New Orleans, for example, and 650 in Chicago.

21. Presbyterian clergyman Joel Parker (1799–1873), pastor of Bleecker Street Church in New York, on May 8, 1852, wrote letters to Harriet Beecher Stowe and her husband, protesting that a statement ascribed to him in *Uncle Tom's Cabin* (1991 ed.), p. 159, was quoted out of context. When replies were unsatisfactory to him, he threatened suit. While this correspondence was being pursued, an exchange of letters affirmed to have been written by Parker and Harriet Beecher Stowe, in which Stowe agreed to withdraw the ascription and Parker to accept the withdrawal as sufficient redress, was published in the New York *Tribune* (June 24, 1852). This exchange was exposed as a forgery by the New York *Observer* on the following Sept. 23, the forger identified to be Stowe's brother, Henry Ward Beecher. See Wilson, *Crusader in Crinoline*, pp. 261, 266, 281, 285–88, 303, 307–22.

22. John Milton, *Comus*, l. 208.

or to threaten suit for $40,000. We presume that the reviewer is ignorant of her ability in composing facts, and thus takes without dispute those which he quotes from her letter. "*The heart-words of this true-hearted woman*"! So goes the world! We will not wish for a "collapse of the firm earth" to swallow up our fair foe, but truly we would counsel her, as she is fond of quoting scripture, to study a little the decalogue. Perchance she may there come across an old law which seems to have slipped her memory: "Thou shalt not bear false witness against thy neighbor."[23]

A propos of misstating facts, the reviewer himself, misled by somebody not more accurate than Mrs. Stowe, falls into some strange blunders. "What is the meaning," he asks, in the midst of sundry quotations, showing what he supposes the condition of our negroes under "the hideous social malady" [236] under which we labor, "what is the meaning of that law of South Carolina, declaring death to be the punishment not only of the runaway slave, but of any person who shall choose to aid him in his escape? or of that of Louisiana, declaring it lawful to 'fire upon any slaves who do not stop when pursued'?" etc., etc. [249]

We will quote no further. Wishing to dispose first of these two clauses, we honestly looked for the authorities to these statements, and find in a note as reference for the first clause, "Brevard's *Digest,*[24] vol. ii., p. 236." We turn to book, volume, and page. The gentleman must have been reading with Mrs. Stowe's spectacles; there is nothing in any way resembling the quotation referred to. For the second clause, the reference is (also in a note) "Brevard's *Digest of the Laws of Louisiana, Code Noir,* vol. i., p. <§> 33." Here we are quite at a stand, Brevard's *Digest of the Laws of Louisiana* being a volume entirely unknown to American lawyers.[25] There is not, and never has been, any such work, Brevard's *Digest* including only the laws of South Carolina. How are such wantonly false assertions to be met? We are not well enough versed in the laws of Louisiana to say what shadow of foundation the reviewer may find in them for his quotation from his imaginary law book.[26]

23. Cf. Matt. 19:18.

24. Joseph Brevard (1766–1821), *An Alphabetical Digest of the Public Statute Law of South-Carolina,* 3 vols. (Charleston, S.C., 1814).

25. Joseph Brevard is not known to have composed a *Digest of the Laws of Louisiana.* "*Code Noir,*" however, refers to *Le Code noir, ou recueil des reglemens rendus jusqu'à présent, concernant le gouvernement, l'administration de la justice, la police, la discipline et le commerce des nègres dans les colonies françoises* (Paris, 1742; frequently reprinted).

26. So far as the reference is to the *Code Noir* of Louisiana, it is also false. No such privilege is recorded in any of the sections of the code. That code was made in 1724 by [Jean-Baptiste Le Moyne, sieur de] Bienville [(1680–1747); governor of Louisiana and founder of New Orleans], and, with many harsh features, has some that are in the highest degree liberal and indulgent. Among them are: (xi.) "Masters shall have their Christian slaves buried in consecrated ground." (xliii.) "Husbands and wives shall not be seized and sold separately

Those of South Carolina we have at hand, and have carefully examined all of them which relate to slaves. In Brevard's *Digest,* vol. ii, p. 245, we find, among our colonial laws, passed A.D. 1754, the following:

> All and every person and persons who shall inveigle, steal, or carry away any negro or other slave or slaves; or shall hire, aid, or counsel any person or persons to inveigle, steal, or carry away, as aforesaid, any such slave, so as the owner or employer of such slave or slaves shall be deprived of the use and benefit of such slave or slaves; or that shall aid any such slave in running away, or departing from his master's <master> or employer's service, shall be, and he and they is and are hereby declared to be guilty of felony; and being thereof convicted or attainted, by verdict or confession; or being indicted thereof, shall stand mute; or will not directly answer to the indictment; or will peremptorily challenge above the number of [twenty of] the

---

when belonging to the same master; and their children, under fourteen years, shall not be separated from their parents. This article shall apply to *voluntary* sales." (xxxii.) This is the only section that seems to justify the charge of the reviewer, as it makes the crime of "running away" punishable with death, but then it must be the third offense, must be continuous, must have been denounced by public authority, and the punishment must be by the constituted authorities. British statutes have made the offence of breaking prison and escape a felony, without clergy, even where the party is innocent of the original offence charged. The *Code Noir,* however, has not been in force in Louisiana since 1806. By the law of 1806—[Henry Adams] Bullard and [Thomas] Curry, [*A New Digest of the Statute Laws of the State of Louisiana: from the Change of Government to the Year 1841, Inclusive* (New Orleans, 1842), one volume only published,] vol. i. (sec. xxxii.)—the runaway slave may be killed, "should the said slave *assault and strike* the person pursuing," a very different case from that of the *North British*! (xxxv.) "It shall be lawful to fire upon *runaway slaves who may be armed.*" Xxxix. gives magistrates the right to fine for improper provision for slaves by their masters, and to seize property of the offender for the purpose. Xvi. imposes death upon all persons wilfully killing a slave, and heavy fine for unusual and immoderate punishment of slaves. In the consolidated statutes of Louisiana, 1852, art. *Slaves,* we see (p. 523) that disabled or old slaves shall be provided for by their masters. "It shall be the duty of the masters to procure sick slaves all spiritual and temporal assistance." Old slaves shall not be sold from their children. Children under ten shall not be separated from their parents, etc., etc. (p. 543.) Evidence of slaves may be received on the trial of slaves. In the Louisiana *Gazette,* as far back as 1805 ["1806" in original], now before us, there is an advertisement of a slave to be sold by public authority, in consequence of her being ill-treated and not properly provided for by her present master. But the whole spirit of the slave system of Louisiana is mild and equitable.—EDITOR.

Sheriff's Sale: Will be sold at the Principal, on Thursday, 5th September, 1805, a negro wench, named Mary, belonging to Mr. De Lavine, in consequence of the maltreatment of her master.

By order of the Judge of the County Court of Orleans.

Geo. T. Ross, Sheriff.

August 13th, 1805.

[*De Bow* note]

> jury, shall suffer death as felons, and be excluded and debarred of the benefit of clergy.

Here is certainly a law stern enough, but not against the slave. Here is punishment for the tempter, but none for the tempted. The punishment for the runaway slave is *never,* and has never been, death. In the act of actual resistance, he is certainly liable to receive death, as is any fugitive from law while resisting constituted authorities; but there is not, and never has been, any law making the act of evasion a crime. The act just quoted against the person inveigling a slave is an old English law, and a strong disposition has existed on the part of the State of South Carolina to repeal it, as too severe for the offence. The action of the state has in this been only checked by abuse and mischievous interference with her legislation. In our own opinion, however, it is an act which, for the *safety and comfort of the slave,* should be kept in force. The object of it is to guard *him* from the attempts of evil-disposed persons, who either with a view of gain would abstract the slave and afterwards dispose of him to their own profit, or else maliciously inveigle him from the protection and direction of his master. In either case, in justice to the slave, and to secure him, as much as possible, from such attempts, the tempter should receive condign punishment. We believe the general opinion is against us, but, as the *friend of the slave,* we would desire to continue the act in force. It is our duty, as far as possible, to protect our slave from all such acts of oppression, injustice, or interference, as his position makes him peculiarly liable to. Therefore, as the guiding and directing power, taking upon ourselves the responsibility in so far as we take the direction of his action, we should save him so far as in our power lies from the snares of the tempter.

Our reviewer gives sundry quotations (or at least purporting to be such) from the laws of other states, all more or less ferocious, and which, not having a general law-library at hand, it is impossible for us either to confirm or refute; but we certainly have a right to conclude, in a series of assertions, that when the first two are so utterly false as we have proved the above to be, there is little faith to be attached to any of them.

The sweeping assertion so constantly made that our laws are, in their general bearing, cruel or neglectful of the slave is entirely unfounded. The truth is, that our laws are most carefully protective of the slave. Our reviewer quotes from a nameless correspondent, "a Barbadian by birth, [and] who has himself owned slaves," to the following effect:

> The picture of American slavery in *Uncle Tom* is not the less faithful because a stranger visiting the country sees so little of it, and because the *general* conduct of slave-owners may be humane. The worst cases no one sees. Slavery was mitigated in our West Indian Colonies by the small size of the islands,

> and the check of public opinion which reaches every corner. But in the remote districts of America, and even of Jamaica, what may and must have taken place when every master was a law to himself? [241]

This reasoning is funny enough. What is the amount of it? When a man gets out of the reach of legal authority, in *remote districts,* where neither law nor public opinion can reach him, it is possible for him to commit crimes for which, were he within the grasp of the law, he would be punished. *Therefore* the laws are bad. *The worst cases no one sees!* (How the gentleman finds out their existence it is hard to determine, but let us see his corollary.) *Therefore* the system is heinous which does not punish them. *The general conduct* of slave-owners is, it is acknowledged, humane—but, as it is possible that there may be some very wicked individuals in some very remote districts, where "the master is a law to himself," *therefore* the laws which endeavor to take such master under their cognizance are heinous and infamous. The *facts* in the gentleman's letter are entirely laudatory of our system. For the *imaginary horrors,* not we, but himself, must be answerable. Those crimes that *no one sees* enjoy, unfortunately, all the world over, impunity from punishment. Would the reviewer and his Barbadian friend invent a remedy for this evil, they would certainly immortalize themselves. Let us imagine such a style of reasoning applied to any system but our own, and where is the egregious fool to receive it? Nothing goes farther to prove the ignorant vehemence of our accusers than such blind argument.

The reviewer then goes on to cite from "the disgusting details of facts [. . .] taken from legal documents," "information[s] sworn before the House of Commons, on occasion of the inquiry into the state of the West Indian Colonies" [242]. We might easily plead here that West Indian slavery is not our slavery, and that the laws of England, not ours, were answerable for the atrocities there described. But we will be more just to human nature. These *facts* are generally as false as those imputed to the working of the system with us. The statements there adduced bear upon their face the impress of irrationality: many of them are *physically* impossible; and, for the rest, it is *morally* impossible that any people should so combine the traits of civilization and brutal barbarism. One or the other must necessarily be put down. A people is civilized or barbarous. In the transition state of semi-civilization they may be neither entirely, but to be both is impossible. A nation must either rise to the one or sink to the other condition. We do not deny that a nation of men may be morally brutes; but we do deny that a nation of civilized and enlightened Christian men, fellow-citizens of Englishmen of the nineteenth century, can be so. Further: has our reviewer ever seen or heard of a work entitled *The West Indian <India> Colonies; the Calumnies and Misrep-*

resentations Circulated against Them by the "Edinburgh Review," Mr. Clarkson, Mr. C[r]opper, etc., Examined and Refuted by James McQueen, and published in London, A.D. 1824?[27] If ever corrupt witnesses and bitter, prejudiced falsehood, were held up to shame and obloquy, here we have damning proof against the so-called reformers, who, to satisfy a malevolent spite, or to gratify a sentimental whim, rushed headlong to the ruin of an innocent and prosperous people. We think it is Sterne who has beautifully remarked that "when it is once determined that a lamb shall be offered up, there may be sticks enough found under any hedge to complete the sacrifice."[28] Jamaica was doomed (*delenda est Carthago*),[29] and the scarce vital wrecks of her once triumphant prosperity now alone remain to show what fanatics can accomplish. "But," says the reviewer, "we cite *legal documents*." Ah! that is distressing, and we must give way before such authority, however the darkest perjury may have been concerned in the concocting of them. We are then condemned in the case of our brethren of Jamaica. *Legal documents* cannot be disputed.

"But," says somebody, "one of the maxims which the devil in a late visit upon earth left to his disciples is, when once you have got up, kick the stool from under you." Our reviewer evidently thinks himself safely mounted now, and, Lord! what a hurry he is in to kick away the stool of legal documents! Some half-dozen pages or so after his remarks upon Jamaica documents, having got his readers into a fine swing of sentimental horrors, he thinks apparently it is high time to follow the advice of the Rev. gentleman from the lower regions, and with a quick glance round—not, we presume, without a furtive wink at the knowing ones—he gives a most vigorous kick at the said stool, just as an unfortunate wight on the opposite side of the argument was triumphantly climbing thereon.

"An American writer," he exclaims indignantly,

> An American writer of a book, entitled *England's Glory and Her Shame,* gives the result of his [(supposed)] observations during a "tour in the manufacturing districts <*manufacturing districts*> of England," and draws a most

27. Reprinted New York, 1969.

28. Laurence Sterne, *The Life and Opinions of Tristram Shandy, Gentleman,* ed. James A. Work (New York, 1940), 1: chap. 12, p. 29: "When, to gratify a private appetite, it is once resolved upon, that an innocent and an helpless creature shall be sacrificed, 'tis an easy matter to pick up sticks enew from any thicket where it has strayed, to make a fire to offer it up with."

29. Plutarch in his biography of Cato the Elder (27.1) records that Cato, toward the end of his life, was so much convinced that Carthage was a threat to Rome that, no matter what the subject under discussion in the Roman Senate, Cato would end his speech with the words *delenda est Carthago* ("Carthage must be destroyed").

appalling picture of the misery and degradation of the manufacturers, to the great consolation, no doubt, of the American slave-owners, who are thus left satisfied that, if slavery is a bad thing, there is no alternative but something worse. Now, we happen to have ascertained, through the medium of a gentleman who personally knew the author, that he [*never*] *set foot* in Europe <*in Europe*>, but concocted his work partly from Blue-books and perhaps partly from imagination.[30]

It must, however, be added, in fairness to the author, that he was probably not aware of the amount of misrepresentation some of these Blue-books contain. They are the Reports of the Evidence taken before the Committee on the Ten-hours' Bill—a work which too much resembled a supposed botanical examination of a certain farm and garden, resulting in a collection of a few nettles out of one field, and four or five thistles out of another, and a handful of groundsel from the garden, representing these as *the produce of the estate*. [255–56]

So much for *legal documents*. Excellent they are against the slave-holder, but o' the other side[31]—bah! kick the stool over, and lo! your antagonist is sprawling on his back. And so Jamaica witnesses were right, and Ten-hours' Bill witnesses were wrong. Documents here—documents there. White, they are; presto, black. True, they are; presto, false. Pretty jugglery! and worthy of all admiration!

Too truly has Mr. McQueen remarked in his work upon Jamaica, of which we but now made mention, that: "The French revolution, which, with its infamous principles, convulsed the world, [. . .] boasted to have been built upon the very foundations <foundation> on which Mr. Clarkson grounds his charge[s] against the <our> West India Colonies, namely, '*Nature* and *Reason*'!"[32] Nature and Reason are truly high authorities, but too often, like the cheating oracles of old, do they render a doubtful response, the erroneous interpretation of which becomes a snare to the feet, and a pit of destruction, to the hasty interpreter of destiny. Long and laborious is the task of him who would read the truth. Like the worshipper at the cave of Trophonius, a life-long sadness, a wearing out of soul and body, in the eager pursuit of the

30. Charles Edwards Lester, *The Glory and the Shame of England,* 2 vols. (London, 1841). Charles Edwards Lester (1815–90), Presbyterian clergyman and author; b. Griswold, Conn., a great-grandson of Jonathan Edwards. The *North British* reviewer is misinformed when saying that the author of *The Glory and the Shame of England* had never visited England: in 1840 Lester came as a delegate to the World Anti-Slavery Convention, held at Exeter Hall, in London.

31. *Macbeth* 1.7.25–28

32. *West India Colonies,* pp. 181–82.

great reality, is the price to be paid for its acquisition.[33] The enthusiast seldom reaches it. Blindly zealous, ignorantly active, in proportion as he has the least certain foundation for his opinions, he defends them with impulsive fervor; stirs, in fanatic haste, the bubbling cauldron of society, little heeding what poisonous scum and froth may thus be floated to the surface; and lauds himself at last, like a Robespierre, or his petty imitators in revolutionizing, a Buxton, a Clarkson, or a Stevens,[34] even in the chaotic ruin which his madness has effected. France rose from her ashes to run a new course of greatness and of madness. For Jamaica, alas! there seems no phoenix life.

Our reviewers and commentators generally lay a constant stress upon the "uncontrolled power" which they suppose the slave-owner to possess. We would fain convince them that in truth no such power exists. This bugbear is the offspring of their own distempered imagination.

> Although slaves, by the Act of 1740, are declared to be chattels personal, yet they are also, in our law, considered as *persons* with many *rights* and *liabilities,* civil and criminal. (*Vide Negro Law of South Carolina,* collected and digested by J. B. O'Neall,[35] chapter 2d, section 11th) [p. 18; LSM's italics]
>
> By the Act of 1821, the murder of a slave is declared to be a felony, without the benefit of clergy. (Ib. ib. section 15) [p. 19]
>
> To constitute the murder of a slave, no other ingredients are necessary

33. The god Trophonius had his shrine and oracle at Lebadea in Boeotia. In his *Description of Greece* (9.39.4) Pausanias (fl. c. A.D. 150) describes the elaborate, arduous, and terrifying ritual required of the petitioner. This ritual became proverbial as causing melancholy, as for example in the first paragraph of Erasmus' *Praise of Folly* and, humorously adapted to Bow Street by Sandy Mackaye, in Kingsley, *Alton Locke,* pp. 195–96.

34. Sir Thomas Fowell Buxton (1786–1845), brewer, member of Parliament (1818–37), and Thomas Clarkson were associates of William Wilberforce in the struggle against slavery in the British dominions. "Stevens" is James Stephen (1758–1832); having practiced law in St. Kitts, he was a member of Parliament (1808–15) and Wilberforce's brother-in-law; wrote *Slavery in the British West India Colonies,* 2 vols. (1824–30). All three are refuted in McQueen's *West India Colonies.*

35. *The Negro Law of South Carolina . . .* (Columbia, S.C., 1848). John Belton O'Neall (1793–1863), lawyer, became a judge on the South Carolina court of appeals in 1830; on the court of law appeals in 1835; its president in 1850; chief justice of South Carolina from 1859; opposed nullification; unionist; author also of *Biographical Sketches of the Bench and Bar of South Carolina* (1859). On July 23, 1853, O'Neall wrote from Springfield, S.C., to the New York *Tribune* a letter (accompanying a copy of his *Negro Law of South Carolina*) listing the legal errors in Harriet Beecher Stowe's *Key to Uncle Tom's Cabin* (1853) and defending South Carolinian treatment of the slave. "Visit Charleston, Columbia, Camden; Gov. [William] Aiken's plantation at Jehossee; Col. [Wade] Hampton's, near Columbia; Col. [James] Chesnut's, near Camden; and then the whole upper part of the State; and if the Institution of slavery be, as depicted in Uncle Tom, or the Key, make it known *far and wide;* but if not, *do us justice. We ask no more.*" The letter is printed in the *Tribune,* Aug. 15, 1853.

than such as enter into the offence of murder at common law. So the killing on sudden heat and passion, is the same as manslaughter. (Ib. ib. section 16) [p. 19]

An attempt to kill and murder a slave by shooting at him, [was] held to be a misdemeanor (State vs. Mann),[36] and indictable as [an] assault with [an] intent to kill and murder. (Ib. ib. section 17) [p. 19]

[The Act of 1821 makes] the *unlawful* whipping or beating of any slave, without sufficient provocation by word or act, is a <act, a> misdemeanor, and subjects the offender, on conviction, to imprisonment not exceeding 6 months, and a fine not exceeding $500. (Ib. ib. section 18) [p. 19]

The Act of 1740 requires the owners of slaves to provide them with sufficient clothing, covering, and food; and if they should fail to do so, the owners, respectively, are declared to be liable to be informed against, subjected to fine, etc. (Ib. ib. section 25)[37]

It is the settled law of this State, that an owner cannot abandon a slave needing either medical treatment, care, food, or raiment. If he does, he will be liable to any one who may furnish the same. (Ib. ib. section 27) [p. 21]

By [the 22nd section of the] Act of 1740, slaves are protected from labor on the Sabbath day. The violation of the law in this respect subjects the offender to a fine of £5 current money, equal in value to $3.70 <equal to $3 7-100> for every slave so worked. (Ib. ib. section 28)[38] [p. 21]

Surely these should suffice to show that the owner's power is not "uncontrolled." However he may evade the law when he hides himself in the "remote districts" of which the Barbadian ex-planter discourses, he is kept in check so long as the arm of the law is long enough to reach him. We presume that every country has some point within its limits, where law penetrates with

36. This parenthesis is a marginal note in the original, reading: "The State vs. Mann, 2 Hill 453."

37. O'Neall, *Negro Law of South Carolina,* p. 20, reading: "The 38th section of the Act of 1740, requires the owners of slaves to provide them with sufficient *clothing, covering, and food,* and if they should fail to do so, the owners respectively are declared to be liable to be informed against to the next nearest Justice of the Peace (Magistrate now), who is authorized to hear and determine the complaint; and if found to be true, or, in the absence of proof, if the owner will not exculpate himself by his own oath, the magistrate may make such order as will give relief, and may set a fine not exceeding £20, current money, equal to $13 66–100, on the owner, to be levied by warrant of distress and sale of the offender's goods."

38. But for the complete slave laws of South Carolina and other Southern States, see De Bow's *Industrial Resources,* Art. "Slavery." [LSM] There is no single article on "Slavery" in De Bow, *Industrial Resources.* Of several articles referring to the subject (including LSM's own "Negro-mania," reprinted in ibid., 2:196–205), the reference here is probably to John Belton O'Neall, "Negroes—Slave Laws of the South," ibid., 2:269–92.

difficulty. England, too, has her moors and her high-roads; aye, and—perhaps worse than either—the purblind alleys of her great cities, where crime boldly treads, or cunningly hides herself. But surely not therefore shall we say, because her laws are sometimes inefficient, that all are iniquitous. Our reviewer triumphantly remarks that the opponents of Mrs. Stowe, in not denying the *possibility,* virtually admit the truth of her statements. Upon the same principle of argument, what fearful pictures might as *possibilities* be deduced from the institutions of every existing state of society! What law, what bond, what tie, might not be abolished if *possible* abuse were sufficient to condemn it? Ruler and subject, servant and master, parent and child, husband and wife, cast all to the winds! These may be, nay, more, these *are* all abused, *daily* abused, *brutally* abused. "Nature and Reason!" cries the old school of god-improvers. "Higher law!" responds the new. On! on! what next? Where shall we destroy? Say ye, "What next?" Ask ye "Where?" Nay, 'tis a foolish prejudice to doubt. Sweep every thing! everywhere! The Goth and the Vandal of old found something to spare, something to respect. Not so our innovators. *Excelsior*! Communism and Fraternity!—Barbarism and Brutality! God of Heaven! pity this world which Thou hast made!

The reviewer says "there is [moreover] a plain admission on the part of the Slave State Legislatures <Legislature>, that there is nothing that can be inflicted on a man, in this life, worse than slavery, in the fact that the punishment affixed to crimes committed by the slaves *is always* <is always> *death.* Cases of arson, theft, and burglary, which would be comparatively lightly dealt with, if committed by white men, are all death, to the slave." And then comes a flourish from the Cincinnati *Herald,* ending with a marvelously ferocious, "He can be killed. [. . .] Let him be killed." [246–47]

"We should very much like to know," as the old song saith, whether our reviewer means to claim exemption from all response and dispute, for himself as well as for Mrs. Stowe, on the plea of the unattackableness of *works of fiction.* Is *his* article, too, a *so-called* work of fiction? Verily, whether or not he claim for it the merit, we must give our mite of approbation to the inventive genius therein displayed. Truly, it is full of "most quaint and admirable inventions." For fear, however, that some simple blockheads should really imagine that our talented brother of the quill meant these witty sallies to be taken as literal truth, we will, for the benefit of such dunderpates, answer his statements seriously. The reviewer will find, by a glance at the statutes of England, that arson and burglary are both in his own happy land punishable with *death.* In most of our states, we believe—and certainly in South Carolina, from which we write—the old English law is for these crimes retained in force, alike for *white and black.* For theft, we have abolished the more severe punishment still retained by English law (which frequently, as the learned reviewer no doubt knows, pronounces death as the penalty for the purloining of a few shillings' worth of property), and have substituted, according to the offence, lighter punishment alike for *white and black*. For *both,* the legal penalty is the same. One difference, however, we must acknowledge. While the law is the same for both, there is, it must be confessed, great inequality in the administering of it. Justice is no longer even-handed. One side may often escape the law which rigorously pursues the other. But which is it? We fear our transatlantic friends will hardly credit us, when we answer: *the negro.* And yet the thing explains itself easily enough! The white man, encroaching upon the rights of society, becomes a public nuisance, which it is necessary to keep in check, and the only means of so doing is by such bodily restraint and suffering as shall hold him in fear of future transgression. It is, therefore, to the interest of society that he should be punished, and he *is* punished accordingly. The negro, under similar circumstances, will often have his master to stand between him and the law. For offences not too notoriously criminal, indemnification from the master to the injured person oftenest ends the affair altogether. Where the state as prosecutor is not forced to take cognizance of the offence, the master can frequently buy off individual prosecution, and both interest and humanity incline him to do so: interest, because the slave, unenfeebled by imprisonment and stripes, is a valuable property for which he is willing to pay; humanity, because the slave, in his childlike, dependent position, becomes to him a part of self, which he would rather correct with the mercy of a father than the severity of a judge. He buys him off therefore. Society is satisfied, because the master thus renders himself the virtual sponsor of the slave, making it his own interest to prevent further misdemeanor. The negro gets his whipping, goes home to warm himself by his fire, and perhaps laugh in his sleeve at "Massa," who thinks, "dat kind o'lashin ebber hut nigga," while the white man bears the double infliction of imprisonment and stripes. In England, for a similar offence, if mercy so tempered justice (as we know it now oftenest does) so far as to spare life, the offender is glad with that to escape, banished from hearth and home, wife and children, a disgraced exile to——he knows not whither.

The reviewer gives what he calls a digest of our slave-laws [256–57], containing thirteen propositions, almost every one of which either places things in their falsest light, or are in their grossest statements utterly untrue. His proposition that "the labor of the slave is compulsory and uncompensated" [256], we answer by saying that he receives a very much larger compensation in actual value, in housing, in food, and in raiment, than the half starved artisan of many a proud metropolis. He is, it is true, obliged, in proper weather and when in health, to do his work. He has *not* the right by idleness or drunkenness to starve his family for the indulgence of his own vices; but he is, in return for this constraint, insured a comfortable maintenance for himself and family under all circumstances, in sickness and in health, in feeble youth and in tottering age, through good report and through evil report. Even in his vices he is saved from that lowest degradation of unprotected misery which the white man must meet. The lowest slave cannot sink to the degradation of the outcast white.

"The amount of toil, the time allowed for rest, are dictated solely by the master." [256]

This is untrue. The law, as we have shown, protects the slave from Sabbath-day labor, and another section (*vide* O'Neall's *Digest,* chap. 2d, section 29[, p. 21]), part of an old English act, limits his labor to from fourteen to fifteen hours per day. The time here allotted for labor is, however, so much more than is now required of the slave that the law is in fact of non-effect. The working hours are in South Carolina from eight to twelve, varying with the season and exigencies of the crop, with occasional intermission of holidays and half holidays, which, if "dictated solely by the master," are not, we presume, on that account to be considered as obnoxious. If the duchesses of Stafford House could be instrumental in giving to each of their tenants an occasional merry holiday, it is scarcely to be presumed that their vassals would take it in dudgeon, because inconsistent with their dignity as men.

"He may be separated from his family." "He can make no contracts, has no legal right to property."[39]

And yet, as a *fact,* there is less separation among negro families than among whites. Starvation drives harder than the hardest master. The property of the slave, for property he always to a certain extent has, he holds by a stronger tenure, upheld as he is by his master's protection, than many a poor freeman who, by taxes and tithes, individual trickery and legal frauds, finds himself juggled out of every right but that of dying unprotected, grateful to the disease which opens his prison door.

"He cannot bear witness against the white man."[40]

39. "American Slavery and *Uncle Tom's Cabin,*" p. 256, reading: The slave "may remain with his family, or be separated from them for ever. . . . Slaves can make no contracts, and have no legal right to any property, real or personal. Their own honest earnings, and the legacies of friends, belong in point of law to their masters."

40. Ibid., reading: "Neither a slave nor a free coloured person can be a witness against any *white* or free person in a court of justice, however atrocious may have been the crimes they have seen him commit, if such testimony would be for the benefit of a *slave;* but they may give testimony *against a fellow slave,* or free coloured man—even in cases affecting life, if the *master* is to reap the advantage of it."

Granted—and properly cannot—nor would the witness of a similar class be taken as of much weight in England against their aristocratic masters. Every man in England is, legally, free to say what he pleases, but dares any man say that there is not a gag upon the mouth of the ignorant and illiterate poor? that his witness is of material weight against his lordly ruler? The word of the law matters little, and whatever its letter may be, the testimony of a lower and therefore of necessity a jealous class—of an ignorant and therefore of necessity an easily corruptible class—is and should always be taken with a reservation. Upon the same judicious principle of guarding against jealousy, corruption, and prejudice, the English law requires that a man should be judged by his peers. A man of the people cannot sit upon a jury to judge the guilt of a noble. The jealousies of rank as well as the prejudice of ignorance must be guarded against. So far we grant, but the reviewer adds, to the clause quoted by us, that slaves cannot bear witness against the white man when "such testimony would be for the benefit of a *slave;* but they may give testimony against a *fellow slave,* or free colo[u]red man—even in cases affecting life, if the *master* is to *reap the advantage* of it." Certainly we are hence to conclude, without any unfair reading, that he *can* give such testimony for the *benefit* of a *white* man, and that he can *only* give testimony against the *slave* when his master *is to reap the advantage*. Both propositions are equally false. He can *never* bear witness against a white man, and can *always* do so against a negro, although in either case his witnessing, or his abstinence from witnessing, might be to the utter ruin of his master.

"The slave may be punished at his master's discretion, without trial, without any means of legal redress, whether his offence be real or imaginary; and the master can transfer the same despotic power to any person or persons he may choose to appoint." [256]

We have above quoted an act showing that whipping without sufficient provocation is a punishable misdemeanor. Another act (*vide* O'Neall's *Digest,* chapter ii. section 21[, p. 20]) prescribes the punishment for *maiming* or "any other cruel punishment." "This provision, it has been held, extends to any cruel beating of a slave."

The slave, says the reviewer, not being allowed to resist a white man "under *any* circumstances, his <*his*> only safety consists in the fact that his owner <*owner*> may bring suit and recover the price of his body, in case his life is taken. [. . .]" [257]

This is wilfully false. Our law necessarily forbids, as a general rule, the striking of a white man by a negro, unless under command, or in defence of his master. The negro, whether bond or free, cannot therefore be guilty of manslaughter. In killing a white man, he therefore becomes always guilty of murder, unless the case falls, as many are judged to do, under the head of excusable homicide. An express act too gives to the courts, trying any negro under the law of murder, the power, when "any favorable circumstances appear," to mitigate his punishment (*vide* O'Neall's *Digest,* chapter iii[, section 5, p. 29]). It is intentional misrepresentation of this law to say that a negro must stand still and be murdered, that his master may recover the price of his body. No negro defending himself against a murderous attack would be held guilty. The case would come under the act as excusable homicide. We have already shown that the murder of a negro is equally punishable with that of a white man, and his master, or any other being proved guilty, may be hung for it.

"The slave is entirely unprotected in his domestic relations." [257]

False again. He is protected by the master and through the master.

"The operation of the laws tends to deprive slaves of religious instruction and consolation." [257]

Utterly false. No law, having to the smallest extent any such tendency, is to be found in our whole collection of statutes. The habit of our country is to admit slaves to all places of worship, certain parts of churches being generally set aside for them, though we have seen, in some of our handsomest and most frequented churches, old family servants seated in front of their masters and mistresses along the aisles or at the foot of the pulpit or the altar. Places of worship are, besides, frequently built by owners for their special accommodation.[41]

"What is a trifling fault in a *white man* <man> is considered highly criminal in a <the> *slave;* the same offences which cost a white man a few dollars only are punishable <punished> in the negro with death." [257]

False as the rest. We have already answered a similar accusation above.

"The whole power of the law[s] is exerted to keep slaves in a state of the lowest ignorance." [257]

False, again. There is a law of South Carolina, we do not know how far extending to other states, forbidding that slaves should be taught to read. For ourselves, we consider this act as one which would be better repealed as useless and of non-effect. Its object was to prevent the circulation of incendiary writings. To this purpose, however, it is worse than ineffectual. It does not prevent, and has the usual effect of exciting, a desire for forbidden fruit. Still, even with this impulse, book-learning is so contrary to negro-nature, that there is the smallest possible disposition to seek it, although it is notorious with us that every negro, who chooses to take the trouble to learn, may be taught to read in spite of the law, and very generally by the

41. There are many in New Orleans. Our planters frequently employ regular chaplains to their slaves. [LSM]

children even of his owners. The law is based upon a false principle, inasmuch as it was intended for an object to which it must necessarily prove inefficient, and, like all such, as an unfailing consequence falls of itself dead, without the legal form of repeal. Granting, however, that it were in full force, would it in fact do more than to place the negro on a level with the corresponding classes of other nations? How much book-learning does a man get, when rest and sleep must be cheated of their dues to fill the hungry stomach by manual toil? Ignorance moreover does not consist in the mere deficiency of knowledge in one's spelling-book. The slave-negro of our United States, in spite of his inferiority of race, stands higher in the scale of being, is better informed in the duties of life, more polished and humanized by association—in short, is the higher man—than the wretched off-casts of a nobler race which crowd the streets and lanes of every densely populated metropolis.

Our reviewer sneers at us that slavery can only be sustained by the help of the law, that law must "come in to defend and maintain it" [250]. If this be so, he only proves that slavery is *not barbarism*—is *not* despotic power—is *not* lawless might. Every institution of civilized society requires to be maintained and defended by law, maintained and defended against lawless barbarism and brutal force. This argument, therefore, works entirely in our favor, but we think that such an assertion claims too much. Slavery does exist quite independently of law, and exists, too, in a form scarcely, we presume, more soothing than ours to the feelings of our friends and advisers the Stafford House ladies and *North British* reviewers. They will hardly contend that it is law which gives his majesty of Dahomy the right to roast his slaves, as we have noticed above. Law is the defence of the weak against the strong. What need of law, where power is supreme? "Thus far shalt thou go and no farther,"[42] is the fiat of law. Bad laws are weak laws, inefficient laws. They do not sufficiently protect, and therefore are they bad. An oppressive law is so, not because there is in the law any power of oppression, but because the individual or party imposing it, has the *might* which he or they choose to abuse, and there is no power in the law sufficiently strong to keep them in check. The despot who makes a law giving to himself the right of confiscating the property of his subjects under certain circumstances, however whimsical or tyrannical, does not exercise his confiscations in right of the power given by the law, but by the power which is inherent in himself, his circumstances or position; and the law, even such as it is, is a virtual acknowledgment of some limit to that power. He does not confiscate under all circumstances, but under such and such. The government imposing an unjust law does so, not through any power of the law, but because, having the superior

42. Cf. Job 38:11.

might which enables it to enforce an unjust demand, it will not allow the law to be made sufficiently strong to check its rapacity. The wolf robs, not through the law, but through want of the law. Law is the voice of reason curbing the rule of might. It is never a bestower of power, but a check, however feeble and inefficient that check may be. The nation which rebels against oppressive laws, combats not for the abolition, but for the better regulating, of law. A revolution which seeks to abolish law, must end necessarily in despotism. Perfect codes of law are not to be looked for in an imperfect world, and ours are doubtless faulty enough. It is something, however, to know, that they are no worse than those of contemporary nations, and that in their results the sum of comfort and enjoyment is at least as great for humanity as under any other system.

Here again we subject ourselves to the sneers of the reviewer, who, because a common ground of defence with us is to show how much the position of our negro is preferable to that of the white slave of other countries, remarks: "The way that this argument is pushed would seem to imply that *better* must mean always <always mean> *good*" [255]. Truly this is laughable enough. If *better* does not mean always good, it certainly does mean always *better;* and it would be the part of a madman to abandon *better* because it was not *good,* and to take *worse* instead. It is a most legitimate and a strong argument to prove that, however we must acknowledge some faults in a system, there is in the casting up of results none other found to surpass it. *Pro optimo est minime malus.*[43]

The reviewer argues that with the freeman (so-called) "no legislative <*legislative*> restriction sets any limit to his <that> improvement" [255]. This is not exactly true; but granting it were so, want, poverty, and starvation set frightful barriers, to overleap which no *legislative* permit gives the power. Where is the master so hard as poverty? where the driver so pitiless as starvation? The average condition of man under any government is a pretty fair criterion of the encouragement which such government gives to his improvement. A strange inconsistency in the arguments of negrophilists generally is a constant lamentation over the degradation of the negro, while, if we are to believe their descriptions of negro character, nothing can approach nearer perfection. Take, for instance, Mrs. Stowe's great work,

43. "Who is least bad is taken for the best." Seneca *De tranquillitate animi (On Calmness of Soul)* 7.4: "In amicorum legendis ingeniis dabimus operam ut quam minime inquinatos adsumamus. . . . Nec hoc praeceperim tibi, ut neminem nisi sapientem sequaris aut adtrahas. Ubi enim istum invenies quem tot saeculis quaerimus? Pro optimo sit minime malus." "In choosing the intellects of our friends we shall make an effort to take up those who are as little as possible corrupted. . . . But I would not instruct you to follow or take to yourself nobody who is not a sage. For where will you find him whom we have sought for so many centuries? Who is least bad, let him be taken for the best."

which, like the little leaven that leaveneth the whole loaf,[44] has set fermenting the entire mass of rabid fanaticism in two hemispheres, and what saintly pictures does it not represent? "If," remarks the *Journal of Commerce,* "these characters are fair types, as the writer doubtless intended them to be, of the mass of Southern slaves, we confess that we have abundant reason for heartily wishing that all Africa were under a tutelage that would develope so much of Christian symmetry of character. Why employ missionaries to spend their years among <amid> the malaria of the African Continent, if the Southern system of slavery brings out such rare and beautiful models of moral excellence?"[45] Laud and glory should, indeed, be to the system which could produce such characters.[46] Mrs. Stowe has, however, mistaken her ground. Her black angels are as hard to find as her white devils, both being creations whose existence belongs to the *terra incognita* of her own brain. The negro is neither the strangely perfect, delicately sensitive being thus described at one moment by the negrophilists, nor yet the degraded brute which in the next breath they would represent him. The negro is not a degraded, but essentially a lower, man. By nature a grown-up child, he requires the authority and the indulgence, the checks and the privileges, accorded to his younger prototype. Such he enjoys under our system, a system not perfect, but perfectionable, and requiring only to be let alone in its natural progress to develop itself to fuller proportions of beauty and symmetry.

Our *North British* reviewer devotes some pages to prove that the slave does not *like* slavery, and adduces advertisements, etc., to convince the world that he frequently attempts to escape from it [248–50]. We should be delighted to discover that there was any locality or condition in life, where every individual in it *liked* his position. Does the Irish beggar, sleeping in his ditch, like his? Does the starving artisan of England *like his*? Does the hungry mother, of the same prosperous land, who poisons her babe, that the survivors may for a time subsist upon the paltry pension of a burial club, *like hers*? Such fearful instances may stand against scores of advertisements, and whole columns of falsehood from abolition papers to boot. Few are satisfied in this world, even amongst the so-called happy.[47]

44. 1 Cor. 5:6; Gal. 5:9.

45. "English Congregational Union—Rev. J. P. Thompson—*Uncle Tom's Cabin,* etc.," New York *Journal of Commerce,* Nov. 20, 1852.

46. "The Communion: Proper Preface," *The Book of Common Prayer* (New York, 1992), p. 255: "Therefore, with Angels and Archangels, and with all the company of heaven, we laud and magnify thy glorious Name."

47. William Makepeace Thackeray, *Vanity Fair,* ed. John Sutherland (Oxford, 1983), p. 878: "Ah! *Vanitas Vanitatum!* Which of us is happy in this world? Which of us has his desire? or, having it, is satisfied?"

Against our peace we arm our will;
Amidst our plenty, something still
For houses, horses, pictures, planting,
To thee, to me, to him, is wanting:
That cruel something unpossessed
Corrodes and leavens all the rest.[48]

It would be strange indeed if the whole body of negro slaves were to form the great exception to this universal longing of mankind. Taking them for all in all, there is no class of men in which a larger proportion can be found to be satisfied. The only wonder is that, with the whole pack of abolition hounds and new-light hunters in full cry after them, there is not tenfold the discontent and uneasiness that really exists. "What American, North or South," triumphantly asks the reviewer, "would like to change places with the slave?"[49] What scaly inhabitant of the deep, O most sapient brother, or the reviewing brotherhood, would like to change places with an oyster? And yet oysters *are,* and God made them; and, although the sportive denizen of the ocean, as he glances to and fro through its briny recesses, might not fancy being suddenly caught by the tail and glued down in some muddy shoal or gloomy submarine recess, yet have we a fair right to conclude that, as the oyster has, as evidently as his more sprightly brother of the deep, his object and destiny in existence, so is he by nature suited to its functions and its contingencies; and yet we might imagine the poor devil of an oyster made exceedingly uneasy in his position, should some whispering demon of mischief set up a submarine school of communism, and lecture on the propriety of general abolition. "Liberty! liberty!" cries the oyster; "am I too not a brother of the deep?" Alas! what knows he of liberty? He fancies that he need but be released from that rock, and, without further effort, he may skim the waves, or plunge, sporting, beneath the billows. "Liberty from these cursed bonds!" exclaims the agitator. "Liberty!" echoes his deluded victim. Behold! if the bond be burst, has he found liberty? Nay, rather destruction. True liberty consists but in the freedom to exercise those faculties which God has given, and the oyster upon his rock is as free as his nature permits him to be.

As regards negro-nature, he who runs may read.[50] The negro (as a

48. Matthew Prior, *The Ladle,* ll. 161–66, l. 163 reading: "For horses, houses, pictures, planting."

49. "American Slavery and *Uncle Tom's Cabin,*" p. 245, reading: "But what American, North or South, would like to be himself exposed to the risk of such abuses as, by their own shewing, slavery is liable to?"

50. Hab. 2:2: "And the Lord answered me, and said, Write the vision, and make it plain upon tables, that he may run that readeth it." William Cowper, *Tirocinium,* ll. 79–80: "Shine by the side of every path we tread / With such a luster, he that runs may read."

people) *cannot* be free. He has not the faculty of freedom. In no age and in no land has he lived free from restraint, except as the savage. Scarcely by the grossest quibble upon words can the imbruted savage, in his native wilds, be called a freeman. Does he promise better under England's pet experiment of enfranchisement in Jamaica? He has been watched over, helped—and what is the result? So long as England will make his clothes and bake his bread, he will wear the one and eat the other; but (we quote from the London *Times*)

> Our legislation has been dictated by the presumed necessities of the African slave. After the Emancipation Act, a large charge was assessed upon the colony in aid of civil and religious institutions for the benefit of the enfranchised negro, and it was hoped that these colored <coloured> subjects of the British Crown would soon be assimilated to their fellow-citizens. From all the information which reaches us, no less than from the visible probabilities of the case, we are constrained to believe that these hopes have been falsified. The negro has not acquired with his freedom any habits of industry or morality. His independence is little better than that of an uncaptured brute. Having accepted few of the restraints of civilization, he is amenable to few of its necessities; and the wants of his nature are so easily satisfied, that, at the current rate of wages <wage>, he is called upon for nothing but fitful and <or> desultory exertion. The blacks, therefore, instead of becoming intelligent husbandmen, have become vagrants and squatters, and it is now apprehended [that] with the failure of cultivation in the island will come the failure of its resources for instructing or controlling its population. So imminent does this consummation appear, that memorials have been signed by classes of colonial society hitherto standing aloof from politics, and not only the bench and the bar, but the bishops <Bishop>, clergy, and ministers of all denominations in the island, without exception, have recorded their conviction[s] that, in [the] absence of timely relief, the religious and educational institutions of the island must be abandoned, and the masses of the population retrograde to barbarism.[51]

Again we ask, will any quibble of words descend low enough to argue that this barbaric license is liberty?

But the most fairly tried experiment of negro independence in modern days, is the great empire of Hayti, concerning which we have lately had some

51. This passage from the London *Times* of Aug. 4, 1852, is quoted also in Henry C. Carey, *The Slave Trade, Domestic and Foreign: Why It Exists, and How It May Be Extinguished* (Philadelphia, 1853; rpt. New York, 1967), pp. 31–32. LSM reviews this book in chap. 13, "Carey on the Slave Trade."

most edifying developments. We refer to the correspondence of R. M. Walsh, Esq., late commissioner of the United States to Hayti.[52] Mr. Walsh, who is a Pennsylvanian, is, we must premise, certainly not to be suspected of any bias in favor of Southern institutions. Not only the locality of his birth and education would incline him to entirely opposite predilections, but, very certainly, no one with such a bias could for a moment think of accepting such a position as the one occupied by this gentleman when writing to our Secretary of State the series of letters from one of which we make our extracts. The whole correspondence is such a *bijou* in its way that it is well worth the study of the world; quite a Koh-i-noor,[53] which we specially recommend to the attention of Stafford House. Let the parliament of ladies pronounce, if they dare, in favor of his supremely disgusting *nigger* majesty, Faustin Soulouque. We have space only for one or two short extracts, showing the impressions of an unprejudiced observer regarding the condition of the country and the general nature and improvability of its inhabitants. Mr. Walsh writes to the then Secretary of State, Hon. Mr. Webster:

> I trust, sir, you will pardon me if I sometimes wander from the serious tone appropriate to a despatch, but it is difficult to preserve one's gravity with so absurd a caricature of civilization before one's eyes as is here exhibited in every shape.
>
> Nothing saves these people from being infinitely ridiculous but the circumstance of their being often supremely disgusting by their fearful atrocities. The change from a ludicrous farce to a bloody tragedy is here as frequent as it is terrible; and the smiles which the former irresistibly provoke, can only be repressed by the sickening sensations occasioned by the latter.
>
> It is a conviction which has been forced upon me by what I have learned here, that negroes only cease to be children when they degenerate into savages. As long as they happen to be in a genial mood, it is the rattle and the straw by which they are tickled and pleased; and when their passions are once aroused, the most potent weapons of subjugation can alone prevent the most horrible evils. A residence here, however brief, must cause the most determined philanthropist to entertain serious doubts of the possibility of

52. Robert Moylan Walsh (1811–72), diplomat, born in Philadelphia; was appointed (January 1851) by Secretary of State Daniel Webster to cooperate with British and French agents in order to bring peace to the island of Hispaniola, where Haiti was attempting to rescind by force the independence, declared in 1844, of the Dominican Republic. During his visit to Hispaniola (February-May 1851), Walsh composed nine dispatches to Webster, and upon his return to the United States a brief report (June 10). See Kenneth E. Shewmaker and Kenneth R. Stevens, eds., *The Papers of Daniel Webster, Diplomatic Papers* 2 (1850–52) (Hanover, N.H., 1987):307–13, 325–32.

53. Diamond, originally of 186 1/16 carats, acquired by the British Crown in 1850.

their ever attaining the full stature of intellectual and civilized manhood, unless some miraculous interposition is vouchsafed in their behalf. In proportion as the recollections and traditions of the old colonial civilization are fading away, and the imitative propensity, which is so strong a characteristic of the African, is losing its opportunities of exercise, the black inhabitants of Hayti are reverting to the primitive state from which they were elevated by contact with the whites—a race whose innate superiority would seem to be abundantly proved by the mere fact that it is approaching the goal of mental progress, while the other has scarcely made a step in advance of the position in which it was originally placed. It is among the mulattoes alone, as a general rule, that intelligence and education are to be found; but they are neither sufficiently numerous, nor virtuous, nor enlightened, to do more than diminish the rapidity of the nation's descent, and every day accelerates the inevitable catastrophe by lessening their influence and strength.

The contrast between the picture which is now presented by this country and that which it exhibited when under the dominion of the French, affords a melancholy confirmation of what I have said. It was then indeed an "exulting and abounding"[54] land, a land literally "flowing with milk and honey";[55] now it might be affirmed without extravagance that, where it is not an arid and desolate waste, it is flooded with the waters of bitterness or covered with noisome and poisonous weeds. [. . .]

The government, in spite of its constitutional forms, is a despotism of the most ignorant, corrupt, and vicious description, with a military establishment so enormous that, while it absorbs the largest portion of the revenue for its support, it dries up the very sources of national prosperity, by depriving the fields of their necessary laborers, to fill the town with pestilent hordes of depraved and irreclaimable idlers. The treasury is bankrupt, and every species of profligate and ruinous expedient is resorted to, for the purpose of obtaining the means of gratifying an insane passion for frivolous expenditure. A great[, if not the greater,] portion of the public revenue is wasted upon the personal vanities of the emperor, and his ridiculous efforts to surround himself with a splendor which he fancies to be preeminently imperial. It is a fact, that the same legislature which voted him several hundreds of thousands of francs for some absurd costume, refused an appropriation of twenty-five thousand francs for public schools. The population for the most part is immersed in Cimmerian darkness, that can never be pierced by the few and feeble rays which emanate from the higher portions of the social system,

54. Byron, *Childe Harold's Pilgrimage* 3.442 (to the Rhine): "But Thou, exulting and abounding river!"

55. Exod. 3:8, and frequently.

> whilst there is a constant fermentation of jealousies and antipathies between the great majority and the only class at all capable of guiding the destinies of the land, which threaten[s] at every moment to shatter the political vessel in which they are so perilously working. As to the refining and elevating influences of civilized life, the influences of religion, of literature, of science, of art, they do not exert the least practical sway, even if they can be said to exist at all. The priests of the altar set the worst examples of every kind of vice, and are universally mere adventurers disowned by the church, who alone can come here in consequence of the assumption by the emperor of ecclesiastical authority which militates with that of the Roman pontiff. The press is shackled to such a degree as to prevent the least freedom of opinion, and people are afraid to give utterance, even in confidential conversation, to aught that may be tortured into the slightest criticism upon the action of the government.
>
> In short, the combination of evil and destructive elements is such, that the ultimate regeneration of the Haytians seems to me to be the wildest of Utopian dreams. Dismal as this picture may appear, its coloring is not exaggerated. It is as faithful a representation as I can sketch of the general aspect of this miserable country—a country where God has done everything to make his creature happy, and where the creature is doing everything to mar the work of God.[56]

What is this but a rapid descent to barbarism, faintly combated by the relics of a fast-dying semi-civilization? Such is and has ever been the fate of the negro when left to his own guidance. Childlike in intellect, he needs a perpetual leading-string. Under the dominion of the white man among us, as formerly in Hayti, with the imitativeness, careless docility, and disposition to dependance, which form a part of his childlike nature, he follows in the track of his master and becomes the half-enlightened, useful, and contented being exhibited under our slave system. Set him free from the wholesome check of authority, and behold what he must be.

We have made throughout this article no reference to the important subjects of cotton, sugar, coffee, etc., without which productions the world would now get on but badly. Cotton is, for England particularly, of such vital importance, that the cessation of two crops from America would set her in the blaze of revolution. Do our philanthropists contemplate this among the results of emancipation? Or do they fancy that the emancipated negro of the United States will grow their cotton better than those of Jamaica and St. Domingo have done their sugar and coffee? We have made no reference to

56. Robert Moylan Walsh to Daniel Webster, April 10, 1851, in *United States Congressional Serial Set, Senate Documents,* 32d Cong., 1st sess., ser. 621, no. 113, pp. 31–33.

this great point in the question, because we have turned our argument principally to combat the accusations of cruelty and abstract injustice brought against our system, and are anxious to show that, quite independently of the benefit accruing to the white man, the negro is happier, *ex necessitate rei,*[57] in his position with us, than is possible in any other circumstances. Amalgamation being put (as we presume the bitterest of our antagonists will allow us to do) out of the question, what must become of him if released from this salutary bondage? Let the ladies of Stafford House deliberate upon this question. Let them contemplate, if they can, the flood of barbarism which, following their wished-for measure of emancipation, would inundate the world. For, strange to say, at this moment, upon the negro and negro slavery depends all that the world has of highest civilization. America in ruins—England in revolution—what becomes of the world? Ladies, at your next meeting think of this, and then, if you dare, send your incendiary appeals across the Atlantic to try whether, like a nation of Tarpeias, we women of America can be either frightened, bribed, or flattered, to our country's ruin.[58]

And now, "glory to God in the highest, on earth peace, and good will toward men."[59] Ladies of Stafford House, thus you end your appeal; thus, too, dare we. Our tongue shrinks not the ordeal. We hold out to you the right hand of fellowship; we say to you, as women, slander not so your sex as to consent to believe, on the blind testimony of careless and misinformed, if not mischievous scribblers, the libels which you have so thoughtlessly accredited. Are we mothers without mothers' hearts? Are we wives, sisters, and daughters, yet have no heart-throb for those mothers, wives, sisters, and daughters whom Providence has committed to our supervising care? Are *we* alone marked out by nature as devoid of that God-given woman instinct whose privilege it is to pity and to soothe? Believe us, no! Woman is woman still, and were this system what you represent it, long since would her heart have risen against it, and with pleading tears and earnest prayer she would have taught the son of her bosom that truth is nobler than gain, and humanity better than power. The outspring of a mother's heart (ladies, though ye be duchesses and countesses, have ye not felt it?) cannot limit itself to her own babes, and we who watch and sympathize with the sick and the mourner, must learn to love (in Christian charity, and human brotherhood, to love)

57. "From the necessity of the thing" (Latin).

58. Daughter of the magistrate holding the Roman citadel, Tarpeia betrayed the fortress to the besieging Sabines, who thereupon killed her (Livy 1.11.5–9). The Tarpeian Rock, from which traitors were hurled to their deaths, was named for her.

59. Luke 2:14.

these our humble friends and close dependents. We cannot shirk our poor, nor bid them betake themselves to asylums and houses of refuge. We dare not (whether in law or conscience, we dare not) shuffle them off upon town-councils, beadles, and constables. We have no deputy work, nor can we ease our consciences that our charity is done by substitute. With our own hand we relieve, with our own heart we sympathize; and, believe us, ladies, if you have never tried it, go amongst the lowly; nurse one poor sufferer through his agony; with your own hand bathe the anguished brow, with your own eye watch the flickering breath, and you will perchance find that one act of practical charity more softens the heart than a thousand theories for foreign missions and slave emancipation. Look, ladies, at the slave at your own door, the Lazarus at the gate of Dives.[60] Though decorously excluded from the princely gates of Stafford House, turn but a few corners and you will find the thronging multitudes of misery. Blind alleys are here, damp cellars, filthy garrets, the stench and the wretchedness and the vice of which are scarcely decent for the investigations of gentle ladies; hells, to which our poorest negro hut would present a cheerful and a blessed contrast. England, your own proud, happy England, teems with wretchedness. We speak not of her Indian coolies crushed by the iron rule of conquest; we speak not of her Kaffir foes fast disappearing from existence to make way for Saxon laws; we speak not now even of her wretched Irish emigrant forced under pain of death to flee from the land that starves him. No! nearer, nearer, ladies! even at your chariot wheels, almost under them, crushed in the dust and groveling in their wretchedness, lie these, the victims of the juggernaut of English aristocracy. Ha! and if you cannot *pity,* ladies, may you not perhaps be forced to *fear* them? These down-trodden millions can think; they can reason; they can rise from their wretchedness and cry aloud against the false sentimentality which casts its sympathy, its tears, and its efforts upon the unknown and imagined evils of far-off lands, while misery shrieks unheeded at its feet. Aye, they may turn those shrieks to thunder. "Liberty and equality" may resound in your ears in other than the gentle tones wherein your ladylike voices speak them. God forbid that this should be! and yet beware that, in your sentimental follies, you do not give the first stroke of the tocsin for your own destruction! Shall liberty be for the negro and not for the white man? Shall bread be for the stranger and not for the brother? Hark! the cry is already on the wind! *Egalité! Fraternité! Droit de travail! La propriété c'est le vol!* What means all this? It means that trampled millions, when they reason, rush from crouching idiocy to rampant madness; it means that an unin-

60. Luke 16:19–25.

formed people governs fiercely when it seizes the reins; it means that sparks may light a flame; it means that your beggars, proud ladies! may yet be your rulers. Beware how you chant the "Marseillaise"!

These are hard words, of which, even as we utter them, we repent—mischievous words, to feed the flame of discontent and rouse to wrathful resistance against irremediable ills. We believe that such works as Mayhew's *Sketches of London, Alton Locke,* and others similar, which are constantly emitted from the English press, are calculated (by pointing out evils for which they have no practicable remedy, thus exciting vague, aimless, and therefore necessarily mischievous effort) to do much harm, and we would not willingly play into the hands of such agitators.[61] But what can we do? We are put upon the defensive, and must show that our system is not the one *monstrum horrendum, informe, ingens, cui lumen ademptum*[62]—is not the great Giant Despair[63] which you imagine it. We mean, therefore, no reproach upon the greatest nation that ever God's light shone upon. We mean but to show that even England—great, glorious England—proud, and justly proud of her people and her institutions, has her running sores too fearfully nauseous to bear the probing. The proverb bids us mistrust the sick physician.[64] He should not pretend to be the physician of others who himself teems with ulcers.

To conclude. We have been induced to the writing of this article principally in the hope of convincing the ladies of Stafford House, and others who may be disposed to join them, that they have mistaken their sisters of America. They have judged, we fear, by some noisy specimens of woman's-rights meetings, that the masses of womankind are ready to set the world on fire for a little notoriety. They have believed on the testimony of certain *âmes damnées* in the abolition service, vouched for by the affidavits of all the *gobes-mouches,* who have written out their tales of horror for the benefit of the world, that the state of affairs was desperate with us of the slavery section, and have supposed that the ranting dames and demoiselles above referred to

61. By "Mayhew's *Sketches of London*" LSM presumably refers to Henry Mayhew, *London Labour and the London Poor* (1851–62); she may be confusing the title with James Grant (1802–79), *Sketches of London* (Philadelphia, 1839). Charles Kingsley's *Alton Locke* (1850) is reviewed by LSM in chap. 6, "Negro and White Slavery—Wherein Do They Differ?"

62. Vergil *Aeneid* 3.658 (of the Cyclops Polyphemus, blinded by Odysseus): "A dreadful monster, hideous, huge, robbed of his eye." The quotation is applied to the Chartist petition of 1848 by Sandy Mackaye, in Kingsley, *Alton Locke,* p. 300.

63. As Polyphemus had imprisoned Odysseus and his men, so, in John Bunyan's *Pilgrim's Progress* (Harmondsworth, Eng., 1965), pp. 151–57, Giant Despair imprisons Christian and Hopeful in Doubting Castle.

64. Luke 4:23.

might sweep us from the world of argument by some decisive "boo to a goose" process. Perhaps our arguments may be of sufficient weight to convince our aristocratic sisters of England, that there is with us of the Southern United States a strong *corps de reserve* of sober, quiet women, who, satisfied to find out duties at home (not for want of thought, but because thought teaches us that therein lies woman's highest task, and the fulfillment of her noblest mission), can nevertheless start up with the true feeling of womanhood in defence of right and property, hearth and home. *Ora et labora*—strive and pray. Such is the lesson of our life, ladies, and it were hard to find a better. With us woman finds her noblest rule, her highest privilege, a privilege which, in the aggregate, her sex has never abused. However individual exceptions are to be found, woman (as a class) never sides with the oppressor. Our system, abhorrent as it seems to your ladyships, has the sanction of our hearts and heads; and in the conscientious exercise of it we find enough to occupy both without the necessity of joining any of the world-improving and God-improving societies which at present are so much in vogue, and each one of which threatens the world with some new *fiat lux* for its regeneration.[65]

Heaven bless you, ladies! Have not we, too, hands and feet? eyes and ears? heads and hearts? What sticks or stones are we that we should contentedly settle down with the barren waste of wretchedness which you have been led to believe around us? If there is misery, can we not see it? If there is wretchedness, can we not hear it?[66] *Our* poor, we have already told you, cannot be shoved into garrets and cellars. They are with us at bed and at board; and when there is woe with them, the wailing of it is in our ears. Believe ye that there is also no pity for it in our hearts? Shall we love—grant us the common feelings of humanity—shall we love the horse, the ox, the cat, and the dog; shall we cling with fond affection to the scenes of our childhood, the house in which we have been reared, the soil which our baby feet have trod, aye, even an old chair or a crippled sofa, because of the holy memories which cling around it; shall we love all these, and yet charity, feeling, conscience suddenly become extinct when, just at the point that we touch upon, humanity, all should become more vivid? Surely this is not in human nature. Strong as are the instincts of race—intensely as we are taught to feel that black men are not white men—and shudderingly as we turn from the impi-

65. *Fiat lux:* "Let there be light" (Gen. 1:3).

66. *Merchant of Venice* 3.1.52–60: "Hath not a Jew eyes? hath not a Jew hands, organs, dimensions, senses, affections, passions? fed with the same food, hurt with the same weapons, subject to the same diseases, healed by the same means, warmed and cooled by the same winter and summer as a Christian is?—if you prick us do we not bleed? if you tickle us do we not laugh? if you poison us do we not die? and if you wrong us shall we not revenge?"

ous and insane idea that would level in one sweeping equality of degradation what God has so distinctly severed, yet can we most acutely feel the human tie between us. We can weep with them, nurse them, and comfort them; we can learn, in this school of the affections, that

> He prayeth best, who loveth best
> All things both great and small;
> For the dear God that <who> loveth us,
> He made and loveth all.[67]

By this exercise of charity, our whole being is the better attuned to love. The affections which pass from the child to the slave, descend still by gradation to the brute. The poor broken-down horse becomes dearer to us, and even the old ass, as we stroke his long ears, is from habit a friend. But, for heaven's pity! gentle ladies, be satisfied that we are kind to him, and do not insist that, because he cannot walk upright, we, for the sake of charity, equality, and so forth, shall creep on all fours to keep him company. The white man may nurse and protect the negro—may pity the negro—may love the negro—but cannot consent to stoop to him. That position which is no degradation to the negro, because therein, as a really inferior man, he but conforms to nature, becomes to the white man a disgrace and a reproach.

We have done. Brethren and sisters, in conformity with the *Christian* tone of your articles we conclude ours. "More in sorrow than in anger,"[68] brother reviewer, have, to use your own words [258], been our remonstrances; and sisters of Stafford House, of you we only beg, in Christian charity, that you will learn to know better both the white man and the negro of America. The chances are that by so doing you will be the better able to strive with us towards that great aim which shall bring, as you (no doubt sincerely) pray, "Glory to God in the highest, on earth peace and good will toward men."

67. Samuel Taylor Coleridge, "The Rime of the Ancient Mariner," ll. 614–17.
68. *Hamlet* 1.2.231.

11.

Charity Which Does Not Begin at Home

Bob. Daddy, Sam's been stealin' lots o' sugar from the great China-dish.

Daddy (much affected at hearing of Sam's immorality). Lord pity the wickedness of this world! But are you sure of it, Bob?

Bob. Sure on it? That I is. I seen him do the darned wicked thing with my own eyes, Dad; and I knows it was no sham, 'case I gin him one o' my old marbles, and I promised him not to make a fuss about it, and then he gin me one-half o' the sweetenin'. Lor' Dad, did you think Sam was so wicked? It hurts my feelin's mightily to think on't, and I hopes the Almighty will punish him like all fire.

Dad, absorbed in meditation, perhaps upon the wickedness of the age, forgets to give Bob any answer to his last pious reflection upon Bob's misconduct.

Now it would seem in Mr. John Bull's opinion, Uncle Sam has been stealing the sugar, i.e., he has been, and is, according to John, indulging himself in the *dolce far niente* of luxurious idleness, making black fingers work for him, and Mr. John's feelin's are mightily hurt to think on't. He is telling Dad of it every hour of the day, now bellowing and now whining out his dolefuls for the benefit and information of the doubting world. Sam is at the sugar,

SLM 19 (April 1853): 193–208. Publications reviewed: [J. F. W. Johnston], "Slavery and the Slave Power in the United States of America," *Blackwood's Edinburgh Magazine* 73 (Jan. 1853): 1–20; [William Edward Forster], "American Slavery, and Emancipation by the Free States," *Westminster Review* 59 (Jan. 1853): 125–67.

and there's no sham about it, and John most righteously hopes to see him yet get "all fire" to pay off the enjoyment.

Dear philanthropic brother John, ought you not to remember that you have had your share of the "sweetenin'"? Are you not indeed daily licking your lips under the enjoyment? Do penance, dear brother. At least deny yourself the privilege of sharing in the results of this iniquity. Touch not our sugar, brother: let your lords and ladies "do their meetings" without their *sweetenin'*. Touch not our cotton, brother: let your manufacturers go starve; let your empty ships return to rot in your docks. Taste not the *sweetenin'*; and then if you have time and disposition for the amusement, you may with more show of justice pitch "all fire" at the guilty Sam.

Fanaticism is a horse apt enough to take the bit in its teeth;[1] but the rabid madness which is at present instilling itself, so to speak, through the veins of the civilized world, is no longer simple fanaticism, but a death-spreading poison. The mad dog is loose! or rather the slow aspic is hissing at your ears. Sleepers, for your lives, awake!

What do these people mean? Is this all talk or earnest? Do they really, seriously, wish to abolish slavery? Scarcely; and yet what mean these constantly renewed attacks? On they come, in spite of argument, reasoning, entreaty. Another and another and another! It seems as though the line would indeed "stretch out to the crack of doom."[2] And worse than the worst of Egypt's plagues, the furrow of its track is sweeping desolation. Piled upon the heap of similar offerings to their goddess of Reason (rather is it not Unreason?), the January number of *Blackwood* throws in its mite of folly. Let us (although weary of similar tasks) glance at its arguments.

> The cotton-shrub which, seventy years ago, was grown only in gardens as a curiosity, yields now to the United States an amount of exportable produce which, in the year ending with June, 1850, amounted to seventy-two millions of dollars, of which from thirty to forty millions were clear profit to the country. With its increased growth has sprung up that mercantile navy which now waves its stripes and stars over every sea, and that foreign influence which has placed the internal peace, we may say the subsistence of millions, in every manufacturing country in Europe, within the power of an oligarchy of planters. [10–11]

Leaving out the side hit at the "oligarchy of planters," which is evidently intended to excite democratic jealousies (not a very wise stroke, by the way, for an English tory), would any body believe that the above extract was taken

1. Cf. *2 Henry IV* 1.1.9–11.
2. *Macbeth* 4.1.117.

from a bitter, anti-slavery article? We take it for granted that no one whose education has passed the first ten pages of his spelling-book is fool enough to imagine that American cotton can be produced without negro-labour in a region where, as the reviewer tells us (in perhaps rather stronger terms than are literally true), that "the climate in the hot season" is "rife with fever, and fatal to the constitution of the white man" [2]. We give his own words to prove his knowledge of the fact that the cotton crop is thus dependent upon negro-labour. How incapable the negro is of managing his own labour without white superintendence, is made sufficiently evident by the history and habits of his race for four thousand years back. Vainly has modern effort endeavored to put him on another footing. A glance at St. Domingo and Jamaica sufficiently proves the futility of such efforts. Luxuriant deserts, these islands stand before us, showing, like tattered robes of royalty, the soiled but costly vestiges of what they have been. Thus, then, the reviewer tells us in almost so many words, that the cotton crop is *dependent upon the institution of slavery.* He tells us that this crop gives to the United States an *immense revenue,* and an *almost boundless foreign influence.* He tells us that it is necessary to the *internal peace* and to the *subsistence of millions in every manufacturing country in Europe,* and with the same breath exclaims, *abolish it! abolish it!*

Once in the history of the world we have heard the insane cry, "Crucify him! Crucify him!" and the good and the holy, the just and the pure, blown upon by the popular breath, misrepresented by envy and bigotry, was adjudged vile and iniquitous! Ye zealots of progress beware that in your folly, ye crucify not again the spirit of Wisdom, the incarnate good! *God* breathes throughout his universe the beautiful law of order: certain beings to certain ends. Such is the invariable and regulating influence of creation. It is not always an easy lesson to read the mystery of God, and ofttimes the object and destiny of the creature is a long time in developing itself to human intellects. Once developed, however, how beautifully does *God's* system justify itself to the querulous fault-finder! The useless becomes useful; the lawless falls into order; the supposed deformity proves itself beautiful; and Reason learns to worship and adore the over-ruling power which it dared to dispute. *Certain beings to certain ends.* God has no higher law in sublunary things, and, stamped upon creation, its beautiful effects are daily more and more developing themselves. Herein consists the world's true progress. "Obey and live."[3]

3. Bernard Barton, "Night Musings," in *Poetic Vigils* (London, 1824), ll. 31–36: "O! hasten, then, that happier hour, / When bright within shall shine / Thy Holy Spirit's teaching power, / With ministry divine, / Whose sacred teachings strength can give, / And bid the soul obey and live!"

Man's reason is given him to *find* the way which Omniscience points, never to *create* a newer track. Its piddling efforts to clear for itself a way in opposition to the Almighty rule of order, produce those mighty cataclysms in the moral world at which we gaze and shudder. Blind moles! thinking to build their tiny homes, how often have men shaken down over their own heads the magnificent structures of ages!

Such a work is now going on in this grubbing about the foundations of negro-slavery. *God* has made this world for use. The alluvial soil of the United States, as well as, no doubt, the ice-bound rocks of those polar regions of which as yet we read not the destiny, have their use and object. Our destiny is at present plainly enough marked. Cotton, the great peacemaker of the world, the destined civilizer of unexplored realms, the link of nations, cotton is our destiny. The negro only can cultivate cotton. He cannot cultivate it without the white man's rule. Then, with the white man's rule, cultivate it he must, cultivate it he will, in spite of lords and ladies, *North British*ers and *Blackwoods*. All the fashionable twaddle, now so prevalent about "free and equal," "human rights," "the dignity of man," etc., must give way to the stringent laws of nature. *Certain beings to certain ends.* The man and woman are not equal. They are different, and created to different purposes and different ends. The white man and the negro are *not* equal; the Anglo-Saxon and his Coolie subject are *not* equal; the philosopher and the idiot are *not* equal; the sage and the madman are *not* equal. All have their destiny in life; all, no doubt, far beyond the perception of our feeble faculties, contribute to the working out of some useful purpose in an all-wise system of creation; but all are different. Some must rule and some must submit. Equality is simply anarchy. At certain periods of excitement, society, or at least an active portion of it, has been frequently seized with a kind of intermittent delirium for progress and, in the wild struggles of its maniac efforts, tramples under foot the very object at which it aims. Through such a phase we are now passing, and "negro-mania" is decidedly at this crisis the prominent form of disease; a form more virulent than any heretofore exhibited. The inventors and propagators of philanthropic aphorisms have oftenest been confined in their aspirations to a *white* Utopia. Even Sir Thomas More, we presume, would have been strangely startled, if in his own dream-land some big "Daddy Cuffee" had come forward to claim a prominent position. Until the last half-century, the negro has, as a people, been literally unknown in the civilized world, and still in the greater part of it is unknown. Men have been legislated for on one broad principle, as though all men were white men; and herein lies the blunder of European philanthropists. They know nothing of the negro, and persist in regarding him as a black white-man. They talk of "the prejudices of colour," as though in colour lay the material difference between the races, and wish to legislate and to force us to legislate according to the wild results of their own ignorant speculations upon the *general nature* of man, entirely ignoring all abstract differences of race. The negro is certainly a man; but as certainly and most emphatically not a white man with a black mask; and no individual or people who has not habitually associated with him and studied him in his habits and nature, can be in any way fitted to legislate for him.

We defend the system of African slavery as existing among us, not upon the ground of *temporary expediency,* but as a *fixed and permanent necessity* from the nature of things and the nature of men, as exhibited in their varieties of race. Negro-slavery is only destined to die out upon this continent, when God destines the race also to die out from among us. Then, and no sooner, will the negro be left (the melancholy refuse of a society to which his existence has become a burden) to pass away as the red man has passed before him. In the mean time his comfort and safety are in slavery, and like every creation of God he is beautifully fitted to his intended position. In every characteristic of mind and body he is suited to it. To him, bodily comfort is the height of enjoyment. The liberty for which the white man longs, the negro never dreams of. The rights for which the white man dies, the negro cannot comprehend. He may be made discontented by injudicious interference, but enlightened upon any abstract point of human rights he cannot be; his nature is not susceptible of the necessary impulses and trains of thought. In the drawing up of our American Declaration of Independence, the negro was evidently considered as *not a man,* in the sense in which the word "man" is there used. "All men are born free and equal" evidently meant: all white men, all men of our own race, possessing our instincts and our inclinations, are born free and equal. Our forefathers no more thought of including the negro in their acceptation of the word man, than they were prepared for a similar admission of the word female-man, as is now and with equal plausibility claimed by our progressive ladies. The assumed position of equality even in the limited sense which we adopt is plainly a false one. There is no such thing as equality possible or desirable among the masses of society. Differences and grades are almost as numerous as individuals. But such we may presume to have been the interpretation which, in the enthusiasm of their struggle for disfranchisement from foreign bondage, our ancestors put upon these words. They claimed liberty for themselves, but certainly *not* for their slaves. Nothing but wilful perversion, or idiotic imbecility, could suppose any application of the words sufficiently comprehensive to include the negro; when, at the very moment of the signing of the Declaration, the larger number of its subscribers and their constituents were holding property in slaves, and so little thinking of abandoning it that, in the formation of our constitution, every arrangement was made for the perpetuation and security of the institution.

The *Blackwood* reviewer goes on, in direct contradiction of his own above-quoted statement with regard to the immense prosperity accruing to the United States from our institution of negro-slavery, to prove by argument the degradation and general condition of pining degeneracy which it entails upon the slaveholding States. It does appear to us that these two results are so palpably incompatible as to bear upon their face the stamp of irrationality. How can the degradation, the semi-prostration of one half, or nearly one half, of a country contribute to the prosperity of the whole? Let us, however, one by one, meet the statements by which he endeavors to prove that we are suffering under a Providential dispensation. "The fathers ate sour grapes, and the children's teeth are set on edge."[4]

First: This retribution is seen in the fact that our negroes are in the course of nature increasing, and thus, although the immense influx of immigration causes the white population to increase still more rapidly, the slave power is, by a very curious *non sequitur,* becoming proportionably stronger in all governmental questions, and the slaves themselves will, in ten years more, become so numerous and dangerous, that "having 'the best blood of the states'[5] flowing in their veins," and all "their interests, hopes, and aspirations [. . .] opposed to those of the white population" [8], they will be disposed and able to eat up their masters, or perform some other such terrible operation. Their masters, meanwhile, with "the constant fear of insurrection" [4] before their eyes, are already frightened half out of their senses, and by way of soothing the irritated slave amuse themselves with various acts of wanton cruelty, which will of course increase in number and atrocity, in equal proportion with their increasing trepidations. Therefore the slave States are ardently desirous of maintaining the Union intact, and, inasmuch as nothing can induce them to leave it, they thus put it in perpetual danger of dissolution (these paradoxes cost nothing to our reviewer); and because it is so important to them in their enfeebled and perilous situation to keep upon good terms with the more powerful free States, they constantly ride over them, with an outrageous assumption of power, "controlling cabinets, influencing diplomacy, and determining the public choice for all the great offices of State" [8].

We have no argument to combat here. The reviewer saves us the trouble,

4. Ezek. 18:2.

5. This constantly repeated slander is about as true as it would be to assert that the brothels of England are the regular and habitual resort of all that is highest and noblest in the land. [LSM]

and as fast as he raises a difficulty, most obligingly knocks it down for us. The thing is black because it is white, is the amount of his reasoning. He then goes on to point out two circumstances in which, he says,

> we seem to perceive the finger of Providence manifestly interfering to maintain for the present and extend this melancholy institution [9].

The finger of Providence *manifestly interferes to maintain* slavery, but the wiser reviewer knows better than Providence, and condemns it as a *melancholy institution*! One of these circumstances he calls the rejection of the bill reported to the Congress of the Confederation in 1781 to exclude slavery from the territory then ceded by Virginia to the United States.[6] The other is the immense increase of the annual cotton produce which has in the space of about sixty years passed from one million to about 1,500,000,000 and made "the subsistence of millions" dependent upon its continued production. "*God* saw that it was good," and blessed the work of his hands, even to the whole world, from land to land, and from generation to generation.[7] But the quick eye of our reviewer detects this Providential blunder, and, as our Daddy Cuffee (head-man and superintendent of our little realm of negrodom) remarks with regard to some lesser concerns, he will electrify[8] things and set all right without troubling *Massa* to look into it farther. Whitney invented his

6. "Slavery and the Slave Power," pp. 9–10, citing *A Chapter of American History. Five Years' Progress of the Slave Power; A Series of Papers First Published in the Boston "Commonwealth," in July, August, and September, 1851* (Boston, 1852), p. 10. On March 1, 1784 (LSM's "1781" is an error transcribed from "Slavery and the Slave Power"), Congress accepted Virginia's cession of its western lands north of the Ohio River. Thomas Jefferson, as chairman of a committee appointed to draft an ordinance for the government of the ceded lands, submitted a report in which it was declared that "after the year 1800 of the Christian aera there shall be neither slavery nor involuntary servitude" in any of the states created from the ceded territory. This clause was deleted, by a vote of seven states to six, when the Ordinance of 1784 was adopted by Congress on April 23.

7. Gen. 1:10, 12, 18, 21, 25. Job 1:10: "Thou hast blessed the work of his hands, and his substance is increased in the land." Rom. 1:8: "I thank my God through Jesus Christ for you all, that your faith is spoken of throughout the whole world." Jer. 12:12: "The spoilers are come upon all high places through the wilderness: for the sword of the Lord shall devour from the one end of the land even to the other end of the land: no flesh shall have peace." "From generation to generation" is a favorite phrase in the Old Testament (Exod. 17:16, etc.).

8. Probably the good old man means "rectify". [LSM] "Drivers love big words, and we ourselves heard a driver . . . say to his master, who had interfered in a quarrel between two of his slaves, 'Neber mind, massa, neber mind—leave dem to me, I will *electrify* dem'; meaning he would settle all matters between them." David James McCord, "Practical Effects of Emancipation," p. 495.

cotton-gin, Arkwright his spinning-roller, and Cartwright his power-loom;[9] and, says the reviewer,

> each of these machines removed obstacles which stood in the way of the increased consumption of cotton, and gave a new impulse to a species of cultivation by which it is intended that slaves should [meanwhile] be multiplied, and slavery itself extended over new dominions [11].

It was *so intended;* but decidedly *Massa's* intentions need *electrifying,* and so we are set to hunt up some "mysterious end" to all this prosperity.

> Is another Toussaint[10] to arise, more pale-faced than the first, the descendant of a Washington, or inheriting in his mixed blood the spirit of a Jefferson, to vindicate the rights of his race? [11]

Truly, if the prayers of these righteous ones could induce such an end, we would not doubt their charitable interference to bring "*all fire*" upon us in the shape of any kind of a Toussaint black, white, or yellow. But let them beware of their own millions, who are confessedly, by their own showing, to be thus turned starving upon the world. May the Almighty find no avenger of his outraged laws among *them*? Too soon, oh! most righteous Pharisees, do you congratulate yourselves upon the "gracious interference" by which Great Britain has "been disposed to shake herself wholly free from the vile contamination" [11].

Free she is *not*. If there be blood upon our robes, the sprinkling of it has fallen largely upon hers. Free she is not, and if slavery be the blight, the canker, and the contamination which you state it, England, like us, lives upon its produce; England, like us, starves in its extinction; England, like us, triple-dyed in her own blood, must rue (if it ever comes) the successful end of these machinations. We believe, however, that this can never be. Our faith in the all-pervading rule of order which governs nature is strong. God has so made the negro that even these mischievous promptings cannot drive him to the end so anxiously anticipated by reformers. He clings to the bonds which nature has fitted him to wear. Horrible instances of individual or limited murder and insurrection may occur, but the tragedy of St. Domingo

9. Eli Whitney (1765–1825), inventor of the cotton gin, which removed seed from cotton fiber (1793); Sir Richard Arkwright (1732–92), whose water-powered spinning frame, patented in 1769, produced cotton thread of a sturdiness sufficient for weaving; Edmund Cartwright (1743–1823) with his power loom (patented 1785–87) applied machinery to weaving.

10. François-Dominique Toussaint-Louverture (c. 1743–1803), slave-born leader of slaves' insurrection in Haiti (1791); attacked and occupied Spanish Santo Domingo, and abolished slavery there (1801); defeated by the French (1802), died in a French prison.

(planned and excited as it was by whites, not blacks) can never be re-enacted on a larger scale. As a nation the negro will continue in slavery; and the only permanent effect of this injudicious interference, if it takes effect at all, must be to painfully tighten the shackles which now lie loose and easy upon the unchafed limbs of this destined victim to philanthropic sentimentality.

Our reviewer continues:

> A second form of this retribution is seen in the influence which slavery already exercises over the moral and social condition of the people. It is a corrupter of morals, both national and individual; an enemy to knowledge; a barrier to progress; a paralyzer of industry; a perverter of religion; a despiser of the restraints of law; an enemy to just social legislation; the mother and nurse of unjust social prejudice. [11]

Whew-ew! why here are a dozen forms of retribution, not one! "I's so awful wicked," as Topsy says, "there can't nobody do nothin' with me."[11] *Blackwood* continues:

> We cannot pollute our pages by describing the immoral grossness to which the system is said to give rise on <in> every plantation [11].

"*Is said*." Very decisive testimony that! Ye righteous judges hang that man; it *is said* that he has committed murder.

Then follow long quotations from abolitionist writers, swearing to their own false witness. Slander backed by slander, falsehood by falsehood. To these we could for every page give volumes of opposite testimony. But what avails it? If you flash the light in a man's face and he persists in swearing that it is dark, think you he can be moved by an argument? The *Blackwood* reviewer has, even among his own not unprejudiced countrymen, testimony to the purity of Southern morals. We have not at hand, and cannot adduce such witness as we would desire on this subject. Two authorities, however, occur to us.[12] Alex. Mackay remarks, among other high praises of the social qualities of our "country gentry," that "throughout the society of the Southern Atlantic states" (he particularly designates Maryland, Virginia, and South Carolina) there prevails

> a *purity of tone* and an *elevation of sentiment,* together with an ease of manner and a general social *aplomb,* which are only to be found [united] in a truly leisure class. Any general picture of American society would be very incom-

11. Stowe, *Uncle Tom's Cabin* (1991 ed.), p. 292.

12. These authorities, together with the particular passages quoted by LSM below, are the same given by David James McCord, "How the South Is Affected by Her Slave Institutions," pp. 355–56.

plete into which was not prominently introduced the phase which it exhibits in the rural life of the South.[13]

Mr. Hamilton (author of *Cyril Thornton*) says of the "opulent and educated" Southerner, that he is

> distinguished by a *high-mindedness, generosity,* and *hospitality,* by no means predicable of his more eastern neighbours.[14]

We have not time for farther research, but here are at least two English gentlemen, who have seen our plantation life and have remarked nothing of the "*immoral grossness* to which the system gives rise on *every plantation,*" and with which the sensitive *Blackwood* "fears to pollute" its pages. Our southern women, much admired by these gentlemen, and found fault with, by their more aspiring northern sisters, for timidity and an even insipidly shrinking modesty—how can *they* pass unpolluted through the fiery furnace of abominations? Or will the reviewer dare to intimate that they, too, join the unholy revels?

It is easy to see upon what kind of authorities the reviewer leans. Mrs. Stowe will tell him endless "tales of wonder,"[15] and abolition meetings will string on dittos in abundance. We have at present under our eye the very edifying details of a meeting recently (Jan[uar]y 27th and 28th) held in Boston, where some fifty to two hundred persons, black, white, and yellow, male and female, under the guidance of Mr. Garrison, give "their experiences."[16] Mr. Edmund Quincy announces that abolitionism

13. Alexander Mackay, *The Western World; or, Travels in the United States in 1846–47: Exhibiting Them in Their Latest Development, Social, Political, and Industrial; Including a Chapter on California,* 3 vols. (London, 1849), 1:207 (LSM's italics). Alexander Mackay (1808–49), Scottish journalist; in 1846 assigned by the London *Morning Chronicle* to report on congressional debates of the Oregon question; sent to India by a group of Manchester merchants to investigate cotton cultivation, perished at sea on the return journey.

14. Thomas Hamilton, *Men and Manners in America,* 2d ed. (Edinburgh, 1843; rpt. New York, 1968), p. 350 (LSM's italics). Thomas Hamilton (1789–1842), journalist and novelist; wrote *Cyril Thornton* (1827); on staff of *Blackwood's Edinburgh Magazine.*

15. Lewis, *Tales of Wonder.*

16. The proceedings of this meeting were published in Garrison's *Liberator* of Feb. 4, 1853, and reprinted in a somewhat revised form as an appendix to the *Twenty-first Annual Report Presented to the Massachusetts Anti-Slavery Society by Its Board of Governors, January 26, 1853* (rpt. Westport, Conn., 1966), pp. 81–100. Cited below: Edmund Quincy (1808–77), corresponding secretary of the Massachusetts Anti-Slavery Society (1844–53); editor of abolitionist journals; wrote short stories. Stephen Symonds Foster (1809–81), fierce abolitionist; wrote *The Brotherhood of Thieves; or, A True Picture of the American Church and Clergy* (1843), attacking organized religion; husband of fellow reformer Abigail Kelley Foster. Charles Lenox Remond (1810–73), agent of the Massachusetts Anti-Slavery Society; lecturer in Great Britain (1840–41). Parker Pillsbury (1809–98), lecture-agent for antislavery societies; editor of *Herald of Freedom* (1840, 1845–46); woman's rights advocate.

> shall sweep over the ruins of the constitution and the Union, when a fairer edifice than our fathers knew how to build, shall arise.

Mr. Foster says:

> that God had sent him into the world to further the cause, and if he was or was not successful it was immaterial to him, as the responsibility did not rest on his shoulders.[17] By the direction of an all-wise Providence, the church has thrown itself across the path of abolitionism, but she would soon have her neck under their heels, when she would be ground to the dust. The power of the church is passing away, and will die when plantation slavery become extinct.[18]

Mr. Quincy will be content to oust the authority of the Constitution and break down the work of our fathers. Mr. Foster is more ambitious and avowedly takes up arms against Providence, upon whom he first lays the responsibility of all abolition failures, and then threatens the All-Wise, who has had the temerity to put his church in their way, that they will soon have her neck under their heels!

Mrs. [Sarah C.] Redlon says:

> She had heard some terrible stories concerning slavery on the plantations—stories which were unfit for repetition; but they were true, and it made her feel that the friends of the slave should lose no time in gaining whatever aid they could.[19]

Mr. Remond (a colored gentleman) is vastly delighted at the deaths of our distinguished senators, Calhoun, Clay, and Webster; utters sundry rejoicings over sundry murders, hopes to see more of them, and is evidently in a most satisfactorily progressive state towards the highest perfection of African Cannibal civilization.[20] Mr. Parker Pillsbury finds great fault because the rec-

17. Do it if you choose, sir, on your own responsibility (says Mr. Foster to *God* Almighty); I wash my hands of the business. [LSM]

18. This is a paraphrase of part of Foster's speech, which was reprinted verbatim in the *Liberator* of Feb. 11, 1853.

19. Mrs. Redlon is here in beautiful sympathy with the *Blackwood* reviewer. The same shrinking delicacy from repeating naughty things, and the same simple and pure-hearted reliance in the truth of *hear say.* [LSM]

20. *Twenty-first Annual Report Presented to the Massachusetts Anti-Slavery Society by Its Board of Governors, January 26, 1853,* p. 84: "I may speak for the colored people of New England, at least, when I say, *We feel encouraged.* We were encouraged by the Jerry rescue, at Syracuse; by the death of Slaveholders at Christiana; and we are encouraged by the deaths of Calhoun, Clay, and Webster, that trio of defenders of Slavery. All these things are helping forward the triumph of freedom." William ("Jerry") McHenry (d. 1853), having escaped from his owner in Missouri, was living in Syracuse, N.Y., when on Oct. 1, 1851, he was arrested under the

reant abolitionist Sumner so far forgets his holy position in warring against Providence, that he speaks

> of Washington as being in heaven, and yet he was a slaveholder and slave-hunter. The speaker thought the pirate on the high seas might as well go to heaven as he, if he only quits his plundering when he can follow it no longer.[21]

The same gentleman winds up his speech of the next day with the pious observation that

> this society would overthrow religion, or religion would overthrow them.

Such are the authorities beloved of *Blackwood, North British* and *Westminster* reviewers, Stafford House Ladies, Lords Shaftesbury, Carlisle, etc. We congratulate them upon the *enlightened* and *christian* fraternity which they have found for themselves.

We should have remarked that, towards the close of this meeting, a negro brother presented himself as a fugitive from bondage, and begged pecuniary aid for the release of his wife and children. But apparently these parti-coloured ladies and gentlemen were not of the opinion that "who steals my purse steals trash." Mr. Parker Pillsbury denounced the application as made in the wrong place.[22]

But let us return to *Blackwood*. Slavery is "an enemy to knowledge, a barrier to progress" [11]. He proves (in his own way) how our press is gagged, and our pulpit restrained; how our children have no schools, but vast means of education in all sorts of moral atrocities. As the simplest way of answering this, we point to the bright names which have illustrated our annals from the days of Washington downwards. Even Mr. Parker Pillsbury (although considering them all as food for the devil) will hardly set them down as proofs of the ignorance of our land. Wherever talent and genius have been called out in the service of our country, the South has always had her full

---

terms of the Fugitive Slave Law of 1850; a mob broke him out of jail the same afternoon and got him safely into Canada. At Christiana, Pa., on Sept. 11, 1851, a slaveholder from Maryland was killed during a riot while trying to recover some runaway slaves; his son was severely wounded, and others of the pursuing posse injured.

21. Ibid., p. 86.

22. Ibid., pp. 91–92. *Othello* 3.3.161. The New York *Daily Times* of Jan. 28, 1853, after remarking that the proceedings of the previous day had been "quite tame and uninteresting," reported that "a colored man, representing himself as a fugitive with a wife and two children in slavery, requested a collection might be taken to purchase their freedom. PARKER PILLSBURY denounced the application as made in the wrong place. He would have nothing to do with buying slaves, and referred the applicant to the editors of the New York *Journal of Commerce*." "Ten to twelve dollars," the *Times* concluded, "were collected among the spectators."

share. Is it of the land of the Washingtons, Henrys, and Jeffersons; the Rutledges and Pinckneys; the Lowndes' and Cheves'; the Randolphs, the Calhouns, and the Clays, that it shall be said, this is the region of besotted ignorance and stagnating imbecility? Nay; with Mr. Parker Pillsbury, send them all to the Old Nick, if you will; or, with Mr. Cuffee Remond, smack your lips over their dead bodies, but give up the task of proving them fools, or the children of fools. These (and how many more bright names!) have been known and made their power felt on both sides of the Atlantic. Even the *Blackwood* reviewer, we presume, must have heard of some of them. By a most conclusive course of *Blackwood* reasoning, however, we are proved guilty of presenting a vast conglomeration of black and white degradation.

> It has been estimated that the number of slaveholding voters does not exceed 100,000; and, allowing six to a family, that not more than 600,000 are directly interested in and supported by the labour of slaves. But the white population of the slave states amounts to 6,169,387, so that of this *poor and degraded class* there are not less than 5,569,387, or they are to the rich and educated as 9 to 1. [4–5; LSM's italics]

The age of miracles, it would seem, is not over; for, wonderful to tell, with this degraded and wretched population of 9 to 1, pauperism is almost absolutely unknown, while death from starvation is only conceived from foreign newspapers, and fearful accounts of wretched Irish, at which our children shudder as over horrible tales

> Of sharp-teethed ogres crunching babies' bones
> Or ghouls and afrites feasting on a corpse.

Where these wretched 5,569,387 outcasts hide themselves, it is hard to imagine. Were *Blackwood* arithmetic true, they should be dying upon our dung-hills and rotting in our streets; for we are told that they have no visible means of existence, and show "all that vulgar brutality of vice which poverty and ignorance render so conspicuous and disgusting."[23] They have neither land, nor intelligence to cultivate it if possessed; neither trade nor handicraft art of any description—5,569,387 of these outcast whites, besides 3,200,380 wretched negroes, making in all a vicious, degraded, ignorant, and starving population of 8,769,767 brutally governed and tyrannized over by 600,000 despots, or rather by the 100,000 planters, whose wives and children make up the 600,000 who compose the whole privileged class. Was it ever attempted to palm so gross a statement upon a thinking world? And

23. "Slavery and the Slave Power," p. 4, citing Richard Hildreth (1807–65), *The White Slave* (London, 1852; a revised version of *The Slave; or, Memoirs of Archy Moore* [1836]).

yet, strange to say, such a statement is accredited by people who think themselves not fools; is circulated by fanatics who believe themselves neither madmen nor hypocrites; and is gulped down and argued from by men who call themselves philanthropists! Where do these wretches shrink to hide themselves and die? Their death-groans should be echoing our every note of laughter; the stench of their carcasses should be poisoning our every meal. By what miraculous interference of the blinded if not iniquitous Providence, against which *Blackwood* and Mr. Foster, while acknowledging its intervention, openly declare war, are the monster 100,000 with their progeny saved from breathing in the awful pestilence scattered by the rotting carcasses of these 8,769,767 beings, as they pass by thousands from this wretched existence. The *Blackwood* reviewer and his coadjutors should have perfected the system of monstrosity which they have invented for us, by imagining some profitable mode for disposing of the dead bodies. We are quite sufficiently ogrish to devour the article, but the supply must be too abundant for home consumption. The 600,000, gorge as they might, could scarcely dispose of the mass. Could the remainder not possibly, through some patent process, be manufactured into *pâtés* for foreign exportation; or, at least, can *Blackwood* ingenuity not imagine some improved crusher which might combine the mass into new species of manure to save the purchase of Guano? It might be a profitable speculation, and abolitionists would not, we presume, hesitate to encourage the manufacture. Do they not daily eat the sugar stained, by their own account, with negro blood? Do they not daily traffic in our cotton spattered with tell-tale gouts of the same? This is the work of Providence, its "manifest interference," says *Blackwood*. This is the work of Providence, echoes Mr. Foster; God Almighty has made himself responsible for this iniquity and must take the blame. It is the work of Providence and wonderful in our eyes:[24] 3,200,380 wretched slaves dying beneath the lash; 5,569,387 outcast whites, unable or unwilling to labour, without the food and clothing which the owner gives to his slave, without the crust that the master throws to his dog; and yet no pauper in our streets, no famine, no pestilence desolating our land!

Blackwood continues:

> Whatever temptations the free states may present to our emigrating population, neither the charms of society, nor the love of knowledge, nor the hope of speedily bettering his condition, can lure a man to leave his paternal home for a residence in the southern states [5].

24. Ps. 118:23: "This is the Lord's doing; it is marvellous in our eyes."

A very remarkable fact this, indicating great research in the propounder of such a proposition. But what are these bulky looking figures that we meet at every turn in our cities, on our wharves and our highways, on our railroads, our canals, and our steamboats? Rather too substantial they are to be spectres, and yet they are not of *us*. There is a rich brogue upon the tongue that smacks wonderfully of the Gaelic. Ghosts look not thus, and yet, 'tis *Blackwood* says, no man is lured to seek his residence on southern soil. We'll speak to them. We'll call them Pat, O'Hara, O'Flannigen, O'Toole! What are ye? Answer! Let us not burst in ignorance.[25] "Arrah! in fait, your honor, we are honest Irishmen, come out to dig your ditches, lay your rails, to sweep, to stand, to run, do what you will, your honor, so you'll only give us bread." Now, we will not dispute that *Blackwood* ought to know an Irishman better than we; but, "in fait," if these be not Irishmen, we can but explain the wonderful appearance by repeating, as we have said above, this must be a new age of miracles. *Aut Patricus aut Diavolo.*[26]

One rather odd characteristic of all arguments against us is, that our opponents in their eagerness to prove some one point of their position, constantly go head-foremost, smashing into and utterly destroying others which they had already, as they supposed, nicely disposed of. For instance, our reviewer, desperately bent upon proving the degradation of our white population, and forgetting entirely how his main business is to wail over the black, seizes upon one of the numerous recent libels published against us (*The White Slave*), and, quoting largely from it to prove the "vulgar brutality of vice which poverty and ignorance render so conspicuous and disgusting" among the great body of our southern people—the whole class which forms the "substratum and basis of our southern civilization, such as it is"—goes on to quote that "these poor white men have become the jest of the slave[s]" [4]. How is this? The poor negro, who is lashed and starved and cut up and murdered by any white man who happens to feel an evil or ogrish disposition towards him; who has, as the *North British* has recently told us, no security for his life but a pecuniary fine which his master may plead against his murderer;[27] has he the heart to jest at anything, and most of all at the white tyrant's dagger-armed hand? It would seem that these brutal and disgusting

25. *Hamlet* 1.4.43–46 (Hamlet to the Ghost): "Thou com'st in such a questionable shape / That I will speak to thee. I'll call thee Hamlet, / King, father, royal Dane. O answer me. / Let me not burst in ignorance."

26. This appears to be a macaronic verse, three words of Latin, the fourth Italian. "Either Patrick or the Devil."

27. "American Slavery and *Uncle Tom's Cabin*," p. 257. This essay is reviewed by LSM in chap. 10, "British Philanthropy and American Slavery."

white tyrants should very soon end the jest, with *nigger-slaughter* (which, according to our English critics, can never be legal murder), and that without even the small check of the fine before their eyes; for what chance would there be of making good a sentence of fine against any one of the brutishly degraded, disgusting, and penniless 5,569,387, who form the substratum of our southern civilization?

Slavery is a "paralyzer of industry," says our reviewer [14], and therefore, it would seem, has produced and is producing the most immense and important agricultural staple which the world has ever known, and has by this wonderful production set our country upon the high pinnacle of usefulness and power which the reviewer himself proves it to possess, by the quotations we have already made from his article.

Against the charge that slavery is a "perverter of religion" [14–15], we hardly know what system of defence to adopt with assailants who, while they accuse us of impiety, openly declare, with *Blackwood,* that they are acting against a manifest Providence; or with Messrs. Foster and Pillsbury, that their society "must overthrow religion, or religion must overthrow them." Are these the champions who are to purify our creed? Lords and Ladies of England, these, and such as these, are your authorities against us. These are Mrs. Stowe's co-labourers; and to these you now (we yet have the charity to believe that you do it blindly) extend the friendly hand in a fraternal grasp of union!

To another remarkable deduction of our reviewer we must draw attention. He certainly deserves *Punch*'s medal to the "calculating boy." Endeavoring to prove the extent and atrocity of our internal slave trade, he quotes from another abolitionist authority (Rev. John D. Choules), to prove that of the exported negro (particular reference is made to the Virginia slave) "*the* <the> *average existence is only five years.*"[28] This he tells us, even at the moment that he is arguing to prove the immense exportation from that State. Now, does he mean to imply that it is particularly the Virginia transplanted negro who perishes so rapidly under the change of climate and labour? If so, he at once proves the comparative worthlessness of the labourer, and disproves what he is endeavoring to establish, regarding the enormous trade

28. "Slavery and the Slave Power," p. 15, citing [Theodore Dwight Weld, comp.] *Slavery and the Internal Slave Trade in the United States of North America* (London, 1841), p. 86. John Overton ("D." is an error copied by LSM from *Blackwood's*) Choules (1801–56), English-born Baptist clergyman; author and editor; pastor variously in Newport, New Bedford, Buffalo, New York City, Jamaica Plain near Boston, and back at Newport; friend of Daniel Webster and Cornelius Vanderbilt.

based upon his exportation. For it is impossible to imagine a comparatively worthless article bearing the market-price of a sound one; and a trade resulting so constantly in the premature death and loss of the object traded for would of necessity be a losing, or exceedingly limited, one. Or does the reviewer mean to say that the average life of the labouring negro is five years? If so, how can he account for an increase of upwards of 29 per cent during the ten years between the census of 1840 and that of 1850, being from 2,478,927 at the first named period, to 3,200,380 at the second. In either case, we think the reviewer is posed.

The winding up of the article we comment upon is a long argument of which the sole and evident object is to excite the mutual and sectional jealousies of the United States against each other. Great Britain certainly reads badly her own interests if she imagines that any dissolution of our Union, which should not be a perfectly peaceable one, could be other than vitally injurious to *her*. We cannot believe that the present commotion, calculated (if it have any effect) to drown our confederacy in blood, can be a national one. The insidious foreign intermeddlings which are of late so constantly launched against us emanate, we hope and believe, from individuals or cliques, but the mischief which they have done is incalculable. We are inclined to think, however, that this last effort of *Blackwood* needs but to be carefully noted, to prove its own antidote. Its object is too plain, its mischief too transparent. The tumbling of the clown is so clumsy, and his jugglery so coarsely managed, that we turn away in disgust at not being more cunningly cheated.

It is a great injustice, he would have us believe, that the slave states have a partial representation of their slaves, thus giving what the reviewer considers a too predominating influence to the "slave power" [17]. Now, we ask, were the provisions of our constitution made to suit the exigencies and conveniences of British reviewers or of the states to which they severally refer? If the last, wherein can consist the injustice of our slave representation, which was at the formation of our government formally demanded by the southern interest, and acceded to by our co-states as a *sine qua non* to the former's entering into any terms of Union. Independent states, combining in a partnership of union, had as full a right mutually to demand and concede terms, as have any other partners in any other business or compact; and, these terms being agreed to, simple honesty requires mutual good faith in the fulfillment of them. The right was honestly and clearly demanded, honestly and clearly conceded, and should be honestly and clearly maintained. The injustice lies in the breach, not in the performance, of the articles of compact.

This right, says the reviewer, has given rise to

> a political power in the States more absolute than [that of] any European aristocracy—almost as uncontrolled by public sentiment as that of an Asiatic potentate—and in the hands of a class of men the idea of submission to whom is most abhorrent to British feelings [17].

We must first remark here, that we really cannot see what *British feelings* have got to do in the matter. Surely the "slave power" has attempted no legislation upon British soil. We have sent neither remonstrances nor appeals across the water and, confining ourselves to our own affairs, have a right to expect that British feelings should be put out of the question. If A. agrees to live with B. on certain terms of mutual convenience, agreeable to both, it is an excessively impertinent act on the part of C. to interfere with their housekeeping; and we could scarcely sympathize with the delicacy of his nerves, should he complain of his feelings being hurt because A. and B. mutually agreed to like bacon and corn-bread for dinner instead of a *dindon aux truffes.* The reviewer forgets, too, in the vehemence of his argument against this exclusive privilege granted to the "slave power," that, according to the statement advanced by him which we have noticed a little above, nine tenths of our white population are not slaveholders; and, as every white man has an equal vote, the vote of the poorest is, by this provision, as much enhanced as that of the richest. A slaveholder does not give a vote for himself and so many of his slaves, as the reviewer appears to imagine. The law gives no such privilege. It merely gives to the *state* an enhanced representation in proportion to her slave property, and this, with reason, as representing an interest and population not existing in the free states. But the vote of the poorest voter counts equally with that of the richest. The largest slaveowner has but one vote, not counting for more at the polls than that of his neighbour who does not own a single slave. If, therefore, the reviewer's computation as given above be correct, the right given by this clause of the Constitution is not given to the *slave power,* but mainly to the *free-power* of the slave states. This the reviewer must allow, or consent to take back his former statements. That or this is false, what Mr. Mantalini would call a "demned fabrication."[29] We leave it to the gentleman to determine which of his fledgling inventions he will abandon. As both seem to have a clumsy alacrity for sinking, we would strongly counsel him to let both fall back into the mire of unclaimed and irresponsible falsehood from which he has endeavored to draw them.

The reviewer's strongest ground of complaint, however, and the one upon

29. From his first word ("Demmit") in Charles Dickens, *Nicholas Nickleby* (chap. 10 [Everyman's ed., 1907], p. 125), Mr. Mantalini shows himself very fond of various locutions incorporating "damn."

which he seems most to endeavour to excite the feelings of our northern brethren against us, is that the slaveholding states always give their support to the candidate upon whom they believe they can most rely to carry out their views. We have always supposed this to be the case in all honestly conducted elections. Why does a voter support any one candidate in preference to another, except that he supposes the one he votes for to be the most likely to carry out his views whatever they may be? Our *Blackwood* judge, however, pronounces this to be a great iniquity. We ought, it would appear, to vote for the man who will go in the most direct opposition to our views of what is right. We ought to vote against our conscience and what we consider the interest of our fellow-citizens. We ought to allow ourselves to be flattered, cajoled, and bribed. So says our *Blackwood* prophet. What else mean such reproaches as the following:

> No matter what court the risen man may pay to the southern goddess, when he begins to fancy the prize of the Presidency not unattainable as the end of his intellectual struggles—no matter what sacrifice of principle he may make to secure the support of the southern lords, what efforts he may put forth in their behalf, measures pass in favor of their views, declarations falsify, opinions recant, or old friends shake off and disgust—when the hour of nomination comes, they will prefer before him a nameless man, whose antecedents bespeak consistency in southern sentiment, and from whose talents or conscientious convictions they have nothing to apprehend. Who laboured longer in their behalf than the popular and beloved Clay? Who sacrificed more than the talented and broken-hearted Webster? Who deserved more at their hands for his actual doings than brave old General Scott? Yet a Polk or a Pierce were lifted at once from comparative obscurity, and without a struggle placed in the high position to which these men had spent their lives in endeavoring to attain. [18][30]

What means all this rigmarole but, in plain words, that, according to the *Blackwood* reviewer, the Southern States have not allowed themselves to be bought or cheated? Though the "risen man" *sacrificed his principles, falsified his declarations, recanted his opinions* to an extent which made his old friends shrink from him in *disgust,* the South preferred to the "risen man" who would

30. Whig candidate for the presidency Henry Clay (1777–1852) was defeated by Andrew Jackson in 1832, by James Knox Polk in 1844. Daniel Webster (1782–1852), as Whig candidate for president in 1836, received the electoral votes of Massachusetts only; in 1848, aspiring to the Whig candidacy, he was defeated by Zachary Taylor. Winfield Scott (1786–1866), Virginian soldier; general in chief of the United States Army (1841–61); commander of American forces in the Mexican War; as Whig candidate for president (1852), was defeated by Franklin Pierce.

stifle his conscience and throw away his honor to buy a vote, one comparatively nameless whom they believed at least to be honest, and from whose "conscientious convictions they had nothing to apprehend." Mr. *Blackwood* Reviewer, you have finished the argument for us, and upon this, your own statement, we are willing to rest the question of southern morals and intelligence—declining, however, to adopt the gentleman (Mr. Seward) whom you particularly recommend to our attention as the model of a "liberty-loving and independent man" [18], too pure to succeed in the arena of Federal politics![31]

Our reviewer makes a farther attempt to interfere in the political differences of the U. States, by taking upon himself to determine upon the propriety of excluding slave property from all unsettled territory. "The slave party," he says,

> are now asserting the *new doctrine,* that all territory—instead of being free till its population is large enough to form a constitution, and pronounce upon the admission of slavery—being the property of all the states alike, is open equally to all citizens for settlement with their property of every description, and that the government is bound to protect them. [20; LSM's italics]

The gross ignorance of these foreign intermeddlers would be laughable, were there not so bitter a poison mixed with their folly. They read our congressional bickerings and, entirely uninformed as they are concerning the nature of our government and provisions of our Constitution, undertake to determine all questions according to their own prejudices, and dictate to us as domineeringly as though they imagined themselves laying down the law for his naked majesty of Musquito.[32] It is a *new doctrine,* it would appear according to the *Blackwood* prophet, that unoccupied territory is *the property of all the states alike,* and that *all citizens* have an *equal right* to the protection of the government in establishing themselves therein with their families and property. This new and iniquitous doctrine ("don't care how you share 'em, so you share 'em right") our tory rulers cannot allow us to assert (it would seem that we have been mistaken in supposing that our struggle of '76, and its consequent three-fourths of a century of self-government, should free us from English tory rule); and we are now informed that we were not set free,

31. William Henry Seward (1801–72), born in Florida, N.Y.; antislavery leader in the Whig party, until joining the Republican party in 1855; U.S. senator from New York (1849–61); secretary of state (1861–69).

32. Since the seventeenth century the British had maintained a protectorate over the Miskitto Indians, who lived in the coastal region of Nicaragua; in 1848 a British force captured San Juan del Norte, at the mouth of the San Juan River in southern Nicaragua. By the Clayton-Bulwer Treaty of 1850, made between the United States and Britain, and establishing the neutrality of northern Latin America, the Americans had thought to negate the British protectorate of the Mosquito Coast, a view not shared by Britain.

but merely let loose, upon a lengthened tether, with a *con-si-de-ra-tion* that we shall *not* "share 'em right." Our citizens are *not* to have equal rights nor equal protection in their rights.

Blackwood and Co. determine that the insolent southrons must be starved down to humility, kept upon low diet, until with humbled spirit and crouching knee we beg them to take our cotton at their own price. They will buy their share of the "sweetenin'" for an old marble, and soothe their consciences by flinging "all fire" at us. The ridiculous assertion that an equal protection to all "would virtually annex to the slave states every territory in which slave-owners might choose to settle" [20], is of a piece with the rest of this precious sample of argument. An equal protection to all would naturally encourage such emigration as would be best suited to the nature, soil, and climate of the territory in question. That territory once settled, it would remain to the inhabitants, whether slaveholders or otherwise, to determine for themselves according to the legal provisions of our Constitution (so far as these provisions leave them free to choose) what form of state government they might prefer for themselves. According to the reviewer's own calculation, which we have given above, of the numerical force, or rather weakness, of the "slave power," it is difficult to imagine how his 100,000 slaveholding voters could so spread themselves over all unoccupied territory as to every where have a majority of votes and establish their favorite system. New York *alone* with its population of upwards of three millions could send out settlers enough to oust them every where. We have heard of a man being between the horns of a dilemma. It does seem to us that our reviewer has fallen among so many horns that there is no resting room at all. Verily, he is consistent only in his endless inconsistencies. The unequal protection that he advocates, i.e., the favoring of certain individuals, factions, or states, to the virtual extinction of the rights of others, must be the first step towards the dissolution of a government which has, in its magnificent prosperity, so excited the envy of certain British would-be legislators that, in the blind zeal of sectional jealousy, they seek to crush the power upon which depends their own existence.

The *Blackwood* reviewer takes credit to himself that he has discussed this matter calmly and "candidly, equally without hard words and <or> home bias"! [20]

O wad some Pow'r the giftie gie us
To see oursels as others see us!

Candidly and without home bias!

My sooth! right bauld ye set your nose out.[33]

33. Robert Burns, "To a Louse," ll. 43–44, 25.

We are charged with every folly, every crime, and judged according to *Blackwood* ideas of morality. Thief, murderer, dastard, dotard, are merely the light skirmishing in the war of words with which we are assailed. All these repeated *ad nauseam,* we are, as a *coup de grâce,* informed, that the worst is too infamous for words. We are accused of daily acting foul scenes which our accusers are too pure even to whisper; and this species of moral torture through which we are dragged (for we confess that our blood boils under the operation) is called a candid examination of our system. Week after week, and month after month, the same process is repeated again and again, by every periodical and every book-writer who hopes to make a successful speculation by pandering to a corrupt public taste, and outranting the filthy imaginations of a Sue or a Dumas. But forsooth the patient on the rack must not dare wince under peril of condemnation; sensitiveness is a proof of guilt. Let his eyelid wink, let his lip quiver, and the quick eye of the tormentor exults. *He,* in truth, is perfectly composed. A Titus Oates can swear coolly enough to every falsehood.[34] Is it a sign of guilt that the indignant blood rushes to the brow of the victim whom he is endeavouring to crush beneath his accumulated slanders?

We thought we had done, but find that we have neglected one point whereon we proposed to ourselves to give our *Blackwood* friends a modest lesson in arithmetic.[35] "The whole free population of the slave states," says the reviewer,

> is actually decreasing instead of increasing, as we are in the habit of believing to be the case all over the Union. Thus, in the two censuses of 1840 and 1850, the total free population in the free and slave states respectively was as follows:

	1840	1850
Free States	9,654,865	13,533,328
Slave States	7,290,719	6,393,758

> So that, while in the last ten years the population of the free states has increased by nearly four millions, that of the slave states, though Texas has been added to them in the interval, has diminished by nine hundred thousand. [5]

From this remarkable decrease, the reviewer argues most feelingly upon the wretched consequences of an institution which first degrades and then

34. Titus Oates (1649–1705) informed against a large number of people (many of whom were executed), including Charles II's queen, Catherine of Braganza, as being implicated in a "Popish Plot" against the king and his government; convicted of perjury and imprisoned for life (1685); pardoned and pensioned (1689).

35. The error to which LSM calls attention here is corrected in [J. F. W. Johnston], "Note to the Article on Slavery in Our January Number," *Blackwood's Edinburgh Magazine* 73 (March 1853): 387–88.

drives away its population, producing "so large a number of restless men in the <these> southern states ready for every emergency, and panting after an outlet, just or unjust, for the exercise of their festering energies" [5]. The reviewer is welcome to his conclusions (although, as we have before remarked, singularly paradoxical throughout), if he can prove his premises. Facts are stubborn things, and the adduced numbers are stated to be facts; but let us see. It is a common school exercise to make the student correct certain arithmetical answers, rendered purposely false, in order to try whether he has properly mastered his multiplication and addition tables, and is thereby fit for the detection of blunders in practice. It is a long time, probably, since the reviewer's school days, and like the old woman who could not count her chickens, he may have "forgotten his larning." Had a school boy of ten years old thus blundered or adopted a blunder, we would, with all our heart (albeit not generally inclined to flagellatory discipline), have adjudged a correction according to Solomon's recipe, to brighten his intellects.

The only authority quoted by the reviewer for this immense decrease of southern population, is the *American Almanac for 1852.*[36] He seems never to have heard of Mr. Kennedy's abstract of the official census for 1850.[37] One would suppose that so startling a fact as a diminution in ten years by nearly one seventh of our whole white population would have created some excitement, or at least serious remark, on our own side of the Atlantic. This startling check to the prosperity of so large a portion of the Union could scarcely have failed to excite some inquiry. Strange, that the whisper of it has not passed among ourselves! Strange, that the cry of it has not echoed over the world! A decrease of population in a proportion unheard of, except in wretched Ireland, is sweeping our Southern lands at a rate which in less than another half century must leave in lieu of our luxuriant fields a howling wilderness, in lieu of our rich harvests a barren desolation; and yet no voice has been raised in pity, in triumph, or in dread! To the great *Blackwood,* it has been left to discover the mare's nest, and to raise *Te Deums* over the desolating effects of slavery. Lo! the avenger cometh![38] The *American Almanac* (a work compiled in Boston, by whom we know not; a very convenient compendium, but certainly due entirely to individual enterprise and unvouched for by any responsible authority) says that the free population of

36. *The American Almanac and Repository of Useful Knowledge for the Year 1852* (Boston, 1852).

37. Joseph Camp Griffith Kennedy (1813–87), superintendent of the 1850 census, supervised several publications arising from his work; the reference here is probably to his *Report of the Superintendent of the Census. Census Office, Washington, December 1, 1851* (Philadelphia, 1851?), which bears at the head of the title: "An Abstract of the Seventh Census."

38. Mal. 4:1.

the slave States, which by the census of 1850 gives a sum total of 6,393,758, gave in 1840 the sum of 7,290,719; and thereupon the learned *Blackwood,* never, we presume, having heard of such a thing as a misprint or a careless miswriting of figures, sets up such a crowing as a six months baby might do over a new rattle. Mamma's darling can't keep its pretty plaything though, for the poor little ignoramus, not satisfied with enjoying its noise, has made sundry ugly attempts to rap its brother over the pate with the new toy. The thing becomes troublesome, dangerous perhaps, and baby must give it up.

Let us examine, then, the reviewer's sole authority, the *American Almanac.* We have mislaid our volume for 1852, but in that of 1853 find the blunder repeated, with some unessential difference of figures from those quoted by him. The statement is evidently the same. A moment's attention suffices to show that the compiler has most carelessly taken the sum total of the *whole* population of 1840, as that of the *free* population. We find his recapitulation, which appears to have been all that was penetrable to the profundity of *Blackwood,* thus stated:[39]

	Total Free Population in 1840	Slaves in 1840
Free States	9,654,865	1,102
Slaveholding States	7,290,719	2,481,532
Districts and Territories	117,769	4,721
	17,063,353	2,487,355

	Total Free Population in 1850	Slaves in 1850
Free States	13,434,559	225
Slaveholding States	6,412,151	3,200,380
Districts and Territories	140,271	3,713
	19,986,981	3,204,093[40]

39. *The American Almanac and Repository of Useful Knowledge for the Year 1853* (Boston, 1853), p. 209.

40. We copy this last summing up of slaves in 1850, although the addition is false, because we are quoting, and wish to do so, literally. The mistake in this case is an immaterial

Now let us add the sum total of slaves in 1840 to that of the here stated free population of the same year, and we find the grand total of 19,550,708, within a small fraction of 20,000,000! Every child knows, and every census report will prove, that we were several millions below this in 1840. The true sum total of our population, at that census, was 17,063,353, which this volume of the *Almanac* has, with great remissness, taken as the total of the *free,* instead of that of the *whole,* population. Casting our eye back a few columns even in this same almanac,[41] we find the total of the whole population in 1840 stated to be what it really was, 17,063,353, which sum has evidently by some slip of the pen, or some blundering, been transferred to its present position in the recapitulation. We do not pretend to excuse this carelessness, but should suppose that a few simple additions would have been no heavy demand upon *Blackwood* scholarship, and the reviewer might have been saved some laughably *mal-à-propos* conclusions. To discover, then, which of the three sums going to form this sum total of 17,063,353 (as given in the recapitulation) is wrong, we add together the several populations of the several States as given by the census of 1840, and find that with no very material difference the amounts given to the free States and to the Districts and Territories accord with those set down in this almanac and adopted by *Blackwood.* As we pass, however, to the slave States, two minutes' calculation sets us right. As the reviewer has particularly selected the *American Almanac* for his authority, we will give him the volume of the same work for 1843, rather than any other publication, to correct himself by. Here we find the populations of the several States, for the census of 1840, to be as follows:[42]

	Free Population	Slave Population
Virginia	790,810	448,987
Tennessee	646,151	183,059
Kentucky	597,570	182,258
North Carolina	507,602	245,817
Georgia	410,448	280,944
South Carolina	267,360	327,038
Alabama	337,224	253,532
Maryland	380,282	89,737

hundred or two; but such mistakes (which by the way are numerous in this volume) are the result of a culpable carelessness, which a work of the pretension and circulation of the *American Almanac* should endeavor to avoid. The compilers should read the January number of *Blackwood* and learn what grave deductions may be based upon false figures. [LSM]

41. *American Almanac and Repository of Useful Knowledge for the Year 1853,* p. 208.

42. *The American Almanac and Repository of Useful Knowledge for the Year 1843* (Boston, [1843]), p. 204.

	Free Population	Slave Population
Missouri	325,462	58,240
Mississippi	180,440	195,211
Louisiana	183,959	168,452
Arkansas	77,639	19,935
Florida	28,760	25,717
	4,733,707	2,478,927

This gives for the thirteen slave States, including Florida (shortly after admitted as a State, though in fact in 1840 still a territory), a free population of 4,733,707; add to this the slave population of the same year amounting to 2,478,927, and we have a total of 7,212,634, nearly equal to that assumed and argued upon by *Blackwood* as the amount of our *free* population *alone*.

The fact is, that the increase of our population, in the slave as well as the free States, is enormous: that of the North, owing to the larger influx of emigration, is indisputably the greatest; but the difference is not so large as we had imagined previous to examination of the subject. To the free States have been added, within a few years, Iowa, Wisconsin, and California. With these additions, we find the increase of the sum total of their population is, between the periods of the two censuses, from 9,654,865 to 13,434,559, an enormous accumulation of 39 per cent. To the slave States has been added only Texas.[43] The emigration to the South is confessedly much less than to the Northern and Western States (*Blackwood* says there is none), and yet we find, in the same ten years, an increase in their free population from 4,733,707 to 6,393,758, which is within a fraction of 35 per cent! So much for the diminishing free population of our slave States. An actual increase of nearly 35 per cent!

As a further proof of the wanton carelessness of the *Blackwood* statements, we find (a page or two beyond the calculation we have just referred to) a comparative statement of the numbers and increase of the free and slave population of the States generally under the various decimal censuses which have been taken [8]. In every one of them our calculating reviewer, who seems to have a singularly halting intellect as to figures, gives as the sum of the *free* population (what the *American Almanac* set him the example of doing in a single case) the sum of the *whole;* and the consequence is, if we add what he gives as the last sum total of our free population, 23,351,207, to his sum total of the slave population, viz., 3,178,055, we have the grand sum total of 26,529,262 for our last census return! And such are the authorities, such

43. Florida we have already classed among the States. [LSM]

the critics, by which, and on whose statements, we are judged and condemned. Is it possible that a work which can wantonly or ignorantly (with no plea but a careless misprint in an almanac) build up such a mound of falsehood as *Blackwood* has done in the article we have reviewed, be received in a country like England as an accredited and favorite periodical, the organ of a powerful party? On quite as slender authority are all such statements against us based. Figures are tangible things, and the man who ventures upon them must take care how he slips in their management—the blundering is easily proved. Not so with the ordinary statement of fact. It is impossible to disprove general assertion, except by counter-assertion, and counter-assertion is neither proof nor argument for those who stop their ears against it. Let this sample of *Blackwood* arithmetic lead our revilers to calculate how much a similar system of logic may be at the bottom of the widely circulated tales of horror with which it is the fashion to illustrate the history of our slave States.

Since writing the above, we have received our January number of the *Westminster* [*Review*], and are by no means surprised to find it in violent conformity with *Blackwood* upon this topic. Extremes meet. The tory and the ultra-radical are here in brotherly communion. The position is a natural enough one for the *Westminster,* which some eighteen months since (July, 1851) took so bold a stand, in the war for progress, as chivalrously to set itself forth the champion for the "enfranchisement of woman," upholding equal rights without distinction of sex or colour.[44] We were therefore quite prepared to find in this noted periodical a devout defender of Mrs. Stowe, Mrs. Folsom, Mrs. Bloomer,[45] and the whole corps of Reverend Misses, Lady Lecturers, and M.D.'s who are the main movers in the abolition reform. But the tory *Blackwood,* and its aristocratic coadjutors, do they notice whose hand they are shaking?

In this *Westminster* article there is nothing new. It is the old ding-dong of abolitionist falsehood, sworn to and verified by abolitionist witnesses. B. swears for C.'s veracity, and C. returns the compliment. It is utterly useless to prove the falsity of these assertions, for who so deaf as he that will not hear? The same worn out tale is repeated again and again. There is no check to a libel but legal punishment, and this form of wholesale libel does not come under the law. The *Westminster,* therefore, must be allowed to retain its happy communion with the choice spirits of abolitionism. "Progress" is the watchword; and, provided these zealous reformers can but get up a

44. *Westminster* "Enfranchisement," reviewed by LSM in chap. 3, "Enfranchisement of Woman."

45. Amelia Jenks Bloomer (1818–94), woman's rights advocate; founder and editor of the journal *Lily* (1849–55); promoted the item of apparel now named for her.

breeze, it seems to be a matter of small import to them whether the motion be God-ward or devil-ward.

To endeavor to answer the *Westminster* article would be but a repetition of such argument as we have already advanced against *Blackwood.* These, our antagonists, all alike assume the truth of certain statements, which they have no means of verifying, which are either entirely groundless or gross exaggerations; and upon a slanderous libel, or even, as we have shown, a misprint in an almanac, they build volumes of hypotheses which, because their own distempered imaginations can conceive them as possible, they therefore argue *are* possible, and, by a strangely irrational logic leaping to the farther conclusion that what is *possible* must be of *habitual occurrence,* they hold us judged, condemned, and (it would appear from these recent articles) gib[b]etted even, or at least pretty nearly so. We have shown how *Blackwood* proves that we are already gnashing our teeth in the hell of a merited retribution. The *Westminster* is not slow in a similar cry. To believe these writers, we are secure of nothing under the terrors of this institution. Property, family, life, are all in such hazard, that the constant dread of some fatal irruption hangs, like the sword of Damocles, ever threateningly over us; and yet, strange to say, this, according to them, fearfully dangerous property bears at present a higher money value than it has ever hitherto done. This does not look as though its possession were considered dangerous or of perilously doubtful tenure.

Another point whereupon the tory and the radical strongly combine forces, is in the very evident determination which they exhibit of interfering in our domestic policy. England loves rule, and the glorious little nation is so used to having her own way, that she cannot keep her fingers from turning the spit for her neighbors, whenever the roast does not proceed in a way exactly to suit her fancy. She doctors India, the Cape, etc., etc., *ad libitum.* China does not like her prescriptions, but like an energetic *Mater familias* she quickly has the *mauvais sujet* on its back, and "swallow or be whipped" is the peremptory sentence.[46] The United States has had of late the good or ill fortune to fall under her special cognizance. It remains to be seen whether we too are prepared for the dose or the rod. The *Westminster* has some pages of instructions by which our Northern States are directed how to deal with us reprobates of the South [154–65]. They are to send the Constitution with all its reservations, grants, and provisions to the devil. They are to cheat, to

46. By the Treaty of Nanking, which concluded the Opium War between China and Britain (1839–42), the Chinese submitted to opening their ports to foreign trade and to ceding Hong Kong to the British. Foreign pressure continued to be exerted, culminating in the Anglo-French or Second Opium War (1856–60) and further Chinese concessions.

hoax, to humbug, and browbeat the fool Southron who fancies that he has a right to be governed by the written law, and to claim the conceded rights which were made by his ancestors an express requisite for their accession to the Union. Those innovators among us who have allowed their heated imaginations to run ahead of reason, have now a fair opportunity to step back. Will they, with Mr. Garrison and his followers, trample upon religion and hoist the flag of rebellion against decency, accepting the lordly dictates of an insolent English interference? Or will they yet take warning and, hearkening to the earnest protestations of their own countrymen, their natural allies, their brethren in home and in interests, fling from them the impertinent interference of these our self-instituted instructors, these preachers of a charity which does *not* begin at home; believe that we of the South are men and women with hearts and heads not inferior to their own, with reason and human sympathies upon which the lights of civilization act probably as truly as upon them; and take us to their hearts as brothers, not as aliens, as those who, having striven with them in the great cause of humanity, in that cause may be trusted? It is sad to see the world gulled by the fictions of a Mrs. Stowe; but let America be true to herself, and we are but the stronger and the wiser for this gust which will blow past us, even as the autumn wind, prostrating the dead leaf and the rotten branch, while over the green tree and the sound in heart the blast whistles harmlessly.[47]

L. S. M.

47. LSM's peroration is modeled upon that of the *Westminster Review* article being answered here. The *Westminster*'s peroration, defining the proper form of alliance between British and Americans in "the cause of freedom" (166), concludes: "No, the only alliance for freedom possible is an alliance between its friends here and its friends there—every other is a lie on our parts, and a sham on theirs; and the friends of freedom there have far too hard a fight at home to be able to afford aid abroad. Let that fight once be finished, let but America herself be free—then, and not till then, England and America together will shield the oppressed against the despots of the world." (167)

12.

A Letter to the Duchess of Sutherland from a Lady of South Carolina

Messrs. Editors:

The letter, of which the following is a copy, has been sent by a lady of this State to the Duchess of Sutherland.[1] The original has the name and address of the writer, clearly given and in full, so that if the Duchess has the smallest desire to exercise her philanthropy, practically as well as theoretically, she will know where and to whom to address her answer. The writer has not chosen to put her name in print, as it can be a matter of no moment to the public. It is enough that a bona fide letter has been written, and a bona fide offer made from a respectable and responsible quarter. Let the Duchess, if her zeal be sincere and earnest, prove it now by action.

Yours, respectfully,

———

The title is that given in Duyckinck and is likely to have been taken from the questionnaire as filled out by the McCords. The text is that published, with the author's name and address removed, in the Charleston *Mercury* of Aug. 10, 1853, and includes the covering letter to the *Mercury,* which from manner and style belongs also to LSM. LSM's letter to the duchess was "deservedly admired for its dignified tone," according to Hale, *Woman's Record,* p. 894.

1. From Stafford House, the London residence of the duchess of Sutherland, was issued "The Affectionate and Christian Address of Many Thousands of the Women of England to Their Sisters, the Women of the United States of America" (also known as the Stafford House Address), which urged the abolition of slavery in the Southern states. It provoked many replies, of which that by Julia Gardiner Tyler, wife of former president John Tyler, was most celebrated (as such being singled out for publication by the New York *Daily Times,* Feb.

——— ———, July 30, 1853

To her Grace, the Duchess of Sutherland:

Madam and Dear Sister: The kind interest some time since manifested by your Grace, in common with the Countess of Shaftesbury, and other noble ladies, in the cause of us women of America, whom you then condescendingly invited to your confidence in terms of christian sisterhood, induces me now to take the liberty of addressing you upon a subject near to every woman's heart, and more particularly near to every mother's.

As a woman, however exalted in rank above a large portion of your sex, your Grace still feels that woman instinct which unerringly assures you that the appeal of charity and christian love, however in individual and exceptional cases it may be spurned, can never be vainly made to the large woman-heart of any age or any country. Woman, as a body, has never sided, and never can side, with the oppressor. Man, burying duty beneath passion, may often deafen his conscience with the arguments of interest, and bustle it even quite from existence in the frantic struggles of ambition: but woman, in the subdued stillness of her usual life, in the quiet of her own self-searchings, finds that calm voice which is not in the storm, which is not in the whirlwind,[2] and which continually whispers to her the God inspired dictates of that all-enduring charity, that self-sacrificing love, of which by her nature she seems destined to be the constant prophet and exponent. If such be (as your Grace doubtless well knows that they are) the natural impulses of woman, how much are these enhanced by the mother's love, which, as she clasps to her breast her baby offspring, pours itself out to her God in the purest and most purifying prayers of which human lips and human hearts are capable; a mother's prayer for the offspring of her bosom! a mother's heavenward appeal for the child of her hope! Even the most erring of our sex, under the inspiration of this purifying, second existence, this being which must draw from us its good or its ill, have, for its sake, often turned from the evil of their ways, and hearkened to that lesson which bids them "go and sin no more."[3]

Your Grace, and the honorable Ladies acting with you, have then shown, in undertaking a great work, only a proper reliance upon your own sex in the appeal which you have addressed to the women and mothers of America. You rightly believe that we cannot coolly stand by, the witnesses and accom-

---

5, 1853, reprinting from the Richmond *Enquirer*). LSM responded to the address also in chap. 10, "British Philanthropy and American Slavery." For the text of the address, see app. 1.

2. Nah. 1:3: "The Lord is slow to anger, and great in power, and will not at all acquit the wicked: the Lord hath his way in the whirlwind and in the storm, and the clouds are the dust of his feet." Cf. Job 38:1, 40:6.

3. John 8:11.

plices of those atrocities which you have heard depicted. I, Madam, a woman, and a mother, moved by your philanthropic appeal—not hastily but with mature deliberation, and after long reflection—(presuming, from the magnificent hospitality lately tendered by you to Mrs. Stowe, as the agent and representative of the woman move which it is your object to excite, that you are really desirous of forwarding, not by words only but by deeds, your charitable aims) now venture to address myself to you, as one who has both the means and the will to forward the herculean task which your Grace, in common with your most praiseworthy and noble sisters in the faith, has indicated a desire to undertake.[4]

I will not ask you, noble Madam, why America particularly has, of all countries of the earth, chanced first to attract your effort for the improvement of mankind.[5] I will not ask you why slavery, which is in one form or another almost co-extensive and co-existent with society, should appear so peculiarly obnoxious among us. I will not ask why, when the great Empire of China, with its three hundred and fifty millions of souls, is systematically drugged under English legislative enactment, your Grace and the honorable

4. Harriet Beecher Stowe had departed for Europe on March 30, 1853. Her tour was triumphant, a high point of it being the levée held for her by the duchess of Sutherland at Stafford House (May 7), to which came a great part of fashionable and titled London. In her *Sunny Memories of Foreign Lands* (London, 1854), Stowe praised the clearances of Sutherland—"an almost sublime instance of the benevolent employment of superior wealth and power in shortening the struggles of advancing civilization" (313)—and defended the conduct of the duchess against charges of cruelty and hypocrisy made both in Britain and in the United States. Stowe was in turn accused of being the paid hack of the duchess, for example by Donald Macleod, *Gloomy Memories in the Highlands of Scotland* (Toronto, 1857); Macleod, now living in exile in Canada, had experienced at first hand the ejection of tenants in Sutherland. But this accusation "was unjust and untrue. She was a simple, impressionable woman, an amateur reporter who did not know how or where to find the truth" (John Prebble, *The Highland Clearances* [Harmondsworth, Eng., 1969], p. 294).

5. "'These periodical paroxysms of philanthropy, these outbreaks of pretended sympathy for slaves, . . . are, in fact, nothing more than significant indications of [British] apprehensions of the consequences ultimately to result from the growth of the United States, and the irresistible energies of freemen. It is a POLITICAL feeling, not a genuine sentiment of humanity, that infuses such warmth and vigor into these reiterated and persevering attempts against the peace and union of the United States, under the hypocritical pretence of a deep interest in the freedom and happiness of the human race.' . . . [Democracy], then, is no doubt the great source of offence to British philanthropists, and American philanthropy is a mere cat's-paw to the British. Otherwise, would that vulgar, ill-bred woman, Mrs. Stowe, have met with such a reception as she has received from the proud, upturned noses of the English aristocracy? They have, no doubt, had their rooms since fumigated and cleansed, as in case of a visitation from the devil." David James McCord, "American Institutions—the Monroe Doctrine—Intervention—etc.," pp. 586–87.

sisterhood have not turned your sympathies towards its perishing millions.[6] I will not ask why, simply because these people are yellow and not black, they should so escape your Grace's sympathies that you calmly, and without remonstrance, see your own government almost force the poison down their throats, condemning millions to a mental and bodily prostration—to a lingering and brutish death, compared to which the ancient punishment of the hemlock bowl were a charity and a mercy. This entire oblivion of the woes and oppressions of other nations presents at first sight a strange contrast to the warm sympathies excited for America. But of this, it surely is not for us to complain. It is, as I interpret it, but a proof of the greater affection which you entertain towards us. As the parent chasteneth his child,[7] as the friend reproveth his friend, your anxieties are naturally most alive where your sympathies are strongest; and great indeed must be the affection which can make you thus turn your whole effort toward us, even to the detriment of the morals of your own beloved England. You leave her groaning under the shame of the Opium trade, until through your generous interference we shall be relieved of our sin and our sorrow. What I can, Madam, individually feel for such disinterested kindness, I am here most anxious to express, and this letter should be a proof to you at once of my confidence in your sincerity, and my firm reliance upon your christian sympathies and assistance.

My position is one of some difficulty, and your Grace will allow me, in the spirit of sisterly affection, to lay open to you its circumstances, that you may the better counsel[8] and aid my decisions. I have not spoken hastily, but, on the contrary, have deliberated long, because I judged that time was necessary both to you and ourselves to think coolly and dispassionately upon this subject. I am, Madam, by birth, parentage, education, marriage, and residence, a South Carolinian. South Carolina, you are perhaps aware, is the heart and centre of the slaveholding States of this Union, and defends with peculiar warmth her rights and privileges upon the slave question. My ances-

6. The Chinese government had banned the opium trade in 1799, a ban ignored profitably but so blatantly that in March 1839 the impatient government sent an imperial commissioner to Canton, who confiscated and destroyed the opium stored by foreign merchants there. The Opium War between China and Britain followed (1839–42), concluded by the Treaty of Nanking, which opened Chinese ports to foreign trade and ceded Hong Kong to Britain. Britain and other foreign powers continued to press for further trade concessions; the Treaty of Tientsin (June 1858) and related negotiations at Shanghai formally legalized the opium trade, but the treaty's provisions were not accepted by the Chinese until compelled by the Peking Convention, so bringing to an end the Anglo-French or Second Opium War (1856–60).

7. Deut. 8:5: "As a man chasteneth his son, so the Lord thy God chasteneth thee."

8. "Council" in *Mercury.*

tors became possessed, while under British rule, of certain lands and slaves which the then institutions of the country, enforced by British law, rendered the only form in which could be invested the little proceeds of their labor. The same land owned by those ancestors when they dared to raise the arm of resistance against the might and power of your noble Lion of England, the same slaves (or rather the descendants of the same slaves) who remained faithful to them through the prolonged and bloody struggle of a civil war, now, Madam, have descended to me by gift and inheritance, forming together the sole means of support for myself and children. So far, I have lived with my sable subjects, the busy but contented petty sovereign over a petty realm, believing that I was fulfilling my duty by staying at home, and devoting to their comfort and maintenance a large portion of my time as well as my moderate income. I have believed that God Almighty had seen fit, in his wisdom, to suit his creatures to the positions which they are intended to occupy. I have believed, dear Madam, that as he has formed you and me to be daughters, wives, and mothers, subject to woman's duties and unfit and unable to those of men, that He has equally formed divers men for divers positions in society, according to their powers of mind and body. And if ever God's seal was set upon the brow of any race with the stamp of inferiority, believe me, Madam, or rather believe the investigations of science and the experience of ages, it is upon that of the negro. Mark me, your Grace, I say not a curse. God creates not with a curse. Inferiority is by no means necessarily a curse. Genius, talent, and fortune, however they may ennoble, give no monopoly of happiness; and as some humble cotter, under your Grace's indulgent rule, may perchance lead an easier and a happier life than can your Grace's self under the accumulated cares, anxieties, and duties of your higher position, so many a woolly head lays itself quietly to sleep, while the aching brow of the master is burdened with watchfulness and care.

Mrs. Stowe has exhibited to you, ladies of England, her fancy picture of American negro slavery. Living in the midst of the institutions against which she has raised the now fashionable hue and cry, I can but smile at the clumsy daub which Europe has consented to receive as our portrait. But let this pass. Mrs. Stowe has luxuriated in the hallelujahs addressed to her, and, like many other false prophets, is rapidly passing to oblivion. The sensible, judicious, and womanly course which your Queen has pursued with regard to her, has done much towards placing this lady in her true position.[9] If you, noble ladies of England, have, in the pardonable excitement of a philan-

9. After a warning from the American minister, Queen Victoria was advised not to receive Harriet Beecher Stowe, lest doing so should seem to sanction the abolitionist movement.

thropic zeal, allowed yourselves to be misled to the strange belief that the women of half a continent could forget their nature to revel in the grossest of imaginable crimes, and to educate their children to inevitable infamy, it is still a woman of England whose cooler judgment has set you right; and your Queen, in defending womankind by her practical condemnation of this slanderer of her sex and country, has vindicated her right to even a nobler title than that of Queen of an Empire upon whose dominions the sun never sets. She has proved herself a sound hearted woman. Although, however, Mrs. Stowe is disposed of, and her "tales of wonder" will probably take their place in future by those of Monk Lewis,[10] the Brothers Grimm, or the yet more celebrated "Mother Goose," the question of our United States system of negro slavery is not so completely set to rest; and it is on this point that I now seek assistance from your sisterly sympathies.

It is not enough, we are told, that we make our negroes comfortable; we must make them free; and then follow dissertations numberless, on the inalienable rights of man, etc. Now, Madam, I have already suggested to you the idea in which I think you must concur, that the inalienable rights of men are very different, according to the character and capacity, mental and bodily, of the individual, kind, or race. Is it possible that your Grace, or myself, for instance, should have the rights of our husbands and brothers? Has the idiot the same rights as the sage? Does not the physical power in the first case, and the mental difference in the last, give inalienable rights and duties to the one side, which are withheld from, or not enjoined upon, the other? Does society, by placing the man and the woman, the sage and the idiot, in different positions, with differing privileges, and under differing restraints, commit a sin and an injustice? or is such action in accordance with the dictates of God's law, as exhibited in the varying nature of his creatures? What must become of our world if women would make themselves soldiers, and idiots be forced forward as lawyers? Surely you must acknowledge that these have their positions and inalienable rights of widely differing nature! What is good for the man is not always good for the woman; what is good for the sage is not always good for the idiot or the madman; man's right is surely not woman's right, nor can wisdom and folly claim the same privileges. Here then, Madam, in the case of the individual and the kind you cannot fail to perceive differing rights and differing necessities. Can you not also perceive it as possible, that differences of race may be at least as strongly distinctive?

I am but one of many, and mean to claim to myself no peculiar merit,

10. Matthew Gregory Lewis, editor of *Tales of Wonder,* received the nickname "Monk" from his Gothic novel *The Monk* (1796).

when I say that I have studied this point deeply, conscientiously, and with the wish to fulfil my duties to God and the world; to my family, to my country, and to mankind. I believe that the negro holds with us the position for which his nature marks him, and that any serious attempt to change this position must result in the final extinction of his race in every country habitable and cultivable by the superior white man. In countries not habitable and cultivable by the white man, the negro may retain possession, but must fall back into his original barbarism. This position you, however, will deem subject to question, and the point stands in discussion. Now, Madam, it would certainly be impolitic in us, pending its at least doubtful decision, to act as though judgment were in favor of our opponents. Our negroes, in spite of Mrs. Stowe's assertions, present a body of the most comfortable peasantry and least corrupt lower class that the world knows. Shall we force them from this position to the fearful experiment of self-government? Or, rather, shall we turn them loose, not to self-government (for of this we believe them incapable), but to misrule? not to liberty, but to the wildest license? Shall we put weapons into the hand of the savage, solely that he may slaughter his civilized lord, without hope of bettering his own condition, but on the contrary with (we believe) the certainty of plunging him back to the lowest abyss of barbarism from which present institutions have raised him, to at least an imitative and semi-civilization?

From our opinions, dear Madam, as to the result of such an experiment, you differ. But is it not possible—nay, even probable—(high-born Duchess though you be), as knowledge comes not by intuition, nor can be made the monopolized prerogative of the rich and great, that you, who have certainly never in your life even looked through your *lorgnette* at a score of black faces, may be less likely to know the nature of this negro people than we, who, born and bred among them, have played with them and sorrowed with them, laughed with them and wept with them, even from our babyhood upward? With the grey hairs beginning to cluster around my brow, I am still cheerfully served by many of the same faithful negroes who watched with hope my tottering baby steps; their children labor for me, and their grand children are cherished and reared by me. Is it likely that you or I should feel the greatest affection for them, the warmest interest and closest sympathy? Allowing to both of us the ordinary feelings of women (I claim no more than the average share which is common and general to the rightminded of our sex), which of us is likeliest to judiciously consider, and to feelingly act for their weal? You are, I do not doubt it, actuated by a laudable spirit of philanthropy, and a general wish for the well-being of humanity. Allow the same to me; and am I not farther moved by the additional and closer feeling of interest in those who are near to me? Such a feeling there is, as may have existed in olden times between the Highland Chief and his kindred subjects; the feeling of protector and dependant; a something approaching the relation of parent and child. Unless, then, I, and all Southern United States women situated like myself (and they are numerous, forming the majority of the female population of nearly half our nation) are utterly devoid of woman and human feelings, we sympathize with the negro more than can your Grace. On the same principle, though certainly more strongly indicated, your Grace, if you be a mother, must necessarily feel more for the son of your home and your bosom, than could I from any philanthropic impulses.

Such reasoning as this should, it might be supposed, be decisive in determining the world to leave to ourselves and our consciences the general management of affairs, and the internal police of our own country. But your Grace, and those cooperating with you, think differently; and I would, so far as my individual effort can, willingly satisfy you in all reasonable and practicable measures. I do not, of course, acknowledge the right of any foreign country, or of any number of the inhabitants of any foreign country, to interfere with our internal legislation. Such an assumption is, on the contrary, so preposterous, that were it not for the christian and sisterly spirit which mutually pervades our communications, believe me, dear Madam, such attempts would deserve the epithets of "impertinent interference," "impudent dictation," etc., which have been, I grieve to say it, rather hastily launched against that philanthropic move, headed by the Countess of Shaftesbury, to which your Grace, as mistress of Stafford House, stood, as it were, sponsor and godmother. The beautiful spirit of christian love which is at the foundation of, and pervades, your whole course of action in this affair, should have saved it from such reproach. Regretting that it should have been so misunderstood, and with a due appreciation on my part of its merits, in a similar spirit of affectionate charity is, dear Madam, dictated the proposition which I am presently about to make to you.

As you appear to regard it as an imperative duty of the civilized world to deliver this negro people from bondage, I presume you would deem it incumbent upon, or at least highly meritorious in, an individual situated as I am, to make a beginning, and set a beautiful example of disinterestedness and self-sacrifice by persuading my husband, or others upon whom I am, as a woman, according to the usages and decencies of society, to a certain degree dependant, to liberate and colonize, or to permit me to liberate and colonize, those whom we now hold in bondage. But here arise some difficulties. My ancestors, hard working colonists, were forced, as I have already said, by the laws of England, imposed by the nobles of your land (your ancestors, gentle lady) into the owning of this property. Shall their descendants (myself and children) go begging their bread in penance for the sin thus forced upon them, while the descendants of the very nobles thus forcing it yet revel in luxuries? If this system be a system of sin, you with me are at least equally guilty, and you with me should bear the expiation. I will not say but that, did I feel it a sin, I might and ought to cast it off without weighing the consequences. But even were I so disposed, the urgings to it, unaccompanied with some substantial sacrifice on your part, would come badly from you, who, with more than equal responsibility through your ancestors in the origin of the sin, should bear your full portion of weight in the removal of it.

Your Grace is willing to help with words and cheer us on. But words do little here. We want acts. Will your Grace, from your immense income, assist? I am quite willing to allow and to forward, for the improvement of these my black subjects, any experiments to which they shall not themselves object; but I believe that your plan is a wrong one. I believe that its end would be certain ruin to my negroes and myself. Would it not therefore be unjust both to them and myself that we should, unsecured of the results, be called upon to bear all the risks of such a venture, upon the simple speculation of those who, like your Grace, are little versed in the character and habits of this people? Believing, as I do, that I have pursued the best possible course for their interests, and having to the extent of my power, and according to the dictates of my conscience, fulfilled my duties towards them, I am not willing to run this risk, unless on the condition that your Grace shall bind yourself, out of the income of your immense property, to preserve from the abject want which is, in my opinion, likely to ensue from your experiment, these helpless creatures, whom I am (supposing always that they are consenting to the change) ready to transfer to you—and, further, on condition also that a certain sum shall be furnished to secure to my own family such maintenance as shall prevent their becoming outcasts from those habits of society to which by education and ancestry they are entitled. Your Grace has, I am informed, in conjunction with your noble husband, an income of some three hundred thousand pounds sterling per annum. One fifteenth part of this your annual income would suffice for the liberation of some one hundred and sixty negroes, who, as I have said, form, with the land which they cultivate (and which without them becomes valueless), my whole property. As your Grace, and the noble ladies who act with you, acknowledge your share in the common sin which we inherit from our ancestors in the establishment of slavery, we must, of course, understand that you are willing to furnish your mite to assist in throwing off the curse which, according to your belief, now sits like an incubus upon the civilized world, scowling vengeance upon the farthest descendant of those in any way (whether by act, complicity, or tacit non-opposition) concerned in so iniquitous a system. Anxious to contribute our share to the happiness of mankind, the women of America (not Mrs. Stowe and her compeers, the Abbe Kellys,[11] Lucretia Motts, etc., but the true and sober women of our western world) will, I believe, be ready to give their aid in setting at rest, by any experiment, or series of experiments, which you may desire, the great question of negro capability, which seems now to be the all important one in your nobly charitable plans for the world's improvement; and what I can individually do, I am now, Madam, and dear sister, most willing and anxious to accomplish.

Here then stand, waiting your decision, one hundred and sixty souls, whom, as the first fruits of your efforts, you can easily free from all those evils, real or supposed, with which you understand them to be overwhelmed. One fifteenth part of one year's income will enable your Grace to do this. I am, as you may perceive, ready to make a very much larger sacrifice in proportion to my means, by the loss which I may suffer from the throwing out, as so much dead capital, of waste lands, which for want of negro labor must become comparatively valueless to me, and also by the inconveniences resulting from an entire and undesirable change of life and habits. This sacrifice I am, however, ready to make in consideration of the tender consciences of the Stafford House sisterhood, and to give you an opportunity first of personally experimenting upon the feasibility of your plans, and next of proving to the world the sincerity of your efforts in the cause which you undertake. I have, as a woman and a mother, been so startled by the curses, both loud and deep, lately showered upon our slave system, that I am anxious, for my own and my children's sake, that every opportunity should be given to the philanthropists of the day, to prove the truth or falsity of their position by any limited process of experiment which can satisfy them, without hazarding the ruin of nations for the verifying of an untried theory.

Try now, Madam, what can be done with these one hundred and sixty candidates for enlightenment. It will be the first step of real earnest endeavor which you will have made in the cause; and, if a wise one, it will assuredly be rapidly imitated. As I cannot doubt of your sincerity, I equally cannot doubt that you will be ready and anxious to accept my offer; and I shall expect soon to hear from you, by the transmission, in any manner or form that may be most convenient to you, of the (to you) almost insignificant sum which will make you absolute mistress to liberate, to colonize, to educate, and to bless, in all manner of conceivable ways, the one hundred and sixty souls whom I now offer to release to you; always with the proviso that you have their own consent to the change. It is probable, Madam, that after

11. Abigail Kelley Foster (1810–87), born in Pelham, Mass.; abolitionist and woman's rights advocate.

having done your best with these one hundred and sixty Uncle Toms and Topsys, you may have a truer appreciation of the negro character and capabilities for improvement than can be obtained from the perusal of Mrs. Stowe's romance, and may be able to guide your co-laborers and imitators, by some valuable hints, in the management of future and similar undertakings. Your Grace cannot, I presume, fail to perceive the merits of a plan which will thus enable you to exercise upon a small scale, and illustrate the merits of, your expansive system of philanthropy, thus setting to your friends and coadjutors an example of the only course which can prove to the world the sincerity of your professions, and to yourselves the truth or error of your opinions.

Should your Grace desire any further communication with me upon the subject for the completion or furtherance of your aims, I shall be happy to hear from yourself or any suitable agent. I have received from my husband full authority to act in this matter as may be most satisfactory to myself for the soothing of any such doubts or scruples of conscience, as might be awaked by the eloquent persuasion of your Stafford House appeal. Your Grace, therefore, need fear no interruption or impediment in the prosecution of the well-intentioned and praiseworthy experiment which I propose for your consideration. Please address ———.[12]

Wishing your Grace all success and happiness in the new career which, with the most sincere feelings of kindness, I have suggested for your effort, and, with the assurance that my one hundred and sixty black martyrs, big and little, shall on demand, and in consideration of the fulfilment of the above named reasonable terms, be promptly forthcoming, I am, Madam, with all respect and assurances of the highest consideration, your Grace's

Humble servant and sincere well wisher,

——— ———[13]

12. Her name and address are in the original given in full. [*Mercury*'s note]

13. Her name and address are in the original given in full. [*Mercury*'s note]

13.

Carey on the Slave Trade

Oyez! oyez! oyez! Give ear, oh! ye nations! The infallible remedy for all the ills of life is found!—the monster humbug cometh. "Morrison's pills," "Swaim's panaceas," "Spanish mixtures," "sarsaparillas," and "ready reliefs," hide your diminished heads. Let us hear no more of your "bad legs cured," your fever sores, your pimples, and your ulcers, your rheumatisms and consumptions, blotches, boils and pustules. Bah! Here is that which, as the serpent formed from Moses' rod demolished its antagonists, shall, in like manner, quickly swallow up your puny inventions.[1] Oyez! oyez! oyez!—here is

SQR, n.s., 9 (Jan. 1854): 115–84. Publication reviewed: Henry C. Carey, *The Slave Trade, Domestic and Foreign: Why It Exists, and How It May Be Extinguished* (Philadelphia: A. Hart, late Carey and Hart, 1853; rpt. New York, 1967). Henry Charles Carey (1793–1879), born in Philadelphia; son of Mathew Carey, in whose publishing firm he became a partner (1817), later head; after his *Essay on the Rate of Wages* (1835), he retired from publishing to devote his full time to political economy, writing several books including *Principles of Political Economy,* 3 vols. (1837–40), and *The Principles of Social Science,* 3 vols. (1858–59); his early adherence to free trade was replaced by a strong commitment to protectionism. Carey, "while a professed free trader, is the most indefatigable advocate of protection in the United States, and [his] extraordinary inconsistencies and false deductions, while they mortify and disappoint his friends here, are the wonder and confusion of his foreign admirers; . . . among other things, [he] has discovered that wonderful theory that is to settle all the unsettled points of Political Economy—the theory that in the pursuit of wealth, the producer and consumer must hunt in couples, like hounds in a chace." David James McCord, "American Institutions—the Monroe Doctrine—Intervention—etc.," p. 593.

1. Exod. 7:9–12.

the great doctor of nations. Have ye sorrow? have ye poverty? have ye tyranny? have ye lethargy? have ye barren lands or sickly swamps, rivers inundating their banks, or sunparched deserts? Behold your cure! Lo! the redeemer cometh, the great medicine man with his charms and his rattles! Mr. Carey has the remedy in his pocket; you may purchase the receipt for just one dollar, warranted to suit all cases. *The Slave Trade, Domestic and Foreign: Why It Exists, and How It May Be Extinguished* will tell you how all these evils may be cured by making the producer hold on tightly to his consumer. Don't let the fellow budge a step. "All the world's a stage," says Shakespeare;[2] all the world, according to Mr. Carey, is a kind of contra-dance. Gentlemen, keep to your partners; you are perfectly free to dance as high as you please, but no meddling with privileges; we'll have no freedom of exchange.

Mr. Carey is the author of several works, which have procured him considerable notice as a political economist; and, in some of his more recent productions, he has already puzzled a little the students of his theories by the peculiar species of free-trade of which he has, of late, made himself the apostle. Everybody knows what, in the ordinary acceptance of the terms, are free-trade and protection; but Mr. Carey's theory of free-trade, like Jacob's streaked and speckled lambs,[3] seems a mysterious existence, which, not coming regularly within the laws of nature, has required some little ingenuity for its invention. It is, at least, a regular half-breed, a hybrid production, which his commentators are puzzled how to class. In his last work, which we have under notice, the writer's opinions take a more decided shape, and, although he flourishes his old standard, and mouths of free-trade and Adam Smith, as Louis Napoleon of his "république française," the mask is pretty fairly dropped. Louis Napoleon's "république" is despotism; Mr. Carey's "free-trade" is protection; i.e., the limiting of commercial exchanges, the check upon what he considers as injurious exportation, is his panacea for every national evil.

Mr. Carey regards himself as having advanced some entirely original theories in political economy. Two letters of his, which have appeared in *Putnam's Magazine*,[4] claim for himself the merit of having reorganized the science, and developed its hitherto concealed mysteries. Verily, Mr. Carey is right, at least in supposing that he has struck out a new track; he has made the marvellous discovery that protection is free-trade. While he claims to fight under the banners of free-trade, the whole substance of his book is an attack

2. *As You Like It* 2.7.139.

3. Gen. 30:31–31:13.

4. *Putnam's Monthly Magazine* 2 (Aug. and Sept. 1853): 229–31, 342–44. The letters are dated July 2 and Aug. 8, 1853.

upon the liberty of foreign exchanges, and an argument in favour of forcing upon consumer and producer, by means of protective tariffs, a local vicinage. He tells us that "the protective tariffs of all the advancing nations of Europe are but measures of resistance to a system of enormous oppression, and that it is in that direction that the people of this country are to look for *the true and only road to freedom of trade and the freedom of man*" (*vide Slave Trade, etc.*, p. 411). They are measures of resistance to what?

A patient just roused from the nightmare still shudders with a fearful horror at the thoughts of the monster of his dream. Mr. Carey appears to have had some restless nap, of which England has been the tormenting incubus, and almost every line of his present work shows his instinctive horror of this bugbear of his imagination. The laws and customs of England, he appears to think, enslave not only her own people and her own dependants, but her kiss is fatal as that of the vampire. Commercial intercourse with her is slavery; and friendship, moral death. *Hers* is the "system of enormous oppression," against which it has become necessary for the nations to guard themselves by "*protective tariffs*" as "*the true and only road to freedom of trade and freedom of man*." Under *her* influence our U. States beneficently protective tariff of 1842 was replaced by the less protective one of 1846.[5] By this latter tariff, or, rather, by the partial freedom of trade which, through it, we enjoy, Mr. Carey contends that we have fallen into that class of nations which exhibit "a daily increasing tendency toward utter barbarism," among whom "education diminishes and intellect declines" (p. 376). "Slavery now travels North, whereas only twenty years ago freedom was travelling South. That such is the case is the natural consequence of our submission, even in part, to the system that looks to compelling <*compelling*> the export of raw products, the exhaustion of the land, the cheapening of labour, and the export of the labourer. Wherever it is submitted to, slavery grows. Wherever it is resisted, slavery dies away, and freedom grows, etc." (p. 375)

Rather a marvellous piece of information this, for progressive America. We are quite willing to join issue with Mr. Carey upon this point; for, although such reasoning does not ill accord with some of the fashionable "*isms*"

5. At least from 1820 protective tariffs were disliked in the slaveholding states, as favoring Northern manufactures against Southern imports and exports. Resistance was frequent (including nullification in South Carolina). Although the Whigs had won most of the South in 1840, eight Whig senators from the South would not support their party when in 1842 the tariff was raised to an average of 33 percent, the highest since 1832. However, in 1846 the tariff was reduced by the victorious Democrats to an average of 26.5 percent, together with other adjustments favorable to the South; the tariff passed the Senate only with the votes of the senators from Texas, lately annexed.

of the day, and the rant about progressive slavery would better suit the style of argument of an Antoinette Brown, or her sister in the faith, Mrs. Sojourner Truth,[6] than that of a grave political economist, we believe that not only the country generally, but the world, must decide against our increasing tendency towards barbarism, and our perishing intellect. In the palmy day of their wonderful and unexampled progress, the United States have but one shoal to fear—one danger to guard against—and that is not to be found in the centralization resulting from the institutions of England—which Mr. Carey seems to regard as a kind of ogre-power, destined to devour the vital energies of the habitable world—but in our own home centralization, a centralization which is the result of protection to our Northern manufactures, Northern coal, Northern iron, and Northern shipping, excluding us, whether wholly or in part, from that very English market which Mr. Carey so much dreads, and thus building up Northern factories and Northern steam engines at the expense of our Southern agriculture, by shutting us out from our fair and natural markets. From such a system of protection, elevating Northern manufacturing privileges in fierce opposition to Southern agricultural interests, results the tendency which exhibits itself, yearly increasing, of the majority to trample upon the law. As the tiger which has tasted blood, the multitude discovers that it can with impunity deface what it hitherto has held sacred; constitutional regulations are forgotten, and "higher laws" called in to sanctify want of faith and breach of contract.

From England we are safe enough, could we but prove true to ourselves. English intermeddling may excite home fanaticism; but only home fanaticism, which seeks to crush one portion of our Union beneath the strongly centralizing tendency of the bloated and unjustly-grasped power of the other, can sound the death knell of our prosperity. No foreign power is destined to prostrate us; our fall will be suicidal. Linked in uncongenial brotherhood, if we of the Southern States shall ever be destined to meet our fate from Northern legislation, the wretched twin, which is joined with us by bonds as essential to its own existence as are to the Siamese brothers those which confine them, must perish with the perishing prosperity of Southern

6. Antoinette Louisa Brown Blackwell (1825–1921), born Henrietta, N.Y.; studied toward a degree in theology at Oberlin College but was refused permission to graduate; lecturer on antislavery, woman's rights, temperance; ordained minister of the First Congregational Church in Butler and Savannah, N.Y. (1853). Sojourner Truth (c. 1797–1883), born a slave and named Isabella, in Hurley, N.Y.; took refuge with a sympathetic family, from whom she took the surname Van Wagener (1827); freed in 1828; claimed to have received divine visitations; took the name Sojourner Truth in 1843; joined the abolitionist movement and traveled widely; active also as a woman's rights advocate.

agriculture.[7] Blind as they seem to the fact, our Northern States prosper by us and through us. The South may prosper without the North States; the North cannot exist without the South, whether in union of government as now, or in the intercourse of friendly and independent states, as time may be destined to develope. Our agricultural produce is essential to their very being, under existing habits and institutions. From this are their store houses filled, and their ships laden; through this do their merchants grow rich, and their farmers flourish; and so much are they instinctively prompted by these facts, even while affecting unconsciousness of them, that, like the greedy boy in the fable, they too often defeat their own objects by attempting to grasp all instead of being satisfied with their natural portion.

To this point tends all Mr. Carey's complex argument in favour of the necessity of vicinage between consumer and producer. We must eat our sugar and work up our cotton at home; i.e., the North States must have a monopoly of our Southern produce, and the command of our market—for it is, as we say at the South, "all talk for Buncombe"[8] when Mr. Carey gravely argues that the South States should manufacture for themselves; that the "spindle and loom" should be "placed in and about the cotton fields;" and when he tells us that "the planters have labour, *that is now wasted,* that would be abundant for the conversion of half their crops, if they could but bring the machinery to the land, instead of taking the produce of the land to the machinery" (p. 254). This remark is made generally of "India, Egypt, Brazil, the West Indies, and our Southern States" [254], which, however dissimilar in habits, institutions, and government, he sees fit to jumble and lump together in argument. We answer for our Southern States alone (having no room in anything less than a volume, at least as large as Mr. Carey's own, to go into an investigation of the varying institutions of each of the above named countries) that, if Mr. Carey is serious in this assertion, no six year old infant fresh from the nursery could be more ignorant than such a statement proves him to be of the condition and habits of our country. "Waste labour" we have not to any important extent. We have an indulgent system of management which prevents us from forcing our negroes to an undue effort in labour;

7. Chang and Eng (1811–74), born in Siam and exhibited in America in Barnum's circus; the first "Siamese twins" because the first in which was recognized the embryological chance of two identical twins being born physically fused together.

8. Buncombe, a county in western North Carolina. "Near the close of the debate on the 'Missouri Question' in the Sixteenth Congress [1820], when the member for this district rose to speak, while the house was impatiently calling for the 'Question,' several members gathered round him, begging him to desist; he persevered, however, for a while, declaring that the people of his district expected it, and that he was bound to *make a speech for Buncombe*" (*OED*[2]).

and, as their capabilities for energetic action are, in general, far inferior to those of the white man, we allow them for their rest, amusement, and arrangements for personal comfort an amount of leisure which may appear wasteful to the uninformed; the old, too, the feeble, and the young, are frequently allowed to pass their time in a *dolce far niente,* which is the negro's paradise. Perhaps Mr. Carey may think this *wasteful.* He would have the decrepit grandmother forced to throw aside her crutch, and her grand child of six or eight called from its nursery pleasures to drudge beside her in the labours of a cotton mill, while the feeble invalid, whose only comfort for the hard treatment received from nature is that sickness gives, under our indulgent system, the almost invariable privilege of rest, must at least half resign that prerogative to give every moment of comparative ease to the whirl of the spindle and the clank of the loom. Is it waste of labour to endeavour to leave the remnant of life a holyday of rest to the infirm, or the first bloom of it a holyday of joy to the young? Is it waste of labour to leave to the toil-driven husbandman his afternoon lounge, or his evening frolic? Is it waste of labour to give him time for his harvest dinner, or his Christmas week of visiting and feasting? If these form the waste of labour to which Mr. Carey refers, we can only say that we more than doubt whether there would be any amelioration in the condition of the slave by the abridgment of it. It is a common remark among us, of the slaveholding States, that foreigners and residents, from our Northern States, are the most exacting masters.[9] Not that these are, we presume, naturally at all inferior in heart or conscience to the Southern-born owner; but that, ignorant at once of the nature both of our tillage and our labourers, they expect of the negro such effort as is by the brawny foreigner easily accomplished. The poor negro, whose life is wretched unless a large portion of it be basked away in his congenial sunshine, sinks under such unaccustomed push of labour, broken in health, or heart, or both.

The physician called in to prescribe to a patient looks at the tongue, feels the pulse, and makes every effort to discover, by attentive observation, the condition of the sufferer, before indicating his remedies. It is only the

9. "We must inform our friends at the North, that it is a notorious fact, that the most cruel masters in this country are Northern men and foreigners; and it is equally true, as to those who most frequently disgrace themselves by illicit amalgamation; and that indecencies and unbecoming connections, of that sort, are held in as much abhorrence here as elsewhere; and that no man can be known to be guilty of them without impairing his respectability in society; and that the public feeling on that subject is what it should be; and we believe our country is freer from adultery and seduction than theirs, and quite as exempt from all kinds of debauchery." David James McCord, "Slavery and the Abolitionists," *SQR* 15 (April 1849): 165–223; 202.

charlatan who pretends by clairvoyance, electro-biology, spiritual manifestations, or other short-cut tracks to the mysteries of science, to prescribe by instinctive or supernatural knowledge. Mr. Carey has, unfortunately for his reputation as a patient student of statistics, jumped to his conclusions in a very clairvoyant style. We were amused some time since at a scene in *Blackwood:*

> A patient is brought into the presence of the *clairvoyant,* who forthwith proceeds to give a diagnosis of the complaint, and a description of its seat, in terms which are certainly oracular, [. . .] the interlocutors being the operator and the possessed one[, of course confederates]. "D'ye see that man?" "Ay, I see him." "Is he weel?" "Far frae it!" "What's the matter wi' him?" "The matter wi him! d'ye no see yon?" "No, but what is't ye see?" "It's that, ye ken—the thing there! Lord save us, how it's louping! It's a red thing, and a'wrang thegither." "Ay, is't a red thing?" "Just that." "Will it get better?" "I dinna ken; there's something coming out o't that's no right. The man's no weel ava!" "Can ye tell onything to mak him better?" "Ay, there's a thing he might tak, but I dinna mind the name o't." "What is it <is't>, Davie, man? Think again!" "O'o <oo> it's a pouther!" "A powder, is it? and what's the colour o't?" "It's whiles a' <ae> coulour <colour> and whiles anither; ye can pit it in your mouth, gin ye like it! <gin ye like!>" "What kind o' a taste has it?" "It's no nice." "If he were to take it, wad it cure him?" "If it did him nae gude, it wad do him nae harm!"[10]

So it is with Mr. Carey. He sees the "red thing louping, and a'wrang thegither," and *nolens volens* would have us swallow his "pouther" (dinna mind the name o't, Free-trade or Protection, he is not quite sure which), while we, feeling by no means safe in his assurance that it shall do us *nae harm,* are disposed to consult a little our own reason upon the subject. Here is an evil, he determines, and "how it may be extinguished" is the question with him. He may be surprised at our response. "Do not extinguish it at all!" We are by no means convinced that the red thing louping is not rather a blessing, and no evil. The great heart perchance of our system, to stop whose *louping* will be death.

As we cannot find the waste labour which is a large part of the *wrang a'thegither* of which Mr. Carey complains, let us see further what he understands of the making of a cotton-crop. In his *beau ideal* sketch of a government for the nascent republic of Liberia, he proposes, as usual, for all evils, his *pouther,* i.e., protective tariffs to force home consumption of home pro-

10. [W. E. Aytoun], "Spiritual Manifestations," *Blackwood's Edinburgh Magazine* 73 (May 1853): 629–46; 632–33.

duce. In the progress of such a system, machinery, etc. being brought into the country, it should be announced, "that at one time cotton was to be picked, and at another it was to be converted into cloth; that in the summer the cane was to be cultivated, in the autumn the sugar was to be gathered,[11] and in the winter it was to be refined; that at one time houses and mills were to be built, and at another roads to be made," etc. etc. (p. 300). Now Mr. Carey is well "posted up," no doubt, upon the subject of building roads and houses, as they do such things considerably in Pennsylvania; and we see, in the nature of things, no possible objection to building a house one month, and working roads the next. Houses and roads are articles which can wait the convenience of the labourer and artificer. If they are not completed in January, they will do as well perhaps in June; at least there is no dead loss of the article by delay. Not so with cotton and sugar. If the laborer is called to convert his cotton into cloth, or to refine his sugar, when he should be saving his provision harvest, preparing his lands for the next crop, scattering his manures, repairing his fences, or putting in his seed, the turn out at the end of the year would indeed be *wrang a'thegither.* What is left undone in January, we may needlessly rue in June. The arrangement and nature of our crops allow but little waste time to the labourer. A constant succession of needful duties follow each other from New Year to New Year, and any manufacturing of cotton goods or refining of sugar could be only effected by planters, without the ruin of their entire crops, by depriving the poor negro of the rest and comfort so necessary to his existence. He would have to work like, or perhaps even harder than, a northern or English factory operative. Mr. Carey's plan could have no other good effect than the depriving the fashionable philanthropic humbug of the day (*negrophilism*) of all pabulum for its existence. The negro race would, under his improved system, die out with us, as rapidly as they do in Mr. Carey's native State. Besides, even supposing us prepared for this wholesale and very facile method of extermination, how could the planter's pocket bear the heavy cost of establishing the extremely expensive machinery of cotton mills and sugar refineries, only for his negroes to work at them on spare afternoons and broken holidays? This stuff, of the spindle and the loom being "placed in and about cotton-fields," converting planters into semi-manufacturers, is as preposterously ridiculous as though we should insist upon it that Wall Street merchants must devote their spare time to medicine and tailoring; that, at one time, goods should be sold

11. By the way, what does Mr. Carey mean by "gathering sugar"? We have been accustomed to hear of gathering cane and boiling sugar, but never before imagined the possibility of sugar growing ripe to the hand, like well-filled corn. Perhaps it does so in Pennsylvania, as the old nurses tell us young babies are gathered in the cabbage bed. [LSM]

and, at another, converted into clothes; that, in the summer, accounts might be collected, and, in the autumn, soothing doses of chloroform administered to the unlucky owners of empty purses.

No doubt, strong protective tariffs, such as Mr. Carey recommends, might, if forced upon us by violent legislation, induce a large portion of our community to abandon what, in the natural arrangement of things, proves itself to be our most profitable labour, and to adopt another which nature condemns, but which government might prop up into an artificial value at the expense of nature; and thus, half the population of cotton-planting countries might be forced into manufacturing; and the spindle and the loom be thus introduced in and about our cotton-fields. But what does this prove? That manufacturing could thus be made more profitable than agriculture? Not at all. It only proves that, our natural means of existence, agriculture, being ruined by insane legislation, we would be thus forced from the natural, and consequently better pursuit, to the false and unnatural expedient of manufacture for a subsistence. It would be no difficult matter, by local legislation, under a sufficiently tyrannical government, to make it absolutely necessary to the comparative comfort, and even existence, of Mr. Carey, that he should take up the pavement in front of his dwelling, to plant potatoes and turnips. Digging and hoeing would scarcely be as agreeable, nor perhaps as profitable, to the accomplished gentleman, as his literary studies; but drive his own theory to its height, and there will be no alternative. This would be going to extremes, Mr. Carey would answer. Granted—but who is to fix the limit? We must keep our hands from picking and stealing, lest they go on to house-breaking and robbery. If Mr. Carey insists that we must be forced from our natural occupation (happening with us to be agriculture) to one which his judgment pronounces better, viz., manufactures—the loom and the spindle—may we not with equal propriety insist, that it will be altogether better for his health and the comfort of society that he shall abandon his special occupation of literature to adopt the hoe and the spade, because our judgment so pronounces best? He does not desire this change, which he considers uncomfortable and injurious, not only to himself, but to the world. We think otherwise, and demand governmental legislation to enforce our opinions. Here, we say, is waste labour and waste land. A portion of this pavement can be spared, as well as Mr. Carey's literary productions. Society will profit more by the turnips and potatoes. Let Mr. Carey be forced to digging. This is tyranny, Mr. Carey might well respond, tyranny of the most oppressive stamp. Equally, do *we* so answer *his* suggestions. Give us back your boasted tariff of '42, and we pronounce it tyranny, tyranny of the most oppressive stamp.

Once admit the system to the smallest extent, allow the principle to be a correct one, and where are its limits? Mr. Carey is as fit for hoeing as are we for manufacturing. Our individual judgment we have the temerity to suppose as good as his. Who shall decide between us? Here is no longer a question of eternal right and justice, which the immutable laws of morality must determine, but a question of judgment. If the truth of the principle be allowed, some sovereign power must be enthroned in order to limit its action, some Lord who shall issue his fiat: thus far shalt thou steal, and no farther; thus far shall thy neighbour's rights be encroached upon, but no farther; thus far shall protective tariffs and monopolies raise the price of your iron and your coal, but here stop.[12] Mr. Carey, no doubt, deems himself a very competent person to decide the proper bounds for his remarkable system of limited free-trade; but from his judgment, we demur. Honest free-trade needs no such intervention to decide its limits. The pubic treasury overflows with specie, which it is most important to once more set in circulation. Let it then be done by lightening our imposts. Nature shows her own resources, and needs no "protective tariffs" to aid her in their development. As well might it be insisted that the cotton-field shall take its place by the loom and the spindle, as *vice versa*. What say our Northern friends to this? Shall we force the cotton-blooms, by a hot-bed growth, among New England rocks? Shall we extirpate the golden harvests of Pennsylvania fields, and plough up her clover-pastures to produce a sickly crop of stunted bolls? Heaven forbid! and grant that our affairs may be guided by clearer-sighted political economists than Mr. Carey! If consumer and producer are to be hitched together, we must be consistent; and the cotton-mill, which is transported from New England to Texas, should drive its expelled cotton-field back from Texas to New England; or, this being impossible, consequent loss must ensue, and the country remains *minus* the extirpated cotton-field, New England and Texas equally suffering from the loss. And yet such is Mr. Carey's system. The loom and the spindle must, in spite of nature, be brought to the cotton-fields of Carolina and Georgia. Equally the cotton-field must, in spite of nature, go to the loom and the spindle of New England, and the yankees must try their hand at cotton-growing. Consumer and producer must retain their juxtaposition, and Mr. Carey, self-instituted viceroy under Providence, will regulate the exact amount of requisite importation in this line. Rather more difficult articles of transport, however, we *calculate* he will find them, than the heaviest cotton crop.

What wordy stuff too, is this of vicinage! Mr. Carey does not use the term in this volume, but his whole argument turns upon the necessity of the thing. Does he mean *local* vicinage or vicinage of accessibility? Does Mr. Carey

12. Cf. Job 38:11.

forget that it is frequently more difficult to surmount a single mile, in some certain neighborhood, than a hundred in another direction? We can more easily (if let alone by protective tariffs) transport our cotton three or four thousand miles to the English manufacturer, than as many hundred to the mountain streams of North Carolina. What is vicinage? "Who is my neighbour?" is a memorable question once answered by the beautiful parable of the "good Samaritan."[13] He that showed mercy, he that aided the sufferer, was his neighbour. So, in all intercourse of men, not actual contiguity, not simple local proximity, but accessibility and facility of intercourse is vicinage. Our commercial neighbours are not simply the inhabitants of such portion or portions of territory as lie at the smallest number of measured feet or miles from us, but those nations whose habits, customs, produce, and daily circumstances of life render it most convenient and profitable for us to hold intercourse with them. The produce of any country will always naturally incline to its most convenient consumer; and this necessary accessibility of producer and consumer Mr. Carey strangely confounds, and endeavours to comprise under the head of mere local vicinage. With such accessible nations the unbiased impulse of events, and the instinctive tendencies of nature, bring us at once, individually and nationally, into intercourse. Commerce is the great aggregate of individual intercourse, extending the hand of friendship from nation to nation, from continent to continent; practically enforcing, in its most expansive signification, that *neighbourhood* which depends less upon inches and miles than upon sympathies and mutual interests. Mr. Carey's belittling theory would drive us back a century. We must cease to be America, to emulate *Russia* and *Spain;* which Mr. Carey places prominently among those countries which he sets before us as legislative models, in which *freedom grows;* classing them as remarkable instances of "great increase of intellectual activity," countries "in which civilization advances;" while we, unfortunate United States of America, are, under the crushing influence of a more unrestricted commercial intercourse, on that unlucky list "in which there is a daily increasing tendency towards <toward> utter barbarism" (pp. 375 and 376). We can scarcely imagine how Mr. Carey could read over his proof sheets without laughing at himself, and sincerely hope that—for the sake of his own far-spread reputation, and that he may not, in his own arguments, furnish at least one somewhat practical proof of this retrograde action which he asserts in American intellect—he will, as soon as possible, write a *requiescat in pace* over this strange jumble of argument.

Could we make up our minds to accept Mr. Carey's *dictum* as gospel, we

13. Luke 10:30–37.

might, under the present circumstances of our cotton crop (which, having suffered first from almost unexampled drought, and then from almost unexampled rain, leaves us reason to hope for a very limited yield), find great comfort in his statement that "the planter becomes rich when crops are short. . . . He is almost ruined when crops are large" (p. 258). This is one of Mr. Carey's discoveries. Could we not, artificially, produce a similar state of affairs, by compelling the labourer to eat up half his sugar and to burn or use for manure half his cotton? In Mr. Carey's system of legislation, an edict to such effect would appear but right and natural, and thus could make us poor demented planters rich at once. This is even a simpler plan for our enrichment, than protective tariffs.

Because, in a supposed case (for which *vide* pages 255 to 259)—a case which could not possibly occur under any natural combination of circumstances, but could only result from the most stringent and tyrannical protective legislation—Mr. Carey proves that a monopoly which would confine mill-power to a single neighbourhood, and force all the corn produce of a large territory to pass through a single confined outlet, would be indisputably ruinous to the producer, he thence argues—with what plausibility it will, we think, require but little penetration in his readers to determine—that we, who willingly choose the market of England, not because there is *no other,* but because we consider this the *better outlet,* are in the same road to ruin, and that we must, like maniacs, be guided, *nolens volens,* to our better destiny. Mr. Carey would shut us out from this large outlet, to confine us to a hundred little ones. We have now the choice between the numerous small and the larger one; and, in so far as we *freely,* and unbiassed by tax or law, choose the larger outlet, he determines that we are in the condition of the corn grower whom he imagines confined, by the contrivance of a combination of corn-millers, to a single limited outlet. In other words, freedom of choice is not freedom of choice—free-trade is monopoly, and protection is free-trade!

The labour of the slave is, Mr. Carey tells us, to a high degree unproductive, and in proof of this statement he quotes from some unnamed letter writer in the New York *Daily Times,* who gives "the result of information derived from a gentleman of [Petersburg,] Virginia, *said to be* 'remarkable for accuracy and the preciseness <and preciseness> of his information'" [395; LSM's italics]. When Mr. Carey seeks statistical information concerning England, France, Germany, or Russia, does he go to French gazettes for the statistics of England, to Germany for those of France, or to Russia for those of England? taking the "say so" of *respectable gentlemen,* quoted at second hand by nobody knows who—or does he enquire of the residents, and look into the literary productions and official reports of the several countries about which he seeks such information? Mr. Carey might find better authority in Southern matters than letter writers in the New York *Daily Times*. We have Southern writers and Southern papers that a student of statistics might find it worth his while to consult.

We have already remarked that Mr. Carey's antipathies to England take so violent a stamp as scarcely to be accounted for on any ordinary grounds. That England has her faults, her blotches, her boils, and her spots of rottenness, so hideous that the eye shrinks from, and the heart sickens in, their investigation, we surely are far from denying; great, glorious, but far from perfect, she bears about her full share of the soil of the earth; sorrow and sin, the voice of agony, and the cry of the oppressed, echo from ocean to ocean under English rule. Not, therefore, are we, however, prepared to see in England the mother of all iniquity; not therefore do we look upon her as some monstrous exception to the laws of the universe, but rather only as one of the many instances of the powerful of earth showing even in resplendent greatness the weakness and the failings of humanity.

Mr. Carey tells us that England continually seeks to establish "a system of commercial centralization," having for "its object to compel all descriptions of raw produce to pass through England on its way from the producer to the consumer <from the consumer and the producer>, even when the latter are near neighbours to each other, and England distant many thousands <thousand> of miles from both." To carry out this system it has been required "that all [other] nations should be prevented from obtaining either the knowledge or the machinery required for enabling them to mine coal, smelt iron ore, or manufacture machines by aid of which they could command the services of the great natural agents," wind, water, steam, etc., etc. (pp. 260 and 261); that she has "determined that the whole earth shall become one great farm, with but a single workshop, in which shall be fixed the prices of all its occupants have to sell or [need] to buy" (p. 291). Now what is the amount of these terrible allegations? Only this: that England, as a manufacturing and commercial country, has not deemed it necessary to refuse the market of producing countries, and has not gone missionarying to force instruction in machinery, etc., upon the nations of the earth generally. What is the sin of England? She manufactures. To satisfy Mr. Carey, she must ruin herself, break up her manufactures, and protect those of other nations. "Has England," he asks, "ever endeavoured to strengthen the Neapolitan people by teaching them how to combine their efforts for the working of their rich ores, or for the conversion of their wool into cloth?" [378] Has she given up Malta and the Ionian Islands? Has she given up Gibraltar to

Spain?—and, because she has not, is she not responsible for the subjection of the Spanish people, for their poverty and their weakness?[14]

We are not about to make ourselves the defenders of England, nor are we at all disposed to take up the cudgels in her cause: her taxes and her monopolies have undoubtedly done much to crush and oppress her dependencies. But, besides that, her efforts to arrest this system, and adopt a more enlarged one of free-trade, become a principal point of attack with Mr. Carey. How, we would ask, except with her actual colonies and dependencies, is her authority exercised, and her system enforced? Mr. Carey tells us (p. 288) that "the nation [of England][15] is gradually losing its independent position among the nations of the earth. It is seen that the whole 'prosperity' of the country depends on the power to purchase cheap cotton, cheap sugar, and other cheap products of the soil, and it is feared that something may interfere to prevent the continuance of the system which maintains the domestic slave trade of this country;"[16] and that to "this feeling of growing dependence, and growing weakness" [289] are[17] to be attributed, he thinks, the conciliatory articles which, from time to time, appear in her gazettes. She "is becoming from day to day less powerful and less capable of the exercise of self-government among the community of nations" (p. 291).

14. Mr. Carey maintains that England "retains Malta and the Ionian Islands, as convenient places of resort for the great reformer of the age—the smuggler, whose business it is to see that no effort at manufactures shall succeed;" and that Portugal and Gibraltar are "the seats of a vast contraband trade, having for its *<its> express object* to deprive the Spanish people of all power to do any thing but cultivate the soil." (p. 378) [LSM] Malta, seized by Napoleon from the Knights of St. John Hospitaler in 1798, was restored to the knights by the Treaty of Amiens in 1802; the Maltese preferred the sovereignty of Great Britain, confirmed by the first Treaty of Paris (1814). The Ionian Islands, off the west coast of Greece, which had been taken from Venice by Napoleon (1797), were placed under a British protectorate by the second Treaty of Paris (1815). Spain ceded Gibraltar to Britain in 1713 by the Treaty of Utrecht, concluding the War of the Spanish Succession.

15. LSM's interpolation.

16. This is a new sin to find in England, and, in the face of recent Stafford House manifestations, and threats of Cuban interference, a rather remarkable accusation. England labouring to maintain our slave system! [LSM] American designs to annex Cuba were promoted vigorously with the election to the presidency of Franklin Pierce, who sent an envoy to Spain to persuade the Spanish government to accede to the annexation. The British (with France) opposed the American plan, both because they were apprehensive of what could be interpreted as American expansionism and because they believed that the abolition of the Cuban slave trade, which they were urging upon Spain, would be less likely under American rule. British resistance was much resented, and its motives suspected, by the Americans, until (October 1853) the British foreign secretary Lord Clarendon judged it prudent to assure the American minister, James Buchanan, that the British did not desire a government of liberated slaves in Cuba, nor did they want Cuba as a colony for themselves.

17. "Is" in original.

"Throughout England there is a deference to rank, a servility, a toadyism, entirely inconsistent with progress in civilization" (p. 324). How, then, does a nation so degraded, so effete, maintain her influence and authority among foreign nations? Are we, of the Southern United States, or are we not, among her *de facto* subjects? Mr. Carey, as we have quoted, says that her whole prosperity depends upon our agricultural produce, and yet again speaks of us as her abject subjects, in progress of ruin through her machinations. Her system of "commercial centralization," he says (p[p]. 127[–28]), "renders the agriculturists of the world mere slaves, dependent for food and clothing upon the will of a few people, proprietors of a small amount of machinery, at 'the mighty heart of commerce.'" "We see the women and [the] children of Jamaica and Carolina, of Portugal and Turkey, of India and of Ireland, compelled to remain idle or to cultivate the land, because of [the existence of] a system which denies to all places in the world but one the power to bring the consumer to the side of the producer" (p. 202). The "free-trade" system, i.e., the system of England, has for its object to prevent all other communities "from doing any thing but raise sugar, coffee, cotton, wool, indigo, silk, and other raw commodities, to be carried, as does the slave of Virginia or Texas with the product of his labour, to *one great purchaser,* who determines upon their value and [upon] the value of the things they are to receive in exchange for them. It is the most gigantic system of slavery the world has yet seen, and therefore it is that freedom gradually disappears from every country over which England is enabled to obtain control, as witness the countries to which reference has just been made." (p. 364) "The English system, based on cheap labour, destroys the value of both labour and land, and therefore it is that there is so large an export of men from [the] countries subject to it—Africa, India, Ireland, Scotland, England, Virginia, and Carolina." (p. 362) Now, we repeat, how is this? Can Mr. Carey, for one instant, gravely contend that Carolina, Virginia, or Texas hold towards England the position of India, Ireland, or her African colonies? His arguments throw us all together in such strange confusion, that there seems no other egress than this conclusion from his labyrinth of words. Is it today that so distinguished a political economist must be taught the difference between compulsory and free action? As colonists of England, we rebelled against the system which her policy then and since inflicted upon her dependencies. As subjects, we rejected the taxed and shackled intercourse which she endeavored to force upon us; but, as free States, we accept her offered commerce, as one equally advantageous to herself as to us, and herein we are no more the subjects of her system than is Mr. Carey the slave of any individual who happens to have the cash to purchase the products of his coal mines. If Mr. Carey should be told, you shall not sell your coal or iron to X, Y, or Z, but must limit your sales to P and Q, then, indeed, by confining his market to P and Q, we put his produce at their disposal; they may fix their own prices, and thus become the virtual masters of himself and his coal mine; but if, in an unlimited freedom of exchange, he may prefer the market of P and Q, having still the liberty of turning to X, Y, and Z when he so desires, then P and Q, even though he[18] should find it convenient to sell them his whole produce, to the exclusion of all other purchasers, have neither power nor influence over him, further than is produced by the salutary bonds of mutual interest. Herein lies the difference between our Southern States and India or Ireland. Surely Mr. Carey, in his abstruse studies, has forgotten the A, B, C of the science of which he announces himself the prophet, or he could not at this day need to have this simple truth recalled to him by so humble an observer as ourselves.

It is Mr. Carey's own theory which would limit his market: as, for instance, were the government to decide that he must not sell his coal to X, Y, or Z, because they are at an inconvenient distance, but must limit his sales to P and Q, whose immediate vicinage should render them the natural consumers of his produce, then, as we said above, P and Q, having the monopoly of his market, might fix their own terms and Mr. Carey becomes *de facto* their servant or slave; and such is the condition to which his protective tariffs would tend to reduce all the consumers of the United States. Exclude us from the English market, which, of our free option, we select as our most profitable mart—limit us to our home consumer, our neighbour by miles and inches—and as inevitably we become his slave, his property, his chattel. Our labour is no longer our own, as its produce is not our own; for that is not fully our own of which the legislation, whether of one or of many, fixes or in any way limits the sale. All protective tariffs are, therefore, under free governments, virtual robbery, inasmuch as they take from, or more or less limit, the right of the legally free man in disposing of his own property; and this, under a free government, none has the right to do—under a despotism, the law which legalizes the act gives the right.

Mr. Carey's perceptions seem to be somewhat obtuse upon this point. In pages 71, 72, and 73 of the volume we are reviewing, in order to prove that the policy of England is always the same towards her dependencies, he quotes first from "Gee on Trade," for the year 1750, and then from Lord Grey's despatch for just a century later.[19] In the first, with the avowed object of giving to Great Britain the entire rough produce of her dependencies, it

18. "They" in original.

19. Joshua Gee, *The Trade and Navigation of Great-Britain Considered* (1729 and later editions). Henry George Grey, third Earl Grey (1802–94), colonial secretary (1846–52).

is broadly stated that "manufactures in American colonies should be discouraged, prohibited [71]"; that

> to stop the progress of any such manufactures <manufacture>, it is proposed that no weaver have the liberty <no *weaver* have *liberty*> to set up [any] looms without first registering them at an office kept for that purpose, and the name and place of abode of any journeyman that shall work for him. But if any particular inhabitant <*particular inhabitant*> shall be inclined to have any linen or wool[l]en made of their own spinning, they should not be abridged of the same liberty that they now make use of, namely to have a weaver who shall be licensed <*licensed*> by the Governor, and have it wrought up for the use of the family, but *not to be sold to any person in a private manner,* [n]*or exposed to any market or fair, upon pain of forfeiture.*[20]

Here, as we argued above, is an absolute enslaving of the colonist. He who has not the right to dispose of his own labour becomes, consequently and necessarily, to a greater or less extent, in proportion to the check put upon him by a system of rule in which he takes no part, and to which he is not consenting, the serf or bondsman of the individual or government thus shackling and limiting his exchanges. Such was, as every schoolboy knows, the policy of England towards her dependencies (causing our separation from the mother country), and such to a greater or less degree it has since continued.

The more enlightened theories, of later days, have dictated a course of improvement, and accordingly we find Lord Grey, in 1850, arguing the necessity of withdrawing from the tariff duties of Canada such as were imposed simply in the view of protecting the interest of the manufacturer, and the propriety of limiting duties to the purpose of revenue. This, he most justly argues, is for the benefit of Canada, as leaving her population free to profit, as they naturally desire, by the producing power of their soil, instead of being forced by protective duties from the tillage of that soil to an unnaturally fostered system of manufactures. There is no limit or check of any kind proposed upon manufactures, as in 1750, but simply a removal of checks upon another branch of industry. The manufacturer is no longer shackled to give an unnatural extension to agriculture, and Lord Grey simply argues that the agriculturist shall, in his turn, equally be set free from the shackles of the manufacturer. Let neither be protected; let neither be forced; let both be free to profit by all advantages of clime and country. One would suppose that it would be difficult to confuse two systems, so entirely distinct as are

20. Carey, *Slave Trade,* p. 72 (LSM's italics) = Joshua Gee, *The Trade and Navigation of Great-Britain Considered,* 4th ed. (London, 1738; rpt. New York, 1969), p. 120.

these; and yet, because Lord Grey argues, as any free-trade man will willingly concede, and even maintain (for therein consist the *real harmonies* of political economy or, as Mr. Carey terms it, "Social Science"), that England, not less than her colonies, will profit by this repeal of duties; because she is willing to abandon the blind policy which drove us to revolution, and at last perceives that beautiful harmony of interests which renders the freedom and profit of her colonies at once her own freedom and her own profit; because in this wiser and juster course she finds, not penance and punishment for past faults, but reward for present well doing; because she sees this, and rejoices to find that, according with the old proverbs, "honesty is the best policy," and "virtue her own reward;" because she is not in sackcloth and ashes over the discovery but, on the contrary, congratulates herself upon having found the true road to profit, for which, a century back, she was blindly groping, Mr. Carey now declares her *policy to be unchanged*! "The phraseology is different, but the object is the same!"[21]

It is only a difference in *phraseology,* whether nature's rule or governmental tyranny regulates our exchanges! It is only a difference of *phraseology* whether a man carries his goods safely to a desired market, or whether in answer to a summons to stand and deliver he hands them over to the highwayman. Perhaps this *phraseological* idea will account for some of the wondrous inventions of modern anti-slavery writers. It is only a difference of phraseology, they may, peradventure, maintain, whether a man eats or starves; whether he is lashed to the bone, or greasy, fat, and comfortable! Only a difference of phraseology! All figure of speech! Words are wondrous things under the management of some logicians. We have heard of a precocious student who proved his puzzled father an ass. "An ass is an animal; you are an animal; *ergo,* you are an ass." Much in the same style, Mr. Carey proves the necessity of protective tariffs for the benefit of Southern agriculture. Heaven forefend that Southern agriculture should ever, like the patient old gentleman just referred to, submit to the ass's harness!

Mr. Carey, in his letters to the editor of *Putnam's Magazine* (August and September), says that his books fail to meet with circulation because they have too much originality of thought. His compeers in the study of political economy he treats, according to French phrase, in a very *haut en bas* style, and tramples over their insignificant labours with a most delightful and

21. "The phraseology of the two is different, but the object is the same—that of rendering it necessary to send all the raw products of the land to a market far distant, and thus depriving the farmer or planter of the power to return any portion of the loan made to him by the earth, and which she is always willing to renew, on the simple condition that, when the borrower has used it, he shall return to the lender the elements of which it had been composed" (72).

amusing self-satisfaction. After having tossed a sneer at "the confused and worthless systems of Wayland[22] and <or> Say" [229], he goes on to lash Mr. Mill, who, he remarks, "has no idea of any enlarged view of man and his actions, nor of the laws by which he and they are governed." Herein, he modestly states, consists "the difference between Mr. Mill and myself" [230]. Malthus, Ricardo, and McCulloch receive one contemptuous *knock down:* Mr. Carey cannot condescend to "regrind" them, and therefore he is not the fashion [231].[23] Of Guizot and De Toqueville,[24] he writes: "Why are they so eminent? Because, having no idea of principles, or laws, they do not offer them to the consideration of their readers. . . . Their readers are beguiled with the idea that they are being taught, but they end as they began—not [in] the least wiser—and *<and> hence it is that their <the> books have had so much success.*" [230]

Will our readers believe that the italics are Mr. Carey's own? Truly he should hug himself in the comparative obscurity of which he seems inclined to complain. He is altogether too wise for his day and generation. One great exception to the class of fools and pretenders of whom he so cavalierly disposes, he however acknowledges in the person of "one of the ablest of European economists, and [among the] most brilliant of French writers," by whom, he says, his own whole system, from beginning to end, has been "reproduced" [229]. Mr. Carey's ideas have travelled to Europe, are there "stolen" and sent back to us in this "rehash" (*vide* August number of *Putnam* [231]). Alas! for Bastiat! the talented! the brilliant! cut off in the prime of life; admired and lamented by thousands to whom his lucid and beautiful illustrations opened, as it were, a new daylight in the studies to which he devoted himself—must all his fame be limited to being an imitator, nay, worse, a literary pickpocket of Mr. Carey's *original* opinions? So says Mr. Carey, and acknowledges, therefore, in Bastiat more talent than in any of his

22. Francis Wayland (1796–1865), Baptist clergyman; president of Brown University (1827–55); among his numerous works, *The Elements of Political Economy* (1837 and later editions).

23. Thomas Robert Malthus (1766–1834), English economist; author of *An Essay on the Principle of Population* (1798; 2d ed. 1803) and *Principles of Political Economy* (1820). David Ricardo (1772–1823), English economist; member of Parliament (1819–23); wrote *Principles of Political Economy and Taxation* (1817). John Ramsay McCulloch (1789–1864), Scottish economist, editor, educator; adherent of Ricardo; author of *Discourse on the Rise, Progress, Peculiar Objects, and Importance of Political Economy* (1824).

24. Alexis-Charles-Henri Clérel de Tocqueville (1805–59), French politician; visited the United States in 1831–32; member of Constituent Assembly (1848) and Legislative Assembly (1849); minister of foreign affairs (1849); imprisoned briefly after the coup d'état of Louis-Napoléon in 1851; wrote *De la démocratie en Amérique* (1835, 1840) and, unfinished at his death, *L'Ancien régime et la révolution* (1856).

contemporaries. He had the talent to *steal,* and to *rehash*! One thing, however, a little puzzles us. In this stealing and rehashing, Mr. Bastiat, like some other thieves, must have mistaken the nature of the articles he was appropriating, and put them to a wrong use. Who that has read his beautiful *Sophismes économiques,* or his *Protectionisme et communisme,* can find any thing there in common with Mr. Carey's "protective tariffs"? "So soon," says Mr. Bastiat (*Protectionism and Communism,* p. 11),[25]

> as the tax, losing its fiscal character, undertakes to repulse a foreign produce, to the detriment, perhaps, of the revenue <au détriment du fisc lui-même>, in order to raise, artificially, the price of a similar national produce—thus committing an act of extortion against society, for the profit of a class—from that instant protection or, in other words, spoliation becomes manifest.

Again (ib. p[p]. 20 and 21):

> To call in the intervention of government, giving to it for object the regulating of profits and equalizing of fortunes, taking away from one individual without his consent, to give to another without compensation, entrusting it with the levelling of society, by means of spoliation—assuredly this is communism. Neither the forms employed by government to effect this end, nor the fine names bestowed upon it, make any difference. Whether this object be pursued by direct means or indirect, by restriction or by taxes, by tariffs or by "the rights of labour"; whether it be heralded under the plea of equality, solidarity, or fraternity, the nature of things is the same: the pillage of property is no less pillage because it is accomplished with regularity and order, systematically and by the action of law.

Again (ib. p[p]. 31[–32]):

> Property does not exist, if I cannot change <*échanger*> as well as consume <*consommer*> it; and permit me to add that the *right of exchange* is at least as precious, as important to society, and as characteristic of property, as the right of *giving* <le *droit de donner*>.

These certainly are not now Mr. Carey's grounds. Vainly we seek him. Here he is *non est inventus.*[26] Has Mr. Bastiat so altered his stolen goods as to make them entirely unrecognizable, or has Mr. Carey, with an unexampled

25. Frédéric Bastiat, *Protectionisme et communisme* (Paris, 1849).

26. Lit. "he has not been found" (Latin). *Non est inventus* signifies "the sheriff's return to process requiring him to arrest the body of the defendant, when the latter is not found within his jurisdiction" (*Black's Law Dictionary,* 5th ed. [St. Paul, 1979], p. 950).

liberality, abandoned his principles in favor of his talented imitator, generously consenting to adopt his own cast-off errors, that Mr. Bastiat may *appear* original? However this may be, certainly Mr. Carey can now claim little in common with the author of *Sophismes,* when he tells us, as he does (*Putnam,* August, 1853), speaking of his own recent work, *The Slave Trade, etc.,* that "*there is no book which throws so much light on the study of social science.*"[27] This volume, as we have already partly shown, and will still further show, aims, throughout, less at supporting a system of free-trade and liberal government than one of universal equality and what the author calls freedom, a system wherein it shall not be asked how, in varying situations, God may have suited man to his varying circumstances, or what capacities he may have given him for acting in those circumstances; but black man and white man, Celt and Saxon, man of every race and every capacity, in torrid and in frigid zone, is equally to be clinched down by the universal laws of Mr. Carey's universal system of "social science," and for this great object his *pouther,* i.e., a patent decoction of protective tariffs, is ready.

Is this communism? There is a strange squinting towards it. "Protection," says Mr. Bastiat, "in extending itself, becomes communism, just as certainly as the young carp grows to be an old one, if God only grants him a long enough life."[28]

The system which requires taxes and monopolies to check the action of nature—the system which aims at making certain men free by protective tariffs which unjustly tax the labour of other men—is but a shuffling of slavery from the shoulders of one to the other. Because *God* has not made all men *free,* i.e., as Mr. Carey uses the word, *equal* (for he classes alike the English labourer, the Irish emigrant, the United States' negro—in short, all who are suffering and oppressed, all who are in want or in bondage—under the name of slaves); because some always have been, and apparently must continue to be, "hewers of wood and drawers of water" to the more fortunate or the more highly gifted,[29] therefore, we must needs alter this God's

27. "Because I chose to call my book *The Slave-trade,* your reviewer would have your readers believe that its object had been little more than the determination of a question relative to the trade in cotton, woollens, and iron! I could not but ask myself if he had read the book. It seemed to me not, for if he had he certainly would have spared himself the trouble of recommending me to study social science. Read it yourself, and then tell me if you know any other that throws so much light on that science." (230)

28. "La protection <Le Protectionisme>, en se généralisant, devient Communisme, comme un carpillon devient carpe, pourvu que Dieu lui prête la vie <prête vie>" (*Protectionisme et communisme,* p. 4). [LSM]

29. "A brief examination of these propositions [of the Ricardo-Malthusian system] will satisfy the reader that they tend inevitably to the centralization of all power in the hands of the few at the cost of the many, who are thus reduced to the condition of slaves, mere hewers

world, to modify it into Mr. Carey's world. We must have protective tariffs to equalize men into what he calls freedom or, rather, into what is, as we have endeavoured to show, one universal bondage—only our masters are those certain individuals for whose benefit such taxes may chance to be imposed. The tariff of '42, which Mr. Carey so much lauds as causing the great prosperity of the United States, and by the repeal of which we are, according to him, rapidly sinking into barbarism, made us virtual bondsmen of the northern United States cotton manufacturer. That which he would now impose would, we are inclined to believe, from certain indications, aim at a coal and iron rule. At least the interests would play into each other's pockets; and, after the manner of the famed Roman triumvirate with their obnoxious citizens, our self-elected masters would consent to the decapitation of one public right after another, until we should be pretty well shorn of all that is worth preserving.[30]

In illustration of the blessings of the tariff of '42, Mr. Carey tells us that, previous to its enactment in the years '39, '40, and '41, "throughout the whole length and breadth of the land," i.e., the Northern States, "there was a <an> universal cry of 'Give me work; make your own terms—myself and family have nothing to eat,' and the consequence of this approach[31] toward slavery was so great a diminution in the consumption of food, that the prices at which it was exported to foreign countries were lower than they had been for many years; and thus it was [that] the farmer paid for the system which had diminished the freedom of the labourer and [the] artisan" (page 366). This was under the "strictly revenue provisions of the compromise tariff." "With cheap cotton and cheap food came so great a decline in the demand for labour, that thousands of men found themselves unable to purchase this cheap food to a sufficient extent to feed their wives and [their] children" (ib.). We suspect exaggeration in this statement of extreme distress; but the more literal it is, the more it proves the enormity of the system which caused it; and this system *was not* that of the strictly revenue tariff.

---

of wood and drawers of water for their masters" (397). Cf. Josh. 9:23: "Now therefore ye are cursed, and there shall none of you be freed from being bondmen, and hewers of wood and drawers of water for the house of my God."

30. After the assassination of Julius Caesar and the consequent confusion in public affairs, the leaders of the Caesarian faction—Caesar's great-nephew Octavian, Marcus Antonius, and Marcus Aemilius Lepidus—were eventually able to have themselves declared a triumvirate for the restoration of the Roman republic. They immediately instituted a proscription of their enemies (43 B.C.). The occasion is famously dramatized in act 4, scene 1, of Shakespeare's *Julius Caesar.*

31. Having *nothing to eat,* is an *approach* toward slavery! Slavery, then, fully developed, is what? Something a step further than nothing to eat. Wonderful creatures these slaves must be, to be able to exist on something less than nothing! [LSM]

Mr. Carey himself, warm admirer and advocate as he is of protective systems, cannot contend that letting people alone forces starvation upon them. A protective tariff may give, but the want of it cannot take away, except in so much as it withdraws what protection has given. Charity may require the almsgiver to give, but there is no robbery in withholding. These starving people were starving from want, Mr. Carey says, of protective duties; from want, that is to say, of charity. Their case certainly was a sad one. But whence this necessity, transforming a whole people into beggars? Whence this extreme need of protective duties? From the fact that they had been educated to them. Like the child in leading strings, they had never been left to their own resources, nor had learned to use them. A protective policy had induced, for years, false applications of industry which, when this protection was withdrawn, became, of course, valueless, and great distress ensued. We grant that here was injustice. These spoiled children of governmental protection, after being for years fondled, petted, and nourished, at the expense of their less favoured brethren, are suddenly turned loose and told to take care of themselves. As a matter of course they *cannot.* But whose was the injustice? Which system is responsible for their condition? Surely not that which says to them, "Take care of yourselves"; but that which has so enfeebled their physical, and bewildered their moral, powers, as to make them not only unable to take care of themselves, but even unable to perceive the absolute justice and indispensable necessity of their learning so to do. As the lounging exquisite who wrings his father's purse to supply his gambling necessities, and in fashionable drawl laments the impossibility of finding a decent maintenance because some diplomatic or other governmental post does not stand ready to pay him for doing nothing, would, instead of taking to the plough, cry "injustice" against the old gentleman as soon as his means for indulging his promising heir run short—so it is with these sturdy beggars. They do not ask *charity,* or we might more patiently listen to their demands. They have so long had their hands in our pockets, that they have ceased to distinguish between *meum* and *tuum,* and because they are hungered, bawl out as lustily for our loaf as does the spoiled baby for its brother's gingerbread. If Mr. Carey meant to teach us a lesson in charity, his argument should have been different; charity is sued for, not forced. If the farmer really suffered in common with the manufacturer, it could only have been in so far as he had profited from the bloated prosperity of the latter. We repeat it: ceasing to give is no robbery. Injudicious giving is mistaken charity; and the gift which is robbed from another is at once injustice to him who is despoiled and to him who receives the result of the spoliation. The one loses in that of which he is actually despoiled, and the other in the false habits of industry to which, by his unnatural gains, he is induced to turn his efforts.

Because suffering results from the withdrawal of an abuse, this is no reason for continuing the abuse. The wise patient will not shrink from the surgeon's knife. Amputation is preferable to disease, and a short penance better than a long sorrow.

Mr. Carey laments that for want of a protective tariff factories are closed, and the building of mills and furnaces has ceased. So be it. If the profits of factories, mills, and furnaces are not self-sufficient for their maintenance, it is full time that they should be closed. Their parasitical growth can bring nothing but extended loss, if not ruin, to the country upon whose sap they are allowed to fatten.

Again, he says: "Local places of exchange decline, and great cities take their place; and with the growth of centralization grows the slave trade, North and South. Palaces arise <rise> in New York and Philadelphia, while droves of black slaves are sent to Texas to raise cotton, and white ones at the North perish of disease, and sometimes almost of famine." (p. 368) One radical error in Mr. Carey's book is that he continually makes the mistake of assuming two or three States to be the whole country. It is quite possible that palaces may rise in New York and Philadelphia, to the detriment of smaller commercial marts; it is quite possible that their "white slaves" may perish of disease, and almost of famine, and none more than ourselves will sincerely lament these disastrous consequences of misplaced legislation: none sooner than ourselves will acknowledge that such may be, nay, to a certain extent, almost must be, the effect of such a system of legislation as this country has pursued. Those States which profited by the monopoly given by our protective system, naturally suffer from its cessation; but not, therefore, can this cessation be pronounced an evil. Because loss must fall upon the wrongdoer, and upon him who, whether knowingly or ignorantly, has profited by the wrong, not, therefore, can we pronounce its cessation a cause of lamentation; and Mr. Carey's mistake is in supposing that New York and Pennsylvania, or rather certain sections of New York and Pennsylvania, are the United States. We hear no cry of "give us work," in the Carolinas, in Georgia, Mississippi, Louisiana, or Texas; we hear of no slaves, whether white or black, "perishing of disease and almost of famine." If an occasional cotton factory be closed (and Mr. Carey is obliged to drag in, more than once, his demonstration of the "Saluda Manufacturing Company"), we make no complaint. The factory is abandoned because our labour is more profitable in the cotton crop. Nature says to us, raise cotton, and I will compensate your labour; spin it, and you will do it at a loss. Mr. Carey would, by a protective tariff, offer a *bonus* to the spinner, that he may compete with the agriculturist. He would force labour, as he cannot force nature. We ask nothing of the kind, but entreat to be saved from such protection. If our manufactures cannot support themselves without the *bonus,* it is the most convincing proof that we had best let manufacturing alone. The mill and the furnace which cannot work without protection, are better abandoned. When they are needed they will find strength to stand alone.

Mr. Carey gives sickening extracts from New York and Philadelphia papers, showing the extent of vice and misery pervading those cities. He holds up to us (p. 369) from the New York *Courier and Enquirer* "the hideous squalor and the deadly effluvia; the dim, undrained courts, oozing with pollution; the [dark] narrow stairways decayed with age, reeking with filth, and overrun with vermin; the rotten floors, ceilings begrimed, crumbling, ofttimes too low to permit you to stand upright, and windows stuffed with rags; . . . the gaunt shivering forms and wild ghastly faces in these black and beetling abodes, wherein from cellar to garret

> All life dies, death lives, and nature breeds,
> Perverse, all monstrous, all prodigious things,
> Abominable, unutterable![32]

He shows us (p. 370), from the Philadelphia *Evening Bulletin,* poor needlewomen living upon the "wages of sin," pawning their clothing for bread, and often "literally without a crust." All this is indeed fearful, and proves that these suffering wretches need charity, need perhaps municipal assistance—but certainly not governmental protection; their case is entirely beyond the sphere of such influence. Because New York and Philadelphia pay the price of their growing magnificence and, midst their palaces, teem with misery and destitution, must Georgia, Texas, and Carolina be taxed to relieve it?—that tax, withal, being so laid that, for every dollar dispensed in the cause of the wretched, hundreds, illegally taken from us, must first go to pile up the gains of their merchant princes. No cries for aid are heard from us. Our negroes, forsooth, are sometimes "sent to Texas to raise cotton." This seems, by Mr. Carey, to be considered the equivalent for *dying of disease, and almost of famine.* What a hell that Texas must be! And the poor negroes to be sent there to *raise cotton!* Fearful fate! And yet, after all, some of those shivering forms and wild, ghastly faces, pawning their clothing for bread, and sometimes literally without a crust, might be glad perchance of a not less comfortable refuge.

Mr. Carey may think that he has done enough to satisfy us by putting upon nearly the same level our system of negro slavery and the white slavery (so called) of other lands. We reject, however, such associations *in toto.* Starvation is not an *approach* towards slavery. The Southern slave is, in spite of Mrs.

32. John Milton, *Paradise Lost* 2.624–26, reading "inutterable."

Stowe, Mr. Carey, and the legion of assertions to the contrary, well clothed, well fed, well treated, in every way comfortable beyond the labouring class of any country, and, although not enjoying the luxuries of life, is as far from starvation as his master. It is, however, necessary to prove that we have our wretchedness too; and, for this purpose, from whom does Mr. Carey quote? He has very properly proved from New York and Philadelphia papers the respective misery of each of these towns. He has not needed, or sought to that effect, extracts from the New Orleans [*True*] *Delta,* the [New Orleans *Daily*] *Picayune,* or the Richmond *Enquirer.* But to prove the parallel in the case of Richmond, what authority does he find? A Richmond paper? No. The New York *Tribune:* a paper notorious North and South for its restless incendiarism, and one the most libellous of the South that the country furnishes [371]. For New Orleans, he crosses the ocean to quote, from a radical British reviewer, the slanders of Dr. Howe, a noted New England abolitionist, who, having prospered in the teaching of deaf and dumb children, and received, as he merited, his meed of praise therefore, forthwith thinks himself a great man and, according to the fashion of the day among little great men and *strong-minded* women, would try his hand at dabbling in *philanthropy* generally.[33] Such authorities are not worth combatting; indeed, cannot be combatted. False assertions cannot be argued against. If a man insists, as a fact in his experience, that the rainbow is black, what argument can be advanced to the contrary? We may talk of decomposed light, refracted rays, etc., etc. It does no good; he still swears that he saw it. You may call him fool and liar if it will comfort you, but that is the mere enjoyment of personal luxury, and in no degree advances your argument. Let a man swear the blackest falsehood in creation, he will always find fools and knaves to believe, or who pretend to believe, him. If Dr. Howe and the New York *Tribune* assert that Southern rainbows are always black, owing to some decomposition of negro exhalations, or some diabolical affinity to the negro's master, there is no use arguing to the contrary. Dr. Howe and the New York *Tribune*'s contributor saw it, and Mrs. Stowe and Mr. Carey will believe it, and *North British Reviews*, and teachers of "social science," if they have a twang of the world-reformer about them, will be sure to quote it.

We will presently return to Mr. Carey's opinions touching slavery, asking our reader's patience for a few words more upon the subject of his peculiar

33. Carey, *Slave Trade,* pp. 372–73, citing "American Slavery and *Uncle Tom's Cabin*" (reviewed by LSM in chap. 10, "British Philanthropy and American Slavery"), pp. 243–44. Samuel Gridley Howe (1801–76), born in Boston, abolitionist and educator; principal of the Perkins School for the Blind (1832–76); famous for his work with the deaf and blind Laura Bridgman.

system of *protective free-trade.* Adam Smith is the only political economist of whom he speaks with respect, and of the system of Adam Smith he declares himself the continuator. Let us see. He quotes from Adam Smith thus:

> An inland country, naturally fertile and easily cultivated, produces a great surplus of provisions beyond what is necessary for maintaining the cultivators; and on account of the expense of land carriage, and inconveniency of river navigation, it may frequently be difficult to send this surplus abroad.

Consequent abundance attracts workmen who

> give a new value to the surplus part of the rude produce, by saving the expense of carrying it to the waterside, or to some distant market. . . . The cultivators get a better price for their surplus produce, and can purchase cheaper other conveniences which they have occasion for. . . . As the fertility of the land has given birth to the manufacture, so the progress of the manufacture reacts upon the land, and increases still further its fertility. . . . Though neither the rude produce, nor even the coarse manufacture, could, without the greatest difficulty, support the expense of a considerable land carriage, the refined and improved manufacture easily may. . . . The corn which could with difficulty have been carried abroad in its own shape, is in this manner virtually exported in that of the complete manufacture, and may easily be sent to the remotest corner[s] of the world.[34]

Here are truths clearly announced, and to which we can see no possible exception—but how Mr. Carey can, from these, deduce his principles, it is hard to imagine. Dr. Smith has supposed a country producing a surplus of provisions, and, with a market of difficult access, goes on to show the natural course of circumstances in such a country. Mr. Carey, as a *parallel case,* takes a region: South Carolina, Texas, Alabama, or Louisiana, for instance, whose more profitable produce is not provisions, but cotton and sugar, and where the facilities of exportation are sufficiently great to enable the producer to export his cotton, at a much larger profit to himself, than he could make by raising provisions for the market. The proof of this is found in the fact that he, unhesitatingly, devotes himself to the cotton culture, limiting his provision crop to his own necessities—and following the suggestion of Dr. Smith, in putting sufficient labour upon his produce to suit it for exportation. As the farmer does not send his corn abroad in the bulk, but has it, first, transformed into flour, not deeming it necessary to finish the operation by baking it all into biscuit, so we do not send our cotton in the pod, nor our sugar in

34. Carey, *Slave Trade,* p. 50 (LSM omits Carey's italics) = Adam Smith, *An Inquiry into the Nature and Causes of the Wealth of Nations,* ed. W. B. Todd (Oxford, 1979), pp. 408–9.

the cane. They are both manufactured sufficiently to suit them to our means of transportation.[35] In such a country, Mr. Carey would *imitate* Dr. Smith, by *forcing* a provision crop, by *forcing* a further home manufacture, by *forcing* a home consumer, and then congratulates himself on his proposed exploits; as though a gardener who should devise a plan, by exterminating the produce of acres, to give, in their stead, a few sickly hot-house plants, should laud himself for his genius and usefulness in saving the labour of importing a bushel of oranges or a basket of pineapples. Will Mr. Carey allow nothing for difference of soil, and difference of natural produce? Will he, we have already asked, force cotton upon New England rocks, or in Pennsylvania iron mines, that we may raise turnips and cabbages in southern swamps? Must New York and New Jersey grow their own oranges and pineapples, that the West Indies may coax a scanty wheat crop from uncongenial soils? Shall China drink up all her tea, and yankee-land live upon its ice, its wooden nutmegs, and its "notions"?

There is, in Brazil, Lieut. Maury informs us,[36] the "ipecacuanha region," an immense plantation of three thousand square miles; its "crop is perennial and may be gathered the year round"—fifteen pounds may be collected, by a single hand, per day, and it is worth one dollar per pound, at Rio [de] Janeiro. But the transportation is tedious and expensive. Mules are the carriers, and one year is consumed in a single trip of the caravan. Now, to say nothing of the rhubarb, jalap, sarsaparilla, copaiva, nux-vomica, etc., etc., etc., of Paraguay,[37] for which delicacies it might be difficult to find a market of home consumers, we would beg Mr. Carey's friendly counsel for these poor Brazilians of the ipecacuanha region. What can be done for them? Transportation is difficult and distressingly tedious. Must their ipecacuanha crop be abolished to grow potatoes? Or will Mr. Carey devise, for them, a system of home consumption? As the loom and the spindle must come to our cotton fields, surely all ipecacuanha consumers might congregate in this three thousand square miles; cottages might be built, and an agreeable place of re-

35. Perhaps Mr. Carey does not know this fact. He has elsewhere spoken of "gathering sugar"; he may not know how much of the manufacture of cotton, also, is actually done by the planter. The ginning and preparation of the cotton-wool is, in fact, no insignificant portion of its manufacture. It should be a relief to Mr. Carey to know that the *poor negroes* are allowed some hand in the manufacture of their produce. [LSM]

36. Matthew Fontaine Maury, *The Amazon, and the Atlantic Slopes of South America: A Series of Letters Published in the "National Intelligencer" and "Union" Newspapers,* rev. ed. (Washington, D.C., 1853), pp. 19–20. Matthew Fontaine Maury (1806–73), born near Fredericksburg, Va.; naval officer and oceanographer; favored free trade with the Amazon basin; agent of the Confederate navy in England (1862–65); professor of meteorology at the Virginia Military Institute from 1868; wrote, among other works, *The Physical Geography of the Sea* (1855).

37. Maury, *The Amazon,* p. 14.

sort spring up. All that is received from the soil, Mr. Carey tells us, "must be regarded as a loan," and must be returned to the earth under penalty of losing her future favours [48]. This ipecacuanha produce would be a particularly convenient one in this respect, being always tolerably certain of being returned with interest. The idea of such a settlement is, we think, a brilliant one; and we shall hope, at no distant period, to hear of Mr. Carey's flourishing village of Ipecacuanaville, which his beautiful system of protective free-trade could, no doubt, soon establish. "The ship that goes to China," says Mr. Carey (p. 245),

> performs no more exchanges in a year than the canal-boat that trades from city to city performs in a month; and the little and inexpensive railroad car passing from village to village may perform almost twice as many as the fine packet-ship that has cost ninety or a hundred thousand dollars.

Still cheaper than canal boats or railroad cars, and still more numerous in its exchanges, would be, may we humbly suggest, the still smaller and more inexpensive wheelbarrow of Ipecacuanaville.

Mr. Carey quotes (p. 121) from certain travellers, with great admiration and approbation, accounts of a Turkish village ycleped Ambelakia. This said Ambelakia, being built on a mountain, had little intercourse with the surrounding world; but "the hearts of the Ambelakiots" were "pure and their faces serene;" and, in short, their village was a kind of "happy valley," perched on a mountain top, where every body, instead of making themselves happy, however, by lying under shady trees, looking at the stars, and moralizing, enjoyed the felicity of living in factories, men, women and children, "like swarms of bees in their hives." The population was four thousand; there were twenty-four factories, and they manufactured "yearly two thousand five hundred bales of cotton yarn, of two <one> hundred cotton okes each." The yarn being sold in Germany, this village thus gave "birth to an *immense commerce* which united Germany and Greece by a thousand threads" [121; LSM's italics]. Alas for these pure-hearted and serene-faced Ambelakiots!—Mr. Carey seems to speak of their system as perfect, but he therein forgets his own system of home-producer and home-consumer—why did they not grow their own cotton on their own rocks? and why go to sell it, when manufactured, to Germany, instead of wearing it out on the happy shoulders which bore their own serene faces? Alas for the Ambelakiots! when in their height of prosperity, England, the ogre England, "invented new machinery for spinning cotton" [122]—actually had the audacity to invent new machinery! This atrocious act was the ruin of Ambelakia. She was "outstripped by Manchester" [122]. The *immense commerce* in cotton yarn kept up by her four thousand inhabitants, dwindled away. Oh! wicked Manchester, shall not the judgment of Sodom and Gomorrah be upon thee for using those mischievous machines, that thou might'st in such base manner undersell the hard-working and serene-faced Ambelakiots! Such are the sins of England. To her system it is due that such "local places [of exchange] no longer exist" [124]. Mr. Carey does not cite for our imitation the little (as it were) toy republic of San Marino. Why not? With its single mountain road, and all other communication with the stranger strictly forbidden by law, we should have supposed it a beautiful model. However, Ipecacuanaville shall outstrip all. Its inhabitants shall be wiser than the Ambelakiots. They must produce and consume at home, and thus be secure from the rivalry of all monster machinery. *Qu[a]ere:*[38] Whether they will be *serene-faced.*

Diogenes broke his cup when he saw from example that the simpler hollow of the hand could replace it.[39] Mr. Carey's system leads the same way: for allow the principle of a check upon foreign importation, in favor of home consumption, as preferable on account of vicinage, or even rapidity of exchange, and at what point shall its simplifying effects be arrested? Mr. Carey would check foreign exchanges in favour of home exchanges. What is home? The civilized world? Our country? Our State? Our district? Our village? Our house? Our chamber? Where is the limit? Exclude or limit European to encourage American produce; and on the same principle the South, bringing home the loom and the spindle, must exclude or limit Northern, to encourage Southern, produce. Each State must exclude or limit the produce of its sister State; each village, each house, should, in turn, limit as much as possible its exchanges, and at last we would find the system perfected only when each individual Diogenes should, like a surly cur, coil himself in his own tub, and bask in his own sunshine. Then might Mr. Carey, as we before suggested, find it convenient to turn his pavement into a potato-patch, and grub roots instead of writing books.

But to return to Adam Smith. "According to the natural course of things," he says,

> the greater part of the capital of every growing society is, first, directed to agriculture, afterward to manufactures, and last of all to foreign commerce. . . . Without the assistance of some artificers, [indeed,] the cultivation of land cannot be carried on but with great inconveniency and continual interruption. Smiths, carpenters, wheelwrights and ploughwrights, masons and bricklayers, tanners, shoemakers, and tailors, are people whose services the farmer has frequent occasion for. Such artificers, too, stand occasionally in need of the assistance of one another; and, as their residence is not, like [that of] the farmers <farmer>, necessarily tied down to a precise spot, they natu-

38. "Query" (Latin).

39. Diogenes of Sinope (d. c. 320 B.C.), Cynic philosopher; famed for the austerity and simplicity of his life.

> rally settle in the neighborhood of one another, and thus form a small town or village. . . . Had human institutions[, therefore,] never disturbed the natural course of things, the progressive wealth and increase of the towns would, in every political society, be consequential, and in proportion to the improvement and cultivation of the territory and <or> country.[40]

All this is very plain English, but it would appear that, like the initials upon Monkbarns' relic, it will bear two interpretations. "Aiken Drum's Lang Ladle" becomes in Latin *Agricola Dicavit Libens Lubens.*[41] So Dr. Smith's *natural course of things* is substituted by Mr. Carey's *protective tariffs.* Dr. Smith's artificers, etc., *naturally settle,* but Mr. Carey's must be frightened and coaxed into it, by taxes and bribes; where nature does not *call,* protective tariffs must *drive* them. Strange that the simple meaning of such plain language can receive such opposite interpretations. "Had human institutions never disturbed the natural course of things, the progressive wealth and increase of the towns would, in every political society, be consequential, and in proportion to the improvement and cultivation of the territory or country." So says Dr. Smith, and unhesitatingly we give our assent to this proposition. But as Mr. Carey quotes it as confirmatory of his system, seeming to imply that something is out of order in the natural course of things, with which *human institutions* must not interfere, but which his protective tariffs can remedy, he would appear to consider protective tariffs as no human institutions. He should have enlightened us as to their origin. Are they perhaps included among the famous Mormon revelations, or has chancellor Bacon *impressed* them upon his intimate friends Judge Edmonds and Dr. Dexter?[42]

We have our artificers, masons, bricklayers, ploughwrights, and others,

40. Carey, *Slave Trade,* pp. 63–64 = Smith, *Wealth of Nations,* pp. 380, 378.

41. In chapter 4 of Sir Walter Scott's 1816 novel *The Antiquary* (ed. Andrew Lang, 2 vols. [Boston, 1893], 1:40–44), Jonathan Oldbuck, laird of Monkbarns and the antiquary of the title, claims to have found the site of "the final conflict between [Gaius Julius] Agricola and the Caledonians"—it is described by Tacitus (*Agricola* 29–38)—from which site he has excavated a stone insculpted with "a sacrificing vessel and the letters A. D. L. L., which may stand, without much violence, for *Agricola Dicavit Libens Lubens*" (trans. "Agricola has dedicated [this] gladly and with pleasure"). But a beggar exposes the truth: twenty years before he and some friends had made the inscription to mock Aiken Drum at his wedding, the ladle alluding to his love of broth.

42. Joseph Smith (1805–44), founder of the Church of Jesus Christ of Latter-day Saints, reported that in 1820 he was visited by God and Jesus Christ and that in 1827 an angel bestowed upon him a text which, with divine help, he translated; it was published as *The Book of Mormon* (1830). John Worth Edmonds (1799–1874), a judge of the New York Supreme Court, and George T. Dexter announced a series of communications made to them, through both direct conversation and spirit writing, from a number of the illustrious dead, Francis Bacon prominent among them; they published these communications, with commentary, in their book *Spiritualism* (1853).

as many as *naturally* belong to us, and as many as suit our interests. There has never been any kind of legislation to check their increase, and we desire none to push it. We have no wish to have their progress stimulated whether by supernatural or other protective tariffs.

Dr. Smith objects to the system of England, in his time, as discouraging home trade, and prohibiting manufactures among her colonists. "*To prohibit a great people[, however,] from making all [that] they can of every part of their [own] produce, or from employing their stock and industry in a <the> way that they judge most advantageous to themselves, is a manifest violation of the [most] sacred rights of mankind.*"[43] Are we dreaming? Is this Hebrew, Sanscrit, or simple English? Mr. Carey quotes it as though favoring his side of the question. What more do we ask than that *we may employ our stock and industry in the way that we judge most advantageous to ourselves*? And what does Mr. Carey ask, but that we shall, by protective tariffs, be *forced* from such employment, to one which *we* deem less profitable, but which *he* deems more suitable? It is he who now proposes to prohibit a great people from making all they can of their produce in their own way, by *a manifest violation of the sacred rights of mankind*. It is he who tells us, you shall cease to grow cotton to an unlimited extent; you must let your plough rest to bring the loom and the spindle near, and among your cotton-fields. It is not we, but he, who complains of "strictly revenue tariffs," and calls for protective, i.e., prohibitory ones.

Our space cannot permit us to follow Mr. Carey's extracts through half a volume; but, at every turn, we find him quoting Dr. Smith, as opposing England's right to tax, and her policy in taxing, whether subjects, nations, or her own people, for the protection of her manufactures; and then, by a strange summerset in argument, endeavouring to show that other countries *ought* to tax their own people (exactly the course that Dr. Smith reprehends in England) to protect their own manufactures.

Archimedes said that, give him a fulcrum, and he could move the world; but he never attempted to imagine a fulcrum. Mr. Carey is bolder; he has imagined a fulcrum. He turns every thing upon the supposed fact, that England has a coercive power over the commerce of all other nations. Because we find the market of England an advantageous one for our cotton and sugar, he assumes the singular ground that England forces our sales, prohibits our manufactures, and that we are her virtual colonists. England

> has sought to restrict her subjects and the people of the world in their modes of enjoyment <employment>; and this she has done with a view to compel them to make [all] their exchanges in her single market, leaving to her to fix

43. Carey, *Slave Trade*, p. 66 (LSM's italics) = Smith, *Wealth of Nations*, p. 582.

the prices of all she bought and all she sold, thus taxing them at her discretion in both time and money. (page[s] 210–11)

This State [Virginia] is not *permitted* to do any thing but grow wheat and tobacco. (page 110 [LSM's interpolation and italics])

Protection looks only to resisting a great scheme of foreign taxation. (page 392)

By what magic might this crushing and absolute power is established and maintained by England, Mr. Carey does not attempt to exhibit. He assumes it as existent; he imagines his fulcrum, and forthwith behold our political Archimedes making a bold attempt to set his machinery in motion. This is alarming. His fulcrum in the air is, fortunately, rather an unsteady concern, or he might chance to exterminate us just as that wicked Manchester did the serene-faced Ambelakiots.

Before leaving, entirely, the subject of Adam Smith, whose acknowledged penetration and sagacity few, we believe, are disposed to dispute, we cannot but express our astonishment at his far-sightedness, as announced by Mr. Carey: "He saw clearly that the man and the easily transported spindle should go to the food and the cotton, and that, when once there, they were there for ever; whereas the bulky food and cotton might be transported to the man and the spindle for a thousand years, and that the necessity for transportation in the thousand and first would be as great as it had been in the first; and that the more transportation was needed, the less food and cloth would fall to the share of both producer and consumer." [249] Now, if Dr. Smith knew anything about cotton—cotton as the staple produce of half a continent—cotton as (what it indeed is) the great basis of the world's commerce and civilizer of nations—he must have seen it in prophetic vision. Dr. Smith wrote before our revolution, when not a bag of cotton was grown in America,[44] when the scanty produce of the East was manufactured by a laborious process, long since discarded. Of the spindle and the loom, with which Mr. Carey insists upon gagging us, of the railroad and the steamboat which so facilitate our exchanges, he equally knew nothing.

No vision of the future, only the solid reason which looked out upon his present, and taught him to read, in the transgressions of his nation, their own certain punishment, inspired the noble lesson which he taught, that "*to prohibit a great nation <people>[, however,] from making all [that] they can of every part of their [own] produce, or from employing their stock and industry in a <the> way that they judge most advantageous to themselves, is a manifest violation*

44. As late as the year 1784, an American vessel that carried eight bags to Liverpool was seized on the ground that so much cotton could not be produced in the United States. [LSM]

of the [most] sacred rights of mankind."[45] England might better have listened to his teachings; and the cry of downtrodden nations needed not then to have been raised against her. Heavy are the sins of England, and we defend her not; but we cannot, with Mr. Carey, acknowledge ourselves among her trampled colonists, and we greet, with pleasure, the dawning of a better system, in her efforts to liberate the commerce of her dependencies. Great are the faults, but glorious the virtues, of the Saxon race. Missionaries of progress, their faults, even, have combined with their virtues to scatter civilization over our globe. Infamously rapacious as she has sometimes proved herself; tyrannical as has been her Indian rule, and unjust her aggressions; foul as are the dark transactions of the opium-trade, still England is the pioneer of progress, and the world which acknowledges her greatness sees in us her noblest offset, but not her subject nation. Inheriting alike her vices and her virtues, the United States may learn from her many an example, both to shun and to imitate. We, for one, are not anxious to place ourselves among her revilers. From English interference, there is, to us, but one point of serious danger; and, if true to ourselves, we have, even there, nothing to fear. The fashion of the day is a crusade against negro slavery; and in this a portion (we believe it but a portion) of the English nation is inclined, not only to join, but to become mischievously active. Had we no traitors in our own camp, we might laugh at their impudent assumption and captious intermeddling; but, when every day brings us damning proof that the enemy has his spies and his coadjutors thick among our ranks; when men like Mr. Carey condescend to place themselves in the ranks with Mrs. Stowe, Lucretia Mott, Gerritt Smith, and all the other old women, breeched and unbreeched, who go into hysterics of agony over the evils of a system of which they know absolutely and literally nothing; then, indeed, we begin to spy English influence, and then we see cause to fear that, what such unaided influence could never effect, home fanaticism may find means to accomplish. Our security from English machinations is to be found principally in that very freedom of exchange which Mr. Carey would destroy. So far as our produce is necessary to her, so far have we some security from her intermeddling with our institutions. If reports be true, with regard to her interference with Cuban legislation, it proves that this security is less strong than we had anticipated. England is emboldened, by our own home cowardice and home treachery, to aim this blow at an institution vitally necessary to our national existence; and, even now, while her doubtful course hangs quivering in the scale, the angel of peace holds out to her the sole and the strongest possible argument to arrest her foolhardy progress, pointing to her ships laden with

45. Carey, *Slave Trade,* p. 66 (LSM's italics) = Smith, *Wealth of Nations,* p. 582.

the growth of our fields—to her factories, rich in the produce of our agriculture—and to her people, whose daily bread is the result of her commerce with us. Subjects of England we neither are, nor are we destined to become; but victims of home fanaticism, stimulated by English cant, we may yet be; and darkly fearful is the fate which such a crisis holds before us. Mr. Carey has, more perhaps than he is conscious of, played into the hands of the babbling crew whose petty mischief and party spite menace such fearful consequences. Very sure we are that he would not join the cry of immediate emancipation. Indeed, he argues to prove the injurious effect of the precipitate course of England towards Jamaica; but in the same breath he is casting his effort toward a worse result among us. *Noli me tangere* is the only security, and should be the motto of the South, in regard to her slave institutions.[46] He whose mock charity cants of the hard necessity which forces us to maintain a system of iniquity to whose abuses we are submissive, but not blind, only attacks us more insidiously, and insults us more grossly, than the noisiest reviler.

With his allies of the New York *Tribune,* and others of similar stamp, Mr. Carey joins in glorifying Russia, by way of contrast to English institutions. "Who," he asks (p. 380 [LSM's italics]), "are our natural allies? Russia, Prussia, and Denmark are despotisms, we are told. *They are so;* but yet so beautiful and so perfect is the harmony of interests under a *natural system,* that that which despots do in their own defence strengthens the people, and carries them on toward freedom." What does this mean if not that despotism is Mr. Carey's natural system for developing his beautiful harmony of interests? This, as our readers know, we have stated frequently, but scarcely expected himself to acknowledge it. Of the Czar he says: "He is a despot, it is true, but he is doing what is required to give freedom to sixty millions of people. . . . We are told of his designs upon Turkey—but what have the people <*people*> of that country to lose by incorporation with[in] the Russian Empire?" [380–81] We cannot exactly define the minutiae of their loss, but as "the *people of that country*" seem to have a very strong antipathy to the transfer, we can only say that it seems an odd way of making freemen to whip them into it. Quite consistent, however, is such a process of liberation with Mr. Carey's *protective free-trade system.* Only call a "protective tariff" an "imperial ukase" (the terms are perfectly synonymous), and Mr. Carey makes as good a despot as Czar Nicholas himself, developing the "*harmony of interests*" in his "*natural system.*"

It is the nature of prejudice to seize crude arguments, or unargued decisions, in favour of foregone conclusions. Mr. Carey, ardent admirer as he is

46. John 20:17: "Jesus saith unto her, Touch me not."

of the free government of Czar Nicholas, never allows himself for one instant to doubt that negro slavery, as existent in the Southern United States, is an evil—an evil, sooner or later, by fair means or foul, to be *remedied.* And to this effect every officious intermeddler, every incendiary publication, is to be listened to and encouraged. "It is right and proper," he says, "to give due weight to all opinions in regard to the existence of an evil, and to all recommendations in regard to the mode of removal, let them come from what source they may" (p. 33).

The extreme communists (there are communists of every grade; our author himself we consider as being on the lower round of the ladder) will think it an evil that Mr. Carey should have a comfortable house appropriated to the use of his wife and children. "You have *no right,*" will such a one say, "to wife and children. Families belong to the State. The interests of society require a community of rights. Herein lies *the true and only road to freedom of trade, and freedom of man.* This isolation of families is an evil which we must get rid of. Here are many suggestions for remedying this evil; some of them a little ultra, perhaps, but *it is right and proper to give due weight to all opinions in regard to the existence of an evil, and to all recommendations in regard to the mode of removal, let them come from whatever source they may.*" And, forthwith, behold Mr. Carey's house invaded by a host of reformers, black, brown, and white; men and women; Bloomers and broomers. Would it be surprising should the proprietor of the invaded mansion lose patience, and send them all to the *devil,* by pistol, blunderbuss, or any other easiest mode of extermination? We are more patient. Our dwellings are invaded; our rights disputed; our property and lives imperilled; and yet, our would-be reformers are surprised that we cannot always argue coolly. They are surprised that we are sensitive to their abuse. Mr. Carey, no doubt, will be astonished that he is not considered as a philosophically charitable defender of the slaveholder. He has even taken up our cause against the advocates of immediate emancipation. He tells us that, in Jamaica, "the landowner has been ruined and the labourer is fast relapsing into barbarism; and yet in the face <in face> of this fact the landowners of our <the> Southern States are branded throughout the world as 'tyrants' and 'slave-breeders,' because they will not follow in the same direction. It is in face of this great fact that the people of the North are invited to join in a crusade against their brethren of the South, because they still continue to hold slaves, and that the men of the South themselves are <are themselves> so frequently urged to consent <assent> to immediate and unconditional emancipation." (p[p]. [34–]35) He acknowledges that "unenlightened enthusiasm has often [before] led almost to crime, and it remains to be seen if the impartial historian will not, at a future day, say that such has been here the case" (p. 94). He not only acknowledges, but urges, the fact that "it would be unfair to attribute to him [the Jamaica planter] the extraordinary waste of life resulting necessarily from the fact that the whole people were limited to the labours of the field [83; LSM's interpolation]."[47] "Master of slaves, he was himself a slave to those by whom the labours of himself and his workmen were directed" (p. 83). "He was a mere instrument in their hands for the destruction of negro morals, intellect, and life; and upon them, [and] not upon him, must rest the responsibility, etc." (p. 86). Speaking of the State policy of Virginia, which he considers objectionable, he asks : "Upon whom[, now,] must rest the responsibility of <for> such a state of things as is here exhibited? Upon the planter? *He exercises no volition*. . . . He is *compelled* to conform his operations to the policy which looks to having but one workshop for the world." (pp. 115–16 [LSM's italics])

Is Mr. Carey surprised when we tell him that these Judas kisses in no way assuage our wrath at his interference? The communist, who is trying to oust him of his family and house, will give him abundance of similar cant. "Dear brother, you are not responsible for this iniquity. Faulty governmental institutions have misled you. Your errors are those of circumstance, not character. We do not hold you responsible; you have been gulled and misled. We do not blame so much as pity you, and will turn our best efforts to the correction of these evils." Again we ask whether, if these intruders will not submit to being quietly kicked out, Mr. Carey will not cry aloud for constables and revolvers, for laws and bludgeons, to eject his self-instituted preceptors. This cant of charity is the fashionable style of the "uppertendom" of abolitionism. It is quite in taste to exhibit pity for the poor, deluded, shackled slaveholder, "the master of slaves," who, as Mr. Carey says (p. 383), "whether wearing a crown or carrying a whip, is himself a slave." Just so talks Mrs. Stowe; and just so talk the most obnoxious of her coadjutors. Mrs. Stowe's charity is religious; Mr. Carey's is philosophical; both are of one school. Off, we say, with this humbug cant! this sugared venom! We defend our system, and he who attacks it attacks us. We are no tools in the hands of any men; no infants in law, to lay our sins on other men's consciences. We know what we do, and do it deliberately, exercising as full a power of *volition* as Mr. Carey, or any other individual in the land. We prefer to meet Mr. Carey with his bolder sneer, upholding the falsehoods of Mrs. Stowe and Dr. Howe, and talking of our Southern negroes as likely to be found among the *dramatis personae* of the horrible scenes invented by the one and the other.

47. This *necessary result* of Mr. Carey is strangely disproved by our census returns, which prove a rapid increase among the negro slaves limited to the labours of the field. [LSM]

"Our people," he says (p. 304), "are becoming from day to day more satisfied that it is 'for their advantage' that the negro shall 'wear his chains in peace,' even although it may cause the separation of husbands and wives, parents and children, and although they know that, in default of other employment, women and children are obliged to employ their labour in the culture of rice among the swamps of Carolina, or in that of sugar among the richest and most unhealthy lands of Texas. This will have one advantage. It will lessen the danger of over-population." Mr. Carey has, we have already remarked, started with the foregone conclusion that *slavery is an evil*. This ground he does not attempt to prove, but dashes onward, seizing, without attempting to weigh them, every authority which appears to prop his argument. The housebuilder will examine his materials before he sets to work, and if his bricks are ill-baked, or his planks flawed and cracked, he will reject them. Not so, Mr. Carey. If his bricks will only stand on top of each other, he does not examine their quality, and, accordingly, his building cannot but crumble to destruction. If he had consulted the ordinary statistical information within the reach of everybody, he would have learned that women and children in the swamps of Carolina, and sugar lands of Texas, do not die out so as to "lessen the danger of over-population." The negro constitution resists malaria to an extent which makes the black man thrive where the white dies; and no class of population in our country increases faster than that of the negro slave. One of the most remarkable instances of exemption from deaths which we have ever known in any population, was on a rice swamp plantation of South Carolina, where, among upwards of two hundred negroes, there was one death in the course of three years. This was undoubtedly a singular instance, but by no means so singular as Mr. Carey's foregone conclusion would lead him to suppose.

"The consumption of cotton," says Mr. C. (p. 252), "on the plantation is very small indeed, because, before being consumed, it has to be dragged through long and muddy roads to the landing, thence carried to New Orleans, thence to Liverpool, [and] thence to Manchester," etc., etc., and hence he argues for loom and spindle and so forth. Here is another of Mr. Carey's bad bricks, which will crumble rapidly. He might as well tell us that the consumption of rain-water upon our earth is very small indeed, because, before being consumed, it has to be drawn up, for miles, by the heat of the sun's rays, to reach the cloud region; then it is wafted about, for leagues and leagues, with great loss of time and labour to the winds, etc.—and then wind up by advising us to get up some great bellows and furnace process, to bring the easily conveyed heat and winds home to the water, and encourage home consumption. In all civility and kindness, we would suggest to Mr. Carey that, as he evidently knows quite as little about our cotton plantations as he does about the cloud regions, he had better leave the management of both to nature, and the Almighty God. Who told him that the plantation consumption of cotton is "very small indeed"? We have been, for the greater portion of our life, resident of a cotton plantation, and, being in the habit of assisting and superintending the distribution of supplies, speak knowingly and experimentally of such. Upon the plantation to which we refer, which is no remarkable instance, but one of many taken from the lower country of South Carolina, our grown negroes, men and women, receive an average, per head, of from eleven to twelve yards of heavy cotton Osnaburghs. Their winter (woollen) cloth, of which they receive, per head, from eight to nine yards, is generally from yankee mills, and our northern friends know better than we how much cotton such goods contain. Avowedly, all the warp is generally cotton. With their blankets, men's hats and caps, and other woollen articles, it is very certain that they get their portion of cotton too. Besides this, the women receive their cotton head kerchiefs, and, moreover, men and women always purchase for themselves, with the proceeds of their chickens, eggs, corn crops, etc., sundry little extras, such as additional shirts, calico and homespun gowns, stockings, cotton-flannel undershirts, bed-quilts, sheets and other cotton articles, besides having the liberty to use what cotton they desire in home-spinning, from which they occasionally, though, we must confess, not often (they apparently approve as little as their masters of home manufacture), knit a pair of gloves, stockings, or other similar luxury. We do not wish to exaggerate, and would not be understood to say that every individual purchases *all* the articles above enumerated; but these are all purchased frequently and habitually, by one and another; and we do not hesitate to say that the average consumption of the grown negro (children in proportion) equals twenty yards per head, of woven cotton, besides the portion of cotton mixed with their woollen goods, which our New England purveyors will, we presume, answer for us is not small. In this calculation, be it remembered, we speak only of the personal uses of the negro, whose position answers to that of the lowest labouring classes of other countries. We make no calculation for the larger use of the whites, nor for the considerable quantities consumed in bedding and, also, for plantation purposes, in the form of cotton-picking sheets, corn sacks, etc. This simple statement of facts Mr. Carey, probably, will never take the trouble to read or, reading, will choose to disbelieve (because it is published not in the New York *Tribune,* or *North British Review,* but in a southern periodical, in a land where folks know nothing about their own affairs); and when the subject happens to be again touched upon, he will repeat the old humbug that "the cotton consumption of plantations is very small indeed," because, etc., etc. His concatenation of reasoning proves to his own satisfaction that "it must be very small," and so, right or wrong, he states that "it is very small"; and the *great political economist* who sides with the fashionable mania of the day will, of course, be quoted; and the tiny voice of truth will remonstrate in vain; and so it becomes a fixed fact, on the *highest American authority,* that our slaves are not allowed to wear the cotton which they raise; and it will need only a stroke or two of imagination, from some travelling Mr. Thompson, or Mrs. Stowe, or Miss Bremer,[48] to convince the world that they go for the most part naked, hiding themselves, of cold nights, in manure heaps, or among cotton seeds, by way of shelter from the pitiless winds. Thus theory makes its facts, and, on these manufactured facts, again, theory builds; and so, like a child's card house, on and on is raised the shaking edifice; and lo! comes the builder to vaunt its symmetry to the world, and fools gape and wonder, and lean upon its fancied strength, and the crowd huzzas; and then, alas! comes the crash, and nations perish because men will not be in earnest to think and believe for themselves, but follow the lead of ambitious book-writers, and penny-a-line scribblers!

It is a remark, we believe, of Locke, that many of our differences in argument proceed from a misunderstanding, or a different understanding, of terms; and that often, on a fair examination of words, differences will disappear.[49] There may be something of this in the question between Mr. Carey and ourselves. *What is slavery?* Does slavery necessarily imply oppression on the part of the master, and suffering on the part of the slave? Is all oppression slavery, and *vice versa*? In other words, are *slavery* and *oppression* synonymous terms? In Mr. Carey's vocabulary, evidently, they are. In the opening sentence of the volume, which we are reviewing, he says:

> Slavery still exists throughout a large portion of what we are accustomed to regard as the civilized world. In some countries, men are forced to take

48. George Thompson (1804–78), English reformer and member of Parliament; his visit to the United States (1834–35), at the invitation of William Lloyd Garrison, was widely censured for malicious interference in American affairs, his *Letters and Addresses* made during the visit being published in 1837; a second visit took place in 1851; his *Lectures on British India,* with a preface by Garrison (Pawtucket, R.I., 1840; rpt. London, 1842), was cited by Carey and as such is mentioned below by LSM. Fredrika Bremer (1801–65), Swedish traveler and novelist; visited the United States, including South Carolina, in 1849–51; her account of this visit was translated as *The Homes of the New World: Impressions of America,* 2 vols. (New York, 1853).

49. The "ill use of words" is often addressed by John Locke in his *Essay concerning Human Understanding,* especially in book 3, chaps. 9 to 11, and book 4, chap. 3, sect. 30. For example: "If we consider, in the fallacies men put upon themselves, as well as others, and the mistakes in men's disputes and notions, how great a part is owing to words, and their uncertain or mistaken significations, we shall have reason to think this no small obstacle in the way

> the chance of a lottery for the determination of the question whether they shall or shall not be transported to distant and unhealthy countries, there most probably to perish, leaving behind them impoverished mothers and sisters to lament their fate. In others, they are seized on the highways <highway> and sent to sea for long term[s] of years, while parents, wives, and sisters, who had been dependent on their exertions, are left to perish of starvation, or driven to vice or crime to procure the means of support. In a third class, men, their wives, and children, are driven from their homes to perish on <in> the road, or to endure the slavery of dependence on public charity until pestilence shall send them to their graves, and thus clear the way for a fresh supply of others like themselves. In a fourth, we see men driven to selling themselves for long periods at hard labor in distant countries, deprived of the society of parents, relatives, or friends. In a fifth, men, women, and children are exposed to sale, and wives [are] separated from their husbands <from husbands>, while children are separated from parents. In some, white men, and in others, black men, are subjected to the lash, and to other of the severest and most degrading punishments. In some places men are deemed valuable, and they are well fed and clothed. In others, man is regarded as "a drug," and population as "a nuisance"; and Christian men are warned that their duty to God and to society requires that they should permit their fellow-creatures to suffer every privation and distress, short of "absolute death," with a view to prevent the increase of numbers.
>
> Among *these various classes of slaves,* none have recently attracted so much attention as those of the negro race. [5–6; LSM's italics]

Here we find classed, as "various classes of slaves," all who are suffering from poverty, all who are suffering from oppression, whether legal or illegal, whether accidental or incidental to their position in life. *All oppressed persons are slaves,* is the position assumed. And then to prove the converse of this position is easy, by precisely the same logical formula which we quoted earlier in our argument. For, "an ass is an animal; you are an animal; therefore, you are an ass," we have, "an oppressed person is a slave; the negro is a slave; therefore, the *negro is an oppressed person.*" Having fairly settled this point to their satisfaction, our antagonist[s] (for Mr. Carey is but one of many, the representative of a class) assume farther that, as the negro is an avowed slave, whereas the other is only proved so by the amount of oppression endured,

to knowledge; . . . I am apt to imagine, that, were the imperfections of language, as the instrument of knowledge, more thoroughly weighed, a great many of the controversies that make such a noise in the world, would of themselves cease; and the way to knowledge, and perhaps peace too, lie a great deal opener than it does" (3.9.21).

the negro, of course, suffers the greater weight of oppression, and thence they talk of *starvation as an approach towards slavery*!

Now, we demur from this given signification of the term in question. What is slavery? We answer: *involuntary legal subjection* of any individual to another. This condition does *not* imply oppression on the part of the ruler, nor suffering on that of the ruled, or slave. The fearful suffering so vividly depicted by Mr. Carey, as existing among many classes of England, our own Northern States, and elsewhere, does not prove that these suffering individuals are any more slaves than their more fortunate fellow-citizens, except so far as *legal* differences may exist, as in the case of the noble and commoner of England, or those classes subjected to religious disabilities, etc. The mere suffering, the wretchedness, to whatever height it may reach, is not, nor does it indicate, bondage. Where all are subject to one code of laws, all are equally free or equally slaves, though one may be starving for a crust of bread, while the other rolls in wealth. The richest Wall Street merchant is no less a slave (if either be so) than the starving inhabitant of the dirtiest cellar of New York's murkiest street. Both are subject to the same legal abilities and disabilities; either might, without any change of rule, by a mere accidental alteration of circumstances, take the place of the other. Misfortune, or imprudence, has placed the one individual in a position to suffer from the action of certain institutions (whether faulty or only imperfect, it is not here the place to examine), from which the better fortune, or better judgment, of the other has exempted him. But, both being under the same rule, subjected to the same legal restraints, and enjoying the same legal privileges, if one is a slave so is the other. Illegal oppression is, we repeat, not slavery. Slavery is a legal institution which may be oppressive, but is by no means necessarily so. *Perfect slavery* implies authority without appeal, in the one individual, and subjection, without right of resistance, in the other. The perfect slave can only resist by rebellion, and the infliction of death upon him can never be a legal crime on the part of the master. In the eye of the law, despotic power is incapable of crime; for, so soon as the law begins to take cognizance of its acts, so soon does it lose its character of perfect despotism. *Our system of negro slavery is not perfect slavery, because the negro has in many cases a legal appeal from the judgment of his master who is responsible to the law for cruel oppression, and must answer with his life for the life of his slave.*[50] A much more perfect system of slavery is to be found under the rule of Mr. Carey's model government of the Russian Czar. *His* subjects can resist the imperial ukase only by rebellion and, as they have no legal appeal, are much more perfectly

50. This argument upon the nature of slavery, we believe has never before been advanced, and may hereafter use it in another form. [LSM]

slaves than our negroes. This unlimited legal right, by no means, however, implies its abuse, nor at all proves oppression on the part of the ruler; and we can perfectly well understand how (in the words quoted by Mr. Carey, p. 338, from a recent writer) it might very possibly be that, under such a system, the Russian serf, without knowing "the meaning of popular franchise," may "enjoy and benefit by privileges by which some of the most civilized nations have proved themselves incapable of profiting."[51]

Mr. Carey very erroneously argues that such a condition of the subject proves an increasing freedom; it proves no such thing. It proves an increasing comfort under a master's rule; it proves that with limitless power a master may still be indulgent; it proves (if such a state of things really exists) that Nicholas, however he may be disposed to trample over his neighbour nations, has the heart of a man for his subjects; but it does not prove that he has the slightest idea of resigning the slightest portion of his power over them. We may give our slave a holiday from Christmas to Christmas—from year to year; we may leave the regulation of his labour entirely to his own judgment, the proceeds of it to his own use; he may enjoy more than the privileges of a freeman; but he is still, so long as we retain the legal right of demanding his service, and regulating his actions, no less our slave than if treated with the lowest brutality. A master may allow every privilege to his slave, but, so long as he retains the right to curtail these privileges, he is none the less the legal master, nor is the slave less his legal slave. A freeman may be brutally oppressed; a slave may be unlimitedly indulged; but such ill-treatment on the one side, or kind treatment on the other, cannot change their condition in law. Slave and freeman they still are, according to the government under which they live, the legal abilities which they enjoy, and the disabilities to which they are subjected.

The term slave, frequently used as it is, as a figure of speech, has come to have a figurative use entirely independent of its simple signification, which implies only *one in a state of legal bondage*. We say of a man, he is the slave of his necessities, the slave of his vices, the slave of conscience, the slave of duty, etc. These are figurative uses of the word, always, as in the nature of figurative language, increasing in intensity the original signification of the term borrowed. No man can, by any possibility, be legally the slave of his conscience, for no law could be imagined capable of coercing him in such obedience. Equally, no man is the slave of his necessities or his vices, for it is not only permitted to him, but enjoined on him, by the law frequently, to resist the first, and always the last. Inasmuch, however, as he is, through his

51. Carey cites: Edward Jerrmann (1798–1859), [*Unpolitische Bilder aus St. Petersburg*] *Pictures from St. Petersburg*, trans. Frederick Hardman (New York, 1852), p. 27.

own weakness, incapable of such resistance, we figuratively speak of him as a slave. The same figure has been used for persons in great suffering or need—he is the slave of wretchedness, the slave of despair; and thence has followed the idea among the great mass of careless and illogical reasoners, that suffering is really and absolutely slavery. But, in truth, the wretched starving figure of a man, breathing out his last in the vilest hovel of the lowest suburbs of Mr. Carey's own great city, is the slave of wretchedness and want only in the same sense in which that gentleman might himself be the slave of an attack of gout or rheumatism, should it please Almighty God to send it to him.

The misery which results from ill government we are far enough from denying, and would be most happy to find some remedy proposed for it, more likely to be effective, and less likely to be injurious, than Mr. Carey's *protective tariffs;* but we wish to repel the idea that such misery has anything to do with legal slavery. Every individual, subjected to the laws of any society, must be more or less the subject or slave of those laws, in so far as he is, to a certain extent, in a state of bondage to them. Perfect freedom, in this sense, could be found only in a condition of perfect isolation. Every human being, living in society, gives up a certain portion of his freedom to the demands of such society. According to the nature of the government adopted by the particular community to which he attaches himself, or is by circumstance attached, he gives up more or less of his perfect freedom, receiving, in return, more or less of the privileges granted to him by that government, or its agents. In all *equal* governments, all are, as we above remarked, equally bond and equally free; but none can be perfectly free. The very act of submitting to any government, is the giving up of certain rights. The despot (*tyrannus*) may rule his slaves with infinite indulgence, but still they have *no rights,* consequently, *no freedom.* England's rule over her colonists was formerly one of perfect despotism. (We waive here all question of injustice or oppression, and use the word despotism in its simple sense, of absolute not cruel power.) Her rule over her dependencies today, is still but little varied from the same system. What rights have India or Hindostan? England grants rather than they require. Whether England has the right to conquer countries, that she may govern them, we do not here stop to ask; we are merely illustrating our argument. In the case of China and the opium trade, there is an evident act of illegal oppression. England has no legal rule over China. China has her indisputable legal rights, and whether these exist in her Emperor, her people, or both, matters not to us, as a question of simple justice. China has her rights, which no principle of justice authorized England in invading; and only after England shall have subdued and made laws for her, can her subjects be the subjects or slaves of

England. All colonies are, in their infancy, necessarily under despotic rule. Like children under the rule of the parent, they must be absolutely, though not of necessity unjustly, oppressively, or unkindly, governed. Only as *freedmen,* ascending from the condition of slave to freeman, gradually progressing towards a higher development, and therewith passing from the condition of colonists, do they attain rights. The colony which asks for rights and not for grants, which requires rather than pleads, is in a state of revolution—peaceable, slow revolution perhaps—but still revolution. It is passing from under the rule of despotism and, as it attains its maturity, claims its freedom. The home government of England is not one of absolute power, her people having rights which they claim and exercise, though individually they are not equally free. In the various grades of society, between the noble and the commoner, the churchman and the layman, the Jew, the Catholic, and the Church of England-man, there are great differences of rights, and consequently great differences in degrees of freedom. Some, therefore, may, with correctness, be said to be more slaves than other some; but all have their rights, according to the class to which they belong, each class equal in the privileges of its individual members; and the poorest manufacturing hand-labourer is, of necessity, as legally free, inasmuch as he has the same legal rights, as the manufacturing millionaire. Here is no room for discussion of the various degrees of freedom of which different races, different nations, or different individuals are susceptible. Many individuals, as the lunatic and idiot, are entirely unfit for freedom, and, accordingly, the laws of all societies deprive them of it, putting them under individual rule and guardianship. Many are fit for it only to a certain extent, and in varying degrees. Whole nations seem frequently to have an inaptitude for it, which would seem, sometimes, to amount to absolute incapacity. France, after the bloodiest struggles, tost like a shuttle-cock from tyranny to tyranny, has finally settled down into an almost absolute despotism, and the opinion of the world would seem to say that this is right—at least that it is best for her.

It is madness to talk, as does Mr. Carey (p. 393), of "all men black, white, and brown," enjoying "*perfect freedom.*"[52] *Perfect* freedom is, we repeat, incompatible with society. *Equal* freedom, a freedom setting all men upon the same footing, has been dreamed of, has been talked of, but never seriously aimed at by any government. Does our own government, or did it at any period of

52. "The men of this country, therefore, who desire that all men, black, white, and brown, shall at the earliest period enjoy perfect freedom of thought, speech, action, and trade, will find, on full consideration, that duty to themselves and to their fellow-men requires that they should advocate efficient protection, as the true and only mode of abolishing the domestic trade in slaves, whether black or white."

its existence, or did its framers in any way, uphold so preposterous an idea? Miss Antoinette Brown, Sojourner Truth and Co., do talk of it; but no reasoning man (we beg the ladies' pardon; we mean no exclusion of them, the term "man" signifying with us "human being"), no reasoning individual ever imagined so anomalous a state of society. Mr. Jefferson's great humbug flourish of "free and equal" has made trouble enough, and it is full time that its mischievous influence should end. The signers of the Declaration never meant it; Mr. Jefferson, himself, never meant it; or he and they were equally impostors against the great truths of which they stood up as exponents. Most of them owned slaves, most of them had wives, and certainly not *one* of them intended the interpretation to which sisters Antoinette and Sojourner have, with a strictly logical deduction, brought their conclusions. If that sentence meant anything, it meant what the pantalooned ladies now claim, and the gentlemen must either resign their prerogative right to the garment in question between them, or throw the "free and equal" overboard. One or the other, gentlemen! "To hold or not to hold, that is the question."[53] If Cuffee's mental and bodily disabilities be no impediment, surely much less so should be those of the fair Antoinette; and as to the amiable Sojourner, she can come in under either wing of the improvement squad. Is Mr. Carey ready to take his stand thus boldly? Or will he defend his pantaloons and his conservative rights? If the last, he must concede to us that equality is out of the question, a dream which the necessities of nature refuse to recognize, and which he himself, the advocate of it, positively refuses to a large portion of his fellow human beings.

In every government, and under every rule, woman has been placed in a position of slavery—actual, legal slavery: not perfect slavery, we grant—not under as perfect a system of slavery, even, as are our negroes—but still in a very decided state of bondage, inasmuch as she is deprived of many rights which men enjoy, and legally subjected to the supremacy of man. There is, as the result of such a system, much hardship, much individual suffering. Many a woman of dominant intellect is obliged to submit to the rule of an animal in pantaloons, every way her inferior. This seems unjust and unreasonable; she, therefore, sometimes deserts the pantaloons, or perhaps, in preference, *assumes* them, and sets up a free and equal independency. But, as we have already remarked, society requires from its members, on condition of certain advantages accorded, an abandonment of certain rights. Woman has been required to abandon more than man, because her nature needs more protection. As she requires a larger protection for her weakness, she gives up a larger portion of her natural rights. She pays for what she

53. *Hamlet* 3.1.56: "To be, or not to be, that is the question."

receives. She needs the arm of man to defend her against man himself. She, therefore, cannot be his equal. In many things his superior, she is still the dependent upon him for that protection which her physical weakness requires. Individual women may sometimes suffer from such a state of things; but society, which consults the good of all, requires it for the good of all; and, however talented may occasionally be the women who thus step out of their woman sphere, it is a defective system of reasoning which has led them to this course, and the "free and equal" theory has vastly helped to blow up this bubble of their imagination.

Equally, and more, with the negro as with the woman: he needs protection, and must pay for it by the abandonment of privileges which otherwise might seem to be his right. The universal rule of nature, by which inferior races have invariably disappeared before the advance of the superior, has, in the case of the negro, been arrested to his advantage; and, instead of extermination, he has, in the Southern United States, met protection. For this protection, he has been required to give up such rights as the superior man claims, under what is usually termed a free government. This protection withdrawn, his fate is as certain as that of the red man, whose ruin has preceded him. Nature, as though tired of the destruction of her feebler offspring, holds out to him this refuge. Here, he finds an average security of life, with an average degree of comfort. But society, which accords to him this protection, requires of him, as in the case of woman, a compensating equivalent. He needs a large protection; he must give an equivalent return. He must pay for what he receives; and the abandonment of many rights, which the stronger, i.e., the superior man may claim, must be the price of his existence. If any think this wrong, they must call the Almighty Creator to account, nor hope to find *protective tariffs* a preventive of *his* necessities. No man who ever lived among negroes but must perceive (and science goes far to confirm individual observation) their entire incapacity for forming an integral portion of any free and equal government, whose equality is not destined to sink into comparative, if not total, barbarism. In individual cases, there may be hardship (though neither as frequently nor as strongly exhibited as in the case of woman) in their fulfilling the necessities of the position in which circumstances have placed them; but society necessarily legislates for the masses, and not for individuals. The individual, therefore, who finds the laws of society irksome to him, has no resource but submission to the discomfort entailed upon him, or the abandonment of that society of the laws of which he complains. Any individual, whose ideas of freedom become injurious to society, must banish himself, and resign the protection of that society, to enjoy in isolation his peculiar ideas.

Perfect freedom, we have said, can exist only in isolation; otherwise the thief and the communist would end by exercising their peculiar ideas of freedom, to the extent of depriving all other men of their own houses, goods, and families. The negro must submit to the laws of society which assign to him an inferior position, or he must leave that society, with the protection and advantages which it offers him, to establish his position elsewhere. In our Northern States he is *called free,* but refused the enjoyment of legal equality. He has more legal rights and less real protection than in our Southern States. He naturally wishes a change. He claims equality and is answered "Emigrate," "Go to Africa." "No," answer Fred. Douglas and Co., "we must have equality *here.* We belong to a civilized nation." That civilized nation turns from them in disgust, refusing, at once, the equality for which they are not fit, and the protection for which they give no equivalent. And then comes nature, with her stern law of necessity, and her *fiat* is, "*Begone ye incompetent!*"[54] And behold, they go. Poverty, disease, helplessness—it matters not by what road they wend their way to annihilation; at least, they obey nature, and *die out,* making way for the higher race, with whom they cannot compete. At the South, for equivalent service, given in such manner as the judgment of the higher and civilized man dictates, they receive an equivalent protection. On that condition, and that condition alone, can the negro continue to form an integral portion of any civilized community.

Among Mr. Carey's wise plans of reform to get rid of the *evil* which he presumes to be existent among us, he proposes that our negroes should be rendered *adscripti glebae.* Tie the poor negro to the soil, there to suffer under the pinching rule of want, for both master and slave, until the master, driven away, starved out, leaves the negro to his freedom and his pursuing fate. "Raise the price of food," says Mr. Carey (p. 393). "Raise it still higher, and the profit would disappear; and then would the master of slaves find it necessary to devolve upon the parent the making of the *sacrifice* required for the raising of children, and thus to enable him to bring into activity all the best feelings of the heart."[55]

Here is progress! The negro is too comfortable in his slavery; make him

54. Cf. [Carlyle], "Occasional Discourse," p. 678: "Depart ye quack-ridden, incompetent!"

55. The paragraph of Carey, *Slave Trade,* p. 393, reads down to LSM's second excerpt: "It will, perhaps, be said that even although the slave trade were abolished, slavery would still continue to exist, and that the great object of the anti-slavery movement would remain unaccomplished. One step, at all events, and a great one, would have been made. To render men *adscripti glebae* ['bound to the land,' i.e., in the manner of a serf], thus attaching them to the soil, has been in many countries, as has so recently been the case in Russia, one of the movements toward emancipation [Alexander II abolished serfdom in 1861]; and if this could

a freeman; let him suffer a *greater sacrifice* for the "raising" of his children (they grow up too easily now); enable him thus to bring into activity the best feelings of the heart. Sorrow maketh wise[56]—but is it therefore the duty of the philanthropist to imagine the means of new sorrows for the world? The best feelings of the heart! What are these, as exhibited among the highest civilized nation of the earth, whose advancement stands in wide contrast to negro barbarism and weakness? Those feelings which drive English mothers to burial clubs, and bring, so soon after, the little corpse to claim the pittance which these clubs pay for its death [231]! Those feelings which (as Mr. Carey himself quotes, p. 229, from English papers to prove) cause "about three hundred children, yearly, to be put to death in Leeds alone, not even registered by the law!"[57] Those feelings which crowd into the *Morning Chronicle* "twenty-two trials for child-murder; . . . and these are <were> stated to be but one-half of those that had taken place in the short period of twenty-seven days!" (p. 230) Such are the feelings which "the sacrifice required for the raising of children" excites among a highly civilized nation; let our readers judge what might be its comparative effect with the untutored negro. May heaven, in its mercy, save us from such freedom as this! The freedom to leave the neglected babe to its lingering death-gasp, because "it is in the club" [231].

No, Mr. Carey! Leave us *our slavery*! Such books as yours show us cause to *glory* in it! If these horrible cases which you draw together be indeed not fearful fables, our system can ill afford to bear comparison with those which produce them. Even the sickening inventions of the authoress of *Uncle Tom's Cabin* fall far behind them in terrific horrors. Leave to the negro that protection for which he now cheerfully pays his labour and his service. Do not call the wretched and unprotected beings who are forced to grope their way, unaided, through such suffering and temptation as you have described—do not call *these, slaves!* Alas! how cheerfully would they change places with our lowest negro! The slave has his master to protect and defend him; these have

be here effected by simple force of attraction, and without the aid of law, it would be profitable to all, both masters and slaves; because whatever tends to attract population tends inevitably to increase the value of land, and thus to enrich its owner. There, however, it could not stop, as the reader will readily see. Cheap food enables the farmer of Virginia to raise cheap labour for the slave market. Raise the price of food, and the profit of that species of manufacture would diminish."

56. Cf. Eccl. 7:3–4: "Sorrow is better than laughter: for by the sadness of the countenance the heart is made better. The heart of the wise is in the house of mourning; but the heart of fools is in the house of mirth."

57. "It was declared by the coroner of Leeds, and assented to as probable by the surgeon, that there were, as near as could be calculated, about three hundred children put to death yearly in Leeds alone that were not registered by the law" (229).

none. Our slave has his daily bread, his comfortable house, his fire, his bed, and his clothing; these have none. Baby corpses, ruined and guilty mothers, and starving fathers, scatter the way which these must travel to their earthly goal; and yet those Dives, who live surrounded by misery like this, dare preach to us; and, sick and rotten to the core as are their own systems, cant to us of the sins of ours!

Mr. Carey lauds the English ladies, for their move against Southern United States slavery. "We have here a movement," he says, "that cannot fail to be productive of much good. It was time that the various nations of the world should have their attention called to the existence of slavery within their borders, and to the manifold evils of which it is <was> the parent; and it was in the highest degree proper that woman should take the lead in doing it, as it is her sex that always suffers most in that condition of things wherein might triumphs over right, and which we are accustomed to define as a state of slavery." (p. 7)

Throughout his work, Mr. Carey feigns to have made a general attack upon all systems of oppressive or defective government, which he has seen fit to class under the head of slavery. Here, however, in the very commencement of his volume, is his particular venom exhibited against our avowed system of negro slavery. Else, surely, he could have found no cause for praise of those ladies who, neglecting the much nearer duties and, by his own showing, the much more stringent sufferings at their own doors, occupy themselves with correcting the faults of strangers, separated from them by thousands of miles of ocean. Nothing could excuse such a course but the supposed fact, for which he thus virtually vouches, that ours is, among all the systems which *he* calls slavery, the most heinous, and, therefore, the first to attack. His volume is, therefore, if there were no proof of it but this endorsement of the Stafford House demonstrations, a particular attack upon us, and as such we have received it.

Is there not enough for these English ladies to do in their Indian dependencies, of which we will transcribe a small part of Mr. Carey's quotations, from Chapman's *Commerce and Cotton of India*? This land "becomes the burying-place of millions, who die upon its bosom crying for bread. [In proof of this,] turn your eyes backward upon the scenes of the past year. Go with me into the northwestern provinces of the Bengal presidency, and I will show you the bleaching skeletons of five hundred thousand human beings, who perished of hunger in the space of a few short months. . . . The air for miles was poisoned by the effluvia emitted from the putrifying bodies of the dead. The rivers were choked with the corpses thrown into their channels. . . . Jackals and vultures approached, and fastened upon the bodies of men, women, and children, before life was extinct. . . . It was the carnival of death!"[58]

From Mr. George Thompson, M.P., Mr. Carey tells us of a certain neighbourhood where, "when the governor-general passed through that part of the country, the roads were lined on either side with heaps of dead bodies, and that they had not unfrequently to remove the <those> masses of unburied human beings, ere the governor-general could proceed onward with his suite."[59] Have English ladies no protest against the system which produces scenes like these? none against the opium traffic, which, as Mr. Carey quotes, "takes with it fire and sword, slaughter and death, and leaves <death; it leaves> behind it bankrupt fortunes, idiotized minds, broken hearts, and ruined souls" [157]. Have they no sympathies for Ireland, where, as their fellow-citizen, Thackeray, tells us: "The traveller is haunted by the face of the *popular starvation.* It is not the exception—it is the condition <*the condition*> of the people"; whose population is "*starving by millions,*" and where "strong countrymen," unable to get work, are "lying in bed '*for the hunger,*' because a man lying on his back does not need so much food as a person on foot";[60] where whole districts, over which the process of eviction has swept, appear like enormous graveyards, "the numerous gables of the unroofed dwellings" rising above them "like gigantic tombstones" [184]. Mr. Dickens, in his *Household Words,* thus describes the effects of *one* of the *fifty thousand* evictions that took place in the single year of 1849, and, adds Mr. Carey, one "of the *hundreds of thousands* that have taken place in the last six years" [184; LSM's italics]:

> Black piles of peat stood on the solitary ground, ready after a summer's cutting and drying. Presently, patches of cultivation presented themselves, plots of ground raised on beds, each a few feet wide, with intervening trenches to carry off the boggy water, where potatoes had grown, and small fields where grew more ragwort than grass, enclosed by banks cast up and tipped here and there with a briar or [a] stone. It was the husbandry of misery and indigence. The ground had already been freshly manured by sea-weeds, but the

58. Carey, *Slave Trade,* pp. 149–50 (LSM omits Carey's italics of the last sentence). Although Carey has just quoted from John Chapman (1801–54), *The Cotton and Commerce of India, Considered in Relation to the Interests of Great Britain; with Remarks on Railway Communication in the Bombay Presidency* (London, 1851), this quotation he takes not from Chapman but from George Thompson's *Lectures on British India,* p. 57.

59. Carey, *Slave Trade,* p. 150, citing Thompson, *Lectures on British India,* p. 185.

60. Carey, *Slave Trade,* p. 182 = William Makepeace Thackeray, *The Irish Sketchbook of 1842,* in *Works* 9 (New York, 1903): 341–42.

> village—where was it? Blotches of burnt ground, scorched heaps of rubbish, and fragments of blackened walls, alone were visible. Garden plots were trodden down and their few bushes rent up, or hung with tatters of rags. The two horsemen, as they hurried by, with gloomy visages, uttered nothing <no> more than the single word—*Eviction!*[61]

A lingering inhabitant thus comments, to the traveller, upon this scene:

> Oh! bless your honour! If you had seen that poor frantic woman when the back of the cabin fell in and <fell and> buried her infant, where she thought she had laid it safe for a moment while she flew to part her husband and a soldier who had struck the other children with the flat of his sword and bade them troop off. Oh! but, your honour, it was a killing sight! . . . I could not help thinking of the poor people at Rathbeg when the soldiers and police cried, "Down with them! Down with them, even to the ground!" and then the poor little cabins came down, all in fire and smoke, amid the howls and cries of the poor creatures. O[h]! it was a fearful sight, your honour—it was indeed—to see the poor women hugging their babies, and the houses where they were born burning in the wind. It was dreadful to see the old bed-ridden man lie on the ground among the few bits of furniture, and groan to his gracious God above![62]

From a recent journal Mr. Carey quotes that:

> The Galway papers are full of the most deplorable accounts of wholesale evictions, or rather exterminations, in that miserable country. The tenantry are turned out of the cottages by scores at a time. As many as two hundred and three men, women, and children, have been driven upon the roads and ditches by way of one day's work, and have now no resource but to beg their bread in desolate places, or to bury their griefs, in many instances for ever, within the walls of the Union workhouse. Land agents direct the operation. The work is done by a large force of police and soldiery. Under the protection of the latter, "the crowbar brigade" advances to the devoted township, takes possession of the houses, such as they are, and, with a few turns of the crowbar and a few pulls at a rope, bring down the roof, and leave nothing but a tottering chimney, if even that. The sun that rose on a village sets on a desert; the police return to their barracks; and the people are nowhere to

61. Carey, *Slave Trade,* p. 184 = [William Howitt], "Two Aspects of Ireland: The First Aspect," *Household Words* 4 (Sept. 27, 1851): 6–10; 7. Charles Dickens was editor of *Household Words.*

62. Carey, *Slave Trade,* p. 185 = [Howitt] "Two Aspects of Ireland: The First Aspect," p. 8.

> be found, or are vainly watching from some friendly covert for the chance of crouching once more under their ruined homes. [189–90]

When these poor wretches, thus evicted, would emigrate, what is their fate? Mr. Carey tells us (p. 199) that "out of ninety-nine thousand that left Ireland for Canada in a single year, no less <loss> than thirteen thousand perished on shipboard, and thousands died afterwards <afterward> of disease, starvation, and neglect; and thus it is that we have the horrors of 'the middle passage' repeated in our day. It is the slave trade of the last century reproduced on a grander scale, and on a new theatre of action."

And have the ladies of England no protest against all this? Again let them turn their eyes, once more, upon their own homes, their own green fields, their own parks, and their own palaces—they may see, there, a people of their own race, a people with God-given powers to be and to do what a great people should be and do; but among whom, on the authority of their own historian, Mr. Alison, crime increases "four times as fast as [the] population. . . . 'In Lancashire, population doubles in thirty years, crime in five years and a half.'"[63] In their great city of London alone, says Mr. Kay, "the filthy, deserted, roaming, and lawless children, who may be called the source of nineteen-twentieths of the crime which desolates the metropolis, are not fewer in number than *thirty thousand*"; and "these thirty thousand are quite independent of the number of mere pauper children, who crowd the streets of London, and who never enter a school." The same writer tells us how, in the same metropolis, "people of both sexes, and [of] all ages, both married and unmarried—parents, brothers, sisters, and strangers—sleep in the same rooms, and often in the same beds." In horrible details, he tells us how these have to "crawl over each other, half naked, to reach <in order to get to> their respective resting places."[64] Ladies, cannot you guess to what all this leads? You are delicate ladies, and fashionable; nice, no doubt, in your

63. Carey, *Slave Trade,* p. 226. "Mr. Alison" (Carey gives no further reference) is presumably Sir Archibald Alison (1792–1867), lawyer, historian, and biographer; frequent contributor to *Blackwood's Edinburgh Magazine;* among his works, *History of Europe during the French Revolution* (1833–42). However, in his *England in 1815 and 1845: or, A Sufficient and a Contracted Currency* (Edinburgh and London, 1845; rpt. Shannon, Ire., 1971), p. 14, Alison says that "crime has augmented *ten times* as fast as the numbers of the people."

64. Carey, *Slave Trade,* pp. 227, 228–29, citing Joseph Kay, *The Social Condition and Education of the People in England and Europe,* 2 vols. (London, 1850; rpt. Shannon, Ire., 1971), 1:394, 472. The second pair of quotations refers not to London, as LSM states, but to agricultural districts. Joseph Kay (1821–78), in 1845 appointed traveling bachelor of Cambridge University; traveled in France, Switzerland, the Netherlands, Germany, Austria (1845–48); wrote also *The Education of the Poor in England and Europe* (1846) and *The Condition and Education of Poor Children in English and in German Towns* (1853).

ideas of propriety; and, moreover, may feel, with Sir Leicester Dedlock, that "it will never do to bring this sort of squalor among the upper classes."[65] In what choice language can we whisper to you the horrors which such dwellings must generate? Prostitution and infanticide are everyday events with creatures born and bred in these dens of infamy. Ladies, you dare not look into such; perhaps, for very blushing, you dare not speak of them; but it is right you should know of them. It is right and needful that you should learn what is passing at your very doors, among your sisters, ladies, of your own country and your own race: whose Saxon blood might blush through cheeks as fair as your own, could you raise them from this degradation. We are told that in Manchester alone "there are fifteen hundred '*unfortunate females,*'" and that "some two hundred and fifty of them die, in horror and despair, yearly. In England it is calculated that there are forty thousand houses of ill-fame, and two hundred and eighty thousand prostitutes" [232; LSM's italics]. "A committee of gentlemen," says Mr. Carey, "who had investigated the condition of the sewing-women of London made a report stating that no less than thirty-three thousand of them were '*permanently at the starvation point*' [LSM's italics], and were compelled to resort to prostitution as a means of eking out a subsistence. But a few weeks since, the *Times* informed its readers that shirts were made for *a penny a piece* by women who found the needles and thread; and the *Daily News* furnishes <furnished> evidence that hundreds of young women had no choice but between prostitution and making artificial flowers at *two pence a day!*" [232]

Every one of our quotations is taken, at second hand, from Mr. Carey's own pages. We have been careful to avoid all other authorities, that from his own words he may be judged. It is himself who has gathered for us this fearful mass of testimony to the misery of the lower classes of England; and yet, after all this summing up, he coolly talks of the great *credit* which is due the women of England for bringing the question of United States negro slavery before the world. Can Mr. Carey coolly maintain that the women of England are right to overlook the thirty thousand outcast children, who crawl and crouch, unprotected, about the streets of their own great metropolis (poor wretches, sunk so low, that even the pauper crowd forms a kind of aristocracy for them), while they spend their time and their money in holding meetings, and making protests, about matters of which they know nothing? Can he praise them that, while their two hundred and eighty thou-

65. Charles Dickens' *Bleak House* was published in 19/20 monthly parts, from March 1852 to September 1853. In chap. 12, Sir Leicester Dedlock accedes to his wife's insistence that lawyer Tulkinghorn be allowed to continue his account of a possible suicide, "though he still feels that to bring this sort of squalor among the upper classes is really—really—" (*Bleak House,* introd. Osbert Sitwell [London, 1948], p. 165).

sand sisters are forced to give life, virtue, and good fame, for bread, they turn all their sympathies to help the far off black, whose condition, by Mr. Carey's own avowal, is much superior to such wretchedness? Strange to say, he can, and he does. What but the bitterest enmity to our institutions could, for a moment, so blind him to the right as to consider such a course as even excusable? The mother who leaves a starving home to its own sorrows, while she courses the world to minister to the wants of others, is surely not praiseworthy. And yet Mr. Carey cheers on these, the *should-be* mothers of England, in their headlong and heartless folly!

Ladies! Ladies! in self-respect, in common decency, if not in charity, listen to the natural dictates of your women hearts, and soothe first the sorrows of your own homes. Give mothers to those thirty thousand outcast babes; give homes to those two hundred and eighty thousand perishing sisters; and then, if you will, come to us, learn to know our negroes as we do, take the subject to your hearts, and we will share with you your earnest counsels. The petty vanity of your recent flippant remonstrances and syllabub effort, is only so far not disgusting, as it is ridiculous.[66] Mrs. Jellaby—leaving her ragged, dirty children to their own devices, of sticking their heads in area-railings, strolling after dustmen's carts, getting lost in the market-place, and tumbling down stairs all day long, her miserable husband finding in his family, as poor Caddy says, "nothing but bills, dirt, waste, noise, tumbles down-stairs, confusion, and wretchedness," while she devoted all her energies in the cause and for the benefit of "the natives of *Borrioboola-Gha,* on the left bank of the Niger"—is scarcely so ridiculous, and far from being so mischievous, as these Stafford House ladies in their misapplied efforts. Her eyes "had a curious habit of seeming to look a long way off, as if [. . .] they could see nothing nearer than Africa," while the sorrows at her very feet were forgotten, the duties of her very home neglected.[67] Mistress of Stafford House, is there no lesson that you may gather here? It might be reasonably supposed that the charitable Duchess might

66. LSM echoes here the diplomat Robert Moylan Walsh (from whose dispatch to Daniel Webster on conditions in Haiti she quotes in chap. 10, "British Philanthropy and American Slavery," pp. 313–15): "Nothing saves these people from being infinitely ridiculous but the circumstance of their being often supremely disgusting by their fearful atrocities."

67. Dickens, *Bleak House* (1948 ed.), pp. 185, 36–37 (LSM's italics). "Jellaby" should read "Jellyby." "Caddy" is the Jellybys' daughter. "Meddling philosophy looks very far, says Mr. Dickens of Mrs. Jellaby; strange, that the same person cannot see how greatly he himself deserves the same censure. There have been, we fear, too many Mrs. Jellaby's for the good of mankind; Jellaby's in breeches as well as petticoats—fools and meddlers, of precious little good, either at home or to those of Borrioboola Gha, to the myriads who need the help of common sense and virtue, rather than that philanthropy which appears to possess so little of either." David James McCord, "Africans at Home," *SQR,* n.s., 10 (July 1854): 70–96; 84.

have some misgivings as to the suitableness of *her mission* to the African, if ever she should condescend to glance her eye over the once *clan* property of Sutherland, from which, in the years 1814 to 1820, fifteen thousand inhabitants were expelled, to transform a whole, once populous, district into sheep-walks—where "all these <their> villages were demolished and burned down, and [all] their fields converted into pasturage"; where "British soldiers were commanded for this execution," and where "an old woman, refusing to quit her hut, was burned in the flames of it"; and "*thus the countess appropriated to herself seven hundred and ninety-four thousand acres of land, which, from time immemorial, had belonged to the clan*. . . . The whole of the unrightfully appropriated clan-land she divided into twenty-nine large sheep farms, . . . and in 1821 the fifteen thousand Gaels had already been superseded by one hundred and thirty-one thousand sheep." [203–4; LSM's italics][68]

Here is wholesale robbery, with occasional murder, burning to death of an old woman, and so forth; and Mr. Carey quotes it all; on *his* authority we give it to you as true—and yet this gentleman can persuade himself that the mistress of these sheep farms, the Duchess of Sutherland, has nothing better to do than, lolling on sofas, amidst the splendours of Stafford House, to dictate to American women the treatment of their slaves! Sisters of Stafford House, be easy! Our slaves shall not be driven out, nor their unroofed cottages burned to the ground, with contumacious old women in them, to make room for sheep farms. The strong man shall not need to lie in bed "for the hunger," nor the starving mother to live upon the proceeds of her baby's corpse—unless, indeed, Mr. Carey's protective tariffs shall ever, as he proposes, succeed in raising the price of food higher, "higher still," to starving point, that the negro may be turned loose, to make the sacrifice for the raising of his children which has so beautifully worked, as Mr. Carey has demonstrated, among a higher race.

Our slaves are safe, so long as they continue useful as slaves. By their services they pay the price which nature requires from her feebler children for protection from such treatment. They are useful, and therefore safe from extermination. The Duchess of Sutherland's free Gaels were useless, and therefore driven to make way for the more useful sheep. The plan of Mr. Carey, and the ladies, could easily reduce our negroes to the same—and

68. Elizabeth Sutherland (1765–1839), *suo jure* nineteenth countess of Sutherland; married (1785) to George Granville Leveson-Gower (1758–1833), then Viscount Trentham; second earl Gower (1786–1803); second marquess of Stafford from 1803; created first duke of Sutherland (1833). The countess was thus the mother-in-law of LSM's "charitable Duchess."

even, in proportion to their capacities, a lower—state of freedom, uselessness, and helplessness. And such a condition Mr. Carey calls an *approach towards slavery.* Such an insult to our system of slavery we reject, and *in toto.* Ours is a legal slavery, bearing with it its own peculiar advantages and disadvantages. Master and slave have each their rights, regulated and enforced by the laws and habits of a civilized and enlightened people. The slave has his place, however humble, and is protected and defended in that position. Not so the poor Gael of the Duchess of Sutherland's clan-lands; not so the thirty thousand lost babes of London city; not so England's two hundred and eighty thousand wretched prostitutes. *These* have no masters. These are free, to be wretched, to suffer, to starve, and to die. Duchess of Sutherland, give to *some* of them a mistress and *a mother.* Do what one woman can do; lay the hand of blessing and of comfort upon the nearest to you, and let the charitable influence, like a ripple in the water, spread in wider and yet wider circles, that the victims of misery and oppression may yet rise up and call you blessed! Believe us, here is a nobler duty than Mrs. Jellaby's far off view into Africa!

To return to Mr. Carey. We cannot too much regret the publication of his present volume. He has some reputation as a political economist, and this unlucky production, with all its prejudice and mis-statements, is to go forth as a sample of American opinion. Of such national disgrace we have already too much; and the higher the reputation of the author, the more injurious, of course, must be the effects of such a work. At home, we can appreciate the prejudice and want of research everywhere apparent through its pages; but abroad, its mis-statements are taken for facts. When Mr. Carey speaks, as he does (p. 106), of the "poverty and weakness of the South," bolstering up his assertion by a drolly lame argument, based on half-stated facts from a respectable Southern periodical, a home reader instantly detects his errors. Not so the foreigner. Here is the work of an American political economist; *the* American economist, says our author himself—vainly, less ostentatious writers, who are not trumpeters of their own merits, may confute and reconfute him. Mr. Carey's book, which so admirably caters to the fashionable fanaticism of the day, will be taken as gospel, while our census returns are unstudied, and such productions as the unostentatious, but closely accurate, pamphlet of Elwood Fisher, for instance, is cast aside, as of no authority.[69] Where a false statement is desired, it is always believed. However low has of late fallen the reputation for veracity of our modern female Mun-

69. Elwood (or Ellwood) Fisher (1808–62), of Quaker descent, born in Lynchburg, Va.; lawyer; ardent advocate of slavery; established (1850) the *Southern Press,* promoting secession; wrote *Lecture on the North and the South* (Cincinnati and Charleston, S.C., 1849).

chausen, Mrs. Harriet Beecher Stowe, the disciples of Mr. Carey's school must in future swear by her. He tells us (p. 111) that, if the reader desires to enlighten himself upon the subject of the working of our system, "he cannot do better than read the first chapter of *Uncle Tom's Cabin,* containing the negotiation between Haley and Mr. Shelby for the transfer of Uncle Tom, resulting in the loss of his life in the wilds of Arkansas." Here, then, we have an American authoress vouched for by *the* American political economist. Authority indisputable. What matters it to the negrophilist that every paper and every periodical in the South has emphatically declared *Uncle Tom's Cabin* a compound of falsehood, and most particularly pointed out this very opening chapter as one outraging all truth of fact and character? Mr. Carey is an American; Mr. Carey is a political economist; and he will serve well to supply quotations and authorities. In the same way, when he talks (p. 116 and frequently elsewhere) of the "light labo[u]r of the North," and "the severe labour of the South and South-west," of women driven to the "severe labour of the fields,"[70] and so forth, he furnishes a fine text for any young lady bloomer who may wish to exhibit her "pants" upon the stage, while her less adventurous grand-dame, with chin on hand, sits rocking to and fro with responsive groans, and a far off glance of dreamy sympathy, towards our United States Africa, of which she knows literally nothing, except from Mrs. Munchausen Stowe and her voucher, Mr. Carey. If we of the South tell them that our negroes, incapable of the extreme of hard labour which the white can endure, are not habitually forced to it; and that the field labour in which negro females are employed is lighter than washing, for instance, and many other usual avocations of women even in civilized countries; and that the song of the shirt,[71] or any equivalent for it, could never be imagined for our negroes by any one who had ever lived among us, and known our institutions and habits—bah! we might as well tell them that we don't eat negro-baby soup! If Mrs. Munchausen says so, and if Mr. Carey says "ditto" to Mrs. Munchausen, why then we *do* eat negro-baby soup. It is proved incontestably, and preposterously ridiculous it is, in us, to deny it!

We must hasten to a conclusion as our article has already reached an unwarrantable length. Our argument has turned principally upon Mr. Carey's model remedy (viz. protective tariffs) for all the ills which nations are heir to, because, among those ills our system of negro slavery standing in his

70. Carey, *Slave Trade,* p. 117, reading "the existing system . . . sends the women to the labours of the field."

71. Thomas Hood's poem, "The Song of the Shirt," representing the misery of a sweated seamstress, was first published in the Christmas number of *Punch,* 1843, and immediately translated into other European languages.

opinion prominent, this appeared our most necessary point of defence, as well as the most legitimate for attack. We have left ourselves no room for discussing his pet discovery, his land theory, of which (as the distinguished Bastiat just before his death happened to strike upon a somewhat similar train of thought) Mr. Carey has been loud in vindication, and infinitely anxious to defend his prior right of discovery. Most cheerfully we resign to him all the glory that he can manufacture out of such a theory. In vindication of Bastiat, we must say that we consider it unfair to judge him from the half developed ideas which his unfinished writings upon this subject indicate. We believe that his system, fully developed, could never have coincided with Mr. Carey's any more than, as we have shown, did his ideas of free-trade. His acute and penetrating mind could never have satisfied itself with so superficial an argument. Bastiat never dealt in foregone conclusions; he needed *facts,* as the solid foundation of any system he embraced.

Mr. Carey's theory—that the least productive lands are always the first cultivated—is based upon the idea that the light growth of sterile lands is easily conquered by the pioneer in cultivation, while the draining of rich swamp lands, or the clearing away of the tangled forest, presents to the unpractised husbandman an almost insurmountable difficulty. To this theory, two obstinate *facts* instantly spring up in opposition. First, the pioneer labourer of our days is far from being always a helpless savage. "The first poor settler," says Mr. Carey (p[p]. 405[–6]), "has no cup, and he takes up water in his hand. He has no hogs or cattle to yield him oil, and he is compelled to depend on pine knots for artificial light. He has no axe, and he cannot fell a tree, either to supply himself with fuel or to clear his land. He has no saw, and he is compelled to seek shelter under a rock, because he is unable to build himself a house. He has no spade," etc. Mr. Carey is an American born and, although, as we have shown, remarkably ignorant of Southern institutions and habits, would, we should suppose, know enough of American pioneer husbandry to remember that a grand exception to such a routine as he describes exists in our own vast territories, as necessarily in all countries settled by the offspring of any civilized and enterprising people. Our Western pioneer is oftenest not a destitute, but an enterprising settler, with not only cup, spoon, and plate, axe, saw, and spade, horse and plough—but experience, capital frequently, and, generally, with a knowledge of the world, which puts him quite above the necessity of selecting his land only for the facility of cultivation. The most difficult lands, we grant, he would not probably select, but equally he would avoid the most facile, if they should at the same time be the most sterile.

The other fact which rears its head against Mr. Carey is that sterile lands are, in truth, not always the most facile of cultivation. We need go no farther than the extensive pine-barrens of our own Southern States to prove this. It was as difficult (or nearly so) to clear the pine, as the oak forests, and, consequently, our first settlers, enjoying some conveniences of a rough comfort, selected the better lands in the vicinity of rivers, etc.; and, avoiding equally the swamps, which nothing but a laborious system of drainage could render productive, and the unpromising pine-barren, they settled upon the richest land which did not threaten to be too difficult of cultivation.

In general, two objects must guide the pioneer cultivator, viz., facility and productiveness of soil. Difficult lands, although productive, he cannot generally undertake. Sterile lands, although facile, unless in abject want he invariably avoids. Occasionally, facile lands, as in some of the Western *prairie* lands, are among the richest, and then, combining both advantages, they are eagerly seized on. But, as a general rule, it is probably the medium quality of land which first falls under cultivation. The difficult rich lands must wait for the monied capitalist; the wretchedly sterile lie until, in the progress of society, all else being monopolized, necessity learns to improve what the right of selection had avoided.

We have done; and if we have dealt a little hardly with the respectable and respected gentleman whose work we have noticed, he must recollect that, if he turns out of his way to tread upon his neighbor's toes, he must not be surprised at the natural and indignant motion which would answer the insult. That he believes himself in the right we have no doubt. Like Luther of old, he fancies that he spies the devil, and has flung his inkstand at him; but, like Luther, deceived by a shadow, his heroism leaves no trace but an ink-blot.[72] One good effect alone can we conceive as resulting from this publication. Most plainly it shows the mischievous tripartite power which, more than all other causes combined, menaces the existence of our republic. Here, protection, communism, and abolitionism plainly class themselves together—the great tribune Demon whose spectral form hovers over us, menacing desolation and ruin.

Mr. Carey, among other causes of complaint enumerated in his *Putnam* letters, is indignant, that, in the twelve years which followed the publication of his first "great work" in which his peculiar theories were announced, instead of receiving countenance from the press he "never saw a single American <*American*> notice of it that might not have been written by a student fresh from college and inflated with [the idea that he had qualified himself

72. This incident in Martin Luther's life is usually placed during his withdrawal, after the Diet of Worms and the ban placed against him and his adherents, to Wartburg Castle, above Eisenach (May 1521–March 1522). Despite frequent replasterings, tourists have clawed a perpetual hole into the wall where the inkstand, or inkhorn, is said to have struck.

for the office of critic by puzzling] himself during the last term, in trying to understand the confused and worthless systems of Wayland and <or> Say" [229].

We anticipate honourable mention in the same category, and can only say, in all humility, that we regret not having more learning at Mr. Carey's service, nor many better authorities than those to which he objects. But he must take our rough facts as the best we can give him. Many years since, we recollect hearing an anecdote related by the Hon. Edward Livingston, of an officer taken prisoner at the battle of New Orleans.[73] This gentleman, striding about his apartment, with an impatient and irritated manner, was heard muttering to himself, "Damned disagreeable, damned disagreeable!" "Have you anything to complain of?" asked his polite custodian. "To complain of! Damned disagreeable! Your officers in command have acted most unhandsomely!" "In what respect?" again enquired his anxious host. "In every respect. Every rule of tactics was neglected; the highest military authorities contemned! Damned disagreeable, to be beaten by such rabble!" "I regret, sir," was the polite answer, "that you should be so annoyed; but the insult was quite unintentional; we have given you the best we had."

L. S. M.

73. Edward Livingston (1764–1836), lawyer and politician; born in Columbia County, N.Y.; settled in New Orleans (1803); member of Andrew Jackson's staff at the battle of New Orleans (1815); U.S. congressman (1823–29) and senator (1829–31) from Louisiana; secretary of state (1831–33); minister to France (1833–35).

14

Slavery and Political Economy

Hailing, as we do, with pleasure, the first number of a new series of the *Southern Quarterly,* issuing from the hands of its highly distinguished and talented editor,[1] we must yet put ourselves in arms against a grave error which appears in its pages. This we do with great deference and some hesitation; but, believing firmly in the necessity of giving to the public mind a proper bias on such questions, we deem it the duty of each to give his effort, however feeble, to the working out of the truth. We must, therefore, express

De Bow 21 (Oct. and Nov. 1856): 331–49, 443–67. Publication reviewed: John Stuart Mill, *Principles of Political Economy, with Some of Their Applications to Social Philosophy,* 3d ed. rev. (London: John W. Parker, 1852).

1. James Henley Thornwell (1812–62), Presbyterian clergyman; professor and (1851–55) president at South Carolina College; professor (from 1855) at Presbyterian Theological Seminary in Columbia. "After Col. Preston left the College, Dr. Thornwell became President and his children were our dear friends and cronies, while he and his wife were kind and devoted friends to my mother, my father then being dead" (Smythe, p. 17). "Mrs. McCord in her outspoken way was denouncing a surgeon for some malpractice at her hospital." The surgeon was a nephew to Nancy Thornwell, who demanded immediate investigation. "Mrs. McCord, nothing daunted, went with Mrs. Thornwell." They found that "the delinquent was not Mrs. Thornwell's nephew but an assistant surgeon." But Mrs. Thornwell's annoyance over the incident was soon removed. "A doctor spoke roughly to a soldier who wanted a wooden leg. 'You can do without it. They are too expensive to give to everybody.' 'Cheer up and be of good heart,' said Mrs. McCord. 'My fine fellow, order your wooden leg and send the bill to me.' Mrs. Thornwell said she forgave her on the spot." (*Chesnut,* p. 402)

our strong dissent from at least a portion of the opinions expressed in the article "Slavery and Freedom," in number for April, 1856.[2]

We grieve to find that the writer, faithfully and honestly bold in defence of Southern institutions, has withal fallen into what we consider a most unlucky error, which, as error always must, obtrudes its weakening influence at every point, making the strongest blow fall weak, and blunting the point of the keenest argument. The reviewer has not hesitated to throw down the gauntlet, challenging to the combat the whole body of advocates of a science among the expositors of which may be found as strong minds and as able reasoners as ever brought logical argument to bear upon and co-operate with facts. That a person of the reviewer's acuteness should thus wantonly, and with an almost Quixotte valor, thus pit himself against a science because that science is not yet perfected, and because its expositors have fallen into some errors, proves an acerbity of enmity which must be rather the result of impulse than philosophical investigation, and therefore we cannot but strongly hope that a little cool thought, rather than our feeble argument, will rectify those aberrations which we so much deplore.

It is our object now to show: first, that an error cannot prove a science false; next, that Political Economy, though many of its advocates, adopting the almost universal prejudice, have exhibited a strong tendency against slav-

2. [George Frederick Holmes], "Slavery and Freedom," *SQR*, n.s., 1 (April 1856): 62–95. George Frederick Holmes (1820–97) was a friend of David James McCord and LSM, having lived (1842–46) in Orangeburg, south of Fort Motte and Lang Syne, in pursuit of a legal career, in which he was disappointed; he later held a number of academic posts, ending at the University of Virginia; he was a various and voluminous contributor to Southern periodicals. Holmes prepared a reply to LSM but was dissuaded by Thornwell from publishing it: "It is a gratification that your view of the inexpediency of replying to Mrs. McCord is so decided. It accords fully with my judgment and feelings. I had only one apprehension—that Mrs. McCord's friends might represent the attack as unanswerable, and might use it to the disadvantage of the Review. There is nothing to be gained in a controversy, or the appearance of a controversy[,] with a lady—

> nullum memorabile nomen
> Foeminea in poena est, nec habet victoria laudem.

Still less is to be gained in irritating a friend, and one meriting the highest esteem. I am relieved at finding that the absence of any necessity for reply permits me to avoid it: and I am glad that you have suppressed my note" (Holmes to Thornwell, Dec. 1, 1856, James Henley Thornwell Papers, SCL). The Latin translates: "There is no memorable name to be gained in punishing a woman, nor does the victory receive praise." Vergil's text (*Aeneid* 2.583–84), which Holmes adapts, reads: "etsi nullum memorabile nomen / feminea in poena est, habet haec victoria laudem"; Aeneas, as Troy is being sacked, catches sight of Helen, the cause of the destruction of his city, and meditates killing her: "Although there is no memorable name to be gained in punishing a woman, *this* victory receives praise."

ery, has never as a science pretended to decide the question between it and free labor; and lastly, that a deeper investigation of the question will, in the end, give us the support of that science.

Our reviewer, commenting upon the work of a Mr. Fitzhugh,[3] remarks (page 65): "His objections to Political Economy are not sufficiently precise in themselves, nor sufficiently developed, explained, or limited, nor so closely connected with his main thesis, as to prove either acceptable or entirely intelligible. That the truth of Political Economy is involved in the decision of the slavery question, is undeniable; but the implication is only partial, as there may be an opportunity of showing."[4]

We have no knowledge of Mr. Fitzhugh's work, and do not care at present to burden ourselves with its consideration. All we would remark upon in this passage is the acknowledgment, or rather assertion, of the reviewer, that the truth of Political Economy is involved in the decision of the slavery question. What does this mean? That, slavery being established as a right, Political Economy as a science ceases to exist. Where the truth of a science is involved, its existence is involved. Prove false the postulates upon which a science is based, and the science is non-existent. This the reviewer can scarcely mean to maintain would be the case with Political Economy: for, quite independent of all ideas, whether of slavery or free labor, men have the instinct of accumulation with notions of value and of wealth. And the production and distribution of wealth must be an object of man's speculation so long as he appreciates the difference between hunger and fullness, clothing and nakedness. We might indeed imagine our world as falling into that crass ignorance which, acting only from animal instincts, ceases to investigate cause and impulse, but such very certainly is not what the reviewer means to express. We think he has fairly lost his compass, and did not himself calculate, in penning the sentence we have quoted, whither he was drifting.

Men may seek to dispute and stumble in their search after any truth, but the truth nevertheless exists. Astronomy is none the less a science because the plurality of worlds is a matter in dispute; nor is chemistry all false because the nature of the miasmatic gases continues a subject of doubt and conjecture. What science ever sprang ready armed into the arena of argument, Minerva-like, from the head of Jove, without crack or flaw in its

3. George Fitzhugh (1806–81), proslavery advocate; author of *Sociology for the South; or, The Failure of Free Society* (1854), reviewed by Holmes in "Slavery and Freedom," and *Cannibals All! or, Slaves without Masters* (1857).

4. In this essay LSM regularly capitalizes "Political Economy," even when quoting Holmes, who does not.

armor of defence? Slow and weary has been the progress of each, and only through clouds of error does the sunlight force itself at last. He who would catch the truth-beam must watch patiently and long. How many *te deums* have been chaunted for victories never won! How many triumphant eurekas died away in the sigh of disappointed aspirations! How many lips, trembling with the excitement of supposed certain triumph, have felt the touchstone of truth, and hushed themselves in despair, feeling that not yet is their's the prophet's mission. *Magna est veritas.*[5] Yes, beautiful Truth! great art thou, and magnificent is thy godlike might; but that might worketh not like the lightning-flash, fearful in danger, quick in destruction, but rather like the gentle dew, ever coming again and again—softly, slowly, almost imperceptibly working its great end. Thou prevailest! Ay, like God's love thou prevailest! But not in the sudden flashing beam, not in the crashing blow which annihilates opposition. Rather in that heaven-sent moisture, ever returning, ever beautifying, making the bud to bloom and the fruit to swell into ripeness, decking the earth in beauty, and teaching wisdom even in the wordless[6] stillness of unwearying beneficences. Slow, though sure, are the victories of truth, and science is but the word which men use to express their search for her. Science is as it were the note-book in which her votaries enter every trace of her supposed presence—every faintest track of her passage. As a matter of necessity they must sometimes err. Other footprints are mistaken for the true. Shall the search therefore be abandoned, and sluggard despair cast aside all that has been accomplished, because the result shows some error in calculation? Were it not wiser rather to retrace our steps and, with fresh spirit to the task, to try again and yet again, with the true courage of unwearying endurance, until error is sifted out, and the pure gold rewards our endeavor? Patient investigation is, in such research, our only philosopher's stone. Thus, then, the general condemnation of a righteous thing (as we sustain slavery under certain circumstances to be) by the entire body of political economists, would no longer crush Political Economy as a science

5. 3 Esd. 4:41: "Magna est veritas, et praevalet" ("Great is truth, and it prevails"). Holmes concludes his article, p. 95, with this quotation (reading "et praevalebit," "and it will prevail"). For her invocation of Truth, which extends over the next sentences, LSM combines reminiscences of other authors, e.g.: "Fear no more the lightning-flash" (*Cymbeline* 4.2.270); "Who is like thee, O Lord, among the gods? who is like thee, glorious in holiness, fearful in praises, doing wonders?" (Exod. 15:11); "The quality of mercy . . . droppeth as the gentle rain from heaven" (*Merchant of Venice* 4.1.180–81); "Thou prevailest for ever against him" (Job 14:11); "heavenly moisture" (*Venus and Adonis,* ll. 64, 542); "Israel shall blossom and bud, and fill the face of the world with fruit" (Isa. 27:6); "decking with liquid pearl the bladed grass" (*Midsummer Night's Dream* 1.1.211).

6. "Worldless" in original.

than was medicine, for instance, condemned by the general prevalent errors concerning the blood, before Harvey made known its laws of circulation.[7]

But we contend, further, that the question has never been clearly made, nor brought before the bar of Political Economy. The general impressions and vague impulses of the world for a century back (and in that century Political Economy as a science has found its birth) have been constantly tending, with a stronger and stronger bias, against slavery. Political economists have, for the most part, followed this general bias; but they have done so as prejudiced men rather than as political economists, the judgment of the science having never yet been sought or pronounced. No stronger proof can be given of this than the sentence of Mr. Mill quoted by our reviewer. Mr. Mill is, the latter remarks, "the highest received standard of the matured views of the political economists in regard to the conditions and relations appropriate to the laboring classes in modern times, and [. . .] may, therefore, be safely consulted as the most distinguished representative of the advanced theories of the science entertained in England and the European continent" [71]. And Mr. Mill (we quote from our reviewer),

> impersonating Political Economy, has no positive arguments to adduce in proof of the absolute and exclusive righteousness of the free labo[u]r system. After a few observations, sometimes acute, usually erroneous, on the effects of slavery, he concludes in not very elegant English, that "more needs not to be said on a cause so completely judged and decided as that of slavery."[8] Strange delusion! The world is only now seriously addressing itself to the philosophical examination of the question. Hitherto, it has been content to act precipitately under the influence of philanthropic fantasies, and conscious or unconscious pecuniary instincts, and to decide without investigation. Like Mr. Mill, other opponents of slavery sustain their positions almost entirely by broad assertions and blind censures, and negative proofs. They have either unsuccessfully attempted to answer the reasoning of Aristotle in favor of slavery, which has never yet been answered, or they have proceeded on the presumption that it had been already refuted. [74–75]

Strange delusion, we grant: showing the strongest prejudice, and resulting in as unscientific a mode of shuffling off an argument as can well be imagined. The author who gives chapter upon chapter to the discussion of the

7. William Harvey (1578–1657), physician to James I and Charles I; proposed theory of the circulation of the blood in *Exercitatio de motu cordis et sanguinis in animalibus* (1628).

8. John Stuart Mill, *Principles of Political Economy, with Some of Their Applications to Social Philosophy,* ed. J. M. Robson (Toronto, 1965), p. 250, reading: "More needs not be said here on a cause. . . ."

peasant proprietary system, the metayer system, and the cottier system, finds nothing more to say on slavery but this. The cause is prejudged, and he casts it aside as unworthy the attention of that science of which our reviewer takes him as the personification.

We beg in this to differ. Mr. Mill is a prominent writer upon Political Economy, but we are far from willing to accept him as its prophet. His work, although classing among the highest on the subject, is far from infallible, and teems with errors. On the question of slavery, he gives us his *ipse dixit,* and nothing more. Surely this is not the last word of science! As our reviewer himself says, the question has been decided *without investigation;* "the world is only now seriously addressing itself to the philosophical examination of the question," and the opponents of slavery sustain their positions "by broad assertions [and] blind censures, and negative proofs." What better proof that the subject has never met the investigations of science? A question decided without investigation is surely not decided scientifically; nor shall the noble science of Political Economy be expunged from the category of sciences because its disciples sometimes act, judge, and are led astray by the common passions and prejudices of common men. Mr. Mill has on this subject allowed himself to be carried away by the tide of vulgar prejudice and ignorant assumption, and has with a most illogical precipitancy of assertion come to his conclusions. "I think it is so because I think it is so," may, according to Shakspeare, serve as a woman's reason,[9] but certainly not as a logician's, and yet this is the sum total of Mr. Mill's position. We grant that to see prejudice thus:

> Mistress of passion, swaying to the mood
> Of what it likes or loathes;[10]

to see passion thus swallowing up reason—to see grave men who should be teachers of something wiser and holier, hallooing on the howl of fanaticism, and condemning, as though their's were God's fiat, things of which they know literally nothing, whether by investigation or experience—is enough to rouse the ire of any man who finds himself thus cast aside as some insensate, unreasoning thing, and smiled down with a cool complacency of superiority, when he feels and knows himself in the right, with justice and good sense on his side. It is enough to excite the bile of a philosopher; and yet it

9. *The Two Gentlemen of Verona* 1.2.23–24: "I have no other but a woman's reason: / I think him so, because I think him so."

10. *Merchant of Venice* 4.1.50–52: "for affection / (Master of passion) sways it to the mood / Of what it likes or loathes." The emendation "mistress of passion" has been suggested by several editors of Shakespeare.

can serve us no good turn to give way to similar prejudice. If a man robs us of our purse, it cannot help us to swear murder against him. He who is in the minority, who has the force of social opinion against him, whether that opinion be true or false, must the more carefully look to his armor of argument, and take heed that no flaw or crack be found in it. The blunder which may be past over in the defender of a favorite creed will be conned and commented upon with bitter exactness in an opponent.

Our reviewer has unfortunately followed Mr. Mill's example, and taken sides from impulse, without sufficient investigation. From the general tone of his argument we are constrained to believe that Political Economy has never been a favorite study with him, and that he condemns it as Mr. Mill does slavery, rather from prejudice than knowledge. By bringing forward Political Economy as the special champion of free labor, he makes an issue which Political Economy itself has never made. The sin of the advocates of that science is (and it is a heavy one) that they have followed in the wake of this prejudice; but certainly they have not led it. They have joined the cry, but they did not start the scent. Political economists have believed in the propriety or otherwise of free labor rather as a question of morals than as a point of their political creed, and have adopted it on authorities entirely distinct from their science. It is true they have generally assumed it to be more productive than slave labor; but this is, we repeat, always on assumption, never on proof. The question in its present form is so new a one they are as yet scarcely awake to it. Political Economy is, moreover, almost entirely a European study, and, in so far as it has noticed slavery, has regarded it as an exploded system, and as preceding an enlightened civilization. This is a limited but, for a European, most natural point of view; such indeed is, or rather was, the slavery of Europe, to which, in default of answering information from us, their observations have been confined. Where slavery lingers in Europe, it is in process of change, showing the beginning of the end. Ours is of an entirely dissimilar stamp, and the European knows as little of the inferior race of men which it has fallen upon our clime and our day to utilize, as he knows of our swamps and our forests. When by chance some politico-economical argument has appeared from our side of the Atlantic, it has invariably been from north of Mason and Dickson's line, where bitter sectional animosity darkens the question even more than European prejudice.[11] To do our Northern brethren justice, however, they have meddled little with the economical argument, and take much more kindly to higher

11. The Mason-Dixon Line was drawn during 1763–67 by the English astronomers and surveyors Charles Mason (1730–87) and Jeremiah Dixon (d. 1767), hired to resolve boundary disputes between Maryland and Pennsylvania. Mason and Dixon's survey of 230 miles

law and other vagaries. The general error of all, however, on both sides of the Atlantic, is that they treat the question as though the negro were a white man, with a black skin, instead of learning the truth that the complexion of the races is among the smallest of their differences.

To return to our reviewer: He has made, we say, an issue which Political Economy never did make, when he brings forward free labor as one of its essential beliefs. Adam Smith, although showing a prejudice mingled with simplicity absolutely amusing in some of its conclusions,[12] has entirely avoided an examination of the subject, and rather speaks of it on hearsay as a thing beyond his ken—as (page 34), after presuming that the expense of slave labor is greater than free, he remarks, "it appears, accordingly, from the experience of all [ages and] nations, *I believe,* that the work done by free men comes cheaper in the end than that performed by slaves." And again (page 159): "the experience of all ages and nations, *I believe,* demonstrates that the work done by slaves, though it appears to cost only their maintenance, is in the end the dearest of any."[13] *He believes,* and so he passes on from this merely incidental topic to more immediate objects of discussion. Adam Smith was before the day of continental abolitionism, but he was also before the day of United States negro slavery, nor could he read in the future its great results. J. B. Say has so entirely ignored the subject of slavery that we cannot recollect any reference to it in his work, although we have, to refresh our memory, patiently perused a very lengthy analytical table of contents attached to our edition, printed at Paris, 1817.[14] We have already remarked

---

was continued farther westward in 1784, completing the survey between Pennsylvania and Virginia. By the time of the Missouri Compromise (1820), slavery had been abolished in all the states north of the Mason-Dixon Line, which henceforth was popularly recognized to mark the division between the North and the South of the United States.

12. As, when he attempted to account for the assumed non-inventiveness of slaves, he says (page 254, Edinburgh edition, 1838 [= Smith, *Wealth of Nations,* ed. Todd, p. 684]): "Should a slave propose any improvement of this kind, his master would be very apt to consider the proposal as the suggestion of laziness, and of a desire to save his own labour at the master's expense. The poor slave, instead of reward, would probably meet with much abuse, perhaps with some punishment. In the manufactures carried on by slaves, therefore, more labour must generally have been employed to execute the same quantity of work, than in those carried on by free men." This childish reasoning, if reasoning it can be called, is a mere shoving aside of the question. [LSM]

13. Ibid., ed. Todd, pp. 99, 387 (LSM's italics).

14. The only place in the whole treatise where we can recall even the mention of the word slavery is in a note ([Jean-Baptiste Say, *Traité d'économie politique,* 3d ed. (Paris, 1817)] vol. 1, p. 136 [= (n.p., 1972), 1.14.133–34]). We translate: "But however sacred be the right of property in industrial talent, and in all personal faculties, natural or acquired, it is ignored not only in slavery which violates this most indisputable of all properties, but in many other cases much more common <beaucoup moins rares>"; and, continuing in the

how Mr. Mill disposes of the subject. These three among the prominent writers on Political Economy will serve as a fair sample of the whole. Do not let us be misunderstood. It is indisputable that we have been violently attacked, and bitterly slandered, by political economists as by men of almost every imaginable grade and profession. We only contend that political economists have so acted not specially and consequently upon their economical creed, but in common with others, and consequently upon an almost universal prejudice. These crude opinions and most lame conclusions belong not to their science, but to the social atmosphere in which they live; and their sin is greater than that of others, precisely because in that science, would they listen to it, they find a truer guide. For ourselves it is sheer madness to throw away our armor at the very moment when we should be girding it on to the defence. This is precisely what our antagonists would desire, and already we can imagine those of them who may have noticed our review triumphantly chuckling over an opponent who just as the fight thickens offers them so palpable an advantage. When in the very heart of a slave State (a State of which the faith and earnestness in defence of the persecuted cause of slavery has not and cannot be doubted) a leading periodical takes such grounds as our reviewer has taken, it is the absolute hoisting of a signal to the enemy, and every gun will be pointed at the wavering ranks. That the mistake has been made in the best faith, we cannot for an instant doubt, but it is none the less a fatal error of which the speediest recantation is the best. To our reviewer, much more a classical scholar than a political economist, we are quite ready to do all honor, and, acknowledging our childlike ignorance where he excels, to offer homage to his superiority on a ground where we have often lamented our own deficiencies. But "this honor due and reverence paid,"[15] we must hold ourselves none the less ready to repulse what we consider mischievous encroachment upon another. Evidently he is a tyro in Political Economy, and half in play we think (trying as it were of new weap-

---

text the subject of general violation of personal property, he remarks: "I know perfectly well that the maintenance of social order which guarantees property must go before property itself, and thus nothing but the necessity of maintaining social order through evident peril can authorize all these different violations of private right." We ask no stronger argument in favor of United States negro slavery, though certainly the author did not intend it as such. [LSM] The second passage cited above reads in the original: "Je sais fort bien que le maintien de l'ordre social, qui garantit la propriété, passe avant la propriété même; mais il ne faut pas que la conservation de l'ordre puisse servir de prétexte aux vexations du pouvoir, ni que la subordination donne naissance au privilège."

15. John Milton, *Paradise Lost* 3.736–38: "Satan bowing low, / As to superior spirits is wont in heaven, / Where honour due and reverence none neglects, / Took leave."

ons), half in impulsive prejudice, has flung this random shot, whereby thinking to startle his enemy he has grazed the heart of his friend.

Political Economy, that science which has so successfully struggled against the prejudices of the dark ages of protective tariffs, duties, drawbacks, and the thousand and one shackles which corroded the limbs of fettered commerce—that noble science which, even in its almost infancy the foster mother of nations, extends their brotherhood from zone to zone and, opening to our view the panorama of future ages, shows us a world exulting in the noblest blessings of a christianized civilization—has yet pronounced no judgement upon the subject which now so intensely engrosses our attention. Our reviewer represents free-labor as the principle of this science; but, as we have shown, this question is yet new to political economy. *Free-trade,* not *free-labor,* has been her aim (that these are things entirely distinct, the history of these States for the last quarter of a century fully exhibits); and it has needed all her energies to fight *that* battle through. Even now she stands with eagle-eye surveying the fields of conquest, breathless in victory, and yet on guard. Even now, as she surveys the rich products of a world daily more and more released from the blundering guidance of an ignorant and selfish policy, she watches for the renewal of attack. "A scotched snake is not killed."[16] The mischievous principle is checked but not extinct.

Slavery, an institution born with society, never attacked until the pseudo-philanthropy, rather than science, of recent years dragged it forward before the tribunal of a sickly new-light philosophy, has, half-stunned by such unexpected assault, hitherto scarcely muttered a word of defence. But this lethargy must be ours no longer. We must speak now, not in hasty declamation, but in logical defence. Slavery is truly and fairly a subject for the investigation of Political Economy. The wonderful development of this western continent, effected only through and by the means of slavery—her immense produce scattered over our globe, carrying food and clothing to the hungry and the destitute; her cotton and her sugar sustaining not only herself but the might of Europe's most powerful nations; her ever increasing expanse of new land, opening an asylum for Europe's starving millions, and staving off menaced revolutions—what are these but the glorious results of American negro slavery? a system which it is recently the fashion to contemn, but which must now come boldly forward to claim its true place in the world's development; and it is before the tribunal of Political Economy that it must claim this place, and prove the justice of its cause. Hitherto we have, as

16. *Macbeth* 3.2.13: "We have scorch'd the snake, not kill'd it." "Scotched" is a conjecture of the editor Lewis Theobald.

it were, played at shuttlecock with the assumed sin of the thing. England has thrown it upon America—America has cast it back upon England—Yankee-land has vociferated, "It is yours"; and the South echoes back indignantly, "Yours." But this is a paltry shuffling off of responsibility which suits not a great people. Where there is sin (with whomsoever originating), it soils the hands which cling to the ill-gotten spoil. We have been asleep, acting as though in a startled dream. Up! and away with it! sin there is none. Once and forever let us disclaim the blot. No sin! no sin! but laud[17] and glory rather: glory, not to man, the hitherto blind instrument, but to the great dispensing Providence, which shows us this light out of the seeming darkness. The pillar of fire is before us, and we acknowledge the hand that guides.[18]

Nothing is easier than a sneer.[19] Happily, however, a sneer is not an argument; neither can it profane that which is holy, nor change the just and the true into the false and unrighteous. It is the fashion with a certain modern school of philanthropists to sneer at Political Economy as the science of wealth; the science of pounds and pence; the spiritualized Shylock; the distilled essence of that spirit which, seeing only what is in the bond, insists always upon its pound of flesh. How our reviewer should have fallen into the category of such declaimers we cannot understand, for certainly he is not of them. These are of the sentimental school, extending from the Wilberforce and Clarkson brotherhood to Mrs. Stowe with her black, white, and yellow fraternity. It has been shrewdly remarked that there are two classes of philanthropists, the feelers and the thinkers.[20] The first, showing its most perfect type in such characters as a Howard, a Mrs. Fry, or a Florence Nightengale[21] (characters whose blessed influence far be it from us to underrate), descends

17. "Land" in original.

18. Exod. 13:21–22.

19. Cf. "Who can refute a *sneer?*" in William Paley, *The Principles of Moral and Political Philosophy,* rev. ed. (London, 1821), p. 302, discussing the attitude toward Christianity of "an eloquent historian" (Edward Gibbon, "Sapping a solemn creed with solemn sneer, / The lord of irony" [Byron, *Childe Harold's Pilgrimage* 3.999–1000]). William Paley (1743–1805), English clergyman and theologian; wrote—besides *The Principles of Moral and Political Philosophy* (1785), which was used as a textbook at Cambridge University—*Horae Paulinae* (1790), *View of the Evidences of Christianity* (1794), and *Natural Theology* (1802). LSM cites Paley's *Principles* below.

20. [Greg], "English Socialism, and Communistic Associations," pp. 3–4. The passage is quoted at length by LSM at the beginning of chap. 6, "Negro and White Slavery—Wherein Do They Differ?"

21. John Howard (1726–90), English reformer; promoted through Parliament bills improving prison conditions (1774); wrote *State of Prisons in England and Wales* (1777) and other books advocating prison reforms. Elizabeth Gurney Fry (1780–1845), English philanthro-

in the mass to a set of sentimental Mrs. Jellaby's and Mr. Stiggins' getting up subscriptions to supply little negroes in the West Indies with flannel waistcoats and moral pocket handkerchiefs, and launching curses and anathemas against all who may venture to doubt the benefit of their procedures.[22] These people never hesitate about the truth of the restless inspiration which pushes them on; they never listen to a suggestion that their new-light doctrines may perchance be not of God, but of the devil, and set up a howl of indignation over all who hint the possibility of their moral pocket handkerchiefs doing more harm than good. The thinkers, on the contrary, cool, quiet, calm, stoical perhaps in action, and little given to demonstrative sympathy, have on their side, doubtless, also their pretenders and their bigots; but, likewise, they have their good Samaritans. The first class have a salve ready for every sore, a bandage for every wound, and rush with their ready remedies to staunch the blood wherever they perceive it to flow. The last, of more deliberate action, inspect the wound before they apply the remedy, painfully probe it, perhaps, or open the bleeding vein, and bid the sufferer often rather to bear the running sore than to heal it at the risk of his life.

With what propriety shall the first, however amiable, under its better developments, may be their ready impulse, exclaim against the last as butchers and miscreants—and yet such is the ground taken by modern philanthropists against Political Economy. Because Political Economy doubts the policy of their proposed expedients, they find no epithet too harsh for its expounders. Because Political Economy asks, doubts, studies, questions, and, seeing what appear hopeless ills, seeks to counteract rather than to cure them, searching for palliatives where it fails to find remedies, they pronounce it accursed—Anathema Maranatha.[23] We repeat, our reviewer is not

---

pist; Quaker minister; active in reform of prisons, hospitals, madhouses. Florence Nightingale (1820–1910), nurse; founded first school for the professional training of nurses (1860); her indefatigable exploits during the Crimean War (1854–56) had recently received much attention.

22. In Dickens' *Bleak House,* Mrs Jellyby devotes herself so fervently to the cause of African emancipation that she neglects her husband and family; her example is reproved by LSM in chap. 13, "Carey on the Slave Trade." In chapter 27 of Dickens' *Pickwick Papers,* Mr. Stiggins, a reforming clergyman, "a prim-faced, red-nosed man, with a long, thin countenance, and a semi-rattlesnake sort of eye," thus deplores Toby Weller to Sam Weller, his son: "He has an obderrate bosom. Oh, my young friend, who else could have resisted the pleading of sixteen of our fairest sisters, and withstood their exhortations to subscribe to our noble society for providing the infant negroes in the West Indies with flannel waistcoats and moral pocket handkerchiefs?" (*Pickwick Papers,* introd. Bernard Darwin [London, 1948), pp. 365, 368).

23. 1 Cor. 16:22: "If any man love not the Lord Jesus Christ, let him be Anathema Maranatha."

of their ranks. Even the article upon which we comment shows noble flashes of a wider range of thought and aims far more philosophic. We regret the more that his unlucky precipitance of judgment has forced us, for the nonce, to class him with the revilers of a science whose aim has hitherto been the going about to do good. This science is not the Shylock it has been represented. It is not the science of dollars and cents. But, because it acknowledges wealth as its object, a sickly sentimentality takes fright at the word, connecting always by a strange perversion of ideas wealth with its abuses—as though to look at wine should nauseate with drunkenness, and the sight of food make one shudder at thought of a surfeit. Truly may all the gifts of life be put to an ill purpose; but not therefore shall we despise them all. And if, in spite of possible drunkenness and surfeit, we may still honestly eat bread and drink wine and not be defiled, even so may we righteously study wealth, i.e., the means of attaining and increasing our earthly comforts, and yet be guiltless of avarice, extortion, and all uncharitableness.[24] And if innocently we may thus seek our own enjoyment, is it not virtue, is it not christian charity, to seek the best means for the extension of these blessings to others? Is it a crime in us that we should endeavor to devise means whereby that bread and that wine may be shared with all? Is it a crime in us that we should ask how can this people, this nation, this world of nations, be made to enjoy the greatest possible proportion of these comforts of life that we call wealth? Surely this is christian charity, christian civilization! And this is the end and aim of Political Economy.

Political Economy professes to investigate (we take Mr. Mill's definition) "the nature of Wealth, and its laws of production <the laws of its production> and distribution: including, directly or remotely, the operation of all the causes by which the condition of mankind, or of any society of human beings, in respect to this universal object of human desire, is made prosperous or the reverse."[25] Surely here is space of almost boundless limit, and research of no belittling kind. The constant progress of man from barbarism to enlightenment, from brutality to civilization, from the crass ignorance of the savage, scratching with his nails roots from the earth, and with his teeth tearing the quivering flesh of his palpitating victims, to the highest improvement which science and philosophy have yet attained, all this and more, all progress, all possible worldly improvement, link themselves with this grand

24. Cf. "The Litany" in *The Book of Common Prayer* (1992 ed.), p. 48: "From all blindness of heart; from pride, vain-glory, and hypocrisy; from envy, hatred, and malice, and all uncharitableness, good Lord, deliver us."

25. *Principles of Political Economy,* ed. Robson, p. 3.

object of investigation. To own, to possess, to understand the *meum et tuum,*[26] is one of the first distinguishing characteristics of reason; and in proportion as man becomes enlightened on this point, he rises above the beast. He learns to own, and to permit others to own; he learns to give and to refrain from taking; he learns at once to be generous and just. Moral progress cannot advance but by improvement in physical condition. Improvement in physical condition can only be insured by accumulation of means of comfort—accumulation of means of comfort is wealth. These are truths so trite as scarcely to bear repetition, were it not that these are the axiomatic postula upon which Political Economy is based. Wealth is studied not to put self-interest above morals and religion, not to bid it clash with duty and charity, but to show how all work together in beautiful concord for man's improvement and progress.

"When" says our reviewer,

> we see political economists so blinded by narrow aims as to ignore or be ignorant of the more urgent wants of society than those embraced in their special investigations, and also of the real effects of the contrasted systems, we are strongly inclined to apply to their science, especially when the attempt is made to carry it rigidly into practice, the words of the last of the Roman poets:
>
> Blanda quidem vultus, sed qua non t[a]etrior ulla:
> Ultrices fucata genas, et amicta dolosis
> Illecebris, torvos auro circumlinit hydros.[27]

Now what does this mean? *We* say that the most urgent wants of society are precisely those which fall under the investigation of Political Economy. It is essentially the science of society, or, as it has been sometimes termed, "social science." The contrasted systems of slavery and free labor are now for the first time, as we have already remarked, brought before its tribunal. The

26. "Mine and yours" (Latin).

27. Holmes, "Slavery and Freedom," p. 93, quoting Claudian *De consulatu Stilichonis (On the Consulship of Stilicho)* 2.135–37, describing Luxury as a Fury in disguise: "Her face is charming indeed, but none is fouler: with her avenging cheeks rouged, and wrapped in deceitful allurements, she smears with gold the fierce serpents [of her hair]." In Holmes, "genus" was printed for "genas," an error transcribed without comment by LSM. LSM, or more likely her printer, imported a second error, "amicita" for "amicta." Claudian (d. c. A.D. 404), born in Alexandria, Egypt; came to Italy before 395; court poet to the emperor Honorius; adherent of the general Stilicho; wrote panegyrics, invectives, epithalamia, historical and occasional poems, and an unfinished epic in three books, *De raptu Proserpinae (The Abduction of Proserpina).*

attempt has been made to cast us in default and decide against us on the grounds of non-appearance in court. But science is not so prompt in her decision. We have yet time, and it is for us now to speak. It is for us now to show Political Economy in its connexion with slavery. It is for us to prove that the general weal of mankind is forwarded by slavery as now established in America. This has been partially and can be fully done. Proof is rife; it needs but that we learn to use it. In such proof lies our justification. Our reviewer has well said: "The question of negro slavery is implicated with all the great social problems of the current age. Originating in considerations of moral propriety and social expediency, it embraces the fundamental enigma of the organization of labo[u]r, and, transcending even this wide sphere, extends to the future destiny of the inhabitants of nearly the whole globe. Such a question cannot be too diligently studied. Its comprehensive examination has only commenced." [95]

Strange that a sentence showing so entirely the relation between slavery and Political Economy should be penned by the same hand as the following: "If Political Economy will transgress the narrow limits which are assigned to it as a specific science, and will meddle with questions which concern much higher interests of society than the augmentation of wealth, distorting facts and perverting instruction to minister to the cupidity of grovelling capitalists, we may regret with Niebuhr that there is not a gallows on which it and its apostles might be gibbetted."[28]

What Niebuhr has said on the subject we do not remember, but shall be much surprised if on investigation he is found to have desired so general a gibbetting. We think he surely would have spared us the science, and we on our part would by no means object to giving up to his bloodthirsty propensi-

28. Holmes, "Slavery and Freedom," p. 82. Barthold Georg Niebuhr to Georg Heinrich Ludwig Nicolovius, Rome, Jan. 22, 1817, in *The Life and Letters of Barthold George Niebuhr, with Essays on His Character and Influence* . . . (New York, 1854), pp. 336–37: "That forestalling is an honest trade, to which the State can offer no opposition; and that by these high prices and their profits, large capitals are created, which contribute much more to the increase of the national wealth than the pennies trickling through the poor man's purse for his daily wants—has been proved to satisfaction by political economy, for which science there is unfortunately no gallows, because it was only in the schools of the rhetoricians that one could bring forward an accusation of *inscripti maleficii* [written wrongdoing]. Our forefathers, however, would have drowned the teachers of this wisdom, and my old Romans would have banished them still more rigorously than the Greek sophists, or at least would have ordered them to cease from their *ludus impudentiae* [school of impudence]." Barthold Georg Niebuhr (1776–1831), German historian and diplomat; patron and adviser to the McCords' friend Francis Lieber; his *Römische Geschichte* (1811–32) was praised for setting new standards of historical scholarship. In a letter of June 12, 1848, LSM appealed to his authority to support her view of Gaius Gracchus.

ties a few of the apostles. There are false prophets in all creeds; and, true to our faith of Political Economy, we are quite ready for a weeding out of the noxious plants that choke the true growth. But we would here once for all entreat our reviewer to review his own opinions, and to know what Political Economy is before he condemns it, whether Niebuhr has or has not set him the example. That science whose special object of investigation is the well-being of society, and whose aim to point out its sources and the streams that nourish it, surely need not be reproached with its narrow limits. Wide as the inhabited globe, co-extensive with society, those limits can only be found in man's earthly destiny. Progress, civilization, enlightenment, even morals and virtue, are so linked and intertwined with man's corporeal comforts, that it is hard to draw the line where such a science could be regarded as an intruder. Is it needful to remind our reviewer how often, how almost invariably, want, hunger, and shivering cold are accompanied with crime and depravity? How constantly and necessarily with brutal ignorance? He may probably answer that it is precisely such depravity and ignorance that he seeks to relieve, and that it is the part of the poor against the wealthy that he would defend. We believe it, and therefore lament that he has thus strangely flung aside his natural ally.

It is the poor and ignorant that Political Economy would assist and instruct. It is the masses that it would sustain against the oppression of the few. It is the wealth (i.e., the means of comfort) of all classes and all ranks, not of a few over-gorged capitalists pampered with Government protection, that she undertakes to defend. To naked and starving nations, blighted under the benighted policy of tyrannical governments, Political Economy came to feed and clothe them. If in so doing she could show, as she has shown, as she will yet in her future progress more clearly show, more beautifully develop (for the apostleship of Political Economy has but just begun), if, we say, she can prove that the good of all is irrevocably linked in the good of each; if she can prove (as she does prove) to the purse-proud capitalist that to preserve or increase his wealth his laborer must be fed, his country and his nation must thrive, or all his wealth, like fairy gifts,[29] turns in his hands to dry leaves and trash; if she can prove (as she does prove) to the hungry laborer that his bread is none the dearer, his labor none the less in demand, because the rich man is accumulating his millions—that on the contrary even the most selfish hoarder hoards for the good of all; if she can prove (as she does prove) that labor and capital are not inimical, but rather, working in unison, assistant handmaids each to the other; if she can prove (as she does prove) the truth of

29. Thomas Moore, "Believe Me, If All Those Endearing Young Charms," l. 4: "like fairy gifts fading away."

all these, at first sight, apparent paradoxes, and reconcile interests hitherto in unnatural and fraternal war, is she not indeed a prophet of peace, the beautiful development of christian civilization? Ever thus she comes before us, the teacher of that most beautiful of christian lessons, "Help ye one another."[30]

The great error of dabblers in Political Economy (we most respectfully beg our reviewer to understand that we apply this term not to him, but to a class with whom he has no connexion otherwise than by accidental, and we believe temporary, oversight) is that they, by a strange misuse of terms, regard this science, which claims to investigate wealth and its causes, as the supporter of the wealthy and the oppressor of the poor, as though a wealthy nation should by necessity be composed of millionaires and beggars. Nothing is easier to demonstrate (did time and space allow) than that the wealth of the masses, and not the wealth of the few, makes a nation's wealth. Nothing is easier (and it would seem to us that even a word suggesting the idea should suffice) than to demonstrate that a nation of beggars, though mingled here and there with overgrown capitalists, is not a wealthy nation. Political Economy does constantly demonstrate this, and, aiming at the wealth of nations, seeks not to robe princes in velvet and jewels, but to give their people cheap bread and abundant clothing. But because it has shown that the same system which brings to the people cheap bread and clothing gives also to the prince his velvet and his jewels, because it has extended over these supposed opposing interests the wand of peace, those who half study its arguments strangely contend that, because it would better the rich, it must oppress the poor. Let them study it more deeply and they will find that Political Economy encourages, not the wealthy, but wealth, wars not against the poor, but against poverty; and surely no sane man will be found to contend that this is an unholy war; that the laborer can be too comfortably clothed, or his child too well fed; that the farmer's cottage is too snug, his cattle too fat, or his land too well tilled. Yet this is what Political Economy teaches us is a nation's wealth. This is what Political Economy teaches us is at once the wealth of the laborer and the wealth of his employer, the wealth of the prince and the wealth of his subject, the wealth of the individual and the wealth of the nation.

We have now to pass to the last branch of our subject, and to prove, or at least suggest the grounds upon which it may be proved, that Political Economy will, when properly appealed to, bring the strongest possible arguments in favor of negro slavery. Political Economy, we have shown, is the

30. The citation is not from the Bible; it seems to be an adaptation of such passages as John 13:34 and 15:12, 17; 1 Cor. 12:25; Gal. 5:13, 6:2.

science which considers wealth and its means of increase. Wealth is not money alone, but all desirable things which may be accumulated and exchanged, which may be lost by one individual or nation and gained by another individual or nation, passing from the possession of one into that of another. Thus individual or national wealth will be found to include all things desirable to a man or a nation which are extraneous from his or its individual or national existence, i.e., all things which he or it can possess, and transfer to another. A man's health, integrity, or industry cannot certainly be called his wealth, but they still fairly fall under the consideration of Political Economy because they are indisputably causes operating upon his condition in respect to wealth, and moreover may perhaps in themselves be considered as national wealth. They are certainly so in so far as the man himself may be considered as the property of the nation, to be lost or gained by one or another society, and capable of passing from the possession of one nation into that of another. Thus, then, Political Economy links itself with religion and ethics; for all that improves man, increasing his power and intelligence, makes him a more capable producer of wealth, makes him the better *wealth machine.* If this manner of enunciating our idea be objected to, as bringing man down to the brute and the steam-engine, let our antagonists remember that we do not degrade man to the machine, but bring every argument (this with the rest) to prove that no man can honestly benefit himself without tending also to benefit his fellows, and that even he of the most selfish and grovelling spirit is the better, morally and intellectually, for his honest efforts to improve his own condition. He is, to speak politico-economically, of higher value to his nation. There are wider and purer motives for action than simple self-interest; but simple self-interest (considering its universal prevalence) does more for the world's progress than any one human passion or desire. It exists in the bosom of every man, and he would be a monster in whom it should not be found. Mingling in some with the noblest virtues, in others with the lowest baseness, it still exists in all, and only is criminal when ministering to crime. It is not a virtue, but certainly not a vice. It is purely an instinct: the hunger of the spirit seeking always to gratify its longings, and exciting to crime or to virtuous effort according to the character and disposition of the individual in whom it exists, precisely as the honest man is pushed by hunger to labor for that bread which the thief in preference steals. But because the thief steals to satisfy his hunger, none surely will argue that hunger is therefore a sin. Political Economy sees in his hunger of the spirit a powerful motive for effort and a powerful incentive to good, except when combining with vice. Then only it becomes vicious, and then Political Economy, again siding with religion and morals, declares that vice and crime are injurious, and in their consequences both mediate and immediate degrading to man, incapacitating him as a producer of wealth, and in their nature tending to the disorganization of society.

Thus Political Economy never opposes but always strengthens the decisions of justice and morality. It does not, like good Paley, commit the terrible mistake, so degrading to humanity, of making self-interest the sole basis of virtue,[31] but it proves that self-interest is not a vice; that God, in giving man instinct and desires, made him not a creature of evil, but capable of both good and evil—that if our desires may be corrupted they may also be purified, and that in their purification consists not our spiritual but our worldly welfare. Religion teaches us submission to God and charity to men; ethics teach us justice to men; and Political Economy teaches us that charity and justice are prudence and wisdom. Thus all combine to the same great end, teaching that the good and the wise are one. The institution of slavery must, to prove its innocence, purge itself from sin before this three-fold tribunal.

The religious side of the question has already been so triumphantly argued, that no man taking the gospel for his guide needs to have it repeated. Accordingly, we find the most violent opponents of the system among the new-light and higher law men with whom any religion, further than the dictates of their own wild fancies, ceases to be even a pretext; and next to them the improved christianity mongers, whose creed is blood and murder, and the gospel according to Sharpe's rifles. In its ethical point of view, the defence of the system which has also been frequently, ably, and we think successfully undertaken, must be based upon the natural proprieties of the institution in particular cases, and upon the relative capacities, powers, and propensities of the men or nations concerned. To those who absolutely shut their eyes and ears to common sense, and insist upon a meaningless formula of words, in opposition to all truth and reason, nothing can be said, and they must go on forever, or until they see fit to turn from their folly, insisting, in the face of common sense, common law, and common practice, that all men are born free and equal. But to those who acknowledge a difference in men,

31. Such is in truth the only interpretation which can be given to Paley's definition of virtue [in *Principles of Moral and Political Philosophy,* p. 27], viz, "Virtue is the doing good to mankind, in obedience to the will of God, and for the sake of everlasting happiness." [LSM] Cf. Hugh Swinton Legaré, "Jeremy Bentham and the Utilitarians," in *The Writings of Hugh Swinton Legaré,* ed. Mary Legaré, 2 vols. (Charleston, S.C., 1846; rpt. New York, 1970), 2:469: "Take this very principle of utility. . . . In the hands of Paley, it is quite harmless—it is even, in one point of view, a beneficent and consoling principle. It presupposes the perfect goodness and wisdom of God; for the rule of moral conduct, according to that Divine, is His will, collected from expediency."

different capacities, character, and tendencies, according to race,[32] and other inalienable natural distinctions; to those who recognize the almost axiomatic truth, that circumstances and varying degrees of development require difference of social position, the sometimes practice and even necessity of slavery can be indisputably proved. It is treading over oft trodden ground to endeavor to show that all men are not fit for all things, and that, wherever the Creator's will for his creature can be discovered in the tendencies and capacities of the creature, there can be no surer rule for man's guidance. The universal practice and judgment of the world have assigned to women and children a subordinate position to men. In the women's case this subordination is permanent, as are the constitutional characteristics which give rise to and justify it. In the child's it is temporary, as are also the peculiar characteristics in him causing its necessity. In either class the rule is general, in spite of exceptional powers existing in occasional individuals, and properly it is so. No general rule can be made to suit exceptional cases. Precisely similar are the causes and proofs of the justification and necessity of slavery in all its phases. The positions of women and children are in truth as essentially states of bondage as any other, the differences being in degree, not kind. They are states of subjection to the supremacy of others, and of greater or less deprivation of the rights of self government. This, the true definition of slavery, applies equally to the position of women in the most civilized and enlightened countries. That there are higher and lower degrees of subjection and deprivation makes no difference in the question of justice (if either is injustice both are injustice, as it is equally robbery whether I forcibly take from a man one dollar or a thousand), except in so far as it is necessary that these higher and lower degrees be in accordance with the peculiar characteristics and capabilities of the class thus held in greater or less subjection for their own benefit and that of society. The permanent natural characteristics, or the temporary condition, of certain classes of human beings indicate them as fitted for a certain position in the social scale and as unfitted for certain other positions, and their own as well as the general good of society requires that this fitness should be considered. The nearer the position of each class can be suited to its capacities, the nearer is the law of nature (that is of God) fulfilled, and the nearer is perfect justice attained. Perfect justice it is scarcely within man's capacities to attain, and all that can be done by the science of morals is to approach nearer and nearer (as does the mathematician in the squaring of the circle) to perfect truth. That system of govern-

32. We specially avoid here the question of unity or diversity of origin, which can make little difference in our argument. An existing difference in races, which centuries cannot eliminate, is equivalent in practice to perpetual difference. [LSM]

ment, then, and that amount of subjection which is needful to the highest development of the peculiar powers, and to the keeping in check the peculiar defects, of any class of men, is the most useful and the most just for that class.

The necessities of each class, race, or nation can only be calculated from its antecedent conditions and its actual developments. In the case of any society of men which have attained a certain degree of enlightenment, it is a just conclusion that themselves are the best judges of the proprieties and necessities of their case; but when a nation or society is in a condition unfit for self-government and inconsistent with its higher development, often the circumstance of contact with or subjection by more enlightened nations has been the means of transition to a higher development. When two nations, enlightened and unenlightened, are thus thrown in contact upon the same soil, nothing but slavery can prevent the destruction of the weaker race. In those phases of society where the developments of corporeal power are of more value, i.e., more useful to existing society, than mental (as in the first beginnings of society, where it is more important to men to know how to dig than to invent steam engines), the muscularly strong man becomes the master, the intelligent one the slave; and thus the functions of both are best fulfilled. Thus the weaker is protected (albeit often oppressed, for everything earthly is faulty), and the stronger aided in the point where he needs aid, i.e., mentally improved. In more advanced stages of society, where mind asserts its supremacy, intellect makes the master; intellect is the true strength, and mere muscular power needs not only the guidance, but the protection, of that mighty power which man's intellect teaches him to sway. The savage cowers before the builder of cities, or the inventor of steam-engines and magnetic telegraphs. The thought which commands the elements is stronger than muscle or fibre. Here, therefore, intellect (now become strength) protects, and muscle serves. In either case the weaker people perishes, but for the protection granted by the stronger, and, in return for that protection, serves. We do not say that this is done by regular compact. It is not so done; no society is formed by compact. Society is the result of instincts. Brutes and insects form societies as men; men, only by afterthought and progressive reasoning, think of compacts. The existence of society is an inherent necessity to man's existence; what therefore is needful to the existence of society cannot be unjust.

Thus, then, slavery is sometimes and to certain extents proved just. Political Economy may now be adduced as a powerful adjunct to define its limits, for we are far from granting that it would prove so frequent a remedy for the evils of society as our reviewer's argument appears to us to imply. And here Political Economy must also bring forward the test of utility. That position in which man is of the greatest utility and highest benefit to himself and to mankind—that position in which all his powers are exerted to the greatest advantage, his deficiencies kept in abeyance, and his faults under check—is by philosophical argument his legitimate duty, his highest interest, and in accordance with the eternal justice of things. The test of the right must be in its results, and surely the tree must be known by its fruits.[33] For although it is very certain that every good deed does not, with the exact measurement of good boy story-books, bring its immediate reward, and every ill one its castigation, it is inconsistent at once with experience, and with every idea that man can form of the goodness of deity, that any regular system of evil can result in permanent and general good. The oppressor of the widow and the defrauder of the orphan may, in the inscrutable wisdom of Providence, be permitted to revel in his ill got gains; the murderer may hide his bloody hand, and unquestioned of justice pass through life high in the world's prosperity; but certain it is that, by the test of utility in result, the actions of such men are most injurious to society. A nation of defrauders and murderers could be nothing but a nation accursed, a people degraded to the lowest savagism, a robber band, in truth true Ishmaelites, whose hand should be against every man and every man's hand against them, "curtailed from all the fair proportions" of civilized society, and condemned to unprogressive barbarism.[34] And even in such condition, to prevent an entire obliteration of the species, some shadow of virtue, some good instinct must remain. At least there must linger that proverbial honor said to exist among thieves; there must survive some affection, some pity, some human passion, some virtue in short, or, worse than brutes, every man would be a Cain to his brother.

While, therefore, religion and morals say to us crime is wrong because it is crime, displeasing to God and hurtful to man, Political Economy confirms their decision on prudential motives. It teaches us that what is hurtful to man is impolitic, degrading him both individually and nationally, and checks progress because it destroys all security. Man is constantly aiming at advancement in his social condition, and in this constant individual effort to better himself, so long as honestly indulged, each pushes forward by his own fractional effort the great wheel of progress. Let crime or injustice intrude, and, precisely in proportion as these prevail, society is disorganized, men's rights become insecure, their energies flag, lethargy displaces effort, want displaces honest accumulation; man makes for himself a scourge equal to those which Heaven in its wrath has sometimes sent; and as, when pestilence

33. Matt. 7:16–20.

34. Gen. 16:11–12; *Richard III* 1.1.18: "I, that am curtail'd of this fair proportion."

or famine makes men insecure of everything but the life of today, they seek to enjoy that only, forgetting all else in a kind of reckless madness—"let us eat, drink, and be merry, for tomorrow we die"[35]—so with the prevalence of crime "all order dies."

> And one fierce spirit of the first-born Cain
> Reigns in all bosoms, that, each heart being set
> On bloody courses, the rude scene may end,
> And darkness be the burier of the dead.[36]

All society in which crime is systematically encouraged must perforce rush more or less rapidly to destruction, and legalized injustice is national suicide.[37]

Political Economy thus takes utility as the test of right. It does not set—this is the libel put upon it—utility above right. It does not say utility *is* right, but only brings utility to prove the right. The sense of right man receives from no argument or system of proof; it is instinctive with his nature. But in so far as it is susceptible of being clouded and misled, no test can be found other than God's approbation; and God's approbation, where man is not guided by special revelation, can only be read in results. All moralists agree, and all common sense confirms, that sound morality must always result in general good; and although we must do right for the love of right, and avoid wrong for the hatred of wrong, although the impulse of conscience is a guide to all men, not entirely extinguishable even in the most depraved, still general results must determine by the rule of cause and effect where and how man's instincts have gone astray. It is a common expression that the good man must act independently of consequences. But this abbreviation of speech, which is a truth only so far as it means that he must act independently of *personal consequences,* has led to many errors, and is, if taken literally, the grossest of fallacies. No sane man ever acts independently of consequences; no good man can for a moment deem it his duty so to do. There can be no virtuous action done without virtuous intent; and criminal intent makes the best action a crime. It is an innocent action to steep opium in alcohol. It is a right action to do this with the object of trade and to gain a livelihood. It is a virtuous action to do it with the intent of relieving the agony of a wounded or suffering creature. It is a criminal action to do it with

35. Eccl. 8:15; Isa. 22:13; Luke 12:19.

36. *2 Henry IV* 1.1.154, 157–60, reading: "Let order die! . . . But let one spirit of the first-born Cain / Reign. . . ."

37. At this point concludes the first of the two instalments of LSM's article as originally published in *De Bow.*

the intent of poisoning a brother. The consequence aimed at makes the deed right or wrong. We do not contend that good intent always makes a good act, and that poisoning our brother with the good intention of sending him to heaven would be a virtuous action. But neither would it be a vicious, though a most lamentable and mischievous, one. It would be simply the action of a madman, of a being whose reasoning powers are ineffectual to his guidance and incapable of properly estimating consequences, and which would thus commit wrong ignorantly. The same man might possibly in another phase of his madness commit the murder without any calculation of consequences, or he might save the victim's life from some unexpected danger, equally without consideration of consequences. In either case the madman is no more a responsible agent than are the inanimate means which he has used. In neither case is he either criminal or virtuous, precisely because he has not the power of calculating consequences or of estimating the importance of so doing. A sane man thus acting (if a sane man could thus act) would be guilty of criminal thoughtlessness; and on the other hand, however beneficial might be the result of his action, has no merit in it, because he has acted independently of consequences. Consequences (not personal but general) are the sanction or condemnation of God upon any course of action. Paley is to be condemned, not because he gives consequences as the aim of virtuous action, but personal consequences. To act from the hope of reward and fear of punishment (i.e., from consideration of personal consequences) is prudence, but certainly no higher virtue. To act with the hope and aim of doing all the good we can to our fellow men, considering and weighing consequences with the best judgment God has given us, is virtue, is the highest reach of morality; and, as we have already remarked, the result, or accomplished consequence, is the truest test we can have of the correctness or faultiness of our judgment. A man may be conscientiously right, and yet being of misguided judgment do what is in itself wrong and leading to evil—thus committing, not a sin, but an error, and being thus, although innocent in intention, the cause of ill. The only corrective of such misguided judgment (except in cases of distinct revelation) is the test of utility or ultimate good.

Herein, then, lies the great defence of American negro slavery which Political Economy (the science which considers the weal of nations) cannot on due investigation fail to pronounce. We do not say what has been done, but what inevitably must in the future be done. Men and prejudices have gone against us; but science cannot be swayed by prejudice or outcry; and however its advocates may, leaping to crude conclusions, often join in the chorused "hip hurrah" or the wild "halloo" of riot and fanaticism, at last she bears aloft the banner of truth, and points her worshippers to the rising sun of knowledge. All that is now needed for the defence of United States negro slavery and its entire exoneration from reproach, is a thorough investigation of fact, an investigation which will force sight into eyes that now will not see, and hearing into ears that now will not hear.[38] We want a broad exposition of fact! fact! fact!—fact without coloring and without distortion; fact whose simple truth shall put slander to the blush, paralyze the tongue of falsehood, and, taking the system and its results in their entire development, expose both in their fullest breadth and depth. So soon as our opponents can be forced to look into the fact of this system, instead of taking it on hearsay from works of fiction and the mawkish sentiment of that class of "feelers" in philanthropy which we have endeavored in the earlier part of our article to depict, so soon as the public mind can be brought to a sufficiently sane condition on this subject to receive such testimony as would be decisive before any court of law or equity, our cause will be conclusively and triumphantly determined in our favor; and Political Economy (call it by what name we may, "social science," "national economy," "political science," what you will, still always the noble science, not, perhaps, too justly named Political Economy) will and must be our judge. Let hasty prejudice declaim as it may, that science, whose object is the weal of nations, itself the physician of social disease, must be called upon to pronounce our system (as we have endeavored to prove it) no disease, but the normal and healthy condition of a society formed of such mixed material as ours.

We think the reviewer of "Slavery and Freedom" has carried quite too far his idea that an established slavery is the preferable condition of all society, for although he says (page 86), "We will not maintain that slavery is the sole, rightful condition of labo[u]r," he tells us elsewhere (page 82), speaking of free labor, "This is comparatively a recent innovation, a social neoterism. It is not one of the universally and necessarily recur[r]ing types of social organization, but, in great measure, a new thing under the sun. The universal and necessary institution is slavery. This has appeared in all ages and in all countries, and apparently refuses to be eradicated from the earth—a strong presumption that it is a natural growth." And again, "Free labo[u]r is, then, the exceptional procedure of some nations in late centuries; the prestige of human experience is adverse to it" [82]. Again (page 84), "It is sustained by no philosophy, but only by the most fallacious and pernicious sophistry; and the works which constitute our text supply the evidence that it can claim no presumption of right from its consequences to individuals and to societies. The first fruits of the general renunciation of serfdom were mendicancy, larceny, vice, crime, and pauperism, to which may be added

38. Jer. 5:21.

Queen Elizabeth's poor laws.[39] Its final fruitage is the destitution of the English labo[u]rer and the French proletaire, and the disintegration of European government and society."

Now we contend that the system of free labor is one of the necessarily recurring types of social organization, not *the* type, *but one of the types,* and the advocate of slavery who defends it to the exclusion of free labor, is as far wrong as he who defends free labor to the exclusion of slavery. Both are necessarily recurring types of social organization, and each suited to its peculiar phase of society. Free labor is a recent innovation, a social neoterism, says the reviewer. Now, in spite of the imposing influence of a rather hard word, there is nothing so bad in a neoterism after all. It signifies only a thing of Northern growth; and such we grant the system of free labor to be. It is progress, an innovation if you will, but no more an innovation than commerce and navigation, than steamboats and railroads.

We endeavored earlier in our article to show that slavery was oftenest a rudimental condition, a state of progression wherein two or more unequally endowed peoples, existing on the same soil, could become, instead of clashing and destructive rivals, the assistants and protectors of each other. With the progress of society these separate peoples became oftenest so commingled in blood, interests, and capacities, that what had been distinct was no more. The serf, both in power of mind and body, was now the equal of his lord. The distinction, now become purely conventional, was no longer in the man, but only in the position of the man. Their relative positions (natural at first as those of child and parent) now became forced, and the inevitable progress of society was gradually, almost insensibly, to efface existing differences. That this progress should be constantly interrupted and impeded by man's passions and interests, proves nothing more than that (as we see with everything earthly) an inscrutable Providence sees fit to allow man's passions and interests to interfere with the natural course of events, the ill consequence of such interference only constantly proving itself by ill results. Still, with more or less impediment, such progress is and must be effected. The man who is by nature the equal of his brother cannot be his slave, except under exceptional circumstances, and no nation or race of men can ever, by any earthly power, be kept in subjection by another nation or race of men which is only its equal. There will need no foreign promptings, no excitements from abroad, such as abolition manufacture constantly circulates

39. Formulated in 1598 and 1601, the poor laws stipulated that individual parishes were responsible for the relief of poverty, supervised by justices of the peace and administered by overseers; funds were to derive from local property rates. The poor laws were superseded by the Poor Law Amendment Act (1834).

among our negroes, to show such a people its natural position. Man to man it will be felt, and man to man the true God-given power will assert its pre-eminence. So long as a people has not the impulse within itself, there is no surer sign of inferiority. We are not here contending for any utopian equality even in the most fully developed nations, nor do we believe in men being born free and equal under any system. We think it not unlikely that in the progress of time, with the fullest development of which man is susceptible, the higher and more perfectible races may attain under a constantly advancing civilization a nearer general equality than has yet been approached, and that, all classes of men being developed to their highest point of perfection, present differences of position may be diminished. A constant progression towards this the world has shown for centuries. But to this end bloodshed and violence alone can effect nothing. The man must be changed. Brute force may destroy, but can effect nothing. The lion may slaughter the man, but does not thereby make a man of himself. Brutal ignorance roused to resistance is brutal ignorance still, and the savage who is excited to murder his master can only be slaughtered or again enslaved, unless he be driven out from association with the civilized man.

Free labor, we contend, is as natural as slavery. Both are necessary institutions and neither universal. Both are sustained by the truest philosophy, and the "mendicancy, larceny, vice, crime, and pauperism" to which our reviewer alludes, "the destitution of the English labo[u]rer and the French proletaire, and the disintegration of European government and society" [84], are not the fruitage of the abolition of serfdom, but rather the result of its imperfect manner of abolition and the obstacles constantly opposed by the man in power to the natural advancement of his equal man. We are no upholders, under any system of society or in any condition of progress, of communism,[40] agrarianism, or any other artificial equalizer of men. Equality must, so far as equality is possible, be from the root in the nature of the man himself, and cannot be forced or coaxed by any hotbed culture. We defend a man's right to property in land with as much tenacity as any other possible right or possession. But it is not only the rights of property which the laws of Europe protect. Look for instance at the laws of England in favor of a privileged class. The laws of entail alone might suggest a more rational cause than free labor for the destitution of the English laborer. Who dares say that

40. The only just and practicable communism which we can imagine, is the one exhibited by our own system of slavery, where the mass of inferior men is subjected to a ruler with whom the idea of competition is by nature impossible. Without such a head communism cannot exist. Louis Blanc and Co.'s communism was impracticable because naturally headless. [LSM]

the laborer is free when no effort on his part, no debt nor extravagance on the part of the landholder, can release land from such a monopoly as the annexed extract exhibits? "Five noblemen are said to own about one-fourth of all the landed property in Scotland. They are the Marquis of Breadalbane, and the Dukes of Argyle, Athol, Sutherland, and Buccleuch. About two thousand proprietors are said also to own one-third of the land and total revenue of the three kingdoms of England, Scotland, and Ireland."[41]

This, if not exact, is essentially correct; and this tenure is not under a simple right of possession which mismanagement on the part of the landholder would set aside by purchase and sale, and the natural process of exchange, but by a stringent law which forbids all possibility of exchange and, condemning the laborer never to be a landholder, puts him at the mercy of the owner of the monopolized article.

Who again dares say that labor is free when the cost of royalty is such as the following extract shows?

> Cost of Royalty. The Liverpool Association, composed of merchants in that city, have published various financial reform tracts. From one lately issued called "The Royal Household, a Model to Parliament and the Nation,"[42] republished in part in the New York *Tribune,* we make some extracts, showing the amount paid to the Queen.
>
> In December, 1837, Parliament settled on the Queen for life the sum of £385,000 a year—with £10,000 additional for "home secret service money." The particular application of the money was provided for by the statute as follows: 1. For her Majesty's private purse, £60,500. 2. For salaries for her household, £131,260. 3. Expenses of the household (i.e., what Paddy would call "the best of eating and drinking"), £172,500. 4. Royal bounty, alms, and special services, £13,000. 5. Pensions to the extent of £1,200. 6. Unappropriated money, £7,040.
>
> What is called "The Civil List" of Ireland and of Scotland add[s] £115,000 per annum to the £385,000 in question—the Duchy of Lancaster also yields £12,000 per annum net addition to the Queen's income; there is £38,000

41. Francis Bowen (1811–90), *The Principles of Political Economy* (Boston, 1856; rpt. New York, 1974), pp. 522–23: "Five noblemen, the Marquis of Breadalbane, the Dukes of Argyle, Athol, Sutherland, and Buccleuch, own perhaps one fourth of all Scotland. I have already quoted [p. 195n] the assertion of M. [Léonce] de Lavergne, that 2,000 proprietors possess among them one third of the land and total revenue of the three kingdoms of England, Scotland, and Ireland." This passage is quoted in the New York *Journal of Commerce,* May 5, 1856, "to show why the laboring classes in England are less wealthy, less intelligent, and less influential than those in this country."

42. Financial Reform Association, Liverpool, *Tracts of the Financial Reform Association,* 2d ser., no. 14 (Liverpool, March 1856).

extra every year from the Duchy of Cornwall (which ought to be, but is not, kept for the future use of the Prince of Wales, to whom it belongs), and there are also annual accessories of revenue from counties Palatine of Chester and Durham, the amounts of which can only be approximated by striking an average. On the whole, however, independent of the waifs which occasionally fall into the Queen's lap from other sources (for instance, she is heir to all persons without legal heirs, who die intestate in any part of her empire), Queen Victoria's annual income is £668,000, or nearly double what even George IV luxuriated upon.

She has likewise the use of various palaces, which are kept in repair at the public cost. When she travels by land it is at no cost, and when by sea the admiralty furnish her a steam yacht, man and provision it.

Prince Albert was allowed by parliament £30,000 as the Queen's husband, in addition to which he receives emoluments from different offices given him by the Queen, amounting to £30,000 more.

By the above figures, it will be seen that the Queen and Prince Albert cost the British Government, for their personal and domestic expenditures, the sum of £977,695, or nearly $4,700,000.

This is not yet perfected free labor. These are the obstacles which men put in the way of the natural progress of events, and the result is a system neither of pure slavery nor pure free labor. All Europe is boiling up in this transition state—a state of slow revolution. Labor is making itself free, but is not yet fully so. We believe that it is to be, for its time has come. When the noble and master has no distinction but the cut of his coat or the fashion of his air to distinguish him from the crowd—when even this distinction is kept up only by legal privileges which can find no foundation in right—when the man can face the man feeling his rights and daring to ask them, the time has come when those privileges must be abolished and those rights listened to.

This progress has been retarded, not more perhaps by the opposition, determined as it may be, of the one class, than by the faults of the other. The hitherto lower classes, as it were a blind man restored to vision, are dazzled by the light, and stumble in their way, even from its excess. They see their rights and, knowing these withheld, fancy them greater than they are, and grasp beyond them. Thus come the outcries for freedom of the soil, right to labor, communism, woman's rights, fraternity, and equality, all men born free and equal, and all the divers follies of the day, which, like vaulting ambition, o'erleap their aim, "to fall o' the other side."[43]

43. *Macbeth* 1.7.25–28: "I have no spur / To prick the sides of my intent, but only / Vaulting ambition, which o'erleaps itself / And falls on th'other—"

Free labor is indeed so new a thing that as yet it scarcely knows itself. Its trial is to come in revolutionized Europe. Great and fearful has been the struggle; great and fearful it may yet be. But one thing is certain. In proportion as the rising classes are fitted for the position which they claim, the horrors of the struggle, which exist only in their weakness, will be diminished. The firm demand which thoroughly knows its own limit, is irresistible and oftenest not resisted. An enlightened civilization is the only equalizer among men and, in as far as it is permitted to act without interference, acts always peacefully. We hope, we believe even, that the world has seen such horrors as no future circumstances can renew, and that the inevitable progress of the system of free labor will be peaceful and prosperous precisely in such proportion as the present and future man of Europe is and will be raised above the past. We speak here of the man of Europe, and only of Europe. For him of Asia little has been dreamed of liberty or free labor. His fate would seem to be bondage; and for him of Africa, savagism. As yet theory has interfered so little with these that in questions such as the one before us they are scarcely counted as of the world whose fate is in discussion. They have apparently accomplished that destiny of which they are capable; and tacitly they are left aside for future ages to determine whether such condition may be permitted to continue in a progressive world, or whether the irresistible impulse of a civilization which they are incapable of following must sweep them to extinction. When we speak of the world of men, Asia and Africa are for the most part forgotten. But the young giant, the offspring of Europe (for the man of America has already met that destiny which we anticipate as possible for him of Asia and Africa, and the transplanted energy of Europe has now become a new world), the young giant of America, shall it too follow in the wake of its parent, and show a unity in the form of modern civilization? Is the system of free labor also our destiny?

Most decidedly we answer: This is impossible, now and forever impossible, except by the total and entire eradication of a race which, transplanted at the same time with ourselves, has grown with us and become a dependent limb of our system, or rather a vital organ, to sever which is death. America has grown to her present point of maturity with the established system of negro slavery. The strong race and the weak, the civilized and the savage, him by nature ruler, protector, master, and him by nature subject, dependent, slave, are here not only cast together, but have been born together, grown together, lived together, worked together, each in his separate sphere, striving for the good of each, and together beautifully exemplifying the developed utility which earlier in our article we endeavored to indicate as the perfect condition of slavery—that condition which, fully exhibited, could not fail to elicit from Political Economy its sentence of approval, as the one in which these two races of men are mutually assistant to each other, and contributing, in the largest possible degree consistent with their mutual powers, to the good of each other and mankind. This system is in no way a laggard from that of Europe. It is a system quite as perfect in its kind, much more perfect in its development.

The results of the free labor system, so far as developed, truly do, as our reviewer has argued [65–69, 76–81, 85–86], teem with a wretchedness and misery, vice and crime, unknown to our quieter social condition. This is precisely because (as we have just remarked) our system, equal in kind, is more perfect in its development. Both are, with a progressive world, in a state of progress. Both are advancing to meet the highest tone of a fully developed christian civilization. Neither is, in itself, better or worse than the other. Each is proper, necessary, inevitable, in the phase of society which has called it forth. To force either into the place of the other is equal madness in either case, and in either case must lead to such fearful atrocities as must inevitably follow all human efforts to resist divine laws. The attempted enslavement of the English laborer would equal in folly (and nothing more) the attempted liberation of the American negro. Either, seriously undertaken, and with sufficient power to oppose the natural current of events, could but produce chaotic anarchy. Either would drown in blood the civilization of the continent wherein it might be attempted. Each of these systems works well its part; each has made noble progress; each is destined to further improvement, each to be perfected in its kind. Let but the unnatural animosity, whose source is ignorance, cease, and the social millennium will show that both are right, for both are in accordance with the laws of nature and necessity (which are the laws of God), and both must work together to the world's great progress. Both have indeed already done so. What century of man's world history developes such forward impulse as the last? And candid investigation must prove that, in this, a strong laborer has been the American negro slave. His labor has opened the new world of American agriculture with its great staples, cotton and sugar, which are the wealth not of his master only, not of one country only, but of the world. Even the lowest peasantry of Europe profits by them. Even benighted Asia, even savage Africa profits by them. Comfort and wealth, circulating through the arteries of commerce, extend from shore to shore; and every pulsation of the world's great heart sends further and further, with new comforts and new joys, the glad tidings of a constantly progressing improvement, of a world ever moving onward, ever happier, better, and more enlightened. These are the results of slavery, thus always blessing the slave even with the increasing abundance and comforts of which he is himself at once the producer and the recipient.

We have said that nothing but the extinction of the negro race in America can eradicate slavery. The negro can never be the white man's equal; and were slavery truly the evil, the moral sore, which our opponents suppose it, its cure could only be in the amputation of the limb. If the negro's fate be worthy of consideration, for his sake slavery should be maintained. But charity is an individual, not a national, virtue. Nations are not and cannot be good Samaritans. The only conceivable national charity is that wise policy which continually seeks the greatest good of the greatest number. The negro's cause then must be pleaded on the grounds of policy; and, as we have already repeated, Political Economy stands here to prove that christian charity is national policy. Slavery, which is the negro's protection, is the world's wealth.

The reviewer of "Slavery and Freedom," had he been a political economist, would have seen the immense power of this argument, and would not have thoughtlessly thrown it aside, confessing thus a weakness in our system which not only does not in truth exist, but which would logically prove its inevitable destruction. After telling us truly that the great moving cause of emancipation has always been the pecuniary interest of the master, and that the slave is only turned loose when his free labor can be purchased more cheaply than his slave labor can be maintained, he, by a most unfortunate *non sequitur,* concludes that, because certain nations have abolished slavery when become less profitable than free labor, that slave labor is therefore in its nature less profitable than free labor. He says (page[s] 84[–85]):

> The principle which occasioned the substitution of free for slave labo[u]r was the prospect of diminished expenditure and increased gain. It is, after all, the sole motive which has upheld and extended the change. It is also, in the ultimate analysis, the sole ground on which the abolitionists have waged the war against slavery, and advocated the exclusive propriety of free labo[u]r. Look into their declamations, contemplate their tactics, survey the whole literature of Political Economy, and it will be manifest that the real argument is simply that free labo[u]r is cheaper and more productive or profitable than slave labo[u]r. This we do not doubt, if the maximum of profit is wrested from the labo[u]rer; but are government, and society, and the human family, created and ordered singly for the production, augmentation, and accumulation of wealth? We think not. The free labo[u]r enthusiasts maintain, practically, that they are; the defenders of slavery assert, both theoretically and practically, that they are not.

Now we assert unhesitatingly (and not only Political Economy but common sense will bear us out) that, if free labor is cheaper and more productive than slave labor, slavery is a wrong.[44] If the slave is kept to a less profitable system of labor than he could exercise being free, there is injury done, not to him only but also to society, of which he is thus made the unprofitable servant. "Government, and society, and the human family," are certainly not "created and ordered singly for the production, augmentation, and accumulation of wealth," and we presume that there never was folly so gross as to assert that they are; but any government or society (individual charity is a thing entirely distinct) which voluntarily chooses a less, in preference to a more, profitable system, thus injuriously affecting the interests and comforts of its citizens of every grade, acts by a peculiar logic of its own, proving the true influence neither of christian charity nor philosophic wisdom.

Such is, however, not our case, as the reviewer, in spite of the incautious admission we have quoted, goes on to prove. He says (page 87), speaking of slavery: "It multiplies and strengthens the links which bind society together, and it affords the largest practicable amount of happiness and comfort to the largest number—nay, to all the members of the community." And again (page 88):

> All the evils which the feverish avidity of the times has occasioned in free communities, would be more rapidly and certainly introduced into slave societies, if the interests of the master ceased to be identified with the comfortable existence of the slave. . . . The interests of each must be advanced by the connected and reciprocal interests of all. Slavery, as any other social institution, is just only so long as it conforms to this law, and advances the interests of the slave concurrently with the interests of the master. We do not contemplate any equality of interests, but only their just proportion, agreeably to the prescription of distributive justice; for in this case, as in all others, the remark of Henry Cornelius Agrippa is perfectly true, that the greatest equality is the greatest inequality.[45] Whatever would diminish the interest, the tender and considerate interest, of the master in his slave, is calculated to frustrate all the alleged advantages of slavery, and would produce, as it has heretofore produced, greater evils than have been occasioned by the ominous conjunction of free competition and free labo[u]r, in the most civilized nations of Christendom, where the progress of events has composed a terrible

44. And if it be cheaper, as the reviewer asserts, when the maximum of profit is wrested from the laborer, it must equally be cheaper under all co-incident circumstances. [LSM]

45. Holmes cites Heinrich Cornelius Agrippa von Nettesheim (1486–1534), German theologian and philosopher, *De incertitudine et vanitate scientiarum et artium (On the Uncertainty and Emptiness of the Sciences and Arts),* published in 1531, chap. 55 ("De politica"): "Cum omnes sibi habeantur aequales, nihil est tam inaequale quam aequalitas ipsa."

commentary on the ancient text, that the nations of Europe were led astray by the fierce appetite for gain.[46]

These, passing over the constantly recurring prejudice of the writer on the subject of the "ominous conjunction of free competition and free labor," are plain truths. A master's *interest* must be in his slave—must be identified with the comfort of the slave. It must be more *profitable* to him to have healthy and happy slaves than sick and wretched ones. It must be more *profitable* to him that they should live than that they should die; and this can only be, so long as the slave's labor is more profitable to him than any other which he can attain. Certainly there may be found individuals (thank God! not a few) whose philanthropy, generosity, or charity would lead to self-sacrifice, often limitless, for the sake of certain other individuals. But (however it may perhaps be a proof of the weakness or limited perfectibility of human nature) it is a very plain truth that, admirable as are the individual Howards and Florence Nightengales, who pass, meteor-like, spreading a benignant and purifying influence through a contaminated atmosphere, a would-be nation of Howards and Nightengales would be but a sickly specimen of human development. If our duty is to do good, it must always be remembered that the good of today is not always the good of tomorrow; that the good of the teacher is not the good of the learner; and that, according to the homely proverb, circumstances alter cases.[47] Men must make bread before they can give it. They must have clothing and food before they can take thought of the wants of others. To make possible the existence of the Howards and the Nightengales, there must have been *workers* before them: hard-handed men, looking into the necessities as well as the charities of life; stern reasoners, who could see that alms giving is rather a beautiful incident in the life than its first duty, and that the stern practicalities of life must come before its sentiment, however amiable the latter may be. Charity covereth a multitude of sins,[48] and none less than ourselves would underrate the beautiful and softening influence of this great christian virtue. But men must labor

46. The "ancient text," which Holmes cites in the original Greek, is John the Lydian (fl. sixth century, reign of Justinian), *De magistratibus (On the Magistracies)* 3.46[.7]: "There are slanderous remarks recorded by the ancient sources concerning almost all the inhabitants of Europe on the score of excessive fondness of money, both in their manner of acquiring and in that of spending what surpluses they had" (trans. T. F. Carney, *Bureaucracy in Traditional Society: Romano-Byzantine Bureaucracies Viewed from Within* [Lawrence, Kans., 1971]).

47. Thomas Chandler Haliburton, pseud. Sam Slick, *The Old Judge, or Life in a Colony* (1849), ed. M. G. Parks (Ottawa, 1978), chap. 15 ad fin., p. 253.

48. 1 Pet. 4:8: "And above all things have fervent charity among yourselves: for charity shall cover a multitude of sins."

and strive before they can assist; they must accumulate before they can give; they must cease to be savages before they can be christians; they must have formed themselves into enlightened societies before the Howards are conceivable. The widest charity, which labors not for individuals but peoples, the truest philanthropy, which would heal the wounds of nations, must look beyond the limits of "men of feeling";[49] and if (as we have contended throughout our article) that which is right must bring the greatest ultimate good, of necessity ultimate good, though it cannot make right, must be a proof of the right. It is God's blessing upon man's actions, the fire from Heaven acknowledging his sacrifice.[50] We say, then, that the world's progress is man's duty as well as instinct; that, were negro slavery really injurious to the world, abolitionists would be right; and, although individual charity would, like angel visits,[51] strive to soothe the sorrows of the doomed race, and to lighten the horrors of its extinction, that the negro's doom would be pronounced, and (horrible as it might be) rightly pronounced; for it would be the lesser evil. Better (did a mysterious Providence make the alternative) a race of savages swept from the world than the world doomed to retrograde barbarism. And the alternative would be presented, were our antagonists right in contending for the comparative unproductiveness of negro-slave labor. Were this labor really comparatively unproductive, it would be in truth an incubus upon society, a burden upon the nation's efforts, and a certain impediment to its progress; and slowly but surely would that nation, held back by such impediment, fall from the civilization of its contemporaries, becoming as it were a running sore among the nations, soiling with its disease their healthier growth.

But thus it is not. The results of United States negro-slave labor are such as no other system of labor yet known upon earth could have accomplished. It has explored regions under whose miasmatic influences the white man sickened and died. It has drained swamps and made habitable the pestiferous marsh. It has conquered the pestilence and opened to a growing world a garden of hitherto unknown comforts and luxuries. It has called the hungry to be fed and the naked to be clothed.[52] It has given a home to the homeless and a new world to progressive and aspiring man. Who dares call this unproductive?

49. In *The Man of Feeling* (1771) by Henry Mackenzie (1745–1831)—important to the history of the sentimental novel and a favorite of Robert Burns—the hero possesses a sensitive moral character offended by the harsh realities of the world about him.

50. Cf. Lev. 9:24.

51. Thomas Campbell (1777–1844), *The Pleasures of Hope* 2.375–78: "Cease, every joy, to glimmer on my mind, / But leave, oh! leave the light of Hope behind! / What though my wingèd hours of bliss have been / Like angel visits, few and far between?"

52. Matt. 25:35–36.

It may well be that the most capable negro may dig a ditch, or run a furrow, or shape a stone, less rapidly and skillfully than the white man of the same grade, and most certainly he will fall far behind him in all work requiring intelligence and continuous effort; but he can stand a sun under which the white man faints; he can be healthy in a swamp where the white man dies; he can make a sugar and a cotton crop where no white power can ever effect it. He does this under the white man's direction, and his labor is (thus employed) not only cheaper than any other, but no other can be found to replace it. No money and no price could buy such labor from the white man; for the white man can no more become a negro than the negro a white man. No money and no price could extract it from the negro himself, he being free; for the negro cannot work without the white man. Each is needed to each, and glorious has been the result of the system under which they have been brought together. Happy it is for the negro that it is so, for so soon as slavery ceases to be profitable, its days as a system are numbered; and with slavery the negro, except as a savage, in his native wilds, perishes. The negro then finds his refuge in slavery, and slavery its justification in utility—in the good which results from it at once to master and slave.

The reviewer of "Slavery and Freedom" may here answer that this is his own argument, and so in many parts of his article it is. He says (pages 93 and 94):

> It is expedient to trace, in the past history of the world, the mode in which slavery has operated as the prime instrument in the civilization and education of the different races of men, and how largely it has contributed to the progress of the human family. In respect to African slavery in particular, many writers have occupied themselves with showing that the Africans have been released from a state of the most savage barbarism, and admitted to the enjoyment of the protection, tranquillity, and other advantages of civilized life (so far as they were competent to participate in the last), by the fact and consequences of their enslavement. The horrid cruelties and beastly depravities from which the negroes have been rescued, and the infinite amelioration of their condition, even under the worst form which slavery has assumed on this continent, have been elucidated in a manner which should have arrested the denunciations of abolitionists, if they had been as willing to listen to reason, as they have been anxious to indulge in calumnies. But hitherto, or at least until the last few months, no sufficient attention has been paid to the prospective advantages and the prospective necessity of negro slavery, for the future welfare of humanity. The rapid increase of population in the older countries of the world has pressed so heavily upon subsistence, and even on the means of production, that it becomes much more essential to enlarge the

> area of cultivation than the area of freedom. New lands must be reclaimed for human use; dense forests must be cleared off, and additional space acquired for the productive industry of men; crowded populations must be dispersed, and distributed over the regions now unoccupied, where the exuberant energies of nature waste themselves in unheeded luxuriance. The richest countries of the globe remain uninhabited and unemployed. They offer an abundant support to all who will avail themselves of their bounty, and a sufficient surplus of production for the sustenance of all the starving myriads of the earth. The interior of South America, which is still almost a terra incognita, despite of the hurried explorations of Messrs. Herndon and Gibbon,[53] would alone support more inhabitants than the population of Europe numbers, and postpone for centuries the irremediable starvation and pauperism which menace annihilation to the millions of that continent. . . . The only agency which can be effectually applied to the cultivation of the feracious lands of the torrid zone is negro slavery. Under its operation, the labo[u]rers would be supplied with the necessaries and necessary comforts of life; the owners of the slaves would be rapidly enriched; and the whole of humanity would be relieved by the diminution of population where it was too dense, and by the simultaneous increase of markets and alimentary products.

Here is sound argument, and we advance with open hand to greet the enunciator of it. But he will none of us, for we are of the politico-economical school, and he will not believe that any good can come out of Nazareth.[54] We would entreat our reviewer to glance over the textbooks of his reviled science, and we think he will find that his sounder argument is always of a good, solid, politico-economical turn, while on the contrary his errors may be easily traced home to the socialistic school.

Hear him, for instance (page 91), on the poverty of the laboring classes in France, after noticing the smallness of the sums appropriated to their maintenance: "Nor is this all: it has been shown that this is not the consequence of any special iniquity, but the legitimate consequence of the operation of the laws of modern society; and that the tendency is daily to abridge these rations." "It has been shown" where? by whom? Would the general reader imagine that his authority, brought so placidly forward as conclusive in judging the operation of the laws of modern society, is the notorious

53. William Lewis Herndon (1813–57), naval officer; born in Fredericksburg, Va.; brother-in-law of Matthew Fontaine Maury; after service in the Mexican War, attached to the Naval Observatory in Washington; with Lardner Gibbon, assigned to explore the Amazon River, the report published as *Exploration of the Valley of the Amazon* (1853–54); lost with his ship *Central America* off Cape Hatteras.

54. Cf. John 1:46

Proudhon? a man of talent doubtless, but strange authority for any but a French revolution[n]aire.[55]

Again (page 78), to prove the deterioration of modern society, he quotes Horace Greeley!

> "Human labo[u]r," says Mr. Greeley, and he speaks truly in this instance, "is efficient beyond example, but the labo[u]ring class is hardly benefitted thereby. Houses multiply with extreme rapidity, but the number of the houseless is not diminished. The prolific earth yields larger and larger harvests, as wilds are reclaimed and science is applied to agriculture, but millions pine and thousands starve for lack of food. Our roads and means of transit are visibly improved from season to season; but our road-makers are no better circumstanced than their grandfathers were. Each year sees the number and value of arable acres increase, while the proportion of those who possess any land in their own right steadily diminishes. Each year produces more and more fuel and cloth, yet witnesses more and more shivering and nakedness. While new inventions and processes are daily rendering material life more smooth and comfortable to the affluent, the number of the destitute, squalid, and miserable is steadily on the increase."[56]

Greeley, the ultra-radical reformer, the advocate of every "ism" of the day, who, as our reviewer says, truly, "is neither a great man, nor the shadow of a great man" [67], tells us, in the face of all authority and of common sense, that food and clothing are scarcer than of old; that, while millions on millions of coarse and cheap manufactures are scattered over the globe, the poor man wears fewer shirts; that, in proportion as corn is abundant, he starves!—and on Mr. Greeley's authority we are required to believe. We must decline throwing ourselves under such wild guidance, and retain our opinion that, if cotton is spun into cloth, and if corn is ground into flour, the cloth is worn, and the flour is eaten; and that, if coarse cloths and cheap breadstuffs are consumed, they are consumed, not by the affluent, but by the needy; and this is what American negro slavery has accomplished to a hitherto unheard of degree, not for every individual man and woman, not for the wretched groups which incumber the streets of over populous cities, not for the brutified populace of a misgoverned Ireland, not, alas! for many and numberless wretched exceptions, but yet for millions on millions of the masses all the world over, slave and free. Suffering and wretchedness must

55. Holmes cites Pierre-Joseph Proudhon, *L'Idée générale de la révolution au XIXe siècle,* 2d ed. (Paris, 1851), p. 52.

56. Holmes cites Horace Greeley, *Hints toward Reforms, in Lectures, Addresses, and Other Writings* (New York, 1850), pp. 180–81.

be; but suffering and wretchedness are daily diminishing wherever an enlightened government, under the guidance of just economical principles, has left free play to the natural action of man's instinct of self-improvement.

One more instance we must be permitted to give of our reviewer's unlucky quotations; and in this case there is even (we are sure from unintentional oversight) a perversion of his quite sufficiently objectionable authority. He says (pages 69–70): "The outrageous denunciations of slavery and slave institutions appear preposterous when uttered from the midst of such free societies as those whence the complaint of the labo[u]rer unable to procure work simultaneously proceeds, declaring in the heart of Paris that the free labo[u]r system 'strangles the whole class, and would let a man die of starvation on a sack of wheat, or of cold on a bale of wool'; and where such a complaint is left without a denial of its truth, without excuse, and without redress."

And in a note he shows us his quotation: "Il (l'argent) nous jugule tous; il laisserait mourir un homme de faim sur un sac de blé, ou de froid sur un ballot de laine; cette anomalie n'est que trop exacte," as cited by the *Journal des économistes,* No. 97, 15 Avril, 1849, p. 104.

Now in the note we perceive that the antecedent of the pronoun "il" is *l'argent* (money), but in the text we have the "free labor system." Surprised at this discrepancy, we refer to the *Journal des économistes* and find that the line quoted is a half sentence taken from a red-hot socialistic pamphlet which the journal notices only to ridicule,[57] and which contends for *mutualité* in the results of labor, declaiming against money in a manner worthy of a Diogenes. The sentence quoted is precisely its strongest fling against that obnoxious article, and the journal cites it to show to what preposterous extremes the rabid and at that time rampant spirit of reform was forcing on its votaries. "Sans la *couardise de l'argent,* le monde eût épargné la moitié au moins de ses ébranlemen[t]s calamiteux. Il nous jugule tous; il laisserait mourir un homme de faim sur un sac de blé, ou de froid sur un ballot de laine; cette anomalie n'est que trop exacte." [104; LSM's italics]

Any further argument here would be out of place. We can only say, in all kindness, that the reviewer has mistaken his authority. Were he serious, we could but recommend him to the charity of the anti-money fraternity for a comfortable tub wherein to indulge his further speculations. The day has long since past when "*la couardise de l'argent*" can become a subject of serious discussion.

This proclivity of our reviewer to socialist authorities accounts for an-

57. [Gustave de Molinari], review of *De la question du travail, ou solution proposée par un travailleur sans ouvrage* (Paris, [1849?]), *Journal des économistes* 23 (April 1849): 103–4.

other constantly recurring weakness in his argument, i.e., a continual harping upon that most mischievous fallacy, the antagonism of labor and capital. It is one of the triumphs of Political Economy to have shown that no such antagonism exists: capital and labor are as essential co-laborers and auxiliaries, as head and hand. There is no antagonism, but constant and mutual assistance which even passion, avarice, and crime cannot force into opposition. The farmer needs his tools, his seed, and his store-houses (which are capital) as much as his power to labor; and to the journeyman who owns nothing but his strength of arm, it is quite as essential that his employer have the means of payment—otherwise his labor is worthless. He starves before its proceeds can be forthcoming. Capital is the nurse and nourisher of labor, and labor in return the builder up of capital. The economy of today feeds the labor of tomorrow, and so beautiful is the connection that even avarice cannot force these into opposition. What God has joined, man cannot put asunder.[58] The miser's hoards, even in his own despite, feed the hungry: for, credit, the necessary accompaniment and consequence of capital, making it more profitable to him to invest his money than to lock it up, even the love of gain induces investment, and investment is the payment of labor.

That a natural jealousy exists between man and man, it were folly to deny. That he who has not, is, and always has been, inclined to covet from him who has, the decalogue forbidding us to covet, as it forbids us to give way to other mischievous passions and impulses, brings proof. But this has nothing to do with antagonism between labor and capital, and only proves that a man's natural impulse to improve his condition may be indulged in an improper way, as when hunger makes him steal rather than work. Let but two men be together, the one having bread and the other not: the breadless one will envy the other and devise means for getting his bread, or a portion of it, whether by honest or fraudulent means. Now, if he having bread have a sufficiency for both, the breadless one may, in exchange for labor or service rendered, receive his neighbor's surplus, and thus is the better of his neighbor's reserved capital; whereas, were the capital reserved too small for the payment of labor, he may starve, though a strong man, for want of such compensation. Again, if there be two breadless to the one owning a reserved supply, and if that supply suffices but for one besides the possessor, is it not evident that the breadless laborers are worse off than if the capitalist were more wealthy? Both now must necessarily give their labor, or so much of it as the capitalist needs, in exchange for a deficient supply; whereas, where there was but one breadless laborer (and his labor sufficiently efficient to

58. Matt. 19:6: "Wherefore they are no more twain, but one flesh. What therefore God hath joined together, let not man put asunder."

induce the exchange), he could receive the whole in exchange for his efforts. Or, again, if the capitalist have enough for two besides himself, they might each receive, for efficient labor, a sufficiency of bread in exchange, instead of one or the other being necessarily doomed to starvation, or both to stinted existence (no matter what their efforts or what their power of labor), until by their labor they may possibly lay up for themselves, or others may lay up for them, a supply of capital.

Thus the real antagonism is in truth between labor and labor, and capital and capital. The greater the accumulation of capital, the better chance is there for the laborer to receive a full proportion in exchange for his labor; and, *per contra,* the greater the supply of labor, and the smaller that of capital, the smaller is the share that falls to the laborer. Precisely as in all other exchanges, where the supply is full, the article is cheap, and *vice versa.* Capital and labor fall under the common law. Whether the article exchanged be hats, shoes, corn, sugar, cloth, land, tools, money, labor, or whatsoever else, it is cheap in proportion as it is abundant, and those giving anything in exchange for it receive a proportionably larger compensation. Like only competes with like. There can be no competition but between similar things, things at least in so far similar that the use or the gains of the one interfere with the use or the gains of the other. Thus there may be competition between jewelry and cashmere shawls, or fine lace, because, according to the veering of fashion, the same class of customers may seek or discard either of these articles; and thus (the number and means of customers being equal), in proportion as cashmere shawls or lace would be purchased, jewelry would be neglected, and *vice versa.* Likewise between coarse woollens and coarse cotton goods there may be rivalry, because the poorer classes who consume them, preferring one, would proportionably reject the other. Even there may be rivalry between coarse cloths and the cheaper breadstuffs, because, when the poverty of a people is such as to prevent a full supply of both food and clothes, the question might arise of preference between them. But between coarse woollens and cashmere shawls, or coarse cottons and jewelry, or lace and cheap breadstuffs, there can be no rivalry, because the same consumers would never seek them; and it could never benefit the lace maker or the importer of jewelry that the vender of coarse goods and cheap breadstuffs should lose his market, while it might much benefit the importer of jewelry that the lace merchant should lose his.

Thus between capital and labor rivalry cannot exist, for the one can never be benefitted by the decline of the other, but on the contrary much injured. That the capitalist tries to get the most labor for his money, and the laborer the most money for his labor, is nothing more than the inevitable result of the common instinct of trade, to buy cheap and sell dear, an impulse perfectly moral, legitimate, and right (to be modified by charity, but never, as indeed it cannot be, discarded); and no more indicates rivalry between capital and labor, than there is rivalry between boots and shirts, knives and plates, or corn beef and gutta-percha walking canes, because the vendors and purchasers of each mutually make with each other the best practicable bargains. We dare not, however, enter further into this discussion, as our article already threatens to exceed all reasonable limit.

In our defense of Political Economy we must now only suggest to its opponents to remember, that no science is responsible for the natural tendencies which it studies and explains, but never produces; that Political Economy, in discovering the laws of society, in no wise creates them; and that it is no more than the ordinary physician responsible for the incurable ills of its patient. Let that impulsive kindness which condemns the coolness of its investigation pause at least to doubt if there be not oftenest truer charity in the action of the steady hand which guides the scalpel, separating vein from vein and nerve form nerve, even while the patient writhes under the infliction, than in the sentimental weakness which shudders and faints, daring not to look upon the anguish, and would, even at the expense of the sufferer's life, shading its eyes from his agony, hand the opiate which brings him at once relief and death.

Political Economy is the physician which the unthinking in his restlessness condemns. Look again, you who in earnest truth have thought him wrong, look again, and you may find a heart quite as warm as your own, a charity quite as true as your own, patiently striving to work out the problem which you have failed to read—to untie that Gordian knot which you have vainly thought to cut asunder. The true question is not, are the positions of Political Economy charitable or uncharitable? but, are they true or false? An inscrutable Providence has made an imperfect world, and, in the exercise of a wisdom incomprehensible to us, has created man a strange bundle of faults and virtues, passion and reason. Governed alternately by truth and error, he gropes his way midst phantoms of darkness. Sophistry parades before him her twilight theories, strutting in the robes of wisdom. Folly peeps from behind her harlequin mask, while fanaticism stabs with a prayer, and hand in hand with hypocrisy dares call down Heaven's blessing upon deeds of Hell. Knee-deep in error, man works out the truth only by patient investigation and laborious research; and society must find its way to the goal of such perfection as earth permits only by the study of itself. Political Economy is this study. Commenced but not accomplished, the investigation needs to be patiently followed up; and, if our predecessors have sometimes erred, we may learn wisdom where they have stumbled.

In defence of slavery our plea is that under certain combinations of circumstances (and United States negro slavery presents all these circumstances) it is defended by the soundest truths of Political Economy; and this is logically shown by the entire failure of proof, and the absurd conclusions to which all political economists have been reduced when attempting anything like argument against us, the science thus convicting its own disciples of error, precisely as geometry sets its blundering student right by showing him, in his imagined solution of a problem, only an absurdity. In an article "Esclavage,"[59] to which we some pages back referred as an example of the abuse sometimes heaped upon us by political economists, the writer, after giving a table of produce showing its falling off after emancipation, remarks (pages 720 to 722):

> These figures prove how fatal emancipation has been to the material prosperity of the West Indies. . . . In the Mauritias alone, production was sustained, thanks to the importation of Indian Coulis. . . .
>
> Looking at the actual prosperity of the colonies and the interests of the metropolis, English emancipation was a disastrous operation. . . .
>
> In France, as in England, emancipation has proved a bad economical operation. . . .
>
> As a compensation for this, liberty has been given to a million of human creatures, and truly we would not say that this had been bought too dearly, if the result of emancipation had not unfortunately been to increase elsewhere, in an equal if not greater proportion, the development of slavery. . . . Thus the emancipation that England and France have with so much effort and so many sacrifices accomplished in their colonies has resulted simply in a *displacement* of slavery, and this displacement has been made in favor of nations the least accessible to feelings of justice and humanity. Lamentable result of so noble and generous an enterprise!
>
> This result has not escaped the attention of the abolitionists, who have strenuously exerted themselves to combat it. No sooner did they perceive that the sugar produced by the labor of Brazilian and Cuban slaves had taken the place of that of the emancipated colonies, than they demanded differential duties in favor of free grown sugar. . . . But, the insufficiency of the supply furnished by the colonies and by the free growing countries having kept up prices, the distinction between free and slave grown sugar was abandoned [l'année suivante], notwithstanding desperate efforts on the part of the abolitionists. . . .

59. We would gladly give pages of extracts, but must, owing to the length of our article, limit ourselves to detached sentences. We refer our readers to the work itself: [Gustave de Molinari, "Esclavage," in] *Dictionnaire d[e l]'économie politique, [. . .] publié sous la direction de MM. [Ch.] Coquelin et Guillaumin* à Paris[, 2 vols. (1854), 1:712–31]. [LSM]

This law,[60] which was a new victory for the principles of free trade, was energetically attacked by the abolitionists, and with reason, for it was in direct opposition to the philanthropic measures adopted for the emancipation of the negro race. What motive had actuated England in devoting, since 1819, large sums to the repression of the slave-trade? She wished to prevent the increase of the number of negro slaves in America. What motive had induced her to spend 500,000,000 to free her colonial slaves? She wished to diminish the number of negro slaves. And now, in suppressing the duty which forbade the entrance of slave sugar into the British market, what was she doing? [. . .] She was undoing for the sake of free trade what she had already done for the abolition of slavery.

The discussions which this question raised in Parliament were of the most animated nature. The abolitionists easily proved that the lowering of the duty would act as a *bonus* to the production of slave grown sugar; but their adversaries, particularly Mr. Macaulay, showed still more forcibly how absurd and injurious would be the maintenance of such a prohibition.[61] . . . Parliament decided in favor of free-trade, refused to continue to legislate in favor of free grown, to the injury of slave grown, sugar, and equality of duties was declared. . . .

Recently opinion has advanced a step further. Some of the most important papers, particularly the *Times* and the *Economist,* solicit Government to take a decided step, and to suppress the cruisers established for preventing the slave-trade. Is it not indeed absurd to continue to oppose obstacles to the trade when there has been granted, by the diminution of the duty on slave grown sugar, an enormous *bonus* to the importation and increase of negro slaves in America?

Thus writes a political economist, who with all the prejudice of the day is arguing against slavery. We would beg the reviewer of "Slavery and Freedom" here to remark, that free labor and free-trade are far from being, as he continually supposes them, part of one and the same system; that they

60. The law and its provisions are specified in the passage immediately preceding, omitted from LSM's extracts: "En vertu de la loi des sucres présentée par le ministère de lord John Russell et adoptée par le parlement, en août 1846, le droit sur le sucre des colonies fut maintenu à 14 shell., et le droit sur le sucre étranger de toutes provenances abaissé à 21. La loi portait, en outre, que les droits sur les sucres étrangers seraient successivement abaissés jusqu'à la limite des droits fixés sur les sucres coloniaux, de telle manière que l'égalité se trouvàt entièrement établie le 5 juillet 1854." (721)

61. Thomas Babington Macaulay (1800–59), speech on "The Sugar Duties" (Feb. 26, 1845), in *The Miscellaneous Writings and Speeches of Lord Macaulay* (London, 1878), pp. 667–80. Immediately following this sentence, Molinari gives a French précis (omitted by LSM) of part of this speech.

were in fact in this struggle in direct opposition to each other; and that the true principles of Political Economy carried the day *in favor of slavery,* and in spite of the strongest prejudice even on the part of those who were thus obliged to acknowledge the folly of their own previous action. Surely it is unnecessary to attempt further to prove that it is only the diseased action of a prejudiced mind which could induce the writer of the *Dictionnaire d[e l]'économie,* from whom we have just quoted, to go on and imagine new devices for the abolition of negro slavery. This is not the effort of science but truly rather of another Paul who kicks against the pricks.[62] "Lamentable result," exclaims the writer, "of so noble and generous an enterprise." Natural result, answers science, of a blindly miscalculated undertaking. To use a quaint comparison we have seen lately, it is like the combat of the bull with the locomotive: "Pluck good, discretion bad."

The great prophet of abolitionism, Wilberforce, a most well-meaning man in his way we do not doubt, was nevertheless, in his ignorant self-conceit, the propagator of a disease fatal to millions, and the whole world is yet sick with the moral taint that he and such as he have scattered through it. From him and such as him comes all this pseudo-philanthropy which at every turn confounds the best reasoned conclusions; from him and such as him comes all the pestiferous tribe of canting sentimentalists which continually butt against common sense ("pluck good, discretion bad"); from him this kind of teething fever that beginners in philanthropy seem nowadays obliged to go through before they cut their wisdom teeth. We cannot too much lament that our Southern reviewer should to the smallest extent have thrown himself on such a side. He will find in the arguments of the abolitionists, and their declamations against the thirst of gain, many of his own, while the political economist, as we have seen, cannot blind the spirit that guides him, and even trying to condemn is obliged to defend us. "In France, as in England, emancipation has proved a bad economical operation." Like Balaam of old,[63] when he tried to curse, the spirit of truth was upon him, and behold he blessed them entirely!

Even now echoing in our ears there comes across the Atlantic the best and unanswerable defence of United States negro slavery. Political Economy, fairly appealed to, pronounces it right by the test of utility, and now behold the proof. A difference arises between England and the United States, which under ordinary circumstances would result in war. The British Minister is dismissed. Expectation is on tiptoe for the result.[64] Will the ministry in

62. Acts 9:5.

63. Deut. 23:4–5.

64. Dislike and distrust already existed between Great Britain and the United States over Cuba and Central America when, on May 28, 1856, the British minister to the United States, John Fiennes Twisleton Crampton (1805–86), was dismissed by President Franklin Pierce for, it was alleged, promoting illegal recruitment of troops (to serve in the Crimean

retaliation dismiss the United States Minister? Will it declare war? What will be its action? The people does not wait for its action. War must not be! War would be their ruin! The cry rises from Manchester: "No war with America!"

NO WAR WITH AMERICA. Fellow Countrymen: You have hardly escaped from war with Russia before you are threatened with a far more serious war with America! How long is this system of diplomatic irritation to go on? How long are the vital interests of the country to be placed at the mercy of men who care for nothing so much as the gratification of official pride?

Consider, for one moment, what ruin a war with the United States would entail upon the greater portion of the trade and commerce of Great Britain. The latest returns from the Board of Trade give the annual imports from that country, consisting chiefly of corn and cotton, at upwards of thirty millions; and the exports at from twenty-five to thirty millions sterling. To carry on this princely commerce between two nations, there are employed more than three thousand ships, with nearly three million tons burden. Of the entire annual imports of Great Britain, that of raw cotton alone amounts to more than twenty millions; and the cotton manufactured goods exported, to upwards of twenty five millions sterling. Upon the trade which this commerce creates there are depending for their daily subsistence nearly or quite three millions of people, chiefly in Lancashire and Yorkshire.

Now, are you prepared to see this hive of industry—this vast population—factory hands, tradesmen, and manufacturers, men, women, and children—thrown out of employment, deprived of their regular resources, and in large numbers driven to beggary or to the commission of crime for their daily resources? Are you prepared to encounter the pauperism, the gaunt famine, the depredations on property, and the civil commotion which less than twelve months war with America would inevitably produce? To say nothing of bloodshed among men of the same race—of the disgraceful carnage between the two foremost Christian nations of the world—or of the squandering of the hard earned money of the people in deeds of mutual destruction over a question that only deserves contempt; to say nothing of these things, are you willing to sacrifice your trade, to sink your country into poverty, crime, and commotion, and to plunge mankind into deadly strife,

War) within American territory. Word of the dismissal, announced on June 11 by the American minister George Dallas to Foreign Secretary Lord Clarendon, and combined with the transfer earlier of four thousand British soldiers to Canada and several ships to the North American squadron, brought much speculation of war, soon dissipated, however, by the attitude of the English press, mindful of Anglo-American trade, and by temperate American proposals concerning Central American disputes.

> simply to gratify the mad ambition of bungling diplomatists? If not, then meet without delay and, with a voice and a determination about which there can be no mistake, declare to your government and to the world, that there shall be no war with America.
>
> William Stokes,
> Secretary to the Manchester Peace Conference.

And this appeal is echoed by millions; an address to the people of America receives in a few hours eight thousand signatures.

> Never in recognized history were two great communities so closely allied by blood, or so intimately blended by their common interests; and never before was [it] given to the world to witness a union where so much was involved of the wealth, the prosperity, and happiness of the distinct <of distinct> States, each having its separate government, and being under the control of its own independent laws. We are, therefore, all the more alive—and allow us to add, tremblingly alive—to whatever may affect this union, and interrupt the harmony that has so long existed between us to our reciprocal advantage, and we believe to the benefit of the whole world. Providence has made us mutually dependent, so much so, indeed, that whatever would seriously injure the one would, to an equal extent, seriously injure the other. As the direct consequence of this providential arrangement, we are equally interested with yourselves in the material that is grown in your fields, the shipping that conveys the cargoes to every market of the universe, and in the endless train of relationships that the most princely commerce of the world has interwoven between us for its own auxiliary support.
>
> . . . A higher than human destiny has made our interests identical, and interwoven the prosperity of the one State with the prosperity of the other; we are, therefore, placed among the nations in a position to show what national friendships may accomplish where rivalry is directed to [a] common good, and where success is equally shared between the rivals. And shall war be permitted to sever us? Shall battle and bloodshed, conflagration and the sword, be allowed to divide those whom God and mutual interest have made one, and to convert into national enemies brethren by blood, by race, and by religion? In the name of humanity and civilization—in the name of our common Maker and of his holy faith, which both nations profess to believe and practice—we say no! There is no sacrifice of time, of wealth, and of influence, that we would not be ready to make to prevent so dire a catastrophe among mankind—a catastrophe that we believe would more directly tend, than any other possible event, to throw the world back into the barbarism of the feudal ages, and to furnish despotism with a plausible pretext for

banishing every form of constitutional government from the face of the earth.[65]

And whence this "princely commerce" with its three thousand ships and three million tons burden? Whence this raw cotton to the amount of more than twenty millions to feed your great manufactures? Whence but from negro slave labor? And the gaunt famine, and the civil commotions which would follow a cessation of this commerce—brothers, believe us, you men of Manchester, who in your ignorance perhaps, misled by the Wilberforce teething-fever, would tomorrow sign an abolition petition and cry out for negro emancipation: you are pulling the ruin upon your own heads. A war of England with America would indeed tend, more than any other possible event, *except one,* to throw back the world into barbarism. But there *is* one still more certainly powerful in its evil influences, and that one is negro emancipation. The white man will never raise, *can* never raise, a cotton or a sugar crop in the United States. In our swamps and under our suns the negro thrives, but the white man dies. That the negro can do nothing as a free man, surely West India experience is enough to demonstrate. Brethren of Manchester, brethren of England, brethren of the world, may your God-given reason guide you to the true solution of this great problem, and forbid that blind passion should lead you to sacrifice life, and more than life, in obedience to an ignorant prejudice, dashing yourselves, brute-like, against a great reality!

65. "Address to the People of America from the Citizens of Manchester," issued on June 11, 1856, and published in the London *Times,* June 13, 1856; in the New York *Daily Tribune,* New York *Daily Times,* and New York *Journal of Commerce,* June 28, 1856; in the Washington *Daily National Intelligencer,* June 30, 1856; in the Charleston *Daily Courier,* July 1, 1856. The Charleston *Mercury* of July 1, 1856, notes, without quoting, peace addresses issued by Liverpool and Manchester and adds that the Manchester address "received eight thousand signatures in a few hours." LSM's excerpts are collated with the text printed in the *Daily Tribune,* which includes the following headnote, from which LSM (and the *Mercury*?) appear, directly or indirectly, to have drawn: "A peace address to the people of the United States was placed for signature in the Manchester Exchange, and received eight thousand signatures in a few hours. The address is appended." (The *Times, Daily Times, Journal of Commerce,* and *Daily Courier* do not mention number of signatures; the *Intelligencer* notes the number in its June 28 telegraphic report of New York news.)

15

To the Editor of The XIX Century

Dear Sir:

In the present condition of our press, you will perhaps permit the use of your magazine for a few words, of which the daily papers should be the legitimate vehicle, were it not that the aggressive action of the "Press Conference" party leaves no outlet for opinions which are of vital importance to our existence as a people.

XIX Century 3 (June 1870): 83–84. On Feb. 14, 1870, the Columbia *Guardian* had suggested a convention to be held of newspaper editors who were opposed to the Radical Republican government of South Carolina but who believed that, if there was to be any chance of replacing that government in the coming October elections, the lately enfranchised black population of the state, viewed as the heart of Republican strength, must be acknowledged and courted. The resulting "Press Conference," convened on March 16 in Columbia, adopted resolutions proclaiming the "legal rights of all citizens of the State, irrespective of color or former condition," and urged that a state convention meet on June 15 to nominate candidates for the October elections. (For LSM's opinion of this convention, see her letter of June 17, 1870, to the Board of Managers of the South Carolina Monument Association.) The *XIX Century,* which took an editorial position against the forthcoming convention, thus introduced this letter to the editor: "The following letter, from a distinguished source, will indicate to the great public whether the position of *The XIX Century,* in respect to the 'so-called' reform party movement, is in harmony with the views of our best people." On the *XIX Century,* see Noel E. Polk, "W. W. Hicks and *The XIX Century,*" in *South Carolina Journals and Journalists,* ed. James B. Meriwether (Spartanburg, S.C., 1975): 121–31.

A pamphlet (scarcely more than a sheet) recently published, and entitled "The Press Conference—Whither does it Lead?" has endeavored to lay open to the public (so far as the limited circulation attainable by individual effort striving against the "Press Ring" can do) the certain destiny to which, under the proposed course, we are veering. Unless treason, not only to honor and all gentlemanly principle, but even to simple truth, is intended by this party which holds out to the negro the flag of brotherhood, he is now invited by them to equality with the white race.

Apparently the Press Ring is not only willing to accept this, but even so anxious to attain it, that a *clique* meeting—recently held in Charleston, and in itself far from a unit—is distorted by their reports into a general and unanimous one. They crave negro equality, while the wily rather than sagacious negro nibbles but very doubtfully at the bait. The result is evident enough: fearful degradation to the white man, without the anticipated benefit expected from negro fraternization. And yet there still are among us, and with us, a majority of Southern gentlemen. By the epithet "gentleman" we would indicate the claimant of no special privileges in birth or fortune, but only the possessor of such honorable principles as may, equally in the plowman, the mechanic, the planter, or the literary and professional man, keep him free from all that is unclean or doubtful to the moral touch. Many a whole-souled gentleman in homespun and in rags has in our State history paid over his life, an intended ransom for his country—more honored thus in poor and roughest garb than the most plausible and polished bearer of a soiled conscience.

There are, we repeat it, Southern gentlemen, many and true, still among us. Will these die, and "make no sign"?[1] Will there not, rather, be a decided opposition, however quiet? a disclaimer of this false action which, assuming to be what it is not, is trying to hurry matters forward to the apparent implication of the whole State, in the fatal blunder of a small fraction of it? Let our true men throughout the country look at the list of names which has been used to summon a meeting and nominate delegates to what *they* propose calling a *State Convention,* and there will be seen a small sprinkling of names which we would have expected to meet in better company, the rest a regular *riff-raff* of the "am I not a man and a brother"[2] stamp, of every shade of color and complexion. And these raise their voices in some sort of fashion, and call the result the voice of Charleston? "Charleston

1. *2 Henry VI* 3.3.29: Cardinal Beaufort "dies, and makes no sign. O God, forgive him!"

2. The motto on the seal of the Anti-Slavery Society of London, taken from a medallion made by Josiah Wedgwood (1730–95).

has spoken," say they. Has it so? Verily our old city does not so recognize her own tones.

And this radical measure—for radical it is, and of the blackest dye; call it by what name its advocates may, they can never wash off the pitchy stain—this radical measure, should it be possible to push it forward, does not, to a careless glance, show the worst features of its case. That we should disgrace our names, not only as a State, but as individuals—all pride, all honor forgotten—is bad enough; and most surely in our own sin would be found our own punishment. But herein is not all. The world does not end with *us;* and "après moi le déluge"[3] is the saying of no honest man. No honest man but must ask himself, What of his country? what to posterity must be the result?

It needs but small sagacity to predict the fate of any semi-negro people. A similar degradation to that of the effete nations of Southern America could, in such case, only be *in part* avoided by the taking back of falsely spoken promises: betraying the negro with the false kiss of peace, and throwing him overboard so soon as he proves useless. Then, with the double stain of treason to his own conscience, and treachery to the abject negro whom he will have deceived, behold the Southern gentleman! "Shame, where is thy blush?"[4]

Be assured, gentlemen—you who have not already tried it—that your heads will ache a little, and your breakfast not be pleasant, with the morning paper that shows your names, by your own consent, "*sandwiched*" with those of negroes for any position whatever.

Great sacrifices may be borne with philosophy, with pride, even with triumph, when honorably met, in an honorable cause. Heroes may fall exulting in their fate, and martyrs die rejoicing. But such support belongs only to the man who nobly plants his foot on honest principles and dies sooner than abandon them. There is a courage greater than the courage of battles; and he who consents, for any consideration, to the degradation of his country, and of his descendants, has it not.

The question before us is one of morals more than of politics. Let no man deceive himself, believing that he may touch pitch and not be defiled.[5] Let every man do his duty, refraining to advance, even by one finger's weight, a cause so soiling as this both to heart and mind. Let him ignore and avoid all

3. This French proverb, also in the form "après nous le déluge," is variously attributed, often to the marquise de Pompadour or to Louis XV.

4. Cf. 1 Cor. 15:55: "O death, where is thy sting? O grave, where is thy victory?"

5. *Much Ado about Nothing* 3.3.55–56: "I think they that touch pitch will be defiled." Also Ecclus. 13:1: "He that toucheth pitch shall be defiled therewith."

possible conventions for the negroizing of our State, and the Press Conference, with its platform and its resolutions, will be blown away in its own smoke.[6]

Carolinian

6. Alexander Pope, *Homer's Iliad* 2.402–7:

Then Nestor thus—These vain Debates forbear;
Ye talk like Children, not like Heroes dare.
Where now are all your high Resolves at last,
Your Leagues concluded, your Engagements past?
Vow'd with Libations and with Victims then,
Now vanish'd like their Smoke: The Faith of Men!

APPENDIXES

BIBLIOGRAPHY

INDEX

Appendix 1

The Affectionate and Christian Address of Many Thousands of the Women of England to Their Sisters, the Women of the United States of America

A common origin, a common faith, and, we sincerely believe, a common cause, urge us, at the present moment, to address you on that system of negro slavery which still prevails so extensively, and, even under kindly-disposed masters, with such frightful results, in many of the vast regions of the western world.

We will not dwell on the ordinary topics—on the progress of civilization, on the advance of freedom everywhere, on the rights and requirements of the nineteenth century—but we appeal to you very seriously to reflect and to ask counsel of God, how far such a state of things is in accordance with His Holy Word, the inalienable rights of immortal souls, and the pure and merciful spirit of the Christian religion.

We do not shut our eyes to the difficulties, nay the dangers, that might beset the immediate abolition of the long-established system; we see and admit the necessity of preparation for so great an event; but in speaking of the indispensable preliminaries, we cannot be silent on those laws of your country which, in direct contravention of God's own law, "instituted in the time of man's innocency,"[1] deny, in effect, to the slave the sanctity of mar-

A. H. Abel and F. J. Klingberg, eds., *A Side-Light on Anglo-American Relations, 1839–1858, Furnished by the Correspondence of Lewis Tappan and Others with the British and Foreign Anti-Slavery Society* (Lancaster, Pa., 1927), p. 40, n. 33, citing the text published in the *Christian Times,* Dec. 3, 1852, p. 769; the text is printed also in Carey, *Slave Trade,* pp. 6–7.

1. "The Form of Solemnization of Matrimony," in *The Book of Common Prayer* (1992 ed.), p. 308: "Holy matrimony . . . is an honourable estate, instituted of God in the time of man's innocency."

riage, with all its joys, rights, and obligations; which separate, at the will of the master, the wife from the husband, and the children from the parents. Nor can we be silent on that awful system which, either by statute or by custom, interdicts any race of man, or any portion of the human family, education in the truths of the Gospel and the ordinances of Christianity.

A remedy applied to these two evils alone would commence the amelioration of their sad condition. We appeal, then, to you as sisters, as wives, and as mothers, to raise your voices to your fellow-citizens, and your prayers to God, for the removal of this affliction from the Christian world. We do not say these things in a spirit of self-sufficiency, as though our nation were free from the guilt it perceives in others. We acknowledge, with grief and shame, our heavy share in this great sin. We acknowledge that our forefathers introduced, nay compelled, the adoption of slavery in those mighty colonies. We humbly confess it before Almighty God; and it is because we so deeply feel, and so unfeignedly avow, our own complicity, that we now venture to implore your aid to wipe away our common crime and our common dishonour.

Appendix 2

Two Accounts of Louisa McCord's Death

Charleston News and Courier, *Thursday, November 27, 1879*

Obituary—White

McCord, Mrs. Louisa S.—Died, at her home in Charleston, S.C., on the 23d day of November, 1879, after a brief illness, in the 69th year of her age, Mrs. Louisa S. McCord, widow of Col. D. J. McCord and daughter of Hon. Langdon Cheves.

Louisa McCord Smythe to Sophia Cheves Haskell

Dear Aunt Sophia, Charleston Dec[ember] 4 [1879]

It was very kind of you and Sophie to write to me, both of you, so soon but you ought to be glad that you did for your letters have helped me. You don't know how utterly lonely I feel. Of course a great part of my day is taken up by the children, for nothing seems to make a difference in their calls upon one's time and attention, but still there are so many times when Mamma and I used to be here alone and when everything was discussed and arranged and her advice asked even if it was not taken and now you don't know what a perfect blank it seems. I have so much time—more than I know what to do with, and yet I cannot settle down to any occupation and so it ends by my sitting here half the day thinking it all over again until I hardly know myself. Every minute of those three days seems to stand out so sharply and distinctly in my mind that it is positive pain to recall them[.] I want to forget a little—at least to lose that unnatural recollection of every step, every chip of wood that fell and still seems to go through me with a shudder at the thought of the pain it would give her. It was so short that I did not have time to get used to it, though I did have time to long and pray for her last breath. She did suffer so, and I could not bear to see it when I was so helpless. Her one thought was to spare me and the only thing she begged was not to be allowed to suffer so that she would become irritable. I could not immagine a more calm and—mentally—peaceful death bed. I do not feel—unless it is God's will to send a sudden death—that we ought to let any one be as it were overtaken by death without a fair warning, so as soon as I saw that the Dr. had no hope I told Mamma that I did not think she would get well and asked her if she felt willing. I wish you could have seen the look of bright, calm surprise as she said "Willing[,] my child? *glad*"—"glad to rest." I said "but what can *I* do without you[?]" At that the tears came in her eyes and she said "Don't talk that way my baby or you will make me break down and I don't want to do that." So I did as she wanted and after that only did what I could to relieve her from the great pain that we could not relieve and to the last she would pat my hand or hold it for a moment to thank me. She spoke much more fully to the Dr. and told him that she trusted to a merciful and Almighty God and was willing to put herself in His hands. Her last distinct utterance was to Gus—She drew him down to her and whispered "I am all right." But her last word was the name of her good friend Dr. Huger and her last smile and look was as he took her hand—long after she had ceased to know my touch.[1] I never can forget his kindness to her.

Her attack came on very suddenly just a few minutes after she had told me that for the first time in months she was free of pain. She recognized it at once and told me it was Gout in the stomach but I do not think that she any more than I did, thought until the ~~second~~ third day that it would be fatal. She was sick five days in all—suffering intensely all the time—but the last three days were terrible. I try to feel that it is all right and I *do* feel so in many ways, but she had been so well lately—so bright and happy, enjoying other people[']s happiness and grieving so in other people[']s troubles quite forgetting her own, that I had made up my mind to years of comparative happiness for her. For the last two months she had been her old self.

You did please me by speaking so kindly of my husband and indeed he de-

1. Probably Joseph Alston Huger (1815–95), physician, master of Murray Hill plantation and a plantation near Flat Rock, N.C.; studied at Harvard College (1835–37); M.D. from the Medical College of South Carolina in 1839. He was married to a sister of LSM's brother-in-law Thomas Pinckney Huger. There is also William Harleston Huger (1826–1909), born in Charleston; M.D. from the Medical College of South Carolina in 1849; served at the battery on Morris Island; returned to practice in Charleston after the war, where he was physician to the Orphan House.

serves it for he has been an affectionate and dutiful son to her from first to last and she leant on him in all her troubles and no son could have closed her eyes and given her last kiss more lovingly than he did. And it does me good to hear him as he did yesterday, looking tired and worn out, wish that he could ask her what she thought about something that was worrying him. He used so often to refer questions of right and wrong to her—as he said—she had old time ideas and such a keen sight into things.

I was fortunate in having at the last, when more was required than I could do, the help of my dear, good sisters. I asked Mamma if she would mind them in the room and she answered "I couldn't mind any one who has been so good to me"—and she tried to kiss her hand as one of them came in the room. They did all that I could not do and attended to every thing for me so that I had nothing to worry about.

Poor Aunt Isabella was so sick that I sent her word not to come on any account but as it was she came to see me when she ought to have been in bed and I have not heard from her since. I ought to have sent to ask after her, and will send tomorrow.

I ought not to have written you this long letter but it is such a relief to be able to speak out what I am thinking of all the time and I cannot talk to people when they come to see me.

I had heard of Alice[']s illness from Miss Murden but the old lady very considerately did not tell me until she had heard better news.[2] What a terrible time it must have been to Alec—worse than to poor Alice herself. What a blow that would have been! She impresses me always as a woman perfectly different from other people and perfectly fascinating to me. I see by the papers that Alec has made a change. How do you like it? I liked him as the Judge.[3]

Much love to Sophie—tell her this long scratch must answer her as well as

2. Malvina Murden, daughter of Charleston poet Eliza Crawley Murden (1784–1847), with her sister Victoria had run a school for girls in Charleston. She is recorded as sixty years old in the 1870 census. "The Little Girl's Lament for the Fairies," *Russell's Magazine* 6 (Dec. 1859): 242–43, is ascribed to a "Miss Murden" in John Russell's copy, presumably Malvina or her sister.

3. "Father's work in the Supreme Court was congenial to him but it was also confining, and the long ride to Columbia and back, in all sorts of weather, was a strain upon him. Gradually his health began to trouble him. At the same time Mother was suffering from the effects of an almost fatal attack of pneumonia in the winter of 1879, from which she never fully recovered. . . . Just at that moment, Father was asked to be president of the Charlotte, Columbia, and Augusta Railroad. . . . He accepted the appointment and resigned from the Supreme Court." (Louise Haskell Daly, *Alexander Cheves Haskell: The Portrait of a Man,* intro. Lee A. Wallace, Jr. [Wilmington, N.C., 1989; rev. rpt. of 1934 ed.], p. 189.) In 1870 Alexander Haskell had married, as his second wife, Alice Van Yeveren Alexander (1848–1902); in 1877 he had been elected associate justice of the Supreme Court of South Carolina, replacing Jonathan Jasper Wright.

you for awhile. Please write to me sometimes for indeed I do feel in spite of husband children and all, very much alone—like the last of my own people. And don't talk of your "following soon"—we cannot spare you. We need the old people to help us with our children. I counted so on Mamma's help with mine—

Most affectionately
Your niece
L. McC. Smythe

Source: ALS, Langdon Cheves III Papers, SCHS.

Appendix 3

William Porcher Miles' "Sketch" of Louisa S. McCord

Louisa McCord Smythe to William Porcher Miles

Dear Cousin William, Charleston S.C. Feb[ruary] 26th, 1880

My mother's warm friendship for you gives me courage to ask a favour which I fear may give you some trouble. I would hesitate to trespass upon your time, but for my own perfect incompetence to do what I want done, and my conviction that you are the one best fitted in every way to do it for me.

Mr. Smythe has received several letters from a Mr. Epes Sargent of Boston who is getting up a Cyclopaedia of English and American poetry and has written repeatedly asking for some selections from my mother's writings and also for any facts in her life.[1] I enclose his last letter[2] that you may see for yourself what he wants. At first I felt inclined to let it alone but he wrote saying that he had a notice of her life in Duykinck's encyclopaedia and wanted the date of her death to add to it. I have so often heard her laugh at the incorrectness of that notice—particularly some anecdote about her setting a negro's broken arm—of which there was not a word of truth—that I do not like to have it repeated. Mr. Smythe suggested to me that as Mr. Sargent was evidently going to publish some sketch of her life I had best send a correct one. I am so ignorant of the happier part of my mother's life, and her friends of that time are so scattered that it

1. *Harper's Cyclopedia of British and American Poetry,* ed. Epes Sargent (1813–80), was published in 1881.

2. Not found.

would be impossible for me to do anything of the kind myself—besides that even if I had the information I would be perfectly unable to put it into anything like a proper form—and so, in thinking it over, it struck me that you would be the one to do it for me. You knew her before the clouds had so settled over her ~~life~~, and you knew her too in her time of greatest trouble—the time that broke her heart and really ended her life, and I know you can in a few words say something that will give an idea of her life and character.

I would like to select for publication the dedications to "My Father" and "My Son" in her two books—"My Dreams" and "Caius Gracchus" and I would like it said that that son's death and the failure of the cause she loved so well ended her life. After that she only waited patiently for the welcome release.[3]

I do not know if you have her books. I will send them to you. Will it be going too far if I ask you to look them over and make what other selections you think best[?]. You will notice that "My Dreams" is very much marked and torn. I have two or three copies but all are so and Mamma often told me that she never liked it to be seen on account of the mistakes made in the printing—and because much of it she did not now think worth printing.

My own judgement and taste in such things I know is not at all to be relied on, but there are some little fugitive pieces cut from newspapers which seem to ~~be~~ me better than some of those in the book. I do not like to enclose the newspaper slips as my letter might be lost, but will copy some of them and send them to you in a few days.[4]

Please excuse my asking so much of you. It is no small favour I know, but you will appreciate my anxiety to have the thing well done if it is done at all, and Mamma always spoke of you with such peculiar kindness and affection that I almost feel I have a right to call on you. Will you forgive me if I have presumed on ~~it~~ this feeling too much, and believe me always

Sincerely your's
Louisa McC. Smythe

As I doubt if you know my husband's initials I give you my address

Mrs. Augustine T. Smythe
25 Legaré St.
Charleston S.C.

Source: ALS, William Porcher Miles Papers, SHC.

Dear Cousin William, Charleston March 16th [1880]

You do not know how much I thank you for what you have done for me. Your sketch is just what I wanted said but did not know how to. I do not know

3. See "Later Poems," introductory footnote, in *PDBL*. Sargent did not print the dedication "To My Father."

4. Not found.

how it will suit Mr. Sargent's taste—he must judge for himself as to that—but my self respect will have been gratified, through you, by a little plain speaking. It shall go to Mr. Sargeant as it is and even if he cuts it down to suit himself he cannot altogether spoil it.

Independently of Mr. Sargent I am so glad to have this sketch for my children's sake and I mean to send away a copy—keeping the original for them until they are old enough to appreciate it.

With renewed thanks for your kindness, believe me

Affectionately your's
Louisa McC. Smythe

Source: ALS, William Porcher Miles Papers, SHC.

Sketch of Mrs. David J. McCord, by the Hon. William Porcher Miles, Mayor of Charleston, Member of the Confederate Congress, and President of the South Carolina College; Written in 1880.[5]

Mrs. McCord inherited much of the force and vigor of intellect, and clear logical faculty, of her distinguished father, Judge Cheves. She was endowed with rare argumentative power, and was singularly happy in her statement of principles, and arranging of facts, when discussing any important question. The bent of her genius was rather for matters of State policy and political economy than for subjects commonly embraced in what is called "General Literature." Nor was this strange when we consider the long public life of her father, during which she was habitually thrown with the leading statesmen of the country (and there were statesmen in those days), and heard so often discussed the then absorbing topics of "States' Rights," "Free Trade," "Tariffs," and "Banks." One familiar with the old *Southern Quarterly Review* can well remember many a vigorous and trenchant article from her pen—chiefly on politico-economic subjects. A translation she made of Bastiat's *Principles of Political Economy* was admirably done, and attracted much attention. Indeed when her first essay in poetry appeared—a little volume entitled *My Dreams*—it took everybody acquainted with her by surprise. So entirely were even her intimate friends accustomed to associate her intellectual [productions?][6] with logical and argumentative efforts, rather than with those of the fancy or imagination. Nor is it often that the poetical afflatus comes upon a writer so late in life as it did in her case. It was not before she had reached the mature age of thirty-seven, was married and the mother of three children, that she made her first—or at least first published—attempt at verse.

5. *FOLS,* pp. 7–10.

6. Ibid., p. 8, reads "profunctions," a word unknown to *OED*^{2}.

Indeed it is doubtful if before her marriage she had ever written anything for the press. Her husband, the Hon. David J. McCord, a prominent lawyer, well known from *McCord's Reports*,[7] a man of bright and versatile gifts and talents—himself a practiced writer and contributor to the *Southern [Quarterly] Review*—doubtless helped to turn her thoughts to a literary occupation and composition. They sometimes would contribute articles simultaneously to the same number of the *Review*. But so far as we remember none of these were of what might be called a purely literary character. As we have already indicated, they were almost entirely of a practical character, dealing with social, political, or economic questions. Hence *My Dreams* was read with much curiosity and interest by all who knew the author, as an entirely new departure in her literary career. While it showed in the structure of its verse, oftentimes, the want of a practiced hand, and in its rhythm a not always very musical ear, still there was originality and depth of feeling and emotion, a true portrayal of human passion, and the human heart, and a bold and fervid imagination that gave unmistakable evidence, as well as promise, of genuine poetical genius.

My Dreams was published in 1848. It was not until 1851 that Mrs. McCord essayed a more ambitious flight in *Caius Gracchus, a Tragedy in Five Acts*. This was evidently a more carefully prepared and matured effort. It abounds with striking passages full of high and noble thoughts, clothed in language well fitted to give them just expression. The characters of Gracchus and Cornelia are given in accordance with their traditional reputations; and the former with due poetic license, as the hero of the play, is portrayed in fairest hues as the ideal patriot and citizen. Some of his speeches are very fine and effective. *Caius Gracchus,* like many plays written by some of the first English authors, is a "closet drama," not intended for the stage. But that [it] shows strong dramatic power, and a high poetic faculty and sentiment, even the casual reader must admit.

Mrs. McCord also, from time to time, wrote fugitive poems, showing increasing powers, and a more facile command of versification. Whether, if fortune had compelled her to embrace literature as a profession, she might not have attained a distinguished place among the poets of America, it is impossible to say.

Magister artis ingenique largitor venter, says the Roman satirist.[8]

Born to affluence and high social position, Mrs. McCord never had that sharpest of all spurs—necessity—"to prick the sides of her intent"[9] and urge

7. David James McCord, *Reports of Cases Determined in the Constitutional Court of South Carolina,* 2 vols. (1820–21), with his law partner Henry Junius Nott; he continued the series on his own in four volumes (1822–30). He also completed Thomas Cooper's *Statutes at Large of South Carolina* (1836–41), adding five more volumes to Cooper's five.

8. Persius *Prologus* 10–11: "The belly [is] the teacher of art and the dispenser of genius."

9. *Macbeth* 1.7.25–28: "I have no spur / To prick the sides of my intent, but only / Vaulting ambition, which o'erleaps itself, / And falls on the other." The speaker is Macbeth.

her on to constant literary effort—almost a *sine qua non* to great literary success. She belonged to the class of planters who were no more inclined to become authors than the gentry of England are. Living upon a large cotton estate, and taking a constant and intelligent interest in its management, looking carefully after the comfort and well-being of a large number of slaves to whom she was ever a kind and attentive mistress; and with a family of children growing up around her—bred, too, to an active interest in politics, which, and its cognate sciences, as we have already said, so often employed her husband's pen and her own—it is not surprising that she "wooed the muse" but fitfully, more as a pastime than with any idea of making it a serious pursuit. No great poet has ever lived that did not give his whole and undivided heart to the muse of poetry. Of all mistresses she is the most jealous and exacting, and allows not even dalliance with any other than herself.

But it is not as a poet that the name of Louisa McCord will be most honoured and cherished in her native South Carolina. It is as a devoted daughter of the State, proud of its history, sensitive of its honour, willing to sacrifice all she possessed and all she held most dear in its defence, that her memory will live longest among her people. No one had stronger convictions as to the right of secession, and the necessity for its exercise. A great confederacy of homogeneous and friendly states—identified in interest as in origin—instead of a so-called "union" of hostile and discordant ones—had long been the dream of some of the greatest of Carolina's sons. Mrs. McCord's own noble father shared it. She received it by inheritance as well as by reason and patriotism. In the great struggle of the South for independence, she contributed from her ample means with no stinted or niggardly hand. She was willing to spend and be spent in the cause. Her contributions to the hospitals for sick and wounded Confederate soldiers—her constant labours with her own hands for their health and comfort—showed an untiring zeal and energy that filled the hearts of her fellow-citizens with admiration and respect.

Her only son, Cheves McCord, a young man of uncommon talent and fine character, full of the brightest promise, lost his life in the war. None but those nearest and dearest to her knew how terribly and stunningly this blow fell upon his mother's heart. It broke it. And when the cause was lost for which she had so long struggled with pen and means, and sacrificed so much, and at last offered up her first born—her dearly cherished boy—her only son—around whom the strongest and tenderest cords of her heart were entwined—she gradually but surely began to fail in health and spirits. She lived long enough to drink with her people the dregs of humiliation and suffering in South Carolina, during the rule of the harpies and carpet-baggers so long fastened upon her vitals by the overwhelming numbers and brute force of "negro suffrage," sustained by the bayonets of a consolidated despotism at Washington—a "Paternal Government" only desirous of "enforcing the rights" of all classes of her citizens. She also lived long enough to see the manhood, intelligence, virtue, and property of the "prostrate State," under the lead of the wise and patriotic Hampton, once more assert their inherent and inalienable right to shape its legislation and control its destinies.[10] But the shaft had been shot. The arrow had sped home, deep into her heart, and rankling there had sapped it of all strength and hope. One dear daughter had been taken from her—gone before her to join the dearly loved brother and son. Still in another daughter equally dear—her only surviving child—and her granddaughter, her dear son's only child, and in his lovely young widow—almost like her own daughter—she had much to comfort and soothe her in their loving care and attention, and to afford some balm to her wounded and weary spirit.

But the mandate had gone forth, and ere long the messenger of death was sent to conduct her in turn to those calm regions of eternal rest, where reunited to her dear ones, in a land that knows no war, or pain, or wrong, she at last reposes "in the bosom of her Father and her God."[11]

10. Wade Hampton III (1818–92), planter, politician, Confederate general, was elected governor of South Carolina in 1876 (although the returns were disputed) and installed in office in 1877 after President Rutherford B. Hayes withdrew Federal troops from the state; reelected governor in 1878; U.S. senator (1879–91).

11. Thomas Gray, "Elegy Written in a Country Churchyard," ll. 125–28: "No farther seek his merits to disclose, / Or draw his frailties from their dread abode / (There they alike in trembling hope repose), / The bosom of his Father and his God."

Appendix 4

Louisa McCord Smythe's "Recollections"

After her own writings, the most copious source for LSM's life is the "Recollections" written by her daughter, Louisa McCord Smythe, for her children, a discursive work to be dated, from internal evidence, to 1896–98. Louisa Smythe had something of her mother's eye for the vivid and telling detail; she sets scenes efficiently, often sharply; but how far is her account accurate? In general, her information, when it can be checked against other sources, can be relied upon. But there will be reservations when a detail, such as the proper name of a place visited once, of somebody met a few times or even often, is recollected after forty years; or, more seriously, when the chronology and the sequence of events are examined.

So Schlangenbad, the spa near Wiesbaden where LSM sprained her ankle during her European tour, becomes "Schanjenbad" in the "Recollections" (p. 35). "Mr. Brown," hired as nurse to Langdon Cheves in his last illness, is to be corrected to Mr. Boyd.[1] Less easily to be emended: "Cardinal Bertoni," whose help to the McCord family while in Rome is recorded (p. 29), is not found among the 124 cardinals in the reign of Pius IX. There were four alive in 1859, likely to be in Rome, and having names which might well be misremembered as "Bertoni" after forty years: Benedetto Barberini (1788–1863), prefetto della Sagra Congregazione dell' Immunità Ecclesiastica and arciprete di S. Giovanni in Laterano; Alessandro Barnabo (1801–74), prefetto della Sagra Congregazione di Propaganda Fide; Giuseppe Bofondi

1. Smythe, p. 37; LSM to Langdon Cheves, Jr., Dec. 20, 1856; Jan. 7, 29, 1857.

(1795–1867), presidente del Censo; and Roberto Roberti (1788–1867), presidente di Roma e Comarca. Louisa Smythe's "Bertoni" was "particularly kind and attentive." The duc de Gramont, French ambassador to the papacy, prepared in 1861 a list of cardinals, noting the characters of each and likelihood to be favorable to French interests: Barberini being a cipher whose age and decrepitude have made him "plus nul que jamais," Barnabo brilliant but with "une violence de caractère qui le rend cassant et quelquefois grossier et brutal," there remain Bofondi, described "d'un caractère extrêmement doux, posé et phlégmatique," and Roberti, assigned "une grande douceur de caractère, beaucoup de simplicité dans ses moeurs." Ear, too, suggests that these two are most likely. Bofondi may take a slight preference, if the Irish Benedictine Bernardo Smith (1812–92), whom we find with Bofondi belonging to a liberal faction in 1865–66, is to be identified with "Bertoni"'s secretary, "a young Irish priest, named Smith," whom the cardinal directed to escort the McCords. However, is Bernardo Smith, two years younger than LSM, likely to have seemed young to her thirteen-year-old daughter?[2]

Chronology also presents difficulties. "We started off early in the summer of '57 and came back in the late fall of '58" (p. 23). So, unusually, Louisa Smythe gives particular dates for an event, here the family's tour of Europe. However, the dates are set a full year too soon, the McCords sailing for Europe on July 7, 1858.[3] Between the death of her father, in May 1855, and the departure for Europe which in fact occurred in 1858, she records events of two summers. Which is the missing summer? The second summer recorded in the "Recollections" is that of 1857, when, at Dog Creek near White Sulphur Springs, "I remember many notabilities who used to call on my Mother—among others Gov[ernor] F. W. Pickens, who was then an elderly widower, and brought with him his young fiancée, Miss Lucy Holcombe" (p. 22)—for this celebrated courtship, ending in marriage in 1858,

2. See Christoph Weber, *Kardinäle und Preläten in den letzten Jahrzehnten des Kirchenstaates: Elite-Rekrutierung, Karriere-Muster und sociale Zusammensetzung der kurialen Führungsschicht zur Zeit Pius' IX (1846–1878),* 2 vols. (Stuttgart, 1978), pp. 321, 334, 421–529, 553–70.

3. LSM to Langdon Cheves, Jr., July 7, 1858. Describing (p. 37) her mother's reaction to news received when, at the end of their voyage back from France, their ship the *Persia* docked in New York (Oct. 26, 1859)—"we heard of the nomination of *Abraham Lincoln* as President of the United States"—Louisa Smythe notices the discrepant chronology and suggests that "maybe it was something about John Brown and the Harpers Ferry affair" which caused her mother's response: "'There goes then this glorious Union.' . . . I remember the shock it gave me and the way my brother looked as he said 'Oh no, don't say that.' . . . She answered him, 'Yes, you will see—this is not the end of it, we will be forced to assert ourselves.'" The raid on Harpers Ferry, Va., and the arrest of the surviving raiders took place Oct. 16–18, 1859; Lincoln was nominated Republican candidate for the presidency on May 18, 1860, and won the election on Nov. 6 following.

was performed at the springs of Virginia in 1857; a letter of LSM's sister Sophia confirms that in the spring of 1857 the McCords were planning a visit there.[4] What, then, of the first of the two summers recorded, to which is assigned the trip to Narragansett, accompanied by "Uncle and Aunt Dulles" from Philadelphia, and to the White Mountains? Is it the summer of 1855 or of 1856? It looks to be the summer of 1855, for "my brother [was] not yet fifteen" when he "was our man who looked after everything" during this trip (p. 22): Langdon Cheves McCord turned fifteen years of age on April 17, 1856. Furthermore—but out of sequence, for Louisa Smythe is describing the difficulty in finding the rings required for her wedding—the "Recollections" tells that "the summer after my father's death" LSM lost her wedding ring while on a steamer and purchased a replacement "as soon as we got to Philadelphia" (p.76), that is, it may be inferred, on the way to collect the Dulles family before proceeding to Narragansett. On the other hand, Louisa Smythe writes (p. 21) that she "was ten years old" when she "went to Nar[r]agansett for the second time" (the first having been when she was four years of age); she did not turn ten until August 10, 1855. But this evidence is ambiguous: the exact day of arrival at Narragansett might have followed her birthday, or she may fix her age at the conclusion of the summer to describe the whole. The difficulty is resolved by a letter of Francis Lieber who, in late September 1856, from Philadelphia reported to his wife that "Mrs. McCord and her whole family spent the summer at Narragansett, because the physician in Columbia told her that Cheves will have the cataract, and that she is threatened with other blindness"; and that Hayne Cheves, who died on August 14, 1856, "is dead at last."[5] The summer missing from Louisa Smythe's "Recollections" is, therefore, that of 1855. The trip to Philadelphia during which LSM lost her wedding ring is not to be combined with the journey to Narragansett (unless Louisa Smythe's "the summer after my father's death" is itself an error); and the reference to Cheves McCord's age, if not Louisa Smythe's mistake, must be applied to other journeys, which, but for the incident of the lost wedding ring, the "Recollections" omits along with the whole of that summer.

After the war well-known events cease by which easily to date and test Louisa Smythe's recollections. When, for example, was Lang Syne sold? The plantation is central to the "Recollections," and so, it might be expected, the

4. "Your Aunt Louisa and Cheves are still suffering from their eyes and I fear there is no improvement in either. I believe they are going to Virginia to the Springs this summer." Sophia Cheves Haskell to William Haskell, May 20, 1857, Langdon Cheves III Papers, SCHS.

5. Francis Lieber to Matilda Lieber, Sept. 24–25, 1856, Francis Lieber Papers, Huntington.

loss of it would be recorded with care. But there is ambiguity. Louisa Smythe's health began to deteriorate.

> We had struggled with the plantation now for a good many months, and it was becoming very evident that there was no money in it—at least plenty went in it and none came out. Your father was already trying to read law, as well as he could, with the constant drudgery of trying to follow up the affairs of the place. In spite of our frolics things were looking blue from a business standpoint and as for me I was a wreck. So I was not consulted. My mother and my husband fixed it all. Taddie for the first of many times packed my trunk and one morning your father picked me up in his arms, for I was too weak to walk, and carried me on the train, where my pillow and my white wrapper, for they had not tried to dress me, excited much sympathy, except from an old woman who would shut the door when I wanted it open! And so the dream of making a home at Lang Syne was over, and my poor mother and Hannah were once more wanderers. [84–85]

It would be reasonable to infer from this that Louisa Smythe's departure as recorded here coincided with the selling of Lang Syne, which must therefore predate March 2, 1869, the day of Hannah McCord's marriage to John Taylor Rhett. But later in the "Recollections," after reporting that the Smythes came to Charleston to live with Augustine's parents, Louisa writes:

> We lived as I have said for three years at your Grandfather Smyth's house—then No. 12 Meeting St.—I was very happy there, though very homesick for the homes forever gone, for "Old Lang Syne" too was sold, we reserving only the family burying ground and a little place in the Pinelands which we gave to Tom and Marianne [former McCord servants] for their own. . . . I saw them once in this home. When your father and I went for the last time to Lang Syne, to gather the few things that were worth bringing away—the books chiefly—remains of my father's and grandfather's libraries—Marianne begged me as a great favor to come out to her house for breakfast one morning. [89]

So it appears that two separate events, two separate departures from Lang Syne, are being recorded. That the second refers to the actual sale (and the former, perhaps, to a leasing or rental of the plantation) is supported by the Mesne Conveyance records of Orangeburg District: on December 1, 1870, for the sum of $14,180, Augustine T. Smythe, "of Charleston," sold to Daniel Zimmerman "of Saint Matthews . . . Planter," the plantations of Lang Syne and Goshen and 277½ acres in the Pine Lands, "the above being the tract conveyed to me by deed of conveyance from Mrs. Louisa S. McCord, dated 27th day of June 1865; Saving and reserving however from and out of the hereby granted premises the family graveyard or tomb, consisting of about one quarter of an acre, and situated and being on the said tract known as 'Lang Syne.'"

That exact chronology is not to be demanded from her "Recollections," Louisa Smythe herself acknowledges. "I cannot," she writes at one point, "fix dates in my own mind or get even all my facts exactly clear, which is not to be wondered at at this lapse of time." Again, "You may find out some time that I have the sequence of events all wrong, but I doubt if you do for there is no one left to correct me or to find fault."[6] Finding fault would be useless, even ungrateful, in return for what Louisa Smythe tells us; we do in fact have evidence which on occasion can correct her; and her purpose, in any case, is not to compose a history fixed firmly by chronological methods, but to gather reminiscences of significant events and persons loosely about general topics, such as childhood, war experiences, early married life, and so on. Her portrait of her mother, not painted as such formally, but sketched in a variety of anecdote and incident, is therefore invaluable; strokes of the pencil, however fugitive, are telling. The funeral of Cheves McCord, who in his last letters home had expressed the intention to be confirmed as an Episcopalian, was held, like his father's, in Trinity Church; but Presbyterian Dr. Benjamin Morgan Palmer (1818–1902), "a faithful friend," performed the graveside service.[7] "At the end of his prayer, I remember my poor Mother falling on her knees at the open grave, and dropping into it, as a last token, one of her gloves—I have the match now, she had never parted with it" (p. 54).

Or preparations for Louisa Smythe's wedding in June 1865 (pp. 74–75). The trousseau challenged the family. The necks and sleeves of undergarments "were frilled with the finest linen cambric frills cut from what had been a cravat of my uncle Hayne Cheves. His trunk had come home after his death in Italy, and in it were these soft linen cambric cravats which had been laid aside ever since." Smythe relations, her sister Hannah and sister-in-law Charlotte, Charlotte's mother, contributed treasures and ingenuity; "Mrs. Herbemont—an old, old friend—tall and big boned, sent me a pair of white silk gloves of hers," which were cut down to correct size, the wounds concealed and embellished with "white gauze and ribbon."

> But still there was no dress and what would all the elegant things be without a dress? Mamma inquired far and wide. Nobody had a white dress. About this time a few shanties were put up in the burnt district by some enterprising Yankees who were keeping shop there. Mamma, anxious to do this one

6. Smythe, pp. 43, 46; cf. pp. 51, 99.

7. "We dined at Mrs. McCord's. . . . How her strength contrasts with our weakness! Like Dr. Palmer, she strings one up to bear bravely the worst." *Chesnut,* p. 677 (entry of Nov. 28, 1864).

thing so much desired, even went to the Yankees and found that one of them, named Jackson, had a few yards of white organdie, but—he asked $10.00 in greenbacks for it, and where could we get greenbacks? So Mamma took the chairs out of her room, and a piece of carpet (too stiff to cut into soldiers' blankets) also from her room, and she sent them to auction. They were sold but not for $10.00. And then, what did my mother do, *my* mother! with all her pride! She went and begged that Yankee to keep the muslin a few days, which he hemmed and hawed about doing, saying that his wife fancied it; and then she had the Merrimac hitched up and its chain harness and she took some lard and butter that had with great difficulty been sent up from Lang Syne, and she drove round town selling lard and butter until she made up the deficiency in the $10.00, bought the dress and brought it home to me! Do you think I can ever forget that?

Bibliography

MANUSCRIPT SOURCES

Charleston County, S.C.
  Probate Court Records

Manuscript Department, William R. Perkins Library, Duke University, Durham, N.C.
  Rachel S. Cheves Papers
  Ann Heatly Reid Lovell Papers

Henry E. Huntington Library, San Marino, Calif.
  Francis Lieber Papers

Library of Congress
  William Lowndes Papers

Orangeburg County, S.C.
  Mesne Conveyance Records

Peabody Institute, Baltimore
  John Pendleton Kennedy Papers

Historical Society of Pennsylvania, Philadelphia
  Edward Carey Gardiner Collection, Henry C. Carey Section
  Gratz Collection
  Sarah Butler Wister Papers

Richland County, S.C.
  Mesne Conveyance Records

Archives of American Art, Smithsonian Institution, Washington, D.C.
  Hiram Powers and Powers Family Papers

South Carolina Department of Archives and History, Columbia
  Will of David James McCord

South Carolina Historical Society, Charleston
  Langdon Cheves I Papers
  Langdon Cheves III Papers
  Dulles-Cheves-McCord-Lovell Papers
  Motte Family Miscellaneous Material
  Smythe-Stoney-Adger Papers

South Caroliniana Library, University of South Carolina, Columbia
  Cheves Family Papers
  Francis Lieber Papers
  James Henley Thornwell Papers

Williams-Chesnut-Manning Families Manuscripts
Louisa McCord Smythe. "Recollections of Louisa Rebecca Hayne McCord (Mrs. Augustine T. Smythe)" (typescript)

Southern Historical Collection, University of North Carolina, Chapel Hill
William Porcher Miles Papers
Pettigrew Family Papers

Virginia Historical Society, Richmond
Preston Family Papers

State Historical Society of Wisconsin, Madison
Lyman C. Draper Manuscripts

PUBLISHED SOURCES

Anderson, Mary Crow, ed. *Two Scholarly Friends: Yates Snowden-John Bennett Correspondence, 1902–1932*. Columbia, S.C., 1993.

Angell, James Burrill. *The Reminiscences of James Burrill Angell*. New York, 1912.

Ashton, Jean W. *Harriet Beecher Stowe: A Reference Guide*. Boston, 1977.

Barnwell, John. *Love of Order: South Carolina's First Secession Crisis*. Chapel Hill, N.C., 1982.

Bastiat, Claude-Frédéric. "Justice et fraternité." *Journal des économistes* 20 (June 1848): 310–27.

[Bass, Robert Duncan.] "McCord, Louisa Susanna Cheves." In *DAB*.

Bennett, Susan Smythe, comp. "The Cheves Family of South Carolina." *SCHM* 35 (1934): 79–95, 130–52.

——, comp. "The McCords of McCords' Ferry, South Carolina." *SCHM* 34 (1933): 177–93.

Bleser, Carol, ed. *Secret and Sacred: The Diaries of James Henry Hammond, a Southern Slaveholder*. New York, 1988.

The Book of Common Prayer. New York, 1992.

Burke, Edmund. *Letter to a Noble Lord* and *First Letter on a Regicide Peace*. 1796. In *The Writings and Speeches of Edmund Burke*. Vol. 9, pt. 1, *The Revolutionary War, 1794–1797*, and pt. 2, *Ireland*, ed. R. B. McDowell, pp. 145–264. Oxford, 1991.

——. *Reflections on the Revolution in France*. Ibid. Vol. 8, *The French Revolution, 1790–1794*, ed. L. G. Mitchell. Oxford, 1989.

Carey, Henry C. *The Slave Trade, Domestic and Foreign: Why It Exists, and How It May Be Extinguished*. Philadelphia, 1853; rpt. New York, 1967.

[Carlyle, Thomas.] "Occasional Discourse on the Negro Question." *Fraser's Magazine* 40 (Dec. 1849): 670–79.

——. *Works*. Ashburton ed. 17 vols. London and Philadelphia, 1885–88.

Conrad, Susan Phinney. *Perish the Thought: Intellectual Women in Romantic America, 1830–1860*. New York, 1976.

Cooper, Thomas, and David James McCord, eds. *The Statutes at Large of South Carolina*. 10 vols. Columbia, S.C., 1836–41.

Daly, Louise Haskell. *Alexander Cheves Haskell: The Portrait of a Man*. Intro. Lee A. Wallace, Jr. Rev. rpt. of 1934 ed. Wilmington, N.C., 1989.

Davidson, Chalmers Gaston. *The Last Foray: The South Carolina Planters of 1860, A Sociological Study*. Columbia, S.C., 1971.

Davidson, James Wood. *The Living Writers of the South*. New York, 1869.

De Bow, James Dunwoody Brownson. *The Industrial Resources, etc. of the Southern and Western States. . . .* 3 vols. New Orleans, 1853.

Duyckinck, Evert A., and George L. Duyckinck. *Cyclopaedia of American Literature*. 2 vols. New York, 1856.

Eacker, Susan A. "'A Dangerous Inmate' of the Antebellum South: Louisa McCord on Gender and Slavery." In *Essays on Southern Writers and Their Worlds*, ed. Christopher Morris and Steven Reinhardt. Walter Prescott Webb Memorial Lectures, vol. 29. College Station, Tex., forthcoming.

Eaton, Clement. *The Mind of the Old South*. Rev. ed. Baton Rouge, La., 1967.

Fladeland, Betty. *Men and Brothers: Anglo-American Antislavery Cooperation*. Urbana, Ill., 1972.

Forrest, Mary [Julia D. Freeman]. *Women of the South Distinguished in Literature*. New York, 1861.

Fox-Genovese, Elizabeth. *Feminism without Illusions: A Critique of Individualism*. Chapel Hill, N.C., 1991.

———. *Within the Plantation Household: Black and White Women of the Old South*. Chapel Hill, N.C., 1988.

Fraser, Jessie Melville. "Louisa C. McCord." M.A. thesis, University of South Carolina, 1919.

Genovese, Eugene D., and Elizabeth Fox-Genovese. "Slavery, Economic Development, and the Law: The Dilemma of the Southern Political Economists, 1800–1860." *Washington and Lee Law Review* 41, no. 1 (Winter 1984): 1–29.

Gillespie, Neal C. *The Collapse of Orthodoxy: The Intellectual Ordeal of George Frederick Holmes*. Charlottesville, Va., 1972.

[Greg, William Rathbone.] "English Socialism, and Communistic Associations." *Edinburgh Review* 93 (Jan. 1851): 1–33.

Hale, Sarah Josepha. *Woman's Record; or, Sketches of All Distinguished Women, from the Creation to A.D. 1854*. 2d ed. rev. New York, 1855.

Hampton, A. F., ed. *A Divided Heart: Letters of Sally Baxter Hampton, 1853–1862*. Spartanburg, S.C., 1980.

Hart, John Seely. *The Female Prose Writers of America*. Philadelphia, 1852.

Haskell, John Cheves. *The Haskell Memoirs*. Ed. Gilbert E. Govan and James W. Livingood. New York, 1960.

[Hill, Alicia, with Richard Whately and Samuel Hinds.] "American Slavery and *Uncle Tom's Cabin*." *North British Review* 18 (Nov. 1852): 235–58.

Hollinger, David A., and Charles Capper, eds. *The American Intellectual Tradition*. 2d ed. 2 vols. New York, 1993.

Hubbell, Jay B. *The South in American Literature, 1607–1900*. Durham, N.C., 1954.

Huff, Archie Vernon, Jr. *Langdon Cheves of South Carolina*. Columbia, S.C., 1977.

Irving, Washington. *The Complete Works of Washington Irving. Letters.* Vol. 1, 1802–23. Edited by R. M. Aderman et al. Boston, 1978.

Jenkins, William Sumner. *Pro-Slavery Thought in the Old South.* Chapel Hill, N.C., 1935.

Jones, Norrece T., Jr. *Born a Child of Freedom, Yet a Slave: Mechanisms of Control and Strategies of Resistance in Antebellum South Carolina.* Hanover, N.H., and London, 1990.

Kingsley, Charles. *Alton Locke, Tailor and Poet: An Autobiography.* New York, 1850; rpt. London, 1910.

———. *Yeast.* London, 1851.

LaBorde, Maximilian. *History of the South Carolina College. . . .* Columbia, S.C., 1859.

Legaré, Hugh Swinton. "Jeremy Bentham and the Utilitarians." In *The Writings of Hugh Swinton Legaré,* ed. Mary Legaré, 2:449–81. 2 vols. Charleston, S.C., 1846. Rpt. New York, 1970.

Lewis, Matthew Gregory, ed. *Tales of Wonder.* London, 1801.

Lounsbury, Richard C., ed. *Louisa S. McCord: Poems, Drama, Biography, Letters.* Charlottesville, Va., forthcoming.

———. "*Ludibria Rerum Mortalium:* Charlestonian Intellectuals and Their Classics." In *Intellectual Life in Antebellum Charleston,* ed. Michael O'Brien and David Moltke-Hansen, pp. 325–69. Knoxville, Tenn., 1986.

McCord, David James. "Africans at Home." *SQR,* n.s., 10 (July 1854): 70–96.

———. "American Institutions—the Monroe Doctrine—Intervention—etc." *De Bow* 15 (Dec. 1853): 584–95.

———. "The Anatomy of the Navigation Laws." *SQR* 16 (Jan. 1850): 416–44.

———. "Barhydt's Industrial Exchanges." *SQR* 15 (July 1849): 460–83.

———. "California Gold." *SQR,* n.s., 5 (April 1852): 301–21.

———. "Civil Liberty and Self-Government." *SQR,* n.s., 9 (April 1854): 300–332.

———. "The Federal Constitution." *Southern Review* 2 (Nov. 1828): 432–54.

———. "How the South Is Affected by Her Slave Institutions." *De Bow* 11 (Oct. 1851): 349–63.

———. "Lieber's Political Ethics." *SQR* 12 (Oct. 1847): 464–504.

———. "Life of a Negro Slave." *SQR,* n.s., 7 (Jan. 1853): 206–27.

———. "Memphis Convention." *SQR* 10 (Oct. 1846): 377–417.

———. "Navigation Laws." *SQR,* n.s., 1 (April 1850): 48–75.

———. "Pennsylvania Iron Memorial." *SQR,* n.s., 6 (July 1852): 1–22.

———. "Political Economy—Manufactures." *SQR* 9 (April 1846): 392–433.

———. "Political Elements." *SQR,* n.s., 10 (Oct. 1854): 383–431.

———. "Practical Effects of Emancipation." *De Bow* 18 (April and May 1855): 474–96, 591–602.

———. *Reports of Cases Determined in the Constitutional Court of South Carolina: Being a Continuation of Nott and McCord's Reports.* 4 vols. Columbia, S.C., 1822–30.

———. "Slavery and the Abolitionists." *SQR* 15 (April 1849): 165–223.

———. "What Is Fair and Equal Reciprocity?" *De Bow* 15 (Nov. 1853): 433–47.

"McCord, Mrs. Louisa Susannah Cheves." In *The South in the Building of the Nation,* ed. Julian A. C. Chandler et al., 12:132. Richmond, 1909.

McCurry, Stephanie. "The Two Faces of Republicanism: Gender and Proslavery Politics in Antebellum South Carolina." *Journal of American History* 78 (1992): 1245–64.

McGowan, Clelia P. "Louisa S. McCord (1810–1879)." In *Library of Southern Literature,* ed. Edwin Alderman and Joel Chandler Harris, 8:3505–7. New Orleans, 1907.

Manly, Louise. *Southern Literature from 1579–1895: A Comprehensive Review, with Copious Extracts and Criticisms.* Richmond, 1895.

May, Caroline. *The American Female Poets, with Biographical and Critical Notices.* Philadelphia, 1848.

Meats, Stephen, and Edwin T. Arnold, eds. *The Writings of Benjamin F. Perry.* 3 vols. Spartanburg, S.C., 1980.

Meriwether, Anne Blythe. "McCord, Louisa Cheves." In *Encyclopedia of the Confederacy,* ed. Richard N. Current, 3:969. New York, 1993.

Nott, Henry Junius, and David James McCord. *Reports of Cases Determined in the Constitutional Court of South Carolina.* 2 vols. Columbia, S.C., 1820–21.

O'Brien, Michael, ed. *All Clever Men, Who Make Their Way: Critical Discourse in the Old South.* Fayetteville, Ark., 1982; 2d ed., Athens, Ga., 1992.

———, ed. *An Evening When Alone: Four Journals of Single Women in the South, 1827–67.* Publications of the Southern Texts Society. Charlottesville, Va., 1993.

Oliphant, Mary C. Simms, et al., eds. *The Letters of William Gilmore Simms.* 6 vols. Columbia, S.C., 1952–82.

Plutarch. *The Lives of the Noble Grecians and Romans.* The Dryden Translation, rev. Arthur Hugh Clough. 2 vols. New York, 1992.

The Proceedings of the Woman's Rights Convention, Held at Worcester, October 15th and 16th, 1851. New York, 1852.

Rable, George C. *Civil Wars: Women and the Crisis of Southern Nationalism.* Urbana, Ill., 1989.

Read, Thomas Buchanan, ed. *The Female Poets of America.* Philadelphia, 1849.

Sargent, Epes, ed. *Harper's Cyclopaedia of British and American Poetry.* New York, 1881.

"S.C. Birthday." Charleston *News and Courier.* Dec. 3, 1945.

Smith, Adam. *An Inquiry into the Nature and Causes of the Wealth of Nations,* ed. W. B. Todd. Oxford, 1979.

Smythe, Louisa McCord. *For Old Lang Syne: Collected for My Children.* Charleston, S.C., 1900.

Stockton, David. *The Gracchi.* Oxford, 1979.

Stowe, Harriet Beecher. *Uncle Tom's Cabin or, Life among the Lowly.* New York, 1991.

[Tardy, Mary T., ed.] *The Living Female Writers of the South.* 1872. Rpt. Detroit, 1978.

Thorp, Margaret Farrand. *Female Persuasion: Six Strong-Minded Women.* 1949. Rpt. n.p., 1971.

———. "McCord, Louisa Susannah Cheves." In *Notable American Women, 1607–1950: A Biographical Dictionary,* ed. Edward T. James et al., 2:450–52. Cambridge, Mass., 1971.

Trent, William P. *William Gilmore Simms.* Boston and New York, 1892.

United Daughters of the Confederacy, South Carolina Division. *South Carolina Women in the Confederacy,* ed. Mrs. Thomas Taylor et al. 2 vols. Columbia, S.C., 1903–7.

Watson, Charles S. *Antebellum Charleston Dramatists.* University, Ala., 1976.

Wauchope, George Armstrong, ed. *The Writers of South Carolina.* Columbia, S.C., 1910.

Wilson, Forrest. *Crusader in Crinoline: The Life of Harriet Beecher Stowe.* Philadelphia, 1941.

Wister, Sarah Butler, and Agnes Irwin, eds. *Worthy Women of Our First Century.* Philadelphia, 1877. Rpt. Plainville, N.Y., 1975.

Woodward, C. Vann, ed. *Mary Chesnut's Civil War.* New Haven, 1981.

———, and Elizabeth Muhlenfeld, eds. *The Private Mary Chesnut: The Unpublished Civil War Diaries.* New York, 1984.

Wunder, Richard P. *Hiram Powers: Vermont Sculptor, 1805–1873.* 2 vols. Newark, N.J., 1991.

Wyman, Mary Alice, ed. *Selections from the Autobiography of Elizabeth Oakes Smith.* Lewiston, Maine, 1924.

Index

A. Names

When a name is followed by more than one page reference, annotation is signified by boldface type. Authors being reviewed by LSM are excluded, apart from the page number where annotation can be found.

B. Authors

Not included below are citations from books and articles being reviewed by LSM.